SOCIAL PROBLEMS
and the quality of life

reviewer acknowledgments

Giovanna Follo
Wayne State University

Rebecca Freilinger
South Dakota State University

Paul Fuller
Knoxville College

Carolyn Gates
Bellevue Community College

Elinor Lerner
Richard Stockton College of New Jersey

Meena Sharma
Wayne State University

SOCIAL PROBLEMS
and the quality of life

Eleventh Edition

Robert H. Lauer
Alliant International University

Jeanette C. Lauer
Alliant International University

Boston   Burr Ridge, IL   Dubuque, IA   Madison, WI   New York   San Francisco   St. Louis
Bangkok   Bogotá   Caracas   Kuala Lumpur   Lisbon   London   Madrid   Mexico City
Milan   Montreal   New Delhi   Santiago   Seoul   Singapore   Sydney   Taipei   Toronto

To Jon, Kathy, Julie, Jeffrey, Kate, Jeff, Krista, Benjamin, David, and John Robert

"... the greatest of these is love."

The McGraw·Hill Companies

 Higher Education

Published by McGraw-Hill, an imprint of The McGraw-Hill Companies, Inc., 1221 Avenue of the Americas, New York, NY 10020. Copyright © 2008, 2006, 2004, 2002, 1998, 1995, 1992, 1989, 1986, 1982, 1978.

This book is printed on acid-free paper.

1 2 3 4 5 6 7 8 9 0 WCK/WCK 0 9 8 7

ISBN: 978-0-07-338012-4
MHID: 0-07-338012-1

Publisher: *Frank Mortimer*
Sponsoring Editor: *Gina Boedeker*
Marketing Manager: *Lori DeShazo*
Production Editor: *Paul Wells*
Production Service: *Newgen-Austin*
Manuscript Editor: *Michelle Chancellor*
Design Manager: *Margarite Reynolds*
Cover Designer: *Margarite Reynolds*
Photo Research: *Emily Tietz*
Production Supervisor: *Randy Hurst*
Composition: *10/12 Palatino by Newgen*
Printing: *PMS 2738, 45# New Era Matte, Quebecor World, Inc.*

Cover: © Digital Vision/PunchStock

Credits: The credits section for this book begins on page 533 and is considered an extension of the copyright page.

Library of Congress Cataloging-in-Publication Data

Lauer, Robert H.
    Social problems and the quality of life / Robert Lauer.—11th ed.
        p. cm.
    Includes bibliographical references and index.
    ISBN-13: 978-0-07-338012-4 (alk. paper)
    ISBN-10: 0-07-338012-1 (alk. paper)
    1. United States—Social conditions.   2. Quality of life—United States.
3. Social problems—United States.   I. Title.
    HN57.L39 2008
    361.10973—dc22   2007024662

www.mhhe.com

brief contents

contents

PART 1 Foundations 1

PART 2 Problems of Behavioral Deviance 33

PART 3 Problems of Inequality 155

6 Poverty 156

7 Gender and Sexual Orientation 186

8 Race, Ethnic Groups, and Racism 220

PART 4

Problems of Social Institutions 251

9 Government and Politics 252

10 Work and the Economy 284

11 Education 312

list of figures

People everywhere want to maximize the quality of their lives. There is widespread agreement that a high quality of life requires such things as a good education, freedom from fear of crime, good housing, meaningful work, and good health. A high quality of life, then, can only be attained if people deal with the social problems that detract from that quality. As we point out in the first chapter of this text, a social problem is, by definition, a condition or pattern of behavior that is incompatible with people's desired quality of life.

To deal with a problem, you must understand it—how it affects one's quality of life, what causes it, what tends to maintain it. Sociologists have used three theoretical perspectives to answer these questions, to analyze and deal with social problems. We discuss the three major perspectives in chapter 1 and show how we use elements from each to analyze individual problems and talk about how the problems can be attacked.

We do not mean to give the impression here that either understanding a problem or attacking it is a simple matter. Even experts disagree on such things. The factors that combine to cause and perpetuate any particular problem are many and complex. We have seen students feel overwhelmed as they study these factors. As one student said: "I don't see how society can ever deal with some of these problems. The more I understand about what causes them, the more hopeless I feel."

It is interesting to note, therefore, that some problems are less serious than they were when this book was in its first edition. Among other things, poverty among the aged has declined, many crime rates have dropped, divorce rates have declined, the cold war and the accompanying arms race between the superpowers have come to an end, and air and water pollution levels have decreased significantly. Other problems, however, are still just as serious—or even more so. For instance, addictions continue to ruin lives and traumatize families; domestic and international terrorism are of the highest concern to citizens and the government; war remains a vexing problem; white-collar crime is more widespread and more of a threat to the economy than previously recognized; health problems afflict great numbers of people, many of whom have no health insurance; racial minorities have lost some of the gains made in previous years; poverty has increased among some groups; increasing numbers of single parents mean increasing problems for children; equitable opportunities remain elusive for homosexuals; and the threats posed by such things as global warming and toxic wastes are more serious than previously thought. These advances and setbacks are all discussed in the text.

Changes in the Eleventh Edition

A social problem is a product of social definition. That is, something becomes a problem, and becomes a more or less serious problem, as it is so defined by the people of a society. People's definitions of problems and the problems themselves continually change. Each new edition of a social problems text, therefore, strives to capture the current status of an ever-changing phenomenon. To achieve this goal, we have updated all materials in this edition with hundreds of new references as well as the most recent data available from the government and other sources.

There are changing concerns among the public as well as changing emphases among researchers. To reflect current interests and concerns more adequately, we have included new or expanded materials on such topics as the role of the mass media in social problems, cybersex, methamphetamine abuse, rape of males, homelessness, the beauty myth's effect on females, historical racism in the United States, the government's response to natural disasters such as Hurricane Katrina, health insurance, stem cell research, terrorism, and indoor air pollution.

Organization

We have divided the book into five parts and 15 chapters. Part 1 introduces students to social problems. Chapter 1 discusses the various tools needed, including the difference between social problems and personal problems, sociological theories and methods, and fallacious ways of thinking.

In part 2, we look at a cluster of problems that involve behavior that deviates from social norms. Chapters 2 through 5 cover the problems of sexual deviance (prostitution and pornography), alcohol and other drugs, crime and delinquency, and violence.

Part 3 examines problems that involve social inequality. Poverty (chapter 6) is inequality in income and wealth. Gender and sexual orientation comprise another area of inequality (chapter 7), as women and homosexuals strive to gain equal rights. Racial and ethnic inequality (chapter 8) includes the multiple ways in which there is disparity in valued things between the various racial and ethnic groups in the nation.

Part 4 focuses on problems of social institutions. Chapters 9 through 13 cover the institutions of government and politics, work and the economy, education, family, and health care. These institutions are factors in other kinds of social problems but are also problematic in themselves.

Finally, part 5 covers two global social problems: war and terrorism (chapter 14) and the environment (chapter 15). These problems pose a threat to civilization itself and cannot be understood apart from their global context.

Learning Aids

We use a variety of learning aids to facilitate understanding of the materials:

- Chapter-opening vignettes personalize the various problems. They make each problem not just a set of facts but a social reality that disrupts and diminishes the quality of people's lives in concrete, understandable ways.
- Chapter objectives and marginal key terms keep students on track as they work through the chapters.
- Global Comparison boxes add dimension to students' understanding of social problems by seeing how they work out in another nation or nations.

- Dealing with the problems is as important as knowing what causes them. Each chapter, therefore, contains a section called Public Policy and Private Action that suggests ways to ameliorate each problem. We have found that most students are like the one quoted at the beginning of this preface—they don't simply want to know about problems, they also want to know what can be done to address those problems. We do not claim that the suggestions will eliminate the problems, but they do demonstrate that problems have solutions and that the solutions are always, to some extent, up to each individual.

- Marginal icons identify places in the text where we show how people use the fallacies of thinking discussed in chapter 1 to draw erroneous conclusions about social problems.

- End-of-chapter summaries, key terms lists, study questions, and Internet resources and exercises provide students with ample review, study materials, and self-learning projects.

Supplements Package

As a full-service publisher of quality educational products, McGraw-Hill does much more than just sell textbooks. The company creates and publishes an extensive array of print, video, and digital supplements for students and instructors. This edition of *Social Problems* is accompanied by an extensive, comprehensive supplements package:

For the Student

- *Online Learning Center Web Site.* An innovative, book-specific Web site featuring PowerWeb, online access to articles from the popular and scholarly press, weekly updates, daily newsfeeds, a search engine, and more. All of this material—plus flashcards that can be used to master vocabulary and a wealth of other review materials—is organized by chapter for ease of use when studying for exams or writing papers.

For the Instructor

- *Instructor's Manual/Testbank.* Chapter outlines, key terms, overviews, lecture notes, discussion questions, a complete testbank, and more.

- *Computerized Testbank.* Easy-to-use computerized testing program for both Windows and Macintosh computers.

- *PowerPoint Slides.* Complete, chapter-by-chapter slide shows featuring text, tables, and visuals.

- *Instructor's Online Learning Center.* Password-protected access to supplements and other important instructor support materials as well as additional resources.

- *Course Management Systems.* Whether you use WebCT, Blackboard, e-College, or another course management system, McGraw-Hill will provide you with a *Social Problems* cartridge that enables you either to conduct your course entirely online or to supplement your lectures with online material. If your school does not yet have one of these course management systems, we can provide you with

PageOut, an easy-to-use tool that allows you to create your own course Web page and access all material on the *Social Problems* Online Learning Center.

- *Primis Online.* A unique database publishing system that allows instructors to create their own custom text from material in *Social Problems* or elsewhere and deliver that text to students electronically as an e-book or in print format via the bookstore.

- *Videotapes.* A wide variety of videotapes from the *Films for the Humanities and Social Sciences* series is available to adopters of the text.

Acknowledgments

Many people are important in the production of a book. The staff at McGraw-Hill has been most helpful and supportive. Time and again, we have been impressed with the quality of work done by the various editors with whom we have worked. We appreciate each of them, particularly Gina Boedeker, who worked with us on this latest edition. We would also like to thank the academic reviewers who are listed facing the title page; their suggestions have, we believe, enhanced this book.

Robert H. Lauer

Jeanette C. Lauer

Social Problems and the Quality of Life, 11e

Coverage of Today's Social Problems

Domestic and international terrorism receive expanded coverage in chapter 14 as does white-collar crime in chapter 2.

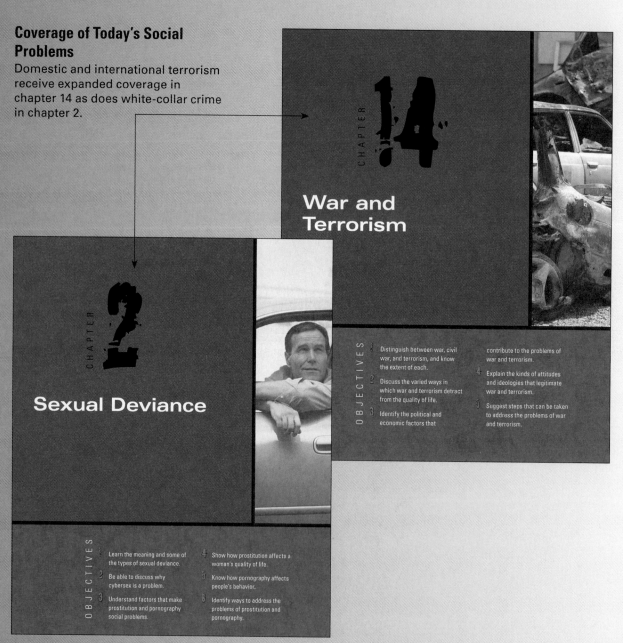

CHAPTER 14

War and Terrorism

OBJECTIVES

1. Distinguish between war, civil war, and terrorism, and know the extent of each.
2. Discuss the varied ways in which war and terrorism detract from the quality of life.
3. Identify the political and economic factors that

contribute to the problems of war and terrorism.
4. Explain the kinds of attitudes and ideologies that legitimate war and terrorism.
5. Suggest steps that can be taken to address the problems of war and terrorism.

CHAPTER 2

Sexual Deviance

OBJECTIVES

1. Learn the meaning and some of the types of sexual deviance.
2. Be able to discuss why cybersex is a problem.
3. Understand factors that make prostitution and pornography social problems.
4. Show how prostitution affects a woman's quality of life.
5. Know how pornography affects people's behavior.
6. Identify ways to address the problems of prostitution and pornography.

Global Comparisons

Fascinating cross-cultural discussions add dimension to students' understanding of social problems by giving them a glimpse into how the problems work out elsewhere.

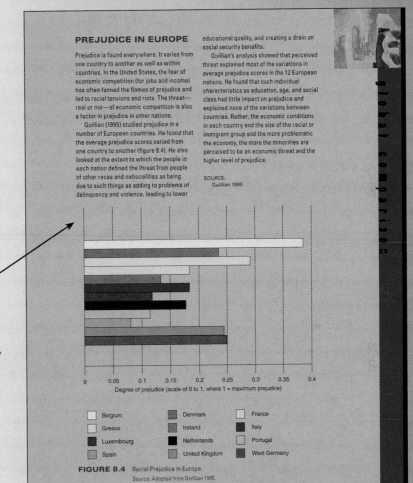

PREJUDICE IN EUROPE

Prejudice is found everywhere. It varies from one country to another as well as within countries. In the United States, the fear of economic competition (for jobs and income) has often fanned the flames of prejudice and led to racial tensions and riots. The threat—real or not—of economic competition is also a factor in prejudice in other nations.

Quillian (1995) studied prejudice in a number of European countries. He found that the average prejudice scores varied from one country to another (figure 8.4). He also looked at the extent to which the people in each nation defined the threat from people of other races and nationalities as being due to such things as adding to problems of delinquency and violence, leading to lower educational quality, and creating a drain on social security benefits.

Quillian's analysis showed that perceived threat explained most of the variations in average prejudice scores in the 12 European nations. He found that such individual characteristics as education, age, and social class had little impact on prejudice and explained none of the variations between countries. Rather, the economic conditions in each country and the size of the racial or immigrant group and the more problematic the economy, the more the minorities are perceived to be an economic threat and the higher level of prejudice.

SOURCE:
Quillian 1995

Degree of prejudice (scale of 0 to 1, where 1 = maximum prejudice)

Belgium Denmark France
Greece Ireland Italy
Luxembourg Netherlands Portugal
Spain United Kingdom West Germany

FIGURE 8.4 Racial Prejudice in Europe.
Source: Adapted from Quillian 1995.

Fallacy Icons

Marginal icons identify how people use the fallacies of thinking discussed in chapter 1 to draw erroneous conclusions about social problems.

Chapter Previews

Chapter-opening vignettes personalize the various problems presented in the text, and chapter objectives keep students on track as they work through the chapters.

When there are poor relationships in the family, parental moral and emotional authority is weakened. The diminished authority tends to weaken children's bonds to the social order and increases the likelihood of delinquency (Browning and Loeber 1999). Don't commit the *fallacy of retrospective determinism* here. Not all children from such families are delinquents. Family background helps you *understand* why some youths become delinquent, but it does not condone delinquency or absolve delinquents of responsibility for their behavior.

Adult criminals are also likely to have had troubled family relationships (Raine, Brennan, and Mednick 1994; Grogan-Kaylor and Otis 2003). We are not saying that the criminal behavior began in adulthood, of course. In fact, virtually all criminal careers (other than white-collar crime) begin before the age of 18. A large number of youths who engage in serious delinquent behavior will continue their criminal activities as adults. In a follow-up study of 99 formerly incarcerated delinquents, the researchers found that 89 had adult criminal records (Lewis et al. 1989). The average number of their offenses as adults was 11.6.

Social Stratification and Crime.   Crime and delinquency are related to the social stratification system in three ways: (1) The kind of behavior considered criminal is defined by those who have power within the system. (2) Different kinds of crime tend to be committed within different strata of the system. (3) Disproportionate numbers of criminals come from different socioeconomic levels.

A good deal of the behavior of relatively powerless people is defined as criminal whereas similar behavior among more powerful people is not defined as criminal. This finding is true especially when the behavior involves monetary exploitation. A corporate executive might support the definition of employee theft as criminal but would not define false advertising and exploitation of consumers as theft or crime. A physician might deplore abuses of the welfare system, labeling them criminal fraud, but think little about prescribing expensive brand-name drugs rather than less expensive generic counterparts because, in part, his or her retirement plan rests on investments in the pharmaceutical industry. In both cases, the people who influence the defining process are the *holders or wielders of power in society,* and they *do not define their own behavior as criminal.*

The second way in which social stratification intersects with crime and delinquency involves the kinds of crime committed. Those in the lower socioeconomic strata are more likely to be both the offenders and the victims of delinquency, violent crimes, and property crimes (Markowitz 2003; Eitle, D'Alessio, and Stolzenberg 2006), whereas white-collar criminals are more likely to come from the middle and upper strata.

fallacy

CHAPTER 12

Family Problems

OBJECTIVES

1. Know the ways in which the American family is changing.

2. Discuss the functions of the family.

3. Identify the kinds and the extent of family problems.

4. Show how family problems affect the quality of life for family members.

5. Explain the ways in which social arrangements, including norms and roles, contribute to family problems.

6. Learn the significance of attitudes, values, and ideologies in perpetuating family problems.

"I Survived the Abuse"

Patricia is a self-confident, middle-aged, professional woman. Yet she could have turned out quite differently, because she grew up in a home in which she suffered ongoing verbal abuse from her mother. To most people, Patricia's mother was a genteel southern lady. Patricia knew a different side of her mother:

My mother was beautiful. She looked like a movie star. I grew up with her and my grandparents after she divorced my father when I was an infant. And I remember the verbal abuse vividly. She never shouted. She never sneered. In her pleasant, soft voice, she simply said things that were gut-wrenching to me. Like the time she took me to buy some shoes, and told the clerk in a giggly voice that he should just bring a shoe box because he probably didn't have shoes that were big enough to fit my feet. Do you know what that does to an adolescent girl?

When I was a teenager, my mother and I were about the same size. She would buy dresses for herself, then try them on me. I didn't say, "Let me try them on," because I never volunteered nor wanted to do it. I knew what her reaction would be. It was always the same—she would look at me in her dress, sigh, and shake her head as though it were hopeless. It was her way of letting me know how ugly I was compared to her. She also let me know this once when we were looking at a picture of us together when I was younger. She said it was too bad I was smiling and showing my big, ugly teeth.

343

90 part 2 • Problems of Behavioral Deviance

chapter 3 review

Summary

The problem of alcohol and other drugs is one of abuse and not merely of use. Various drugs have various effects, and the effects depend on the method of administration, the amount taken, and the social situation as well as the chemical composition of the drug. Alcohol is the most widely used drug, and its effects can be extremely deleterious. Many experts consider alcohol abuse much more serious than abuse of other drugs.

Around 1980, drug use of all kinds began to decline for the first time in two decades. In the 1990s, patterns of use fluctuated. Although less than in the peak years, use and abuse are still quite high. More than one-half of all Americans drink, and more than a third say that drinking has been a source of trouble in their families. Millions of Americans indicate that they are current users of marijuana. Many users tend toward multiple drug use. Most alcohol abusers are young and male but not poor, whereas other drug addicts tend to be young, male, and poor.

The meaning of the drug problem for the quality of life is seen in the consequences for physical health, psychological health, interpersonal relationships, and economic costs. Abusers suffer various undesirable effects in all areas, and they inflict suffering on others. The nation as a whole also suffers great economic cost because billions of dollars per year are involved in lost services and in efforts to combat the deleterious effects of abuse.

Various structural factors contribute to the problem. An important one is group norms. Integration into a group that approves drug use is one of the most reliable predictors of use. Role problems, including role conflict and undesirable role change, create stress in the individual and that stress can lead to abuse. Abusers are more likely to come from homes in which family members are abusers, from broken homes, or from homes with problematic relationships. The government's definition of many drugs as illegal has several implications: more people are classified as criminal; previously classified criminals become deeply involved in the drug traffic; the criminal justice system is strained; and users and abusers are led into various kinds of undesirable behavior. Finally, the suppliers of illegal drugs are organized effectively and take advantage of corruption, so that a supply will always be available when there is a demand and profits are high.

Among social psychological factors is the alienation of users from the larger society. Many people believe drug use produces desirable psychic effects. These positive attitudes toward drug use combine with group norms and various ideologies that develop in groups. The ideologies explain and validate drug use.

In treating the problem, efforts to help the individual abuser or reduce the supply available to users have far exceeded efforts to get at the social roots of the problem. If it is to be dealt with effectively, both approaches are needed—attacks on the social factors as well as treatment of individual abusers.

Key Terms

Abuse
Addiction
Detoxification
Placebo
Role Conflict

Study Questions

1. What is meant by the fact that Americans have had ambivalent feelings about alcohol and other drugs throughout their history?
2. Identify the various types of drugs and briefly note their effects on people.
3. Who are the most likely users and abusers of alcohol and other drugs?
4. How do the use and abuse of alcohol and other drugs affect physical health?
5. What are the consequences of alcohol and other drugs for psychological health?
6. How does alcohol affect interpersonal relationships?
7. Indicate the economic costs of drug use and abuse.
8. In what ways do group norms affect patterns of drug use?
9. What kind of role problems enter into drug use and abuse?
10. How do social institutions contribute to the problem?
11. What are the attitudes and ideologies that are important in understanding the drug problem?
12. Name some steps that can be taken to alleviate the problem of alcohol and other drugs.

chapter 3 • Alcohol and Other Drugs 91

Internet Resources/ Exercises

1. Explore some of the ideas in this chapter on the following sites:

http://www.nida.nih.gov The National Institute on Drug Abuse site contains news, publications, and links to other sources.

http://www.casacolumbia.org Site of the National Center on Addiction and Substance Abuse at Columbia University, with a focus on studying and combating substance abuse. Has publications and links to other resources.

http://ash.org The Action on Smoking and Health home page provides information on nonsmokers' rights, smoking statistics and information, and help for stopping.

2. Look at figure 3.1 in the text. Select five drugs and get detailed information on them from the National Institute on Drug Abuse site. If everyone had this information, how many people would still experiment with the drugs? Give arguments both for maintaining that nobody would be a user and for asserting that some would still be users.

3. Search the Internet for "drug use" and "tobacco." Find sites that defend people's right to be users. List the reasons, and respond to them with materials in the text.

For Further Reading

Clawson, Patrick L., Rensselaer W. Lee III, and Rensselaer W. Lee. *The Andean Cocaine Industry.* New York: St. Martin's, 1998. An examination of cocaine, beginning with its cultivation in South America to its sale on American streets. Includes an analysis of the economic and political effects of the drug business on Andean nations.

Dodes, Lance M. *The Heart of Addiction: A New Approach to Understanding and Managing Alcoholism and Other Addictive Behaviors.* New York: HarperCollins, 2002. Identifies myths about addiction and discusses the common elements in addictions of all types. Includes addiction problems of particular groups and ways to get help.

Engel, Joel. *Addicted: Kids Talking about Drugs in Their Own Words.* New York: Tom Doherty Associates, 1989. Ten young people tell in their own words how drugs overtook their lives and controlled them. Most began with alcohol and marijuana before they were 13 years old.

Erdmann, Jack. *Whiskey's Children.* New York: Kensington, 1997. An account of the personal trauma endured by a man whose drinking resulted in both personal and professional disasters.

Gahlinger, Paul M. *Illegal Drugs: A Complete Guide to Their History, Chemistry, Use, and Abuse.* Las Vegas, NV: Sagebrush Press, 2001. A professor of medicine provides a comprehensive account of all aspects of drug use and abuse for the nonspecialist general reader.

Jersild, Devon. *Happy Hours: Alcohol in a Woman's Life.* New York: HarperCollins, 2001. Both statistics and personal stories highlight the increasingly serious problem of women's abuse of alcohol, including the unique challenges women face as they try to overcome their addiction.

Kluger, Richard. *Ashes to Ashes: America's Hundred-Year Cigarette War, the Public Health, and the Unabashed Triumph of Philip Morris.* New York: Vintage Books, 1997. A comprehensive examination of the American tobacco industry and the complex social, medical, economic, and psychological factors in the industry's growth and the current controversies and legal battles.

chapter 3 review

Chapter Reviews

End-of-chapter summaries, key terms lists, study questions, and Internet activities provide students with ample review and study materials.

152 part 2 • Problems of Behavioral Deviance

chapter 5 review

Summary

Violence is a problem that concerns most Americans. Generally, violence refers to the use of force to kill, injure, or abuse others. Interpersonal violence occurs between individuals or a number of individuals. Intergroup violence involves identifiable groups, such as different races or religions.

In estimating the amount of violence, we find an impressive amount based on self-reports, newspaper accounts, and police statistics. The United States has one of the highest homicide rates in the world. Virtually all Americans are exposed to a vast amount of violence in the mass media.

The meaning of violence can be summed up in terms of human destruction and injury, psychological disruption and dehumanization, economic costs, and "seductive self-destruction." These factors all diminish the quality of life, and their impact can be both severe and long-term.

Violence has been linked with a human need for aggression, yet this explanation is not sufficient. Various sociocultural factors contribute to the problem. One structural factor is group and societal norms, which make violence more likely among members of those groups. An important factor in intergroup violence is exclusion from the political process. People who are unable to exert power through legitimate political means may resort to violence. An important factor in interpersonal violence is the lack of adequate gun control. Inequality is related to violence; political and economic inequalities between groups in a society increase the likelihood of violence.

Among the social psychological factors in violence are a number of attitudes that legitimate violence. The majority of Americans agree that physical force is sometimes justified, including the use of force in intimate relationships. A frequent explanation of violence involves the notion of relative deprivation, which means that attitudes toward deprivation rather than the objective condition are the critical factor.

Certain values support violence, including retributiveness and self-defense. Such values can be internalized, along with attitudes, through exposure to the mass media. The extent to which the mass media socialize people into violent attitudes and behavior is a matter of controversy. However, the bulk of the evidence indicates that violence portrayed and conveyed in the mass media is related to aggressive attitudes and behavior.

Rape is a form of interpersonal violence that afflicts tens of thousands each year. Fear of rape is one of the more common fears of women. All rapes involve both physical and emotional trauma. The rape trauma syndrome involves several weeks of acute symptoms and disorganization, and a long period of painful emotional readjustment.

The more men agree with traditional norms about sex roles, and the more they are integrated into a culture whose norms support male dominance and superiority, the more likely they are to be sexually aggressive and to minimize the harm of rape.

The mass media contribute to the problem of violence against women in general and rape in particular through portrayals of sexual violence. These portrayals increase the tendency of males to engage in antisocial attitudes and behavior. Studies of offenders show that they had negative family experiences and are psychologically disturbed. All have extremely high levels of aggression.

Key Terms

Aggression
Catharsis
Domestic Terrorism
Forcible Rape
Incest
Post-traumatic Stress Disorder
Relative Deprivation
Retributiveness
Statutory Rape
Violence

Study Questions

1. How would you define violence? How much violence is there in America?
2. What are the physical and emotional consequences of being a victim of violence?
3. What social structural factors contribute to the level of violence in America?
4. What role do the mass media play in violent behavior?
5. How common is rape?
6. Discuss the physical and emotional consequences of being a victim of rape or attempted rape.
7. Why do men rape?
8. What can be done about the violence, including rape, in American society?

chapter 5 • Violence 153

Internet Resources/ Exercises

1. Explore some of the ideas in this chapter on the following sites:

http://www.vpc.org Site of the Violence Policy Center, with an emphasis on gun control in order to reduce violence in America.

http://www.ncadv.org The National Coalition Against Domestic Violence offers surveys, discussions of public policy, and ways for victims to get help.

http://www.rapecrisis.com Has information, services, and links for sexual assault victims and their families.

2. Investigate a group involved in domestic terrorism, such as a right-wing militia, the Earth Liberation Front, or the Animal Liberation Front. How does the group justify its stance? How do law enforcement officials and other observers define the activities of the group? What social structural and social psychological factors do you think contribute to the existence and work of the group?

3. Find stories of rape victims. Compare their accounts with the discussion in the text about the rape trauma syndrome. How does the text's description of the syndrome capture or fail to fully capture the victims' experiences?

For Further Reading

Allison, Julie A., and Lawrence S. Wrightsman. *Rape: The Misunderstood Crime.* Newbury Park, CA: Sage, 1993. Uses data from both research and the news media to discuss every aspect of rape, from the offense to the treatment of the victim to the prevention of rape.

Bergen, Raquel Kennedy, Jeffrey L. Edleson, and Claire M. Renzetti, eds. *Violence Against Women.* Boston: Allyn & Bacon, 2004. Essays from a broad range of perspectives that address the issue of sexual and physical violence against women, including commentaries by the authors about their research and its impact.

Hofstadter, Richard, and Michael Wallace, eds. *American Violence: A Documentary History.* New York: Vintage Books, 1970. Provides a wealth of primary materials (original documents) describing various kinds of violence throughout American history.

Kleck, Gary. *Point Blank: Guns and Violence in America.* New York: Aldine de Gruyter, 1991. A thorough look at the major issues involving guns, gun control, and violence, including suggestions for a national weapons policy.

Newman, Katherine, Cybelle Fox, David Harding, Jal Mehta, and Wendy Roth. *Rampage: The Social Roots of School Shootings.* New York: Basic Books, 2004. An extensive investigation of school shootings, including various factors that help explain why students resort to such violence.

Raine, Nancy Venable. *After Silence: Rape and My Journey Back.* New York: Crown Publishers, 1998. A personal account of rape by a stranger who was never caught, detailing the reactions of police, family, and friends as the victim sought to cope with the trauma.

Scheper-Hughes, Nancy, and Phillipe I. Bourgois, eds. *Violence in War and Peace: An Anthology.* Malden, MA: Blackwell, 2004. Two anthropologists put together a collection of essays that explore social, literary, and philosophical theories of violence, ranging from violence in everyday life to genocide to war.

chapter 5 review

subculture

CLICK TO SEE DEFINITION

Online Learning Center Web site

An innovative, book-specific Web site featuring unique interactive exercises that give students the opportunity to explore some of the most compelling issues faced by today's families. The Web site also features PowerWeb, online access to articles from the popular and scholarly press, weekly updates, daily newsfeeds, a search engine, and more. All this material—plus flashcards that can be used to master vocabulary and a wealth of other review materials—is organized by chapter for ease of use in studying for exams or writing papers.

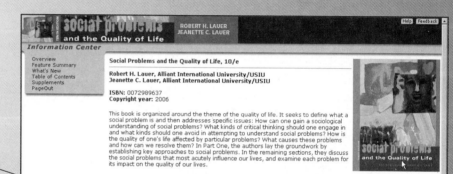

subculture

CLICK TO SEE DEFINITION

a group within a society that shares much of the larger society while maintaining certain distinctive cultural elements of its own

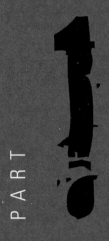

Foundations

1 | **Understanding Social Problems**

A Chinese philosopher remarked that one should not attempt to open clams with a crowbar. In other words, any task demands the proper tools. Part 1 of this book is about the proper tools for the study of social problems. What kind of perspective should you bring to the study? What kind of information do you need, and what are the proper ways to gather it? Unless you answer such questions appropriately, you cannot answer the vexing question of how to deal with social problems. This part, then, prepares you to delve into particular problems. It shows you how to use the proper tools to open the "clams."

Understanding Social Problems

"Why Is It My Fault?"

Marie, her husband Jim, and their two children had a good life until he lost his job. Stress built up, their marriage fell apart, and he moved to another state. Marie's life has never been the same:

I've never gotten any financial help from Jim since we were divorced. I went to work. It was really hard, raising two kids by myself and working full-time. But we were making it. And I enjoyed working—having people tell me I was doing a good job. Then the company downsized and I was laid off. It's been awful since then.

For the first time in my life, I know what it's like to be poor. I know what it's like to try to get help from the government. And you know one of the worst things? It's feeling ashamed. It's feeling like for some reason it's my fault, like there's something I could have done to avoid it. Why is this my fault? I keep telling myself I shouldn't feel that way, but I can't help it.

Introduction

Who is at fault if you are poor? Are you responsible because you are lazy and unwilling to work or because you are a spendthrift and refuse to properly manage your finances? If so, you have a personal problem. Or are there other factors such as the state of the economy that are responsible for your situation? If so, you are caught up in a social problem. Later in this chapter we will define social problems precisely. As a preliminary definition, however, think of social problems as behaviors or conditions that are caused by factors external to individuals and that detract from the quality of life.

Actually, "we are all part of some social problem" (Lopata 1984:249). In fact, we are all part of the biggest social problem of all—the race to save the planet (Brown 2000). These assertions will become increasingly clear in subsequent chapters. In addition, many individuals are wrestling with several problems at once. For example, the stress of poverty may lead to health problems, both mental and physical. If the impoverished individual is a woman or a minority, the stress may be intensified. The individual also may have to deal with unemployment or underemployment, poor performance at school by a child, and the threat of victimization by criminals. Indeed, social workers deal with families who are coping simultaneously with the majority of problems discussed in this book!

It is important, therefore, to understand the difference between social and personal problems. Americans tend to turn social problems into personal problems and to deal with them by trying to identify *who is at fault.* So your first task in this chapter is to understand the distinction between personal and social problems as well as the difference it makes when a particular problem is defined as personal or as social.

We also look at the sociological approach and explain a model for understanding problems as *social* rather than *personal.* Finally, we discuss two important tools of analysis for social problems—critical thinking skills and methods of research.

Personal versus Social Problems

personal problem
a problem that can be explained in terms of the qualities of the individual

social problem
a condition or pattern of behavior that contradicts some other condition or pattern of behavior; is defined as incompatible with the desired quality of life; is caused, facilitated, or prolonged by social factors; involves intergroup conflict; and requires social action for resolution

institution
a collective pattern of dealing with a basic social function; typical institutions identified by sociologists are the government, economy, education, family and marriage, religion, and the media.

We define a **personal problem** as one whose causes and solutions lie within the individual and his or her immediate environment. A **social problem,** on the other hand, is one whose causes and solutions lie outside the individual and the immediate environment. This distinction is not based on the individual's experience of suffering, because a certain amount of suffering may occur in either case.

C. Wright Mills (1959:8–9) made a similar distinction, calling personal problems the "personal troubles of milieu" and social problems the "public issues of social structure." He offered many illustrations of the difference between the two. If one individual in a city is unemployed, that individual has a personal trouble. The person may have personality problems, may lack skills, or may have family difficulties that consume all of his or her energy. But if there are 100 million jobs in a society and 150 million people are available for work, this is a public issue. Even without personal problems, a third of the people will be unemployed. Such a problem, thus, cannot be resolved solely by dealing with individual personalities or motivations.

Similarly, a man and woman may have personal troubles in their marriage. They may agonize over their troubles and ultimately separate or divorce. If theirs is one of few marriages that experience such problems, you may conclude that they have personal problems and their marriage broke up because of some flaw in their personalities or in their relationship. But when the divorce rate soars and millions of families are broken up, you must look for causes and solutions beyond the personalities of individuals. The question is no longer "What is wrong with those people?" but "What has happened to the **institution** of marriage and the family in our society?"

Whether you define a problem as social or as personal, then, is crucial. The distinction determines how you perceive the causes of the problem, the consequences of the problem, and *appropriate ways* to cope with the problem.

The Causes of Problems

When asked why there is poverty in affluent America, a 31-year-old female bank teller said the poor themselves are to blame because most of them "are lazy and unreliable . . . and the little money they do make is spent on liquor and nonnecessities rather than for their economic advancement" (Lauer 1971:8). This is a common approach, namely, that problems are personal. *The victim is blamed as both the source and the solution of the problem.*

Similarly, African Americans are said to have problems because they don't work to advance themselves. If you accept such an individualistic explanation, you are not likely to support government programs designed to raise the status of African Americans. Polls show that while a majority of whites agree that racial minorities have equal job opportunities, 82 percent of African Americans and 62 percent of Hispanics say they do *not* have equal opportunities (Polling Report 2007). It's understandable, therefore, that 44 percent of whites but 70 percent of African Americans and 63 percent of Hispanics favor affirmative action programs to help racial minorities. Thus, the way problems are defined—as social or personal—has important consequences for identifying causes. In turn, the kind of causes identified affects the way problems are handled.

A word of caution is in order here. We are not arguing that *all* problems are social problems, nor that personal problems have no social factors, nor that social problems are free of any personal elements. There are certainly psychological and, in some cases, physiological factors at work. The point is that if you do not look beyond such factors, you will have a distorted view about the causes of problems.

The Consequences of Problems

Viewing a problem as either personal or social leads you to identify very different consequences as well as different causes. Consider, for example, a father who can obtain only occasional work and whose family, therefore, lives in poverty. If the man defines his problem as the result of his own inadequacies, he likely will despise himself and passively accept his poverty. Sennett and Cobb (1972:96) told of a nearly illiterate garbage collector who placed the blame for his lowly position entirely on himself: "Look, I know it's nobody's fault but mine that I got stuck here where I am, I mean . . . if I wasn't such a dumb— . . . no, it ain't that neither . . . if I'd applied myself, I know I got it in me to be different, can't say anyone did it to me." This man defined his problem as personal and, consequently, viewed himself as inadequate.

The *sense of inadequacy*—blaming or downgrading oneself—is not uncommon among those victimized by social problems. Some children who grow up in impoverished homes view themselves unfavorably, believing that their impoverishment is proof of their inferiority. Some women who are beaten by their husbands feel they have done something to deserve the abuse. Some people who lose their jobs during an economic crunch believe they are failures even though they had no control over what happened.

If a problem is defined as personal, *individual strategies* are employed to cope with the problem. Thus, the individual looks inward for a solution. Sometimes that solution is found in an *escape mechanism,* such as neurosis, physical illness, heavy drinking, or self-destructive behavior. At other times a solution is sought from specialists such as psychotherapists or religious advisors who help the person to change. These specialists may facilitate adjustment to the problem but not ultimately resolve it. If America's troubled families sought the help of counselors, they might learn to cope

FIGURE 1.1
Some Possible Differences When a Problem—Rape in This Case—Is Defined as Social or Personal.

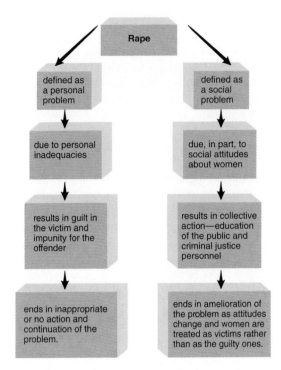

with or endure their troubles. But troubled families would continue to appear just as frequently.

Helping individuals deal with personal problems is important; however, it is only a stopgap approach to social problems. Identifying something as a social problem presents it from a much different perspective and leads to far different conclusions and actions. Thus, if a man defines his poverty as the result of a declining economy, he may join in collective action such as a social movement, a rent strike group, or an organization set up to relieve the plight of the poor. Rather than blame himself for his poverty, he sees it as a *social* problem and takes action to redress it.

Or consider the problem of rape. Whether rape is defined as a social or personal problem makes a great deal of difference (figure 1.1). Defining it as a personal problem either *blames the victim or castigates the offender.* Defining it as a social problem recognizes the need for *collective action* that attacks factors outside the individual.

Several cases of rape (as reported in the news media) illustrate the need to consider it a social rather than a purely personal problem. A physician, 39 years old, married, and the father of two children, confessed to raping 22 women and sexually attacking at least 10 other women, one of whom was a nun. The doctor was a respected member of his community by day but an attacker of women by night. A teenage girl, who decided to follow others and cool off in a park fountain on a hot July day, was raped by two young men while at least three adults ignored her screams for help. Another young woman met a man at a New Year's Eve party. The man's sister, whom the young woman knew, introduced them. The man drove the two women home, dropped his sister off first, then asked if he could come up to the young woman's apartment for coffee. He was a genial, polite man, and since she had no reason to suspect him, she agreed. Once in her apartment, however, the man forced her to participate in various sex acts. When she prosecuted, she discovered that the man was on parole for a prior rape conviction. Yet people who had been at the party testified on the man's behalf, claiming that they had seen the couple talking and that the woman had been drinking. The man was acquitted. Subsequently he was brought to trial again for the alleged rape of a 13-year-old girl.

How can we account for these rapes? Were the victims at fault in the preceding cases? Did they bring it on themselves by luring their attackers? A female student told us, "My father always said that if a woman was raped, it was her fault, that she somehow provoked the guy to do it." Or can the rapes be attributed to mentally ill or evil males? Are the rapists "sick" individuals who need therapy? Or are they evil men who ought to be castrated? You can blame the victims and say that they have personal problems—their wayward behavior. Or you can accuse the rapists of having personal problems—disturbed or evil natures. Neither will resolve the problem. Women who fight, scream, and risk their physical well-being (and even their lives) to ward off an attacker can hardly be said to be luring the man—and there was no evidence that the attackers were mentally ill.

Nor would castration solve the problem. Contrary to popular belief, castration does not prevent a man from having sexual relations. Castration has been used in a number of European countries to punish sex offenders (Incrocci et al. 2002); but of 39 offenders in West Germany who had voluntarily agreed to castration, 11 could still have sexual relations a number of years afterward, and four of the men had sex one to three times a week (Heim 1981).

Rape, in sum, is not a personal problem that can be solved by individual efforts. Like other social problems, rape requires collective action to attack such things as the social attitudes that legitimate exploiting women and a legal system that may treat the victim as harshly as the rapist does. Important differences, thus, result from defining a problem as social rather than personal. Unless problems like rape are defined as social, causes may not be identified nor solutions found.

A Model for Understanding

Given that problems are social and not merely personal, how do we go about understanding them? First let's define precisely what we mean by a *social problem:* It is *a condition or pattern of behavior that (1) contradicts some other condition or pattern of behavior and is defined as incompatible with the desired quality of life; (2) is caused, facilitated, or prolonged by factors that operate at multiple levels of social life; (3) involves intergroup conflict; and (4) requires social action to be resolved.* We explain this definition in the following pages. It uses major insights of sociological theories and is the basis for the model we use in discussing each of the problems in this book.

A Theory-Based Model

There are three major theoretical perspectives in sociology: **structural functionalism, conflict theory,** and **symbolic interactionism.** Each theory has distinctive emphases that are useful for understanding social phenomena. Structural functionalism focuses on social systems and the way in which their interdependent parts maintain order. Conflict theory focuses on contradictory interests of groups, inequalities in society, and the resulting conflict and change. Symbolic interactionism focuses on the **interaction** between individuals, the importance of knowing individuals' perspectives to understand their behavior, and the ways in which social life is constructed through interaction.

structural functionalism
a sociological theory that focuses on social systems and how their interdependent parts maintain order

conflict theory
a theory that focuses on contradictory interests, inequalities between social groups, and the resulting conflict and change

symbolic interactionism
a sociological theory that focuses on the interaction between individuals, the individual's perception of situations, and the ways in which social life is constructed through interaction

interaction
reciprocally influenced behavior on the part of two or more people

	Structural Functionalism	Conflict Theory	Symbolic Interaction
Assumptions of the theory	Society is an integrated system of interdependent parts, bound together by shared values and norms.	Society is a system of diverse groups, with conflicting values and interests, vying with each other for power, wealth, and other valued resources.	Society is an arena of interacting individuals who behave in accord with their definitions of situations and who create shared meanings as they interact.
How the theory might explain social problems generally	Problems arise out of social disorganization, a state in which consensus about norms has broken down.	Problems are the result of dominance over, and exploitation of, some groups by others.	A situation or form of behavior becomes a problem when people define it as such.
How the theory might explain poverty	Political, economic, and educational institutions are not functioning adequately (often because of rapid social change), so that old arrangements are obsolete before new arrangements are in place.	The upper and middle classes oppress and exploit the poor through such things as using political and economic institutions for their own benefit and creating ideologies that blame the poor and justify their poverty.	Poverty in the U.S. became a social problem when people accepted the influential media's definition of it as such; people remain poor when they define their poverty as the result of their own deficiencies.
Illustration of the explanation	Schools train increasing numbers of students for jobs that are diminishing in number as firms adjust to the changing global economy and "outsource" many of those jobs.	Upper- and middle-class lawmakers regularly support corporate welfare (e.g., subsidies and tax breaks) but reject such welfare ideas for the poor as a guaranteed minimum annual income.	The public did not consider poverty as a social problem until the publication of Michael Harrington's influential book *The Other America* in 1962.

FIGURE 1.2   Theoretical Explanations of Poverty.

To illustrate these three approaches, consider the problem of crime. A structural-functional approach would point out the way that rapid change has weakened social solidarity and social institutions like the family, so that insufficient order is maintained. A conflict approach would note that the powerful groups in society define the kind of behavior that is crime (resulting in higher rates among the poor), and that much crime results from the lack of opportunities for the poor and for racial or ethnic minorities. A symbolic interactionist approach would stress the fact that people learn criminal behavior by interacting with, and accepting for themselves the perspective of, others who approve of such behavior. Figure 1.2 briefly summarizes the theories, how they are used to understand social problems, and how they can be applied to another problem—poverty.

Some sociologists use only one of the theoretical approaches to analyze social problems. We believe that all three approaches are necessary. Each of the theoretical approaches to crime is valid. Our model, therefore, incorporates emphases of each perspective (figure 1.3). In essence, the model posits mutual influence between social structural factors, social psychological/cognitive factors, and social interaction. Social problems arise when people define **contradictions** among these various elements as incompatible with their quality of life.

contradiction
opposing phenomena within the same social system

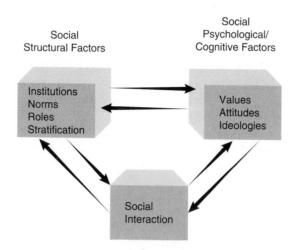

Social Structural Factors

Social Psychological/ Cognitive Factors

Institutions
Norms
Roles
Stratification

Values
Attitudes
Ideologies

Social
Interaction

FIGURE 1.3
A Model for the Analysis of Social Problems.

Each of the three theories contributes to this model. In structural functionalism, a problem involves a system of interdependent parts, including institutions (collective means of dealing with basic social functions such as government, the family, and the economy), **norms** (shared expectations about behavior), **roles** (behavior associated with particular positions in the social structure), and **values** (things preferred because they are defined as having worth). The parts are interrelated and exert pressure to maintain the system.

According to conflict theory, however, contradictions and inequalities exist between the parts of the system that generate conflict between groups. This is manifest in the **stratification system,** the pattern of inequality of wealth, power, and prestige that exists in all societies.

And according to symbolic interactionism, social interaction and the perspectives of individuals, including their **attitudes** (predispositions of individuals toward something) and **ideologies** (sets of ideas that explain or justify some aspect of social life) are important components of the system. Only as you understand how an individual perceives his or her social world can you understand that individual's behavior.

The pairs of arrows in the model indicate *mutual influence.* For example, social structural factors affect the way people interact. Norms and roles may lead a white person and a black person to treat each other as equals at the factory but not in other settings. The influence can go both ways: patterns of social interaction can alter the social structural factors. In recent years, for instance, women have interacted with men in ways that have altered the female role. Similarly, African Americans have persisted in interacting with whites in ways that have changed traditional roles. An ideology of white supremacy can help to create and maintain blacks in a subservient role; but as minorities refuse to accept the role and assume instead the same kinds of roles as whites, the ideology will be rejected by increasing numbers of people.

By the very nature of social life, there are numerous *contradictions* among the elements in figure 1.3. This means that opposing phenomena exist within the same social system. The phenomena are opposed in the sense that both cannot be true or operative. When the contradictions are defined as incompatible with the *desired quality of life,* you have a social problem. For example, the limited opportunities available in the economy are a contradiction to the ideology that all people should support themselves

norm
shared expectations about behavior

role
the behavior associated with a particular position in the social structure

values
things preferred because they are defined as having worth

stratification system
arrangement of society into groups that are unequal with regard to such valued resources as wealth, power, and prestige

attitude
a predisposition about something in one's environment

ideology
a set of ideas that explain or justify some aspect of social reality

by working. The contradiction, as we shall see in chapter 6, is incompatible with the desired quality of life of the poor.

By our definition, not all societal contradictions signal social problems, only those defined as detracting from the quality of life. In other words, objective data alone do not compose a problem. In accord with symbolic interactionism, only when people define a situation as problematic and persuade others to view it in the same way is there a social problem (Fine 2000). For instance, religion tends to be a unifying force, proclaiming a duty to love, make peace, and establish brotherhood. Recent terrorist acts by Islamic extremists and religious conflict in various nations contradict this peaceful role. Still, religion generally is not considered a social problem by most observers.

Whether people generally define something as detracting from their quality of life depends upon such things as how the problem is presented in the media, how the problem squares with people's experiences, how readily people can understand the various facets of the problem, and how political leaders shape public opinion on issues (Hawdon 2001; Sacco 2003).

Finally, consider gender equality as another example of the usefulness of the model. Among the opposing phenomena involved in the problem are:

1. The *ideology* of equal opportunity versus the *reality* of limited opportunities for **female participation in the economy.**
2. The *value* of the pursuit of happiness versus the *narrowness* of the traditional female *role.*
3. The *value* of human dignity versus male-female *interaction* in which females are treated as intellectual inferiors.

Each of these oppositions has consequences that are incompatible with the desired quality of life of many women.

Quality of Life

What is this *quality of life* that plays so prominent a role in determining whether a contradiction is defined as a social problem? Thoreau captured its meaning in his desire to avoid discovering, at the point of death, that

> I had not lived. I did not wish to live what was not life, living is so dear; nor did I wish to practise resignation, unless it was quite necessary. I wanted to live deep and suck out all the marrow of life. (Thoreau 1968:113)

The desire to "live deep," to maximize the quality of life, is reflected in a proliferation of studies in recent decades. In quality-of-life studies, cities and states are evaluated in terms of such aspects as equality of opportunity, agriculture, crime rates, technology, education, climate, the economy, cultural opportunities, and health and welfare. They are then ranked according to their overall "quality of life."

After decades of these studies, there is considerable agreement about what Americans define as important to the quality of their lives (Ferriss 2000). In essence, they evaluate their quality of life according to how well they are doing financially, physically, emotionally, socially, and culturally. Americans want well-paying and meaningful work and financial security. They want good health, access to good health care facilities, opportunity for a good education, opportunity to participate in cultural activities, and opportunity to live and work in areas with minimal crime. Americans also want respect from others, self-respect, and a sense of personal worth. Finally, they want to live without fear and with reasonable freedom from stress.

To the extent that these things are missing, Americans perceive the quality of life to be diminished. Thus, the quality of life is reduced by such issues as personal health problems (Woodruff and Conway 1992; Alonso et al. 2004), work demands that interfere with nonworking time (Rice, Frone, and McFarlin 1992), and environmental problems (Tickell 1992).

Americans are not unique in their view of what constitutes a high quality of life. Studies of other nations show that people everywhere value many of the same things that Americans do (Ventegodt et al. 2005; Liu 2006). Quality of life, then, involves far more than income. You may be able to purchase security devices for your home, but you can't buy total peace of mind when the newspapers regularly remind you of the pervasiveness of crime. You may be able to afford the best seats in the house, but that's meaningless if your community lacks cultural opportunities. You may live in the most expensive area available, but you can't shut out the polluted air that engulfs your property.

Moreover, undesirable conditions that diminish the quality of life affect you both directly and indirectly. For example, some people are the direct victims of criminal activity: assaults, muggings, robberies, rapes, swindles, and so forth. But everyone has some *fear of criminal victimization,* even people who have never been directly victimized. This fear may put limits on where they go or what they do or how secure they feel—limits that reduce the quality of their lives.

In sum, there are numerous contradictions in society that create conditions incompatible with the desired quality of life. Everyone is affected, though some suffer far more than others. Because of the diminished quality of life, we define these contradictions and the conditions they create as *social problems.*

Multiple Levels of Social Problems

Social problems are manifested at *multiple levels of social life.* The factors that cause, facilitate, and help to perpetuate social problems are found at the individual level (e.g., attitudes), group levels (e.g., ideologies of terrorist groups), societal levels (e.g., the government), and in some cases, global levels (e.g., globalization of the economy).

Think, for example, about the problem of racial and ethnic relations (for brevity's sake, we shall refer to this problem by the commonly used phrase "race problem," though the "problem" is not race per se, but the relationships between people of diverse racial and ethnic backgrounds). We could analyze the problem in terms of a stratification system in which racial minorities are disadvantaged, kept in inferior roles, and systematically subjected to discrimination. Such arrangements restrict interaction between the races and justify prejudice and claims that the disadvantaged group is naturally inferior.

Or we could analyze the problem in terms of attitudes of prejudice combined with a value of individualism (meaning that the government should not force people to interact with other races). Add to this an ideology that defines the oppressed race as inferior and therefore deserving of an inferior position. These values, attitudes, and ideology explain and perpetuate a structure where the oppressed race remains in the least desirable roles, institutional positions, and socioeconomic stratum. Furthermore, interaction between the races is restricted, permitting little opportunity for reevaluation and change.

The point is, as our model indicates, *mutual influence* exists among the various factors at differing levels of social life. Prejudice restricts interaction and restricted

Multiple factors, including roles and attitudes, enter into social problems.

interaction fosters prejudice. The two feed on each other. Similarly, education can be structured in such a way as to deprive minorities of adequate learning, thereby justifying an ideology of racial inferiority; but the ideology can also justify inaction in securing adequate education for minorities.

The multiple-level factors, in sum, work together to maintain the problem. Meantime, inequalities in the system lead people to act in their own behalf to bring about change; and interaction is never so confined as to prevent the development of new values, attitudes, and ideologies. Eventually, there may be changes in interaction patterns and in the social structure.

The pressure to change may arise as members of the oppressed race react to the contradiction between an ideology of the free pursuit of happiness and the realities of their situation. They may use the ideology and the contradiction to shape new attitudes and values among the oppressed and the oppressors. They may create new ideologies, such as a myth of their own superiority. They may strive to alter patterns of interaction and elements of the social structure. They may try to change the content of education, the power structure of government, and the practices and policies of the economy.

Thus, understanding and dealing with a social problem is never a simple matter. A social problem cannot be reduced to one thing, such as the race problem's being due merely to prejudice or poverty's being due merely to people's failure to work. All the factors in our model enter into each problem.

Social Action for Resolution

Social problems often give rise to *protest groups* and intergroup conflict as expressions of social action. Protest groups arise because not everyone in the society defines a particular situation the same way. For example, the contradiction between the ideals of American life and the reality of life for most African Americans is not defined by all Americans as incompatible with the quality of life. Some deny that African Americans have less access than whites to the desirable aspects of American life. In other words, they deny the existence of a contradiction.

If all Americans denied the contradiction, there would be no racial problem in this country (even though a foreign observer might see the contradiction). On the other hand, if all Americans affirmed the contradiction and demanded change, the problem might be quickly resolved. Because the contradiction is defined differently by different collectivities, intergroup conflict plays a part in resolving social problems.

We use the term *collectivity* here in reference to members of opposing groups in the conflict who agree on particular issues. The race problem, for example, is not simply a matter of white versus minority. The abortion problem is not just a case of Catholics versus Protestants. Gender inequality is not simply men versus women. Poverty is not merely rich versus poor. In each case there are members of both groups on either side of the issue.

All social problems are characterized by opposing groups with differing ideologies and contrary definitions of the contradiction. One side will argue that the contradiction is incompatible with the desired quality of their lives, while the other side will argue that there is no contradiction, that the contradiction is necessary, or that the contradiction exists but is not rooted in the social system (in other words, the victims of the contradictions are blamed for their plight). Such conflict is the context in which efforts to resolve problems take place.

In subsequent chapters we discuss the ways in which problems may be attacked by social action (both public policy and private action). There are many reasons why resolution of most social problems through social action are slow and agonizing: problems are manifested at multiple levels of social reality; numerous factors are involved in causing and maintaining problems; intergroup conflict surrounds most problems; and efforts to resolve a problem may ameliorate one problem but create new problems (Fine 2006).

The Changing Nature of Social Problems

One additional factor adds to the difficulty of resolving social problems—both the definition and the objective aspects of a particular problem change over time. Sometimes the change may be so rapid that an issue barely has time to be a problem. Until the exceptionally hot and dry summer of 1988, the public did not respond much to the warnings of scientists about global warming (Ungar 1992). That summer brought the problem to the public's attention. When the summer passed, the problem's importance waned in the public mind as other issues rose to the fore.

Thus, problems may *rise and decline in perceived importance,* as illustrated by the problem of poverty. Views of poverty have changed over time. A 1952 edition of a social problems text omitted the two chapters on poverty that had appeared in the original 1942 edition (Reinhardt, Meadows, and Gillette 1952). The omission reflected the belief in the 1950s that poverty was largely a problem of the past. (Even the 1942 edition reflected more the opinion of sociologists than that of the public.) Gallup opinion polls about the most important problems facing the nation, taken since November 1935, show that the public did not consider poverty an important problem until 1965 (Lauer 1976). Concerns about poverty peaked in the 1960s and 1970s. By 2006, concern about the poor had diminished. More people rated national defense, education, the economy, Medicare, crime, health care, energy, and the environment as problems that should be a "top priority" of the government than did those rating poverty as a top priority (Polling Report 2007).

The objective conditions of poverty also have changed over time: the amount of poverty has changed (as measured by some standard such as family income); the composition of the poor has changed (such as the relative proportions of racial, ethnic, and age groups); and the organization of antipoverty efforts has changed (such as the vigor and focus of protest groups and official attitudes and programs).

Recognizing such changes in problems is important for both understanding and action. For example, many people continue to identify poverty as essentially a problem of work—the poor are unemployed. As you will see, the problem of poverty would be little changed even if every able-bodied person in America had a job. It is true that during the depression of the 1930s a considerable number of the impoverished were unemployed. Many people who lived through that period continue to associate poverty with unemployment, failing to recognize the changed nature of the problem. Today, a large number of poor people are working but still live in poverty. Therefore, to continue associating the two concepts is to misunderstand the contemporary problem and thereby fail to take appropriate action.

As you study the various problems, you will see fluctuations in all of them. Some appear to be getting better, and some appear to be getting worse. It is important to remember that improvement does not mean that the problem is resolved (gains can be quickly lost in the ongoing struggle for justice and equality), nor does deterioration mean that the problem is hopeless (lost ground may be regained and new ground may be gained dramatically when appropriate social action is taken).

Analyzing Social Problems

The definition of the term "social problems" that we presented earlier in this chapter shapes our approach to each problem considered in this book. First, we "get the feel" of the problem by seeing how it affects people's lives and examining how the problem involves a contradiction and is defined as incompatible with the desired quality of life. Second, we analyze the multiple-level factors involved in the problem. We do not relate every factor identified in figure 1.3 to each problem: Research has not yet identified the components of every problem. Yet in each we see the multiple-level components that show how the problem arises and is perpetuated. Third, we consider various ways to attack the problem. Our examination is sketchy (any adequate treatment would require a book in itself), but we do discuss some kinds of both public policy and private action that can ameliorate each problem.

Before we turn to specific problems, we need to address an additional issue. Seemingly reasonable statements are made about every social problem. For example, following the series of highly publicized killings by preteens and teenagers in the 1990s, explanations ranged from the pampering of criminals by the legal system to violence in video games and movies to mental illness. How do you know which of these explanations, if any, are correct? Or to put it another way, how do you distinguish opinion from valid analysis?

critical thinking
the analysis and evaluation
of information

First, you need to *develop critical thinking skills*. **Critical thinking** is the process of carefully attending to spoken or written information in order to evaluate its validity. Make sure you understand the information, then evaluate it by asking such questions as whether it is logical and reasonable. One important way to evaluate information is to look for *any fallacies of thinking*. These fallacies are commonly used when people analyze social problems. You will find illustrations throughout this book on how fallacies lead to misunderstandings.

Second, you need to examine how sociologists research social problems by gathering data to test various explanations. The data may lead you to revise your explanations. Remember, the study of social problems is not an exercise in speculation; it needs explanations that are supported by evidence. Let's look, then, at fallacious ways of thinking and at methods of social research.

Critical Thinking: Recognizing Fallacies

Nine different fallacies have been used to analyze social problems. An important aspect of critical thinking is the ability to recognize these fallacies. This ability enables you not only to assess the validity of information and arguments presented by others but also to make your own analyses with logic and clarity.

Fallacy of Dramatic Instance

The **fallacy of dramatic instance** refers to the tendency to *overgeneralize,* to use one, two, or three cases to support an entire argument. This mistake is common among people who discuss social problems. It may be difficult to counter because the limited number of cases often are a part of an *individual's personal experience.* For example, in discussing the racial problem in the United States, a man said to us: "Blacks in this country can make it just as much as whites. I know a black businessman who is making a million. In fact, he has a better house and a better car than I have." We pointed out that this successful businessperson is an exception. The man dismissed the point: "If one guy can make it, they all can." The fallacy of dramatic instance mistakes a few cases for a general situation.

> **fallacy of dramatic instance**
> overgeneralizing

This fallacy is difficult to deal with because the argument is based partly on fact. There are, after all, African Americans who are millionaires. Does this mean there is no discrimination and that any black person can attain success? To use another example, many Americans believe that welfare recipients are "ripping off" the rest of us, that we are subsidizing their unwillingness to work and supporting them at a higher standard of living than we ourselves enjoy. Is this true? Yes, in a few cases. Occasionally, newspapers report instances of individuals making fraudulent use of welfare. But does this mean that most welfare recipients are doing the same? Do people on welfare really live better than people who work for a living?

The point is, in studying social problems, you must recognize that exceptions always exist. To use such cases in support of your argument is to fall into the trap of the fallacy of dramatic instance, because social problems deal with general situations rather than with individual exceptions.

As this fallacy suggests, the fact that you hear about a lazy poor person or a rich African American or a corrupt politician does not mean that such cases represent the typical situation. Millions of people are involved in the problems of poverty, race, and government. *Systematic studies* are needed to determine whether the one or two cases you know about represent the norm or the exception. For instance, the fact that there are black and Hispanic millionaires may be less important than the fact that in 2005 the median annual per-capita income for non-Hispanic whites was $25,036, while the amount for African Americans was $16,874 and for Hispanics was $14,483 (DeNavas-Walt, Proctor, and Lee 2006:7). And over the three years from 2003 to 2005, 8.4 percent of non-Hispanic whites were poor, compared to 24.7 percent of African Americans and 22 percent of

Hispanics (DeNavas-Walt, Proctor, and Lee 2006:15). Such figures are more pertinent to the race problem than are cases that represent exceptions to the general pattern.

We are not saying that individual examples or cases are unimportant or unusable. At various points throughout this book (including the chapter opening vignettes) we use examples of people's experiences. These examples are not given as proof or even as evidence. Rather, we use them to *illustrate the impact of social problems on people's quality of life*. These examples may dramatize better than statistics the ways in which people's lives are adversely affected by social problems.

fallacy of retrospective determinism
the argument that things could not have worked out any other way than they did

Fallacy of Retrospective Determinism

The **fallacy of retrospective determinism** is the argument that things could not have worked out any other way than the way they did. It is a *deterministic* position, but the determinism is aimed at the past rather than the future. The fallacy asserts that what happened historically *had* to happen, and it *had* to happen just the way it did. If you accept this fallacy, the present social problems are inevitable. Whether the issue is racial discrimination, poverty, war, or the well-being of the family, the fallacy of retrospective determinism makes it unavoidable.

This fallacy is unfortunate for a number of reasons. History is more than a tale of *inevitable tragedies*. History is important for understanding social problems. You cannot fully understand the tensions between America's minority groups and the white majority unless you know about the decades of exploitation and humiliation preceding the emergence of the modern civil rights movement. Your understanding will remain clouded if you regard those events as nothing more than an inevitable process. Similarly, you cannot fully understand the tension between the People's Republic of China and the West if you view it only as a battle of economic ideologies. It is vital to know that the tension is based in the pillage and humiliation to which China was subjected by the West. Yet your understanding will not be enhanced by the study of history if you regard the Western oppression of China in the 19th century as inevitable.

If you view the past in terms of determinism, you have little reason to study it and are deprived of an important source of understanding. Furthermore, the fallacy of retrospective determinism is but a small step from the stoic *acceptance of the inevitable*. That is, if things are the way they have to be, why worry about them? Assuming that the future also is determined by forces beyond your control, you are left in a position of apathy: There is little point in trying to contest the inevitable.

Those who are born poor are likely to remain poor. Their poverty, however, is caused by social conditions, not fate.

This fallacy is probably less common in discussions about social problems than the fallacy of dramatic instance, but it does appear in everyday discussions. For example, in responding to the question about the causes of poverty in America, a 64-year-old service station owner told us: "Go back through history, it's traditional; there's no special reason, no cause for it. We can't get away from it. It has just always been this way." A businessman expressed a similar fatalism: "I don't actually know the cause of poverty, but it's here to stay and we must learn to live with it. We have to take the good with the bad."

An individual might view social problems in deterministic terms for reasons other than intellectual conviction. Determinism can relieve you of responsibility and can legitimate a lack of concern with efforts to effect changes you do not want. Whatever the basis for affirming determinism, the outcome is the same: You may as well accept the problem and learn to live with it, because it is inevitably and inextricably with you.

Fallacy of Misplaced Concreteness

Some people have a tendency to explain some social problems by resorting to **reification**—making what is abstract into something concrete. "Society," for example, is an abstraction. It is not like a person, an animal, or an object that can be touched. It is an idea, a way of thinking about a particular collectivity of people. Yet we often hear people assert that something is the fault of "society" or that "society" caused a certain problem. This is the **fallacy of misplaced concreteness.** In what sense can society "make" or "cause" or "do" anything? To say that society caused a problem leaves you helpless to correct the situation because you haven't the faintest notion where to begin. If, for example, society is the cause of juvenile delinquency, how do you tackle the problem? Must you change society? If so, how?

reification
defining what is abstract as something concrete

fallacy of misplaced concreteness
making something abstract into something concrete

The point is that "society" is an abstraction, a concept that refers to a group of people who interact in particular ways. To *attribute social problems to an abstraction* like "society" does not help resolve the problems. Sometimes people who attribute the cause of a particular problem to society intend to *deny individual responsibility.* To say that society causes delinquency may be a way of saying that the delinquent child is not responsible for his or her behavior.

You can recognize the social causes of problems without either attributing them to an abstraction like society or relieving the individual of responsibility for his or her behavior. For instance, you could talk about the family's role in delinquency. A family is a concrete phenomenon. Furthermore, you could say that the family itself is a victim of some kind of societal arrangement, such as government regulations that tend to perpetuate poverty, cause stress, and create disruption in many families. You could say that families can be helped by changing the government regulations that keep some of them in poverty and, thereby, facilitate delinquent behavior.

Society, in short, does not cause anything. Rather, problems are caused by that which the concept of society represents—people acting in accord with certain social arrangements and within a particular cultural system.

Fallacy of Personal Attack

A tactic among debaters is to attack the opponent *personally* when they can't support their position by reason, logic, or facts. This tactic diverts attention from the issue and focuses it on personality. We call this the **fallacy of personal attack** (philosophers call it *ad hominem*). It is remarkably effective in avoiding the use of reason or the consideration of evidence in discussing a social problem. In analyzing social problems, this

fallacy of personal attack
argument by attacking the opponent personally rather than dealing with the issue

fallacy can be used either to attack an opponent in a debate about a problem or to *attack the people who are the victims of the problem.* Ryan (1971) called this "blaming the victim" and said it involves nearly every problem in America.

Historically, the poor have suffered from this approach. Instead of offering sympathy or being concerned for the poor, people may label the poor as disreputable and, consequently, deserving of or responsible for their plight. People who are not poor are relieved of any responsibility. In fact, government efforts to alleviate poverty are even thought to contribute to the problem by taking away any incentive of the poor to help themselves, and leading them instead to become sexually promiscuous, irresponsible, and dependent on others (Somers and Block 2005).

The meaning and seriousness of any social problem may be sidestepped by attacking the intelligence or character of the victims or of those who call attention to the problem. A few of the labels that have been used illustrate how common this approach is: deadbeats, draft dodgers, niggers, kikes, bums, traitors, and perverts.

Fallacy of Appeal to Prejudice

fallacy of appeal to prejudice
argument by appealing to popular prejudices or passions

In addition to attacking the opponent, a debater may try to support an unreasonable position by using another technique: **fallacy of appeal to prejudice.** (Philosophers call it argument *ad populum.*) With this fallacy, debaters use popular prejudices or passions to convince others of the correctness of their position. When the topic is social problems, debaters use *popular slogans* or *popular myths* to sway people emotionally rather than using reasoning from systematic studies.

Some slogans or phrases persist for decades and are employed to oppose efforts to resolve social problems. "Creeping socialism" has been used to describe many government programs designed to aid the underdogs of society. The term is not used when the programs are designed to help business or industry, or when the affluent benefit from the programs. As someone remarked, "What the government does for me is progress; what it does for you is socialism."

In some cases, the slogans use general terms that reflect *traditional values.* Thus, the various advances made in civil rights legislation—voting, public accommodations, open housing—have been resisted in the name of the "rights of the individual." These slogans help to perpetuate the myth that legislation that benefits African Americans infringes on the constitutional rights of the white majority.

Myths, in turn, help to perpetuate social problems. In the absence of other evidence, people tend to rely upon popular notions. Many Americans continue to assume that rape is often the woman's fault because she has sexually provoked the man. These Americans either have seen no evidence to the contrary or have dismissed the evidence as invalid. Unfortunately, myths tend to become so deeply rooted in people's thinking that when people are confronted by new evidence, they have difficulty accepting it.

Myths are hard to break down, but if you want to understand social problems, you must abandon popular ideas and assumptions and resist popular slogans and prejudices that cloud your thinking. Instead, you must make judgments based on evidence.

Fallacy of Circular Reasoning

fallacy of circular reasoning
using conclusions to support the assumptions that were necessary to make the conclusions

The ancient Greek physician Galen praised the healing qualities of a certain clay by pointing out that all who drink the remedy recover quickly—except those whom it does not help. The latter die and are not helped by any medicine. Obviously, according to Galen, the clay fails only in incurable cases. This is an example of the **fallacy of**

circular reasoning: using conclusions to support the assumptions that were necessary to draw the conclusions.

Circular reasoning creeps into analyses of social problems. Someone might argue that Hispanics are inherently inferior and assert that their inferiority is evident because they hold only menial jobs and do not do intellectual work. In reply, you might point out that Hispanics are not doing more intellectual work because of discriminatory hiring practices. The person might then counter that Hispanics could not be hired for such jobs anyway because they are inferior.

Similarly, you might argue that homosexuals are sex perverts because they commonly have remained secretive about their sexual preference. But, we counter, the secrecy is due to the general disapproval of homosexuality. No, you reply, homosexuality is kept secret because it is a perversion. Thus, in circular reasoning people bounce *back and forth between assumptions and conclusions*. Circular reasoning leads nowhere in the search for an understanding of social problems.

Fallacy of Authority

Virtually everything you know is based on some authority. You know comparatively little from personal experience or personal research. The authority you necessarily rely on is someone else's experience, research, or belief. You accept notions of everything from the nature of the universe to the structure of the atom, from the state of international relationships to the doctrines of religion—all on the basis of some authority. Most people accept a war as legitimate on the authority of their political leaders. Many accept the validity of capital punishment on the authority of law enforcement officers. Some accept that use of contraceptives is morally wrong on religious authority. Most rely on the authority of the news media about the extent and severity of various problems.

The knowledge that you acquire through authority can be inaccurate and can exacerbate rather than resolve or ameliorate social problems. The **fallacy of authority** means an *illegitimate appeal to authority*. Such an appeal obtrudes into thinking about social problems in at least three ways.

First, the *authority may be ambiguous*. Thus, appeal is made to the Bible by both those who support and those who oppose capital punishment. Supporters of capital punishment point out that the Bible, particularly the Old Testament, decreed death for certain offenses. Opponents counter that the death penalty contradicts New Testament notions of Christian love. An appeal to this kind of authority, then, is really an appeal to a particular interpretation of the authority. Because the interpretations are contradictory, people must find other bases for making judgments.

Second, the *authority may be irrelevant to the problem*. The fact that a man is a first-rate physicist does not mean he can speak with legitimate authority about race relations. Most of us are impressed by people who have significant accomplishments in some area, but their accomplishments should not overwhelm us if those people speak about a problem outside their area of expertise.

Third, the *authority may be pursuing a bias* rather than studying a problem. To say that someone is pursuing a bias is not necessarily to disparage that person, because pursuing it may be part of a job. For example, military officers are likely to analyze the problem of war from a military rather than a moral, political, or economic perspective. This is their job—and this is why decisions about armaments, defense, and war should not be left solely to the military. From a military point of view, one way to prevent war

fallacy of authority
argument by an illegitimate appeal to authority

We rely on authorities for information, but authorities are not always right.

is to be prepared to counter an enemy attack. The nation must be militarily strong, according to this argument, so that other nations will hesitate to attack—and military strength requires the most sophisticated technology, a stockpile of weaponry, and a large, standing military force.

The shortcomings of this line of reasoning were dramatically illustrated by the incidents of September 11, 2001, when terrorists seized jetliners and crashed them into the World Trade Center towers in New York City and the Pentagon in Washington, D.C. At the time, the United States was clearly the strongest military power in the world. Nevertheless, the terrorists struck and they struck effectively. As we discuss in chapter 14, the notion of defending against enemies must now be reexamined in the light of a new face of war in the world.

Although some people pursue a bias as a normal part of their work, others pursue it because of *vested interests*. That is, the authority may deliberately or unconsciously allow biases to affect what he or she says because it is personally advantageous. The head of a corporation that builds private prisons and argues that the private sector can deal with prisoners more effectively than can the government will obviously benefit from public policy that privatizes state and federal prisons. The corporate executive who talks about federal overregulation would clearly benefit if the government withdrew from consumer protection programs. Political leaders credit their own policies when crime rates fall and point to uncontrollable circumstances when crime rates rise. Their policies may have no effect on crime rates, but they benefit if they can persuade people that their actions have lowered the rate or will do so in the future.

Finally, *the authority may simply be wrong*. This problem often occurs when one authority cites another. For example, in 2003, the Census Bureau issued a report on the foreign-born population of the United States (Schmidley 2003). The report showed the years of entry of the 32.5 million foreign-born people now living in the nation: 4.1 million came before 1970, 4.6 million came during the 1970s, 7.96 million came during the 1980s, and 15.8 million came after 1990. Suppose that we wanted information about immigration patterns, and we consulted newspapers instead of the Census Bureau. We examined three respectable sources and found the following interpretations of the report. A national financial paper said that the number of immigrants continued to grow at "a blistering pace." An urban newspaper reported that immigration continued at a steady pace during "the past two years." And a national newspaper claimed that the Census Bureau report stated that the number of foreign-born coming to live in the United States has "slowed considerably"! Clearly, when one authority cites another, it is best to check out the initial authority before drawing any conclusions.

Fallacy of Composition

That the whole is equal to the sum of its parts appears obvious. That what is true of the part is also true of the whole likewise seems to be a reasonable statement, but the former is debatable, and the latter is the **fallacy of composition.** As economists have illustrated, the notion that *what is valid for the part is also valid for the whole* is not necessarily true. Consider, for example, the relationship between work and income. If a farmer works hard and the weather is not adverse, the farmer's income may rise; but if every farmer works hard and the weather is favorable, and a bumper crop results, the total farm income may fall. The latter case is based upon supply and demand, while the former assumes that a particular farmer outperforms other farmers.

In thinking about social problems, *you cannot assume that what is true for the individual is also true for the group.* An individual may be able to resolve a problem insofar as it affects him or her, but that resolution is not available to all members of the group. For example, a man who is unemployed and living in poverty may find work that enables him to escape poverty. The work may require him to move or to work for less money than someone else, but still he is able to rise above poverty. As you will see in our discussion of poverty, however, that solution is not possible for most of the nation's poor. Thus, something may be true for a particular individual or even a few individuals and yet be inapplicable or counterproductive for the entire group of which the individuals are members.

fallacy of composition
the assertion that what is true of the part is necessarily true of the whole

Fallacy of Non Sequitur

A number of the fallacies already discussed involve non sequitur, but we look at this way of thinking separately because of its importance. Literally, non sequitur means *"it does not follow."* This **fallacy of non sequitur** is commonly found when people interpret statistical data.

For example, data may show that the amount of welfare payments by state governments has increased dramatically over the past few decades. What is the meaning of such data? You might conclude that the number of people unwilling to work has increased and that more and more "freeloaders" are living off the public treasury, but there are other explanations. The increase may reflect adjustments due to inflation, better efforts to get welfare money to eligible recipients, or a rise in unemployment due to governmental action to control inflation.

Daniel Bell (1960) showed how statistics on crime can be misleading. In New York one year, reported assaults were up 200 percent, robberies were up 400 percent, and burglaries were up 1,300 percent! Those were the "facts," but what did they mean? A crime wave? Actually, the larger figures reflected a new method of crime reporting that was more effective in determining the total amount of crime. An increase in reported

fallacy of non sequitur
something that does not follow logically from what has preceded it

HOW, AND HOW NOT, TO THINK

"Use it or lose it" is a common saying. We might paraphrase that and say "Use it and learn it." That is, one of the best ways to learn something is to use it and not simply to memorize it. For this involvement, therefore, we are asking you to learn the fallacies by using them.

Select any social problem in which you are interested. Show how people could use each of the fallacies to "explain" that problem. Construct nine different explanations that are one or two sentences long. Try to make your explanations sound reasonable. Test them by sharing them with someone and seeing how many you can get

the other person to accept. If the entire class participates in this project, gather in small groups and have each member share his or her explanations. Group members should then try to identify the fallacy in each of the explanations. Be sure not to present the fallacies in the order in which they appear in the book.

As an alternative, use simple observation to test the accuracy of common (or your own) notions about people involved in particular social problems. For instance, visit a gay bar. Or attend a meeting of gay activists, a feminist group, Alcoholics Anonymous, or an ecology group. Ask a number of people to describe the typical member of the group you visit, and compare their responses (and your own preconceptions) with your observations.

crime rates can mean different things, but it does not necessarily signify an actual increase in the amount of crime.

One other example involves studies of women who work. Some employers believe that women are not desirable workers because they are less committed to the job than men, as indicated by their higher turnover rate. Women do indeed have a higher rate of turnover than men. But what does this mean? Are women truly less committed to their jobs?

When you look at the situation more closely, you find that the real problem is that women tend to be concentrated in lower-level jobs. Also, women who quit a job tend to find another one quickly. Thus, women may be uncommitted to a particular low-level job but strongly committed to work. Furthermore, if you look at jobs with the same status, the turnover rate is no higher for women than men.

These illustrations are not meant to discourage you from drawing conclusions. Instead, they are reminders of the need for thorough study and the need to avoid quick conclusions, even when those conclusions seem logical on the surface. Contrary to popular opinion, *"facts" do not necessarily speak for themselves.* They must be interpreted in the light of the complexities of social life and with the awareness that a number of different conclusions can usually be drawn from any set of data.

Fallacies and the Mass Media

In subsequent chapters, we shall discuss how the mass media contribute to particular social problems. Here we want to point out how the media contribute to misunderstandings by committing or facilitating the various fallacies.

In some cases, the media may inadvertently create fallacious thinking by the way something is reported. For instance, a newspaper story about someone who is guilty of welfare fraud, which omits the fact that such fraud represents only a tiny minority of recipients, can lead readers to commit the fallacy of the dramatic instance: The story proves that those on welfare are cheats who want handouts rather than responsibility. Or a story in a religious magazine about a formerly gay man who is now married to a woman, which omits any mention of the numerous gays who have tried and failed to change their sexual orientation, can lead readers to commit the fallacy of non sequitur: If one man can do it, they all can.

Because the media represent authority in the matter of information, they are particularly prone to the fallacy of authority. That is, they might provide information that is misleading or wrong. It may be a case of bias on the part of those gathering and/or presenting the information. It may be a case of misunderstanding the original source of the information. Or it may be a case of the original source itself being wrong. For example, in 2006 a survey commissioned by the American Medical Association found a startlingly high rate of binge drinking and unprotected sex on the part of female college students while on spring break (Rosenthal 2006). The study, reported widely on TV and in newspapers, was based on a "random sample." It turned out, however, that the sample was not random. Those who participated were volunteers, and only one-fourth of them had actually been on a spring break trip. In essence, then, no conclusions about college women in general could be drawn from the survey.

We do not intend to commit the fallacy of dramatic instance ourselves by suggesting that such incidents are typical or even very common. Rather, they illustrate the need to be alert, thoughtful, and cautious about the things you read and hear about social problems.

The Sources of Data: Social Research

The various "intellectual blind alleys" that we have described create and help to perpetuate myths about social problems. *Social research* is designed to gain information about social problems so that you can have a valid understanding of them and employ realistic efforts in resolving them.

Not everything called research is scientifically valid. Therefore, you need to use critical thinking skills as well as information and arguments to evaluate research. Some so-called social research aims to shape rather than gain information. For example, we once received a letter from a U.S. congressman inquiring about our attitudes toward labor unions. Actually, the letter attempted to shape information, and the questionnaire that accompanied it was designed to enlist support for the congressman's antiunion stance. The letter began by saying, "What will happen to your state and local taxes—your family's safety—and our American way of life, if the czars of organized labor have their way in the new Congress?" It used such phrases as "henchmen," "power hungry union professionals," "rip-offs which enrich the union fat cats at your expense," and "freedom from union tyranny." The questionnaire itself requested yes-or-no responses to questions such as "Do you feel that anyone should be forced to pay a union boss for permission to earn a living?" Clearly, this inquiry resorted to *the fallacies of personal attack and appeal to prejudice*. A critical-thinking approach would treat the results as little else than an illustration of people with biases against labor unions.

If you want to gain information and discover the nature of social reality, you must use scientific social research. Scientific research is both rational and *empirical*. That is, it is logical and comes to conclusions based on evidence rather than speculation or feelings. The stages of such research typically include a clear statement of the problem or issue to be researched; formulation of *hypotheses* so that the problem or issue is in researchable form; selection of the appropriate method, including the sample; collection of the data; analysis of the data; and interpretation and report of the conclusions.

A guiding principle throughout the foregoing stages is the desire to discover evidence, not to confirm preconceptions.

Many different methods are used in social research. We look at four methods that have yielded important information about social problems: survey research, statistical analysis of official records (particularly of government data), experiments, and participant observation.

Survey Research

survey
a method of research in which a sample of people are interviewed or given questionnaires in order to get data on some phenomenon

socioeconomic status
position in the social system based on economic resources, power, education, prestige, and lifestyle

variable
any trait or characteristic that varies in value or magnitude

The **survey** uses interviews and/or questionnaires to gain data about some phenomenon. The people from whom the information is gathered are normally a *sample* (a small number of people selected by various methods from a larger population) of a *population* (a group that is the focus of the study). The data include everything from attitudes about various matters to information such as gender, age, and **socioeconomic status.** You can learn two important aspects of social reality from surveys. First, you can discover the *distribution of people along some dimension*. For example, you can learn the proportion of people who say they will vote Republican or Democrat in an election; the proportion of people who favor, oppose, or are neutral about capital punishment; or the proportion of people who believe that homosexuals should be allowed to marry. Second, you can discover *relationships among* **variables.** (A *variable* is any trait or characteristic that varies in value or magnitude.) For instance, you can investigate the relationship between people's positions in the stratification system (socioeconomic status) and their attitudes toward the race problem, gender inequality, or the plight of the poor.

Survey research is probably the most common method used in sociology. Let's examine one piece of such research that deals with the problem of wife rape. The example illustrates both the technique of survey research and the kind of information that survey research can yield about a social problem.

Can a man rape his wife? In our experience, students have diverse opinions. Some believe that wife rape is as serious an offense against a woman as rape by a stranger. Others believe that rape makes no sense in the context of marriage, and they are supported by a long legal tradition. The so-called marital rape exemption goes back to 17th-century England, when Chief Justice Matthew Hale declared that a husband cannot be guilty of raping his wife "for by their mutual matrimonial consent and contract the wife hath given up herself in this kind unto the husband which she cannot retract" (quoted in Russell 1982:17). This decision was based on the idea that wives are property and that sex is a wife's duty. It was the prevailing legal guideline in the United States until the 1970s. In 1977, Oregon deleted the spouse-immunity clause from the rape statute, and a man was tried (though not convicted) for wife rape the next year.

Apart from public and legal opinions, is it reasonable to speak of wife rape? Does the wife suffer the same kinds of trauma as other rape victims? Diana Russell (1982) investigated the question of wife rape by surveying a random sample of 930 women in the San Francisco Bay area. ("Random" does not mean they were chosen at random, but that they were carefully selected using a method that gave every woman in the area an equal chance of being chosen.) She interviewed the 644 women who were or had been married. About 14 percent, or one in seven, told about "sexual assaults" by their husbands that could be classified as rape. The wives were raped by force, by the threat of force, and by their inability to consent to sexual intercourse because of being drugged, asleep, or somehow helpless. The forced sex included oral and anal sex as well as sexual intercourse.

Some of the women said their husbands threatened to beat them if they did not submit. Others said they were held down forcibly. In a few cases, weapons were used to intimidate them or they were beaten with fists or objects. Overall, 84 percent of the wives indicated that some kind of force was used. Pushing and pinning down were the most common kinds of force employed by the husbands, but 16 percent of the women said that their husbands hit, kicked, or slapped them, and 19 percent said they were beaten or slugged. About one out of 10 of the women pointed out, without being asked, that they had been injured during the attack, ranging from bruises to broken bones and concussions.

The husbands also made verbal threats and even used weapons: 13 percent of the husbands had guns and 1 percent had knives. Twenty-one percent threatened to kill their wives. These wives were obviously and understandably intimidated.

What about the argument that forced sex with one's husband cannot possibly be as traumatic as forced sex with a stranger? Russell compared the responses of her sample with those of women who had been raped by strangers; acquaintances; authority figures; and friends, dates, or lovers. In terms of the proportion of women who reported being "extremely upset" by the incident, the proportions were 65 percent of those raped by a relative other than the husband (usually a childhood rape), 61 percent of those raped by a stranger, 59 percent of those raped by a husband, 42 percent of those raped by an acquaintance, 41 percent of those raped by an authority figure, and 33 percent of those raped by a friend, date, or lover (Russell 1982). Further, the same percentage—52 percent—of women who were raped by their husbands and women who were raped by a relative other than the husband indicated "great long-term effects" on their lives, compared to 39 percent of those raped by a stranger, and smaller percentages of those involved in the other kinds of rape.

Clearly, wife rape is no less traumatic than other kinds of rape and is more traumatic than many kinds. Women who had been raped by their husbands suffered, among other effects, increased negative feelings toward their husbands and men generally; deterioration of the marriage (including divorce); changed behavior patterns (drinking more, or never remarrying if a divorce resulted); increased fear, anxiety, anger, or depression; and increased negative feelings about sex. Two of the raped women tried to commit suicide.

Russell's research has clear implications for dealing with the problem. Many states still have various forms of the marital rape exemption on their statute books. In some cases, a distinction is made between rape by a husband and rape by someone else, with the former being a less serious offense; but Russell's research shows that rape by a husband is a serious offense from the victim's point of view. Such research not only provides insight but also suggests realistic ways of resolving a problem.

Statistical Analysis of Official Records

Suppose you want to see how *self-esteem* enters into various social problems. For instance, you might want to see whether prejudice and discrimination affect the self-esteem of minorities, whether negative attitudes about growing old affect the self-esteem of the aged, or whether rapists or other offenders have low self-esteem. You could use a questionnaire to measure self-esteem, then compute the **mean** (average) scores of your respondents.

mean
the average

Let's say that the mean score of a random sample of offenders was 8.9 and the mean score of a random sample of average citizens of the same age, gender, and socioeconomic status was 10.2. The offenders have lower self-esteem. But is the difference between 8.9 and 10.2 a significant one? If not, how much difference would be required before you could say that it was significant—that is, before you could say with some confidence that the two groups differ in level of self-esteem?

test of significance
a statistical method for determining the probability that research findings occurred by chance

The question can be answered by using a **test of significance,** which is a technical way of determining the probability that your findings occurred by chance. That is, if the difference is not significant statistically, then you cannot say that offenders have a lower self-esteem than nonoffenders. A different set of samples might yield scores of 9.4 for both groups, or a slightly higher mean for offenders than for nonoffenders. If the difference is statistically significant, however, you can say with some confidence that offenders generally have lower self-esteem than nonoffenders.

We will not examine details of tests of significance; they require greater knowledge of statistics. Note, however, that many of the findings about social problems discussed in this book—whether gathered through survey research, experiment, or official records—have been subjected to statistical tests. This gives you confidence that the results reflect significant differences between the groups and, if the samples were adequate, that the results apply to more groups than the ones tested. Thus, you can make general statements about, say, women in America without having surveyed the majority of American women.

frequency distribution
the organization of data to show the number of times each item occurs

Some other questions can be asked about data gathered in research. For example, you might want to know how many of the offenders scored high, medium, and low in self-esteem. To get this information, you need a **frequency distribution,** which we use in subsequent chapters. The frequency distribution provides information not available in the mean.

As table 1.1 shows, you can have different frequency distributions with the same number of cases and the same mean. If the scores in the table represented thousands of income dollars of women in an organization, you would draw different conclusions about the women's economic well-being in the two cases even though the means were the same.

median
the score below which are half of the scores and above which are the other half

Another question that can be asked is, "What is the **median** score?" The median is the score below which half the scores fall and above which the other half fall. This furnishes important information for dealing with things such as income distribution. For instance, if A and B represent two communities in table 1.2, the mean incomes of the two are quite different. You might conclude that the people in community B are better off than those in community A. Actually, the median income is the same for both A and B, and the higher mean for B is due to the two families with very high incomes. Thus, *extreme figures* will affect the mean but not the median. When you find a big difference between the mean and the median, you know extremes are involved.

Statistical analysis is useful for several types of research. Suppose you want to see whether women are discriminated against with respect to income. You will need a frequency distribution of male and female incomes as well as mean and median income for the two groups. This information can be obtained from government census data: The analysis has already been made, and you need only interpret it. You do not need to make a test of significance because census data involve the entire population; tests of significance are used only when you want to know the probability that your findings about a sample are true for the population.

Score	Number In:	
	Set A	Set B
1	10	3
2	2	10
3	2	7
4	6	0
Mean score	2.2	2.2

TABLE 1.1
Frequency Distribution of Two Sets of Hypothetical Data

Income Level	Number of Families	
	Set A	Set B
$ 1,000	2	1
2,000	1	2
3,000	1	1
4,000	1	0
5,000	2	1
10,000	0	2
Mean	$3,000	$4,714
Median	3,000	3,000

TABLE 1.2
Frequency Distribution, Mean, and Median of Two Sets of Hypothetical Income Data

Not all official records are analyzed statistically, and not all are as complete as census data. Yet many data are available that you can use to improve your understanding of social problems. An example of the utility of the statistical analysis of official records is provided by Jacobs and Carmichael's (2002) study of the death penalty. The researchers raised the question of why the death penalty exists in some states but not others. Is it simply a matter that some people believe the penalty is an effective crime deterrent while others do not? Or are other factors at work as well?

Using various theoretical considerations, the researchers set up hypotheses about the impact of economic, political, and racial factors on the death penalty. They tested the hypotheses by using official records, including whether a state had the death penalty, the extent of economic inequality in the state, the unemployment rate, the proportion of African Americans and Hispanics, the proportion of families headed by a woman, the extent of public conservatism (measured by the ideologies of the state's elected congresspeople), and the strength of the Republican party (measured by whether the governor was Republican and the proportion of Republicans in the state legislature).

In accord with their hypotheses, the researchers found that states with the largest black populations, the greatest economic inequality, Republican dominance in the state legislature, and stronger conservative values were more likely to have the death penalty. In accord with our model, the researchers identified multiple social factors associated with the death penalty—institutions, stratification, values, and ideologies; and they showed that whether a state has the death penalty is not simply a matter of believing in its value as a deterrent to crime. Economic threats, racial divisions, and ideologies all enter into the matter.

Experiments

In essence, the *experimental method* involves manipulation of one or more variables, control of other variables, and measurement of the consequences in still other variables. The manipulated variables are called the **independent variables,** while those that are measured to see the ways they have been affected are called the **dependent variables.** To see whether the independent variables cause change in the dependent variables, the experimenter uses *both an experimental group and a control group.* Measurements are taken in both groups, but the control group is not exposed to the treatment (the independent variable).

Suppose you want to set up an experiment to test the hypothesis that prejudice is increased by negative interpersonal encounters with people of other races. You get a group of white volunteers, test them on their level of prejudice, and select 20 who score about the same (that is, you control for level of prejudice). You then divide them into two groups and give each group the same brief lecture by an African American. One group is treated kindly by the lecturer, while the other group is treated in an abusive manner. Following the lecture, you again test the 20 subjects for their level of prejudice.

If the 10 who hear the abusive lecturer increase their level of prejudice while the 10 who listen to the kindly lecturer show no increase, the hypothesis is clearly supported. In practice, experiments never come out this neatly. Some people who listen to the abusive speaker will not increase their level of prejudice, and some who listen to the kindly speaker will show more prejudice afterward. In other words, factors other than just the interpersonal contact are at work. The experimenter tries to control the setting and the subjects in order to minimize the effect of these other factors.

The utility of experiments is illustrated in a study of how using a cell phone while driving affects other drivers (McGarva, Ramsey, and Shear 2006). One-third or more of all drivers use cell phones while driving, and cellphone users are more likely than others to be involved in collisions. Is it possible that using cell phones increases the amount of hostility and road rage in others when users are seen driving in ways that are frustrating or hazardous? If so, then cellphone usage while driving may be a factor in the total amount of violence in our society.

How could we find out? McGarva, Ramsey, and Shear (2006) set up two experiments to observe reactions to drivers on cellphones. In the first experiment, one of the researchers drove an older car on some two-lane roads within the city limits of a Midwestern town. The car was equipped with a hidden camera that recorded drivers behind the researcher's car. When a car approached from the rear, the researcher slowed down to 10 miles per hour less than the posted speed limit. In some cases, the researcher appeared to talk on a cell phone while driving slowly (the experimental group); in other cases, the researcher drove with both hands on the wheel (the control group).

In the second experiment, when the researcher's car was at a red light and another car was waiting behind it, the researcher's car paused approximately 15 seconds after the light had turned green. Again, in some cases the researcher appeared to be talking on a cell phone (the experimental group) while in other cases the researcher simply sat in the car with both hands on the wheel.

In both experiments the researchers found that when the driver appeared to be talking on a cell phone, men in other cars honked their horns more quickly and frequently

independent variable
the variable in an experiment that is manipulated to see how it affects changes in the dependent variable

dependent variable
the variable in an experiment that is influenced by an independent variable

Drivers on cell phones increase the amount of roadway aggression.

than when the driver was not on a cell phone. Women in other cars tended to use their horns less, but judgments of their facial expressions concluded that they were more angry when the researcher was on a cell phone than when the researcher had both hands on the wheel.

The researchers concluded that the use of cell phones by drivers adds to the growing problem of roadway aggression. It would be useful to know whether those frustrated drivers with elevated levels of hostility act more aggressively or violently afterward. Such a question illustrates why researchers invariably point out that additional research is necessary.

Participant Observation

Participant observation, the last method we consider, involves a number of elements, including interaction with subjects, participation in and observation of pertinent activities of the subjects, interviews, and use of documents and artifacts. In participant observation, then, the researcher directly participates in and observes the social reality being studied. The researcher is both a part of and detached from the social reality being studied.

However, there are differences in the extent to which the researcher is involved in the social reality being studied. The relative emphasis on participation versus observation, and whether the researcher reveals his or her identity to the subjects, are decisions that must be made (and are matters of ethical debate). For instance, if a researcher uses observation to study poverty, he or she might live in an impoverished community and pretend to be a poor person. Or the researcher might acknowledge that research is being conducted while he or she participates in community activities. The researcher might decide to participate only in selective community activities that he or she specifically wants to observe. Or the researcher could choose to be primarily an observer, watching poor children in a schoolroom behind a one-way mirror. Which will yield

participant observation
a method of research in which one directly participates and observes the social reality being studied

the best information? Which, if any, would be considered unethical? Researchers must answer such questions.

As an example of participant observation research, we looked at Gwendolyn Dordick's (2002) research into a transitional housing program for the homeless. Numerous programs exist to deal with the problem of homeless people. How effective are these programs? This question needs to be addressed in order to frame public policy and provide guidelines for private efforts to attack the problems.

Dordick pointed out that the initial emphasis on setting up emergency shelters and giving monetary assistance for housing has given way to programs that combine temporary shelter with a variety of social services. The services are designed to address the basic causes of homelessness, such as substance abuse, mental illness, and chronic unemployment. Homeless individuals or families are given temporary shelter while they take advantage of the services to deal with the cause of their homelessness. The goal is to make the homeless "housing-ready."

Dordick spent 18 months as a participant observer in On the Way, a transitional program for homeless, single, substance-abusing men. Her goals were to determine the meaning of "becoming housing-ready" and to see how effective the program was in making people housing-ready.

Dordick did not live in the home where the program was run, but she visited it nearly 100 times, spending two to six hours there each time. She joined in staff and community meetings, observed group therapeutic activities, and hung out with people in the home and in the residents' rooms. She also conducted interviews with current and past staff members and residents.

The services provided by On the Way included mental health counseling, education, job training, and training in independent living skills. Basic questions Dordick tried to answer were: How does one know when a resident is housing-ready, prepared to live on his or her own? How do the staff know when to tell a resident that he or she is ready to move on? The ability to pay rent or the eligibility for government subsidy were not among the criteria used. Rather, the staff used very subjective means such as the "quality of sobriety." A staff member found it very difficult to define precisely what he meant by quality of sobriety. He just had a sense of it from his own experience.

So how well did the program work? While Dordick was there, and during the year following her research, seven residents and two resident managers left On the Way. One secured his own apartment and another moved to a permanent subsidized housing facility. The others moved in with relatives or girlfriends. As Dordick summed it up, there was no transition to independent living for most of them. It was just a matter of substituting "one set of dependencies for another" (Dordick 2002:27).

By the use of participant observation, then, Dordick was able to evaluate the effectiveness of one program designed to help the homeless. The minimal success of this program does not mean that the homeless are hopeless. It means that we must keep searching for effective ways to help.

Summary

You need to distinguish between personal and social problems. For the former, the causes and solutions lie within the individual and his or her immediate environment. For the latter, the causes and solutions lie outside the individual and his or her immediate environment. Defining a particular problem as personal or social is important because the definition determines the causes you identify, the consequences of the problem, and how you cope with the problem.

The model we use to analyze social problems treats them as contradictions. It emphasizes that multiple-level factors cause and help perpetuate problems. You must understand social problems in terms of the mutual influence between social structural factors, social psychological or cognitive factors, and social interaction.

In addition to attending to the multiple factors involved, two additional tools are necessary for an adequate understanding of social problems. One is to use critical-thinking skills to identify fallacious ways of thinking that have been used to analyze social problems and that create and perpetuate myths about those problems. The other is to understand the methods of social research. An adequate understanding of social problems is based on research and not merely on what seems to be reasonable.

Nine different fallacies have been used to analyze social problems. The fallacy of dramatic instance refers to the tendency to overgeneralize, to use a single case or a few cases to support an entire argument. The fallacy of retrospective determinism is the argument that things could not have worked out differently. The fallacy of misplaced concreteness is the tendency to resort to reification, to make something abstract into something concrete. The fallacy of personal attack is a form of debate or argument in which an attack is made on the opponent rather than on the issues. Appeal to prejudice is the exploitation of popular prejudices or passions. Circular reasoning involves the use of conclusions supporting assumptions necessary to make those conclusions. The fallacy of authority is an illegitimate appeal to authority. The fallacy of composition is the idea that what is true of the part is also true of the whole. Finally, non sequitur is drawing the wrong conclusions from premises even though the premises themselves are valid.

Four methods of social research that are useful for understanding social problems are survey research, statistical analysis of official records, experiment, and participant observation. Survey research employs interviews and questionnaires on a sample of people in order to get data. Statistical analysis of official records may be simple (computing means, medians, and frequency distributions) or relatively complex (computing tests of significance). Experiment involves manipulation of one or more variables, control of other variables, and measurement of consequences in still other variables. Experiments frequently take place in a laboratory setting, where the researcher has a high degree of control over what happens. Finally, participant observation involves both participation and observation on the part of the researcher; the researcher is both a part of and detached from the social reality being studied.

Key Terms

Attitude	Independent
Conflict Theory	Variable
Contradiction	Institution
Critical Thinking	Interaction
Dependent Variable	Mean
Fallacy of Appeal to	Median
Prejudice	Norm
Fallacy of Authority	Participant
Fallacy of Circular	Observation
Reasoning	Personal Problem
Fallacy of	Reification
Composition	Role
Fallacy of Dramatic	Social Problem
Instance	Socioeconomic
Fallacy of Misplaced	Status
Concreteness	Stratification
Fallacy of Non	System
Sequitur	Structural
Fallacy of Personal	Functionalism
Attack	Survey
Fallacy of	Symbolic
Retrospective	Interactionism
Determinism	Test of Significance
Frequency	Values
Distribution	Variables
Ideology	

Study Questions

1. Using rape or some other problem as an example, how would you distinguish between a personal and a social problem?

2. What difference does the distinction between personal and social problems make in understanding the causes and consequences of problems?

3. Define each of the concepts in the authors' model and illustrate how each can enhance understanding of social problems.

4. What is meant by "quality of life," and in what way is it a part of social problems?

5. Illustrate each of the nine fallacies of thinking by showing how each can be used to "explain" a social problem.

6. How is survey research used to study social problems?

7. In what ways are official records useful for the study of social problems?

8. How do you set up a scientific experiment to research a social problem?

9. What did participant observation teach you about a program designed to help the homeless, and how did the researcher go about being a participant observer?

Internet Resources/ Exercises

1. Explore some of the ideas in this chapter on the following sites:

http://www.asanet.org   The official site of the American Sociological Association. Includes press releases and other information of value to students of social problems.

http://www.sssp1.org   Official site of the Society for the Study of Social Problems, with access to the *SSSP Newsletter.* Links to other sites relevant to social problems.

http://www.le.ac.uk/education/centres/ATSS/sites .html   A guide to sociology sites on the Internet, including links to many sites useful in dealing with social problems.

2. The journal *Social Problems* is published by the University of California Press. Go to its site: **http://caliber .ucpress.net.** Find the journal and examine the table of contents over the past year. Compare the kinds of problems dealt with in the articles with those explored in this text, with those you think are of concern to most Americans, and with those of most concern to you per-

sonally. Is the journal dealing with the issues of most concern?

3. Input the term "fallacies" into your search engine. Select a number of sites and compare their materials with those in the text. Are there other fallacies that should be included in the text? Are there fallacies that seem more appropriate than some of those described in the text for understanding social problems? In addition to those dealt with in the text, what other fallacies do you find helpful for understanding patterns of thinking?

For Further Reading

Diestler, Sherry. *Becoming a Critical Thinker: A User Friendly Manual.* 4th ed. New York: Prentice-Hall, 2004. A comprehensive but accessible survey of critical thinking on controversial issues, including exercises to hone your skills.

Gilbert, Nigel, ed. *Researching Social Life.* 2nd ed. Thousand Oaks, CA: Sage, 2002. Shows how qualitative and quantitative methods can be used to research social phenomena.

Huff, Darrell. *How to Lie with Statistics.* New York: W. W. Norton, 1993. A readable, fascinating exposition of proper and improper use of statistical data. Shows how statistics as well as myths can impart incorrect information.

Kingdon, John W. *Agendas, Alternatives, and Public Policies.* 2nd ed. New York: Longman, 1995. Explores the ways that agendas are set and public policy is formulated in the government. Underscores the complexity of dealing with social problems.

Lindblom, Charles Edward. *Inquiry and Change: The Troubled Attempt to Understand and Shape Society.* New Haven, CT: Yale University Press, 1990. A discussion of the ways people gather and analyze information as they deal with social problems.

Rapley, Mark. *Quality of Life Research: A Critical Introduction.* Thousand Oaks, CA: Sage, 2003. A critical introduction to the concept of quality of life and the ways in which people research it. Uses an interdisciplinary approach in its analysis.

Shreve, Susan Richards, Porter Shreve, and James Reston. *How We Want To Live: Narratives on Progress.* Boston: Beacon Press, 1998. Essays on the notion of progress and how Americans' pursuit of progress affects their quality of life.

PART 2

Problems of Behavioral Deviance

What do such actions as prostitution, drug addiction, and arson have in common? They all involve behavior that deviates from social norms. As such, most Americans view the behavior as within the individual's control and responsibility. That is, if a person engages in prostitution, uses drugs, or robs a store, it is a matter of his or her free choice. Further, because it is a choice that violates social norms, the person who engages in any kind of behavioral variance is likely to be (1) condemned and punished, (2) defined as "sick" and given therapy, or (3) both.

As you will see, the matter is not as simple as this view suggests. If, for example, you define crime as any infraction of the law—including such activities as speeding or failing to report income on tax returns—few if any Americans are innocent of crime. Like all problems discussed in this book, problems of behavioral deviance are complex issues that involve social contradictions, are defined as having adverse effects on the quality of life, and have multilevel causes.

Sexual Deviance

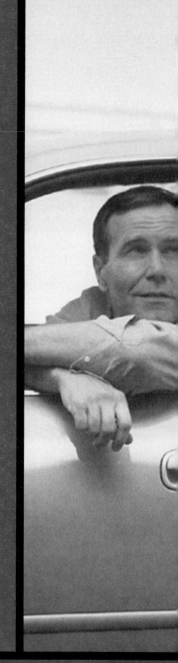

"My Husband Is a Porn Addict"

Kathy is a 26-year-old woman who has been married for four years. She was quite happy in her marriage for the first two years. Then she happened to catch her husband viewing pornographic sites on his computer. The last two years have been a struggle for her:

When I accidentally caught Jake watching porn, I was shocked. I had no idea he was into that kind of thing. I knew he liked sex a lot. But so do I. Or at least, I did. Our sex life hasn't been much to talk about these past couple of years. It's really tough for me to feel aroused by him when I know how much time he's spending watching that stuff on his computer.

That's the thing that shocked me the most—the amount of time he spends at it. I didn't realize it at first because he would watch it late at night after I was asleep or when I was out of the house. However, one night I caught him watching porn when he thought I was in the shower. After a quick shower, I decided to sneak up on him before I dressed and invite him to go to bed, but I stopped dead in my tracks when I saw his computer screen. He tried to convince me that it was all harmless. That it only increased his desire for me and made our sex life better.

That didn't make sense to me. "You mean you have to watch other naked women to feel sexy toward me?" I asked him. He couldn't give me a satisfactory answer. Then I asked him how long and how often he had been watching the porn. He tried to weasel out of a direct answer, but he finally admitted that he had been into it for years—even before we were married. At that point, I realized that my husband is a porn addict!

Previously, I had thought that all porn addicts were perverts, but I've discovered that a lot of seemingly normal men are addicted to porn. And some of them are a lot worse than Jake. I've been attending a small support group for wives of porn addicts. One woman told us about how her husband was into the violent stuff and would act it out with her. She got tired of the above, and refuses to have sex with him any more. They'll probably get divorced soon. Another woman said that her husband convinced her to watch with him. He said it would spice up their sex life. She tried, but she couldn't take it. And when she refused to watch any more, he got verbally and emotionally abusive.

Jake hasn't gone that far. But to be honest about it, that doesn't make it any easier for me. I feel like he's having affairs. He's investing himself emotionally in other women. And I just can't feel the same way about him while he's doing it. At this point, I think I still love him. I certainly love the man I thought I married. But I'm not sure how much longer I can stay married to a porn addict.

Introduction

There's an old story about an expert who was scheduled to give an after-dinner speech on sex. At the appointed time, he arose and said: "Ladies and gentlemen. Sex. It gives me great pleasure." Then he sat down.

Clearly, sex is a source of great pleasure to humans. It is also a source of pain and controversy. Whether it is one or the other depends on whom you're talking to and what kind of sex you're talking about. In this chapter, we look at what is meant by sexual deviance. Then we expand on two kinds of sexual deviance that are regarded as social problems: prostitution and the use of pornography.

Examples of Sexual Deviance

What is sexual deviance? The answer depends on which society you are talking about. All societies regulate sex, but not all regulate it in the same way. In their study of 190 different societies, Ford and Beach (1951) concluded there are wide variations in normative sexual behavior and considerable permissiveness for some kinds of sexual behavior that Americans have historically considered deviant (such as extramarital sex and homosexuality). Of course, people everywhere take their own norms seriously, but the point is that sexual behavior, like all other behavior, is social. No particular type of sexual behavior is "natural" or "normal" in contrast to other types.

Nevertheless, there are certain kinds of sexual behavior that are considered deviant in most societies. Some of these behaviors characterize only a very small proportion of the population. For example, it is likely that *exhibitionism* (exposing one's genitals to a stranger) and *voyeurism* (spying on people who are having sexual relations) are practiced by only a small proportion of people. We don't know the figures for America, but two Swedish researchers have estimates for their nation (Langstrom and Seto 2006). They used results from a survey on sexuality and health that was administered to a representative national sample. They found that 3.1 percent of the respondents admitted at least one incident of being sexually aroused by exposing their genitals to a stranger and 7.7 percent reported at least one incident of being aroused by spying on others having sex. More men than women engaged in the behaviors.

Another type of sexual behavior considered deviant in most societies is **promiscuity,** sex between an unmarried individual and an excessive number of partners. Both men and women say that they prefer sex within the context of a caring relationship, and women say that they enjoy intercourse most when in a committed as well as a caring relationship (McCabe 1987). Although men are often portrayed as having sex whenever they can get it, a national survey reported that two-thirds of the single men said they didn't like a woman who was willing to make love on the first date (Arrington 1990). And an experiment that used college students as subjects reported that the students considered people who are promiscuous less desirable as potential dating or marriage partners (Perlini and Boychuk 2006).

promiscuity
undiscriminating, casual sexual relationships with many people

Extramarital sex also varies from American norms. From a list that included such events as divorce, gambling, having a baby outside of marriage, abortion, suicide, and cloning humans, the item that the fewest people regarded as morally accepted was an extramarital affair (Bowman 2004:48). Behavior doesn't always reflect attitudes, however, and in point of fact a substantial number of Americans engage in extramarital sex. We don't know exactly how many. One national survey reported that about 25 percent of married men and 15 percent of married women admit to ever having an affair (Laumann et al. 1994), while another found that 8.5 percent of men and 4.3 percent of women reported an affair within the past five years (Leigh, Temple, and Trocki 1993). Clearly, most Americans practice fidelity, though not as many as say they disapprove of infidelity.

Still another form of deviant sex is **cybersex**, sexual activity conducted via the Internet. A forerunner of cybersex was telephone sex, which involved a per-minute charge to engage in a sexual conversation with someone (Ross 2005). Telephone sex never attracted as many customers, however, as has cybersex.

cybersex
sexual activity conducted via the Internet

Cybersex can be carried on in a number of ways. In one form, the individual uses online pornographic sites for sexual pleasure. In a second form, two or more people engage in sexual talk while online in order to gain sexual pleasure. A Swedish study found that those who engaged in this form of cybersex also tended to have more offline sexual partners (Daneback, Cooper, and Manisson 2005).

A third form of cybersex is the online game in which the participants can do such things as create their own characters (who can resemble themselves) and have those characters engage in whatever kinds of sexual behavior they desire (Biever 2006). In some of the games, people can go beyond the online sex and use the site to date those with whom their characters have had sex.

Is such online sex just harmless fun? In one study, 41 percent of a sample of people engaged in cybersex did not consider what they did to be cheating on a relationship partner at all (Ross 2005). But the story at the beginning of this chapter gives one woman's account of the harm done to her marriage by a husband involved in cybersex.

And a survey of 91 women and 3 men whose partners had been heavily involved in cybersex found a good deal of hurt—feelings of betrayal and rejection, jealousy, and anger—as well as adverse effects on their children (Schneider 2003). Nearly a fourth of the respondents had separated from or divorced their partners, and they claimed cybersex addiction as a major factor.

Finally, many Americans view *strip clubs* as a form of deviant sex. In both male and female strip clubs, patrons can watch people strip and engage in erotic dancing and, in some cases, chat with the strippers. Men and women seem to have different reasons for going to strip clubs, however. For women, the shared experience of being at the club with friends and bonding with other women may be more important to them than the show itself (Montemurro, Bloom, and Madell 2003). For men, on the other hand, regular attendance at strip clubs is associated with their sexuality and masculinity. Katherine Frank (2003; 2005) worked as a dancer in a strip club while she was a graduate student. Using participant observation and interviews, she probed the reasons that some men are regular patrons. She found a variety of motivations among the men for going to strip clubs, including a desire to express a masculine self free of obligations and commitments; experience adventure; feel desirable; and have a sexualized interaction with a woman that is without risk.

Let's look in greater detail at prostitution and pornography. Both have been both strongly condemned and vigorously defended—and continue to survive every attempt to completely suppress them.

Prostitution

prostitution
having sexual relations for remuneration, usually to provide part or all of one's livelihood

Prostitution is a paid sexual relation between the prostitute and his or her client. Male prostitutes are often young boys—mostly from impoverished homes. They have run away or been thrown out of their homes and offer themselves as sexual partners to gay men. The boys often consider themselves heterosexuals who are only engaging in homosexual prostitution temporarily in order to survive. Since research on male prostitution is sparse, our focus here is on the female prostitute and her clientele.

fellatio
oral stimulation of the male genitalia

cunnilingus
oral stimulation of the female genitalia

Although not every prostitute agrees to perform every sexual act, prostitutes are available for a variety of sexual services. These include **fellatio** (oral stimulation of the male genitalia), **cunnilingus** (oral stimulation of the female genitalia), and anal intercourse as well as standard intercourse (figure 2.1).

How much prostitution exists in the United States? Official records depend on arrests. In 2005, there were 84,891 arrests for prostitution (Federal Bureau of Investigation 2006), but an unknown number of these were repeat offenders and not all prostitutes are arrested. The Web site for the Prostitutes' Education Network claims that more than a million American women have worked as prostitutes. Part of the problem of estimating is that there are *various kinds of female prostitutes,* from streetwalkers to high-paid call girls to brothel workers to prostitutes who use the Internet to solicit customers (Roane 1998). Some work full time, while others use prostitution to supplement their incomes. Some work for decades, while others quit after a short time. On the average, it is estimated that the work life of American prostitutes is four to five years (Potterat et al. 1990). Whatever the total number who have ever been a prostitute, it seems safe to say that at any one time hundreds of thousands of prostitutes are at work in the nation. Some of them are adolescents, usually runaways or "throwaways."

Hundreds of thousands is a reasonable figure in light of the amount of prostitution in other parts of the world. Researchers who examined data from around the world

Type of activity:

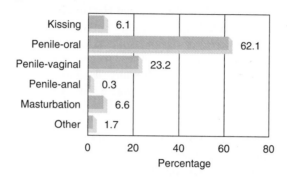

FIGURE 2.1
Sexual Activity of
20 Prostitutes.
Source: Adapted from Freund,
Leonard, and Lee (1989):475.

reported that the proportion of the female population engaged in prostitution ranged from 0.7 percent to 4.3 percent among nations in sub-Saharan Africa, from 0.2 percent to 2.6 percent among nations in Asia, from 0.1 percent to 1.4 percent in Western Europe, and from 0.2 percent to 7.4 percent among nations in South America (Vandepitte et al. 2006). If we assume there are 200,000 to 300,000 prostitutes in the United States, the comparable figure would be somewhere between 0.1 percent and 0.2 percent of the female population, which is comparable to that of other industrial nations.

How frequently do prostitutes have sex? In a "good week," a full-time prostitute might have 15 or more clients (Davis 1993). In a small sample of 20 street prostitutes in New Jersey, researchers reported that the women worked four to five days per week and averaged four clients per day (Freund, Leonard, and Lee 1989). Interestingly, the researchers also found that nearly half the contacts were with repeat clients. The prostitutes had a number of regular customers over a period of years.

Who uses the services of a prostitute? Again, it is impossible to give exact figures. Yet considering the number of prostitutes available and the number of times they have sex each day, it is clear that a substantial portion of the male population has sex with prostitutes. The *typical customer,* or "john," is a married, middle-aged white male (National Victims Resource Center 1991; Lowman, Atchison, and Fraser 1997). Only a small proportion of the men limit their use of prostitutes to one time. In a survey of 120 customers, 25 percent of the men reported using prostitutes 51 or more times, and 16 percent said they had purchased sex more than 100 times (Lowman, Atchison, and Fraser 1997).

Those who use prostitutes tend to do so over an extended period of time rather than having a single encounter. A study of 101 clients of street prostitutes found that they had used prostitutes an average of 5.3 years (Freund, Lee, and Leonard 1991). Nearly two-thirds of the men reported using a prostitute once a week or more, and over half said they had sex with the same prostitute or the same small group of prostitutes.

Surveys of men in various other nations have found that roughly 9 to 10 percent admit that they used the services of a prostitute in the past year (Carael, Slaymaker, Lyerla, and Sarkar 2006). The proportion varied considerably by region, however: 13 to 15 percent in central Africa, 10 to 11 percent in Eastern and southern Africa, 5 to 7 percent in Asia and Latin America.

Prostitution and the Quality of Life

Prostitutes typically prefer their profession to other perceived options. This preference is not so much evidence of the high quality of life for prostitutes as it is testimony to the *low quality of life endured by the women before they decided to become prostitutes.*

We must distinguish, however, between different kinds of prostitutes. Prince (1986) interviewed 300 prostitutes in California and Nevada. Her sample included 75 streetwalkers, 75 call girls, and 150 Nevada brothel workers. When she asked about the major advantages of their work, all the streetwalkers gave money as the answer. Only 18 percent of the call girls and 21 percent of the brothel workers mentioned money. Other advantages they mentioned included adventure, flexibility of time, and learning about themselves and others. Whatever the advantages, however, there are serious problems with the quality of life.

Physical Problems. In the first place, *prostitution contradicts our value of physical well-being.* Americans cherish good health and value the youthful physique. Most prostitutes, however, face certain occupational hazards that may lead to physical problems. In the past, *venereal disease* was a prominent problem. Today it is less frequent because many prostitutes get regular medical checkups and also carefully examine each customer for signs of venereal disease. Juvenile prostitutes, however, rarely seek medical help because they are afraid of attracting the attention of authorities (National Victims Resource Center 1991).

Another common physical problem "is a chronic pelvic congestion characterized by a copious discharge from the cervix and vaginal lining, and a sensation of tenderness and fullness of the side walls of the pelvis" (Winick and Kinsie 1971:70). The congestion results from the prostitute's avoidance of orgasm. She may try to get relief through narcotic drugs.

Finally, prostitutes face the hazard of contracting acquired immune deficiency syndrome (AIDS) (Quadagno et al. 1991). They run the risk both from their clients and from the tendency of some to become intravenous drug users. In the United States, prostitutes not only contract but help spread AIDS (Stine 1998). Rates of infection are particularly high among male prostitutes. A study of young male prostitutes in San Francisco reported that 12 percent of them were infected (Bacon et al. 2006). Fewer than half of the prostitutes required their clients to use condoms, and only 41 percent of those infected were even aware of their condition. In nations in which AIDS is more rampant, even higher rates of infection are found. A study of 426 female prostitutes in West Africa, for instance, reported that 58.2 percent were infected with the AIDS virus (Lankoande et al. 1998), while a survey of Cambodian prostitutes reported an infection rate of 54 percent (Ohshige et al. 2000).

A different problem is the *physical abuse that threatens the prostitute* (Raphael and Shapiro 2004). The abuse is most likely to come from customers. A survey of 325 prostitutes in Miami reported that over 40 percent had experienced violence in the preceding year: 24.9 percent had been beaten, 12.9 percent had been raped, and 13.8 percent had been threatened with a weapon (Surratt et al. 2004).

A prostitute may also suffer abuse at the hands of her husband or boyfriend and her **pimp** (one who earns all or part of his or her living by acting as a manager for the prostitute) (Dalla 2000). The highly paid call girl, who serves a more affluent clientele, is not likely to endure physical abuse, but the streetwalker must be constantly alert.

The constant threat of abuse is one reason why a prostitute needs a pimp. As one prostitute reported, "if you're gonna whore you need protection: a man's protection from other men. All men are in the protection business . . . If men didn't beat us up we wouldn't need half the husbands we got" (Millett 1971:95). Ironically, Norton-Hawk (2004) found that, among the 50 jailed prostitutes she interviewed, pimp-controlled prostitutes were more likely to be victims of customer violence than were those without

pimp
one who earns all or part of his or her living by acting as a manager or procurer for a prostitute

pimps. The pressure to make extra money to support the pimp may lead these prostitutes to take more risks, exposing themselves to a greater chance of violence.

At the same time, the pimp himself inflicts physical abuse (Williamson and Cluse-Tolar 2002). Sometimes the pimp will beat a prostitute when he begins his relationship with her in order to establish his dominance and ensure the woman's loyalty. If the prostitute does not behave in a way the pimp deems appropriate, he may continue to abuse her. One prostitute explained the pimp's behavior in terms of the master-slave relationship. The master seems to have total power but lives in fear because of the uncertainty of how the slave will react to his or her bondage. Like the master with his slave, the pimp fears the loss of his property. In addition, the pimp may feel compelled to maintain his ideal of masculinity before other men:

> Pimps do rotten things. I guess they have to. You've got to prove everything all over every day, right? You've got all the guys watching you. What do they do? . . . I saw a girl walk into a bar and hand the pimp a $100 bill. He took it and burned it in her face and knocked her down on the floor and kicked her and said, "I told you, bitch, $200. I want $200, not $100." Now she's gotta go out again and make not another hundred, but two hundred. I know of some pimps who killed a whore with an overdose of heroin and then fucked her dead body. They're sick. (Millett 1971:101–3)

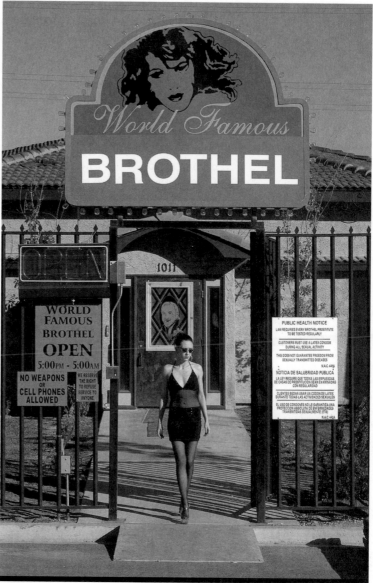

There are different kinds of prostitution, with differing consequences for the prostitutes.

We do not know how frequently prostitutes endure physical abuse from customers or their pimps, but the threat of abuse is constant. It is unlikely that any prostitute can ply her trade for many years without suffering abuse (Nixon et al. 2002). A study of 130 prostitutes in San Francisco reported that 82 percent had been physically assaulted; 83 percent had been threatened with a weapon; and 68 percent had been raped while working as a prostitute (Farley and Barkan 1998). Such violence in their lives, along with the drug use that is common, is a major reason for the higher rate of mortality among prostitutes (Potterat et al. 2004). Compared with other women of their age, prostitutes are nearly twice as likely to die.

Psychological and Emotional Problems. A psychological problem reported by prostitutes arises from the contradiction between the value of sexual fulfillment and the role of the prostitute. The problem is a psychological counterpart to the previously mentioned physical ailment that can result from the prostitute's avoidance of orgasm. Far from achieving sexual fulfillment, the prostitute often becomes *virtually asexual* with respect to her own sexual functioning (Dalla 2001). Again, however, we have to distinguish between different kinds of prostitutes. Prince (1986) found that two-thirds of the streetwalkers agreed that they should avoid orgasms, but only a little over a third of the brothel workers and 4 percent of the call girls agreed.

There is also a contradiction between the value of *human dignity* and the prostitute's role. The continual exposure to violence, along with other aspects of the prostitute's work, may lead to various kinds of emotional trauma, drug use and abuse, feelings of isolation and worthlessness, attempted suicide, and sexually transmitted diseases including AIDS (Norton-Hawk 2002; Romero-Daza, Weeks, and Singer 2003; Roxburgh, Degenhardt, and Copeland 2006). Emotional problems are intensified by the fact that prostitutes generally do not form a cohesive group among themselves because they are competing for customers. They mainly have contempt for their customers and do not establish bonds with them. They often cannot form close relationships with people not connected with "the life" because of the stigma attached to their role. Therefore, prostitutes are barred from a sense of community with anyone.

One way prostitutes cope with this problem is to seek *refuge in drugs* (Gunn et al. 1995; Dalla 2000; Degenhardt, Day, Conroy, and Gilmour 2006). A considerable number of prostitutes need help with addiction (Valera, Sawyer, and Schiraldi 2001). In many cases, the prostitutes were drug users before they began to engage in sex work (Bletzer 2005). Once they started working as prostitutes, however, their drug use tended to escalate.

When the drugs no longer are sufficient to make their existence bearable, prostitutes may try to end their lives. The rate of *attempted suicide* is quite high among prostitutes. In Prince's (1986) study, 68 percent of the streetwalkers, 25 percent of the call girls, and 19 percent of the brothel workers admitted trying to kill themselves.

Finally, there is a *higher rate of emotional problems among prostitutes*. Research shows that about two-thirds of prostitutes suffer serious emotional problems, including anxiety, hostility, depression, and guilt (Farley and Barkan 1998; Zuger 1998).

There is, then, ample evidence of psychological and emotional problems among prostitutes. Moreover, these problems are built into the role of the prostitute, making escape difficult. For some women, prostitution seems to be more desirable than other available options, but the psychological and emotional quality of the prostitute's life is low.

Exploitation.   Quality of life is further diminished by the *contradiction between the roles of the prostitute and the people with whom she must deal and the ideal of "I-Thou" relationships* in which people relate to each other as person to person and not as person to thing. The role of prostitute involves exploitation. Pimps, madams, bellboys, taxi drivers, lawyers, disreputable medical examiners, abortionists, police officers receiving hush money—the prostitute must deal with them all, and they all treat her as a "thing" rather than as a person by using her to make or to supplement their own living. Silbert and Pines (1981) noted that 88 percent of the 200 prostitutes they studied reported themselves as poor. Nearly half of them said they were victimized by an unfair split of money with their pimps, and 41 percent reported victimization by the police (including forced unpaid sex with a policeman).

Thus, the women offer their sexual services to men, pay their fines to men, and return to the streets only to be arrested again by men—all to satisfy the public's sense of "decorum."

CHILD PROSTITUTES

In the United States, women may become prostitutes because, among other reasons, they come from impoverished backgrounds. In some other countries, the relationship between poverty and prostitution takes a different twist—children sell themselves, or are sold by their parents, into prostitution in order to survive. The United Nations estimates that 1.2 million children are trafficked across international borders every year, most of them destined for prostitution.

We should note that not all child prostitution comes out of impoverished settings. Cultural norms also play a role. For example, in Thailand girls sometimes go into prostitution because it appears to be the only choice they have in order to fulfill the norms of their culture. Those norms dictate that the young should repay their parents for the sacrifices the parents have made and should help improve their parents' financial standing. They have the obligation to do so even if the family is relatively well off. But females have little opportunity to make enough money to enhance the family's income and status. Consequently, some of them opt for prostitution as a "bearable" way to fulfill their cultural obligations.

Most child prostitution, however, is tied up with poverty and the need to survive. The close link between child prostitution and survival is illustrated by the account of a 17-year-old Chilean prostitute, who told how the first effort she and her brothers made to get food was to go out and beg, or pick up leftovers at the market. Then they started selling celery, but when they couldn't sell enough to get the food needed by the family, "my mom almost beat us to death." After that, the girl began to sell herself. A Chilean sociologist has estimated that as many as 50,000 children in Chile engage in prostitution in order to survive.

Southeast Asia is another area with child prostitutes. No one knows just how many, but estimates run into the hundreds of thousands and as high as a million. One-fifth of prostitutes in Thailand begin their work between the ages of 13 and 15, and girls as young as 8 are in the brothels of Thailand, Cambodia, India, China, Taiwan, and the Philippines. Many of the girls were sold to the brothel owners by their parents in order to get money for food or other essentials for their families. Once sold, the girls are considered the property of the brothel owners and must work until they pay off their purchase price—or until they get AIDS.

In some cases, the family may run its own prostitution business. A mother with four daughters in Manila looked for clients for the two youngest daughters, ages 8 and 12. When the 12-year-old resisted, the mother held her down while the men raped her.

The clients of child prostitutes come from many different nations, including America. Why do they want children? No doubt they have various motivations, but one seems to be the fear of AIDS. The AIDS virus is spreading rapidly among prostitutes in Asia. The younger the prostitute, so the reasoning goes, the less likely she is to have AIDS. As a result, hundreds of thousands of Asian girls are living in sexual slavery.

SOURCES
Chicago Tribune, March 17, 1996; *New York Times,* April 14, 1996; Kuo (2000); Willis and Levy (2003); Bower (2005); Mathews (2006).

Arresting prostitutes satisfies the public because the appearance of police safeguarding morality is maintained. The prostitute is exploited by many different people, all of whom regard her as an object to serve their own interests.

Perhaps the most exploited of prostitutes are those who are "sex slaves," women forced unwittingly into prostitution by men who kidnap them or who lure them into another country with the promise of work or husbands (van Hook, Gjermeni, and Haxhiymeri 2006). In some cases, the women fled into another country trying to fend off extreme poverty and even starvation. Once there, however, they were forced into prostitution as the only way to survive.

There are probably hundreds of thousands of sex slaves throughout the world. Asian nations have particularly high rates of sex slaves, but there are tens of thousands of them in the United States (Field 2004). Most of those enslaved in America come from Latin America and Southeast Asia. Like the sex slaves in other countries, they are typically deceived and forced into prostitution by those exploiting them for personal gain.

Contributing Factors

If the quality of life for the prostitute is so low, and if many Americans believe the very presence of prostitutes offends traditional morals, why does prostitution continue?

Social Structural Factors.   Social structural factors help explain both why men seek prostitutes and why women enter into the life. American society has traditionally held to the norm of sex only within marriage. In addition, sex has not been openly discussed through much of the nation's history. These two factors—*rejection of nonmarital sex and no open discussion of sex*—were set forth by Winick and Kinsie (1971) as crucial determinants of the amount of prostitution in a society. They pointed out that among the Tokopia of the Solomon Islands, both nonmarital sex and open discussion of sex are accepted, and there is practically no prostitution. They hypothesize that in societies in which social norms forbid either or both of these conditions, there will probably be prostitution. This line of reasoning is supported by the fact that open discussions about sex have become more acceptable, and nonmarital sex (especially premarital) has become more widely accepted in American society. At the same time, although roughly the same number of men appear to use the services of prostitutes, fewer are young men, and the number of visits by each man may have declined.

In addition to traditional norms about nonmarital sex and discussion of sex, the *institution of marriage* does not provide sufficient sexual gratification for some males (Monto 2004). Married men may go to prostitutes to experience variety, to compensate for a lack of gratification with their mates, or to avoid concern about pregnancy (Weiss 1990; McKeganey 1994; Lowman, Atchison, and Fraser 1997). Married men who give and receive oral sex report that they are happier with their sex lives and their marriages, but wives are more likely than their husbands to be embarrassed and inhibited about oral sex (Blumstein and Schwartz 1983). Desire for fellatio is an important reason men go to prostitutes (Monto 2001). The 20 New Jersey prostitutes reported that 62 percent of their sexual contacts involved fellatio (see figure 2.1).

Men may also go to prostitutes because their wives do not desire sexual relations as often as they do. The prostitute then provides a sexual outlet that does not require the time and emotion that would be involved in an extramarital affair.

The nature of the economy also facilitates male use of prostitution (Davis 1993). Workers such as male truck drivers and salesmen must spend a considerable amount of time away from home. Symanski (1974) reported that tourists, traveling salesmen, and truck drivers were among the major sources of business for the Nevada brothels. And a study of Chinese men who used prostitutes reported that one type of client was the man who was required to work far away from his wife or girlfriend (Pochagina 2006). To the extent that *the economy requires travel,* there will likely be clientele for the prostitute.

Structural factors help explain why women enter the life. They tend to come from a *low position in the stratification system.* They usually have little education and few job skills, and resort to prostitution out of what they regard as economic necessity (Dalla 2000; Kramer and Berg 2003). Young, homeless male and female prostitutes also resort to this way of life in order to survive (Tyler and Johnson 2006). Some of these youth view prostitution as nothing more than a desperate attempt to get the necessities of life. They see no other alternative.

Studies of prostitutes in other nations reveal a similar pattern: prostitutes tend to come from impoverished backgrounds and feel compelled to engage in prostitution in order to survive. Often, perhaps most of the time, it is not only a matter of the individual's survival but also that of her family (Wong, Holroyd, Gray, and Ling 2006).

In addition to their position in the socioeconomic system, prostitutes frequently come from backgrounds of *disturbed family experiences and participation in groups with norms that accept prostitution.* Prince (1986) reported that the prostitute's relationship with her father seems to be the most important family factor. In particular, the prostitutes tended to describe a father who abandoned the family, who lost contact after a divorce, or who treated the girl abusively or with indifference. About 9 out of 10 of the streetwalkers said that they did not have a close or happy relationship with either their mother or father while growing up. The call girls tended to have a good relationship with their mother, but fewer than half had one with their father. Among the brothel workers, the proportions reporting good relationships were 43 percent with their mother and 39 percent with their father.

Similarly, interviews with 33 parents of teenage prostitutes reported that the parents were stressed from a history of failed intimate relationships and financial hardships (Longres 1991). They also raised their daughters in neighborhoods conducive to easy entry into prostitution.

In many cases, the disturbed family experiences go beyond mere deprivation. Prostitutes come disproportionately from families involved in physical and/or sexual abuse, alcoholism, and use of other drugs (Davis 1993; Widom and Ames 1994; Farley and Barkan 1998; Dalla 2001; Nixon et al. 2002; Lung et al. 2004). Prince (1986) found abuse, including incest, particularly common among the streetwalkers. A study of 72 Australian prostitutes found that all but one of them had traumatic experiences that typically began in early childhood, including child sexual abuse (Roxburgh, Degenhardt, and Copeland 2006). Abuse, exploitation, and deprivation combine to lead many young women to run away from home. Faced with the urgency of getting food and shelter, and possessing little or no money, they are lured into prostitution in an effort to survive. Even if they do not run away, early sexual abuse increases the chances of their becoming prostitutes (Simons and Whitbeck 1991).

Social Psychological Factors. Although "respectable" people are frequently thought to abhor prostitution, the bulk of the prostitute's clientele are so-called respectable people. Their psychological and social adjustment may be somewhat less than that of others. A study of 1,672 men arrested for trying to hire a street prostitute reported that they, compared to men generally, were less likely to be married, less likely to be happily married if they were married, and more likely to report being generally unhappy (Monto and McRee 2005). But, as the researchers pointed out, the differences tended to be small, suggesting that the customers differed from others by degree rather than by significant amounts.

A study of Chinese men found eight different motivations for using prostitutes (Pochagina 2006). First, some young men with no sexual experience or who have difficulty forming a lasting intimate relationship engage prostitutes. Second, because there are millions more men than women in China, some men gain sexual satisfaction through prostitutes. Third, some men, who find it difficult to find sexual satisfaction with a wife or girlfriend use prostitutes. Fourth, others use prostitutes when age, appearance, or psychological makeup make them unable to form a meaningful sexual relationship. Fifth, some men engage prostitutes as a way to bolster their self-esteem. Sixth, others turn to prostitutes when they are required to work away from wives or girlfriends. Seventh, some use prostitutes to reduce tension in their lives. And finally, some are married but are looking for diversity while on a trip or a vacation.

Other social psychological factors that maintain prostitution include the tolerant attitudes of officials and public acceptance of the ideology that male sexuality needs the outlet. With regard to the former, it is often noted that prostitution could not continue if the authorities were determined to eliminate it. Although this is an overstatement, it is true that police seldom make a determined effort to stop all prostitution. Of course, as long as there is a demand for the services of prostitutes, it is unlikely that the police can eliminate the practice even if they wished to do so.

Tolerance about prostitution is partly rooted in the ideology about male sexuality. In Nevada towns where prostitution is legal, law enforcement people favor brothels because "they have fewer complaints of disorderly conduct from the houses than from other establishments which serve alcohol. . . . Brothels are not so much good in and of themselves as they are better than alternative institutions" (Symanski 1974:376). Parents say that prostitution kept their sons from marrying early and their daughters from getting into trouble. The Nevada brothels were credited with decreasing the amount of rape and other violent crime. Implicit in such statements is the ideology that male sexuality, in contrast to female sexuality, must find expression and that traditional values about marriage, the family, and the purity of women are contingent on men's having a sexual outlet. People who accept this ideology will tolerate prostitution.

Finally, social psychological factors enter into a woman's decision to become a prostitute. In particular, prostitutes tend to have had a series of interaction experiences that are negative and indicative of a deviant lifestyle. A comparison of a sample of 152 prostitutes with 117 females convicted of other offenses showed that the former were significantly different in a number of ways (Vitaliano, James, and Boyer 1981; James and Davis 1982). The prostitutes were more likely than the offenders to have had negative sexual experiences in adolescence, to have withdrawn from school, to have used drugs before the age of 16, and to have had incomplete pregnancies. The cumulative effect of such experiences was to lower the woman's self-esteem and facilitate the "slide into prostitution" (James and Davis 1982:348).

Public Policy and Private Action

Prostitutes and civil rights activists argue that prostitution should be decriminalized, that all sex relations between consenting adults should be considered legal (see, e.g., San Francisco Task Force on Prostitution 1996). Among organizations that support decriminalization are the North American Task Force on Prostitution, an umbrella organization that includes a number of other groups such as COYOTE (an acronym for "Call Off Your Old Tired Ethics"). The North American Task Force publishes papers, encourages research, and provides speakers in an effort to educate the public and to promote and support the rights and well-being of prostitutes.

These various groups, along with some social scientists, advocate the decriminalization of prostitution. Prostitution, they argue, is not a sin and should not be a crime. Instead, it falls in the realm of work, choice, and civil rights (Miller and Jayasundara 2001). Women who choose prostitution as their work have their civil rights violated because of existing laws. Indeed, where prostitution is legal, as in certain counties in Nevada, prostitutes are able to work without fear of arrest and are better able to protect their health (Campbell 1991; Brents and Hausbeck 2005). However, since the majority of Americans oppose the legalization and regulation of prostitution, it is unlikely that there will be a widespread change in public policy in the near future.

Even decriminalization will not completely solve the problem. If prostitution were decriminalized, there would still need to be regulation of the business (Kuo 2002). One reason for regulation is health. Current efforts to suppress prostitution are based in part on the effort to control the spread of venereal disease (Ness 2003). There is also the issue of the prostitute's own health—regular checkups are needed.

In addition, because of potential abuse from customers, prostitutes may still feel the need for pimps. If the prostitutes work in brothels, thereby avoiding the need for pimps, they will still be treated as objects rather than as people and will confront the various psychological and emotional problems inherent in the life.

The problem can also be attacked by lessening the demand rather than punishing the supply. In many cities the police have begun to arrest johns and even to publish their names. In San Francisco, a First Offender Prostitution Program allows men arrested for solicitation to pay a fine and attend a class in which they hear a lecture about the law, watch slides that depict the effects of venereal disease, and listen to ex-prostitutes tell how much they despised their customers (Nieves 1999). In return, the arrest for soliciting sex is removed from their records. Of the 2,181 men who participated in the program in the first 4 years, only 18 were re-arrested for solicitation. Although such programs may be effective, the fact is that most states and municipalities ignore laws that allow them to arrest pimps, traffickers, and customers and focus instead on the prostitutes themselves (Miller and Jayasundara 2001).

Finally, a good part of the problem of prostitution could be resolved if women from lower socioeconomic positions had opportunities to gain some measure of success in other kinds of work. The problem could also be alleviated if women with drug habits and/or women who come from abusive homes had other ways to support themselves and to get the help they need to deal with their problems.

Follow-Up. Set up a debate in your class on the question "Should prostitution be decriminalized? Yes or no?"

Pornography, Erotica, and Obscenity

One person's pornography is another person's literature. It is no surprise, then, that this subject generates strong feelings and great disagreement. What exactly are we talking about when we speak of pornography and how extensively does it penetrate society?

Nature and Extent of the Problem

What comes to mind when you see or hear the word *pornography?* What, if anything, do you think should be done about materials that you would personally label as pornographic? Read the following materials, then return to these questions and see whether your answers have changed in any way.

Definitions. People tend to label as pornographic any kind of *sexual materials that they find personally offensive;* but a finer distinction is required, one that differentiates between pornography, erotica, and obscenity (Hyde 1986). Generally, social scientists define **pornography** as *literature, art, or films that are sexually arousing.* You can further distinguish between so-called soft-core pornography, which is suggestive but does

pornography
literature, art, or films that are sexually arousing

not depict actual intercourse or genitals, and hard-core pornography, in which sexual acts and/or genitals are explicitly depicted.

Some people are aroused by sexual acts that others would consider degrading, such as forced sex or sex involving children. **Erotica** refers to *sexually arousing materials that are not degrading or demeaning to adults or children.* Erotica, for example, may involve a depiction of a husband and wife engaged in sex play and intercourse. To be sure, some people will find this erotica offensive and degrading. Yet for many, including scholars who research this area, there is an important distinction between erotica and pornography. A woman being raped is pornographic. Two mutually consenting adults engaged in sexual intercourse is erotica, not pornography.

Obscenity is the legal term for pornography that is defined as unacceptable. It refers to those materials that are *offensive by generally accepted standards of decency.* A 1957 Supreme Court decision, *Roth v. the United States,* attempted to establish precise guidelines for deciding when a book, movie, or magazine would be considered obscene (Francoeur 1991): The dominant theme of the material as a whole must appeal to a prurient (lewd) interest in sex; the material must be obviously offensive to existing community standards; and the materials must lack any serious literary, artistic, political, or scientific value. The 1973 *Miller v. California* decision reaffirmed the position that obscenity is not protected by the First Amendment.

However, the decisions did not resolve a number of vexing questions: Who decides what is a prurient interest? What is the "community" whose standards must be followed? Who decides whether something has literary, artistic, political, or scientific value? What about the Internet? Should the government regulate Internet content to protect children from pornographic materials? The struggle between opposing positions continues in both public forums and the courts.

Extent of the Problem.   Erotica, pornography, and obscenity appear in many places—books, magazines, videos, telephone messages, and the Internet. It's difficult to know just how much is available overall. The Internet alone offers more than 260 million pages of pornography (about 7 percent of all pages) (Paul 2004). As much as 20 percent of the pornographic Internet pages involves child pornography (Klein, Davies, and Hicks 2001). A study of 1,501 young users of the Internet reported that about one in five had gotten a sexual solicitation, and dozens said they had been asked to meet with or telephone the solicitor, or had received mail, money, or other gifts (Bowker and Gray 2005).

In addition to the Internet, each year Americans rent 800 million or more pornographic videos and DVDs, and the porn movie industry produces 11,000 new films. The videos and DVDs range from the erotic to the sexually violent and degrading (Duncan 1991). A study of magazines and videos available in a New York township reported that 25 percent of the magazines and 26.9 percent of the videos contained some kind of sexual violence (Barron and Kimmel 2000). Estimates of the number of pornographic videos rented each year range as high as 800 million (Oliver 1995).

Moreover, as technology continues to advance, new outlets for pornography appear. The increasing capabilities of cell phones have opened the way for mobile porn (Tanner 2006). *Playboy, Penthouse, Hustler,* and others now have mobile divisions in their organizations. And an estimated 20 percent of mobile Google searches involve pornography.

Lebeque (1991) reviewed the 3,050 magazine and book titles surveyed in the 1986 Attorney General's Commission on Pornography to see whether the titles themselves

erotica
sexually arousing materials that are not degrading or demeaning to adults or children

obscenity
materials that are offensive by generally accepted standards of decency

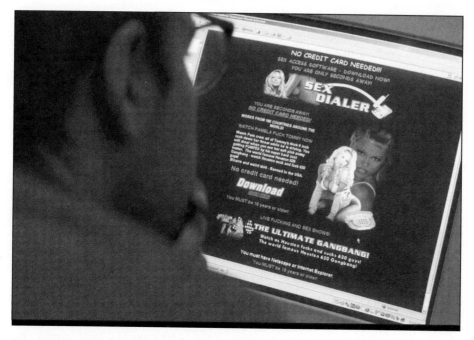

Erotic and pornographic materials are easily accessible, including the violent pornography that increases male aggression.

fulfilled the criteria for an act of **paraphilia** (the need for a socially unacceptable stimulus in order to be sexually aroused and satisfied). Paraphilia is a disorder listed and described by the American Psychiatric Association. Using their criteria, Lebeque found that 746 (one-fourth of all the titles) fit the definition of paraphilia. **Sadomasochism** is the most common kind of paraphilia. It includes such behavior as being tied up, gagged, whipped, or beaten and using verbal abuse as part of a sexual encounter.

We cannot say exactly how much of this type of material is consumed by Americans. Much child pornography used by **pedophiles** (adults who depend on children for sexual stimulation) is underground. We do know that Americans spend hundreds of millions of dollars every year to buy erotic and pornographic magazines and billions of dollars to rent or buy hundreds of millions of X-rated videos, and that a substantial number subscribe to porn television stations (Schlosser 1997; Paige 1998).

Like prostitution, pornography is a global problem, not merely an American one. For example, a study of a random sample of Norwegians found that 82 percent of those responding admitted that they had read pornographic magazines (Traeen, Nilsen, and Stigum 2006). A slightly higher proportion, 84 percent, had seen pornographic films, and 34 percent had looked at pornography on the Internet. Significantly more men than women made use of the pornography (this is also true in the United States).

Pornography, Erotica, Obscenity, and the Quality of Life

With most social problems, there is some consensus about the ways in which a particular problem affects the quality of life. Researchers in the area of pornography, erotica, and obscenity, however, proceed from different premises (Francoeur 1991). Some assume that pornographic materials provide people with an outlet for sexual feelings and needs. The materials are like a safety valve, allowing people to reduce sexual tension without harming others. A different premise is that the materials do just the opposite: They offer models of behavior that lead people to act in sexually aggressive and

paraphilia
the need for a socially unacceptable stimulus in order to be sexually aroused and satisfied

sadomasochism
the practice of deriving sexual pleasure from the infliction of pain

pedophile
an adult who depends on children for sexual stimulation

offensive ways that are harmful to others. Thus, researchers, like the general population, are divided in their assumption about and approaches to the problem.

It is our position that pornography and obscenity do have adverse effects on the quality of life, including some yet not known because there is no supporting research. For example, there is no research that addresses such questions as how the use of pornographic materials affects an individual's day-to-day intimate relationships, including those with friends, spouse, and children. There is evidence that extensive use of pornography produces negative attitudes about the value of marriage, and that wives who discover such use by their husbands struggle with the meaning of their marriage and their own worth and desirability (Linz and Malamuth 1993; Bergner and Bridges 2002). Physically abused wives are also significantly more likely to be sexually abused when their husbands are into pornography (Shope 2004). There is also evidence that exposure to televised pornography has potential negative effects on children, including the modeling of the behavior; interference with normal sexual development; emotional problems such as anxiety, guilt, confusion, and shame; stimulation of premature sexual activity; and the development of harmful attitudes and beliefs about sex and sexual relationships (Benedek and Brown 1999). Consider a few other consequences.

Exploitation of Children.   At one point, at least, there is consensus—child pornography is exploitation. Films and pictures that depict sexual acts with children clearly victimize the children: "Children, by virtue of their developmental level, cannot give true informed consent to participate in such activities, and the potential for doing psychological damage to them is great" (Hyde 1986:514).

Such exploitation is a contradiction with the value of *a child's right to dignity and protection.* A study of 66 children who had been in sex rings found various kinds of psychological damage, including being conditioned to use sex to get attention in the future and/or to boost a low self-esteem (Burgess 1984).

Children are caught up in pornography in various ways, but *frequently the exploiter is a relative,* even a parent. When a porn magazine ran an ad for young girl-child models, dozens of parents responded. An 11-year-old girl was accepted and told to have sex with a 40-year-old man. She ran to her mother and said she couldn't do it, but her mother told her she had to do it because they needed the money (Hyde 1986:514).

Degradation of Women.   American ideology says that all people should be treated with dignity and respect, but much pornography contradicts that ideal. This degradation seems clear in obscenity or pornography that portrays, for example, rape or men urinating on women. Many women feel that pornography generally is degrading because, even if there is no violence, there is a depiction of women as sex objects whose bodies can be purchased and used for male pleasure.

stereotypes
an image of members of a group that standardizes them and exaggerates certain qualities

Pornography also reinforces certain **stereotypes**. Mayall and Russell (1993) analyzed pornographic magazines, books, films, videos, games, and cards to see how women of various ethnic groups were portrayed. Generally, they found that Asian women were depicted as pliant dolls, Latin women as sexually voracious but also completely submissive, and African American women as dangerous sexual animals.

Because most pornography and obscenity involve male dominance and female subordination, it is not surprising that women would react negatively even if no violence was involved. When erotic and pornographic slides were shown to a group of female undergraduates, they reacted positively to the erotica (Senn and Radtke 1990) but they disliked the pornography and strongly disliked the pornography that included violence.

SEXY OR DISGUSTING?

Looking at an erotic picture of a scantily clad young woman, a man responded: "That is the sexiest thing I've ever seen." A woman evaluated the same picture with: "I think it's disgusting." Do men and women always react so differently to erotic materials? Take a survey of a number of students at your school. Enlist the aid of at least one other student of the opposite sex, or make this a class project.

Interviewers should interview a minimum of 10 subjects of their own gender. Ask the following three questions:

1. Do you see any positive value to magazines like *Playboy* and *Playgirl*? What? (List as many as respondents can think of.)

2. Do you see any negative consequences from such magazines? What? (Again, list as many as possible.)

3. Have you ever looked at, or do you now look at, such magazines? Why or why not?

Analyze your results. What positive values do students see in such materials? What negative consequences? Do men and women differ in their opinions? If so, how? Did nonreaders have very strong opinions? Did nonreaders differ from readers? How? Finally, if the positive values and negative consequences identified by your respondents represented the thinking of all Americans, including researchers, what recommendations would you make about the availability of such materials?

Measures of mood before and after watching the slides showed that the pornography led to significant mood disturbance.

Violence. One of the more controversial aspects of the problem is whether the use of pornographic and obscene materials leads to violent behavior. Some researchers find no relationship between the use of pornography and sexual violence (Gentry 1991; Becker and Stein 1991). Others argue that there is a significant relationship between the use of pornography, hatred of women, and rape (Russell 1998). Research supporting the latter includes the work of Boeringer (1994), who distinguished between different types of pornography in his testing of 477 college men. Those who watched pornography that included violence and rape were more likely to be sexually aggressive. Those who watched soft-core pornography were less likely to approve of or engage in rape, but more likely to use sexual force and other kinds of coercion.

Boeringer's research is consistent with that of others who have found an association between violent pornography and men's aggressive attitudes and behavior (Donnerstein 1984; Golde et al. 2000; Malamuth, Addison, and Koss 2000; Shope 2004). In fact, two researchers who gathered data from 100 female victims of sexual violence reported that 28 percent of the victims said the abuser used pornography and 12 percent said that the abuser imitated the pornography during the abusive incident (Bergen and Bogle 2000).

Violent pornography, then, *contradicts our value on human well-being as well as the norm that sexual behavior should be voluntary and not coerced.* Violent pornography affects not only the women who are directly involved. The existence of violent pornography is a threat to all women. Every time a woman sees a store that sells such materials, she is reminded that she is a potential victim.

Contributing Factors

Clearly one of the big factors in maintaining the supply of pornographic and obscene materials is the demand. By the nature of the industry, it is not easy to know who the customers are. An analysis of hundreds of users of Internet pornography reported that the strongest predictors were weak religious ties and an unhappy marriage (Stack,

Wasserman, and Kern 2004). Some women are consumers of pornography, but the majority of consumers are men. Social structural and social psychological factors help guarantee a continuing supply of materials for those men.

Social Structural Factors.   From an institutional perspective, *the economy and the legal system both work to maintain the supply of materials.* Economically, the porn business is extremely profitable. The profit margin on magazines is high; a store with a brisk business can bring in hundreds of thousands of dollars in gross sales a year. Overall, Americans spend billions of dollars on pornographic materials each year, and it has been estimated that about 40 percent of the money is spent on children's pornography (Hyde 1986:515). Even telephone sex is a multimillion-dollar business. In one year, Pacific Bell earned nearly $25 million from the 1-900 porn lines (Francoeur 1991:641).

The legal system presents an extremely difficult issue: *Does any effort to suppress materials, to exercise censorship, violate First Amendment rights?* As we noted earlier, a continuing series of court cases following the 1957 case have attempted to define what is obscene. The reason for the ongoing cases is that the battle over pornography and obscenity involves a *conflict of values.* Some people value openness in sexual matters. They believe that the worst thing that could happen would be to pass any laws infringing on the constitutional right of free speech, and they point out some of the extremes to which people go as they try to guard their own version of morality—such as the removal of a copy of Goya's masterpiece *The Nude Maja,* from a classroom wall at Pennsylvania State University on the grounds that it made some of the female students uncomfortable (Strossen 1995) or the order of Attorney General John Ashcroft in 2002 to cover the bare breast of the statue *Spirit of Justice* in the Justice Department's Great Hall.

Others contend that society must be responsible and responsive to the needs of people whose quality of life is depressed by the materials. They argue, for instance, that to protect the right of pornographers in the name of free speech is a violation of the more basic right of women to freedom from exploitation and inequality (Leidholdt and Raymond 1990).

fallacy   Each side tends to use the *fallacies of dramatic instance and personal attack.* For example, those who argue for regulation may cite a newspaper article about sexual violence by someone who read pornographic magazines and call their opponents the destroyers of personal and social morality. Those who stand for openness, on the other hand, may offer Nazi Germany as an example of a repressive society and argue that Americans are heading in the same direction when they suppress materials simply because some people find them offensive. They may call their opponents prudes or narrow-minded people who are willing to sacrifice the basic rights of all Americans to alleviate their own fears.

In essence, *the legal system has helped both sides.* By its ongoing effort to specify what is obscene, the Supreme Court has made the production and distribution of some offensive materials a criminal matter. In the effort to maintain the right of free speech, on the other hand, the courts have allowed the continued production and distribution of materials that women find offensive and degrading, as well as some materials (violent pornography) that increase the aggressiveness of men against women.

Social Psychological Factors.   *Americans are divided in their attitudes toward pornographic materials.* In a nationwide poll, 29 percent said yes and 64 percent said no when asked whether pornography is generally harmful to adults (Francoeur 1991). On the other hand, 41 percent said that magazines showing adults having sexual relations should be banned from their communities, 48 percent said it is appropriate for stores to remove magazines like *Playboy* and *Penthouse* from their newsstands, and 8 out of 10 Americans want Internet obscenity laws vigorously enforced (Pierce 2002). Perhaps this ambivalence reflects a conflict between the value of personal freedom and a particular ideology of sexual morality.

Public Policy and Private Action

A number of steps can be taken to reduce the flow of pornographic materials in general and violent pornography in particular. One is to provide *education at an early age about the ways in which pornography degrades women*. If boys understand how such materials affect females, they may be less prone to consume them.

A second step is the *mobilization of groups to picket, boycott, and protest in other ways the sale of materials they find offensive*. Boycotts against stores that sold materials offensive to people in a community have led to the removal of the materials. Economic pressure may be effective where other attempts at persuasion fall short.

Third, citizens can mobilize to press for *stricter enforcement of existing obscenity laws*. They can urge more stringent regulation or even a ban of porn cable programs and dial-a-porn telephone services. Such efforts, however, will likely be stymied unless people distinguish between erotica, pornography, and obscenity. Efforts at regulation should begin with those materials most clearly offensive—violent pornography.

Fourth, government at all levels can take action, including the passage of legislation. Local governments have engaged in a number of successful campaigns to reduce the amount of pornography in their communities. For example, New York City officials closed down an entire block of businesses in Manhattan, including porn movie houses, bookstores, and strip joints (Kirby 1996). The city helped bring in retail stores and more wholesome forms of entertainment to the area.

Congress enacted laws in the late 1990s to punish people who make obscene materials available to minors via the Internet. The laws ran into problems in the courts because they violated the First Amendment right of free speech. The challenge, therefore, is to enact laws that regulate obscenity without violating the First Amendment. Children, who have access to some of the worst pornography available, need protection. One such law was the 2000 Children's Internet Protection Act that required libraries receiving federal technology funds to install pornography-blocking software on their computers. The American Civil Liberties Union and a number of librarian groups challenged the law as a violation of free speech, but it was upheld by the Supreme Court in 2003.

Clearly, laws are needed that address the problem of pornography without raising allegations of First Amendment violations. Knee (2004) has suggested enacting laws that make illegal the giving or receiving of payment to perform sex acts. Such laws, he argues, would put some of the largest pornographers out of business because they could no longer pay people to perform in hard-core pornographic films.

Finally, there is a need for *research on the customers of pornographic materials*. What needs do such materials fulfill? Why and how are they used? Answering such questions will point to ways for reducing the demand. This approach is crucial. For as long as there is demand, there will be a supply—whether legal or not.

Follow-Up.   Apart from legislation, what other effective ways can you think of to protect children from pornography on the Internet?

Summary

Sexual gratification is an important part of American life. Some kinds of sex are considered "deviant" rather than "normal." Deviant sex includes such things as exhibitionism, voyeurism, promiscuity, extramarital affairs, cybersex, and strip clubs. Prostitution and pornography are two additional ways of gaining sexual gratification that deviate from the norm. Both involve contradictions and incompatibility with the desired quality of life, and both are sustained by multiple-level factors. At any one time, hundreds of thousands of prostitutes are at work in the nation. The prostitute's quality of life is diminished by physical problems inherent in "the life," as well as by psychological, emotional, and economic problems, including fear, alienation, isolation, and exploitation.

Prostitution is maintained because of (1) norms about nonmarital sex and open discussion of sex; (2) lack of sexual gratification in marriage; and (3) characteristics of the economy, such as jobs that require men to travel and discrimination against women in job opportunities and income. The tolerance of prostitution on the part of both the public and officials is rooted in American ideology about sexuality—the notion that male sexuality, in contrast to female sexuality, must find expression.

It is important to distinguish between pornography, erotica, and obscenity. Such materials are available in multiple forms and are widely consumed in America. Pornographic and obscene materials have a negative impact on the quality of life by exploiting children; degrading women; and in the case of violent pornography, increasing aggressive attitudes and behavior of men toward women.

The materials continue to be widely available for a number of reasons. They are extremely profitable; efforts to suppress them raise the issue of First Amendment rights; and public attitudes are divided, perhaps reflecting concern over censorship.

Key Terms

Cunnilingus
Cybersex
Erotica
Fellatio
Obscenity
Paraphilia
Pedophile
Pimp
Pornography
Promiscuity
Prostitution
Sadomasochism
Stereotype

Study Questions

1. What is meant by sexual deviance?
2. Name and explain six kinds of sexual deviance.
3. What problems do prostitutes face?
4. Why do women and men become prostitutes?
5. What factors help maintain prostitution in American society?
6. How would you differentiate between pornography, erotica, and obscenity?
7. How do pornographic and obscene materials affect men? Women? Children?
8. Discuss the factors that contribute to the problem of pornography.

Internet Resources/Exercises

1. Explore some of the ideas in this chapter on the following sites:

http://www.prostitutionresearch.com Has numerous materials on various aspects of prostitution; sponsored by the San Francisco Women's Centers.

http://www.asacp.org Home page of the Association of Sites Advocating Child Protection, an organization devoted to eliminating child pornography from the Internet.

http://aclu.org The American Civil Liberties Union site that posts warnings on the abridgment of free speech.

2. Good arguments can be made both against and in defense of prostitution. Use the prostitution and ACLU sites listed above, along with a search engine to find additional materials on prostitution, and construct a list of arguments on both sides of the issue. The results can be used for a class debate.

3. Pornography, including child pornography, is a global problem. Search the Internet for materials that discuss the extent of the problem. Compare what you find with materials in the text on pornography in the United States.

For Further Reading

Albert, Alexa. *Brothel: Mustang Ranch and Its Women.* New York: Random House, 2001. Interviews with prostitutes at a legal house of prostitution in Nevada, telling how they came to be there and how they feel about what they do.

Barry, Kathleen. *The Prostitution of Sexuality: The Global Exploitation of Women*. New York: New York University Press, 1995. A discussion of the abuse suffered by prostitutes and an argument that the only appropriate response is to be outraged and to punish men who use prostitutes.

Jenkins, Philip. *Beyond Tolerance: Child Pornography Online*. New York: New York University Press, 2001. A study of the men who participate in on-line pornography that involves adolescent and pre-pubescent girls; includes the men's justifications for their behavior.

Kuo, Lenore. *Prostitution Policy: Revolutionizing Practice through a Gendered Perspective*. New York: New York University Press, 2002. A review of various public policies that deal with prostitution from a feminist point of view, favorable to de-criminalization and the regulation of prostitution.

Raphael, Jody. *Listening to Olivia: Violence, Poverty, and Prostitution*. Boston: Northeastern University Press, 2004. Tells the life story of an American prostitute, from the time she first entered the life until she left it.

Stark, Christina, and Rebecca Whisnant, eds. *Not for Sale: Feminists Resisting Prostitution and Pornography*. North Melbourne, Australia: Spinifex Press, 2004. Using a feminist perspective, various authors cover aspects of the experience of prostitution; includes pornography as a form of prostitution.

Williams, Linda. *Hard Core: Power, Pleasure, and the Frenzy of the Visible*. Berkeley: University of California Press, 1999. New edition of a ground-breaking study of the nature and effects of hard-core film pornography.

chapter 2 review

Alcohol and Other Drugs

1   Learn the types and effects of alcohol and various other drugs.

2   Identify the patterns of use in the United States.

3   Explain the personal, inter-personal, and societal con-sequences of the use and abuse of alcohol and other drugs.

4   Understand the varied social structural factors that facilitate and help perpetuate the problem.

5   Describe the kinds of attitudes and ideologies that underlie America's problem of alcohol and other drugs.

Despair and Hope

Two voices illustrate the trauma of drug abuse. The first is a cocaine addict, a man mired in despair. The second is the parent of an alcoholic, a mother who has hope after years of despair.

• Mark, the cocaine addict, grew up in a small southern town. After two years of college, he found a good-paying job in a large city. For a while, his life seemed to be on a fast, upward track:

But I lost it all because I got hooked on crack. I wanted to hang out with the fast people. But crack is a double-edged sword. It makes you feel great, but it tears your life apart. I was always able to meet every challenge of my life. But I can't beat this drug thing. My company paid tens of thousands of dollars to send me through two rehabilitation programs. I didn't get any better, so they fired me.

I've had a heart operation, but I'm still smoking. Coke is a cruel mistress, man. She don't care who she takes from. And she doesn't give anything back.

Mark, now homeless, is resigned to a dismal existence. In his own mind, he will never be anything other than a cocaine addict.

• Betty, the mother of the alcoholic, is also a victim of the drug problem. Her years of pain underscore the fact that it is not only the abusers who suffer destructive consequences. Her son, Curt, is sober at the present time. But Betty vividly remembers the years of abuse:

He was only 14 when he started drinking. I don't know why. But he began avoiding us, and skipping school. He spent a lot of time alone in his room when he was at home. For years I cried for my boy. But I refused to admit that he had a drinking problem. My husband told me that Curt was getting drunk, but I insisted it was just his allergies.

When he was 18, he left home. You can't imagine the pain I felt. But three months later, he suddenly appeared at the kitchen door. He was dirty, hungry, and thin. I gave him some food. He stayed home, but a year later he came home drunk again and was foul-mouthed. My husband told him to go to bed, and when he sobered up he should leave our house. He did, but three months later he called. He was desperate. We got him into a short-term treatment center, then brought him home again. My husband died shortly after that. I was afraid Curt would go off on another binge, but he's stayed with me and is working now and helping support me.

Betty is hopeful but also apprehensive about Curt's long-term prospects. Like everyone connected with a person who abuses alcohol, she can only live day by day. The grimness on her face as she tells her story powerfully expresses her uncertainty.

Introduction

Americans have had ambivalent feelings about alcohol and other drugs throughout their history. In general, the colonists regarded alcoholic beverages as one of God's gifts to mankind. As Furnas (1965:18) noted, our forebears "clung long to the late medieval notion that alcohol deserved its splendid name, *aqua vitae*, water of life." Drunkenness was punished, but drinking was generally considered one of life's pleasures. Yet by the 19th century a growing temperance movement began urging its members to abstain from all alcoholic beverages (Furnas 1965:67).

Until the beginning of the 19th century, the use of opium and its derivatives was less offensive to Americans than smoking cigarettes or drinking. After the Civil War, however, some Americans began to warn about the dangers of **addiction**. Eventually these warnings became part of national policy as seen in the war on drugs that began in the 1980s.

This ambivalence about drugs is based partly on the distinctions among use, **abuse**, and addiction. The abuse of alcohol and other drugs, not the use, creates the problem. We define *abuse* as the *improper use of alcohol and other drugs to the degree that the consequences are defined as detrimental to the user or to society*. Addiction is a form of abuse. Addiction has been called a "brain disease" because continued abuse of a drug causes changes in brain function that drive the addict to compulsive seeking and use of the drug (Leshner 1998).

addiction
repeated use of a drug or alcohol to the point of periodic or chronic intoxication that is detrimental to the user or society

abuse
improper use of drugs or alcohol to the degree that the consequences are defined as detrimental to the user or society

Not every case of abuse involves addiction. A man may not be an alcoholic, but he may get drunk and kill someone while driving his car. A woman may not be hooked on any drugs, but she may be persuaded to try LSD, have a "bad trip," and commit suicide.

Our focus in this chapter is on abuse, including addiction. We look at alcohol and other drugs, discussing their effects on users, patterns of use, effects on the quality of life, multiple-level factors that create and perpetuate the problems, and ways people have attempted to cope.

Alcohol

The use and abuse of alcohol is the nation's most serious health problem. We examine first the effects of this troublesome drug.

Effects

All alcoholic beverages contain the same drug, ethyl alcohol or ethanol, but the proportion varies in different beverages. An individual can consume about the same amount of alcohol by drinking a pint of beer, a glass of wine, or a shot (1.5 ounces) of whiskey. What happens when that alcohol is ingested? The alcohol is burned and broken down in the body at a relatively constant rate. If an individual drinks slowly, there is little or no accumulation of alcohol in the blood; but if an individual consumes alcohol more quickly than it can be burned in the body, the *concentration of alcohol in the blood increases*.

A small amount of alcohol can result in changes in an individual's mood and behavior, and the effects become more serious as the concentration of alcohol in the blood increases (National Institute on Alcohol Abuse and Alcoholism 2001). A blood alcohol level of about 0.05 percent (one part alcohol to 2,000 parts blood) can make the individual feel a sense of release from tensions and inhibitions. This mild euphoria is the aim of many people who drink moderately. As the alcohol level increases, however, there is an increasing loss of control because alcohol acts as a depressant on brain functions. At the 0.10 percent level, the individual's motor control is affected—hands, arms, and legs become clumsy. At 0.20 percent, both the motor and the emotional functions of the brain are impaired, and the individual staggers and becomes intensely emotional. This is the level at which someone is defined as drunk.

At 0.30 percent, an individual is incapable of adequately perceiving and responding to the environment and may go into a stupor. At 0.40 or a higher percent, the individual lapses into a coma and may die.

What do these numbers mean in actual drinks? Suppose you are a 150-pound individual who drinks on an empty stomach. After drinking two bottles of beer or the equivalent (11 ounces of wine, two highballs, or two cocktails), you will feel warm and relaxed. After three bottles of beer or the equivalent, you will start experiencing more intense emotions and are likely to become talkative, noisy, or morose. Four bottles of beer or its equivalent produces clumsiness and unsteady walking and standing. At this point, you are legally drunk in most states. If you drink four bottles of beer or the equivalent on an empty stomach, it takes about eight hours for all the alcohol to leave your body.

The damaging effects of alcohol abuse are most obvious in the *alcoholic*—the individual who is addicted to alcohol. Alcoholism is defined in terms of four symptoms (National Institute on Alcohol Abuse and Alcoholism 2001): (1) a craving or compulsion to drink; (2) loss of control to limit drinking on any particular occasion; (3) physical dependence, so that withdrawal symptoms (nausea, sweating, shakiness, anxiety) are experienced if alcohol use ceases; and (4) tolerance, the need to drink increasingly greater amounts in order to get "high." Because the effects can be so deleterious and the use of alcohol is so widespread, many experts consider alcohol abuse the major drug problem in the United States today.

Patterns of Use

About 63 percent of Americans identify themselves as drinkers, 25 percent say they sometimes drink more than they should, and 37 percent say that drinking has been a source of trouble in their families (Maguire and Pastore 2006:269–72). A national survey found that alcohol use and impairment affects 15 percent of the workforce (Frone 2006). Some drink before work and some during work. Millions work while under the influence of alcohol, and millions more work with a hangover. By their own admission, then, tens of millions of Americans have a problem with alcohol abuse.

Drinking patterns vary across different groups, though all groups are affected to some extent. American Indians probably have the highest rates of use and abuse of alcohol. Compared to the general population, they begin drinking at an earlier age, drink more frequently and in greater amounts, and have a higher alcohol-related death rate (May and Moran 1995). Alcohol is involved in nearly 17 percent of all American Indian deaths.

Whites drink more than African Americans or Hispanics. And across racial and ethnic lines, men drink more than women (Maguire and Pastore 2006). Gender differences are decreasing, but *alcohol abuse and alcoholism are primarily male problems.*

Alcohol abuse is also more common among the young. A national survey reported that 44 percent of college students were binge drinkers, consuming five drinks in a row (or four in a row for women) on at least one occasion in the two weeks prior to the

Alcohol use and abuse are most likely to take place in groups.

survey (Wechsler 2002). Binge drinkers are far more likely than others to have unprotected sex, to drive after drinking, to fall behind in school, to be aggressive, and to be involved in property damage. Interestingly, going to a four-year college is associated with higher rates of heavy drinking for whites, but with lower rates for African Americans and Hispanics (Paschall, Bersamin, and Flewelling 2005).

A substantial proportion of children and young adolescents also drink. A national survey of 8th-, 10th-, and 12th-grade students found that 75.1 percent consumed alcohol by the end of high school and 41 percent consumed it by eighth grade (Johnston, O'Malley, Bachman, and Schulenberg 2006). In another national survey, 8 percent of seventh graders and 17 percent of eighth graders admitted to binge drinking in the last year (Guilamo-Ramos, Jaccard, Turrisi, and Johansson 2005). Such patterns are important because the earlier someone begins drinking, the more likely that person is to become alcohol-dependent (Hingson, Heeren, and Winter 2006).

Thus, the skid-row image of the alcohol abuser is false. Those most likely to drink frequently and to consume higher quantities of alcohol per drinking session are young, white, male, and comparatively well-to-do (Moore et al. 2005).

Alcohol and the Quality of Life

Alcohol, like other drugs, has some medical benefits when used in moderation. In fact, there is evidence that moderate drinkers, compared to both abstainers and heavy drinkers, have a lower rate of coronary heart disease and are less likely to have a heart attack (Mukamal and Rimm 2001). Alcohol abuse, on the other hand, is highly deleterious to the quality of life.

Physical Health.   The physical consequences of alcohol abuse contradict the American *value of physical well-being.* As mentioned earlier, the immediate effects of intoxicating levels of alcohol include impaired motor performance. The long-range effects of heavy drinking involve impairment of the major organs of the body, including the heart, brain, and liver (National Institute on Alcohol Abuse and Alcoholism 2001). Cirrhosis of the liver, one of the more widely known effects of heavy drinking, is an occupational disease of the alcoholic. A lesser-known effect is the premature aging of the brain (Noonberg, Goldstein, and Page 1985). At any given time, the neuropsychological functioning of the alcoholic—as measured by such things as eye-hand coordination and spatial ability—will be equivalent to that of someone about 10 years older. *In terms of cognitive ability,* in other words, alcoholism costs the user about 10 years of life.

Heavy drinking also may result in muscle diseases and tremors. Heart functioning and the gastrointestinal and respiratory systems may be impaired by prolonged heavy drinking. Whereas moderate alcohol consumption protects the heart, heavy consumption increases the risk of strokes (Reynolds et al. 2003). The ills of the gastrointestinal system range from nausea, vomiting, and diarrhea to gastritis, ulcers, and pancreatitis. Problems of the respiratory system include lowered resistance to pneumonia and other infectious diseases. Among women, alcohol abuse can result in menstrual cycle irregularity, inability to conceive, and early onset of menopause (Gavaler 1991). Among men, alcohol can lead to impotence and sterility (Wright, Gavaler, and Van Thiel 1991).

Alcohol abuse can lead to early death (Costello 2006). A study of male veterans found that the death rate among alcoholics was 2.5 times higher than that of nonalcoholics, and that alcoholics in the 35- to 44-year-old age group were 5.5 times as likely to die as were nonalcoholics of the same age (Liskow et al. 2000).

Alcohol plays a role in various kinds of physical trauma. Consider the following (Rivara et al. 1997; Thun et al. 1997; Greenfeld 1998; Vinson et al. 2003):

Alcohol use is associated with an increased risk of injury and violent death (suicide or homicide) in the home.

Alcohol abuse leads to higher rates of death from cirrhosis, injuries, and various kinds of cancer.

About 35 percent of violent victimizations involve an offender who had been drinking.

Two-thirds of the victims of intimate violence report that alcohol was a factor in the attack.

Nearly a third of fatal accidents involve an intoxicated driver or pedestrian (mostly a driver).

As in the case of other drugs, the health problems of alcohol include effects on the unborn children of pregnant women who drink. The most severe cases are called the *fetal alcohol syndrome* (Burd et al. 2003). Tens of thousands of babies are born each year with alcohol-related defects, and the most serious of them are those with the fetal alcohol syndrome.

Among the health problems of children born with fetal alcohol syndrome are head and face deformities; major organ problems that result in heart defects, ear infections, hearing loss, poor eyesight, and bad teeth; and problems with the central nervous system, leading to such problems as mental retardation, hyperactivity, stunted growth, learning disorders, epilepsy, and cerebral palsy (Streissguth 1992; Aronson and Hagberg 1998; Burd et al. 2003).

Alcohol abuse generally, and the fetal alcohol syndrome in particular, illustrate an important point—social problems have consequences at the community level as well as the individual level. In a real sense, a community can become the victim of a problem, for social problems can strain the community's resources and deprive it of the positive contributions that could otherwise be made by people caught up in the problems.

This point is dramatized in American Indian communities. Alcohol is a factor in nearly 17 percent of all American Indian deaths. A study of the fetal alcohol syndrome among American Indians pointed out some of the consequences, including an overload on community institutions (such as sheltered care), dramatic increases in health care costs, and problems of adoption and foster home placement (May 1991). Add to those costs the loss to the community of positive contributions that could be made by those who are abusing alcohol or those suffering from the fetal alcohol syndrome. Thus, the community at large, as well as individuals, suffers.

Psychological Health.   The *desire for psychological well-being* is contradicted by the various degrees of impairment that result from alcohol abuse. Even a small amount of alcohol can reduce the individual's sensitivity to taste, smell, and pain. Vision can be affected by large amounts of alcohol (one factor in the dangers of driving while drinking). Such problems occur because alcohol adversely affects the brain. In the alcoholic, the adverse effects are severe (National Institute on Alcohol Abuse and Alcoholism 2001). At least half of all alcoholics may have difficulty with problem solving, abstract thinking, memory tasks, and psychomotor performance. Severe alcoholics may succumb to *alcohol amnestic disorder* (short-term memory impairments) or *dementia* (general loss of intellectual abilities, impaired memory, and possible personality change). Some alcohol abusers take the final solution to their despair: Alcohol abuse is associated with a substantial proportion of suicides (Roy 2003; Mann et al. 2006).

ALCOHOLISM IN EASTERN EUROPE

In the 10th century, a Slavic prince noted that drink was the joy of the people. "We cannot live without it," he asserted. Time appears to have borne out his observation. Slavs and other Eastern European people drink, on the average, far more than Americans and have high rates of alcoholism. The problem worsened considerably after the breakup of communism began in 1989.

In Russia, for example, the average adult consumes about four gallons of pure alcohol per person per year. In contrast, the French drink about 3.4 gallons, and Americans drink about two gallons per year. Russians purchase 250 million cases of vodka a year. This is three times the amount sold in all the rest of the world and more than the total amount of hard liquor sold in the United States.

It is not surprising, then, that the average life span for Russian men is only 58. Nor that Russia has about eight million alcoholics; the rate is more than double that of the United States.

Other Eastern European nations face similar problems with alcoholism and consequent health problems and premature death. In Poland, the annual per capita consumption of pure alcohol is around three gallons, a figure twice as high as the 1987 rate. In Hungary, cirrhosis of the liver is the leading cause of death of men age 36 to 60. The number of alcoholics in Hungary doubled from 1989 to 1992.

Why do the Eastern Europeans drink so heavily? There is no simple answer. During the communist era, it was popular to blame the alcoholism on the repressiveness of the regimes. But as we just noted, alcoholism increased rapidly after the breakdown of communism.

A number of factors seem to be at work. In the new market economies, alcohol is much cheaper than it was under communism. In the mid-1980s, the average Polish worker's monthly salary could buy 11 liters of vodka. By the mid-1990s, it could buy 35 liters! In the transition to capitalism, Eastern Europeans have also faced high rates of unemployment and considerable insecurity about the future, conditions that tend to breed higher rates of alcohol abuse. Finally, the Eastern Europeans have a long tradition—stretching back hundreds of years—of heavy drinking. The combination of all these factors has created the highest rates of alcoholism in the world.

SOURCES
Chicago Tribune, April 23, 1995; U.S. News & World Report, April 15, 1996; McKee and Shkolnikov 2001.

One popular belief is that alcohol "releases inhibitions," so that the person who drinks "loosens up" and may, for example, be more motivated toward sexual activity. Actually, heavy drinking inhibits sexual performance, and alcoholics report a deficient sex life or even impotence (Peugh and Belenko 2001). Another belief is that a drink in the evening helps the individual to relax and thereby to sleep better. Whatever the value of one drink, having several drinks before going to sleep decreases the amount of dreaming, which can impair concentration and memory and increase anxiety, irritability, and a sense of tiredness.

Interpersonal Problems. Alcohol abuse leads to *problems of interaction* both within and outside the family. Pregnant women who drink put their unborn children at risk even if they do not drink heavily enough to induce the fetal alcohol syndrome. In a small study, children aged 10 to 18 who were exposed prenatally to alcohol had lower levels of moral maturity and higher rates of delinquency than those not exposed (Schonfeld, Mattson, and Riley 2005).

Early use of alcohol by children is likely to lead to early sexual activity, with all its potential hazards, including pregnancy and disease (Rosenbaum and Kandel 1990). Al-

"I'D KILL BEFORE I'D DRINK"

We once attended a meeting of Alcoholics Anonymous with a friend who had been "dry" for a short time. As we drove through the countryside to the small town where the group met, the friend kept commenting on the beauty of the scenery. He was enchanted by what we thought was a fairly common view on a warm spring evening. But his years as an alcoholic had been a living hell, and in the course of rediscovering what life can be like when you are free of addiction, he was finding beauty in the commonplace. "I really think," he told us, "that if someone tried to force me to take a drink I would kill them." The thought of ever returning to alcohol terrified him.

One of the best ways to understand the impact of addiction on an individual is to talk with an ex-addict. If you do not know an ex-alcoholic, contact Alcoholics Anonymous and attend one of their open meetings. Ask one or two members if they would be willing to discuss their understanding of why they became addicted, what their life was like when they were addicted, and what finally led them to seek the help of AA.

List the adverse effects on the quality of life discussed in this chapter that apply to your informants. Based on your interviews, make a report, oral or written, of your recommendations for dealing with the problem of alcoholism.

cohol use is also associated with risky sexual behavior and is more of a risk factor for sexually transmitted diseases than are other drugs (Ericksen and Trocki 1994). Adult alcoholics have poorer relationships generally with friends, co-workers, spouses, and children (McFarlin et al. 2001). Alcohol increases aggression for males, though not for females (Gussler-Burkhardt and Giancola 2005). This aggression can lead to ill will and conflict with others (Harford, Wechsler, and Muthen 2003; Verdurmen et al. 2005; Graham, Osgood, Wells, and Stockwell 2006), and the conflict can take a violent turn. Homes in which one or both spouses abuse alcohol have higher rates of both verbal and physical abuse (Stuart et al. 2003, 2004; Snow et al. 2006). Even if the drinker is not an alcoholic and is not intoxicated, serious violence can result. A study of homicides in the state of New York reported that alcohol use was likely in homicides that arose spontaneously from personal disputes, and in some cases the alcohol was probably a causal factor in the killing (Welte and Abel 1989).

Even if an alcoholic does not become abusive, his or her behavior is certain to cause *stress* within the family. Mates and children of alcoholics tend to develop physical and psychological problems of their own. Husbands and wives endure painful frustration (trying to cope) and guilt (blaming themselves for their spouse's problems) and may require treatment themselves (Wiseman 1991; Asher 1992). Children tend to develop behavior disorders and, as compared to those from nonalcoholic homes, are more likely to have poorer self-concepts; higher rates of drug use; and higher rates of anxiety, depression, alcoholism, and other disorders when they become adults, as well as lower rates of marriage and of marital quality when they do marry (Rearden and Markwell 1989; Tween and Ryff 1991; Tubman 1993; Obot, Wagner, and Anthony 2001; Watt 2002). The intensity of the stress in an alcoholic home is illustrated by a widow who declared herself to be the happiest person alive because her husband had finally drunk himself to death and thereby set her and her children free.

Economic Costs. Alcohol abuse is costly to the nation. A study of underage drinking alone put the cost higher than the price of the drink (Miller, Levy, Spicer, and Taylor 2006). In one year, underage drinking resulted in 3,170 deaths and 2.6 million other harmful events, costing around $61.9 billion in medical expenses, work loss, and lost quality of life.

The costs for adult abuse also runs into tens of billions of dollars. The costs include the expenses of the arrest, trial, and imprisonment of people who are drunk (in some cities, more than half of all arrests are for drunkenness). They include business losses: people with drinking problems are absent from work about two and a half times as often as others. Moreover, when they are on the job, they may have problems of interaction. Costs to industry are as much as $10 billion a year because of lost work time and lowered productivity of alcoholic employees. All these costs represent resources that could be channeled into activities and programs to enhance the nation's quality of life.

Contributing Factors

The factors that contribute to the alcohol problem both maintain demand and guarantee supply. The problem is embedded in the American way of life.

Social Structural Factors.   Being a part of a *group whose norms and behavior condone drinking* is the most powerful predictor of an individual's drinking (Ames, Grube, and Moore 2000; Thombs, Ray-Tomasek, Osborn, and Olds 2005). Males, in fact, use alcohol to bond with each other and to enhance their sense of importance and power (Liu and Kaplan 1996). Some groups establish a tradition of periodic heavy drinking. For example, about half of those people who drink and attend fraternity or sorority parties engage in heavy drinking in those settings (Harford, Wechsler, and Seibring 2002). Off-campus parties and bars are also settings in which heavy drinking takes place among college students. The hazards of such drinking go beyond any immediate effects. A national study of college and university students found that those who were drunk prior to the age of 19 were significantly more likely than others to become alcohol dependent and frequent heavy drinkers, to report that they drove after drinking, and to sustain injuries requiring medical attention after drinking (Hingson et al. 2003).

Integration into a group in which the use of alcohol is approved does not mean the individual will abuse it. Many people use alcohol without becoming addicted. A lower rate of alcoholism is correlated with the following characteristics (National Institute on Alcohol Abuse and Alcoholism 2001):

1. Children are given alcohol early in life in the context of strong family life or religious orientation.
2. Low-alcohol-content beverages—wines and beers—are most commonly used.
3. The alcoholic beverage is ordinarily consumed at meals.
4. Parents typically provide an example of moderation in drinking.
5. Drinking is not a moral question, merely one of custom.
6. Drinking is not defined as a symbol of manhood or adulthood.
7. Abstinence is as acceptable as drinking.
8. Drunkenness is not socially acceptable.
9. Alcohol is not a central element in activities (like a cocktail party).
10. There is general agreement on what is proper and what is improper in drinking.

Under such conditions, a group or an entire society could have high per capita rates of alcohol consumption and relatively low rates of alcoholism. Group norms are an important factor in alcohol use and abuse, but they need not demand abstinence to prevent abuse. Both Jews and Italians in the United States use alcohol as part of a traditional way of life, but alcoholism in those groups is extremely low. The norms of many religious groups also make abuse less likely. Thus, active participation in religion is associated with lower levels of drinking (Bjarnason et al. 2005; Jessor, Costa, Krueger, and Turbin 2006).

Role problems that generate emotional distress can lead to alcohol abuse (Holahan et al. 2001). People trying to cope with role conflict may resort to alcohol for relief. Those under stress at school or work and those who believe that alcohol relieves stress are more likely to drink (Park, Armeli, and Tennen 2004; Crosnoe 2006). Undesirable role changes also may lead to alcohol abuse. A major loss (for example, divorce or death of a spouse) or separation can result in alcohol abuse, particularly for men (Horwitz and Davies 1994). Furthermore, the loneliness that accompanies moving or loss of intimate relationships is associated with alcohol abuse (Akerlind and Hornquist 1992).

Three kinds of *family experiences* are involved in alcohol abuse. First, alcohol abusers are more likely to come from *homes where other family members are abusers* (Jennison and Johnson 1998; Chermack et al. 2000). Second, alcohol abusers are more likely to come from *broken homes* (Flewelling and Bauman 1990; Wolfinger 1998; Bjarnason et al. 2003). Third, alcohol abuse is associated with various *problematic relationships within the family*, including dysfunctional marriages and troubled parent-child relationships (Silberg et al. 2003; Whisman, Uebelacker, and Bruce 2006). Problem drinking among adolescents is associated with homes in which the parents express hostility to the adolescents or in which there is severe family conflict (Conger et al. 1991; Smith, Rivers, and Stahl 1992).

The *mass media also contribute to alcohol abuse.* Researchers who examined 601 popular movies found that 92 percent depicted drinking (Sargent et al. 2006). The researchers surveyed thousands of adolescents to determine the relationship between watching movies and drinking. There was an association between higher exposure to movie alcohol use and drinking by the adolescents. The researchers concluded that exposure to movie alcohol use is a risk factor for early-onset teen drinking. Similarly, television programs show a great deal of drinking with no negative consequences; adolescent viewers of such drinking are more likely to drink themselves (Pinkleton, Fujioka, and Austin 2000). Finally, a survey of alcohol advertising on radio showed that nearly half of the ads were placed in programs for which the local audience was disproportionately underage youth, thus adding yet another influence of the media on underage drinking (Centers for Disease Control 2006b).

Finally, any social structural factors that increase stress levels are likely to increase the prevalence of alcoholism. In the United States, a *rapidly changing structure* has been associated with increased alcoholism. Both the high rate around 1830 and the increased consumption in the 1960s and 1970s have been associated with stresses induced by a rapidly changing society (Rorabaugh 1979). Another source of stress is a sense of *powerlessness*. You are not comfortable when you feel powerless. Yet the world situation, national problems, your work, and other organizations with which you are involved may induce a sense of powerlessness. If you feel powerless, you are more likely to drink heavily and to have a drinking problem (Seeman, Seeman, and Budros 1988).

Social Psychological Factors.   *Attitudes* toward drinking and drunkenness tend to be different from attitudes toward use and abuse of other drugs. Although alcoholism is a major factor in death and disease, there is little public outcry. Parents who would be horrified to find their children smoking marijuana have allowed them to drink spiked punch or other alcoholic beverages at parties.

The importance of attitudes is underscored by the fact that heavy drinkers have more positive and more indulgent attitudes about the use of alcohol. They are likely to believe that their drinking is no different from that of others in the groups to which they belong and that their own drinking is not enough to be called a problem (Wild 2002). For example, a large proportion of college students overestimate the amount of drinking by their peers (Perkins, Haines, and Rice 2005). And their misperceptions are strongly related to the amount of alcohol they consume: they drink as heavily as they believe that others are drinking.

The problem of alcoholism is further complicated by ideologies—by *the ideology that transforms it into a personal rather than a social problem, and the campus ideology that heavy drinking at parties is both acceptable and the way to maximize one's fun.* Many Americans believe that the alcoholic can recover if he or she "really wants to change"—that alcoholism is basically a problem of individual self-control. And many students believe that heavy drinking, drinking contests, and hangovers are all legitimate ways to maximize their pleasure and prove their mettle.

Public Policy and Private Action

Instead of asking what can be done for an alcoholic, you need to ask first what kind of alcoholic you are dealing with. Experts are attempting to sort out the special needs of the alcoholic with psychiatric problems, the chronically relapsing alcoholic, the alcoholic's family members who may be both victims of and contributors to the problem, and addicted adolescents and women (Abbott 1987). Special programs are being developed for these special needs. For example, the chronically relapsing alcoholic may be placed in a group with other relapsers and undergo group therapy that focuses on ways to confront and overcome the tendency to relapse.

Whatever the special needs may be, of course, the alcoholic is likely to need one or more of the following: *individual therapy, drug therapy, behavior therapy, or group therapy.* Drug therapies involve administration of either a nausea-producing agent along with an alcoholic beverage or a "deterrent agent" that causes intense headaches and nausea when alcohol is consumed. Obviously, drug therapy requires close supervision by a physician.

In group therapy, the alcoholic is in a group with other alcoholics and with a therapist as facilitator. The task of the group members is to attain insight into their individual reasons for drinking and to get control over drinking. The task is achieved by frank and open discussion of each alcoholic's life, feelings, and thoughts. A form of group therapy that is quite successful and does not utilize a professional therapist is Alcoholics Anonymous (AA), which was started by alcoholics. Members gather regularly in small groups to share their experiences and to sustain each other in sobriety. Each member is available to every other member at any time help is needed—when, for example, a member needs to talk to someone in order to resist the urge to drink. Those who join AA begin by admitting they are powerless over alcohol and lack control of their own lives. This admission is significant because it opposes the ideology discussed earlier (an ideology, incidentally, held by alcoholics as well as by others). New members also agree to surrender to a Higher Power (as they understand it), to make amends to those harmed by their drinking, and to help other alcoholics become sober.

Thousands of alcoholics have sought help through AA, which is still one of the most effective ways to deal with alcoholism (Connors, Tonigan, and Miller 2001; McKellar, Stewart, and Humphreys 2003; Moos and Moos 2004). Of course, not everyone who comes to AA will break the habit; no form of help can claim 100 percent success rates.

Two spin-offs of AA that are designed to help family members of the alcoholic are Al-Anon and Alateen. Al-Anon is for the alcoholic's spouse or significant other. It helps the person both to deal with the problems caused by the alcoholic and to see his or her own contribution to the interpersonal problems that may be a factor in the alcoholism. Members of Al-Anon learn to take care of their own needs and to stop focusing their lives around the alcoholic's problems. Alateen uses the same principles to help the teenaged children of alcoholics. Frequently, the sponsor of an Alateen group is a member of Al-Anon.

Behavior therapy is based on the principle of rewarding desired behavior in order to reinforce behavior. The reward can be quite simple, such as the pins given at Alcoholics Anonymous meetings to recognize extended periods of sobriety. Or the rewards can be more substantial, such as the vouchers or tokens given by some therapists for each week or month of sobriety; these vouchers or tokens can be exchanged for various kinds of retail goods or entertainment (gift certificates for stores, restaurants, etc.). The use of voucher or tokens is a form of behavior contracting (also called contingency contracting or contingency management), which is more effective than methods designed to educate, confront, or shock the alcoholic (Miller and Wilbourne 2002).

A somewhat recent trend is the so-called brief therapy. Rather than attending therapy sessions over an extended period of time, the alcohol abuser has only a few sessions with a therapist. At a minimum, brief therapy with alcohol abusers involves a 15-minute initial contact and at least one follow-up. A survey of research studies done of brief behavioral interventions for risky and harmful alcohol use reported that twelve months after the counseling, the clients had reduced their average number of drinks per week from 13 percent to 34 percent more than those who did not have the therapy (Whitlock et al. 2004). During the counseling, the patient receives an assessment of his or her health status, advice, help in goal setting, a motivational message, and other kinds of help.

The problem of alcoholism also has been attacked through various other programs and facilities. Among these are community care programs, which allow alcoholics to remain in their homes and communities while undergoing treatment. Other programs remove alcoholics from their environments. Throughout the nation, there are hundreds of *halfway* houses for alcoholics, places where they can function in a relatively normal way while receiving therapy. Most of these locations have Alcoholics Anonymous groups, counseling, and other services available to the alcoholics. Alcoholics who are acutely ill may have to be hospitalized for a period of time before going to a halfway house or returning to their homes.

Ultimately, to resolve the problem, the social bases of alcoholism must be attacked through public policy. As with other drugs, *enforcement as well as prevention and education programs* are needed. Research has shown that raising the minimum legal drinking age to 21, increasing alcohol taxes, and intensifying the enforcement of drinking-and-driving laws all reduce the number of alcohol problems (Moskowitz 1989; Hollingworth et al. 2006).

Prevention and education programs face difficulty because group norms and alternative means of coping with stress are involved. Nevertheless, there is evidence that educational programs can help reduce the negative effects of alcohol (Flynn and Brown 1991).

Educational programs must help people understand not only the dangers of alcohol but also ways they can deal with the pressure to drink. For instance, adolescents, who are most likely to give in to peer pressure, can resist drinking even in high-pressure situations by using a number of cognitive and behavioral techniques (Brown, Stetson, and Beatty 1989). These techniques include defining themselves as nondrinkers and defining drinkers in negative terms (e.g., drinkers are weak), developing strong refusal skills, finding alternative activities (such as volunteering or religious activities), and limiting direct exposure to high-risk situations (such as not going to a party at which heavy drinking will occur and may even be expected) (Weitzman and Kawachi 2000; Brown et al. 2001; Guo et al. 2001).

Finally, both informal and formal measures can be taken to help those victimized by alcohol-impaired driving and to ameliorate or prevent further victimization. At an informal level, peer intervention—trying to stop a friend or acquaintance from driving drunk—has been shown to be effective in the bulk of cases (Collins and Frey 1992).

At a formal level, campaigns against alcohol-impaired drivers began in the 1980s when a California woman founded Mothers Against Drunk Drivers (MADD). She took action after her teenaged daughter was killed by a man who was not only drunk but out on bail from a hit-and-run arrest for drunken driving just two days prior to the accident. Within two years, the group had chapters in more than 20 states. Other groups formed as well—Students Against Driving Drunk (SADD) and Remove Intoxicated Drivers (RID). As a result of the work of these organizations, a number of states have taken measures to reduce the risks to citizens from alcohol-impaired drivers, including raising the drinking age, using roadside sobriety tests, and suspending licenses of offenders. In some states, a driver with a blood-alcohol content of more than 0.10 automatically loses his or her license for 90 days, regardless of the outcome of the court case. As a result of these varied formal and informal measures, the proportion of fatal crashes that were alcohol-related declined from 60 percent of all fatal crashes in 1982 to 40 percent in 2003 (Maguire and Pastore 2006:278).

Follow-Up. Has anyone close to you—a family member or friend—ever had a problem with alcohol? How did it affect the person's behavior and relationship with you? Describe any efforts or programs that didn't help, and any that did.

Other Drugs

Although alcohol abuse is the major drug problem, the use and abuse of other drugs affect nearly all Americans directly or indirectly. We begin our examination of the problem by looking at the different kinds of drugs and their effects.

Types and Effects

Seven main types of nonalcoholic drugs and some of their possible effects are summarized in figure 3.1. We should note that these do not include all drugs, only some of those that are more commonly abused. New *designer drugs* continue to appear, some of which are performance-enhancing drugs for athletes while others are used for their intoxication effects. We will discuss the health consequences of drug abuse later in this chapter. Here we want to focus on the intoxication effects.

For some drugs, the intoxication effects vary depending on the chemical composition, the amount taken, the method of administration, and the social situation in which

FIGURE 3.1
Some Commonly Abused
Drugs and Their Effects

Substance: Category and Name	Examples of Commercial and Street Names	*Intoxication Effects/ Potential Health Consequences*
Cannabinoids		*Euphoria, slowed thinking and reaction time, confusion, impaired balance and coordination*/cough, frequent respiratory infections; impaired memory and learning; increased heart rate, anxiety; panic attacks; addiction.
Hashish	Boom, chronic, hash, hemp, gangster	
Marijuana	Dope, grass, joints, pot, weed	
Depressants		*Reduced anxiety; feeling of well-being; lowered inhibitions; slowed pulse and breathing; lowered blood pressure; poor concentration*/fatigue; confusion; impaired coordination, memory, judgment; addiction; respiratory depression and arrest; death.
Barbiturates	Amytal, Seconal, Phenobarbital; barbs, reds, yellows, yellow jackets	
Benzodiazepines	Ativan, Librium, Valium, Xanax; candy, downers, tranks	*Also, for barbiturates— sedation, drowsiness/ depression, unusual excitement, fever, irritability, slurred speech, dizziness, life-threatening withdrawal*
Flunitrazepam*	Rohypnol; Mexican valium, R2, roofies, rope	*For benzodiazepines— sedation, drowsiness/ dizziness*
		For flunitrazepam— visual and gastro-intestinal disturbances, urinary retention, memory loss for the time under the drug's effects

Substance: Category and Name	Examples of Commercial and Street Names	*Intoxication Effects/* Potential Health Consequences
Hallucinogens		*Altered states of perception and feeling; nausea/persisting perception disorder (flashbacks)*
LSD	Lysergic acid diethylamide; acid, boomers, cubes, yellow sunshines	*Also, for LSD and mescaline—increased body temperature, heart rate, blood pressure; loss of appetite, sleeplessness, numbness, weakness, tremors*
Mescaline	Buttons, cactus, mesc, peyote	
		For LSD—persistent mental disorders
Psilocybin	Magic mushroom, purple passion, shrooms	*For psilocybin— nervousness, paranoia*
Opioids and Morphine Derivatives		*Pain relief, euphoria, drowsiness/constipation, confusion, sedation, respiratory depression and arrest, addiction, unconsciousness, coma, death*
Codeine	Empirin with Codeine, Robitussin A-C; Cody, schoolboy	
Heroin	Diacetylmorphine; brown sugar, dope, H, smack	*Also, for heroin— staggering gait*
Morphine	Rosanol; M, Miss Emma, monkey	
Oxycodone HCl	Oxy, O.C., killer	
Hydrocodone bitartrate	Vicodin; vike	
Stimulants		*Increased heart rate, blood pressure, metabolism; feelings of exhilaration, energy,*

FIGURE 3.1
Continued

(continued)

FIGURE 3.1
Continued

Substance: Category and Name	Examples of Commercial and Street Names	Intoxication Effects/ Potential Health Consequences
Amphetamine	Dexedrine; bennies, black beauties, speed , uppers	*increased mental alertness*/rapid or irregular heart beat; reduced appetite, weight loss, heart failure, nervousness, insomnia
Cocaine	Cocaine hydrochloride; blow, bump, C, candy, coke, crack, snow	*Also, for amphetamine— rapid breathing*/tremor, loss of coordination, irritability, anxiousness, restlessness, delirium, panic, paranoia, impulsive behavior, aggressiveness, addiction, psychosis
MDMA (methylenedioxy- methamphetamine)	Adam, clarity, ecstasy, Eve, lover's speed, X, XTC	
Methamphetamine	Desoxyn; chalk, crank, crystal, glass, ice, speed	*For cocaine—increased temperature*/chest pain, respiratory failure, nausea, abdominal pain, strokes, seizures, headaches, malnutrition, panic attacks
Methylphenidate	Ritalin; JIF, R-ball, Skippy, the smart drug	
Nicotine	Cigarettes, cigars, smoke- less tobacco, snuff, chew	*For MDMA—mild hallucinogenic effects, increased tactile sensitivity, empathic feelings*/impaired memory and learning, hyperthermia, cardiac toxicity, renal failure, liver toxicity
		For methamphetamine— aggression, violence, psychotic behavior/ memory loss, cardiac and neurological damage; impaired memory and learning, addiction

Substance: Category and Name	Examples of Commercial and Street Names	Intoxication Effects/ Potential Health Consequences
		For nicotine—adverse pregnancy outcomes, chronic lung disease, cardiovascular disease, stroke, cancer, addiction
Other Compounds		For anabolic steroids: No intoxication effects/ hypertension, blood clotting and cholesterol changes, liver and kidney cancer, hostility and aggression; in males, prostate cancer, reduced sperm production, shrunken testicles, breast enlargement; in females, menstrual irregularities, development of masculine characteristics (e.g., a beard)
Anabolic steroids	Anadrol, Oxandrin, Equipoise; roids, juice	
Inhalants	Solvents (paint thinners, gasoline, glues), gases (butane, propane, aerosol propellants), laughing gas, poppers, snappers	For inhalants Stimulation, loss of inhibition/headache; nausea or vomiting; slurred speech, loss of motor coordination; wheezing/ unconsciousness, cramps, weight loss, muscle weakness, depression, memory impairment, damage to cardiovascular and nervous systems, sudden death

FIGURE 3.1
Continued

*A rape drug, associated with sexual assaults.
SOURCE: National Institute on Drug Abuse, "Commonly Abused Drugs," NIDA Web site, 2006.

the drug is administered. In other words, you need to know more than the physiological effects of a drug to understand the experience of the individual taking it.

There are no intrinsic and automatic effects of a particular drug on every individual who takes it. Rather, the *effects vary according to how they are defined* (Becker 1953). A famous experiment by Schachter and Singer (1962) found that individuals who have a physiological experience for which there is no immediate explanation (e.g., you find your heart racing but don't know why) will *label the experience* with whatever information is available. Thus, one person may label a sensation as joy, while another labels the same sensation as anger or fear.

In this experiment, some students received an injection of the hormone epinephrine, and others received a **placebo**. Among the physiological effects of epinephrine are palpitation, tremor, and sometimes accelerated breathing and the feeling of being flushed. All the students were told they had received the drug in order to determine its effects on their vision. Some were given no information on any side effects, some were correctly informed of those effects, and others were misinformed about the effects. While waiting for the effects, each student was sent to a room where a student who was an accomplice of the experimenter created a situation of euphoria for some of the students and of anger for others. Students who had been injected with the epinephrine and who had received either no information or misinformation about side effects "gave behavioral and self-report indications that they had been readily manipulable into the disparate feeling states of euphoria and anger" (Schachter and Singer 1962:395).

Similarly, based on 50 interviews, Becker (1953) found that *defining the effects of marijuana as pleasurable is a learning process*. First, the person must learn the technique of smoking marijuana. Then he or she must learn what the effects of the drug are and learn to associate those effects with its use. For example, if intense hunger is an effect, the user must learn to define that hunger as a sign of being high. Finally, the person must learn to define the effects as pleasurable rather than undesirable. Effects such as dizziness, thirst, and tingling of the scalp can be defined as undesirable or as symptoms of illness. Yet by interacting with others who define those effects as desirable, the user can learn to define them as desirable.

Legal drugs can harm or kill you just as effectively as illicit ones. In addition to alcohol, tobacco is one of the deadliest drugs in American society. In 1997 the Liggett Group, the maker of Chesterfield cigarettes, openly acknowledged that smoking is both addictive and deadly (Vedantam, Epstine, and Geiger 1997). Being legal does not mean that a drug is harmless.

Patterns of Use

It is difficult to know the number of drug users in the United States. Not all users are addicts, and not all addicts are known to the authorities. There is wide variation in use, depending on such factors as the type of drug and the age, sex, race/ethnicity, and social class of the user. Alcohol is the most widely used drug, followed by tobacco and marijuana. About 25 percent of adult Americans use tobacco, a considerable decline from the more than 40 percent who smoked in the 1960s (Centers for Disease Control 2006). Non-narcotic drugs such as marijuana, hallucinogens, stimulants, and depressants are more widely used than are narcotics.

Drug use is higher among the young. The highest usage rates of marijuana, cocaine, hallucinogens, and stimulants, including methamphetamine, occur among people 18 to 25 years of age (Maguire and Pastore 2006:263). They also have the highest rates of usage of legal drugs such as painkillers, tranquilizers, and sedatives. In addition to age differences, rates are higher among men than women. However, gender differences are lessening. Since 2002, more adolescent girls than boys started using marijuana and more of them misuse prescription drugs (Office of National Drug Control Policy 2006). Use also varies by race/ethnicity. American Indians have the highest rates of abuse, fol-

placebo
any substance having no physiological effect that is given to a subject who believes it to be a drug that does have effect

Substance	Total	Age Group		
		12–17 Years	18–25 Years	26 Years and Older
Any illicit drug	8.2	11.2	20.3	5.6
Marijuana and hashish	6.2	7.9	17.0	4.0
Cocaine	1.0	0.6	2.2	0.8
Crack	0.3	0.1	0.2	0.3
Inhalants	0.2	1.3	0.4	0.1
Hallucinogens	0.4	1.0	1.7	0.1
Methamphetamine	0.3	0.3	0.6	0.2

TABLE 3.1
Use of Selected Drugs (percent who used in last 30 days)

SOURCE: Maguire and Pastore 2006:263.

lowed by whites and Hispanics. African Americans and Asian Americans tend to have lower rates (Johnston, O'Malley, Bachman, and Schulenberg 2006). Finally, drug use is higher in the lower than in the middle or upper social classes (Substance Abuse and Mental Health Services Administration 2003; Barbeau, Krieger, and Soobader 2004). In general, then, *the highest rates of drug use and abuse occur among those who are young, male, and poor.*

Table 3.1 shows the proportion of current users of various drugs. These proportions, of course, are smaller than the proportions of those who have ever used the drugs. For example, compared to the current users in table 3.1, the proportion who have ever used the drugs are: any illicit drug, 46.4 percent; marijuana and hashish, 40.6 percent; cocaine, 14.7 percent; crack, 3.3 percent; inhalants, 9.7 percent; hallucinogens, 14.5 percent; and methamphetamine, 5.2 percent (Maguire and Pastore 2006:262).

Trends. Drug use rose rapidly after 1960 and peaked in 1979 (U.S. Department of Health and Human Services 1995). During the 1980s, the upward trend stopped and even reversed for most drugs. Since then, drug use has fluctuated. For example, the proportion of 8th graders who are current users of any illicit drug was 5.7 percent in 1991, rose to 14.6 percent in 1996, and fell back to 8.5 percent in 2005 (Johnston, O'Malley, Bachman, and Schulenberg 2006:52). For 12th graders, the proportions were 16.4 percent in 1991, 26.2 percent in 1997, and 23.1 percent in 2005.

To some extent, the variation in rates of usage may reflect changing definitions of the effects. For instance, when cocaine became popular during the 1980s, one of the appealing aspects was the claim that it gave users a great "high" without undesirable physical effects. However, most people now seem to realize that cocaine and crack (an especially dangerous form of cocaine that can be smoked) may lead to both physical and mental health problems, including chronic sore throat, hoarseness, chronic coughing, shortness of breath, depression, hallucinations, psychosis, and death from overdose (Smart 1991).

Multiple Use. A question often raised is whether the use of one drug leads to the use of others. A number of studies have investigated the question, and in general they support the conclusion that there is a *tendency for multiple use* (Martin, Clifford, and Clapper 1992; National Center on Addiction and Substance Abuse at Columbia University 1998). The likelihood of using marijuana, for instance, is 65 times higher for those who have ever smoked or drank than for those who have done neither, and the likeli-

Because of the expense, many cocaine users are relatively well-to-do.

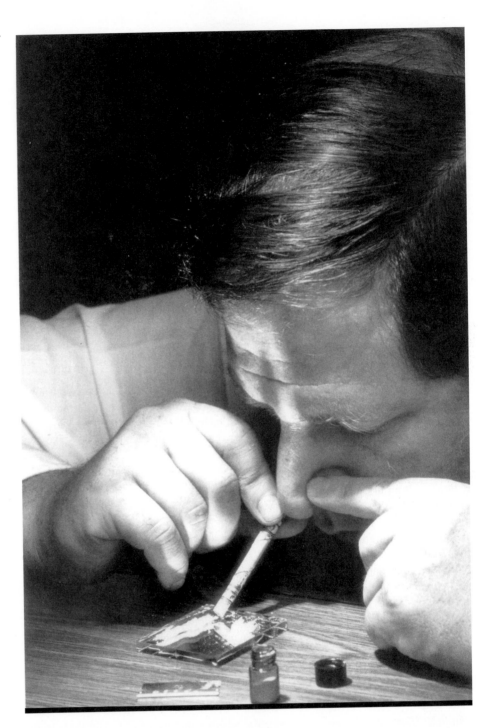

hood of using cocaine is 104 times higher for those who have smoked marijuana than for persons who have not (Leshner 1998:4).

Nevertheless, we cannot say that the use of one drug causes the individual to experiment with another drug. To do so would be the *fallacy of non sequitur*. At this point, we can only say that whatever leads an individual to experiment with one substance may lead that individual to experiment with others.

fallacy

Age of Initiation. Drug use is beginning at an increasingly earlier age (Johnson and Gerstein 1998). Among those born in the 1930s, for example, only alcohol, cigarettes, and marijuana were used by more than 1 percent of people before the age of 35. For those born between 1951 and 1955, 10 drugs were used by more than 5 percent of people before the age of 35.

In both rural and urban areas, children begin experimenting with drugs as early as the third grade (McBroom 1992). Periodic news stories dramatize the problem. For example, two third-graders in Florida were caught with 12 bags of marijuana, and a four-year-old in Massachusetts brought her Head Start teacher a small bag of marijuana as a gift (Sausner 2003). Inhalants are more likely the first drugs with which children experiment (Fritz 2003). As many as 6 percent of American children have tried an inhalant by the fourth grade.

A dramatic change occurs, however, between ages 12 and 13 (National Center on Addition and Substance Abuse at Columbia University 1998). The proportion of those who say they can buy marijuana if they want more than triples (from 14 to 50 percent), and the proportion who say they know a student at their school who sells illegal drugs almost triples (from 8 to 22 percent).

Throughout the teen years, then, young people have increasing exposure to, and opportunities for, drug use. Few users begin experimenting as adults. Adults who smoke, for example, typically become daily smokers before the age of 20 (Centers for Disease Control 1995b). Similarly, adults who use other kinds of drugs, including heroin, typically begin at an early age (Epstein and Groerer 1997).

Drugs and the Quality of Life

It is clear that drug abuse is a widespread problem in America and affects both abusers and nonabusers. Residents in drug-trafficking neighborhoods are often terrorized by and fearful of dealers and users. As we discuss the effects of *abuse on the quality of life of individuals*, keep in mind how whole communities are impacted.

Physical Health. Drug abuse contradicts the American *value of physical well-being*. A person may experiment with drugs because they seem to hold the promise of fulfillment, but the fulfillment is elusive; greater and greater quantities are consumed, and ultimately the person suffers physical and psychological deterioration.

The *physical harm resulting from the use of illegal drugs includes* (U.S. Department of Justice 1992:10):

1. Death.
2. Medical emergencies from acute reactions to drugs or toxic adulterants.
3. Exposure to HIV infection, hepatitis, and other diseases resulting from intravenous drug use.
4. Injury from accidents caused by drug-related impairment.
5. Injuries from violence while obtaining drugs in the drug distribution network.
6. Dependence or addiction.
7. Chronic physical problems.

This list is greatly abbreviated, of course. For example, consider the *multiple consequences of using a drug such as methamphetamine* (National Institute on Drug Abuse 2005). Even small amounts can result in increased wakefulness, decreased appetite, increased respiration, hyperthermia, irritability, insomnia, confusion, tremors, convulsions, anxiety, paranoia, and aggressiveness. Methamphetamine also can cause irreversible damage to blood vessels in the brain, producing strokes, irregular heartbeat, and, ultimately, cardiovascular collapse and death. The point is, drug use involves a long list of physical, psychological, and social consequences that are destructive.

Drug abuse is now the main preventable cause of illness and premature death in the United States. Each year hundreds of thousands of Americans die from smoking, alcohol abuse, and the use of illicit drugs. Early death from illegal drugs is often associated with an overdose of the drug. Heroin slows the vital functions of the body, and if a sufficient amount of the drug is ingested, those vital functions will completely stop. The addict can never be sure how much of the drug constitutes an overdose, nor can he or she be sure about the purity of the drug. Also, the *addict's tolerance level can vary* from one day to another, depending on how much of the drug has been used. If the addict manages to avoid death by overdose, he or she still may die from infections carried by the needle. Thus, the user *is at risk not merely from the drug itself but from other factors associated with drug use.* Crack cocaine use, for example, is spreading the AIDS virus because addicts sell sex for drugs (Edlin et al. 1994).

The health consequences go beyond the addict herself in the case of a pregnant woman. Cocaine and tobacco use are both associated with a significant risk of spontaneous abortion (Ness et al. 1999). Children who survive the risk and are born to addicted mothers have a significant number of perinatal medical problems, behavioral problems in early infancy, and developmental deficiencies in their cognitive and psychomotor skills (Singer et al. 2002). In later childhood, the children may exhibit disturbances in their activity levels, attention spans, and sleep patterns (Householder et al. 1982). Cocaine addiction has a devastating effect, including "strokes while the baby is still in the womb, physical malformations, and an increased risk of death during infancy" (Revkin 1989:63).

Tobacco use is a global problem.   In the United States, it causes more physiological damage than any nonalcoholic drug and is the leading cause of preventable death (Fellows et al. 2002; Bombard et al. 2004). Worldwide, tobacco dependence is responsible for about 4 million deaths each year (Prokhorov et al. 2006). And the number of users increase each year, particularly in developing nations. Among the known consequences of smoking are increased probability of lung cancer and other respiratory diseases, increased risk of heart disease, and increased probability of complications during childbirth. *Mortality rates of older adults from all causes are highest among current smokers* (LaCroix et al. 1991). As many as 85 percent of lung cancer deaths and a third or more of deaths from heart and blood vessel disease are directly related to smoking. There are, of course, people who smoke regularly and live to a "ripe old age," but using them to counter the systematic evidence is the *fallacy of dramatic instance.* What matters is not the few exceptions, but the great numbers who support the conclusions.

fallacy

Moreover, nonsmokers who are exposed to a smoking environment also may suffer. Nonsmokers who live or work in a smoking environment are more likely than those not in such an environment to develop coronary heart disease (Howard et al. 1998; He et al. 1999). Thus, thousands of nonsmokers die each year as a result of inhaling secondhand smoke. Researchers also have found that babies are more likely to develop a respiratory tract infection and to die of sudden infant death syndrome when they are exposed to smoke (Pollack 2001; Blizzard et al. 2003). Smoking parents also increase the chances of their children developing asthma and, in later life, lung cancer (Scott 1990b; Sturm, Yeatts, and Loomis 2004). As a result of such findings, smoke-free environments at work and in public places are becoming common.

Some consequences of other drugs are briefly noted in figure 3.1. We need to examine in more detail, however, the effects of marijuana, which have been a matter of controversy.

Marijuana. Early in the controversy over the use of marijuana, some people insisted that it causes nothing more than slight physiological changes in the user and that it is not as dangerous a drug as alcohol, but numerous studies underscore the fact that marijuana has undesirable consequences that are both acute (brief and severe) and chronic, and both physiological and psychological (National Institute on Drug Abuse 1998; Office of National Drug Control Policy 2003b). In brief, those consequences are

1. Acute effects of marijuana intoxication:
   a. Impaired memory, thinking, speaking, and problem solving.
   b. Impaired time perception.
   c. Increased heart rate (as high as 160 beats per minute).
   d. Reddening of the eyes.
   e. Impaired psychomotor performance (resulting in automobile accidents and deaths).
2. Chronic effects:
   a. Adverse effects on the respiratory system, similar to those of cigarettes.
   b. Reduced sperm count in males.
   c. Possible adverse effects on children when the mother uses the drug, including lowered birth weight and more fetal abnormalities.
   d. Interference with the normal pattern of sex hormones, impairing their release from the brain.

Although it appears that marijuana poses a greater threat to well-being than was once believed, it also may have more medical uses than previously thought—including treating glaucoma patients, relieving the pain of cancer patients, ameliorating the side effects of chemotherapy, and relieving the suffering of asthmatics. Undoubtedly, research on the effects of marijuana will continue.

Psychological Health. Americans value psychological as well as physical health. The search for "happiness," "peace of mind," or "contentment" is common. The short-range euphoria that follows drug use is misleading because the long-range effects of drug abuse contradict the *quest for psychological well-being.* For example, the high that is produced by a drug such as crack can be followed by severe depression. You need only listen to the stories of addicts or ex-addicts to realize the devastation to psychological health that results from drug abuse (Engel 1989). You also should note that, in contrast to the common belief that people turn to drugs for relief from distress, a study of adolescents found that users did not start drugs because of preexisting psychological distress; rather, the drug use led to both physical and psychological impairments (Hansell and White 1991).

The greater the use, the more intense the problems. A study of 161 adolescents reported that increased drug use was associated with increased depression, decreased self-esteem, and a deterioration of purpose in life (Kinnier et al. 1994). Even smoking is associated with psychological problems. Nicotine-dependent individuals are more likely to have problems with depression, anxiety, and lower self-esteem (Croghan et al. 2006; Hu, Davies, and Kandel 2006). By midlife, heavy smoking can lead to cognitive impairment and decline (Richards et al. 2003). And a mother who smokes while pregnant can decrease her baby's IQ by as many as four points (Olds, Henderson, and Tatelbaum 1994).

Similarly, there are serious mental health consequences of using marijuana (Office of National Drug Control Policy 2003b). Regular use by adolescents impairs memory, attentional ability, learning, and psychomotor performance (U.S. Department of Justice 1992; Solowij et al. 2002). Workers who use marijuana are 1.6 times as likely as nonusers to quit or be fired, 1.5 times as likely to have an accident, and 1.8 times as likely to be absent (U.S. Department of Justice 1992:14). A study of Italian men who used only marijuana found that 83 percent were dependent on the drug, 46 percent abused it, and 29 percent of occasional users had at least one emotional disorder (Troisi et al. 1998).

The dangers of marijuana have increased because the drug is stronger than it used to be (Office of National Drug Control Policy 2003b). Marijuana with 2 percent tetrahydrocannabinol (THC) can result in severe psychological damage, including paranoia and psychosis. Currently, however, average levels are 6 percent THC, or three times the amount that can cause serious damage to the user.

Interpersonal Difficulties.   In addition to a sense of physical and psychological well-being, the desired quality of life for Americans demands harmonious relationships. That is, Americans value the ability to "get along well" with others. This value is contradicted by relationship problems that tend to result from drug abuse.

A variety of interpersonal problems are associated with drug use and abuse (U.S. Department of Justice 1992; Office of National Drug Control Policy 2003b). They include arguing with family and friends, feeling suspicious and distrustful of people, encountering troubles at school or work, and getting into trouble with the police. Among adolescents, the greater the involvement with drugs, the higher the rate of delinquent behavior, including felony crimes (Johnson et al. 1991). Young adults who are heavy marijuana users have unstable lives and work histories (Bourque et al. 1991). Married men who abuse drugs have higher rates of wife abuse (Kantor and Straus 1989). Children whose parents abuse drugs are almost three times more likely to be abused and more than four times more likely to be neglected than are children of nonabusing parents, and they are also likely to have emotional, academic, and interpersonal problems (Reid, Macchetto, and Foster 1999; Wilens et al. 2002).

Interpersonal problems may continue for addicts even after they no longer abuse drugs. The ex-addict may attempt to compensate for past failures and assume a role of leadership. The outcome may be a power struggle between the ex-addict and his or her mate. In other cases, there may be unrealistic expectations about the outcome of treatment. The mate of an ex-addict may expect immediate and dramatic changes, and when such changes do not appear, the result can be disillusionment or bitterness. Also, the ex-addict may find that long-term or permanent damage has been done to his or her relationships. The fear and resentment built up over years of coping with an addicted individual may preclude healthy interpersonal relationships.

Economic Costs.   All social problems involve certain *economic costs*, and these affect the quality of life. The more money required to deal with a social problem, the less money there is for other desired services and programs.

Determining the exact dollar cost of any social problem is difficult. The costs of the drug problem include some that can be measured and some that can only be estimated.

There is, of course, a cost to the user: the expense of maintaining the habit (for some, hundreds of dollars a week or more) and the loss of earnings over their life span (Kandel, Chen, and Gill 1995).

The measurable costs to the nation are staggering. Federal funding for various drug control programs is nearly $13 billion a year (Maguire and Pastore 2006:17). State and local expenditures and other costs cannot be easily estimated. They include (U.S. Department of Justice 1992:127):

Criminal justice expenditures on drug-related crime.

Health care costs of injuries from drug-related child abuse and accidents.

The cost of lost productivity due to absenteeism and inefficiency and errors of users at the workplace.

Loss of property values due to drug-related neighborhood crime.

Property damage from drug-related activities.

Loss of agricultural resources, which are used for cultivation of illegal drugs.

Toxins introduced into public air and water supplies by drug production.

Emotional and physical damage to users as well as their families, friends, and co-workers.

Overall, estimates of the economic cost of drug abuse in the nation amounted to $180.9 billion in 2002 (Office of National Drug Control Policy 2004). And the costs continue to rise.

Contributing Factors

The various contributing factors have a double-barreled effect: They maintain demand by encouraging use of drugs, and they guarantee a supply.

Social Structural Factors.   As with alcohol, *group norms* are one of the most important factors in the problem of other drugs, creating *peer pressure* that leads individuals to drug use. For the most part, young people do not take drugs to relieve emotional distress but to be accepted by their peers—and the pressure begins in elementary school.

Group Norms.   Group norms are important for adults as well. Being *integrated into a group in which drug use is approved* is one of the strongest factors associated with drug use at all ages (Leatherdale, McDonald, Cameron, and Brown 2005; Kilmer et al. 2006). The "group" may be your family, your friends, or your peers at school or work. A survey of 1,802 fourth- and fifth-grade pupils found perceived family use to be the strongest influence on the children's drug use (Bush, Weinfurt, and Iannotti 1994). A study of employees who abused drugs reported that they tended to come from families with substance abuse problems and that they, in turn, associated with substance-abusing friends (Lehman et al. 1995).

Some Americans who regard themselves as respectable citizens find it difficult to imagine following group norms when those norms are illegal. They need to realize that people all follow the norms of their groups and follow them for basically the same reasons. The respectable citizen who abides by the norm that the appearance of one's house and yard should be neat and clean derives satisfaction and a sense of acceptance from that normative behavior. Similarly, the youth who uses drugs finds certain *rewards*—including admiration, respect, and acceptance—in that usage when it is the norm of his or her group.

Role Problems.   *Role problems* are a second social structural factor in the drug problem. *Role problems create stress* in the individual, who may then use drugs to deal with the problems and their consequent stress (Goeders 2003). Indeed, when you consider that the first use of a drug like tobacco is likely to be a highly unpleasant experience, it is reasonable that strong forces are at work to develop the habit. Once a youth tries a cigarette, either peer pressure or stress can lead to subsequent tries, but stress seems to lead the individual more quickly to develop the habit (Hirschman, Leventhal, and Glynn 1984).

What kinds of role problems create such stress? One type of role problem is **role conflict**. Two or more roles may be contradictory—as, for example, when a woman experiences a contradiction between her role as a physician and her role as a wife because she does not have time to meet the expectations of both her patients and her husband. Contradictory expectations may impinge upon a single role, as when a physician's patients demand the right of abortion and his or her peers and friends define abortion as illegal and immoral. An individual may define the expectations of a role as somehow unacceptable or excessive, as when a physician feels overwhelmed by the multiple demands made upon his or her time and professional skills.

Physicians have been deliberately used in the examples here because of the high rate of drug addiction among doctors. The actual cause of addiction is not known, but it probably is rooted in a combination of easy access to drugs and the stresses of the role. Drug abuse is a symptom of stress, and role problems do generate stress in the individual. To the extent that particular roles are especially likely to create problems, people who occupy those roles will be particularly vulnerable to stress and perhaps to using drugs to deal with stress.

An important point here is that role conflict is a social phenomenon, not an individual phenomenon. It is not a particular doctor who is oppressed by the demands of the role; rather, all doctors must come to terms with the role of a physician in American society. The expectations attached to the role tend to create the same problems for everyone who occupies the role.

Another role problem that can generate stress and increase the likelihood of drug abuse is a *role change that is defined as undesirable*. Such a role change occurs when a spouse dies. Suddenly a person is no longer a husband or a wife—that role has been lost.

After the loss (which may be the result of separation or divorce as well as death), the individual must work through the grief process. A person copes with a significant loss by passing through a series of emotional phases. The process may take as long as two or more years. Typically, the initial phase is shock, followed by a period of numbness, or lack of intense emotion. In the next phase, the individual wavers between fantasy and reality, overcomes fantasies, and then experiences the full impact of the loss. A period of increasing adjustment follows, punctuated sporadically by episodes of painful memories. Finally, if the full grief process has been experienced, the individual accepts the loss and reaffirms his or her life. The grief process is painful, and some individuals may resort to drugs.

Family Experiences.   *Family experiences* also are involved in the use and abuse of drugs. Families that are strong, healthy, and highly cohesive tend to inhibit the use and abuse of drugs (Wilens et al. 2002; Dorius et al. 2004). Family values and practices such as religious involvement and eating dinner together are associated with less likelihood of drug abuse (Hardesty and Kirby 1995; National Center on Addiction and Substance Abuse at Columbia University 1998).

---

role conflict
a person's perception that two or more of his or her roles are contradictory, or that the same role has contradictory expectations, or that the expectations of the role are unacceptable or excessive

However, the three kinds of family experiences that contribute to the alcohol problem also are involved in the abuse of other drugs. First, as noted earlier in this chapter, drug abusers are more likely to come from homes in which other family members are abusers (Petoskey, Van Stelle, and De Jong 1998; Kilpatrick et al. 2000).

Second, drug abusers are more likely to come from broken homes than are nonabusers. Adolescents who grow up in single-parent homes are more likely to use tobacco and illegal drugs than those who live with both parents (Flewelling and Bauman 1990). Looking at overall drug involvement (including alcohol), rates are higher among those whose homes are disrupted by divorce than those who grow up in intact homes (Wolfinger 1998).

Third, drug abuse is associated with various problematic relationships within the family. The problems may be severe, such as sexual abuse (Kang, Magura, and Shapiro 1994). Even parental conflict and *alienation between youth and their parents* can lead both to the use and abuse of drugs. In their study of adolescents, Simcha-Fagan, Gersten, and Langner (1986) looked at factors associated with the use of marijuana, of drugs other than marijuana, and of heroin. Youths in a home with a traditional marriage and a traditional, restrictive type of mother were less likely than others to use marijuana. Those who used drugs other than marijuana were more likely to come from a home with an unhappy marriage, to report parental coldness, and to have conflict with their parents. Another study reported that adolescents with authoritarian fathers (which typically results in parent-child conflict) are more likely to use drugs (Bronte-Tinkew, Moore, and Carrano 2006). Heroin users also reported an unhappy parental marriage, parental coldness, and conflict with parents. In addition, they were likely to have mothers with some kind of physical or emotional illness. Thus, the use and abuse of all kinds of drugs are likely to be associated with disturbed family relationships.

Of course, the sense of rejection and alienation from parents can follow from drug use rather than precede it. Even if it is true, for instance, that a young person first uses drugs because of his or her group's norms and then becomes alienated from his or her parents, this alienation is likely to perpetuate the drug use. Thus, even if alienation is not one of the causes of initial use, it is likely to be a cause of continuing use.

Government. A fourth structural factor is the government, and especially the *government's definition of drug use as illegal*. For some drugs, the illegal status is the consequence of social and political processes rather than of scientific evidence. Why, for example, is tobacco legal while other drugs are not? Once a drug is declared illegal, criminal elements enter the drug traffic in order to profit from black-market dealings. In essence, illegality raises the cost of maintaining the drug habit, deeply involves criminals in the drug traffic, strains the criminal justice system, and leads the addict to undesirable behavior. Criminal involvement results from the potential for high profits. For example, the street value of heroin may be 50 times or more its wholesale cost and 10,000 times the amount paid to the farmer who supplies the opium! Similar profits are realized in the sale of other illicit drugs and is one reason pushers risk prison to ply their trade.

Economy. A fifth structural factor is the *economy*. The economy supports the drug problem in at least two ways. First, many people who get involved in the distribution, sale, and/or use and abuse of drugs come from the margins of the economy. That is, they are from the more impoverished families and have little hope of achieving any kind of financial success apart from that which drugs appear to offer them. Second, the legal drugs—alcohol and tobacco—are marketed freely and openly, and the industries are so

Ads portray drug users as happy people leading glamorous lives.

profitable that they exert enormous pressure on the government to remain a legitimate part of the economy. The success of the marketing efforts is underscored by the fact that ads are more influential than peers on adolescents' decisions to start smoking (Evans et al. 1995). Research over a three-year period in California concluded that a third of all experimentation with smoking resulted from advertising (Pierce et al. 1998).

Supply.   Although the structural factors that create the *demand for drugs* are crucial, there is also a *powerful organization of supply.* Massive amounts of coca, marijuana, and opium, for example, are grown in Latin America, processed in refineries, and smuggled into the United States. Hundreds of tons of cocaine alone are produced and smuggled into the United States each year (Office of National Drug Control Policy 2003a). About three-fourths of the coca grown for processing the cocaine is from Colombia. Of all the cocaine that enters the nation, 72 percent passes through the Mexico/Central America corridor, 27 percent moves through the Caribbean, and the other 1 percent comes directly from South America. The main ports of entry are central Arizona, El Paso, Houston, Los Angeles, Miami, and Puerto Rico.

Some of the drug suppliers have their own armies and use terrorist activities to intimidate officials. In addition, smugglers exploit the massive corruption that exists at all layers of government (including law enforcement agencies) and among business-people (who may "launder" drug money) in the United States and Latin America.

The supply network in Latin America and elsewhere is so powerful and the potential profits are so enormous that efforts to cut off supplies have been fruitless. Cut off at one point, smugglers find alternatives. Efforts to stop the supply should not be abandoned, but many experts agree that as long as there is demand and profits are high, the suppliers will find a way to provide drugs.

Social Psychological Factors.   People *who have positive attitudes* toward drug use are more likely to become users. Both adolescents and adults underestimate their risks from using legal or illegal drugs (Strecher, Kreuter, and Kobrin 1995; Ayanian and

	Psychic Effects	Dependence	Self-Destruction	Other
All mentions	38	22	33	7
Age				
15 and under	60	7	22	10
16–19	57	17	20	6
20–29	36	28	30	7
30–39	23	24	46	9
40–49	16	21	53	10
50 and over	13	14	61	12
Race				
White	39	18	35	8
Black	33	35	24	7
Other	41	27	26	6
Sex				
Male	46	29	19	6
Female	31	15	45	9

TABLE 3.2
Motivation for Drug Abuse by Age, Race, and Sex of Abuser and Selected Drugs (*percent of mentions*)

SOURCE: U.S. Department of Justice, Drug Enforcement Administration, Drug Abuse Warning Network, Phase II Report, July 1973–March 1974 (Washington, DC: Government Printing Office).

Cleary 1999). Other attitudes are noted in table 3.2. Keep in mind that the data in this table only represent cases of abuse that have resulted in a crisis. Among those people who reached a crisis, a number of *different motivations for abuse* were reported. Some abusers sought certain psychic effects—euphoria, pleasure, and change of mood. Some were dependent on the drug, and some intended to commit suicide.

As table 3.2 shows, 38 percent of the cases involved the quest for psychic effects, especially by the younger abusers and those using marijuana and speed. The quest for psychic effects, incidentally, may be rooted in problems of low self-esteem, low self-confidence, and lack of purpose in life (Dukes and Lorch 1989). In other words, for some users it isn't just a matter of seeking quick gratification through drugs, but of grasping at the one source of gratification that appears to be available.

Two motivations not specifically noted in table 3.2 are *boredom and curiosity;* these are likely to be factors particularly among adolescents (De Micheli and Formigoni 2002; Adams et al. 2003). Adolescents with too few demands on their time may find themselves attracted to experimenting with drugs simply to relieve the boredom. Others may have a natural curiosity that spurs them to want to know what the drug experience is like. Unfortunately, if they define that first experience as highly gratifying, they may continue to use and ultimately abuse the drug.

Motivations may change over the years. A study of 60 clients of a clinic reported that most said they began drug use because of its popularity during their school years (Johnson and Friedman 1993). Once they reached the point of using heroin, however, the motivation became mainly physiological survival.

Finally, *ideology* is a factor in the drug problem. In fact, positive attitudes, group norms, and ideologies about drug use reinforce each other. Friedenberg (1972) identified the following ideology about marijuana:

1. People who are enjoying themselves without harming others have an inalienable right to privacy.
2. A drug whose effect is to turn its users inward upon their own experience, enriching their fantasy life at the expense of their sense of need to achieve or relate to others, is as moral as alcohol, which encourages a false gregariousness and increasingly pugnacious or competitive behavior.
3. Much of the solicitude of the older generation for the welfare of the young merely expresses a desire to dominate and control them for the sake of adult interests and the preservation of adult status and authority.

This ideology, like all ideologies, serves the purpose of explaining and validating certain behavior, thereby reinforcing the behavior.

The attitudes and ideology that support drug use may themselves find support in popular movies and music (Chen, Miller, Grube, and Waiters 2006). A study of 200 popular movies and 2,000 popular songs reported that illicit drugs appeared in 22 percent and alcohol and tobacco appeared in more than 90 percent of the movies (Roberts, Henriksen, and Christenson 1999). A fourth of the movies that included illicit drugs had explicit information about the preparation and use of the drugs. Illicit drugs or alcohol was mentioned in 27 percent of the songs. References to drugs were particularly heavy in rap lyrics: 63 percent mentioned illicit drugs and almost half mentioned alcohol.

The researchers did not look at the effects that the movies and music had on actual drug usage, but you have seen in other chapters that the mass media do influence people's behavior. Furthermore, a study of adolescents who took up smoking found that a third of the adolescents nominated a movie star who smoked on-screen as one of their favorites (Distefan, Pierce, and Gilpin 2004). At least some experimentation with, and continued usage of, drugs, then, stems from popular music and the movies.

Public Policy and Private Action

Is it possible to eliminate the drug problem? No society we know of has completely solved the problem. Even China, which seemed to have eradicated the problem, has experienced renewed drug trafficking (Tyler 1995).

Still, progress can be made, and the severity of the problem can be lessened. For that to happen, programs must attack the social bases as well as treat individual addicts and also focus on *reducing demand rather than stopping the supply*. For example, as noted in this chapter, demand and use are highest in the lower social classes. Public policy that enables those in the lower strata to better their lot will also reduce the demand for illegal drugs. We are not saying that enforcement is useless but only that treatment as well as programs of education and prevention must be given at least as much, and perhaps more, attention and support.

Enforcement Programs.   Enforcement programs involve efforts to prevent drugs from entering the country or from being produced within the country. It also includes the capture, prosecution, and imprisonment of users, dealers, and pushers. A controversial form of enforcement is mandatory testing of employees at the workplace. Some people feel that such testing is a violation of an individual's civil liberties. Yet federal law now requires railroads, airlines, and trucking companies to develop and administer drug-testing programs, and many other firms are setting up programs on their own. Federal law also bans smoking on all domestic airplane flights. Many states have passed laws restricting smoking in restaurants and regulating smoking in private workplaces.

Group therapy can be effective in the treatment of some addicts.

Some local-level strategies are enforcing the laws on drugs other than tobacco (Mazerolle, Kadleck, and Roehl 2004). In street enforcement programs, police watch the hot spots for drug sales and arrest both the seller and the buyer. In some cases, police will seize the assets of a buyer, such as the buyer's car. They also may use a *reverse sting*. Undercover police pose as dealers and arrest users who ask to buy drugs.

Some communities use citizen policing. Knowing that the police alone cannot solve the problem, citizens organize to eliminate conditions that facilitate drug sales. For example, citizens in Seattle set up a drug hotline, lobbied for new abatement laws and jail space, and engaged in neighborhood cleanup projects (Hayeslip 1989).

Treating Addicts. The purpose of treating an addict is to reduce or eliminate his or her dependence on the drug. Because there is no single cause for all addictions, however, there is no single treatment that will work for everyone (Rodgers 1994). One method that has claimed some success with cocaine addicts is a form of behavioral therapy—contingency contracting (Petry and Martin 2002). In contingency contracting, the addicts make an agreement with the therapist to pay a severe penalty if urine tests reveal that they have ingested any of the drug during the week. For instance, a nurse signed a contract in which she agreed that she would write a letter to her parents confessing her drug habit and asking that they no longer give her any financial support. She would write a second letter to the state board of nursing in which she would confess her habit and turn in her license. A Jewish man agreed to write out a check to the American Nazi party. Some cocaine addicts have broken the habit through such contracts.

With heroin addicts, a first step is **detoxification** (see page 93), *the elimination of dependence* through supervised withdrawal. One of the more common methods of treating heroin addiction is *methadone maintenance*. In methadone maintenance, the addict orally ingests the drug methadone, which is considered less dangerous than heroin and

detoxification
supervised withdrawal from dependence on a drug

has a number of properties that allows the addict to lead a more normal life than is possible with heroin. Methadone may also be used in the detoxification program, but detoxification involves the elimination of all drug use—including the methadone after it helps mitigate withdrawal symptoms.

Although there is some disagreement as to whether methadone maintenance is more effective than drug-free treatment programs, it is clear that the methadone program reduces the use of heroin (Marsch 1998). Unfortunately, methadone cannot be prescribed by a physician but must be dispensed at a licensed clinic (Wren 1997). A number of states have no such clinics and thus make methadone harder to obtain than heroin. In addition, methadone is itself becoming an abused drug (Belluck 2003). The number of cases of overdose and death is increasing.

A more recent form of treatment is *brief intervention therapy* (Rodgers 1994). In a relatively few sessions, the therapist seeks to establish a warm and supportive relationship with the addict, while giving advice, exploring various ways to deal with the addiction, and helping the addict see that he or she must take responsibility for getting free of the addiction. The therapist also instills a sense of empowerment in the addict—not only "I *have* to do this," but "I *can* do this."

Addiction is more than physiological, of course. Relationships are involved. Consequently, successful treatment must enable the individual to cope with the conditions that led to the addiction. For many people, this treatment involves group therapy.

One type of group therapy is *family therapy*. Because, for example, adolescent drug abuse is a symptom of family problems in many cases, family therapy may be the most effective mode of treatment (Reilly 1984). For adults, small-group therapy may be helpful. Cocaine Anonymous emerged in the 1980s (Cohen 1984). It is run by former addicts and provides group support to the addict as a means of breaking the habit.

Another variation of group therapy that may be combined with individual therapy is the *drug-treatment center*. The efficacy of the centers is a matter of debate. However, one study showed that 80 percent of the treated addicts were off hard drugs after completing a program at an inpatient or an outpatient center (Biden 1990).

A form of group therapy that is effective for some people involves *religious or religious-type experiences*. A religious orientation enables many people to abstain from experimenting with drugs or to stop using drugs. Adolescents who are high in religiosity are less likely to use drugs (Bahr et al. 1998; National Survey on Drug Use and Health 2004). In a nationwide survey, the National Center on Addiction and Substance Abuse at Columbia University (1998) found that 8 percent of teenagers who attend services at least four times a month, compared to 22 percent of those attending less than once a month, smoked cigarettes. For marijuana, the figures were 13 percent of those attending at least four times a month and 39 percent of those attending less than once a month.

Finally, a more recent form of group therapy involves the use of peer support (Levy, Gallmeier, and Wiebel 1995). Peer support is not new, of course, but the program—"outreach-assisted peer support"—is unique in that it targets active addicts who are not in treatment and who may decide to continue drug use while in the group. Whether they opt for total abstinence or for reduced or controlled usage, addicts may join the group.

Education and Prevention Programs.   Most of the money allocated to the drug problem goes into enforcement, but many people believe that education and prevention are as important—if not more so—because they reduce the demand. Significant declines in tobacco use have occurred in cities and states that have implemented tobacco prevention and education programs, including an increase in the tax on cigarettes, requiring smoke-free work sites, and placing antismoking ads in the mass media (Bauer et al. 2005; Frieden et al. 2005; Netemeyer, Andrews, and Burton 2005; Sung et al. 2005). Programs in schools, of course, must begin early because drugs are available even in elementary schools. In fact, the National Institute on Drug Abuse (2004) recommends that prevention programs begin in preschool. It recommends that programs from first grade through high school increase the academic and social competence of students so that they gain the skills needed to resist drug use.

Much of what young people learn, of course, occurs outside the schools. Antidrug advertising has helped make youth attitudes less favorable toward drugs and less likely to use them (Johnston, O'Malley, and Bachman 2003). Pressure can be exerted on the media to portray drug use, if at all, negatively. For example, smoking shown in movies declined from 1950 to the early 1980s, but in 2002 it was at the same level it was in 1950 (Glantz, Kacirk, and McCulloch 2004).

Decriminalization of drug use is an additional step that can be taken to attack the social bases of the problem. Although decriminalization would reduce the demand for illegal drugs, it is a controversial issue. Advocates claim that it would resolve many aspects of the problem; drug traffic would no longer be profitable (making it useless for organized crime), the courts would not be overwhelmed with cases of drug violators, addicts would not be required to engage in criminal activity to support their habits, and the money now spent on enforcement could be used for better purposes. Opponents claim that decriminalization would only exacerbate the problem: cheap, readily available drugs would increase the rate of addiction; the health costs of dealing with abuse would skyrocket; and the citizenry would get the wrong message (namely, that drug use is OK).

Some state laws regarding marijuana already have been revised. Have the changes resulted in massive increases in the use of the drug, as critics of decriminalization anticipated? Studies of the situation in three states that decriminalized marijuana usage—Oregon, California, and Maine—show that while some officials and citizens believe the problem has worsened, there was little increase in the number of users (Maloff 1981; Petersen 1981).

Follow-Up.   Do you favor the decriminalization of drugs as a way to ease the problem? Why or why not?

Summary

The problem of alcohol and other drugs is one of abuse and not merely of use. Various drugs have various effects, and the effects depend on the method of administration, the amount taken, and the social situation as well as the chemical composition of the drug. Alcohol is the most widely used drug, and its effects can be extremely deleterious. Many experts consider alcohol abuse much more serious than abuse of other drugs.

Around 1980, drug use of all kinds began to decline for the first time in two decades. In the 1990s, patterns of use fluctuated. Although less than in the peak years, use and abuse are still quite high. More than one-half of all Americans drink, and more than a third say that drinking has been a source of trouble in their families. Millions of Americans indicate that they are current users of marijuana. Many users tend toward multiple drug use. Most alcohol abusers are young and male but not poor, whereas other drug addicts tend to be young, male, and poor.

The meaning of the drug problem for the quality of life is seen in the consequences for physical health, psychological health, interpersonal relationships, and economic costs. Abusers suffer various undesirable effects in all areas, and they inflict suffering on others. The nation as a whole also suffers great economic cost because billions of dollars per year are involved in lost services and in efforts to combat the deleterious effects of abuse.

Various structural factors contribute to the problem. An important one is group norms. Integration into a group that approves drug use is one of the most reliable predictors of use. Role problems, including role conflict and undesirable role change, create stress in the individual and that stress can lead to abuse. Abusers are more likely to come from homes in which family members are abusers, from broken homes, or from homes with problematic relationships. The government's definition of many drugs as illegal has several implications: more people are classified as criminal; previously classified criminals become deeply involved in the drug traffic; the criminal justice system is strained; and users and abusers are led into various kinds of undesirable behavior. Finally, the suppliers of illegal drugs are organized effectively and take advantage of corruption, so that a supply will always be available when there is a demand and profits are high.

Among social psychological factors is the alienation of users from the larger society. Many people believe drug use produces desirable psychic effects. These positive attitudes toward drug use combine with group norms and various ideologies that develop in groups. The ideologies explain and validate drug use.

In treating the problem, efforts to help the individual abuser or reduce the supply available to users have far exceeded efforts to get at the social roots of the problem. If it is to be dealt with effectively, both approaches are needed—attacks on the social factors as well as treatment of individual abusers.

Key Terms

Abuse	Placebo
Addiction	Role Conflict
Detoxification	

Study Questions

1. What is meant by the fact that Americans have had ambivalent feelings about alcohol and other drugs throughout their history?
2. Identify the various types of drugs and briefly note their effects on people.
3. Who are the most likely users and abusers of alcohol and other drugs?
4. How do the use and abuse of alcohol and other drugs affect physical health?
5. What are the consequences of alcohol and other drugs for psychological health?
6. How does alcohol affect interpersonal relationships?
7. Indicate the economic costs of drug use and abuse.
8. In what ways do group norms affect patterns of drug use?
9. What kind of role problems enter into drug use and abuse?
10. How do social institutions contribute to the problem?
11. What are the attitudes and ideologies that are important in understanding the drug problem?

12. Name some steps that can be taken to alleviate the problem of alcohol and other drugs.

Internet Resources/ Exercises

1. Explore some of the ideas in this chapter on the following sites:

http://www.nida.nih.gov The National Institute on Drug Abuse site contains news, publications, and links to other sources.

http://www.casacolumbia.org Site of the National Center on Addiction and Substance Abuse at Columbia University, with a focus on studying and combating substance abuse. Has publications and links to other resources.

http://ash.org The Action on Smoking and Health home page provides information on nonsmokers' rights, smoking statistics and information, and help for stopping.

2. Look at figure 3.1 in the text. Select five drugs and get detailed information on them from the National Institute on Drug Abuse site. If everyone had this information, how many people would still experiment with the drugs? Give arguments both for maintaining that nobody would be a user and for asserting that some would still be users.

3. Search the Internet for "drug use" and "tobacco." Find sites that defend people's right to be users. List the reasons, and respond to them with materials in the text.

For Further Reading

Clawson, Patrick L., Rensselaer W. Lee III, and Rensselaer W. Lee. *The Andean Cocaine Industry.* New York: St. Martin's, 1998. An examination of cocaine, beginning with its cultivation in South America to its sale on American streets. Includes an analysis of the economic and political effects of the drug business on Andean nations.

Dodes, Lance M. *The Heart of Addiction: A New Approach to Understanding and Managing Alcoholism and Other Addictive Behaviors.* New York: HarperCollins, 2002. Identifies myths about addiction and discusses the common elements in addictions of all types. Includes addiction problems of particular groups and ways to get help.

Engel, Joel. *Addicted: Kids Talking about Drugs in Their Own Words.* New York: Tom Doherty Associates, 1989. Ten young people tell in their own words how drugs overtook their lives and controlled them. Most began with alcohol and marijuana before they were 13 years old.

Erdmann, Jack. *Whiskey's Children.* New York: Kensington, 1997. An account of the personal trauma endured by a man whose drinking resulted in both personal and professional disasters.

Gahlinger, Paul M. *Illegal Drugs: A Complete Guide to Their History, Chemistry, Use, and Abuse.* Las Vegas, NV: Sagebrush Press, 2001. A professor of medicine provides a comprehensive account of all aspects of drug use and abuse for the nonspecialist general reader.

Jersild, Devon. *Happy Hours: Alcohol in a Woman's Life.* New York: HarperCollins, 2001. Both statistics and personal stories highlight the increasingly serious problem of women's abuse of alcohol, including the unique challenges women face as they try to overcome their addiction.

Kluger, Richard. *Ashes to Ashes: America's Hundred-Year Cigarette War, the Public Health, and the Unabashed Triumph of Philip Morris.* New York: Vintage Books, 1997. A comprehensive examination of the American tobacco industry and the complex social, medical, economic, and psychological factors in the industry's growth and the current controversies and legal battles.

Crime and Delinquency

A Victim Recovers

Marcia, in her 20s, is one of the few survivors of an attack by a serial killer and rapist. After her assailant was sentenced to die for the murder of five young women and the rape of two others, Marcia told her story publicly. Like others, she felt a kind of double victimization:

I was only 22 when he appeared in my bedroom doorway, a bandanna covering his features, a knife raised high as he leaped toward my bed. A week before, he had been a visitor in my home, passing the time during the week he stayed as the houseguest of a neighbor.

Nothing could have prepared me for the viciousness I would experience in the following hours, reduced from a human being to an "it" in the mind and actions of this man. He dragged me around my house by the neck for several hours, forced me to do unspeakable things and twice strangled me into unconsciousness.

I fully expected to die before the night passed, hoping only to die with some dignity. He is 14 inches taller than me and twice my weight. I began to fight him with my mind. It became critical that I showed no fear because when I showed fear, he fed on it. I told him excuses for his behavior. Each time he hurt me, I chastised him almost cheerfully as though I was his friend. Four and a half hours after it started, he walked away of his own accord. I had managed to convince him that he had nothing to fear from me.

Just as nothing could have prepared me for him, nothing prepared me for the seven years ahead, in which I would keep alive these hideous memories for the appeasement of an overburdened and overindulgent criminal defense system. I remember being disheveled and in shock in my living room and the policeman asking me how committed I was to prosecuting my assailant. I told him that I would do whatever I had to do. I could not have known that it would take seven years and three trials. I had to describe to three juries in painful detail the kind of agony he meted out to his victims. Despite my anger that the families of the victims and myself have been further victimized to this extent by a system that gave him every reasonable—and unreasonable— concession and delay over the years, I do not regret my decision to testify.

In the end, I can only mourn at the tragic waste he represents, not only in his victims—and I am no longer one of them—but in himself. However, I'm not so noble as to keep back some satisfaction that this random killer should find that the blood on his hands is also his own.

Introduction

Americans frequently get upset or angry about the problem of crime. A small child is killed, a mother is strangled by her estranged husband, or a businessman cheats people out of their retirement. Such crimes enrage people and can lead to an increased demand for law and order.

Indeed, current statistics on crime rates underscore the need for concern. In 2005, the FBI reported that a violent crime occurred every 22.7 seconds and a property crime occurred every 3.1 seconds (figure 4.1). At those rates, almost everyone will be a victim of a crime at some point in his or her lifetime, and nearly five out of every six will be the victim of a violent crime.

In contrast to this emphasis on major crimes like murder, robbery, and theft, historian Herbert Butterfield suggested that a society can be destroyed by crimes involving "petty breaches of faith" of "very nice people" (Butterfield 1949:54). These two contrasting points of view form the theme of this chapter: Crime is a social problem that pervades American society, and it *includes both respectable and nonrespectable citizens.*

First, we look at the varieties of crime and define crime and delinquency. We then examine the extent of crime in the United States, the effects that crime and delinquency have on the quality of life, and the kinds of sociocultural factors that contribute to the problem. Finally, we discuss measures that can be taken and have been taken to resolve the problem.

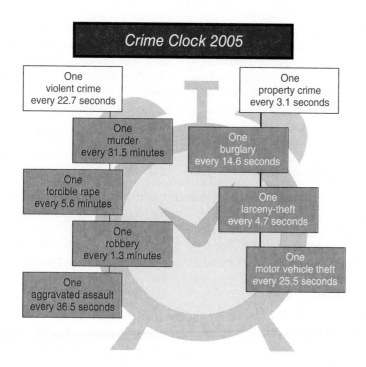

FIGURE 4.1
The FBI "Crime Clocks"
Dramatize the Extensiveness
of Crime in the United
States.

Source: U.S. Federal Bureau of
Investigation, Web site, 2006.

The Varieties of Crime

Technically, crime is any violation of the criminal law. However, as you will see when we examine white-collar crime, this definition is inadequate. Nevertheless, we begin with a discussion of the kinds of acts embodied in the criminal law—acts that are defined as threatening to the state or to citizens whom the state is obligated to protect.

Predatory Crime

When the word *crime* is mentioned, people generally think of **predatory crimes**—*acts that have victims who suffer loss of property or some kind of physical harm.* Property crimes are more common, but the public generally defines crimes against persons as more serious. Less than 10 percent of all crime involves acts such as murder and rape, but these violent acts are the ones that arouse the greatest public apprehension.

The most commonly used measure of *crime rates*—the *Federal Bureau of Investigation Crime Index*—covers eight major felonies, all serious violations of the criminal law, and all predatory crimes. The FBI defines them as follows (Federal Bureau of Investigation 2000:407): (1) *Murder and nonnegligent manslaughter* are willful killing of a person. Not included are deaths by negligence, suicide, accident, and justifiable homicide. (2) *Aggravated assault,* "an unlawful attack by one person upon another for the purpose of inflicting severe bodily injury," usually involves a weapon. (3) *Forcible rape* is defined as actual or attempted sexual intercourse "through the use of force or the threat of force." (4) *Robbery* is the use of force or threat of force to take something of value from a person. (5) *Burglary*—by definition the "unlawful entry of a structure to commit a felony or theft"—does not necessarily mean force was used to gain entry. (6) *Larceny-theft* is the "unlawful taking or stealing of property or articles without the

predatory crimes
acts that have victims who
suffer loss of property or
some kind of physical harm

use of force, violence, or fraud." It includes shoplifting, picking pockets, purse snatching, and the like. (7) *Motor vehicle theft* includes both actual and attempted theft of any motor vehicle. (8) Finally, *arson* is any "willful or malicious burning or attempt to burn, with or without intent to defraud, a dwelling house, public building, motor vehicle or aircraft, personal property of another, etc."

Because not all predatory crimes are included in the FBI Index, the Index cannot be used as an indication of the total amount of crime in the society. Fraud, for example, is not counted, nor are many of the white-collar crimes that we discuss.

Illegal Service Crimes

Illegal service crimes do not involve a definite victim but rather *a relationship between a criminal and his customer.* The illegal service rendered might be drugs, gambling, prostitution, or high-interest loans. Although these relationships violate the law, they are not likely to be reported, because the criminal and the customer probably prefer to have the service available.

Public Disorder Crimes

Public disorder crimes also have no definite victim. They involve behavior that *is treated as criminal only when it occurs before some audience that will be offended.* These crimes include behavior such as disorderly conduct, drunkenness, and indecent exposure. Public disorder crimes are more common than predatory or illegal service crimes, according to arrest figures.

Crimes of Negligence

Crimes of negligence involve an *unintended victim or potential victim.* They include actions such as reckless driving and other infractions of the law by automobile drivers. The "criminal" in this case is not deemed to be deliberately trying to harm anyone. Rather, the behavior is a threat or a nuisance from which the public should be protected. Negligence crimes and public disorder crimes compose the bulk of police work in the United States.

Computer Crime

Computer crime is growing rapidly (Holt 2003). In the workplace alone, computer crime costs businesses more than a billion dollars each year (Goodman 2001). In essence, computer crime is "any illegal act for which knowledge of computer technology is used to commit the offense" (Conly and McEwen 1990:3).

There are five basic types of computer crime (Conly and McEwen 1990:3): *Internal computer crimes* are alterations to computer programs to change the outcome in some way. For example, financial records can be systematically changed or even deleted. *Telecommunication crimes* involve the use of telephone lines to gain illegal access to computer systems or to misuse the telephone system. In one case, a man found a way to avoid the tracking system for long-distance calls. He sold time to friends and made international calls for them. The company lost more than $100,000 before the man was caught.

Computer manipulation crimes involve changing data or creating records in a system for the purpose of engaging in some illegal activity. Embezzlers use this technique; they create false accounts or modify the data in existing accounts. *Support of criminal enterprises* involves the use of databases for drug trafficking, money launder-ing, or other activities. A prostitution ring with at least $3 million yearly income used a microcomputer system to monitor its operations in a metropolitan area. Prostitutes and clients could call the central office, which checked the names and arranged the meet-ings. Client information on file included name, credit card number, and preferred type of prostitute. Finally, *hardware and software theft* includes such actions as software piracy (making a copy of software rather than paying for it) and thefts of microproces-sor chips and trade secrets.

White-Collar Crime

White-collar crime is the crime of "respectable" people. The term was coined by Edwin Sutherland (Sutherland and Cressey 1955), who said that white-collar crimes are *committed by respectable people in the course of their work*. White-collar crimes include consumer fraud, which may be the most widespread of all the crimes (Rosoff, Pontell, and Tillman 2002); environmental offenses; insider trading in stocks; securi-ties fraud; government corruption; computer crime; and misleading advertising.

white-collar crime
crimes committed by respectable citizens in the course of their work

In an effort to categorize the various kinds of white-collar crime, Edelhertz (1983) suggests four types. First are "personal," or "ad hoc" crimes. The individual in this case generally does not have a face-to-face confrontation with the victim. Cheating on federal income taxes and identity theft are examples of such crimes. *Identity theft* includes the unauthorized use of someone's credit card or bank or business account, and using someone's personal information to get a loan or commit other kinds of crime (Baum 2006). In 2004, 3.6 million households, representing 3 percent of the total, had at least one member of the household who was a victim of identity theft during the previous six months.

A second type of white-collar crime involves "abuses of trust," which are crimes committed by people who have custody of someone else's wealth (e.g., embezzlement) or who have the power to make decisions (e.g., accepting a bribe to make a favorable decision). Third are crimes that are "incidental to and in furtherance of organizational operations," though they are not part of the purpose of the organization. Violations of antitrust laws and the federal Corrupt Practices Act fit in here. Or on a smaller scale, Edelhertz says that this "most troublesome" of the four categories involves such issues as fraudulent Medicare or Medicaid claims and the false weight on purchases at the grocery.

Edelhertz calls this third category the most troublesome because the offenders do not think of themselves as criminals and generally have high status in their communi-ties. Nevertheless, the outcome is victimization of people. Consider, for instance, the problem of deceptive advertising. The advertising agency and the corporate executives who pay for ads do not think of themselves as engaging in criminal activity. Yet mil-lions of Americans buy products based on this deceptive advertising.

The fourth category is white-collar crime carried on as a business by full-time con artists. This category includes actions from stock swindles to street games in which people are cheated out of their money.

White-collar crime abounds at all levels: individuals, small businesses, large cor-porations, and governmental agencies. Examples of individuals include computer criminals, some of whom work out of their homes to defraud companies. At the small business level, an example is insurance fraud in auto body repair shops. A study in Massachusetts found that estimates of the shops were significantly higher for customers

White-collar criminals
are usually high-status
individuals who appear to be
successful and respectable.

with insurance coverage than without, independently of the type of car or extent of the damage (Tracy and Fox 1989).

Large corporations also get involved in white-collar crime, including, in recent years, a brokerage firm that committed 2,000 felonies, a health-care organization that paid bribes and kickbacks to doctors, a health maintenance organization that defrauded government health programs, an accounting firm that set up fraudulent shelters to help rich clients evade billions of dollars in taxes, and the Enron corporation's "creative" accounting practices and manipulation of energy markets (Eichenwald 2002; McClam 2005). The Enron case illustrates how far-reaching the effects of corporate crime can be. Among other things, the actions of the Enron executives resulted in California energy costs that soared when markets were manipulated, hurting countless individuals and businesses that could not afford the higher rates; investors lost huge sums of money and many, including Enron employees, lost their life savings and retirement when the corporation collapsed; and many Enron employees lost their jobs.

Although some Enron officials received prison sentences, in many cases of corporate crime the only punishment meted out is a fine. In fact, some of the "crimes" are not defined as illegal by the law. Corporate lawyers are skilled at advising business executives on ways to avoid breaking the law while engaging in questionable practices. Sometimes their advice may be counterproductive: Many of the Enron accounting practices and trading strategies were approved by law firms advising the corporation (France 2004). In other situations, such as a tax shelter that the Internal Revenue Service declares illegal, the fact that the individual or company was advised by a lawyer that the shelter was legal often means no criminal prosecution and lower civil liability (France 2004).

Because of such abuses, Sutherland argued that many practices of respectable people that are not defined by the law as crimes should be treated as crimes. He asserted, in fact, that businesspeople were more criminalistic than people of the ghettoes. A major difference is that criminal law distinguishes between the two groups, so that some acts that logically could be defined as crime are not in the criminal law. Further, some acts involving businesses and corporations are handled by governmental commissions rather than the criminal justice system. You can reasonably argue that when a company advertises a 6 percent interest rate on installment payments and actually collects 11.5 percent, it is committing fraud. The executives of the company will not be charged with fraud; the company will merely be ordered by the Federal Trade Commission (FTC) to stop advertising the false rate.

Even when the offense is covered by the criminal law, white-collar criminals may receive less severe punishment or escape punishment altogether. For one thing, the number of white-collar crimes prosecuted declined 28 percent in the early 2000s as concern shifted to homeland security and prosecution of illegal immigration (Marks 2006). For another thing, when fines are levied against companies, they may have their fines reduced later or the fines may go unpaid (Mendoza and Sullivan 2006). Still, the courts have sentenced a number of executives to prison terms in recent years, ranging from 1 to 25 years. Experts applaud such convictions, arguing that white-collar crime is at least as serious as, or even more serious than, the violent acts of street criminals. Street criminals tax the patience and resources of society, but white-collar criminals are like an insidious corrosion that slowly but surely destroys.

Organized Crime

The term "organized crime" brings up images of Al Capone, machine guns, the Mafia, the Mob, La Cosa Nostra, the Syndicate, and films like *The Untouchables* and *The Godfather*. Is organized crime such a phenomenon in the United States? Are there groups that control the criminal activities of cities, regions, or even the entire nation? Criminologists themselves do not agree on the exact nature of organized crime, but there is some consensus on five characteristics of **organized crime**: the determination of a group of people to make money by any means necessary; the provision of illegal goods and services to people who want them or can be coerced into taking them; the use of political corruption to maintain and extend the activities; the persistence of the activities by the same organizations over successive generations of people; and a code of conduct for members (see, e.g., Berger 1999). There is also likely to be some involvement in legitimate business, which is used to launder illegal funds or stolen merchandise. For instance, profits from drug sales may be claimed as legitimate profits of a legitimate business by manipulating its accounting records.

organized crime
an ongoing organization of people who provide illegal services and goods and who maintain their activities by the aid of political corruption

The activities of organized crime include gambling, prostitution, drugs, extortion, loan-sharking, and various legitimate enterprises (such as restaurants) that are used to launder money received from the illegal activities (Motivans 2003). There is, however, no single organization that controls all organized crime at the international or national level. Rather, there are numerous and diverse groups.

In addition to groups like the Mafia and La Cosa Nostra, there are some new faces in organized crime in the United States (Delattre 1990; Ostrow 1991; Ianni 1998). White supremacist outlaw motorcycle gangs deal in drugs, weapons, extortion, prostitution, and contract murder. Asian organized crime, particularly the numerous Chinese gangs, tends to specialize in drugs. Chinese criminal gangs have taken over some of the heroin trafficking from the Mafia. Colombian cartels specialize in cocaine. Jamaican posses control a portion of the traffic in crack and have been implicated in thousands of drug-related murders. Some of the groups originated in America, and others involve immigrants who may still have ties to foreign-based criminal organizations. Organized crime is no longer the province of any particular racial or ethnic group. Rather, it involves diverse groups who use it to gain economic and social mobility.

Juvenile Delinquency

The concept of juvenile delinquency is a modern one. Until the late 19th century, juvenile offenders were regarded as incapable of certain crimes or were treated as adults in the criminal justice system. This concept changed in the 19th century when a group of reformers set out to redeem the nation's wayward youth (Platt 1969). These "child savers" helped establish the juvenile court system in the United States. As a result, juveniles were treated differently from adults, and certain behavior that was once ignored or handled in an informal way came under the jurisdiction of a government agency. Thus, the *concept of delinquency* was "invented" in America in the 19th century.

The nation's first *juvenile court* was established in 1899 in Illinois. All states now have juvenile court systems. The court's primary responsibility is to protect the welfare of youth, and its secondary task is to safeguard the community from youthful offenders. This orientation has given juvenile judges considerable discretion to make whatever decisions they deem necessary for the juveniles' protection and rehabilitation.

Three types of juveniles come under the court's jurisdiction. (A *juvenile* is typically defined as someone between the ages of 7 and 17.) *Youthful offenders* are those who engage in behavior for which adults can be tried in a criminal court. All predatory crimes are included here. Further, in the mid-1990s most states overhauled their laws so that more youths can be tried as adults in a criminal court and offenders are no longer protected by the confidentiality of juvenile court proceedings. The second type of juvenile handled by the juvenile court is the *status offenders,* those who violate the juvenile court code rather than the criminal code. Behavior such as truancy, running away from home, and breaking the curfew is included in this category. Finally, the court deals with *minors in need of care*—those who are neglected or abused and in need of the court's care. They do not fall into the category of delinquent, but they are the responsibility of the juvenile court.

The range of behavior defined as delinquent tends to be broad. Perhaps as many as 90 percent of all young people have engaged in behavior that would fall under the jurisdiction of juvenile court, including activities such as fighting, truancy, and running away from home. In some states, statutes define delinquency so broadly that virtually all juveniles could be categorized as delinquent. Delinquency, then, includes a much greater range of behavior than does crime.

Juvenile Violence and Juvenile Gangs

Perhaps "delinquency" is a term that does not sufficiently capture the *severity of the problem of youth crime.* Youths under the age of 18 account for 15.6 percent of all arrests for violent crime and 27.5 percent of all arrests for property crime (Maguire and Pastore 2006:358).

Part, but not all, of the problem of juvenile violence stems from juvenile gangs. *The proliferation of gangs, along with involvement in drugs and the ready availability of guns, has exacerbated the problem of violent crime by youths.* Gang members account for a disproportionate number of arrests for serious offenses (Thornberry, Huizinga, and Loeber 2004; Harrell 2005).

Youths join gangs for a variety of reasons, among them being the desire to gain status and escape poverty.

Juvenile gangs are now pervasive, appearing everywhere from the large metropolitan areas to the rural areas of the Midwest that were once thought to be immune to urban problems (Egley and Major 2004). The great majority of youths do not become gang members, and most of those that do join are members for a relatively short time, as little as a year (Esbensen and Huizinga 1993). As many as a fourth or more of gang members are females, and increasing numbers of females are joining gangs (Howell 1998). They join because of such problems as family abuse and the appeal of being an integral part of a group (Miller 2001).

One reason for the increasing number of gangs is that the conditions that spawn the gangs—poverty, discrimination, and lack of legitimate opportunities—continue to exist throughout the nation. Once gangs appear in an area, they *tend to perpetuate themselves by setting models for each succeeding generation.* They also are perpetuated by a small number of members who stay in the gangs into adulthood and even parenthood.

Youths who enter gangs may be *socialized quickly into violence* (Sanchez-Jankowski 1991). Entry into the gang itself may require the new member to be beaten by the others. Fighting among members is common and may be even more frequent than fighting with outsiders. Such violence has a number of purposes, including disciplining, demonstrating courage and toughness, establishing individual status within the group, and gaining the skills necessary to defend the gang's "turf" (Sanchez-Jankowski 1991; Kennedy and Baron 1993).

Youths tend to join gangs for a variety of reasons, including the desire to gain status and income—two goals that otherwise may be very elusive to young people in impoverished areas. Middle-class areas also have gangs; youths may join them for status or for security against other gangs in their neighborhood or school. Once in a gang, youths' rates of drug use and delinquent behavior tend to rise dramatically (Fagan 1990; Thornberry et al. 1993). Among young people who are involved in delinquent or criminal behavior prior to gang membership, then, involvement is even higher while they are members of the gang (Esbensen and Huizinga 1993).

The extent to which gangs are involved in drug use and trafficking varies considerably, however. A government study concluded that two Los Angeles gangs controlled about 30 percent of the crack cocaine market in the nation. The more common pattern is for individual gang members to be involved in drug trafficking rather than for the gang to be organized around the activity (Joe 1994; Howell 1998). Thus, a study of Asian gangs in San Francisco concluded that about a third of the members sold drugs to raise money, and participation in drug sales "has been overwhelmingly as individuals and has not involved a concerted group effort" (Joe 1994:407).

The Extent of Crime and Delinquency

How widespread are crime and delinquency? The question is difficult to answer because of certain problems with official statistics. Here we examine ways to gather data, look at problems with official records, and then draw conclusions about the extent of crime and delinquency.

Sources of Data

The three basic sources of data on crime are *official records, victimization studies,* and *self-reports.* A frequently used official record is the *Uniform Crime Reports* published annually by the FBI. As noted previously, the FBI's Crime Index includes only eight major felonies. A great deal of crime—indeed, most crime—does not appear in this annual report. Other official sources include municipal police records and the records of juvenile courts. Because juvenile courts have no uniform system of reporting, we can only estimate the number of delinquency cases processed annually.

Victimization studies, a newer approach to gathering crime data, attempt to secure information from the victims of crime rather than from officials or official records. A victimization study usually involves interviews at a representative sample of homes. People in those homes are asked whether they or members of their families have been the victims of a crime or crimes during the previous year. The major source of victimization data is the National Crime Victimization Survey conducted annually by the Department of Justice.

In contrast to the *Uniform Crime Reports,* which are based on statistics gathered from thousands (but not all) of law-enforcement authorities in America's cities and towns, the National Crime Victimization Survey includes both a greater range of crimes and crimes never *officially reported.* Because of nonreporting, the Victimization Survey data are sometimes twice as high as those of the *Uniform Crime Reports.*

Self-reports are usually used with youths. The youths are asked whether they engaged in any of a number of different kinds of criminal activity. Various techniques are used to try and ensure honesty and accuracy, and there is evidence that self-reported crime by young people is fairly accurate.

Problems with Official Records

If you attempt to estimate the crime rate from official records, you encounter a number of problems. First, quite a number of crimes are *undetected.* There are two ways to get an estimate of the amount of undetected crime. One is by asking people whether they have ever committed various crimes. When allowed to respond anonymously, people will often admit to a number of felonies for which they were never convicted as a crim-

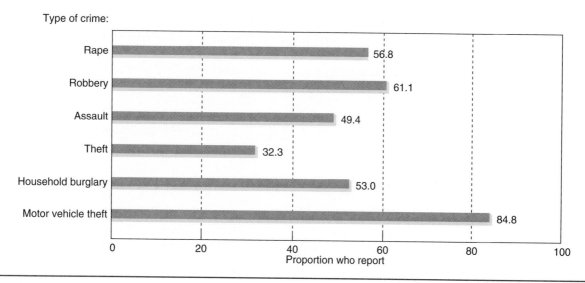

FIGURE 4.2   Reporting Victimizations to the Police.
Source: Maguire and Pastore 2006:209.

inal. The other way is to ask people whether they have been victims of the various crimes and then compare their responses with official records.

Second, *only about a third of all crimes are reported to the police.* The rate of reporting varies with the type of crime (figure 4.2), and the reasons for not reporting also vary (table 4.1).

Official figures, then, underreport nearly every kind of crime.

A third problem with official records is that *definitions of crime change* and the *methods of reporting crime change.* Because a crime is a violation of the criminal law, any change in the law changes the amount of crime. In the early 1930s a considerable number of inmates in federal prisons were there for crimes that would not have been crimes a few years earlier. They were serving time for violating laws related to the Eighteenth Amendment to the Constitution—the amendment that established Prohibition.

Changes in the method of reporting crime can result in an apparent crime wave that may really be a "crime reporting" wave. For example, some years ago the FBI discovered that police were reporting only about half the number of property crimes that insurance companies were reporting. A new system was implemented, and during the next year there was an enormous increase in the police-reported rate of assaults, robberies, and burglaries. The rates reflected the new reporting methods but not necessarily any increase in the actual rate of crime.

A fourth problem with official records involves *police procedures.* Whether some behavior is defined officially by the police as criminal depends on factors other than the behavior itself. For instance, the police may be caught in political cross-pressures when they decide whether to report offenses (Selke and Pepinsky 1982). If they report offenses, they may be blamed for failing to stem the rising tide of crime. If they fail to report them, they may be blamed for being unresponsive. There also may be pressure to keep reported offenses low in order to make areas more attractive to business, residents, and tourists.

Reason	All Crimes, Total	Crimes of Violence		Property Crimes		
		Robbery	Assault	Burglary	Auto Theft	Theft
Reported to another official	13.9	4.7	15.2	4.3	2.8	9.5
Personal/private	19.2	8.7	20.5	6.6	8.2	6.6
Object recovered, offender unsuccessful	20.3	15.1	21.1	22.8	32.7	29.1
Not important enough	6.7	6.5	7.0	3.6	3.5	3.5
Lack of proof	2.5	10.0	1.1	14.1	14.3	11.2
Police wouldn't want to be bothered	4.8	7.0	4.4	9.4	11.0	8.2
Police ineffective or biased	3.0	8.9	2.5	4.4	4.5	2.3
Fear of reprisal	4.6	10.0	3.7	0.9	0.0	0.4
Inconvenient	4.1	8.4	3.8	3.8	5.2	3.4
Other reasons	19.9	15.7	20.7	13.9	11.1	12.4

TABLE 4.1
Reasons for Not Reporting
Crimes to the Police
(in percent not reported)

SOURCE: Maguire and Pastore
2006:210.

A final problem with official records relates to *changing expectations* in society. At one time in U.S. history, many crimes in slum areas and sections of cities populated by minority groups were unreported. Indeed, the police were not necessarily even notified when criminal offenses occurred. In recent decades, the poor and minority groups expect and demand adequate protection. Although a great many crimes are never reported, there is evidence that more are now being reported than in the past, thus making the rate of crime appear to be increasing.

These qualifications to the reliability of official records suggest that the amount of crime in the nation is considerably greater than official records indicate. They also suggest that caution must be exercised when comparing rates across time and drawing a quick conclusion that a "crime wave" is in process. However, when official records are used in conjunction with victimization studies and other evidence, the conclusions are more reliable.

The Amount of Crime and Delinquency

What do the data reveal about the amount of crime and delinquency in America? The amount differs depending on whether you look at FBI or victimization data. According to FBI data, rates of serious crime fluctuate over time; they declined throughout the 1990s and early 2000s, then began to increase again in 2005. By the end of 2005, as table 4.2 shows, the rates were much higher than those of the 1960s.

Victimization data also show that rates fluctuate over time. Table 4.3 gives the rates for 2005. Overall, there were 21.2 violent victimizations for every 1,000 people age 12 or older and 154 property crimes for every 1,000 households. About one of every seven households, therefore, experienced some kind of crime in 2005.

Obtaining information about white-collar crime is difficult, but evidence indicates that it is extensive. *Unethical and illegal behavior abounds in business and industry.* Overall, organizations lose about 6 percent of their revenues to fraud and abuse (Gips 1998). In a survey of 198 businesses, nearly three-fourths reported being victim-

| Year | Violent Crime | | | | Property Crime | | |
	Forcible Murder	Rape	Aggravated Robbery	Assault	Larceny/ Burglary	Auto Theft	Theft
Number (1,000)							
1960	9.1	17.2	108	154	912	1,855	328
1970	16.0	38.0	350	335	2,205	4,226	928
1980	23.0	82.1	549	655	3,759	7,113	1,115
1990	23.4	102.6	639	1,055	3,074	7,946	1,636
2005	16.7	93.9	417	863	2,154	6,777	1,235
Rate (per 100,000)							
1960	5.1	9.6	60	86	509	1,035	183
1970	7.9	18.7	172	165	1,085	2,079	457
1980	10.2	36.4	244	291	1,668	3,156	495
1990	9.4	41.2	257	424	1,236	3,195	658
2005	5.6	31.7	141	291	727	2,286	417

TABLE 4.2
Crime and Crime Rates by Type, 1960 to 2005 (rate per 100,000)

SOURCE: U.S. Census Bureau (1975:153) and Federal Bureau of Investigation Web site (2006).

Type of Crime	Number (1,000)	Rate
Crimes of violence	5,174	21.2
Rape/sexual assault	192	0.8
Robbery	625	2.6
Assault	4,357	17.8
Aggravated assault	1,052	4.3
Simple assault	3,305	13.5
Property crimes	18,040	154.0
Household burglary	3,456	29.5
Motor vehicle theft	978	8.4
Theft	13,606	116.2

TABLE 4.3
Victimization Rates, Personal and Household Crimes, 2005 (per 1,000 persons age 12 or older or per 1,000 households)

SOURCE: Catalano (2006a).

ized by cybercrime (Rantala 2004). Nearly two-thirds had been victims of a computer virus, a quarter had experienced denial of service attacks, and a fifth reported that their computer systems had been vandalized or sabotaged.

The problem is worldwide. A survey of small businesses in the European Common Market nations reported that 41 percent of the companies said their business was a victim of crime in the past year (Weston 2004).

Much of the business crime, however, involves insiders, including businesspeople in the higher ranks. In fact, the median loss caused by owners and executives is 16 times greater than that caused by rank-and-file employees. Bank employees steal more from banks than do robbers. And businesses are offenders as well as victims, engaging in criminal activity against consumers and customers. Indictments for criminal activity and fines for serious misbehavior occur regularly among both small businesses and the nation's largest corporations.

Finally, this nation has an enormous amount of delinquency. Keep in mind, however, that delinquency by definition includes some relatively trivial kinds of behavior. Juveniles may be arrested for conduct that would not be defined as criminal on the part of an adult (e.g., violation of curfew, running away from home, and possession of an alcoholic beverage). But juveniles also are involved in serious crimes. In 2004, 5.1 percent of all arrests involved those 14 years old or under (Maguire and Pastore 2006:349). And 20.4 percent of the arrests were those aged 15 to 19 years. That represents nearly three times their proportion in the population.

The Distribution of Crime

Crime is unequally distributed in the United States. There are variations by region, by state, and by population size. For example, firearm-related murders varied among the states in 2003 from a low of 0.46 per 100,000 in Maine to a high of 10.5 in Louisiana (Maguire and Pastore 2006:306). The overall rate for the United States was 4.1, and the highest rate of any area—27.64—occurred in Washington, D.C. Rates of motor vehicle theft per 100,000 in 2004 varied from a low of 92.5 in Vermont to a high of 970 in Nevada (Maguire and Pastore 2006:287). Washington, D.C. again had the highest rate—1,519.

Group variations also exist. In general, males, young persons (particularly teenagers), racial/ethnic minorities, and the poor have higher rates of victimization than others (Catalano 2006a). Looking at rates of victimization by violent crime, for example, the rates are: 18 times higher for those 19 years and under than for those 65 or older; 2.3 times higher for the poorest than for the richest Americans; 1.5 times higher for males than for females; 1.4 times higher for African Americans than for whites; and 1.2 times higher for Hispanics than for whites. American Indians are not often included in the data, but one government investigation reported that their rate of violent victimization is double that of the population as a whole (Perry 2004).

The Criminal Justice Process

To understand the problem of crime in the nation, it is important to know about the criminal justice process. What happens when you report a crime to the police? The path from the reporting to the final settlement is long and complex. Here we can only give you a sketch of the process to illustrate its complexity.

After a crime is reported and law enforcement officers verify that it has indeed been committed (a proportion of incidents reported to the police are not defined by them as crimes), a suspect must be identified and apprehended. Frequently, extensive investigation is required to properly identify the suspect. After an arrest is made, information about the suspect and the case is given to the prosecutor, who will decide whether to file formal charges with the court. If they are not, the suspect is released.

A suspect who is charged is brought before a judge or magistrate without any unnecessary delay. The judge or magistrate informs the accused of the charges and decides whether there is probable cause to detain the suspect. If the offense is a minor one, a decision about guilt and penalty can be made at this point. If the offense is serious, the process continues. In many jurisdictions, the next step is a preliminary hearing, which is an effort to decide whether there is probable cause to believe that the accused committed a crime within the jurisdiction of the court. If the judge does not find probable cause, the case is dismissed. If the judge finds probable cause, or if the accused waives the preliminary hearing, the case can be turned over to a grand jury. The grand jury hears the evidence and decides whether there is enough to justify a trial. If so, the grand jury issues an *indictment,* which gives the basic facts of the offense charged against the accused.

Once the indictment is filed, the accused is scheduled for *arraignment,* at which time the accused is informed of the charges, advised of his or her rights, and asked to enter a plea to the charges. In most cases, the accused will plead guilty in order to take advantage of *plea bargaining.* Generally, plea bargaining means that the prosecution and defense agree to a lesser offense or to only one of the original charges. Plea bargaining allows the offender to get a lighter sentence, assures the prosecutor that the offender will not be totally acquitted, and saves everyone the time and expense of a court trial. If the plea is "Not guilty," or if the plea is "Guilty" but is refused by the judge (the judge may believe that the accused was coerced into the plea), the case proceeds to trial. The trial can be by jury, or the accused may request that the case be decided by a judge.

If the trial results in conviction, the defendant may appeal to a higher court. If no appeal is made, or if the appeals are rejected, the offender must submit to the sentence imposed by the judge or jury. Sometimes a sentence is handed down only after a sentencing hearing in which the defense presents mitigating circumstances to help minimize the severity of the sentence.

This process is not followed exactly in every jurisdiction, and the juvenile justice system differs in a number of important ways. Yet this explanation outlines the basic process and shows how decisions are made at a number of points in the process. Decision at each point may result in the release of the accused. The system reflects the American belief that the accused is presumed innocent until proven guilty. The result is, as figure 4.3 shows for federal cases, that half or fewer of those arrested for crimes are ever convicted and incarcerated.

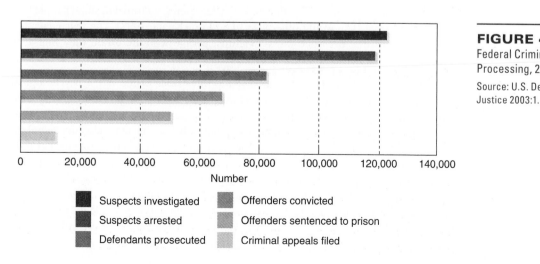

FIGURE 4.3
Federal Criminal Case Processing, 2001.
Source: U.S. Department of Justice 2003:1.

Crime, Delinquency, and the Quality of Life

Widespread crime contradicts American values of freedom from fear, of well-being, and of the right to keep personal property. Crime, by definition, often involves exploitive or violent relationships and thereby contradicts both the *values and ideology* about America being a land of opportunity for all. The "land of opportunity" notion loses some of its appeal for those who fear that their success can make them victims if it attracts criminal activity. Thus, crime diminishes the quality of life by exacting high physical, psychological, and economic costs.

Physical and Psychological Costs of Crime

Crime causes physical and psychological suffering. Although it is difficult to measure, there is evidence that this suffering is considerable. Crime affects physical and emotional health, increases fear, and fosters alienation.

trauma
physical or emotional injury

Physical and Mental Health.   The victim of a crime experiences **trauma.** The victim may be temporarily or permanently injured (either physically or emotionally) or even killed. A fourth of all violent crime victims, and half of rape victims, are injured (Simon, Mercy, and Perkins 2001). Emotional trauma such as anxiety, depression, shame, humiliation, or despair is also likely. As a result, millions of Americans who have been victimized receive mental health counseling or therapy every year (Cohen and Miller 1998). Crime victims represent between a fourth and a fifth of all clients of mental health care professionals.

White-collar crime also takes its toll on Americans' physical and mental health. Some people have lost their businesses or life savings because of fraud. Identity theft can cause severe stress because victims may be denied loans, housing, education, or job opportunities and can even be arrested for crimes they did not commit (Morton 2004). Consumers have suffered financial and health losses because of corporate practices. For example, the suppression of negative information about the defects and dangers of silicone breast implants resulted in health problems and emotional trauma for many women who had implants (Chapple 1997).

Fear and Its Consequences.   Widespread crime can produce pervasive fear in a society. With the falling crime rates since the early 1990s, the fear of crime also diminished. Still, 38 percent of Americans say they are afraid to walk alone at night (Maguire and Pastore 2006:127). Because they fear being victimized, some people will abstain from what they would otherwise like to do (Keane 1998). The fear generated by crime means that everyone loses—victims, people who are afraid they might be victims, and residents and businesspeople in high-crime areas.

Alienation.   Sutherland (1968) argued that white-collar crime has a psychological impact that cannot be measured in monetary terms alone. He pointed out that such crimes create an atmosphere of distrust in a society, lowering social morale and creating widespread social disorganization. People not only become cynical about social institutions (illustrated by the common belief that all politicians are crooked), but they also have a tendency to develop a social Darwinist approach to life ("It's a dog-eat-dog world and you have to look out for yourself above all else"). In a sense, then, white-collar crime may be more damaging to a society than predatory crime. It indicates that the whole society is corrupt—that fraud, theft, and exploitation pervade the paneled offices of professionals as well as the littered streets of the slums. White-collar crime, thus, produces a pervasive sense of distrust and **alienation** and suggests that the society is sick.

Economic Costs of Crime

A great many factors must be taken into account when we try to assess the economic losses due to crime. These factors include the personal loss of property; expense of insurance; cost of loan sharks, false advertising, and shoddy workmanship on consumer goods; work absences and lost wages resulting from physical and emotional trauma; medical cost for treating injuries; cost of maintaining security systems and other crime prevention measures; and cost of maintaining the criminal justice system. The criminal justice system alone (including local, state, and federal levels of government) cost $165 billion in 2001 (Butterfield 2004). The loss to businesses from identity theft is more than $1 billion (Morton 2004). Losses of victims add tens of billions more to the total cost.

Some costs cannot even be measured. Consumers pay higher prices because of organized crime's involvement in legitimate business and because of business losses from crimes (including employee theft). Shoplifting adds to the cost of retail items. Many crimes of fraud, embezzlement, and arson-for-profit are never detected. Some crimes go unreported because the victims are afraid (blackmail or retaliation), embarrassed (con games), or involved in illegal activity (gambling).

When the costs are added, including direct losses due to personal and household crime and the cost of maintaining the criminal justice system, crime costs Americans hundreds of billions of dollars every year.

Contributing Factors

Like crime itself, the factors that generate and sustain crime involve both respectable and nonrespectable elements of society.

Social Structural Factors

Age Structure of the Population. As we noted earlier in this chapter, a disproportionate amount of crime is committed by young males. Males account for slightly more than three out of four of all arrests and eight out of ten arrests for violent crime (Maguire and Pastore 2006:347). Of those arrested for violent crime, about one of six are under the age of 18. It follows that the amount of crime should reflect the age structure: the higher the proportion of young males, the greater the amount of crime. Thus, a partial explanation for the decreasing crime rates of the 1990s and early 2000s is the decline in the number of young males (Bryjak 1999; Phillips 2006).

As the age structure of the nation shifts, with smaller or larger proportions falling into the lower age categories, crime rates should vary accordingly; but we must be cautious about predictions, because no single factor is involved in the amount of crime. Although the current younger generation is more violent than previous ones, the homicide rates have fallen for them also, in part because of the shrinking urban market for crack cocaine (much of the increased killing in the late 1980s and early 1990s occurred in urban crack markets) (Rosenfeld 2002).

alienation
a sense of estrangement from one's social environment, typically measured by one's feelings of powerlessness, normlessness, isolation, meaninglessness, and self-estrangement

Hot Spots. Cohen and Felson (1979) developed a "routine activities" approach to crime. They focused on circumstances rather than the characteristics of offenders. In particular, they emphasized the importance of *likely offenders, suitable targets,* and *a lack of capable guardians* occurring at a particular place and time. "Capable guardians" can include anything from the presence of police to alarm systems. The convergence, or lack of convergence, of these three factors can explain changing crime rates, and why certain areas become "hot spots," or locales of high crime rates (Weisburd and Mazerolle 2000).

Van Koppen and Jansen (1999) used this approach to explain daily, weekly, and seasonal variations in robbery rates. Robbers' expectations of the amount of money available at a particular time and place constitute the suitable target, whereas the increased number of dark hours during the winter mean less adequate guardianship. Bryjak (1999) explained the drop in burglary rates in the 1990s in terms of increased guardianship of suitable targets, namely, the fact that more people are spending time in their homes because of personal computers, cable television, VCRs, and video games.

Other research, covering 52 nations over a 25-year period, suggests that this approach may apply more to property crime than to personal crime (Bennett 1991). At any rate, the convergence of offenders, suitable targets, and inadequate guardianship helps explain a certain amount of crime (Hipp et al. 2004). It follows that changing any one of the three factors may alter crime rates. For example, convenience stores are targets for robbery. Some local governments have passed ordinances requiring convenience stores to have at least two clerks on duty at all times. These additional clerks may reduce the amount of armed robbery by increasing the number of capable guardians.

differential association theory
the theory that illegal behavior is due to a preponderance of definitions favorable to such behavior

Norms.   The **differential association theory** of crime and delinquency emphasizes the importance of *norms*. The theory states that potential or actual criminals or delinquents have their significant interactions with people whose norms violate the criminal law. Consistently with the theory, researchers have found that delinquents tend to spend more time in unsupervised social activities and more leisure time with peers than do nondelinquents (Agnew and Petersen 1989). Those delinquents who grow up in the slums are likely to live with one rather than two parents, to be unemployed, perhaps to be a school dropout, and to be a member of a gang.

Thus, the lower-class delinquent has few or no experiences with people who would lead him or her to accept the norms of the larger society (Paternoster and Mazerolle 1994). The delinquent is drawn to a group because of the need for companionship, and the group develops norms that violate the law. Because *group membership* is more meaningful to this youth than anything else he or she has experienced, those norms are accepted and followed. Those youths, on the other hand, who have their significant interactions with people who affirm the norms of the larger society—family, religious groups, and so on—are much less likely to engage in delinquent behavior (Johnson et al. 2001; Pearce and Haynie 2004).

Norms are involved in white-collar crime also. Certain practices in business and industry may be justified on the basis that everyone does them, that they are necessary for continuing one's enterprise, or that they are acceptable by those in authority. News accounts have reported corporate executives justifying illegal behavior on the grounds that their competitors engaged in the behavior; so if they did not, they would lose business and profits. American businessmen have paid off influential foreigners in order to secure contracts for business, and then shrugged off the practice by pointing out that the alternative was to not do business in those foreign countries. Such practices are learned early. A study of 133 MBA students found them likely to decide to further market and produce a hypothetical drug that was about to be recalled by the Food and Drug Administration when coworkers and the board of directors agreed with that decision (Piquero, Tibbetts, and Blankenship 2006).

The Politics of Control: The Prison.   The United States has a higher proportion of its population incarcerated than does any other Western nation, and the proportion is increasing. In 1985, 744,208 Americans were in prisons and jails, a rate of 313 per 100,000 population; by 2005, the number had soared to 2.19 million and the rate was 738 per 100,000 population (Maguire and Pastore 2006:492).

This high and growing rate of incarceration is a political decision. There are alternative ways of dealing with criminals (see Global Comparison). Some people believe that **rehabilitation** should be the focus of the criminal justice system, whereas others believe criminals should be put into prisons for *punishment* and *isolation from society*. Still others believe that rehabilitation should be combined with the punishment of imprisonment. To address the issue, we examine what happens in the nation's prisons and jails. (A jail is a locally administered institution that has authority to retain adults for 48 hours or longer. A prison is a state or federally administered facility for correction only.)

Not all prisoners have *access to rehabilitation programs.* This fact is particularly true in the nation's jails, where only a fraction of the total jail population has access to any programs other than religious services (Freudenberg et al. 2005). The need for programs of support and rehabilitation is underscored by the fact that *people in jails have high rates of infectious and chronic diseases, substance abuse, mental health problems, and suicide rates that are far higher than those in prisons and in the larger society* (Freudenberg et al. 2005; Mumola 2005). On the average, a prisoner stays in jail about 17 days, though some may remain for a year or more because of the shortage of prison space. The prisoner, who may be frightened, confused, or emotionally disturbed, has no one to talk with except other prisoners.

Among those jails that do have rehabilitation programs, basic adult education is the most common, followed by vocational training. Only the larger jails (those with 250 or more inmates) are likely to have such programs.

The *nature of prison life* also makes rehabilitation unlikely. In fact, *longer time spent in prison can increase the likelihood of* **recidivism** (repeated criminal activity and incarceration) (Orsagh and Chen 1988). For one thing, jails and prisons are *seriously overcrowded* (Gilliard 1999; Welsh 2002). Because there are too many prisoners for the amount of space available, nearly two-thirds of prison inmates are confined to units with less than 60 square feet of space, and a third spend 10 or more hours a day in that space. Such conditions are *stressful* and make any efforts at rehabilitation difficult.

Far from serving as a deterrent to further crime or as a place of rehabilitation, the jail or prison at best keeps criminals away from the public for a period of time. At worst, the prison becomes a *training ground* for making criminals more competent and more committed to a life of crime. If the abnormal circumstances of the prison, including extended, close association with hardened offenders, does not ensure continued criminal behavior, the stigma of having been in prison probably will. The prison itself is a *dehumanizing institution,* and people who enter it are unlikely to escape being brutalized, hardened, and better trained in criminal behavior. The same kind of threats to well-being found in the larger society must be faced by those in prison. Homicides, sexual assault, and gang formation and violence characterize prison life (Allender and

rehabilitation
resocializing a criminal and returning him or her to full participation in society

recidivism
repeated criminal activity and incarceration

ALTERNATIVES TO IMPRISONMENT: GERMANY AND ISRAEL

The fact that the United States has a higher proportion of its population in jails and prisons than any other country in the world does not mean that the nation also has higher crime rates or more effective policing (which would catch greater numbers of criminals). The high incarceration rate reflects the societal attitude that criminals should be removed from society and punished. Would alternatives to imprisonment be beneficial for both the criminal and society? Evidence from Germany and Israel suggest that they would.

German courts make use of suspensions, probation, fines, and community service. Judges have lifetime appointments and sole authority to sentence offenders who are 18 to 20 years old. Hard-line judges continue to use imprisonment, whereas liberal judges try to use alternatives. Researchers found that offenders sent to prison had higher rates of recidivism than did those given alternative sanctions. Even if the imprisonment included job training, offenders had a harder time getting a job after release than did those who had an alternative sanction. A study

of regions reported that the proportion of offenders increased over a period of four years by 7 percent where imprisonment was the norm, and fell by 13 percent where alternative sanctions were the norm.

In Israel, the Kibbutz Resocialization Program is an effort to put offenders into a close-knit society that will change them into respectable citizens. The offenders are placed with an adoptive family, put into a cohesive work group, and expected to become productive members of the kibbutz.

A study of 27 long-term offenders assigned to a kibbutz found that, three years after being assigned, three-fourths of them had no additional criminal activity: nine were working full-time, five served in the army, five were engaged or married, and eight remained in the kibbutz as members.

Thus, programs in both nations offer evidence that alternatives to imprisonment may be a more effective way to deal with some kinds of criminals. If the goal is to rehabilitate, alternatives may work better than imprisonment.

National Institute of Justice 1996a; Fischer and Geiger 1996.

Marcell 2003; Beck and Harrison 2006). The gangs formed in prison may be even more powerful than street gangs, controlling significant aspects of prison life and even directing (through messengers) the activities of street gangs.

Normal behavior and feelings are impossible in prison. The prison is a **total institution**, a place where the totality of the individual's existence is controlled by various external forces. Offenders who enter the maximum security prison are immediately deprived of valuable things: liberty, goods and services, heterosexual relationships, autonomy, and security (from attacks of other prisoners). Moreover, they are in a place with a high proportion of disturbed individuals. Over half of those in state prisons, 45 percent of those in federal prisons, and 64 percent of those in local jails have or have had some kind of mental health problem (James and Glaze 2006). The constraints of prison life are so severe that an individual must focus on survival rather than personal development or change.

The combination of the inmate code and the demands of the authorities virtually eliminates any possibility of individual growth or personal lifestyle. There is a popular notion that "stone walls do not a prison make" and that even in a cell the individual's mind is free to roam and explore; but only a rare individual can transcend the forces that impinge on him or her and thereby avoid the dehumanization of the prison.

total institution
a place in which the totality of the individual's existence is controlled by external forces

CODDLING CRIMINALS

Many Americans believe that one way to deal with the problem of crime is to stop "coddling" criminals. Actually, it is true that some criminals are coddled. Consider, for example, the following cases from the American system of justice:

Item: The portfolio manager of two mutual funds cheated investors out of almost $10 million. He was sentenced to six months in prison and put on five years' probation.

Item: The manufacturer of drugs watered down an antidote for poisoned children with a useless substance. He was given one year's probation and a $10,000 fine.

Item: A judge in a state supreme court was involved in receiving and transporting $800,000 in stolen U.S. Treasury bills. He was fined $10,000 and sentenced to one year in prison.

These cases are just a few examples of the numerous white-collar crimes in which the offenders received very light punishment.

In this chapter we have stressed the seriousness of white-collar crime. How aware are the people in your area of the extent and corrosiveness of this crime? For one week, note any articles in your local newspaper that talk about crime. Assuming that the newspaper gave an accurate picture of the problem of crime in your area, how much and what kind of a crime problem exist? Do you think your paper is sensitive to the significance of white-collar crime? Make a list of various crimes, including street crimes and white-collar crimes. Ask some people in your community to rank them by seriousness, and ask them why they ranked them as they did. How do they feel about the different kinds of crime?

The *inmate code* contributes to the **dehumanization**. The code requires that an inmate must never report infractions of rules by another inmate and must never notice anything. For example, an inmate walking down a prison corridor saw a fellow inmate lying on the floor, bleeding. He had an impulse to help the man on the floor but went to his cell instead. Other inmates who discussed the incident with the prison psychiatrist agreed with the behavior. They pointed out that if the man had called a guard, the guard would have suspected him of having struck the man on the floor or would have intensely questioned him. Further, any other inmate who saw him call the guard would have accused him of "snitching." Had he stopped to help the fallen man, he might have been beaten by the man's attacker. Also, to personally help would suggest a homosexual relationship between the two inmates.

Finally, to survive in such an inhuman context, inmates practice and hone the same skills they used in their criminal careers. The most likely outcome of a prison sentence, then, is an improvement of criminal skills and thus the high probability of a continued criminal career and an eventual return to prison.

The Family Background of Offenders. Because the *family plays a significant role in the socialization of children,* much attention is focused on family background to discover why young people become delinquents. Many family factors have been associated with delinquency, but the most important is the *quality of the relationships between parents and children.*

In essence, there is less delinquency among those youths whose parents value, love, accept, and spend time with them (Warr 1993; Brody et al. 2001). In contrast, rates of delinquency are higher among youths in abusive, troubled, or disrupted families (Demuth and Brown 2004; Thornberry, Huizinga, and Loeber 2004; Fagan 2005). Rates of homicide are higher in cohorts of youth with a higher percentage born to unwed mothers, suggesting again the importance of the family in crime rates (O'Brien, Stockard, and Isaacson 1999).

dehumanization
the process by which an individual is deprived of the qualities or traits of a human being

113

When there are poor relationships in the family, parental moral and emotional authority is weakened. The diminished authority tends to weaken children's bonds to the social order and increases the likelihood of delinquency (Browning and Loeber 1999). Don't commit the *fallacy of retrospective determinism* here. Not all children from such families are delinquents. Family background helps you *understand* why some youths become delinquent, but it does not condone delinquency or absolve delinquents of responsibility for their behavior.

fallacy

Adult criminals are also likely to have had troubled family relationships (Raine, Brennan, and Mednick 1994; Grogan-Kaylor and Otis 2003). We are not saying that the criminal behavior began in adulthood, of course. In fact, virtually all criminal careers (other than white-collar crime) begin before the age of 18. A large number of youths who engage in serious delinquent behavior will continue their criminal activities as adults. In a follow-up study of 99 formerly incarcerated delinquents, the researchers found that 89 had adult criminal records (Lewis et al. 1989). The average number of their offenses as adults was 11.6.

Social Stratification and Crime.   Crime and delinquency are related to the social stratification system in three ways: (1) The kind of behavior considered criminal is defined by those who have power within the system. (2) Different kinds of crime tend to be committed within different strata of the system. (3) Disproportionate numbers of criminals come from different socioeconomic levels.

A good deal of the behavior of relatively powerless people is defined as criminal whereas similar behavior among more powerful people is not defined as criminal. This finding is true especially when the behavior involves monetary exploitation. A corporate executive might support the definition of employee theft as criminal but would not define false advertising and exploitation of consumers as theft or crime. A physician might deplore abuses of the welfare system, labeling them criminal fraud, but think little about prescribing expensive brand-name drugs rather than less expensive generic counterparts because, in part, his or her retirement plan rests on investments in the pharmaceutical industry. In both cases, the people who influence the defining process are the *holders or wielders of power in society,* and they *do not define their own behavior as criminal.*

The second way in which social stratification intersects with crime and delinquency involves the kinds of crime committed. Those in the lower socioeconomic strata are more likely to be both the offenders and the victims of delinquency, violent crimes, and property crimes (Markowitz 2003; Eitle, D'Alessio, and Stolzenberg 2006), whereas white-collar criminals are more likely to come from the middle and upper strata.

Delinquency, violence, and property crime are more characteristic of those people struggling to survive the deprivations of a seriously unequal society. A study of youths concluded that hunger leads to theft of food, problems of hunger and shelter result in serious theft, and problems of unemployment and shelter foster prostitution (McCarthy and Hagan 1992). Basically, the more impoverished an area and the fewer opportunities it offers for dealing with economic deprivation, the higher the rates of crime (Lee and Ousey 2001; Weiss and Reid 2005).

The third way the stratification system is related to crime is in the disproportionate number of criminals who come from the lower socioeconomic strata (Thornberry and Farnworth 1982; Western, Kleykamp, and Rosenfeld 2006). As suggested earlier, part of the reason is that the powerless and deprived are more likely to be defined as

Prison life is dehumanizing.

criminals. Several studies over the last few decades have revealed many consistencies in the characteristics of people *labeled as criminals.* Their general *powerlessness* and their location in the stratification system are clear. Criminals are more likely to (1) lack *social anchorage* in the sense of growing up in a stable family that is integrated into the community, (2) come from a lower-income family, (3) be young, (4) be male, and (5) come disproportionately from a minority group.

In sum, *the powerless are more likely to be defined as criminals throughout the criminal justice system.* They are more likely to be suspects and more likely to be arrested. In some states, judges have the option of withholding **adjudication** of guilt from people placed on probation. The judge's decision, then, determines whether *the individual will carry the stigma of being a convicted felon.* Those people most likely to carry that stigma are the powerless—the poor and minorities. We are not saying that these people are innocent; rather, we are pointing out that the criminal justice system does not treat equally people who commit the same kinds of crime; those in the lower strata are treated more severely.

adjudication
making a judgment; settling a judicial matter

Social Psychological Factors

Respectable people define crime as reprehensible—but how do criminals define it? According to Katz (1988), part of the explanation of crime is found in the fact that criminal acts possess certain "sensual dynamics." Each kind of crime has a certain appeal, one that results in the criminal's feeling good or even exhilarated. For example, robbery is a crime that, on the average, entails considerable risk and minimal gain. What makes robbery attractive, according to Katz, is not just the money gained, but the excitement, adventure, and sense of conquest in the act. "In virtually all robberies, the offender discovers, fantasizes, or manufactures *an angle of moral superiority* over the intended victim" and makes "a fool of his victim" (Katz 1988:169, 174).

Other kinds of crimes have their own emotional rewards. The murderer may gain a sense of righteous revenge. Youths in street gangs may gain a sense of triumph over a destructive and dehumanizing environment. The point is that crime has *both emotional and material rewards for people* (Meadows and Anklin 2002). In part, motivation to continue a criminal career may lie in the emotional rewards.

Attitudes as well as emotions are important in crime. We noted earlier that the attitudes that prison conditions generate in inmates help to perpetuate crime. *Attitudes of respectable people* also contribute to the problem by providing necessary support for much officially defined crime, even though they don't view themselves as culpable or as contributors to crime. The assertion has been made that prostitution could not continue without official support. Certainly it could not continue without the support of the respectable clientele it serves or without the overt or covert support of the police.

Automobile theft is another example of crime supported by respectable people. Upwardly mobile young men in business and the professions sometimes buy stolen luxury cars for a fraction of their retail cost. They may know, or at least suspect, that they are buying a stolen car. Such crimes would have no payoff without these respectable customers ("After all," they reason, "if I don't buy it, someone else will").

Attitudes of respectable people that stigmatize criminals contribute to continuation of the criminal careers (Pager 2003; Davies and Tanner 2003). Often, the very people who decry crime resist providing any help to the criminal. They get mired in the *fallacy of circular reasoning.* They believe that criminals can't be trusted in respectable jobs, then condemn criminals for not becoming respectable people. The ex-criminal who sincerely wants to become respectable becomes the victim of the process.

Attitudes toward white-collar criminals are ambivalent. Generally, unless the acts are flagrant and overt violations, white-collar criminals may not be prosecuted as criminals. However, white-collar criminals are not as invulnerable to the criminal justice system as they once were, in part because of a reaction to the Watergate scandal of the Nixon administration. Some white-collar criminals receive stiff penalties and sentences for their offenses. Nevertheless, their chances for leniency are far greater than are those for other criminals. A study of the prosecution of offenders arrested for savings and loan fraud found that the average sentence was 36.4 months, while the average for burglars and car thieves was 55.6 months and 38 months, respectively (Reckard 1994). In addition, white-collar criminals do not face the same kinds of hurdles when they try to reenter society following imprisonment (Kerley and Copes 2004). Unless such criminals have multiple arrests or are arrested and imprisoned before the age of 24, they are able to secure stable employment much easier than are other offenders.

Finally, in looking at the social psychology of *committed criminals or delinquents,* you find a distinctive set of attitudes, values, and other attributes. For these individuals, delinquency or crime has become a way of life. They have a *"subterranean" set of values*—hedonism, a focus on immediate gratification, and the ability to outwit and con others. They appear to be untouched by punishment, continue their deviant ways, and account for much of the crime in the nation. For them, deviance is a way of life. This finding is illustrated by studies that have examined the *self-concepts of delinquents.* Typically, the studies reveal congruence between attitudes toward the self and behavior. Low self-esteem fosters delinquent behavior, and the behavior, in turn, may raise the individual's self-esteem (Mason 2001). The delinquent behavior is a protection of the self as well as a rejection of law-abiding society.

fallacy

Public Policy and Private Action

Our discussion of the causes of crime suggests the kinds of actions that will reduce the amount of crime. For example, whatever ameliorates economic deprivation reduces crime rates (Hannon and Defronzo 1998; Rosenfeld 2002). Intensive police patrolling of target areas increases guardianship and reduces crime rates (Loeber and Farrington 1998; Rosenfeld 2002). Reducing drug use brings a decline in crime (Blumstein and Rosenfeld 1998). Youth curfew laws cut down on the number of offenders in hot spots and reduce burglary, larceny, and simple assault (McDowall, Loftin, and Wiersema 2000). Finding employment for older offenders reduces recidivism (Uggen 2000). Prevention programs that help youths by fostering a healthy family life, making communities safe, encouraging the young to stay in school, and developing skills and healthy lifestyle choices can reduce the number who begin a life of crime (Coolbaugh and Hansel 2000). Stronger laws can aid the fight against white-collar crime (Goldsmith 2004). In addition, a variety of other programs hold promise; but first we examine the issue of punishment versus rehabilitation.

Punishment or Rehabilitation?   Will crime be reduced by punishing or by rehabilitating criminals? Should criminals be required to reimburse their victims? Are criminals themselves victims, people who can be rehabilitated with the proper methods, or are their offenses unjustified acts that demand punishment? Can you trust a criminal to become a law-abiding citizen again? Such questions are behind the various solutions proposed for the problem of crime.

For many centuries the societal reaction to crime was simply one of punishment in order to deter others who might consider the same acts. Now more people advocate *rehabilitation instead of punishment*. In this view, the criminal has the potential to become a law-abiding citizen and should be given the opportunity to do so. Even if this view is true, some people would argue that *criminals should make restitution* to their victims, and in recent years some courts have required offenders to do so. Usually, the restitution is a cash payment large enough to offset the loss, and the payment may be reduced to fit the earning capacity of the offender. But what kind of payment can be made to compensate for emotional trauma? Sometimes services that benefit the victim directly or indirectly also may be required or substituted for the cash payment.

Experts who advocate rehabilitation face the problem of the offender's *reintegration* into the community. How can offenders be reintegrated into society? Because many offenders got in trouble because of the environment in which they lived, reintegration requires community resources such as vocational counseling and employment to restructure the offender's life. The goal is to help the offender find a legitimate role in the community.

That goal will not be easy. As Talbot (2003) notes, about 1,600 people leave state and federal prisons each day. Most come out with nothing more than a small amount of money ($20 to $200) and a one-way bus ticket. Some are drug abusers who received no treatment. Some are sex offenders who received no counseling. Some are high-school dropouts who took no classes and received no training in job skills. Many are sick (HIV, tuberculosis, and hepatitis C). And only about one in eight received any kind of prerelease program to prepare them for life outside the prison. Clearly, the task of reentry is massive. More options need to be offered to prisoners during their time of imprisonment, including work-release programs, and more programs need to be implemented in the immediate aftermath of release, including halfway houses.

In recent decades, pressures have mounted for a *get-tough* policy—more and longer prison terms. As noted earlier, however, the United States already has an unusually high and growing proportion of the population that is incarcerated.

Another aspect of the get-tough policy is capital punishment. Twelve states and the District of Columbia do not allow the death penalty, even though it was reinstated as constitutional by the Supreme Court in 1976. Since 1977, about 1,000 prisoners have been executed, a third of them in the state of Texas (Maguire and Pastore 2006:531). At the beginning of 2006, an additional 3,373 prisoners were under a death sentence, over half of them racial/ethnic minorities (Maguire and Pastore 2006:535).

Although a majority of Americans favor the death penalty, capital punishment is controversial from both a moral and a criminal justice point of view. From a moral point of view, the question is whether the state has the right to kill someone as punishment for murder. Opponents of capital punishment view it as extreme and inhumane—an official form of the same heinous crime committed by the individual. What is the difference, they ask, between an individual or the state committing murder? Furthermore, they argue, keeping an individual on death row is a form of torture, as underscored by the fact that suicide and natural causes, rather than execution, are the leading cause of deaths of prisoners on death row (Locke 1996). The appeals process can take so long that some prisoners literally die of natural causes, and the process of waiting is so agonizing that many commit suicide or become mentally ill.

Religious groups take varying positions on the moral issue (Falsani 1996). Protestants and Jews are divided. The official Roman Catholic position, as defined in a 1995 encyclical by Pope John Paul II, is one of opposition. The Pope argued for nonlethal means of combating crime.

From the criminal justice point of view, is capital punishment an effective deterrent for murder? Experts disagree. Stack (1990) found a 17.5 percent drop in homicide rates in South Carolina in months with publicized executions. In contrast, Bailey (1990) examined national monthly rates over a 12-year period. He found no drop in homicide rates in months with nationally publicized executions. Sorenson, Wrinkle, Brewer, and Marquart (1999) found no evidence of deterrence in Texas (the most active execution state in recent times) from 1984 through 1997. A *New York Times* survey reported that states without capital punishment have no higher homicide rates than states with it (Bonner and Fessenden 2000). There is also the problem of executing innocent people. DNA tests led to the release of 12 prisoners from death row from 1989 to 2001 (Dwyer and Wilgoren 2002).

Arguments about the effectiveness of punishment versus rehabilitation go on. Advocates of punishment and isolation are correct when they contend that prisons do not rehabilitate. But rehabilitation programs can be effective. In fact, rehabilitative efforts may need to be combined with punishment. There is strong evidence that punishment is a deterrent to crime. However, it is not the harshness of punishment but the *certainty of punishment* that is effective (Paternoster 1989). To the extent that people are convinced that, if caught, they will be punished (rather than avoiding punishment through legal maneuvers), crime rates fall.

Thus, the criminal justice system in the United States should be revamped in two ways: First, punishment for crime must be made more certain. Second, efforts must be made, through reform of prisons or through innovative alternatives, to establish effective rehabilitation programs. Certainty of punishment will act as a deterrent for some criminals and will remove others from society, whereas more effective rehabilitation programs will effect change in others and help them live socially useful lives.

Innovative Alternatives   Some innovative alternatives to the present system, including some that are popular with citizens and law enforcement officials, are ineffective in reducing crime. In a comprehensive study of crime-prevention programs, researchers concluded that the following are among the programs that do not lower crime: gun buy-back programs, drug prevention classes that focus on fear or on building self-esteem, increased arrests or raids on drug market locations, correctional boot camps using military basic training, "Scared Straight" programs in which juvenile offenders visit adult prisons, intensive supervision on parole or probation, and community mobilization against crime in high-crime poverty areas (Sherman et al. 1998).

In contrast, the researchers identified about 30 programs that show promise for dealing with crime, including community policing with meetings to set priorities, greater respect by the police for arrested offenders (may reduce repeat offending), higher numbers of police officers in cities, monitoring of gangs by community workers and law enforcement officials, mentoring programs for youths, prison-based vocational education programs for adult inmates, enterprise zones to reduce unemployment, drug treatment in jails followed by urine testing in the community, and intensive supervision and aftercare of juvenile offenders.

Private prisons (that is, prisons that are privately owned and operated) may also help reduce repeated offending. There is little research as yet to test their effectiveness, but one study of 198 male releases from two private Florida prisons and 198 matched releases from public prisons found that the private prison group had lower rates of recidivism and committed less serious subsequent offenses than did the public prison group (Lanza-Kaduce, Parker, and Thomas 1999). Private prisons are *not* more cost-effective, however (Pratt and Maahs 1999).

Community Action and Involvement   Crime prevention is not just a matter of official action. A number of community programs can reduce crime (Loeber and Farrington 1998; Sherman et al. 1998). Parents, neighborhood groups, and school personnel can work together to teach children values and to encourage and reward law-abiding behavior. Community-based after-school recreational programs may help reduce local juvenile crime. Organized community projects and employment opportunities diminish problems with juvenile gangs (Spergen and Curry 1990).

Even the physical arrangements in a community affect crime. Greener surroundings in the inner city and increased lighting reduce both the fear of crime and the amount of actual crime (Vrij and Winkel 1991; Kuo and Sullivan 2001). Always having two workers in convenience stores at night lessens the likelihood of robbery, and neighborhood parks and recreational facilities can provide alternatives to gang activity.

Finally, whatever can be done to enhance cohesion in a community will deter crime. Three researchers who examined violent crime in urban neighborhoods concluded that the more that residents trust each other, share values, and are willing to intervene in the lives of children (e.g., to stop truancy and graffiti painting), the lower the rate of crime will be (Sampson, Raudenbush, and Earls 1997).

Aid to Victims   An important public-policy effort involves *aid to the victims*. Aid to victims is provided by governments to prevent a double victimization—once by the offender and again by the criminal justice system. Some problems faced by the victim of a crime include a lack of transportation to court, difficulty in retrieving stolen property from the police, threats by defendants if the victim testifies, and the amount of time consumed by the various procedures in the criminal justice system. An aid program can compensate for some of these losses incurred by the victims.

Does the get-tough approach to crime reduce crime rates or dehumanize criminals?

Most states now have compensation programs to help the victims of violent crime. Awards vary from small amounts to tens of thousands of dollars. Some states require the victim to show financial need, and most require that the crime be reported to police and the claim filed within a specified time period (ranging from a few days to a number of months).

The compensation programs provide for the recovery of medical expenses and lost earnings. In a number of states, money to aid victims is accumulated through penalties assessed against offenders or by expropriating the money earned by offenders resulting from their crimes (e.g., by writing a book).

Follow-Up.   Do you think that prisons should primarily punish or primarily rehabilitate inmates? Based on your answer, design the "perfect" prison to achieve your goals.

Summary

Crime is one of the problems about which Americans are most concerned. Technically, crime is any violation of the criminal law. Therefore, the acts defined by law as crime vary over time. We classify crime into four broad types: (1) Predatory crime, which includes white-collar crime, is an act that causes a victim to suffer loss of property or physical harm. (2) Illegal service crimes involve offenses such as drugs or prostitution. (3) Public disorder crimes have no definite victim but are acts that offend the public. (4) Crimes of negligence involve an unintended victim or potential victim. Computer crime may be either predatory or illegal service, whereas white-collar crime is primarily predatory. Organized crime involves groups of people in an ongoing organization who provide illegal goods and services and who use predatory crime and political corruption to maintain their activities. The term "juvenile delinquency" covers a broad range of behavior, frequently including fighting, truancy, and running away from home. Juvenile gangs may get involved in a range of criminal activities, from predatory crime to illegal goods and services.

Crime and delinquency are widespread, as measured by various indexes—official records, victimization studies, or self-reports. Crime is not uniformly distributed, however; the likelihood of being a victim depends on the kind of crime; where the person lives; and his or her sex, race, age, education, and income.

Crime diminishes the quality of life and exacts physical, psychological, and economic costs. Crime threatens physical and mental health. It generates fear, which restricts the activities of people. White-collar crime can lead to pervasive cynicism and alienation. Crime costs the nation billions of dollars yearly, and the costs are increasing because the amount of crime is increasing.

Norms are an important sociocultural factor contributing to the problem of crime and delinquency because they encourage members of certain groups to engage in criminal behavior. In particular, norms that are counter to the law have developed among lower-class youths and groups of businesspeople and professionals.

The political aspects of crime control contribute to the problem, especially through the nation's prison system. Prisons make rehabilitation unlikely because they tend to dehumanize offenders, remove them further from noncriminal social control, and make them more competent in criminal activity.

The family may be a factor in crime. A disproportionate number of delinquents come from families with poor relationships between parents and children or from broken homes. Adult offenders are likely to have had troubled family backgrounds.

The stratification system also relates to crime. Monetary exploitation of others is more likely to be defined as crime among lower-class people than among middle- and upper-class people. The lower class has a greater proportion of violent crime and delinquency, whereas middle and upper classes have more white-collar crime. A lower-class individual is more likely to be defined as a criminal by the processes of the criminal justice system.

Emotionally, crime may provide a certain thrill or reward to offenders. Many attitudes tend to perpetuate crime. Crimes are facilitated by the attitudes of respectable people about their own behavior—especially their use of the services offered by criminals. Stigmatizing criminals tends to keep them in criminal careers. Minimizing the seriousness of white-collar crime also encourages it. Finally, the attitudes, values, and other social psychological characteristics of some criminals and delinquents form a consistent set that makes for a way of life. Having deviant values and attitudes and thinking of themselves as people who engage in criminal or delinquent behavior, they tend to maintain their way of life even when they are punished.

Key Terms

Adjudication	Predatory Crime
Alienation	Recidivism
Dehumanization	Rehabilitation
Differential	Total Institution
Association Theory	Trauma
Organized Crime	White-collar Crime

Study Questions

1. Define and illustrate the various types of crime.
2. What are the problems in obtaining accurate data on the amount of crime?
3. How much crime is there in America, and where is a person most likely to be a victim?
4. How does crime affect physical and psychological well-being?
5. What is the cost of crime in economic terms?

6. How is the amount of crime affected by the age structure of the population?

7. What is the role of norms in criminal activity?

8. How do prisons help or worsen the problem of crime?

9. In what ways do the family and the social stratification system contribute to the problem of crime?

10. How do the attitudes of respectable people bear on the amount of crime in the nation?

11. What can be done to reduce crime?

Internet Resources/ Exercises

1. Explore some of the ideas in this chapter on the following sites:

http://www.fbi.gov   The FBI site offers current crime news, information about the most wanted criminals, and crime data.

http://www.usdoj.gov   The Department of Justice site gives information about all kinds of crime and crime prevention, and includes a link to the Bureau of Justice Statistics.

http://talkjustice.com   Talk Justice is a forum for the discussion of all aspects of the criminal justice system. Includes a "Cybrary," a list of links to numerous other sites.

2. Log on to the Talk Justice site and go to a chat room or the message board. Select a topic that interests you and join in on the discussion. Evaluate the kinds of things that others are saying with the materials in your text.

3. Investigate how victimization rates have varied over time. The Department of Justice site has the data. Chart the data for various crimes over a period of three decades. How do the patterns of the crimes compare with each other? How do they compare with the FBI data in table 4.2? What are some possible explanations for the patterns?

For Further Reading

Bedau, Hugo, and Paul Cassell. *Debating the Death Penalty: Should America Have Capital Punishment?* New York: Oxford University Press, 2003. Gives the pro and con arguments for the death penalty, including the perspectives of judges, lawyers, philosophers, and a state governor who put a moratorium on the death penalty in Illinois.

Calhoun, Keith Benton. *400 Hours: A Father's Journal of His Daughter's Kidnap and Murder.* New York: Graystone, 1999. Shows the intensity of the trauma suffered by a victim of one of the worst kinds of crimes an individual can experience.

Elliott, A. Larry, and Richard J. Schroth. *How Companies Lie: Why Enron Is Just the Tip of the Iceberg.* New York: Crown Business, 2002. Two corporate consultants argue that a new business culture has arisen that justifies any means used to increase profits, including those that are illegal or unethical. The notorious Enron case is but one example.

Muncie, John, and Eugene McLaughlin, eds. *The Problem of Crime.* Newbury Park, CA: Sage, 1996. An interdisciplinary examination of such topics as changing conceptions of crime, white-collar crime, crime and the family, and politics and crime.

Ross, Jeffrey Ian, ed. *Varieties of State Crime and Its Control.* Monsey, NY: Criminal Justice Press, 2000. Case studies of government crimes in the United States and other nations, including political corruption and various kinds of violence and repression by governments against their citizens.

Sanders, W. B. *Gangbangs and Drive-Bys: Grounded Culture and Juvenile Gang Violence.* New York: Aldine De Gruyter, 1994. Analysis of patterns of gang violence, based on data over a 12-year period. Also discusses lifestyles and perspectives of gang members.

Walters, Glenn D. *The Criminal Lifestyle.* Newbury Park, CA: Sage, 1990. Addresses the issue of why some individuals pursue crime as a lifestyle and shows how biological, psychological, and sociological factors all contribute to the problem.

Whitman, James Q. *Harsh Justice: Criminal Punishment and the Widening Gap between America and Europe.* Oxford, England: Oxford University Press, 2003. Shows the many different ways in which American justice is harsher than that of Europe, including the U.S. prison system, the number of punishable kinds of behavior, and the length of sentences.

Violence

1   Gain a sense of the extent of violence in the United States.

2   Understand the human consequences of violent behavior.

3   Identify the factors that lead people to be violent, including societal factors that impinge on the violent individual.

4   Explain the consequences for the victim of both completed and attempted rapes.

5   Know the varied causes of rape.

6   Suggest ways to deal with violence, including rape.

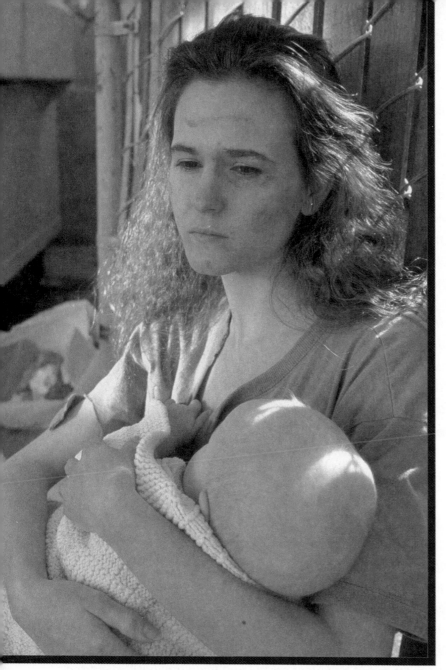

"I Felt Guilty"

The trauma of rape is described by Tammi, a 20-year-old woman who was raped while walking to the parking lot of a college:

It happened about 10 p.m. I had been doing some research at the library and I was in a hurry to get home because I wanted to see a movie on TV. I was standing next to my car, looking in my purse for my keys. I didn't see the man or hear him until all of a sudden he grabbed me from behind and had me on the ground before I knew what had happened. He held a knife to my throat and told me to do what he said and I wouldn't get hurt. I was too scared to move anyway because I could feel the knife pressing against my neck. He was disgusted that I had on jeans and made a derogatory remark about the way girls dress today. He made me take off my pants and perform oral sex on him. Then he raped me. He kept asking me if I liked it, but I was too scared to answer him. He got angry because I wouldn't answer him and he hit me in the breast with his fist. I started crying and he got off of me and let me get dressed. He told me if I told anyone he would come back and rape me again. He said that he knew who I was and where I lived. I started crying harder and shaking all over. He patted me and told me to grow up, that he'd done me a favor and that I was old enough to enjoy sex with a man. He finally left and I got into my car and went home.

I felt so dirty I took a shower and scrubbed myself all over and got into bed. At 12:30 my roommate came home and I told her what had happened. She insisted I call the police, so I did. Two policemen came to our apartment. They asked such things as where did it happen, and what did he look like, and what time did it happen. They acted like I made it up when they found out it happened two hours ago. The young cop asked me if I had an orgasm and if he had ejaculated. I didn't know what to say as I didn't know, since this was my first encounter with sex. I don't think they believed that either. They told me to come down to the station the next day if I wanted to press charges, but that since I had taken a shower and waited so long I probably didn't have a case. No one told me to go to the hospital to be treated for V.D. or that they could give me something to prevent pregnancy until I talked to a friend the next day. She went with me to the emergency room of a hospital and they told me they didn't treat rape victims. I started crying and she took me home. I was pretty shook up. For three or four days I stayed in bed. I cut all my classes. Finally, I went back to school and everything seemed to be fine until I saw a story about rape on TV. I got so upset my roommate called the Rape Crisis Center and had me talk to them about my feelings. I called them eight or nine times in all.

I felt guilty. I thought it was my fault because my mother had been against my leaving home to go to college and against my having an apartment. She had also warned me never to go out alone at night. I didn't tell her I had been raped because I was afraid she'd make me leave school and come back home. So instead of blaming the guy, I blamed myself for being so dumb and naive. It took about three months to get my head together. I feel I have now, but I still am uneasy if a guy comes on too strong, or stops to talk to me in an isolated place, or even if he gets too close in an elevator. I haven't dated since it happened. I guess I shut everyone out and went on my own head trip, but I've started going places with my girlfriends lately and I think I have it together now.

Introduction

In April 1999, two teenage boys shot and killed 12 students and a teacher and wounded a number of other students at Columbine High School in Littleton, Colorado. The boys then committed suicide. During a three-week period in October 2002, two snipers randomly shot people in the region around Washington, D.C., killing 10 and wounding three others. In October 2006, a man went into an Amish school in Pennsylvania and shot ten girls before killing himself. Five of the girls died. In April 2007, a student went on a violent rampage at Virginia Tech University. He killed 32 people, wounded numerous others, and then killed himself. And this is just a sampling of what one student called "the horror stories that keep popping up in the news." In addition to such dramatic and terrifying incidents, Americans are confronted by stories of violence daily in the news media.

Because social problems involve *intergroup conflict,* violence enters into nearly every social problem at some point. The conflict often becomes violent, as illustrated by gangs of straight youths who beat up homosexuals, by race riots, by murders when a drug dealer tries to move in on someone else's market, and so on.

In this chapter we deal with various kinds of interpersonal and intergroup violence, all of which concern Americans and all of which are widely believed to detract from the quality of life. We begin by discussing the meaning, the kinds, and the amount of violence in the nation. We show the ways that violence detracts from the quality of life and identify the various sociocultural factors that contribute to the problem. We discuss ways in which violence can be minimized or eliminated from human life.

We then discuss rape. Although some people have thought of rape as a form of sexual deviance, it is essentially an act of violence. The victim may be further victimized by the reactions of family, friends, police officers, and male jurors.

What Is Violence?

In general, **violence** implies *use of force to kill, injure, or abuse others.* It occurs between two or more individuals as *interpersonal violence,* or it involves identifiable groups in the society and erupts as *intergroup violence* between two or more different races, religions, or political groups. In intergroup situations the violence ultimately means confrontation between individuals whose actions are legitimated by their group affiliation. Interpersonal violence often occurs between people who knew each other prior to the violent confrontation. Intergroup violence, however, is likely to involve people who were strangers prior to the confrontation.

violence
the use of force to kill, injure, or abuse others

How Much Violence Is There?

It is difficult to estimate the amount of violent behavior in the United States. Much is never reported, and for some kinds of violence—riots, gang beatings, violent demonstrations, and terrorist activities—there is no systematic effort to record all incidents. But evidence indicates that there is and always has been a considerable amount of violence in America.

For example, the following incidents were reported over a period of a couple of months in a western city:

A distraught man walked into the emergency room of a hospital and began shooting randomly, killing two people and wounding two others.

Militant antiabortion protestors tried to shut down an abortion clinic, resulting in a violent confrontation that required police intervention and numerous arrests.

A confrontation between two rival youth gangs resulted in a number of injuries, including knife wounds.

Several women who were out jogging were caught and raped by a man who may be a serial rapist.

A brawl erupted between police and members of a religious sect after a police officer attempted to arrest a member of the sect for a routine traffic violation.

A university decided to cancel an annual festival that had taken place for more than 50 years because a weekend of rioting caused more than 100 injuries.

Add to this list numerous other victims—businesspeople robbed and beaten, battered wives and children, women raped by a date, children beaten by a school bully, people harassed because of racial prejudice, jail and prison riots, and countless others—and it quickly becomes obvious that the level of violence is high in American society. In fact, the United States is one of the most violent nations in the world. More than three-fourths of Americans are victims of some kind of violence during their lifetimes, and more than 90 percent will witness some kind of violence (Scarpa 2003).

Interpersonal Violence

Violence occurs in all kinds of settings. A good deal of violence occurs on college campuses. Except for rape and sexual assault, college students experience fewer crimes of violence than do nonstudents. In addition, rates of violent victimization, including those against college students, generally decreased from the early 1990s through the early 2000s (Catalano 2006a). Still, college students experience hundreds of thousands of acts of violence each year, including rape, robbery, and assault (Baum and Klaus 2005). The workplace also has much violence. Between 1.5 and 2 million violent victimizations per year occur against people at work or on duty (Duhart 2001). The majority of victimizations in the workplace are simple assault, but the violence can also be as severe as rape and murder. Law enforcement officers, taxi drivers, and bartenders experience the highest rates of victimization.

Children also experience a great deal of violence. The highest rate of nonfatal violent victimizations each year occurs among youths between the ages of 12 and 17 (Klaus and Rennison 2002). Their rate is more than double that of people aged 35 and above. Rates also vary by such factors as race and social class. A survey of 104 fourth- and fifth-grade children in an impoverished inner-city area found that 89 percent had heard the sound of gunfire; 65 percent had been slapped, punched, or hit by someone; 65 percent had seen someone beaten up or mugged; 16 percent had seen someone killed; and 11 percent had been shot at (Ceballo et al. 2001). Much of the violence experienced by children occurs in the school setting (see chapter 11).

Intimate relationships also are often marked by violence (Catalano 2006b). Violence by an intimate accounts for about one of five of all violent victimizations of women and 3 percent of violent victimizations of males. This translates into hundreds of thousands of incidents each year against a current or former spouse, boyfriend or girlfriend, or cohabiting partner.

Violence claims victims of both sexes, all racial and ethnic groups, and all ages.

Rates of intimate partner violence are higher among dating teens than they are among adults (Office of Juvenile Justice and Delinquency Prevention 2006). Rates of victimization are similar for males and females, but females are more likely to yell, threaten to hurt themselves, pinch, slap, scratch, or kick. Violent males, on the other hand, injure their dates more severely and more often. About one in five female high-school students reports having been physically and/or sexually abused by a dating partner. Overall, women in the 16- to 24-year-old age group have rates of victimization by an intimate partner that are nearly three times the national average.

For adults, rates of intimate partner violence are highest among black women, but the violence occurs in all races. A small survey of Chinese American women found that 8 percent had experienced severe intimate partner violence in their lifetime (Hicks 2006). Among those ever married, the rate was higher and nearly a third of those abused had physical injuries that affected their work or education.

Intimate partner violence is a problem in other nations. A New Zealand study reported that domestic conflict (ranging from minor emotional abuse to severe assault) occurred in nearly 70 percent of intimate relationships, with men and women equally likely to be both the perpetrators and the victims of the violence (Fergusson, Horwood, and Ridder 2005).

Intergroup Violence

How much intergroup violence is there? Ted Gurr (1969:576) attempted to estimate the amount of civil strife in the United States from June 1963 through May 1968, a time of intense conflict. He identified more than 800 events that were either civil rights demonstrations, black riots and disturbances, or white terrorism against blacks and civil rights workers. There were more than two million participants and more than 9,400 casualties. The most common type of violence was interracial.

In 1995, antigovernment militants used a truck bomb to destroy a federal building in Oklahoma City, killing 168 and wounding more than 500. Americans became aware of the problem of **domestic terrorism** (we discuss international terrorism in chapter 14). *Domestic terrorism* is the use, or threatened use, of violence by people operating entirely within the United States to intimidate or coerce the government and/or citizens in order to reach certain social or political aims (Watson 2002). The FBI reported 247 incidents or suspected incidents of domestic terrorism between 1980 and 2000 (Watson 2002).

The Oklahoma City incident was not the first encounter between the federal government and right-wing militias (Smolowe 1995). In 1983, a shootout resulted in the death of Gordon Kahl, a tax resister, militia member, and suspected killer of two U.S. marshals. A number of other incidents occurred in ensuing years, including the FBI attack on the Branch Davidian compound in Waco, Texas, in 1993. More than 70 members of the cult were killed as their buildings burned. Many militia members viewed the attack as the final straw in federal oppression.

All the militias view the government as a tyrannical enemy (Pitcavage 2001). However, *the militias vary according to purpose* (Smolowe 1995). The Aryan nation is a white-supremacist group. The Survivalists are expecting, and preparing for, the breakdown of the economy and the government by preparing to defend and support themselves in the resulting chaos. The Patriots stress the rights of states and the people over the federal government. Posse Comitatus is a tax-resistance group that is also anti-Semitic. Various militias (more than a dozen scattered throughout the nation)

domestic terrorism
the use, or threatened use, of violence by people operating entirely within the United States to intimidate or coerce the government and/or citizens in order to reach certain social or political aims

accumulate weapons to promote and defend the kind of society they believe the Constitution was meant to create (Witt 2004). Other forms of domestic terrorism include extremist groups that engage in direct action (such as arson and destruction of property) to protect animals and the environment from what they regard as exploitation and destruction of the natural world.

As long as such groups operate, there is a strong potential for violence. Many groups not only have sophisticated weapons but also engage in regular training exercises in their use. Their members are deadly serious about what they see as their mission and are prepared to engage in violent measures to achieve it.

Violence and the Quality of Life

You can get a feel for how violence detracts from the quality of life by looking at both objective and subjective evidence. As will be evident, the negative impact of violence on the quality of life can be severe and long term.

Human Injury and Destruction

Violence results in *human destruction* and is, therefore, a *contradiction* to American values of well-being and freedom from fear. Violent crime, riots, and other forms of interpersonal and intergroup violence can lead to both injury and death. Labor-management and interracial confrontations are the kinds of intergroup conflict most likely to result in deaths and serious injuries. One of the worst riots in modern U.S. history occurred in Los Angeles in 1992 following the acquittal of white police officers who had severely beaten a black man who had resisted arrest (Pringle 1997). Three days of rioting left 55 people dead, 2,300 injured, and 1,093 buildings damaged or destroyed. The injured or killed in such situations include spectators or people who are traveling through the area.

People who are injured as the result of violence may suffer various kinds of long-term health problems. Abused children have a higher rate of health problems in adulthood than do nonabused children (Thompson, Kingree, and Desai 2004). A substantial number of battered women sustain brain injuries (Valera and Berenbaum 2003). A large number of homeless families are headed by women who fled from violent husbands (Mason 1993); they escaped the domestic violence only to face the health-debilitating life of the streets.

Psychological Disruption and Dehumanization

Victims of violence endure various kinds of *psychological trauma*. Sexual and/or physical abuse at the hands of a parent or other close relative is a particularly difficult experience (Dyer et al. 2000). Adolescents exposed to violence by an intimate have higher rates of depression, running away from home, thoughts of suicide, dropping out of school, and teenage pregnancy (Hagan and Foster 2001). Victims of intimate partner violence are likely to suffer depression, impaired ability to function normally, thoughts of suicide, and lower self-esteem and life satisfaction (Fergusson, Horwood, and Ridder 2005; Zlotnick, Johnson, and Kohn 2006).

Depending upon the relationship between victim and abuser, *the victim may come to see himself or herself as a bad person who somehow deserves the abuse.* For example, you—like the rest of us—want to believe that your parents are good, loving people, so if they abuse you, you may feel that it is because you deserve it. The outcome of the abuse, then, can include such problems as low self-esteem or even self-hatred, emotional instability, behavior problems, and disturbed relationships with an inability to trust others (Rieker and Carmen 1986; Litrownik et al. 2003). Even if parents do not abuse their children, the *children may be harmed by witnessing violence between the parents*. They may become depressed or emotionally distressed in other ways and are more likely than other children to grow up to be either perpetrators or victims of violence themselves (McCloskey and Lichter 2003; Whitfield et al. 2003). In fact, witnessing violence between parents can be as damaging to children as being physically abused themselves (Kitzmann et al. 2003).

For the victims of abuse, the psychological damage can be severe enough to require hospitalization. A study of 51 teenaged patients at a state psychiatric hospital found that more than half of them had been physically or sexually abused or both (Hart et al. 1989). They were hospitalized for various problems, including self-destructive behavior and drug abuse.

Moreover, *the consequences can be long term, enduring even after the individual is no longer in the abusive situation*. Both adolescents abused by parents or peers and women abused by husbands or boyfriends may develop **posttraumatic stress disorder** (Dutton et al. 2005; Lawyer et al. 2006). This disorder involves emotional and physical difficulties after a traumatic experience. The difficulties can last for years—even a lifetime. They include such symptoms as nightmares, recurring thoughts about the traumatic experience, a lack of involvement with life, and feelings of guilt.

Both violent victimization and exposure to violence can produce posttraumatic stress disorder and other emotional problems (Ceballo et al. 2001; Scarpa 2004). For example, the Oklahoma City bombing resulted in the disorder among some people who were exposed to, though not directly involved in, the violence (Sprang 1999). Although Oklahoma City residents were most likely to be adversely affected, even people who lived hundreds of miles away reported emotional problems six months afterward.

Interpersonal violence not only traumatizes the victim, it also perpetuates the violence. Parents who abuse their children typically were beaten as children. Thus, the *dehumanization process* continues. In addition, childhood sexual abuse leads to higher rates of disrupted marriage and of dissatisfaction with sexual relationships when the victims become adults (Finkelhor et al. 1989).

Intergroup violence is no less disruptive and dehumanizing than interpersonal violence. For example, adolescents exposed to the ongoing violence between Catholics and Protestants in Northern Ireland have more mental health problems and lower self-esteem than youths more insulated from the conflict (Muldoon and Wilson 2001).

posttraumatic stress disorder an anxiety disorder associated with serious traumatic events, involving such symptoms as nightmares, recurring thoughts about the trauma, a lack of involvement with life, and guilt

Violence as Seductive Self-Destruction

Throughout American history, groups have resorted to violence either to bring about certain changes or to try and maintain the status quo. In either case, violence often has been defined as the "only way" to reach the desired goals but instead has facilitated the victory of the opposition. Because expectations and outcome often have been contradictory, violence has frequently been a kind of *seductive self-destruction*.

A survey of violence associated with the labor movement concluded that when laborers resorted to violence, it was almost always harmful to the union (Taft and Ross 1969). In general, violence did not bring the advantages the workers had wanted.

Historian Richard Hofstadter (Hofstadter and Wallace 1970) agreed with this conclusion, pointing out that one of the more effective tactics of labor was the series of sit-down strikes in the 1930s. These strikes were designed to avoid rather than instigate violence.

Hofstadter also made the point that violence has seemed more effective in maintaining the status quo than in bringing about change, at least in the short run. The long history of violence by whites against blacks to maintain blacks in a subordinate status was seductively self-destructive. Whites did not keep blacks subjugated; nor did management, which employed violence far more than workers did, prevent unionization of workers.

Violence, in sum, can appeal to people as a means either to bring about or to resist certain changes, but violence typically turns out to be counterproductive. Not only does the group using violence fail to achieve its goals, but it also may ensure victory for its opponents.

Economic Costs

Violence carries a high price tag. The costs of interpersonal violence include maintaining the criminal justice system and family service agencies. There are also medical costs. It is estimated that the medical costs of gunshot injuries alone in just one year exceed $2 billion, about half of which is borne by taxpayers (Cook and Ludwig 2000).

Intergroup violence involves not only medical costs but also the cost of repairing damaged property. The 1992 Los Angeles riot resulted in an estimated loss of $1 billion from the damages (Pringle 1997). In addition, businesses lose considerable sums of money while damaged stores are closed.

Contributing Factors

Violence has been linked with a *human need to be aggressive*. Early psychologists said that human beings are aggressive animals by nature. More recent psychologists argue that **aggression** is related to *frustration*. Aggression is a common way to deal with frustration, and because frustration is virtually inevitable, you can expect a considerable amount of aggression in social life. Certainly, the frustrations produced by firings and other stressors in businesses have contributed to a rise in the level of violence in the workplace (Johnson and Indvik 1994).

But frustration-generated aggression does not adequately explain violence, for aggression can be channeled into such outlets as competitive sports, hobbies, or hard physical labor. To fully explain violence, let's look at various sociocultural factors that contribute to the problem.

aggression
forceful, offensive, or hostile behavior toward another person or society

Social Structural Factors

Norms.   *Group norms legitimate various kinds of violent behavior* (Reitzel-Jaffe and Wolfe 2001). If you have abusive friends, you are more likely to be abusive in your own relationships. In some families, children observe their parents using violence to settle disagreements or they are taught to employ violence in defending themselves or asserting their rights. This may be based on the *fallacy of non sequitur:* "If I hit you, you will stop doing the things I dislike." It does not follow that violence stops further violence. In fact, violence is likely to elicit more violence.

fallacy

The point is underscored by another norm that involves children—*the norm of physical punishment*. In the short term, physical punishment may lead children to conform to adult expectations. But what happens subsequently? Studies using national samples have concluded that over time, *the use of physical punishment increases the likelihood of delinquent and antisocial behavior by children and is associated with violent crime in adulthood* (Straus, Sugarman, and Giles-Sims 1997; Straus 2001). The more severe the abuse, the more severe the adult crimes are likely to be. A study of juvenile child molesters reported that the molesters, compared to other kinds of offenders, were more likely to have been physically and sexually abused themselves as children (Ford and Linney 1995).

Historically, American norms have legitimated official violence—against radicals and striking laborers, for instance. This official violence is supported by attitudes that approve the use of violence for social control. Throughout the nation's history, groups defined as radical or as a threat to social order also have been defined as legitimate objects of suppression by violence.

An example is the violence of the Chicago police against young antiwar demonstrators during the Democratic Convention of 1968. The committee that investigated the situation called it a "police riot." The police injured many innocent bystanders, including some reporters and news photographers (Hofstadter and Wallace 1970:382). One witness said the police acted like "mad dogs" looking for something to attack. Many people were horrified by the brutality of the police, but public opinion polls showed that the majority of people supported the police. This support came not only because some of the young people had baited the police by taunting them with obscenities, but also because Americans tend to expect and approve violence in the name of social order.

Political Arrangements. Certain political factors affect the level of violence in American society. United States history is characterized by the *exclusion of minorities from the core benefits of and participation in American life.* (*Exclusion* here means both lack of access to economic opportunities and denial of access to the political power by which grievances can be redressed.) This exclusion was maintained and continues to exist to some extent because of political action or inaction. The exclusion has been an important factor in race riots and other interracial violence.

Paige (1971) examined the relationships between *political trust, political efficacy, and riot participation* among 237 African American males in Newark, New Jersey. Political trust was measured by a direct question: "How much do you think you can trust the government in Newark to do what is right—just about always, most of the time, some of the time, or almost never?" Political efficacy was measured by the amount of information the respondents had about local and national political figures. Riot participation was measured by asking the respondents whether they had been "active" in the 1967 Newark riot and what they had done.

Respondents who scored high on political information and low on political trust were most likely to have participated in the riot, whereas those who scored low on information and low on trust were least likely to have participated. In other words, the rioters did not trust the government to be responsive to their needs.

In more recent years, the antiabortion movement has been associated with violence. In 1998, Dr. Barnett Slepian, a physician who performed abortions, became the seventh person killed in the United States by antiabortionists (Gegax and Clemetson 1998). In addition, arson and bombing of abortion clinics and violent confrontations between

Riots are one form of violence that erupts periodically in the United States.

anti- and pro-abortion groups have characterized the struggle over abortion. People who oppose abortion feel that the rights of the unborn have been legislated away by court decisions and that politicians seem to ignore their cause. Thus, they resort to militant and even violent actions to influence the political process and bring about new laws that restrict a woman's right to have an abortion.

In essence, then, *political arrangements virtually guarantee a certain amount of violence* in a society that has groups with diverse and strong beliefs, interests, and demands, and in which violence is defined as a legitimate way to pursue group interests. If blacks make political gains, the Ku Klux Klan or other white-supremacist groups may become more militant and violent. Violence against Asian immigrants has occurred both from white supremacists and from people who feel economically threatened (such as the commercial fishermen in Texas who tried to stop Vietnamese immigrants from fishing). The government can never fully satisfy all the diverse interests of the people. Whatever decisions are made are likely to generate adverse reactions and even violence from people who feel cheated, deprived, or oppressed by these decisions.

The Politics of Gun Control.   Government policy on *gun control* bears on violence in America. Gun control is highly controversial, with strong arguments on both sides of the issue (including the debate about whether the Second Amendment guarantees citizens the right to own firearms). Let's begin with some data. America is a land full of guns; we are one of the *most heavily armed people on earth.* In 2005, 40 percent of American homes had guns, and many had more than one (Maguire and Pastore 2006:156). Thus, between one and two hundred million Americans have access to guns in their homes.

The *government's ability to guarantee security* to the citizenry affects the number of handguns. The less confidence that citizens have in the federal government, the

TABLE 5.1
Weapon Usage in Selected Crimes

Weapon Used	Percent in Which Weapon Used		
	Homicide	Robbery	Assault
Firearm	70	27	8
Knife	13	13	6

SOURCE: Perkins 2003:2.

more likely they are to own firearms (Jiobu and Curry 2001). The important point here, incidentally, is not whether the government protects citizens well by some objective standard but whether the citizens perceive a secure social order.

The significance of the number of guns is underscored by their role in violence. As table 5.1 shows, guns are the most common weapon used in violent crimes.

Since 1960, more than a million Americans have died from gun-related homicides, suicides, and accidents. The homicide rate in the United States is four times higher than that of western Europe and seven times higher than that of Japan (Doyle 2000). The rate of children killed by guns is higher in the United States than in any other industrialized nation. Access to guns has been shown to be an important factor in the killing of intimate partners, gang violence, and school rampage shootings (Braga 2003; Campbell et al. 2003; Newman et al. 2004). And don't overlook the large number of injuries. For every person killed, nearly three others are wounded by firearms (Annest et al. 1995).

In addition to numbers, there is the sheer horror and senselessness of the incidents. A man goes to a school and wounds and kills children whom he does not know. A man and a boy are snipers who kill people they have selected at random. A man walks into his place of employment and starts shooting at everyone, including those who had no part in whatever grievances he has. The point is, the victims of the violence are frequently innocent adults and children who just happened to be where the assailant chose to carry out the attack or attacks.

In spite of tragic incidents like these and in spite of the relationship between the number of gun-involved crimes and gun-control legislation, the issue of gun control is hotly debated. Many people insist that the widespread existence of guns does not contribute to the amount of violence in the nation. One argument is that it is people, not guns, that kill; if a gun is not available, a person will find a different weapon. Professionals dispute the relationship between the number of guns and the amount of violence. Some argue that this society is a violent one and that violence will not be reduced simply by controlling the sale and possession of guns. Many Americans agree that the effort at control would be frustrating at best and counterproductive at worst. As a popular slogan puts it, when guns are outlawed, only outlaws will have guns. This slogan illustrates the *fallacy of appeal to prejudice*. It taps into popular passions in this country about citizens' rights to defend themselves. However, evidence, not emotional slogans, is needed to make a reasonable decision about the issue.

fallacy

In the first place, guns are the weapon most frequently used in homicides. Contrary to the argument that killers would simply find alternative weapons, the gun is the deadliest of weapons; the fatality rate for shootings is about five times higher than the rate for stabbings. Moreover, murder frequently is an act of passion that the killer himself or herself might later regret. At least in some cases, without the gun there would be no murder.

VIOLENTLY OPPOSED TO VIOLENCE

At one time, most of the states had laws prohibiting abortions except when necessary to protect the mother's life. Initially, physicians led the way in calling for a reform of abortion laws. Some lawyers also pressed for change. Abortion should be allowed, they argued, when the mother's mental health or life was jeopardized by the pregnancy or when the pregnancy resulted from rape or incest. Women's groups joined the movement, ultimately resulting in the 1973 Supreme Court decision to legalize abortion.

The Right-to-Life movement then began to work vigorously to reverse the effects of the 1973 decision. Members have pressed for such changes as a constitutional amendment to ban abortions and legislative action to stop funding welfare abortions. Some members became more aggressive, picketing abortion clinics or trying to block people from entering the clinics. Beginning in the 1980s, the efforts have included acts of violence. Arson, bombing of clinics, and even murders have occurred. Some members of the movement—probably a very small number—have resorted to violence to oppose what they define as violence against human life.

Arrange an interview with workers in one or more abortion clinics in your area. Ask them what effect the activities of the Right-to-Life movement has had on their work. Do they fear violence? How do they respond to the charge that they are violently ending human life?

Also interview some members of the Right-to-Life movement. Ask them if they approve of bombing clinics. Is violence against a clinic justifiable? Why? How far would they go in opposing abortions? What answer do they give to people who charge that they are trying to impose their morals on others?

Second, guns are the most frequent weapons used in armed robberies. A gun often seems essential for armed robbery, because without it the offender is unable to produce the necessary threat of force. The fatality rate in armed robberies involving guns is about four times as high as the rate involving other weapons.

Some citizens believe that firearms are necessary to defend their home. This argument has little substance. Many murders occur in homes, but seldom do they involve strangers. The most frequent kind of offender-victim relationship in homicide in homes is that of husband and wife. There is also the possibility of accidental injury or death because of a gun in the home. Ironically, you may face greater danger from a weapon purchased for defense against intruders than from an actual intruder.

A study of firearm-related deaths in the state of Washington was one of the first to examine the issue of deaths caused by guns kept in the home (Kellermann et al. 1992). The researchers found that the guns were rarely used to protect the owners. In fact, for every instance of a homicide for self-protection, there were 43 deaths of residents by suicide, criminal homicide, or accidental gunshot. Only one-half of 1 percent of the cases involved the shooting of an intruder. The researchers concluded that the presence of firearms in the home increases danger to the family more than it increases protection.

Finally, it may be true that people, rather than guns, do the killing; but it is also true that people with guns are more likely to kill than are people without guns. Berkowitz (1981) conducted research that suggests that the mere presence of a gun increases aggressiveness, so that although it is true that "the finger pulls the trigger," it also appears that "the trigger may be pulling the finger." In the research, each student was paired with a partner, ostensibly another student but actually a confederate of the researcher. The two were to come up with ideas to improve record sales and boost the image of a popular singer. Each student was to explain his or her ideas to the partner, who would then administer electric shocks—one shock if the partner thought the ideas were good and up to 10 shocks if the partner thought the ideas were relatively poor. Some of the students became angry after being given seven shocks. Those students then evaluated their partners. They were taken to the room containing the electric-shock machine and a telegraph key that administered the shocks. Some saw nothing but the key lying on a table. Others saw a badminton racket and shuttlecocks, and a third group saw a shotgun and a revolver. Those students who saw the firearms gave their partners a greater number of shocks and administered each for a longer period of time. Berkowitz notes that other studies have shown the same effect; the mere presence of a firearm increases aggressive behavior.

The evidence suggests, then, that gun control could reduce some kinds of violence (murder and armed robbery) and minimize the destructiveness of other kinds (assaults and arguments). Public opinion polls show that most Americans favor the *registration of firearms*. There are two important reasons for the existence of political inaction in the face of the evidence and the will of the people. One is that the evidence is still ambiguous; legislators are not convinced of the value of control. The other reason is the strong *lobbying efforts* of the National Rifle Association (NRA). The NRA has a large, paid staff and thousands of local clubs in every state. It spends millions of dollars a year on direct lobbying efforts. Consequently, as of this writing, apart from some limitations on the importation and sale of semiautomatic and automatic weapons, little has been done to reduce the number of guns in American society.

The Stratification System.   In an effort to put violence in America in historical perspective, Graham and Gurr (1969) identified certain *political and economic inequalities* between various groups that have been associated with violence. The early Anglo-Saxon settlers gained the political and economic leverage necessary to resist *efforts by subsequent groups of immigrants to share fully in the nation's opportunities.* Difficult economic times have been particularly fertile for fueling violence, as illustrated by the mob violence against African Americans in the South during inflationary shifts in the price of cotton (Beck and Tolnay 1990).

Inequalities also have been identified as factors in urban riots. In the 1992 riot in Los Angeles, inequality *formed the motivating basis for many of the participants.* Using interviews with 227 African Americans living and/or working in the area at the time of the riot, researchers compared participants with nonparticipants (Murty, Roebuck, and Armstrong 1994). Participants tended to be younger males with lower incomes and lower amounts of education. They also had more arrest records than nonparticipants. But *nonparticipants as well as participants indicated general acceptance of the rioting.* It wasn't that they approved of rioting as such but that they believed collective violence is the only way to get the larger society to address their grievances (poverty, discrimination, unemployment, and police brutality).

At an interpersonal level, boys whose fathers have a history of unemployment are more likely to engage in violent behavior than are sons of fully employed fathers (Brownfield 1987). Violent behavior here refers to beating up or hurting someone on purpose (other than a brother or sister). Of course, unemployed fathers are more likely to be found in the lower socioeconomic strata. Unemployment generates strains in the family life of lower- and working-class youths. In turn, these strains seem to be conducive to greater violent behavior. Thus, both children and adults who live in economic deprivation are more prone to violent behavior and aggression, including murder (Walter et al. 1995; Benson et al. 2003; Pollock, Mullings, and Crouch 2006).

Clearly, then, *certain kinds of inequality are related to violence.* Inequality generates frustrations and rage in individuals when they find themselves powerless to resolve their situation, and the probability of violence goes up. Some people may engage in the collective violence of riots and public disorder. Others may vent their rage by fighting on their own. In any case, the violence is the consequence of a stratification system that leaves some Americans in the gutters of the economy.

Social Psychological Factors

Attitudes.   *Certain attitudes legitimate violence.* One is the attitude of approval of violence itself. To be sure, people have a tendency to be selective about what circumstances justify violence (Bethke and DeJoy 1993). Still, most Americans accept violence as a problem solver, and about "two-thirds think that the use of physical force is often justified" (Patterson and Kim 1991:132). In particular, many Americans accept intimate partner violence if the circumstances warrant it (Sacks et al. 2001). A study of high-school students reported that 77 percent of the females and 67 percent of the males endorsed some form of sexual coercion, including unwanted kissing, genital contact, and sexual intercourse (Office of Juvenile Justice and Delinquency Prevention 2006:4).

relative deprivation
a sense of deprivation based on some standard used by the individual who feels deprived

One explanation of violence is **relative deprivation**, which means that people have a *sense of deprivation in relation to some standard.* Here, the attitudes people have toward their deprivation are more important than any objective assessment of that deprivation. This observation goes back at least as far as de Tocqueville (1955), who pointed out that the French were experiencing real economic gains prior to the Revolution. An observer could have told the French that, objectively, they were better off at the time of their revolt than they had been at other times in the past. Yet what if the people used a different standard than their past to measure their deprivation? They might then perceive themselves to be less well off than they *should* be and rebel, which is precisely the idea of relative deprivation.

Davies (1962) used the notion of relative deprivation to explain revolutions. He constructed a *"J-curve" theory of revolution.* In essence, the theory states that a *widening gap between what people want and what they get leads to a revolutionary situation.* People do not revolt when the society is generally impoverished. Rather, people develop a revolutionary state of mind when they sense a threat to their expectations of greater opportunities to satisfy needs.

You will always experience a gap between your expectations and the satisfaction of your needs. Some degree of gap is tolerable, and although over time both your satisfactions and your expectations tend to increase, something may happen to suddenly increase the gap. Expectations continue to rise while actual need satisfactions remain level or suddenly fall. The gap then becomes intolerable, and a revolutionary situation is created.

According to Davies' theory, the deprivation of people in a revolutionary situation is relative. Actual satisfaction of their needs may be higher at the time of a revolution than earlier, but their expectations are also higher. The people may be better off in terms of their past, but worse off in terms of their expectations. Their attitudes rather than their objective condition make the situation revolutionary.

Relative deprivation has been identified as a factor in racial militancy and the approval of violent protest by northern blacks. Interviews with 107 riot-area residents of Detroit in 1967 showed that those who were most militant in their attitudes and who believed the riots helped the black cause were those who felt relatively deprived rather than relatively satisfied (Crawford and Naditch 1970).

A survey of 6,074 young adults found that those who saw themselves as economically deprived compared to their friends, neighbors, and Americans generally were more likely to engage in violent behavior (Stiles, Liu, and Kaplan 2000). The sense of deprivation led to negative feelings about themselves, which motivated them to use violent means to cope with their situation.

Finally, *attitudes about firearms help maintain the large number of guns in American homes.* A slight majority (54 percent) of Americans favor stricter gun-control laws (Polling Report 2007). But this number represents a significant decline since 2000, when 67 percent favored stricter control. In addition, 73 percent agree that the Second Amendment guarantees the right of individuals to own guns.

Values.   Attitudes that justify violence are often reinforced by certain values. In American society, people are likely to agree on the values of **retributiveness** and self-defense.

retributiveness
paying people back for their socially unacceptable behavior

Retributiveness, or retributive justice, is summarized by the notion of "an eye for an eye and a tooth for a tooth." It is a value of punishment, of paying people back for their antisocial behavior. This value comes into play when people insist on the death penalty and other harsh forms of punishment.

Self-defense as a value means an *affirmation of the right to violence, including killing, in order to defend yourself or your family.* Some people would extend the value to include the defense of your home as well. In part, these values are maintained through the mass media. We need to look, therefore, at the controversial question of the media's role in teaching values that support violent behavior.

Role of the Mass Media.   *The mass media expose Americans to an enormous amount of violence.* It would be interesting to record the number of violent incidents that impinge on your life in a week's reading, listening to the radio, and watching television. Concern about violence on television began in the 1950s when it became evident that television programming contained a high degree of violence in everything from children's shows to late-night adult entertainment. From time to time, television executives have promised to scale back the amount of violence, but the level remains high.

A child who watches television regularly is likely to witness thousands of violent deaths and an untold number of violent incidents during his or her growing-up years. An analysis of television commercials aimed at young children reported that more than one-third of those that featured children showed acts of aggression (Larson 2003). A study of 443.5 hours of programs for children aged 5 to 10 on broadcast television and cable found a "staggering" amount of violence (Parents Television Council 2006). There were 3,488 violent incidents, an average of 7.86 per hour, a figure considerably higher than the amount seen on programs for adults! In addition, the study found hundreds of incidents of verbal aggression, problematic attitudes and behavior, and sexual content.

Perhaps as disturbing as the amount of violence is the way that the violence is handled. A group of researchers at four universities analyzed 2,500 hours of television (Farhi 1996). They found violence in 57 percent of the programs. They also found that perpetrators of violent acts went unpunished 73 percent of the time, and that 47 percent of the violent incidents showed no harm to the victims.

What are the consequences of all this violence? In brief, the answer is that *violence breeds further violence.* Researchers have found that aggressive attitudes and behaviors increase in people who read violent comic books, listen to songs with violent lyrics, and play violent video games (Kirsh and Olczak 2002; Anderson and Carnagey 2003; Anderson 2004).

Television, including children's programs, exposes children to an enormous amount of violence.

catharsis
discharge of socially unacceptable emotions in a socially acceptable way

Some observers argue that the effect of television violence is an increased amount of violent behavior. Others argue that watching violence on television provides a kind of **catharsis**, *a discharging of aggressive emotions* through vicarious participation in violence. For example, a man who has become extremely hostile toward his wife can discharge his aggression and avoid violence against his wife by watching violent acts on television.

But displacement of aggression and vicarious discharge of aggression are not the same thing. Contrary to the idea of catharsis, portrayal of violence in motion pictures and on television increases the level of violence in society. There is evidence to support this conclusion.

Studies indicate that watching violence on television *socializes* people into the norms, attitudes, and values for violence. The more that people watch television, in other words, the more likely they are both to approve of and to engage in violence (American Academy of Pediatrics 2001; Huesmann et al. 2003). Thus, Eron (1987) found a strong relationship between the amount of violent television a child saw at age 8 and aggressive behavior when the child reached the age of 30. Johnson and his associates (2002) assessed 707 individuals over a 17-year period. They found a significant association between the amount of time spent watching television as adolescents and young adults and subsequent aggressive behavior.

In addition to aggressive behavior, watching televised violence leads to a more jaundiced view of the world:

> [B]eliefs about the prevalence of violence in American life have been correlated with
> amount of television viewing. . . . People who look at a great deal of television tend
> to believe that there is more violence in the real world than do those who do not look
> at much television. . . . Exposure to televised violence has also been found to lead to
> mistrust, fearfulness of walking alone at night, and a desire to have protective weapons,
> and alienation. (National Institute of Mental Health 1982:61)

Such a jaundiced view of the world may lead people to be less concerned about the victims of violence. In an experiment with fourth- and fifth-grade students, Molitor and Hirsch (1994) found that children who watched violence were afterward less likely to be concerned about two other children who engaged in a violent confrontation. The subjects watched a TV monitor that supposedly showed two children in an adjacent room. The subjects were told to get help if anything happened. Those who had watched clips from a violent movie were less likely to, or slower to, get help when the children on the monitor became violent with each other.

These negative effects of watching violence on television affect children at a very early age. Three researchers set up an experiment in which they observed 63 four-year-olds during play (Singer, Singer, and Rapaczynski 1984). They scored the children for amount of aggression. The parents kept logs of the amount and kind of television programs the children watched. The researchers then kept track of the children for six years and measured some of their beliefs and behavior. They found that the children who spent more time watching television, especially violent programs, were less able to behave with self-restraint, more likely to be aggressive, more restless, and more prone to believe that the world is a frightening place.

Finally, note the possibility that even watching violent sports can increase aggression. Researchers who investigated the rate of violent assaults on women in the Washington, D.C., area reported an increase in admissions to hospital emergency rooms following victories by the Washington Redskins football team (White, Katz, and Scarborough 1992). The researchers speculate that viewing the success of violence—even in a sporting event—may give some fans a sense of license to try to dominate their own surroundings by the use of force.

Admittedly, even with all the research we have noted, it is difficult to state unequivocally that exposure to the mass media leads to specific effects because of the many other factors that operate within our lives. However, the evidence is growing and overwhelmingly supports the position that mass media violence is associated with aggressive attitudes and behavior. The evidence suggests that mass media violence teaches people how to be violent and tends to create violent behavior in viewers.

Public Policy and Private Action

We already have discussed some steps for reducing violence, because whatever effectively deals with the problem of crime also reduces the level of violence. In addition, the various norms, attitudes, and values that support violence need to be changed. Early intervention in the lives of children can teach them alternatives to violence and aggression in solving their problems and gaining their goals in life. In families, schools, and churches, children need to learn how to employ nonviolent methods to survive and to find fulfillment. For example, a violence prevention program called Peace Builders has been shown to decrease aggression and increase social competence in children in kindergarten through fifth grade (Vazsonyi, Belliston, and Flannery 2004). Such programs cost relatively little and reach children at an early age.

American norms and attitudes about when violence is legitimate also need to change. In particular, no one should be taught that he or she deserves violent treatment from another person. Many women abused by a male partner remain in the relationship for years in the belief that they somehow brought the violence on themselves. Or they are convinced that they will eventually change the partner into a nonviolent individual. Women who break away from such relationships have learned to reject the notion that they deserve abuse or that they are responsible for helping their partner to change (Rosen and Stith 1995).

Second, *gun-control measures* may reduce the violence in our society. Homicide is the leading cause of death in Colombia, South America; but when two cities—Cali and Bogotá—banned the carrying of firearms on weekends, holidays, and election days, the homicide rates went down (Villaveces et al. 2000). A comparative study of Seattle, Washington, and Vancouver, British Columbia, provides additional evidence (Sloan, Kellermann, and Reay 1988). Vancouver has much stricter firearm regulations than Seattle. During the period of the study, robbery and burglary rates were similar in the two cities, but Seattle had a higher assault rate and 700 percent more assaults using firearms (which means greater risks to the victims). Seattle citizens also were 4.8 times as likely to be murdered with a handgun. In another study, researchers found, in states that passed laws making gun owners responsible for storing firearms so that they were inaccessible to children, unintentional shooting deaths of children younger than 15 declined by 23 percent (Cummings et al. 1997). Similarly, the 1994 federal ban on assault weapons contributed to lower gun murder rates and murders of police officers by criminals armed with assault weapons (Roth and Koper 1999).

Third, violence in the mass media should be reduced. The reduction is needed in cartoons as well as other kinds of programming. An experiment with third- and fourth-grade children found that cutting back on the amount of time children spent watching television and playing video games reduced the amount of aggressive behavior (Robinson et al. 2001).

Not only should violence be reduced, but the programs should include a greater amount of modeling of desirable behavior. *Television could become a medium for promoting more prosocial behavior.* In an experiment with 40 children in a private preschool, the researchers showed a number of prosocial videos (Forge and Phemister 1987). After seeing the videos, the children engaged in more prosocial behavior: sharing toys and play space, cooperating with others, taking turns, and interacting in a positive way.

Finally, violence will lessen as we deal with some of the inequalities in our society. We will discuss this further when we consider poverty and other problems in Part 3.

Follow-Up.   Would you like to see a ban on corporal punishment of children become a matter of public policy? Why or why not?

The Violence of Rape

We know of no society that completely lacks rape or that fails to punish it (Palmer 1989). The definition of rape, however, varies. The American legal code distinguishes between two kinds of rape: forcible and statutory. **Forcible rape** is defined as the "carnal knowledge of a female forcibly and against her will" (Federal Bureau of Investigation 2002:454). The victim of forcible rape can be of any age, and attempts or assaults to rape are included. **Statutory rape** refers to sexual intercourse with a female who is under the legal age for consenting.

Rape is an extremely *traumatic experience* for victims. For the perpetrators, rape is typically an expression of violent aggression against women, not an act of sexual passion.

forcible rape
the carnal knowledge of a female forcibly and against her will

statutory rape
sexual intercourse with a female who is below the legal age for consenting

Racial/Ethnic Background	Percentage Raped in Lifetime	
	Women	Men
Non-Hispanic white	17.9	2.8
Hispanic	11.9	*
Black	18.8	3.3
Asian/Pacific Islander	6.8	*

TABLE 5.2
Racial/Ethnic Background of Rape Victims

*Insufficient number in sample to calculate a percentage.
SOURCE: Tjaden and Thoennes 2006.

How prevalent is rape in the United States? It is difficult to say because an unknown number of rapes are *never reported*. In a national survey of women, 47 percent took at least five years after a childhood rape to tell someone and 28 percent *never told anyone* about it before the research interview (Smith et al. 2000). Adult victims are often reluctant to report a rape because of fear that the rapist will try to get even with them or will attack them again. They also fear publicity, embarrassment, and the way they may be treated by police and prosecutors (Monroe et al. 2005).

However, the proportion of victims who do report rape is increasing. And the rate of forcible rape has been declining. In 2005, the FBI reported nearly 94,000 rapes, representing the lowest rate since 1978. Victimization data also show a decline, but a somewhat higher number and rate: over 115,000 rapes or attempted rapes (Catalano 2006a). A national survey of rape victims, which included male victims (mostly homosexual rapes) for the first time, reported that 17.6 percent of women and 3 percent of men say they have been raped at some time in their lives (Tjaden and Thoennes 2006). This means that more than 20 million Americans have been rape victims.

Not everyone is equally likely to be a rape victim. Table 5.2 shows how the rates vary by racial/ethnic background. American Indians/Alaskan Natives have the highest rates of female victims, followed by African Americans and non-Hispanic whites. Rates also vary by age, with higher rates in younger age groups. In fact, in the national survey, 21.6 percent of women and 48 percent of men were younger than 12 years when they were first raped, and 32.4 percent of women and 23 percent of men were between the ages of 12 and 17 (Tjaden and Thoennes 2006:18). Rates are also higher among the poor than the well-to-do, and among the divorced/separated and never married than those married or widowed (Catalano 2006a:8).

Contrary to popular belief, there is little interracial rape, and most rapes *do not* involve strangers. In the national survey, only 16.7 percent of female victims and 22.8 percent of male victims were raped by a stranger (Tjaden and Thoennes 2006:21). Female victims tended to be raped by a current or former intimate partner, while male victims tended to be raped by acquaintances such as friends, teachers, or neighbors.

Finally, there is the form of rape known as **incest,** which refers to exploitative sexual contact between relatives in which the victim is under 18 years of age. Russell (1986) reported that 19 percent of women she interviewed had been victims of *incestuous abuse*. A study of more than 300 male and female victims of child sexual abuse reported that 88 percent had been abused by a family member (Faller 1989). On the

incest

exploitative sexual contact between relatives in which the victim is under the age of 18

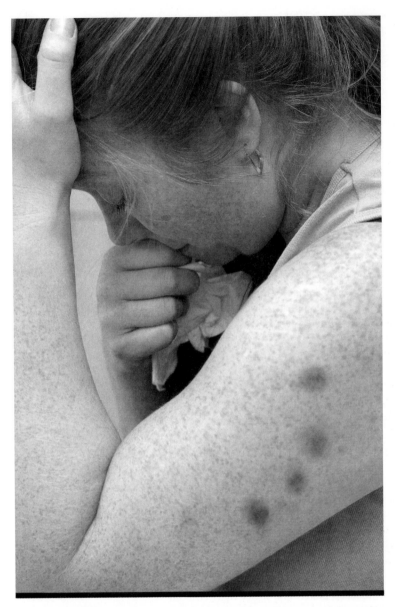

Rape is one of the most traumatic experiences a woman endures.

average, the boys were 6.3 years old and the girls were 5.5 years old when the abuse began. These experiences can be psychologically devastating and can have the same kind of long-term effects as rape. Many of the victims are prone to what Russell called "revictimization," getting involved as adults with men who abuse or rape them.

Rape and the Quality of Life

Regardless of the background characteristics of the victim, the consequences for the quality of life are similar: Rape is a highly traumatic experience, and fear of rape probably causes uneasiness in most women at some time.

Emotional and Physical Trauma

Rape victims suffer *intense emotional trauma*. Rape contradicts the ideal of healthy, voluntary, and nonviolent relationships. The emotional trauma that results from rape is incompatible with the desired quality of life.

Incest victims are likely to have long-term problems. As adolescents they may be characterized by depression, suicidal tendencies, promiscuity, and unplanned and unwanted pregnancies (Beitchman et al. 1991; Boyer and Fine 1992). When they become adults, they are more likely than the nonabused to suffer from depression and various kinds of psychological and physical problems as well as social maladjustment and difficulties in relating intimately (Parker and Parker 1991; Alexander et al. 1998; Filipas and Ullman 2006).

Adult victims of rape experience what Burgess and Holmstrom (1974) delineated as the *rape trauma syndrome*. The syndrome involved two phases of reaction of the victim: *an initial, acute phase of disorganization and a long-term phase of reorganization*. The acute phase, which lasted for a few weeks after the incident, involved both physical and emotional reactions. The *physical reactions* included soreness and bruises resulting from the violence of the offender; tension headaches, fatigue, and disturbance of sleep; various gastrointestinal disturbances such as nausea, stomach pains, and lack of appetite; and genitourinary problems such as vaginal itching and pain. The *emotional reaction* during the acute phase ranged "from fear, humiliation, and embarrassment to anger, revenge, and self-blame. Fear of physical violence and death was the primary feeling described" (Burgess and Holmstrom 1974:983). Although it may seem surprising that victims should feel guilty or blame themselves, such feelings are common (see "I Felt Guilty," at the beginning of this chapter). A young woman reported strong guilt feelings in these terms:

> I'm single but I'm not a virgin and I was raised a Catholic. So I thought this might be some kind of punishment to warn me I was doing something against the Church or God.

Another victim remarked, "My father always said whatever a man did to a woman, she provoked it" (Burgess and Holmstrom 1974:983).

The long-term phase of reorganization included *motor and emotional consequences.* Common motor consequences included actions such as changing residence, changing telephone numbers, and visiting family and friends to gain support. Among the emotional consequences were nightmares; the development of various phobias, such as the fear of being indoors, outdoors, alone, in a crowd, or hearing but not seeing people walking behind one; and sexual fears. One victim reported that five months after the incident she could still get hysterical with her boyfriend: "I don't want him near me; I get panicked. Sex is OK, but I still feel like screaming" (Burgess and Holmstrom 1974:984).

In a follow-up study of 81 victims, reinterviewed from four to six years after they were raped, Burgess and Holmstrom (1979) found that less than a full recovery was reported by 71 percent of the victims who had never had sexual relations, 27 percent of those inactive at the time of the rape, and 35 percent of those sexually active when they were attacked. More than two-thirds of the victims said they had decreased sexual activity, and many of them said that they experienced pain and discomfort and had difficulty reaching an orgasm when they resumed sexual activity.

Subsequent studies confirm and extend the findings of Burgess and Holmstrom (M. B. Stein et al. 2004). Virtually every area of a woman's life is negatively affected by the experience of rape. The majority will suffer from posttraumatic stress disorder at some time in their lives, and some of these sufferers will develop various kinds of chronic medical conditions (Solomon and Davidson 1997; Ullman and Brecklin 2003). Relationships, work, health habits, and sense of personal well-being may be adversely affected (Thompson et al. 2002). And if a woman was sexually abused as a child, she is at increased risk as an adult of rape or sexual assault, domestic violence, self-inflicted harm, and various other kinds of trauma (Noll et al. 2003).

Much less attention has been paid to the consequences of being the victim of an *attempted rape.* One study of 40 victims of attempted rape found that the women had roughly the same short-term and long-term reactions as did women who were raped (Becker et al. 1982). The attempted rape victims were likely to experience feelings of embarrassment, fear, humiliation, and anger; to have sleep disturbance problems; and to experience some physical ills such as gastrointestinal problems and headaches. They were as likely to experience some degree of self-blame as were the rape victims.

Finally, most women experience trauma because of the *fear of rape* (Mesch 2000). As one female student told us, "Every woman knows that she is a potential victim of a rapist." Such fear takes a toll on free movement and peace of mind. A survey reported that murder is the only crime feared more by women than rape (Gordon and Riger 1989). The major fears in the women's lives were losing a job, divorce, cancer, and rape.

Physical Abuse

Although most female victims who report being injured have relatively minor kinds of physical injuries, rapists may use weapons, beat or choke the victim, and use strength or threats to subdue her (DiMaio 2000). Some victims require medical treatment for their physical injuries. The *force and brutality so commonly involved in rapes* lead us to conclude that rapes are acts of violence rather than sexual passion. The rapist is not someone with an overwhelming sex drive; he is, typically, a man who feels compelled to assault and humiliate women. He uses rape as a weapon to express his hatred of females. Physical abuse, therefore, is an inevitable consequence for the female victim.

Contributing Factors

Most of the factors that contribute to other kinds of violence also contribute to rape as a particular form of violence. Other factors distinctively associated with rape tend to *encourage offenders* and to *oppress the victims.*

Social Structural Factors

Certain *traditional norms about sex roles* may be factors in rape. That is, in the traditional roles, males are aggressive and females are submissive. The more strongly that men adhere to traditional rather than egalitarian roles, the more likely they are to have victim-callous rape attitudes (Whatley 2005). For some men, it may be acceptable to rape an assertive woman so that she learns her "proper place."

In general, it seems *the more that men are integrated into a culture where the norms support male dominance and superiority,* the more likely they are to find rape acceptable (Locke and Mahalik 2005). The locker-room talk of athletes tends to treat women as objects, encourage sexist attitudes, and promote rape (Curry 1991). Such talk seems to correlate with behavior, for *athletes are more likely than other men to be sexually aggressive* and to participate in gang rapes (Koss and Gaines 1993).

The *college norm of heavy drinking at parties* is also a factor in rape (Mohler-Kuo et al. 2004). A survey of thousands of women in 119 colleges and universities over a three-year period reported that 1 in 20 (4.7 percent) reported being a victim of rape (Mohler-Kuo et al. 2004). And nearly three-fourths of them were raped while they were intoxicated. The researchers concluded that a female student's chances of being raped are far greater on campuses in which the student body as a whole has a high rate of binge drinking and in which individuals consume large amounts of alcohol.

Finally, *negative family experiences can foster the development of a rapist.* Kruttschnitt (1989) interviewed 38 convicted rapists; 59 convicted nonsexually violent offenders; and 65 nonoffenders who were similar to the others in age, race, and area of residence during adolescence. The rapists were more likely than the others to have a history of sexual abuse. In addition, they tended not to be close to their siblings. In some cases of abuse within families, a victim at least may find support from other family members. The rapists tended to lack that support.

Other research also shows that *a lack of involvement of family members with each other* (in terms of emotional support, closeness, and shared activities) increases the likelihood of family members being the victims of sexual abuse (Ray, Jackson, and Townsley 1991). As with most social problems, the quality of family life is an important variable.

Social Psychological Factors

Attitudes. Are the following statements true or false?

Rape tends to be an unplanned, impulsive act.

Women frequently bring false accusations of rape against men.

Most women fantasize about being raped and find erotic pleasure in the fantasy.

A woman who is raped is usually partly to blame for the act.

It is not possible for a man to rape a healthy woman unless she is—consciously or unconsciously—willing.

What are your answers? If you said that any of the previous statements is true, you have accepted one of the *myths about rape*. In point of fact, many people—even a minority of college women—accept one or more of these beliefs (Holcomb et al. 1991; Carmody and Washington 2001). An analysis of a number of studies on attitudes toward rape concluded that men, older people, political conservatives, and people from the lower socioeconomic strata are more likely than others to accept the myths about rape (Anderson, Harris, and Okamura 1997). They also are more inclined to commit rape and less likely than others to be sympathetic toward rape victims or to blame offenders (Chiroro et al. 2004). They thereby not only lend support to those who rape but also help perpetuate injustice in the efforts to prosecute rapists.

It is important, then, to deal with the attitudes expressed in the myths. In contrast to the notion that rape is impulsive, significant proportions of convicted rapists have admitted that they intended to find a victim prior to the rape and that they looked for women who they thought could not or would not resist the attack (Stevens 1994). As for the fantasy myth, only a small proportion of women report that they fantasize about being forced to have sex.

The myth that women frequently bring false charges of rape against men has no factual basis. There is a good deal of evidence that women frequently do not report rape to the authorities, but no evidence that they frequently make false accusations.

Let's look in more detail at the other two myths, for they are more difficult to answer definitively. First, the humiliating treatment to which a rape victim is often subjected during a trial follows from the *attitude that the victim was somehow to blame* for provoking the offender. This is the *fallacy of personal attack* at its worst. Instead of receiving help and support, the victim of violence becomes the defendant of her own integrity. The attitude that "the victim was asking for it" ignores three things. One, women are socialized to make themselves attractive to men by their dress and mannerisms. Two, provocative dress cannot be considered sufficient justification for inflicting the physical and emotional brutality of rape upon a woman. As Horos (1974:12) argued,

fallacy

> Does a woman's dress or mannerisms give any man the right to rape her? Because you carry money in your pocket, does it mean that you're asking to be robbed? Perhaps this myth arose because rape is the only violent crime in which women are never the perpetrators, but always the victims.

Three, provocative dress is not even involved in all rapes. The victim may be an elderly woman in a long robe, a woman wearing a coat, or a young girl in modest school clothes. In any case, to focus on dress is simply another way of *blaming a victim for an injustice*.

The attitude that a healthy woman can always prevent rape also may help acquit an offender and oppress the victim. This attitude may reflect the *fallacy of retrospective*

ATTITUDES OF TURKISH STUDENTS TOWARD RAPE

Is it rape if the woman lures him on? Is it rape if she agrees to go with him to his apartment? Is it rape if the woman is his wife? Should the rape be reported to the police regardless of the circumstances? Americans have had differing opinions about the appropriate answer to such questions. People in other nations also differ in their attitudes about rape.

Four researchers who investigated the attitudes of Turkish university students toward rape found a high degree of condemnation by both male and female students but also some interesting variations depending on gender and the circumstances. The sample consisted of 432 females and 368 males from a number of universities in Istanbul.

Each student was presented with three different rape scenarios. The first was of a young man and woman who knew each other for two years and had been dating for six months. On a date that involved drinking and dancing until 2 A.M., they went to his house for a cup of coffee. They kissed and stroked each other, but the woman didn't want to go any further. She asked to go, but he ignored her and engaged in physically forced sex.

The second scenario was of a woman who was followed home by a stranger after shopping at the supermarket. She heard him as she was walking down the dark and empty street toward her house. She walked faster, but he caught up with her, put a knife to her throat, and raped her.

The third scenario also involved a stranger, but rape myth information was added. The young woman was returning home alone at 1 A.M. wearing a miniskirt, a low-cut blouse, and high boots. She was raped after getting off a bus and walking to her house.

The students were asked, for each of the scenarios, whether the rape should be reported to the police, whether a crime was committed, and what kind of punishment (if any) should be meted out to the offender. Figure 5.1 shows the proportion of students who agreed that the rape should be reported. Nearly all the students agreed that the rape by a stranger should be reported. The great majority agreed that the rape by a stranger of the woman wearing the provocative clothing should be reported,

determinism. In essence, people may be saying to the victim: "The situation could have had no other outcome. The man is not to blame, because you allowed it to happen—and you allowed it to happen because of the kind of person you are."

This attitude ignores the *paralyzing fear* that can grip a woman. Perhaps a third or more of rape victims exhibit *tonic immobility,* which is an involuntary, reflexive response to a fearful situation, a response in which the victim "freezes" as though paralyzed (Galliano et al. 1993).

This attitude also ignores the *amount of force* used by rapists. Recall that rape typically involves the use of a weapon. Furthermore, beating, choking, and the threat of death may be effective even though no weapon is visible.

We already have pointed out the lack of sympathy and help a victim may experience in encounters with the police. The *attitude of the police* may be that the woman provokes the attack and that a healthy woman cannot be raped. In addition, the police may suspect the woman is merely using the charge of rape to punish a man or get attention for herself. To be sure, there are rare cases in which a woman charges rape to retaliate against a man or fulfill some pathological need.

Furthermore, the police know that not all victims of rape are respectable citizens with backgrounds free of suspicious behavior. In part, then, the attitudes of the police reflect a genuine need for caution. Nevertheless, a past police record, provocative clothing, or minimal resistance do not give a man license to forcibly rape a woman.

though slightly more women than men agreed. And a majority would report the date rape, though significantly more of the women than the men agreed. More women than men also agreed that the date rape was a crime (22.6 percent of the men said "no"). And in all three scenarios, women would mete out greater punishment than would the men. Thus, in Turkey, as in most societies, men are less likely than women to view rape as a serious, violent crime when they can use circumstances to justify the rape.

SOURCE:
    Golge et al. 2003.

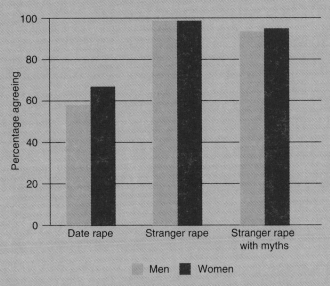

FIGURE 5.1   Proportion Agreeing Victim Should Report Rape to Police.

Considerable improvement has occurred in recent decades in the treatment of rape victims. Yet it is still true that the police, along with legal and medical personnel, can fail to give victims needed services (Campbell et al. 2001). Victims who go to formal authorities for help receive more negative reactions than those who rely on informal sources such as friends and family (Ullman and Filipas 2001).

Mass Media.   As they do with violence in general, the mass media also play a role in the problem of rape. Some movies and magazines "portray women as mindless, undifferentiated, anonymous beings with strong masochistic urges" (Vivar 1982:53). One magazine had an article entitled "Rape Me, Rape Me Not." The author claimed that women train in the martial arts to slow down the rapist so that the sexual experience is more fulfilling. Another magazine had an article on the "joy" of rape for men. Movies are sold for private consumption that show women being sexually abused, tortured, and murdered. Do such portrayals have any effect on the readers or viewers? What about milder forms of media, such as R- and X-rated movies with sexual violence in them?

A number of experiments (Donnerstein 1980; Donnerstein and Linz 1984; Weisz and Earls 1995) show that men who watch movies that portray sexual violence, including those shown in theaters around the country, are more likely to engage in bizarre or anti-social behavior. Even a few minutes of watching a sexually violent movie can lead to antisocial attitudes and behavior. The men in the experiments were more likely afterward to accept the myths about rape (that, for instance, a woman really wants to be raped), to indicate a willingness to commit rape, to engage in aggressive behavior against a woman in a laboratory situation, and to have less sensitivity to the trauma of rape for women. In another experiment, men who watched a film that was sexually degrading to women were more likely than other men to believe that a rape victim found the experience pleasurable and "got what she wanted" (Milburn, Mather, and Conrad 2000).

Justification and Values.   Finally, we raise the question of the social psychology of the offender. What kind of man is a rapist? Is he mentally ill? Two researchers who questioned incarcerated rapists found that some of the offenders gave reasons for the rape that justified or minimized the significance of the act (Scully and Marolla 1984). The various justifications they used were that the women were seductive; that women say "no" but they really mean "yes"; that most women eventually relax and enjoy the experience; that women who are "nice" will not get raped; and that the act was at best a minor offense that did not merit the penalty the offender was now suffering. In other words, the men appeared to accept the rape myths. As we noted earlier, men who accept the myths are more likely to be sexually aggressive and to approve of rape.

Other offenders, however, admitted their guilt and viewed their behavior as morally wrong. They claimed that the rape was either the result of their use of alcohol or drugs, or the result of their emotional problems. They also tended to try to present an image of themselves as "nice" guys whose "true" self should not be judged on the basis of the rape.

Macho values also seem to be a factor in the tolerance of, and proneness to, rape. In one experiment, young men were asked to listen to the tape of a simulated rape and imagine themselves in the role of the rapist (Mosher and Anderson 1986). The tape described an encounter between a man and a woman stranded on a lonely road because of a flat tire. The man forced the woman to have sex with him. Some of the listeners found the tape repugnant, but others found it interesting and sexually arousing. In particular, those with macho values (real men engage in violence and find danger exciting) were more likely to have a positive reaction to the tape.

Finally, whatever else he may or may not be, the rapist and the man who accepts the myths about rape have a high level of hostility toward women (Lonsway and Fitzgerald 1995). Every rape involves aggression.

Public Policy and Private Action

Four lines of attack can be pursued in dealing with the rape problem. First, *programs of prevention* need to be established (Bryant-Davis 2004). We have noted the high rate of date rape. Many colleges and universities have established programs to make students aware of date and acquaintance rape. Research has shown that rape-education programs can change attitudes of both men and women (Fonow, Richardson, and Wemmerus 1992).

Some cities also have set up prevention programs (Harvey 1985). These programs include a variety of services such as self-defense training, public education activities, and support services to professionals in the sexual assault field. The programs may prepare and provide booklets on prevention and self-defense and work with the mass media to gain a wide audience for their educational materials.

The idea of self-defense presents women with a dilemma. On the one hand, the woman who does not struggle may find the police or some jury members unsympathetic to her case. On the other hand, the research on physical resistance has come up with mixed results in terms of recommendations (Ullman 1998). A study of 274 women who were raped or avoided rape concluded that forceful fighting and screaming were likely to reduce the severity of the sexual abuse without increasing the physical injury (Ullman and Knight 1992). Other research found that physical resistance increases the likelihood of physical injury (Ruback and Ivie 1988), and that serial rapists had increased pleasure and prolonged the duration of the rape when the victim resisted (Hazelwood, Reboussin, and Warren 1989). Perhaps the best advice we can give at this point is that self-defense should include thorough training and not just a determination to struggle.

Second, *sex-role norms, legal processes, and attitudes* need to be changed. Some changes will occur only through a painfully slow process of education, for even knowledgeable and well-educated people can be deeply ignorant about rape. A male graduate psychology student told us, "There is a simple way for women to avoid the trauma of rape. They should just decide to relax and enjoy it." Such attitudes encourage offenders and oppress the victims. The fact that a graduate student could hold this kind of attitude illustrates the point that changing attitudes is going to be a painfully slow process. But changing such attitudes, including attitudes about the various rape myths, will reduce the amount of sexual assault (Lanier 2001).

Rapists need treatment. Rapists tend to be psychologically disturbed in some way. As such, they need therapy, some kind of rehabilitation, and not simply punishment. Punishment may remove the rapist from society for a period of time, but it will not deter him from future offenses.

The fourth line of attack is to *provide help for the victims* of rape (Kalmuss 2004). In recent years a number of *rape crisis centers* have been established in urban areas to help victims. The centers offer assistance in dealing with (often unsympathetic) authorities, information about available legal and medical care, and counseling to facilitate recovery from the emotional trauma. The centers also frequently have prevention programs and offer courses in self-defense.

The centers may also offer the services of a rape victim advocate. A study of 81 rape victims in two urban hospitals reported that those who had the help of a rape victim advocate were more likely to have police reports taken and less likely to be treated negatively by police officers (Campbell 2006). They also reported less distress with the legal and medical systems, and they received more medical services such as emergency contraception and sexually transmitted disease prophylaxis. *Rape victim advocates should be available* in all areas.

The attitudes of authorities seem to be changing in the direction of greater sympathy for the victims of rape. A number of cities have established *rape squads* of male/female police teams with the specific responsibility of dealing with rape cases. The female member of the team interviews the victim while the male helps gather evidence. Various states have reformed their laws on rape, and hospitals are beginning to open rape reception centers instead of refusing to treat victims. Ultimately, the aim is prevention rather than sympathetic treatment of victims. Meanwhile, the new types of services for the victims and potential victims are a welcome help for women. They suggest that men finally may be realizing that the rape victim should be helped and not oppressed further by humiliating encounters with the authorities.

Follow-Up. With volunteers from your class, explore, and then report back to the class, any programs you have on campus for educating students about date rape and for aiding victims when date rape occurs.

chapter 5 review

Summary

Violence is a problem that concerns most Americans. Generally, violence refers to the use of force to kill, injure, or abuse others. Interpersonal violence occurs between individuals or a number of individuals. Intergroup violence involves identifiable groups, such as different races or religions.

In estimating the amount of violence, we find an impressive amount based on self-reports, newspaper accounts, and police statistics. The United States has one of the highest homicide rates in the world. Virtually all Americans are exposed to a vast amount of violence in the mass media.

The meaning of violence can be summed up in terms of human destruction and injury, psychological disruption and dehumanization, economic costs, and "seductive self-destruction." These factors all diminish the quality of life, and their impact can be both severe and long-term.

Violence has been linked with a human need for aggression, yet this explanation is not sufficient. Various sociocultural factors contribute to the problem. One structural factor is group and societal norms, which make violence more likely among members of those groups. An important factor in intergroup violence is exclusion from the political process. People who are unable to exert power through legitimate political means may resort to violence. An important factor in interpersonal violence is the lack of adequate gun control. Inequality is related to violence; political and economic inequalities between groups in a society increase the likelihood of violence.

Among the social psychological factors in violence are a number of attitudes that legitimate violence. The majority of Americans agree that physical force is sometimes justified, including the use of force in intimate relationships. A frequent explanation of violence involves the notion of relative deprivation, which means that attitudes toward deprivation rather than the objective condition are the critical factor.

Certain values support violence, including retributiveness and self-defense. Such values can be internalized, along with attitudes, through exposure to the mass media. The extent to which the mass media socialize people into violent attitudes and behavior is a matter of controversy. However, the bulk of the evidence indicates that violence portrayed and conveyed in the mass media is related to aggressive attitudes and behavior.

Rape is a form of interpersonal violence that afflicts tens of thousands each year. Fear of rape is one of the more common fears of women. All rapes involve both physical and emotional trauma. The rape trauma syndrome involves several weeks of acute symptoms and disorganization, and a long period of painful emotional readjustment.

The more men agree with traditional norms about sex roles, and the more they are integrated into a culture whose norms support male dominance and superiority, the more likely they are to be sexually aggressive and to minimize the harm of rape.

The mass media contribute to the problem of violence against women in general and rape in particular through portrayals of sexual violence. These portrayals increase the tendency of males to engage in antisocial attitudes and behavior. Studies of offenders show that they had negative family experiences and are psychologically disturbed. All have extremely high levels of aggression.

Key Terms

Aggression	Posttraumatic
Catharsis	Stress Disorder
Domestic Terrorism	Relative Deprivation
Forcible Rape	Retributiveness
Incest	Statutory Rape
	Violence

Study Questions

1. How would you define violence? How much violence is there in America?
2. What are the physical and emotional consequences of being a victim of violence?
3. What social structural factors contribute to the level of violence in America?
4. What role do the mass media play in violent behavior?
5. How common is rape?
6. Discuss the physical and emotional consequences of being a victim of rape or attempted rape.
7. Why do men rape?
8. What can be done about the violence, including rape, in American society?

Internet Resources/ Exercises

1. Explore some of the ideas in this chapter on the following sites:

http://www.vpc.org   Site of the Violence Policy Center, with an emphasis on gun control in order to reduce violence in America.

http://www.ncadv.org   The National Coalition Against Domestic Violence offers surveys, discussions of public policy, and ways for victims to get help.

http://www.rapecrisis.com   Has information, services, and links for sexual assault victims and their families.

2. Investigate a group involved in domestic terrorism, such as a right-wing militia, the Earth Liberation Front, or the Animal Liberation Front. How does the group justify its stance? How do law enforcement officials and other observers define the activities of the group? What social structural and social psychological factors do you think contribute to the existence and work of the group?

3. Find stories of rape victims. Compare their accounts with the discussion in the text about the rape trauma syndrome. How does the text's description of the syndrome capture or fail to fully capture the victims' experiences?

For Further Reading

Allison, Julie A., and Lawrence S. Wrightsman. *Rape: The Misunderstood Crime*. Newbury Park, CA: Sage, 1993. Uses data from both research and the news media to discuss every aspect of rape, from the offense to the treatment of the victim to the prevention of rape.

Bergen, Raquel Kennedy, Jeffrey L. Edleson, and Claire M. Renzetti, eds. *Violence Against Women*. Boston: Allyn & Bacon, 2004. Essays from a broad range of perspectives that address the issue of sexual and physical violence against women, including commentaries by the authors about their research and its impact.

Hofstadter, Richard, and Michael Wallace, eds. *American Violence: A Documentary History*. New York: Vintage Books, 1970. Provides a wealth of primary materials (original documents) describing various kinds of violence throughout American history.

Kleck, Gary. *Point Blank: Guns and Violence in America*. New York: Aldine de Gruyter, 1991. A thorough look at the major issues involving guns, gun control, and violence, including suggestions for a national weapons policy.

Newman, Katherine, Cybelle Fox, David Harding, Jal Mehta, and Wendy Roth. *Rampage: The Social Roots of School Shootings*. New York: Basic Books, 2004. An extensive investigation of school shootings, including various factors that help explain why students resort to such violence.

Raine, Nancy Venable. *After Silence: Rape and My Journey Back*. New York: Crown Publishers, 1998. A personal account of rape by a stranger who was never caught, detailing the reactions of police, family, and friends as the victim sought to cope with the trauma.

Scheper-Hughes, Nancy, and Phillipe I. Bourgois, eds. *Violence in War and Peace: An Anthology*. Malden, MA: Blackwell, 2004. Two anthropologists put together a collection of essays that explore social, literary, and philosophical theories of violence, ranging from violence in everyday life to genocide to war.

chapter 5 review

The next three chapters address inequalities in the distribution of things that Americans value. These inequalities are so significant that major segments of the population suffer from serious deprivations. We look first at the unequal distribution of wealth in the United States and discuss the problems of the poor in some detail. Then we examine inequalities experienced by three groups in the population: women, the gay/lesbian community, and racial/ethnic minorities.

The people we focus on in this part are largely victims of inequality because of the circumstances of their birth. That is, they did not choose the socioeconomic status of the family into which they were born, or their gender, or their sexual orientation, or their race or ethnicity. And in contrast to the problems discussed in Part 2, in which people were acting in ways that are contrary to and disapproved of by the vast majority of Americans, those who cope with the problems discussed in this part are more likely to face inequitable treatment by a society whose norms and values they affirm and strive to follow.

Poverty

"We Feel Like Deadbeats"

Marlene is in her late 30s, married, the mother of two, and poor. Poverty is something new in her life. For some years, her married life resembled the middle-class home in which she was raised. Then an accident forced her to go on long-term disability leave, her husband's business failed, and for the past three years they have lived deep in poverty. Savings, credit, friends, and relatives helped for a while, but now they have reached "the year I lost 25 pounds without even trying":

We've hit bottom. We have no insurance. We are continually harassed by collection agents. They tell us we're deadbeats. Actually we feel like deadbeats. The first time I really got angry was a few months ago when I saw a guy with a toy attached to his car window. I knew that toy cost around $15, and I could feel the anger rising in me as I thought about how much food I could buy with $15.

I thought about my kids, who now are getting used to strange combinations of vegetables and rice or noodles, and how much they would enjoy the meal I could buy. And all of a sudden I was enraged at someone I didn't even know for spending so much money on a joke. Then it made me mad that $15 seemed like so much money. Then it made me mad that I had gotten mad.

I started watching the expensive cars go by when I was walking or taking a bus. It's like they were advertising the fact that they made it and I haven't. I've never had that kind of car, but it bothered *me that other people did. Suddenly I began to take their arrogance personally. And when I read about a guy paying $20,000 for a watch, I wondered if he was part of the human race. How could he do that when there were hungry kids living just a few miles away?*

I've gotten to the point where I see that without money, a person just doesn't matter. I thought I was a pretty knowledgeable person, but I had no idea of the violent, demoralizing effect of poverty. I had no idea how it would feel to have no food in the house, no gas to drive to buy food, no money to buy gas, and no prospect of money. My husband and I believe we'll pull out of this. But I have a dread in my bones that the worst is not over yet, and that even when it is over, it will never be altogether in the past for any of us.

Introduction

Someone once pointed out that a man who stores money is like the squirrel who stores acorns; both are trying to provide for basic needs. Yet the squirrel is superior to the man in one respect—he seems to know when he has enough acorns, while the man never seems to know when he has enough money. Indeed, studies have shown that the majority of Americans feel that they need more money, regardless of their income. Even if most people do need more, some are clearly far needier than others. The truly needy spend their entire lives at the edge of desperation, barely able to gather sufficient money to exist.

In this chapter we examine that segment of the population for whom the American dream has been elusive and see how the difficulties of the poor are related to the behavior of the nonpoor. To understand why the poor are poor, it is important to understand why the rich are rich.

We discuss what is meant by poverty, identify who the poor are and how many there are, and examine how poverty affects the quality of life. After we identify the structural and social psychological factors that contribute to poverty, we consider what has been done and what might be done to address the problem.

What Is Poverty?

Poverty in America is old and new. It is old in the sense that it has always existed, and it is new in the sense that it was not *commonly defined* as a problem until more recently. As late as the 1950s, economists assumed that, economically, Americans were consistently improving. They were producing more and incomes were increasing. The question about poverty was not *whether* but *when* it would be eliminated. Although sociologists have always identified poverty as a problem, the Gallup poll showed that not until 1965 did the public begin to identify it as one of America's serious problems (Lauer 1976). An influential factor in creating an awareness of the problem was a book by Michael Harrington (1962), *The Other America*. Harrington portrayed the plight of millions of impoverished people in affluent America.

What, exactly, is poverty? **Poverty** is a state in which income is insufficient to provide basic necessities such as food, shelter, medical care, and clothing. *Absolute poverty* means that the insufficiency is so severe that it is life-threatening. *Relative poverty* means that the insufficiency is substantially greater than that of most others in the society.

Why did Americans generally fail to identify poverty as a social problem until the 1960s? One reason is that the poor were largely invisible to many Americans. Another reason is many people failed to make the distinction between absolute and relative poverty; they insisted that even the lowest-income groups in America were not really poor because they fared better than the starving people in other countries.

To be sure, many of America's poor have more food, more clothing, better shelter, and so on than the poor in other nations; but the standard for evaluating America's poor cannot be the starving people in other nations. Rather, poverty in the United States must be evaluated in terms of the *standard of living* attained by the majority of Americans. To tell a poor American whose family suffers from malnutrition that people in other nations are starving to death is not consoling, particularly when the poor person knows that millions of Americans throw away more food every day than that person's family consumes.

In discussing poverty in the United States, then, we are talking about people who are better off than some others in the world but who have much less than most Americans. But less of what? And how much less? The federal government answers these questions in terms of *income*. In the 1960s, the Department of Agriculture developed an "economy food plan" for temporary or emergency use when a family's financial resources were minimal. At the time, the poor spent an estimated one-third of their total budget on food. The government, therefore, simply multiplied the cost of the economy food plan by 3 and came up with the dividing line between "poor" and "nonpoor." In 1964, that meant a family of four with an income below $3,000 per year was officially classified as at the **poverty level.** By 2005 the figures were $10,160 for an individual under the age of 65 and $19,806 for a family of two adults and two children under 18 (DeNavas-Walt, Proctor, and Lee 2006:45).

This method of defining poverty is considered woefully inadequate by many social scientists. For one thing, it ignores the cost-of-living differences between various areas. For another, it puts millions of Americans above the poverty level even though they cannot afford what most of us would regard as a minimal standard of living. Three researchers have plotted a "Dream Line," which is the approximate cost for an urban or suburban family of four to have a no-frills version of the American Dream (Block, Korteweg, and Woodward 2006). This means a home, full health-insurance coverage, quality child care, and enough savings to send their children to a four-year public college or university. The amount of income needed to realize this "Dream" is a little more than double the poverty level.

Finally, the official poverty level uses a nutritionally inadequate food plan as a primary criterion, bases any increases on the **consumer price index,** and maintains the ratio of food to nonfood costs at one-third. Ruggles (1990) has pointed out that Americans on the average now spend only about one-sixth of their income on food. The relative costs of other items, such as housing, have increased considerably since the 1960s. Thus, you could argue that the poverty level should be six times the cost of food, which would raise substantially the proportion of Americans who are poor.

poverty
a state in which income is insufficient to provide the basic necessities of food, shelter, clothing, and medical care

poverty level
the minimum income level that Americans should have to live on, based on the Department of Agriculture's calculations of the cost of a basic diet called "the economy food plan"

consumer price index
a measure of the average change in prices of all types of consumer goods and services purchased by urban wage earners and clerical workers

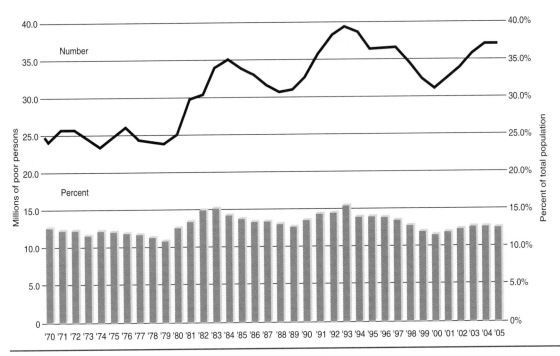

FIGURE 6.1   The Number and Proportion of the Poor, 1970–2005.
Source: DeNavas-Walt, Proctor, and Lee 2006.

In other words, many people are officially not poor today but would have been in the 1960s. Some of the decline (figure 6.1) since the 1960s is due to the definition rather than to progress in helping people out of poverty. Another way to make the same point is to note how the numbers change if alternative definitions of poverty are adopted (Proctor and Dalaker 2003). For example, the National Academy of Sciences has suggested a number of alternatives that would use after-tax income; include as income noncash benefits such as food stamps and housing subsidies; deduct from income some work-related expenses such as transportation and child care expenses; and take into account such matters as out-of-pocket medical expenses, the effects of increasing numbers of children, and geographic location. Each of the six alternatives suggested by the National Academy would add to the number of poor in the nation, ranging from an additional 700,000 to an additional 2.3 million. Thus, depending on how you define *poverty,* the number of poor will vary considerably. The *official definition excludes many people who define themselves, and whom most of you would define, as poor.*

Consider now three questions concerning the *extent of poverty* in the United States: How many poor are there? Who are the poor? Are the majority of the poor better off or worse off now than they were in the past?

Extent of Poverty

The proportion of Americans officially defined as poor has fluctuated over time. The rate declined substantially during the 1960s and 1970s, then rose again and has fluctuated ever since (figure 6.1). By 2005, 37 million Americans, representing 12.6 percent of the population, were categorized as poor. These figures are higher than they were during the *War on Poverty* in the 1960s and 1970s. In fact, the United States has one of the highest rates of poverty among the rich, industrial nations of the world (Smeeding 2005).

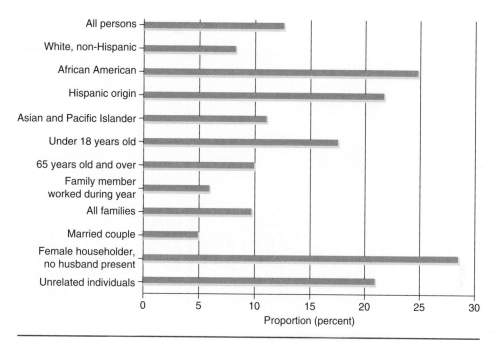

FIGURE 6.2   Proportion of Poverty for Different Kinds of People.
Source: DeNavas-Walt, Proctor, and Lee 2006.

A caution—one dealt with in the previous section—is that the official figures minimize the number of poor. Many of you would probably consider yourselves poor if your income were just above the official poverty level. In addition are people who are not now poor but will be and people who are not now poor but have been. In other words, there is always movement into and out of poverty, so the number of poor at any given time does not reveal the total number of people who will be affected by the problem during their lifetime. Mark Rank (2003) has calculated the proportion of Americans who will spend at least a year in poverty or near the poverty level (defined as between the official level and 1.25 times that level). By the age of 50, 42 percent of Americans will have been in poverty for at least a year and 50 percent will have been near poverty. By the age of 75, the figures are 59 percent and 68 percent, respectively. Poverty is clearly a problem that will afflict a majority of Americans at some point in their lives.

Who Are the Poor?

Wealth and poverty are not *distributed equally* among various social groups. Most Americans are neither wealthy nor impoverished, but the chances of being in one of these categories are greater for certain social groups. For example, the probability of being poor is greater for families headed by a female, for racial and ethnic minorities, and for unrelated individuals (see figure 6.2). Single-parent families headed by mothers are the most impoverished group in the nation. One survey of single mothers found that most had at least a high school education, were in their mid-thirties, and had an average of two children (National Coalition for the Homeless 2000).

Among racial/ethnic minorities, African Americans have the highest poverty rate (24.9 percent). If we look at absolute numbers rather than rates, the majority of the poor are white (because the white population is so much larger than that of other races).

The high rate of poverty among children is a recent development.

In 2005, for example, the numbers (and rates) in poverty were: non-Hispanic whites, 16.2 million (8.3 percent); Hispanic origin, 9.4 million (21.8 percent); African Americans, 9.2 million (24.9 percent); and Asian and Pacific Islander, 1.4 million (11.1 percent) (DeNavas-Walt, Proctor, and Lee 2006).

Thus, the *number* of poor whites is substantially higher than the number of poor Hispanics or poor African Americans, but the *rate of poverty* among whites is substantially lower than that among the other groups (see figure 6.2). These data are the basis for what sounds like a paradoxical statement: If you are white, you are less likely to be poor than if you are nonwhite, but if you are poor you are more likely to be white than nonwhite.

Figure 6.2 also shows the high rate of poverty among youths under age 18. This *high rate of poverty among children* is something new in American history, and it is the highest rate among the industrial countries of the world, with one of every five American children living in poverty (Block, Korteweg, and Woodward 2006).

Finally, the rate of poverty is higher outside (14.5 percent) than inside (12.2 percent) metropolitan areas (DeNavas-Walt, Proctor, and Lee 2006). Extensive rural poverty is one reason many Americans are unaware of the seriousness of the problem. The rural poor are even less visible than those in urban **ghettoes.**

ghetto
an area in which a certain group is segregated from the rest of society; often used today to refer to the impoverished area of the inner city

An additional fact about the identity of the poor is important. Contrary to popular opinion, people are not poor primarily because of their *unwillingness to work*. In 2005, about a third of those 16 and older who were in poverty engaged in paid work during the year, and a small percentage worked full-time (DeNavas-Walt, Proctor, and Lee 2006). Among those who didn't work were people who couldn't find a job, the disabled, the elderly, and single parents who would have to pay more for child care than they would earn in the jobs available to them. As a young single mother told us:

> I know the stereotype of a welfare mother. Well, that's not me. I don't sit around watching
>   TV. I work 40 hours a week, go to college at night, and have worked and paid taxes since

I was a teenager. I don't intend to be on welfare all my life, but I just don't have a choice right now.

We noted earlier that people move into and out of poverty; but there is also a core of people who remain in poverty, an *underclass that experiences chronic hunger and* **malnutrition,** *unemployment, and substandard housing.* Insufficient food, in turn, increases depression and suicide attempts and it inhibits cognitive and psychosocial development (Alaimo, Olson, and Frongillo 2001, 2002). The underclass is only a minority of the poor, but it presents the nation with poverty's most serious challenge—how to deal with those who seem caught in the throes of poverty on a more or less permanent basis (Devine, Plunkett, and Wright 1992; Jencks 1992).

malnutrition
inadequate food, in amount or type

The Homeless.   The homeless are those who live in their cars or on the streets because they cannot afford any kind of housing. The very lack of a stable, identifiable residence makes it difficult to know exactly how many Americans are homeless. One careful study, using data from service providers for the homeless across the nation, concludes that in any given year about 3.5 million Americans, 1.35 million of them children, will experience homelessness (National Coalition for the Homeless 2006c). The number is probably increasing each year, because the demand for shelter in cities has been growing dramatically.

The homeless are a diverse group of people, including all ages, both sexes, every kind of marital status, all racial and ethnic groups, and with a full range of emotional and physical health problems (Kushel et al. 2005; National Coalition for the Homeless 2006d). As many as 4 of 10 are children under the age of 18, and about a fourth are between 25 and 34 years old. More males than females are homeless, but about 17 percent of the homeless are single females. The number of homeless families with children has increased substantially over the past decade, comprising about a third of the total homeless population. African Americans make up nearly half of the homeless. About 35 percent are white, and the rest come from other racial and ethnic groups.

Many homeless women are on the streets because they fled from domestic violence (National Coalition for the Homeless 2006d). One survey reported that a fourth of the homeless mothers had been physically abused in the past year. Some researchers estimate that half of all homeless women and children were escaping from domestic violence.

The homeless differ from the general population in a number of other ways (National Coalition for the Homeless 2006d). A disproportionate number of the homeless are veterans. About 22 percent of single adults who are homeless have serious mental illness. Estimates of the proportion who are addicted vary, but at least a third have some kind of addiction. Finally, a survey of 24 American cities reported that 25 percent of the urban homeless were employed but did not make enough money to afford housing.

As with poverty generally, there is movement in and out of homelessness. Some people are chronically homeless and will die on the streets. But others are homeless for varying lengths of time, ranging from months to a few years. Those who are homeless for a shorter period of time are likely to be younger, earn income, have family support, and lack a history of arrest and of addiction (Caton et al. 2005).

People are not homeless, then, simply because they prefer the streets to gainful employment. Some, like the children and the mentally ill, cannot support themselves. Others are victims of the economy. Home and rental costs have soared in recent decades. Millions of Americans now spend more than half their incomes on housing (National Coalition for the Homeless 2003a). The homeless who work can't get any kind

TABLE 6.1
Distribution of Money
Income of Households,
Ranked According to Income
Received, 1929–2005
(percent of aggregate
income)

	1929	1941	1950	1960	1970	1980	1990	2000	2005
Lowest 40%	12.5	13.6	16.4	17.0	17.6	16.7	15.4	14.1	12.0
Next 40%	33.1	37.6	40.8	41.8	41.4	41.8	40.4	38.3	37.6
Highest 20%	54.4	48.8	42.8	41.3	40.9	41.6	44.3	47.4	50.4
Top 5%	30.0	24.0	17.3	15.9	15.6	15.3	17.4	20.8	n.a.

SOURCES: *Historical Statistics of the United States,* 1961 ed., p. 166; 1976 ed. p. 292; and U.S. Census
Bureau Web site.

of housing even if they could spend half their income. In order to rent a two-bedroom
home in an average area, a worker would have to receive nearly three times the federal
minimum wage (National Coalition for the Homeless 2003b). Some states have minimum wage requirements higher than the federal level, but none are sufficient to cover
housing costs. Thus, families throughout the nation are at risk of homelessness if they
are supported by a single, low-wage worker.

The Changing Nature of Poverty

How has the lot of the poor changed over time in the United States? Certainly the proportion of Americans who are poor is lower than it was in the past—but are those who
are poor now in better or worse condition than the poor of other generations? Although
we have no systematic evidence on the question, it seems reasonable that poverty is
more difficult when the proportion becomes smaller. It is one thing to be poor when
the majority of people, or even a substantial minority, share your poverty. It is another
thing to be poor when most people are living comfortably or in affluence.

Still, if the poor are making gains relative to the rich, poverty might be less stressful
than in the past. Unfortunately, they are not. Table 6.1 shows the percentage of income
received by people in various income brackets. In 2005, for example, those in the top
20 percent got half of the income, or 2.5 times the amount they would have gotten if
there had been perfect equality (no "top" or "bottom"). Moreover, their share of the
total income has increased since 1970. Note, in contrast, what has happened to the bottom 40 percent. Their share of income has dropped substantially. In other words, the
poor have lost ground relative to the rest of the population for nearly four decades.

In fact, an analysis by two economists of the years from 1966 to 2001 concluded that
while median income, after adjusting for inflation, increased by 11 percent overall, it increased nearly six times as much (58 percent) for those in the top 10 percent (Dew-Becker
and Gordon 2005). And for those in the top 1 percent, the increase was 121 percent!

Although the richest, in spite of such gains in recent decades, are getting a smaller
proportion of income than they did before World War II (see table 6.1), it is important
to keep in mind that money income is only a part of the wealth of the rich, and for
some it is not the most important part. Consider the following (Mishel, Bernstein, and
Allegretto 2006):

- The top 1 percent of wealthy Americans hold more than one-third of all the
  wealth.
- The bottom 80 percent of Americans have only 15.3 percent of all the wealth.
- Since the early 1960s, the bottom 80 percent's share of wealth has decreased
  nearly 4 percent.

- Although the United States is one of the wealthiest nations in the world, the gap between the rich and the poor is greater than in any other industrial nation.

In sum, in terms of income there has been a redistribution, but it has not benefitted the poor. Rather, the middle- and upper-middle groups are the beneficiaries of income redistribution. Since the late 1960s, the upper 20 percent have made gains in both income and total wealth at the expense of the lower 80 percent. By 2004, the average wealth held by the top 1 percent was nearly $15 million, while about 30 percent of households had a net worth of less than $10,000 (Mishel, Bernstein, and Allegretto 2006). When you try, therefore, to assess the extent of poverty in the United States, you must recognize that although the proportion of the poor is less than it was earlier in the 20th century, the lot of the poor is worse when compared with the rest of society. Americans who are poor today may have more possessions than the poor of 1920, but they are worse off relative to others in the society than were their counterparts in 1920.

Poverty and the Quality of Life

Some sense of the trauma of living in poverty, even if you assume that it is only a temporary state, may be seen in the account of Marlene (see "We Feel Like Deadbeats," at the beginning of the chapter). In essence, the trauma arises from the fact that the poor get less of everything considered important and necessary for a decent life (less money, food, clothing, and shelter). The *deprivation of the poor is pervasive* (Corcoran 2000; Samaan 2000; Rank 2001). Compared to infants of the nonpoor, infants of the poor are more likely to die. Their children are more likely to fail in school even when they are intelligent. Their children are more likely to drop out of school. They are more likely to become mentally ill. They are more likely to lose their jobs and to drop out of the labor force. They are more likely to experience hostility and distrust rather than neighborliness with those around them. They are less likely to participate in meaningful groups and associations. They are more likely to get chronic illnesses. In the face of more health problems, they are less likely to own health insurance (a problem only partly relieved by Medicaid). In the ultimate deprivation, they are likely to die at a younger age. Thus, poverty diminishes the quality of a person's life in many ways.

The *ravages of poverty* and the way in which *poverty intersects with other social problems* are illustrated in the plight of the homeless. Many of the homeless are former mental patients who were put out onto the streets as a result of the deinstitutionalization movement (see chapter 13) (King 1989). Life on the streets only intensifies their emotional problems. Homelessness can also create mental health problems among people who had no disorders before living on the streets (Hall 1987). Moreover, the homeless face a whole array of hazards and threats to their physical well-being. For example, the homeless experience more sexual victimization and more violence (including severe violence leading to death) than do other Americans (Lee and Schreck 2005; National Coalition for the Homeless 2006b).

The Right to Life and Happiness

The position of the poor in the economy contradicts the American value of the right to life and the pursuit of happiness. The inadequacy of their financial resources deprives the poor of freedom to pursue a full and happy life. Some people argue that lack of money should not be equated with lack of happiness, that many of the poor are carefree, spontaneous, and even better off without the worries that accompany possession of money. It's generally only people with money who use this argument. There is, in fact, a positive correlation between income and *perceived happiness.* Surveys of attitudes both in the United States and in 55 other nations show that the proportion of people who describe themselves as very happy is lower among those in the lower-income than those in the middle- and upper-income groups (Mitchell 1983; Diener, Diener, and Diener 1995; Pew Research Center 2006a). Poverty brings *more despair than happiness and more fear than fullness of life.*

gross national product (GNP)
the total value, usually in dollars, of all goods and services produced by a nation during a year

Discontent and Despair.   When deprivation was widespread during the Great Depression of the 1930s, unrest was also widespread. People marched and demonstrated, demanding food and expressing a willingness to fight rather than starve. In a 1932 Chicago demonstration there were "no bands" and "no quickstep," only "rank after rank of sodden men, their worn coat collars turned up, their caps . . . pulled down to give as much protection as possible" as they marched in driving rain (Hutchinson 1962:274).

The multitude of problems and frustrations of poverty—crowded, dilapidated housing in crime-ridden neighborhoods; inadequate health care; constant financial strain; poor-quality and inadequate food; lack of opportunities for betterment; and so on—are so overwhelming that the impoverished individual may suffer from chronic depression. Low-income mothers, for example, are likely to be depressed, which adversely affects the development of their children (Petterson and Albers 2001).

Despair is not the lot of all the poor, but it is much more frequent among the poor than among the nonpoor. When the despair comes, it can be devastating, and it can strike even the young. Consider Elaine, a teenager whose mother is a chronic alcoholic. Elaine lives in poverty with her grandmother in an urban apartment. She watches television 10 or more hours a day, even though the television only increases her depression because it continually reminds her of how much she lacks. Despite her superior intelligence, Elaine has always felt extremely ashamed in school:

> "If I only had some clothes." Today Elaine . . . [is] dressed in neatly ironed jeans that
> are badly frayed at the cuffs and worn thin. On top she wears a stained cheerleader's
> sweater, out in one elbow, which she has had since she was thirteen. Despite its holes
> and stains, Elaine wears the sweater every day. It reminds her, she says, of a time when
> she was happy. (Williams and Kornblum 1985:8)

The despair that always threatens to overcome the poor is manifested in what Rainwater (1967) called *survival strategies*—ways of living that enable the poor to adapt to their "punishing and depriving milieu." The *expressive strategy* involves manipulating others and making oneself appealing through means such as bettering someone in a rap session, gaining the affection of a female, wearing dramatic clothes, or winning a gambling bet. The expressive strategy leads some nonpoor to define the poor as natural, spontaneous, and carefree; but, as Rainwater pointed out, this strategy, like the others, enables the individual to gain some measure of status and retain some degree of stability and sanity in the midst of an oppressive situation. The *violent strategy* involves actions such as fighting, shoplifting, or making threats. It is a dangerous strategy for everyone, and not many of the poor adopt it. The *depressive strategy,* which involves withdrawal and isolation, characterizes a great number of the poor as they grow older. An individual may alternate among the strategies as he or she grows older, but all three strategies have the same purpose—to enable the individual to cope with a punitive situation. As such, they dramatize the despair that always hovers near the poor.

POVERTY IN THE WORLD SYSTEM

Gross inequalities exist not only within most nations but also between the nations of the world. There are various ways in which we could characterize the inequalities: average family income, average life span, expenditures for health care or education, and so on. Figure 6.3 shows one measure—the **gross national product (GNP)** per capita for a number of countries. The gross national product is the total value of goods and services produced by a nation during a year. To a large extent, people's standard of living is related to the gross national product per capita.

As figure 6.3 illustrates, there are enormous differences in the gross national product per capita of various nations. Switzerland's per capita GNP is 384 times higher than Ethiopia's! People in the richer nations have seven or more times as many physicians per capita as those in the poorer nations. The infant mortality rates in the poorer nations are five or more times higher than those in the richer nations. At least 1.2 billion people suffer from hunger and malnutrition in the poorer nations, and the life expectancy of people in the richer nations is, on the average, 15 to 20 years higher than in the poorer nations. A child born in the United States in 2000 could expect to live to age 77; a child born the same year in Afghanistan, Angola, Haiti, or a number of other poor countries could expect to live less than 50 years.

In other words, the people of poorer nations suffer the kinds of deprivations that afflict the very poorest people in the United States. The number of the poor throughout the world is staggering. Of the world's 6 billion people, more than 1 billion live on $1 a day or less, particularly in South Asia and sub-Saharan Africa. Those who earn $2 a day or more are in the top half of the income distribution! And the disparity between the rich and the poor nations is increasing. The richest 10 percent of people in the world now get over half of all the income, while the poorest 50 percent get less than 10 percent. Even though many of the poor live in agricultural societies, hundreds of millions have inadequate shelter, food, and medical care. They lack safe drinking water and educational opportunities for their children. And millions die every year simply because they are too poor to survive.

SOURCES:
Lauer 1991; Gardner and Halweil 2000; Bowles, Durlauf, and Hoff 2006.

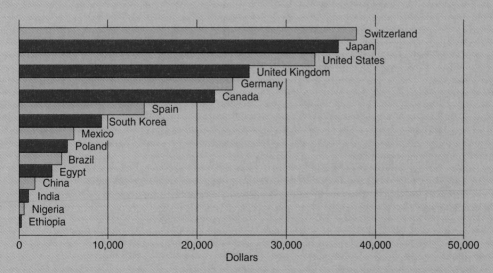

FIGURE 6.3 GNP per Capita for Selected Countries.
SOURCE: U.S. Census Bureau 2003:851.

	Type of Crime			
				Property Crimes (rates per 1,000 households)
	Crimes of Violence (rates per 1,000 persons)			
Household Income Level	Rape/Sexual Assault	Robbery	Aggravated Assault	Total
Less than $7,500	2.4	6.4	7.3	200.6
$7,500–$14,999	0.4	4.4	7.8	174.3
$15,000–$24,999	1.6	2.1	5.6	170.4
$25,000–$34,999	0.6	2.1	5.0	173.9
$35,000–$49,999	0.9	1.4	4.3	159.9
$50,000–$74,999	0.6	1.3	4.9	155.9
$75,000 or more	0.6	1.3	2.5	171.0

TABLE 6.2

Victimization Rates, by Income

SOURCE: Maguire and Pastore 2006:194, 202.

Freedom from Fear.   We mentioned in chapter 5 that freedom from fear is a condition of the right to life and the pursuit of happiness. The poor live in a *capricious world.* The chronic uncertainty of their lives means they have much to fear. We discuss this topic further under the subheading "Dilemmas of Poverty" later in this chapter. Here we will look at two kinds of fear that affect the poor more than others—the *fear of being the victim of a crime and the fear of being harassed by law enforcement officers.*

As table 6.2 shows, the poor are more likely than other people to be victims of crime. Their rates are higher for both violent and property (burglary and theft) crimes. They are, of course, aware of the high crime rates in the areas where they live, and so they typically express a greater fear of walking alone at night than do the well-to-do.

The fear of being harassed by law enforcement officers is particularly a problem for the homeless (National Coalition for the Homeless 2006a). We noted earlier that the number of homeless has been growing, and the number of shelter beds available for them is inadequate. Faced with the growing numbers, many cities have now criminalized the problem of the homeless by prohibiting such things as sleeping, camping, eating, sitting, or begging in public places and using the ordinances to punish the homeless. Some cities even use laws against loitering or having open containers against the homeless. Finally, there have been sweeps of areas where the homeless live. The homeless are driven out and their personal property may be destroyed.

The Right to Dignity as a Human Being

For the poor, the *right to dignity as human beings* is violated by the *contradiction between the American ideal of the worth of every individual and the pattern of interaction between the poor and the nonpoor.* At best, the poor tend to be treated paternalistically. At worst, they tend to be subjected to contempt and rejection, and blamed for their plight (Cozzarelli, Wilkinson, and Tagler 2001). The loss of dignity is manifested

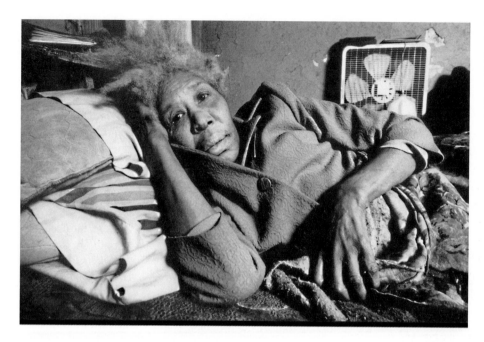

The problems and frustrations faced by the poor can be so overwhelming that the poor individual suffers from chronic depression.

in a number of myths about the poor, myths that employ the *fallacy of personal attack* to discredit the poor and legitimate an unwillingness to support programs to help them.

fallacy

"The Poor Are Lazy."   It's a myth that the poor are lazy; they are willing to work, and in fact, most male heads of poor families do work. To say that the poor are lazy justifies the nonpoor's contempt and disavowal of personal or societal responsibility for dealing with poverty. No evidence supports the myth, but it is still prevalent, and it robs the poor of human dignity.

"People on Welfare Have It Good."   The expressive style of coping may have helped create the myth that people on welfare often live at higher standards than do people who work. A few "con artists" may manage to get a substantial living by *welfare fraud,* but the majority of people on welfare (and the majority of the poor in general) live in circumstances that would be repugnant to most Americans. What dignity is there, for instance, in not being able to buy adequate food for your children, or in living in a rat-infested apartment, or in huddling inside your apartment at night in fear of thieves and drug addicts?

And what kind of dignity is there in trying to survive on welfare payments that may mean an income far below the poverty level? Edin (1995) studied single mothers on welfare in four U.S. cities and found that the welfare benefits were so low that the women had to supplement their income with unreported work or gifts from boyfriends, friends, or relatives. On the average, welfare payments and the cash value of food stamps amounted to just 60 percent of their basic monthly expenses. Whatever else you may say about welfare, it is clearly not true that people on welfare "have it good."

"Welfare Is Draining Us."   One myth by which the poor are humiliated is that they are social leeches. This myth asserts that the cost of maintaining the poor is depriving the nonpoor by raising taxes and reducing the standard of living. As we noted,

however, the poor receive a lower share of national income now than they did in the early 20th century. Historically, welfare payments have done little to reduce the inequity, and the standard of living for middle- and upper-class Americans is higher than ever. A large number of Americans now possess two or more automobiles and television sets, items that were luxuries in the not-too-distant past.

"Welfare Turns People into Lazy, Dependent Deadbeats."   "Welfare bums" is the term used by some Americans to show their contempt for people who rely on welfare rather than on their own earnings. Even with the change to "workfare" (discussed later in this chapter), people who receive government aid may still be regarded as lazy and unmotivated, preferring a "free ride" at the expense of Americans who work (Seccombe, Walters, and James 1999).

This myth ignores certain important facts. First, most of the people on welfare are not able-bodied workers. Well over half of welfare recipients are children, the aged, the disabled, or mothers of small children (some of whom work).

Second, as shown by a number of studies, the able-bodied workers generally prefer to work rather than to be on welfare. In-depth interviews with 47 recipients of Temporary Assistance to Needy Families (TANF), the new name for Aid to Families with Dependent Children (AFDC), found that the recipients were eager for welfare reform and were supportive of work requirements (Seccombe, Walters, and James 1999).

Third, there is very little long-term dependency among welfare recipients. In fact, as we pointed out earlier, there is a *good deal of movement in and out of poverty*. Only one of four children who spend most of their growing-up years in poverty is still poor at age 25 to 29 (Corcoran 2000). Edin (1995) found that 86 percent of the welfare mothers planned to leave welfare for work. Their plans were tempered, however, by their previous work experience in the low-paying labor market. This experience taught them two things: They were no better off financially by working than by being on welfare; and no matter how long or diligently they worked, their low-paying jobs did not lead to better jobs.

Poverty and Health

The circumstances under which the poor are required to live cause higher rates of mental and physical illness among the poor than among the rest of the population (Jackson and Mustillo 2001; Chen, Matthews, and Boyce 2002). The *homeless are particularly prone to ill health*. A substantial proportion of the homeless suffer from various physical ailments, drug addiction, and mental illness (Jencks 1994; Menke and Wagner 1998; Stratigos and Katsambas 2003).

Even the poor who are not homeless suffer a disproportionate amount of ill health. Compared to those of the nonpoor, the health problems of the poor are manifested in higher rates of physical illness, infant mortality, clinical depression and other problems with mental health, and difficulty with such daily living tasks as cooking, shopping, managing money, walking, eating, and dressing (Lynch, Kaplan, and Shema 1997; Alaimo et al. 2001; Belle 2003; Wheaton and Clarke 2003). In fact, even spending a short time in poverty damages people's health, and getting out of poverty later does not repair all the damage done (McDonough and Berglund 2003), perhaps because people develop poor health habits while they are in poverty (skipping medical checkups and eating cheap but unhealthy food) that tend to persist when their income rises above the poverty line.

FROM RICHES TO RAGS

In a now-famous experiment, a reporter had his skin darkened and his hair shaved close, and then he began traveling through four southern states to see what it was like to be a black man. It was a revelation to him. Some nights, he reported, he was so upset by the way people treated him that he cried himself to sleep.

There are times when the only way to understand what a social problem means for the victims is to "walk a mile in their shoes." This project will involve you in a personal experience of poverty, but you will find it easier to do if you work with someone else.

First, try to live for two weeks on a poverty-level food budget. In the latest edition of the *Statistical Abstract of the United States,* find the current poverty-level income threshold. (Remember, this is the most you can have to be classified as living in poverty.) Use the figure given for a nonfarm family of two and divide it by three to get a yearly food budget comparable to the way the poverty level was originally defined. Divide the figure by 26 to get the two-week budget. For example, in 2005 the poverty level for two people was $13,078—about $4,359.33 for food. For the two weeks of the experiment, that amounts to $167.67 for food for you and your partner.

As a second part of your experiment, dress in some shabby clothing. Try to achieve a poor though clean look. Then, go to a public place and ask directions. Also go into a department store and ask for help in finding some relatively expensive clothes.

Record your experiences. Describe in detail your experiences and feelings about grocery shopping, cooking, and eating on a poverty budget. Discuss the reactions you received when asking for directions and when seeking to look at some expensive clothing. Compare the way people related to you with the way you normally experience relationships.

The problem of poverty has received less attention from the mass media in subsequent decades than it did in the 1960s. As a final part of your project, you might share your experience by writing an article that reminds people of the great numbers of poor in the United States. Submit it to the features editor of a local newspaper or a general magazine.

The health problems of the poor are compounded by the fact that they are less likely to have health insurance. Overall, 15.9 percent of Americans have no health insurance (DeNavas-Walt, Proctor, and Lee 2006). But the proportion goes up with each step down the income ladder; for families earning less than $25,000 per year, the proportion without health insurance is 26.7 percent. The lack of insurance, combined with insufficient medical care facilities in poor areas, means that many of the poor get no medical help until their situation becomes critical or unbearable (Kirby and Kaneda 2005).

Some of the health problems of the poor result from poor nutrition, which, in turn, is related to inadequate income. According to the Department of Agriculture, about 12 percent of Americans are food insecure—they suffer from hunger and haven't the money for an adequate diet (Nord, Andrews, and Carlson 2005). That means that more than 38 million Americans have a hunger problem, and a disproportionate number of them are children—nearly one out of every five children is food insecure.

The consequences of inadequate food or of malnutrition are serious (Alaimo et al. 2001). Food-insecure adults tend to suffer from depression as well as various physical problems (Wu and Schimmele 2006). Food-insecure children are vulnerable to a variety of physical and mental problems. In recent decades, American children have suffered from pellagra, scurvy, rickets, parasitic worms, and mental retardation as a result of prolonged malnutrition. Children who receive an inadequate amount of protein in the first year of life can develop problems of various kinds, including an inability to concentrate in school (Galler and Ramsey 1989). Even mild undernutrition can have long-term adverse effects on children's development. Opponents of the welfare system sometimes ask how many children have starved to death in America. The answer is few, if any; but this is little solace to the mother who watches her child grow up with mental or physical deficiencies because of inadequate diet.

Clearly, poverty contradicts the value of good health. The relationship between poverty and health, in fact, is another of the *vicious circles* that often characterize social problems. Because health problems put additional strains on a family's meager financial resources, illness can be perpetuated. Poverty can generate stress that leads to illness that intensifies the stress, and the circle continues.

Dilemmas of Poverty

autonomy
the ability or opportunity to
govern oneself

Americans *value **autonomy** and equal opportunity*. They want to control their own destinies and they want opportunities for advancement. These values are *contradicted* by the realities of poverty. People at the lower end of the stratification system have little control over their lives and have few, if any, opportunities compared to people at the upper end. Poverty is an ongoing series of *dilemmas*. Even when a poor person can choose between options, all the options may have undesirable aspects.

Consider the problems of existing on a poverty budget. Even Americans with incomes that are low but somewhat above the poverty level have to deal with frustrating dilemmas. Matters that would be an inconvenience to people with higher incomes—car problems, illness, appliance breakdowns—can become a crisis for low-income families (Shipler 2004). In fact, anything that adds to the expense of living presents a dilemma to the poor. An unexpected spell of cold weather that raises heating bills means less food for poor parents and their children (Bhattacharya et al. 2003).

Even if a poor family is able to spend the full third of its income on food, how adequate would the food be? What kind of a diet would you have if you existed on the food budget allocated to the poor? The exercise in the Involvement box challenges you to try eating on a poverty-level food budget for two weeks. If you conduct this experiment by yourself rather than with a partner, the 2005 poverty-level figure ($10,160 per year for one person) will allot you $9.28 per day for food. Keep in mind that this figure is for people who are at the top of the poverty scale. Since most of the poor are not at the top, most have less money for food. How much of what you like to eat now would you be able to have? Another way to look at it is that the poor person's food budget for a whole day could be spent at one meal at a fast-food hamburger restaurant. For some of the poor, the choice may be between adequate nutrition and clothes, or between adequate nutrition and medical care. Most students do not face such limited choices.

One of the key dilemmas of the poor is the *choice between security and change*. Should poor individuals maintain whatever security they have or take some risks in order to change their lot? For instance, the ghetto child may be told that the only way to escape poverty is to stay in school and use the education to get a good job; but the only security the child's family may have against utter deprivation is for the child to drop out of school and earn money to add to the family income. At the same time, perhaps the only way the child can be *psychologically secure* is to accept the negative judgments of his or her peers about school. The low value that many of the poor place on intellectual achievement threatens ostracism to any young person who is serious about education. Furthermore, the child has grown up in an unpredictable world and has felt the powerlessness of the individual to change his or her lot in life. Why should the child risk years of schooling (which involves a loss of income) when the payoff is vague and uncertain?

Adults also face dilemmas and the *frustrations of powerlessness*. A woman who grew up in a ghetto related an incident in her life: "When I was a girl, I was given a part in the school play. I was as happy as I could be, and proud to think of my parents watching me perform. But on the night of the play my father got drunk instead of coming to school. I was terribly upset at the time, but later on I realized why he had gotten drunk. He was ashamed to come to the play in the clothes he had, and he didn't have enough money to buy anything new. He didn't know what to do; so he got drunk."

It is easy enough to condemn the man, but remember, the poor live with an agonizing mixture of ambition and powerlessness, of the need for security and the need for change. The security is meager, but the risk of change may appear to be great.

Contributing Factors

It is true that there always have been poor people. It is also true that poverty is a global problem and that the poor of other nations are worse off in absolute terms than are the poor of America. But why is there any poverty at all in affluent America? The United States has sufficient resources to eliminate poverty. Of course the elimination of poverty would require some shift in public policy (see the Public Policy and Private Action section). Nevertheless, poverty in America is not an inevitable outcome of something like overpopulation or inadequate resources. Why, then, do millions of Americans continue to suffer an impoverished existence? Because, in part, a number of structural and social psychological factors that operate to create poverty also tend to perpetuate it.

Social Structural Factors

The structural factors that bear upon the problem of poverty include the institutional arrangements of government, the economy, the family, and education. We examine each in turn.

Political Decision Making. Poverty continues in America, in large part, because of the *distribution of power*. The people who control the wealth are among the most powerful, whereas the poor are among the most powerless in America. As a result, governmental decisions typically reflect the interests of the well-to-do rather than of the poor.

In addition, the political structure is detrimental to the poor because of the *multiple decision-making centers*. The term *"multiple decision-making centers"* refers to the federal, state, and local governmental levels and also to the multiple branches—executive, legislative, and judicial—at each level. All these facets of government have certain decision-making powers, and all have different constituencies. Most categories or organizations of citizens can exercise influence at some point, but there are also many points at which a program or a policy initiative can be stopped. However, some categories of the population have little influence at any point in this complex, and one such category is the poor.

The political arrangements, therefore, mean that programs designed to help the poor are particularly vulnerable to variation, veto, sabotage, or atrophy through neglect. One such example is the 1967 Medicaid program that was intended to ensure adequate health care for the poor. The program was to be operated by the states, which would set up its own schedules of benefits and definitions of eligibility. The federal government would pay half or more of the costs of the program. States could choose not to participate or to provide fewer benefits than other states. Some states were unwilling to assume any financial responsibility for health care of the poor, so they did not partici-pate. Others set up programs with limited benefits. The majority of the poor are still not covered by Medicaid.

Many other programs have been set up to help the poor. Unfortunately, the failure of these programs to sufficiently reduce or eliminate poverty led to a backlash in the 1990s. The largest assistance program for poor families with children—Aid to Fami-lies with Dependent Children—was replaced in 1996 with Temporary Assistance to Needy Families (TANF), which included limited help and work requirements. The ex-act requirements for receiving help were left to the various states. The amount of help was so small in many cases that the combined value of TANF benefits and food stamps fell far below the poverty level. Thus, a poor family of three in Florida can receive $303 a month for a maximum of 36 consecutive months (Swartz 2002). In Minnesota, one of the more generous states, the same family would receive $532 for a maximum of 24 months. Even with a family member working, if the work is low skill and minimum wage, the family could be in poverty in either state. And once the benefits ran out, the poverty would be severe.

Class Composition of Government.   Regardless of the intentions of the various pro-grams and policies, the work of interest groups and the middle-class composition of government make it unlikely that the poor will greatly benefit or that the middle strata will be greatly hurt by governmental action. Consider housing. The federal govern-ment loses four times as much in revenue by allowing people to deduct mortgage inter-est from income taxes as it spends on housing programs for low-income Americans (National Coalition for the Homeless 2003a). In 2001, 59 percent of mortgage interest deduction savings went to households with incomes of $100,000 a year or more.

Another fact that underscores the *class composition of the government* is that the nonpoor generally benefit as much from the programs designed to help the poor as the poor themselves do. Programs that would help the poor at the expense of other groups are unlikely to be implemented or even proposed. Medicaid helps some of the poor, but it also makes a number of physicians wealthy. Job-training programs help some of the poor, but they also provide high-salaried positions for a number of middle-class administrators.

Who Benefits from Government?   Given the multiple decision-making centers and the class composition of government, it is not surprising that the middle and upper classes benefit far more from government programs than do the lower class generally and the poor in particular. Some of the poor do not even benefit from programs that were created specifically to help them. And one reason is the cumbersome and often bewildering application process. Similarly, other kinds of programs never reach the in-tended recipients because of inadequate staffing of governmental offices, complex ap-plication processes, and inadequate communication of the availability of the programs. In a survey of low income parents in Los Angeles County, 51 percent said they were never informed about child care services for which they were eligible, and 52 percent said that the lack of child care caused them to lose a job (National Coalition for the Homeless 2000).

Some benefits do filter down to the poor, but the primary beneficiaries of governmen-tal decisions and programs are (and always have been) the well-to-do. It is ironic that the people on welfare are castigated as "freeloaders," whereas the well-to-do have used their power since the beginning of the Republic to secure handouts from the federal government; but the handouts that the well-to-do secure are referred to as **subsidies**, or

subsidy
a government grant to a private person or company to assist an enterprise deemed advantageous to the public

tax benefits to stimulate business. From extensive gifts of land to the railroads, to guaranteed prices for various farm products, to tax concessions and research money for industry, the federal government has been engaged in a long history of acts that have benefited the well-to-do. In many cases the benefits received by the well-to-do are not as obvious as those given to the poor, even though they are greater.

Consumer advocate Ralph Nader (1990) identified four areas of abuse in the American "corporate welfare state." The first area of abuse is *bailouts,* the federal government's guaranteed loans or guaranteed restitution for corporate mismanagement. In the 1970s, the government guaranteed loans to Lockheed Corporation and Chrysler Corporation to prevent bankruptcy. In the 1990s, hundreds of billions of dollars were needed to deal with the ravages of fraud and speculation in the savings and loan industry and cleanup costs for nuclear weapons plants managed by private firms.

Resource depletion is a second area of abuse. The government has leased at "bargain-basement prices" the rights to minerals and timber. In Alaska, taxpayers paid to build the roads into some timberland that would reap huge profits for those companies that had been given the low-cost lease.

A third area of abuse is *taxpayer-funded research and development.* The government has funded research, including studies in government labs, and then given patent rights to private business. The National Cancer Institute developed the application of the drug AZT to the problem of AIDS. A private drug firm then secured an exclusive patent to market AZT without paying royalties to the government and without agreeing to any price restraints on the drug.

Finally, *subsidies to profit-making businesses* is the fourth area of abuse. The federal government has subsidized everything from private golf clubs to farm crops to giant corporations. **Corporate welfare** refers to governmental benefits given to corporations that are not available to individuals or to other groups. Federal, state, and local governments all contribute to the welfare, which takes the form of such benefits as tax exemptions and tax reduction, training grants, investment credits, infrastructure (roads, water and sewer lines, etc.) improvements, and low-rate loans. Corporate welfare has been on the increase in recent decades. Thus, in the 1950s, corporate taxes were 28 percent of all federal taxes collected, while by 2005 they were less than 10 percent (Kuttner 2005).

corporate welfare
governmental benefits given to corporations that are unavailable to other groups or to individuals

Why is it immoral to feed the hungry and moral to pay for private golf clubs? Is the president of an airline, whose high salary is possible partly because of government subsidies, more moral than the child who has no father and receives paltry sums of money through welfare? If the government can pay millions of dollars to rescue a corporation from bankruptcy, why is it wrong to rescue people from poverty? The answer is that the poor are powerless to secure what the well-to-do secure with relatively little difficulty. Ironically, through the structure and functioning of government, the well-to-do and powerful give to each other that which they say is immoral to give to the poor.

Probably few people in the middle class are aware of how many benefits they receive from government programs. For example, a young man attends a public school, rides on a free school bus, and eats a free or subsidized (and therefore cheap) lunch. If he later spends time in the armed forces, he may pursue a subsidized college education. He then may buy a farm or a home with a loan that is subsidized and guaranteed by the federal government. He may go into business for himself with a low-interest loan from the Small Business Administration (SBA). The young man may marry and have children who are born in a hospital that was built in part with federal funds. His aged parents may have serious and expensive health problems, which are largely covered by the federal Medicare program. This program enables him to save his own money, which he banks in an institution protected and insured by the federal government. His community may benefit economically from an industrial project underwritten by the government, and his children may be able to go to a college because of financial assistance from the government. Then the man, like many good Americans, may rebel against federal programs and high taxes and assert that this country was built on rugged individualism, unaware that his whole existence is enriched and subsidized by various government programs.

The interests of the middle and upper strata are also reflected in the *tax structure*. Presumably, the tax structure is an equalizing mechanism that takes disproportionately from the rich in order to benefit the poor. This equalization has not happened. Both wealthy individuals and corporations continue to be adept at finding loopholes in federal tax laws that reduce their tax burden. And most state and local tax systems severely penalize the poor (Institute on Taxation and Economic Policy 2003). Nationwide, the richest Americans pay 5.2 percent of their income in state and local taxes, compared to nearly 10 percent for middle-income families and more than 11 percent for the poor. In some of the worst states, poor families pay as much as 5.5 times the proportion of their earnings in taxes as do the wealthy. Even when federal taxes are added in, the proportion of income paid in taxes declines consistently from the poorest to the wealthiest.

Although the wealthy do enjoy advantages, we do not mean to imply that they pay no taxes. Most do, in fact, pay a considerable amount in taxes. The question is whether they have paid a proportionately larger amount of their income than the nonwealthy. The answer depends on whether only federal taxes or the total taxes paid—federal, state, and local taxes—are included. When all taxes are considered, the poor have paid a higher proportion of their income than have the nonpoor.

Poverty and the Economy.   The American economy works for the rich and against the poor in various ways. A capitalist economy, which is supported by government policies, allows *concentration of wealth*. The fact that the share of income of the richest Americans has declined during this century (see table 6.1) is misleading unless you recognize that a large part of the wealth of the very rich does not come from personal income. *Stocks, bonds, and real estate are important sources of wealth* for those at the top of the socioeconomic ladder. This is why it is important to consider wealth and not merely income when assessing the amount of inequality.

A second way the economy works against the poor is by *entrapping them in a vicious circle.* Consider, for example, a woman whose job pays her only poverty-level wages. She cannot get a better-paying job because she lacks education or skills. She cannot afford to quit to gain the skills or advance her education because she has a family to support. There is no union, and she is unwilling to risk her job and perhaps her physical well-being to try and organize her fellow workers or even to support a move to unionization. Meanwhile, her debts mount, she may accumulate medical bills, and the rate of inflation may far surpass any wage increase she gets. As she sinks more deeply into debt, she is less and less able to risk the loss of the income she has. Ultimately, she may reach the point of despair that we described earlier. Perhaps she will cling to the hope that at least some of her children can escape the poverty that has wrung the vigor out of her own life.

A third way the economy hurts the poor is by *guaranteeing that a certain proportion of the population will be unable to find employment or unable to find jobs that pay more than poverty-level wages* (Rank, Yoon, and Hirschl 2003). Although most of the poor are not unemployed, a substantial number of families are poor because the family head is either squeezed out of the job market or can find only low-paying jobs. This "squeezing out" can occur when companies close down or downsize, recessions occur, and technological changes make jobs obsolete (Venkatesh 1994). Some of these people will spend time on welfare as they struggle against economic forces that are beyond their control (Rank 1994).

The low-paying jobs that keep the working poor impoverished are most likely to be found in the service industry, particularly in food preparation and service jobs (Bureau of Labor Statistics 2006a). A person working full-time, 52 weeks a year at the minimum wage would earn $10,700 a year—a little higher than the poverty level for a single person under 65 but less than the poverty level for two or more. Clearly, no one can be an adequate breadwinner for a family and work for minimum wages. Yet, in 2005, 1.9 million workers reported wages at *or below* the minimum wage of $5.15 per hour. (Some who made less than minimum were not paid by the hour, but when translated into an hourly rate their income was less than minimum.) These minimum-wage workers tended to be young (under the age of 25). More of them were women than men. Many worked part-time jobs. And many were immigrants.

Immigrants are prime targets for companies that pay low wages. A New York reporter went into a Brooklyn garment factory that had a sign posted in Chinese: "Earnestly, urgently looking for workers" (Lii 1995). Because the reporter spoke Chinese, the owner assumed that she was an immigrant seeking her fortune in America. She accepted the job and took her place in a long line of Chinese women bending over sewing machines and working diligently in silence. At the end of seven days and 84 hours of work, she was told that in three weeks she would be paid $54.24—which came to 65 cents an hour! She walked away "from the lint-filled factory with aching shoulders, a stiff back, a dry cough and a burning sore throat."

Similar stories could be told of Asians and Hispanics in various parts of the country. Both legal and illegal immigrants are exploited. Lacking language skills and/or legal status and desperate for income, they may fall prey to managers who pay only the minimum wage or less.

One way to deal with low-paying jobs is to *unionize* the workers. Unfortunately, as we point out in chapter 10, unions have had their own problems in recent years in organizing the workforce. The problem of low-paying jobs is likely to continue for some time.

Immigrants are prime targets for low-paying jobs.

The same economy that allows low-paying labor furthers the disadvantage of the poor in regard to the purchase of consumer goods and services, including everything from groceries to health care (Brookings Institution Metropolitan Policy Program 2005). Thus, low-income families in Philadelphia paid at least $500 more than other families for the same kind of car and $400 more per year for insurance for the car. Similarly, a study of the cost of being poor in Gary, Indiana, reported that stores in the poor neighborhoods charged more for food and clothes than did stores in other areas (Barnes 2005). Why don't the poor simply go to the other stores, then? They may have neither the time nor the resources to travel to cheaper but distant stores. And some who did found themselves being watched with suspicion in grocery stores when they used food stamps or treated discourteously when shopping for clothes.

To be sure, it is more costly to do business in ghetto neighborhoods than elsewhere because of greater losses through theft and higher insurance premiums. Although higher prices may be legitimate from a business perspective, they do contribute to keeping the poor impoverished.

Patterns of Family Life.   One aspect of family life that tends to perpetuate poverty is the size of the family. The rate of poverty among large families is two to three times that of two-person families.

Even in small families, however, the family is likely to perpetuate its own poverty because of *certain social-class differences in family life* (Heymann 2000; Pittman and Chase-Lansdale 2001; Lareau 2003). Family life among the poor can discourage intellectual achievement (and, therefore, the higher levels of education that are vital for upward mobility). Among the factors that are important for a child's intellectual growth are parents' willingness to give time to the child, parental guidance, parental aspirations for the child's achievement, provision of intellectual stimulation, and the use of external resources such as nursery schools and advice from experts. Children who live in poverty for a period of time are less likely to receive this kind of family help than are those who are not poor (Evans 2004). Those who live in persistent poverty are even more disadvantaged than those who experience temporary poverty (McLoyd 1998).

Why? Can't poor parents provide the same kind of help and motivation as the nonpoor? In theory, yes. Yet consider the circumstances of living in poverty. A poor mother likely has relatively little education herself. In general, the more highly educated a mother, the less she engages in strictly routine kinds of interaction with her infant and the more she smiles at and makes eye contact with her infant (Crockenberg 1983). Such mother-infant interaction is crucial to intellectual development.

Furthermore, in a poor family *interaction of children with adults generally, and parents in particular, tends to be minimal* (Heymann 2000). The home of the poor child is likely to be crowded, busy, and noisy. There are likely to be many people, including a number of children, living in the home, though it is less likely that there are two parents. No single child gets much attention. The children watch television, listen to music, and see movies, but do little reading. Moreover, they have little sustained interaction with adult members of their families.

Evidence also shows that consistent mothering by one person facilitates development of children's ability to express themselves verbally. Children in poor families are less likely to have such a relationship in their early years. Instead, responsibility for child care tends to be assumed by a number of people, including adults and other children. TANF policy, which requires single mothers to find work and become self-supporting, exacerbates the problem.

The interaction that does occur may hinder rather than facilitate intellectual growth because there is a *greater proportion of nonverbal compared to verbal interaction* among the poor. The emphasis on the nonverbal rather than the verbal and on the physical rather than the mental is why children from poor homes tend to move their lips while reading and to use their fingers while counting.

Because the verbal ability of poor adults is generally low, increasing the amount of verbal interaction between adults and children would not resolve the problem. Many language differences have been found between the lower and the middle and upper socioeconomic strata. These language differences involve grammatical distinctions; pronunciation, stress, and intonation; range of vocabulary; and style and taste in the selection and use of words and phrases. Differences in these linguistic features mean differences in how the world is experienced and communicated. In general, poor parents are equipped with neither the financial resources nor the intellectual tools necessary to maximize the intellectual growth of their children. The parents' own opportunities to acquire these resources and tools are minimal, and hence the family environment they provide will tend to perpetuate the limitations in their children.

Another aspect of family life that bears crucially on the problem of poverty is the *high rate of divorce.* Recall that persons in female-headed families have the highest rates of poverty in the nation (see figure 6.2). Divorce is likely to have negative economic consequences for women and may be particularly severe for women with children (Morgan 1991). Indeed, nearly half the increase in child poverty in recent years is due to changing family structure (more children born to single women and greater numbers of single-parent families because of separation, death, or divorce).

The Education of the Poor.   In general, the lower the income, the lower the educational achievement of children (National Center for Educational Statistics 2000a). Even the *educational expectations of poor children are lower than those in the middle and upper classes.* Among those who have reached the senior year of high school, only about half of those in the lower socioeconomic strata, compared to 66 percent of the middle strata and 87 percent of the higher strata, expect to earn a college degree (National Center for Education Statistics 2006b). This educational disadvantage, in turn, exacerbates the worst aspects of poverty, depressing well-being and shutting people out of many economic opportunities.

Unfortunately, the educational environment itself contributes in a number of ways to the low academic achievement of the poor. Chapter 11 considers the problem of the inequitable distribution of quality education and shows that schools in poor neighborhoods tend to have meager facilities and inexperienced or inadequate teachers. Here we focus on the ways *school personnel affect poverty-level students* at the interpersonal level.

Children of poor families may experience **discrimination** when they attend school with children of nonpoor families. In a classic study, Hollingshead (1949) found that high school students in a small midwestern town were treated differently by teachers and administrators, depending on the social-class level of the students' parents. Students from the lower levels received less consideration and harsher punishments. Becker (1952) also identified social-class variations in aspects of the teacher-pupil relationship such as teaching techniques, discipline, and moral acceptability of the pupils.

Other studies have corroborated these findings and extended them to show that *teachers have different expectations for students from different socioeconomic backgrounds* (Kozol 1967; McLoyd 1998). Expectations can significantly retard or stimulate intellectual growth (Rosenthal and Jacobson 1968). Hence, when middle-class teachers

discrimination
arbitrary, unfavorable treatment of the members of some social group

expect students from poor families not to perform well, this expectation can lead the children to perform below their capabilities.

In essence, the poor are less likely than the nonpoor to have gratifying and encouraging experiences in school. They are, therefore, more likely to drop out. Children from lower socioeconomic levels, compared to those from the middle and upper strata, also tend to be more dissatisfied with school, report more interpersonal problems (such as not being popular), feel more difficulty in expressing themselves well, and are more likely to express difficulties concentrating and studying. It is not surprising, then, that the majority of school dropouts are from the lower strata.

In sum, the poor are less likely than the nonpoor to perform well in school or to seek more than minimal education—not necessarily because of innate ability, but because of sociocultural factors. Even when ability levels of poor and nonpoor are equated, the poor are less likely to pursue higher education.

Social Psychological Factors

fallacy

Some attitudes and values held by both the nonpoor and the poor help perpetuate poverty (Rogers-Dillon 1995). For example, many nonpoor accept the *fallacy of retrospective determinism* with regard to poverty: They believe that poverty is inevitable—"There have always been poor people, and there always will be poor people." This kind of attitude may manifest itself as opposition to governmental antipoverty programs, pitting the nonpoor against the poor as various interest groups vie for funds.

Disparagement and Discrimination.   As we pointed out earlier, *the nonpoor tend to disparage the poor.* Through history, and in virtually all societies, the poor have been considered disreputable in some sense. Such attitudes seriously undermine self-respect among the poor and at the same time perpetuate the political and economic processes

Many people are poor even though they work.

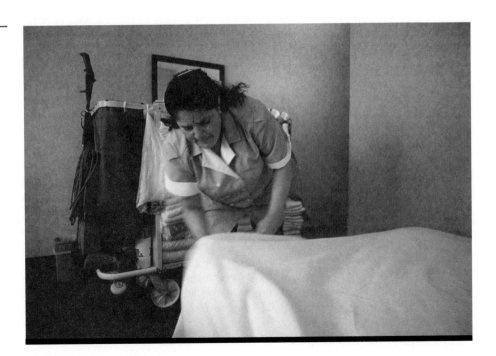

that maintain poverty. You might think that people's disparagement of the poor would lessen during times of more general economic hardship; but beliefs about the causes of poverty and attitudes toward welfare change little—even when the entire society is in an economic recession (Kluegel 1987).

Negative attitudes toward the poor may become **self-fulfilling prophecies**. If a man is poor because he is out of work, he may find that when he secures work, hostility is directed toward him because he comes from an impoverished background. We once lived in a community in which a manufacturing company placed a full-page advertisement in the local newspaper, pointing out that a program to bus inner-city workers to the plant had failed. The ad asked what was wrong with the workers. Why were the jobs still open? The company implied that what many people think is actually true: The poor are too lazy to work and will not accept an opportunity even if it is offered to them. A subsequent investigation showed that the chronically unemployed, who were all black, were unwilling to work because of pressures, hostility, and racial bias.

The Ideology of Wealth and Poverty. Many Americans *believe strongly in an ideology of individualism, attributing both wealth and poverty to the qualities of individuals rather than to the social system.* A *New York Times* survey reported that 80 percent of the respondents believed that people can start out poor, work hard, and become rich (Scott and Leonhardt 2005). This is in accord with an individualist ideology of wealth and poverty, which argues that each individual is responsible for his or her own status because the system itself allows opportunities to all. Clearly, such an ideology allows no basis for political action that would alleviate poverty. It is understandable, therefore, that Americans, compared to those in some European nations, are less concerned about establishing a minimum income level for all citizens (Osberg and Smeeding 2006).

Public Policy and Private Action

There have, of course, been attempts to resolve the problem of poverty. The so-called War on Poverty initiated in the 1960s was a multifaceted attack on the problem. The Economic Opportunity Act of 1964 set up several programs intended to benefit the poor, including the Job Corps (to train young people who have little education or skills), the College Work Study Program (to help college students from low-income families), and the Community Action Program.

The failure of the War on Poverty to eliminate the problem is used by some Americans to disparage any government efforts and to insist that, ultimately, the poor themselves must take advantage of the opportunities in the land to lift themselves from poverty. This argument not only ignores the fact that the war was often more rhetoric than support but also ignores the genuine gains that were made. The poverty rate fell from more than 22 percent in 1959 to a low of 11 to 12 percent in the 1970s. The subsequent rise occurred with the cutback in government programs. Without the programs that exist now, the rate would be much higher than it is. You must also realize that some programs will fail; the study of human behavior is not sufficiently scientific to be able to put together an infallible solution to a problem. Some programs have worked well. Head Start and other early childhood education programs have provided impoverished children with skills that have enabled them to reach higher levels of academic achievement and success (Barnett 1998). Kenworthy (1999) examined the effects of social welfare programs in 15 affluent nations, including the United States, and found that the programs have reduced poverty rates in all of them.

self-fulfilling prophecy
a belief that has consequences (and may become true) simply because it is believed

To eliminate poverty, some attitudes and ideologies among people generally, and political leaders in particular, must be altered. Typically, the more information people have and the more they are exposed to impoverished individuals, the more positive their attitudes are likely to be toward the poor (and, therefore, the more likely they are to support programs that help the poor). Three researchers who studied attitudes toward the homeless found that people who were most exposed to homelessness—including everything from television shows and articles to having been in or worked in a homeless shelter—had the most favorable attitudes (Lee, Farrell, and Link 2004). Whatever governments and community organizations can do to increase exposure is likely to increase support for programs that help.

The attitudes and ideologies of political leaders are also crucial, and the commitment of the federal government is essential. Unfortunately, federal commitment varies enormously from one administration to another. New policies and programs are needed, but the emphasis in the early 2000s was on cutting back on old programs.

Because single mothers have the highest rate of poverty in the nation, strategies to help them must have priority. One way to help mothers who work and are still in poverty would be to create a system of fringe benefits for low-wage workers (Jencks 1992). The benefits could include an increase in the Earned Income Tax Credit, tax credits for child care expenses, and a tax credit for housing expenses.

Some of the poor also could be helped by raising the minimum wage. An individual worker cannot support a family above the poverty level by working full time at the minimum wage level.

Another important step is *to continue to search for antipoverty programs, including welfare programs,* that work. It appears that workfare, introduced in the 1980s, is going to be the policy for the foreseeable future. Under the TANF program, the federal government does not provide long-term aid to the poor. Instead, states are given block grants to run their own programs. Each state has considerable flexibility, but certain guidelines must be followed. Generally, the guidelines are that no family will be given welfare payments for more than five years, and if the head of a family does not find work within two years, the family will lose benefits.

How effective has workfare been so far? First, the program has greatly reduced welfare rolls and moved many former recipients into work (Grogger and Karoly 2005). Second, however, *the reduction in welfare benefits has been far greater than the reduction of poverty.* The earnings from the kinds of jobs available to those moving out of welfare (who are likely to have minimal skills) are frequently no more than the benefits they were receiving from welfare. Thus, they are working, but they are no better off financially than they were while on welfare. And some are even worse off.

It is not surprising, then, that studies of workers who have participated in TANF programs show that *the majority are not able to escape from poverty* even though they follow through to the end of the process that is supposed to rescue them (Cancian et al. 2003; Blalock, Tiller, and Monroe 2004). Moreover, there are some recipients, particularly those with less than a high-school education and a poor work history, who are unable to secure a job within the time limits set by the state (Taylor, Barusch, and Vogel-Ferguson 2006). They are left with nothing.

In addition, another problem has plagued the poor under workfare. Although one of the goals was to strengthen family life by encouraging parents to be responsible breadwinners, workfare has had no effect on the living arrangements of poor white children, has increased the proportion of Hispanic children living with a married parent, but has actually decreased the proportion of black children living with any parent (Bitler, Gelbach, and Hoynes 2004). And a study of low-income single mothers who moved from welfare to work found that the conditions of employment (long hours, erratic work schedules, lengthy commutes, etc.) resulted in a variety of emotional and interpersonal problems among the children (Dunifon, Kalil, and Bajracharya 2005).

In short, workfare may not even be a solution for all the able-bodied workers who have been on welfare, much less for those who are not able to work. A writer who tried to survive by working for a month at low-paying jobs put it this way:

> I lost almost four pounds in four weeks, on a diet weighted heavily toward burgers and fries. How former welfare recipients and single mothers will (and do) survive in the low-wage workforce, I cannot imagine. . . . I couldn't hold two jobs and I couldn't make enough money to live on with one (Ehrenreich 1999:52).

What, then, is to be done at the level of public policy? A number of steps need to be taken at both the federal and state levels of government, including:

- Provide benefits for as long as it takes (rather than the current limits) to enable families to escape poverty.
- Spend all unused TANF money. (Billions of unspent dollars are available to the states.)
- Simplify the process of getting available benefits such as food stamps, child care, health care, and transportation so that the poor are both aware of and able to get the help they need.
- Set a federal minimum wage that enables workers to be self-supporting and able to afford housing.
- Expand educational and training programs so that workers can secure better-paying jobs.
- Provide more supportive services for low-income families.

Finally, various forms of private action can help the poor. One example is Habitat for Humanity, which has built more than 100,000 homes for poor people in the United States and other countries. Interested Americans can volunteer to help in the construction or can donate money to support others who do the work. Other programs include the work of various civic and religious groups in repairing and renovating homes, providing food for the hungry, offering health care to the poor, and giving scholarships to poor children. Such programs reach a portion of the poor, but they cannot replace the broader public policies that are needed to help the millions of poor Americans.

Follow Up.   Think about actions that you as a private citizen have taken to help alleviate the problem of poverty. What more could you do in the future?

Summary

Poverty may not be as bad in America as it is in some parts of the world, but America's poverty must be evaluated in terms of the standard of living attained by the majority of Americans. The government's definition of poverty is based on the cost of a basic diet called the "economy food plan." It is revised to account for inflation and varies according to location (farm or non-farm), size of the family, and sex and age of the head of the family. In 2005, a family of four with an annual income of $19,806 or less was officially poor. This official definition is challenged as inadequate or unrealistic because it sets the poverty level quite low.

The proportion of people who are poor varies over time. Poverty is not equally distributed among the population, however. Your chances of being poor are greater if you are in a female-headed family, are a member of a minority group, are under 18 years of age, and are living in a rural area. Contrary to popular opinion, poverty is not basically a problem of unemployment. Many of the poor work, and some work full time. Some of the poor are homeless. Homelessness is associated with many other problems, such as mental and physical health.

The quality of life for the poor can be characterized as pervasive deprivation: The poor get less of everything that is valued in American society, including rights to life and the pursuit of happiness. Poverty brings despair and fear, including the fear of being victimized by crime. Various myths that disparage the poor diminish their dignity as human beings. Their health is poorer than that of most Americans, and their poverty and ill health can become a vicious circle. The individual living in poverty is forced to choose between limited, undesirable alternatives.

Among the structural factors that contribute to poverty, the distribution of power is of prime importance. People who control the wealth are the most powerful, and their interests are typically reflected in governmental decisions. Both the structure and the functioning of American government tend to work to the detriment of the poor. Multiple decision-making centers, the middle-class composition of the bureaucracy, and the complexities of getting aid all work to the detriment of the poor. Ironically, the well-to-do and powerful give to each other through government actions what they say is immoral to give to the poor. The economy works against the poor in three ways: by allowing the concentration of wealth, by entrapping the poor in a vicious circle, and by guaranteeing that a certain proportion of the population will be unable to find employment or jobs that pay more than poverty-level wages.

The family environment tends to perpetuate poverty when there are many children in the family. Even when there are few children, poor families tend to transmit poverty by anti-intellectual attitudes and patterns of interaction that inhibit intellectual development. Disrupted families are also an important source of poverty, and many widows and divorced women spend a part of the time after disruption in poverty. Educational arrangements themselves contribute to the problem because quality education is much less likely to be available to poor children than to nonpoor children. Also, poor children tend not to have gratifying and encouraging experiences in school or to pursue higher education even when they have the ability to do so.

Attitudes and values of both the poor and the nonpoor contribute to the poverty problem. The attitudes and values of the nonpoor legitimate their disparagement of and discrimination against the poor. The American value of individualism and ideology of equal opportunity combine to justify negative attitudes toward the poor and programs designed to help them.

Key Terms

Autonomy	Malnutrition
Consumer Price	Poverty
Index	Poverty Level
Corporate Welfare	Self-Fulfilling
Discrimination	Prophecy
Ghetto	Subsidy
Gross National	
Product (GNP)	

Study Questions

1. What do we mean by "poverty"? How many Americans are poor?
2. Who is most likely to be poor in America?
3. How have the problems of poverty and the lot of the poor changed over time in our country?
4. Explain the various ways in which poverty affects the basic rights and needs of people.
5. What is meant by the "dilemmas of poverty"?

6. How do social institutions contribute to the problem of poverty?

7. How do attitudes and ideologies help perpetuate poverty?

8. What are some steps that could be taken to eliminate or at least minimize poverty?

Internet Resources/ Exercises

1. Explore some of the ideas in this chapter on the following sites:

http://www.census.gov   The U.S. Census Bureau offers regular reports and the latest data on poverty in the United States.

http://ssc.wisc.edu/irp   The University of Wisconsin's Institute for Research on Poverty offers a wealth of information, including a newsletter with reports from their researchers.

http://jcpr.org   Site for the Joint Center for Poverty Research, offering working papers, newsletters, and links to other resources.

2. TANF requirements vary from state to state. Choose four states and get information on their TANF programs. Also gather, if possible, any data on the effectiveness of the programs (numbers of people moved off welfare, numbers of those out of poverty, etc.). Which of the programs do you think is most effective? In which state or states would a poor person get the most help?

3. European nations tend to have lower rates of poverty than the United States. Investigate what various European nations are doing to alleviate poverty and ensure at least a minimally adequate income for all citizens.

For Further Reading

Belle, Deborah, ed. *Lives in Stress: Women and Depression*. Beverly Hills, CA: Sage, 1982. Observations and interviews with 43 low-income mothers and their children, showing the way in which poverty creates depression. The book underscores the helplessness of people in the face of overwhelming circumstances.

Danziger, Sheldon H., and Robert H. Haveman, eds. *Understanding Poverty*. Cambridge, MA: Harvard University Press, 2002. Various experts address the causes and consequences of poverty, antipoverty policies, and efforts by local communities and neighborhoods to ameliorate the problem.

Fine, Michelle, and Lois Weis. *The Unknown City: The Lives of Poor and Working-Class Young Adults*. Boston: Beacon Press, 1998. An in-depth examination of the lives of poor and working-class men and women, explained by the people themselves as they talk about their struggles with work, school, family life, and sexuality.

Lareau, Annette. *Unequal Childhoods: Class, Race, and Family Life*. Berkeley, CA: University of California Press, 2003. A participant observation study of 12 families in which there were children who were nine or ten years old. Shows how parenting and daily routines differ between the middle-class families and those that are working-class or poor.

Noble, Charles. *Welfare as We Knew It: A Political History of the American Welfare State*. New York: Oxford University Press, 1997. Discusses various factors about American culture and institutions that account for the fact that the United States is the least generous welfare state among Western industrial nations.

Rank, Mark Robert. *One Nation, Underprivileged: Why American Poverty Affects Us All*. New York: Oxford University Press, 2004. A leading poverty researcher explores the basic causes of poverty, the extent of poverty, and the reasons why poverty is an issue of vital concern to the nation.

Shipler, David K. *The Working Poor: Invisible in America*. New York: Alfred A. Knopf, 2004. A thorough study of people who are working but still poor or nearly poor by the official poverty level. The author spent as many as seven years working with some of his subjects; he well understands their struggles.

chapter 6 review

Gender and Sexual Orientation

1 Discuss the issue of biological versus social bases for gender differences.

2 Show how inequalities between the sexes affect women's lives.

3 Explain the social structural and social psychological factors that contribute to gender inequality.

4 Learn various explanations of homosexuality.

5 Identify how homophobia affects the quality of life of homosexuals and how to address the problem of homophobia.

"I Didn't Need the Extra Hassles"

Sandra, a high-ranking university administrator in her 50s, started her graduate work when the youngest of her two children began school. In a sense she has it all—family and a successful career—but, as she notes, it has at times been a "journey of outrage":

When I had the chance to go to graduate school, I was deliriously happy. Most of the other students were younger, but I could tell they accepted me and enjoyed having me around. I'm sure part of it was my enthusiasm for the program. I soon discovered, however, that I was embarking on a journey of outrage as well as one of a new career. My first inkling was when one of my fellow students hit on me one day in the library. He wanted to take me out somewhere. I must admit that I was rather flattered, since I was 10 years older than he was. So I just smiled and reminded him that I was married. He smiled back and said, "I don't mind." I told him that I did mind and that I had to get on with my studying.

I could have easily shrugged it off. But every time I tried to study in the library, he would sit at a table nearby and stare at me. I complained to the librarian, but he said that the student had broken no rules. I reminded him that this was really threatening to a woman. How could I be sure that the guy wouldn't try to do something crazy? The librarian looked sympathetic but helpless. I did the only thing I could. I stopped studying at the library and studied at home whenever I could find a quiet moment. Shortly after that, one of the faculty members started making overtures to me. This was really threatening, because I knew he could blackball me. I had to do a dance around him for three years. He did a good job of quenching a lot of my enthusiasm for school.

I could tell countless stories, but one more will illustrate why I call all this a journey of outrage. I came up for tenure in my first academic position. They turned me down. I hadn't published a whole lot, but I had published as much as a male colleague who got tenure. A friend told me that they rejected me because they thought my productivity would decline because of my family commitments. So all the way along, I faced one outrage after another. And just because I'm a woman. It was hard enough to do graduate work and start a career while raising a family. I didn't need the extra hassles. And what makes them so outrageous is that if I were a man they wouldn't have happened.

Introduction

What does it take for a group to suffer from inequality in the United States? It isn't size, because while one of the groups we examine in this chapter is comparatively small (homosexuals), the other represents a majority (women comprise nearly 51 percent of the population). In other ways, the two groups are similar in the extent to which biological versus social factors affect their behavior. Moreover, both have a long history of suffering from both discrimination and oppression.

Gender Inequality

innate
existing in a person from birth

sex
an individual's identity as male or female

gender
the meaning of being male or female in a particular society

gender role
the attitudes and behavior that are expected of men and women in a society

Do you believe there are more advantages to being a man or a woman in American society today? Your answer may depend on whether you are male or female (Polling Report 2007). In a national poll 41 percent of men and 57 percent of women agreed that men have more advantages, while 14 percent of men and 6 percent of women said that women have more advantages. Most of the rest stated that neither has more advantages. Why would a majority of women and 4 out of 10 men agree that men have more advantages? Apparently they agree that the ideal of equal opportunity for all Americans has been elusive for women.

Because women suffer from inequality as a result of an **innate** characteristic (their sex), women are called the *largest minority* in America even though they are a slight majority of the population. As we discuss gender inequality, we use a number of important terms. The terminology is not yet standardized, but the following definitions are consistent with usage adopted by most social scientists. **Sex** refers to an individual's biological identity as male or female. **Gender** is the meaning of being male or female in a particular society, and **gender role** refers to the attitudes and behavior that are expected of men and women in a society.

The terminology indicates that *some aspects of men and women are determined by social rather than biological factors.* This social aspect is the first issue we examine. Contrary to the argument that gender inequalities are the necessary outcome of biological differences, we show that the problems are sociocultural in origin and how they affect the quality of life for women. Finally, we look at structural and social psychological factors that contribute to gender inequality and suggest some ways to address the problems.

Biology or Society?

There are numerous differences in the attitudes and behavior of the sexes (Marano and Strand 2003; Goldman et al. 2004). Among other aspects, men and women differ in their attention span, their aspirations, the strategies they use in competitive games, the amount they smile, their vulnerability to particular diseases and to addictions, the structure and functioning of their brains, and their sexual interests. The question we want to examine here is, what accounts for those differences? Are they rooted in biology or in society? The questions are important because people who hold to a strong biological position are likely to fall into the *fallacy of retrospective determinism,* arguing that whatever has happened to women in American society is inevitable because people are determined by their own biological makeup to behave and function in certain ways.

fallacy

Gender and Biology.   The "damsel in distress" and "white knight" of folklore illustrate the longstanding notion that men are the independent and women the dependent creatures. This notion was given a pseudoscientific legitimacy in the writings of Sigmund Freud, who argued that biology is critically important in sex-related behavior. Freud's arguments were summed up in his famous idea that *anatomy is destiny.*

Nurturing is a significant part of the traditional role of women.

Freud claimed that girls reach a point in their development at which they recognize that they are anatomically different from boys. They lack a penis and therefore feel short-changed. They develop "penis envy." According to Freud, only in the act of conceiving and giving birth to a child can a woman find fulfillment for her desire to have a penis. He also concluded from his observations that women are naturally more passive, submissive, and neurotic than men (Freud 1949).

Freud's arguments are based on questionable evidence at best. Essentially, he developed his psychoanalytic theories by observing middle-class behavior of his day and then explained the relationships between the sexes in terms of his theories. There is a high degree of circularity involved, so that people who use his arguments often fall into the *fallacy of circular reasoning.*

fallacy

A more empirical basis for asserting the natural subservience of women is claimed by people who draw on research in the areas of sociobiology (the use of biological factors to explain social phenomena), the brain, and human hormones (Wilson 2000; Pfaff 2002). These researchers claim, on the basis of various kinds of evidence, that human behavior must be understood in terms of *innate biological differences between the sexes.* Some stress humans' continuity with other animals and argue that male and female behavior reflect the imperatives of the evolutionary process—the struggle to survive and to perpetuate one's kind.

People who draw on research on the brain and hormones also stress the biological differences but do not necessarily talk about them in terms of evolutionary imperatives. Rather, the differences are used to explain such factors as the higher levels of aggression among males, the greater verbal abilities of females, and the tendency of women to be more stressed than men by emotional conflict (Brizendine 2006).

Clearly, there are differences between males and females in both the structure and functioning of the brain (Kreeger 2002), but the implications of these differences are controversial. First, many of the differences are relatively small or even trivial (Hyde 2005). Second, research continues to modify some of the conclusions about differences. For example, it is not true, as many have believed, that boys are inherently better at math than are girls (Spelke 2005). The two sexes have equal capacity for doing math and science.

Thus, the implications for behavior of the differing brain and hormonal structures of males and females are uncertain and controversial. It is best, we believe, to accept the conclusion of a biologist that social interaction affects biological processes as well as vice versa, so that mind, body, and culture interact with each other (Fausto-Sterling 1985). Behavior is always a function of multiple factors, and no one can say with certainty how much of any particular behavior is biologically driven and how much is socially formed.

Men's Issues.   In the late 1980s, a *men's movement rapidly gained momentum.* In the University of California reference system, the number of books related to men and masculinity increased sevenfold between 1989 and 1995 (Newton 1998). During the period, the number of scholarly essays in the area tripled and the number of popular magazine articles increased tenfold.

We look briefly at this movement for two reasons. First, we don't want to give the impression that men have all the advantages and none of the problems. Men's issues are as legitimate as women's. Second, the men's movement illustrates our point that gender behavior is sociocultural and not merely biological.

Issues of concern to men include (Throop 1997; Newton 1998):

- The meaning of masculinity in a time of changing gender roles.
- The meaning of being a father and a husband in the face of feminist assertions and cultural expectations.
- The rights of divorced and single fathers.
- Perceived discriminatory treatment by lawyers and the courts in divorce and child custody hearings.
- Reverse bias in hiring and promotions when women are chosen over men who are more qualified.

Some segments of the men's movement take the position that men, not women, are the truly oppressed group today (Ferber 2000). They argue that men have been "de-masculinized," that women and the women's movement are responsible, and that men must reclaim their masculinity and their rightful authority.

Others in the movement are concerned with more specific issues such as fatherhood (Ranson 2001). In the past, fathers were thought of as breadwinners who had limited time to spend with their children. Today, fathers are expected to be much more involved in their children's lives; but they are also expected to be successful in the workplace. How can they meet the competing demands? What do they do when parenting and work requirements contradict each other? What is the role of the wife and mother in all this?

Clearly, such questions arise not out of biology but out of the social milieu. Men's issues, like women's, are a reflection of the sociocultural context—or, to put it another way, gender roles result from sociocultural, not merely biological, factors.

Gender Inequality and the Quality of Life

Although men as well as women have problems and complaints, our focus is on the inequality faced by women. As noted earlier, the majority of women and four of 10 men agree that men have more advantages. In this section, we examine those advantages. In essence, they are *contradictions between the ideology of equal opportunities and the reality of life for women.*

Career Inequality.   After World War II, the ideal pattern for women was to marry and become a homemaker and stay-at-home mother. Both the ideal and the reality have changed. The proportion of married women in the labor force rose from 23.8 percent in 1950 to 60.5 percent in 2004; the proportion of women with children under 6 years who were in the labor force increased even more dramatically, from 11.9 percent to 62.2 percent (Bureau of Labor Statistics Web site). It might appear that this means increasing equality in the labor market, even when women have small children at home. Such a conclusion would be further buttressed by *unemployment rates* (table 7.1). The rates are a measure of the number of people who desire employment but who are out of work. Until the 1990s, the rates were nearly always higher for women than for men, a contradiction of the *ideology of equal opportunity.* Since 1990, however, the rates have been more equal.

Yet equal economic opportunities only begin at the point of employment. What about women's opportunities for advancement? What about their income? Are they also equal to those of men?

TABLE 7.1
Unemployment Rates, by
Sex, 1948–2005
(persons 16 years and over)

Year	Male	Female
1948	3.6	4.1
1950	5.1	5.7
1955	4.2	4.9
1960	5.4	5.9
1965	4.0	5.5
1970	4.4	5.9
1975	7.9	9.3
1980	6.9	7.4
1985	7.0	7.4
1990	5.6	5.4
1995	5.6	5.6
2000	3.9	4.1
2005	5.1	5.1

SOURCES: U.S. Census Bureau, *Statistical Abstract of the United States,* various editions; and
Department of Labor Web site.

Unfortunately, the ideology of equal opportunity is *contradicted by the discriminatory treatment of women in various occupations.* Women experience discrimination in hiring, in on-the-job training, in promotions, and in the way they are treated by supervisors and coworkers (Knoke and Ishio 1998; Yoder and Berendsen 2001). And this is not only an American problem. A study of 22 industrialized nations reported that while developed welfare states (such as Sweden) have a high proportion of women in the labor force, those women tend to be concentrated in female-typed occupations and are less likely to be in managerial occupations (Mandel and Semyonov 2006). The consequences of discrimination in pursuing a meaningful career include increased physical and emotional health problems (Pavalko, Mossakowski, and Hamilton 2003).

Consider the following facts about the amount and kind of discrimination women encounter. In many occupational categories, women are found disproportionately in the lower-echelon jobs. Although far more women than men are teachers, the proportion of women in top administrative jobs in education (superintendents, assistant superintendents, principals, and assistant principals) is low (Skrla, Reyes, and Scheurich 2000). Increasing proportions of admissions to medical schools are female, but women may be encouraged to pursue the traditional "female" specialties such as pediatrics, psychiatry, and preventive medicine. Moreover, although women compose 43 percent of all medical students, only 27 percent of full-time medical faculty are women and less than 11 percent of women faculty are full professors (compared to 31 percent of men) (Bickel 2000).

The proportion of women in traditionally male-dominated areas such as science, math, and engineering has increased considerably in recent decades. But female college students majoring in these areas still report discriminatory practices and gender-based obstacles in the pursuit of their chosen careers (Steele, James, and Barnett 2002).

Table 7.2 illustrates the fact that many occupations continue to be male or female dominated, what social scientists call a *segregated labor market.* Such segregation has detri-

Occupation	Percent Female	Occupation	Percent Female
Total	46.4		
Managerial and Professional		*Service Occupations*	
Chief executives	23.8	Dental assistants	96.1
Managers, medicine/health	71.2	Firefighters	3.3
Architects	24.4	Chefs and head cooks	20.4
Civil engineers	13.2	Waiters and waitresses	71.8
Math and computer occupations	27.0	Child care workers	94.8
Physicians and surgeons	32.3	Pest control workers	2.6
College/university teachers	44.4	Police officers/sheriffs	14.3
Elementary school teachers	82.2	*Natural Resources and Construction*	
Librarians	84.9	Farming, fishing, forestry	22.5
Lawyers	30.2	Carpenters	1.9
Announcers	12.2	Electricians	2.6
Social workers	80.1	Highway maintenance	4.6
Sales and Office Occupations		*Production and Transportation*	
Cashiers	75.9	Bakers	54.0
Secretaries	99.3	Machinists	10.3
Receptionists	92.4	Laundry/dry cleaning	62.8
Postal clerks	41.7	Tool and die makers	1.1
Bank tellers	87.3	Pilots/flight engineers	5.2
Wholesale sales reps	27.2	Taxi drivers/chauffeurs	15.5

SOURCE: "Employed persons by detailed occupation, sex, race, and Hispanic or Latino ethnicity," Bureau of Labor Statistics Web site.

TABLE 7.2
Employed Persons, by Sex and Selected Occupation, 2005

mental consequences for women. The occupations that have a high proportion of women tend to be lower in status and lower in pay (Cohen and Huffman 2003). In some cases, the occupations are also less desirable from the point of view of meaningful work.

In other words, in a segregated labor market, people tend to evaluate jobs and careers in terms of the predominant gender of the workers as well as the education and skills required. An apparently obvious solution would be for women to choose male-dominated occupations if they want to maximize their status and their income. Unfortunately, women do not gain the same prestige as men when they enter predominantly male occupations. Many women in male-dominated careers feel that they not only must prove their competence but must do so by performing their job even better than a man would. Yet when men enter predominantly female occupations, their competence is more likely assumed (Williams 1995). Ironically, a study of 404 medical technologists, a female-dominated occupation, found that the women reported more gender discrimination than did the men (Blau and Tatum 2000).

Finally, women face career discrimination because they are more likely than men to experience conflict between their work and their home responsibilities, a conflict that is intensified if the woman has more responsibility for child care (van Vianen and Fischer 2002; Hill et al. 2003). Work-family conflict is common for women in other parts of the world as well (Lo, Stone, and Ng 2003).

Income Inequality.   Slower advancement means that women tend to cluster in the lower levels of virtually all occupational categories and are, therefore, accorded less prestige and lower salaries than men. The demand of the women's movement for *equal pay for work of equivalent value* reflects the fact that women are not rewarded equally with men even when they are equally prepared, equally qualified, and equally competent. There is a "glass ceiling," a term used to refer to the arbitrary and often invisible barriers that limit women's advancement. The glass ceiling on income exists in all occupational categories (Cotter et al. 2001).

Overall, from the 1950s until the late 1970s, women received about 60 percent of the income men received. Then the disparity began to shrink; by 2005, the median earnings of women who worked full-time year round was 77 percent that of men (DeNavas-Walt, Proctor, and Lee 2006). As figure 7.1 shows, the disparity holds for all races.

Even when taking into account such factors as education, occupational category, and proportion of time worked, there is still a substantial wage gap that is not explained. For example, Roth (2003) examined a group of Wall Street securities professionals who were similar to each other in terms of such factors as education and ability. She found significant gender differences in earnings that could not be explained by anything other than discrimination. Similarly, a study of University of Michigan law school graduates reported that 15 years after graduation the men earned 52 percent more than the women, 17 percent more than women with similar characteristics, and 11 percent more than women with similar characteristics in the same job settings (Noonan, Corcoran, and Courant 2006).

The Beauty Myth.   The "beauty myth" involves a *contradiction between the belief in the dignity of all humans,* on the one hand, and the *ideology about a particular group,* on the other hand. According to the beauty myth, a woman must be beautiful to be acceptable and attractive (Sullivan 2001). It's a destructive myth. Women spend billions of dollars a year on cosmetics and cosmetic surgery in an effort to appear more beautiful. Teenage girls use a variety of surgical procedures to enhance their beauty, including breast augmentation, eyelid surgery, liposuction (to remove fat), reshaping of the nose, and the "tummy tuck" to tighten the abdomen (Gross 1998). Beauty is a trap. Women who feel homely cannot enjoy their accomplishments because they are haunted by their failure to be beautiful, and women who are beautiful and successful may attribute their success to their beauty rather than to their abilities.

A particularly destructive aspect of the beauty myth is the current ideal of a slender figure for women. Bombarded by media depictions of thinness as the ideal, many women develop *a problem of body image.* They become dissatisfied with the shape and size of their bodies. White women are slightly more likely than black women to experience body dissatisfaction, but the problem occurs among all races (Grabe and Hyde 2006). And it can develop quite early in life. A study of 128 girls who were 5 to 8 years old found that by the age of 6 a large number already wanted a thinner figure (Dohnt and Tiggemann 2006).

Body dissatisfaction can result in a variety of negative consequences for well-being. It can lead to lowered self-esteem, problematic sexual functioning (including risky sexual behavior), depression, and anxiety (Davison and McCabe 2005; Gillen, Lefkowitz, and Shearer 2006). It also leads some women, in an effort to get thinner, to succumb to eating disorders, such as *anorexia nervosa (a form of self-starvation)* and *bulimia (repeated binge eating followed by vomiting or laxatives)* (Hesse-Biber 1996). The disorders are associated with a variety of physical and emotional health problems. For

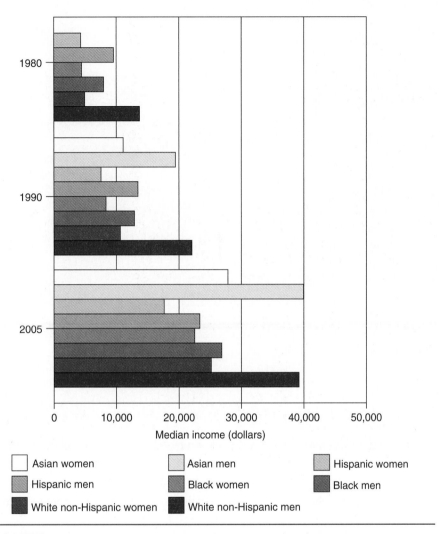

FIGURE 7.1 Median Income of Persons in Constant (2001) Dollars, 1980–2005.
Source: U.S. Census Bureau 2003:462 and 2005 (1980 data not available for Asian women and men).

example, anorexia nervosa is associated with the loss of the menstrual period, anemia, loss of hair and bone density, and kidney failure (Torpy and Glass 2006). Eating disorders are also associated with depression (Stice and Bearman 2001).

In extreme cases, some young women have died from these eating disorders. A woman can go to such an extreme because the disorders involve a disturbed body image (Mazzeo 1999). That is, the woman does not see herself as thin even when others see her as emaciated. Unfortunately, the number of women with poor and distorted body images has been increasing in recent decades (Feingold and Mazzella 1998).

Body image is an issue for men also (Grogan and Richards 2002). For men, a well-toned, muscular body provides confidence and a sense of power in social situations. Like women, men may engage in unhealthy dieting behaviors in an effort to realize

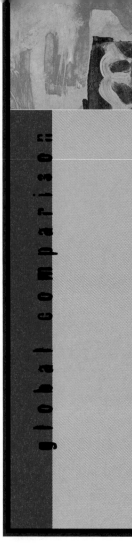

OCCUPATIONAL SEX SEGREGATION IN DEVELOPING COUNTRIES

As noted in the text, occupational sex segregation is detrimental to the interests of women in the job market. In a highly segregated job market, women's income and status, compared to those of men, both tend to be depressed. Although researchers have found such segregation not only in the United States but also in other industrial nations, little has been done to examine it in developing countries. Chang's (2004) recent work, however, not only examined the patterns and extent of sex segregation in a number of developing nations but also identified the effects of government policies on the segregation.

Occupational sex segregation exists in all countries, though the extent of the segregation varies considerably (figure 7.2). Interestingly, Chang found that government policies were the strongest predictor of variations in the extent of segregation. In particular, the lower levels of segregation occurred in nations that have maternity leave legislation. When women must be given maternity leave, increased numbers of them are able to enter the otherwise male-dominated managerial and production occupations.

On the other hand, a surprising finding was that those nations whose governments had enacted antidiscrimination legislation had the highest levels of segregation! Because Chang did not have data both before and after the legislation, it is possible that the legislation did reduce the amount of segregation. But because the levels were so high prior to the legislation, those nations still had higher levels of segregation than the others. It is also possible that antidiscrimination legislation is less effective because it is difficult to enforce and may not be enforced because of cultural restrictions on male-female interaction.

Finally, Chang found that the levels of occupational sex segregation in the developing nations that she studied were higher than the levels found by other researchers in the developed nations. With increasing development, the amount of segregation—and, consequently, the detrimental consequences for women—may diminish. But no nation yet has achieved sexual equality in the job market.

their ideal (Markey and Markey 2005). But the problem of body image is more severe among women, who expressed more dissatisfaction than do men about their body shape (Demarest and Allen 2000).

sexual harassment unwelcome sexual advances, requests for sexual favors, and other sexual behavior that either result in punishment when the victim resists or creates a hostile environment or both

Harassment and Violence. A different form of assault on dignity is the **sexual harassment** to which so many women have been subjected. Sexual harassment refers to unwelcome sexual advances, requests for sexual favors, and other verbal or physical conduct of a sexual nature that result in some kind of punishment when the victim resists or that creates a hostile environment. Although both men and women may be sexually harassed, the proportion of women who experience it is higher. For example, a survey of military personnel found that 70.9 percent of the women and 35 percent of the men who participated in the survey said that they experienced sexually harassing behavior during the previous 12 months (Antecol and Cobb-Clark 2001). And a national survey of college students reported that 35 percent of females and 29 percent of males said they had been physically harassed (touched, grabbed, pinched in a sexual way), while 57 percent of females and 48 percent of males were harassed by sexual comments and jokes (American Association of University Women 2006).

Sexual harassment occurs in all kinds of settings and among all ages. Not only students, but workers in all occupations from professionals (e.g., lawyers, professors, scientists) to blue-collar workers (e.g., autoworkers) report experiences of sexual harass-

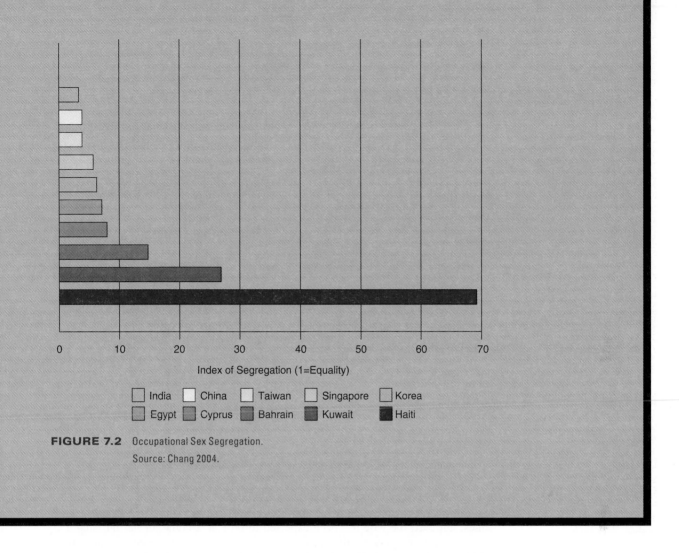

FIGURE 7.2 Occupational Sex Segregation.
Source: Chang 2004.

ment (Piotrkowski 1998; Bronner, Peretz, and Ehrenfeld 2003; Menard et al. 2003; Hinze 2004; Settles et al. 2006). Harassment occurs via e-mail as well as face to face (Finn 2004). Overall, estimates are that at least half of all women will be harassed at some point during their academic or working lives and that harassment will be experienced as degrading, frightening, and sometimes violent (Fitzgerald 1993; Wyatt and Riederle 1995).

The perpetrator of harassment is most likely to be someone in a position of authority over the victim (Uggen and Blackstone 2004). In fact, perhaps the most destructive harassment occurs in the *sexual exploitation of women by men of authority in the helping professions.* Such male power figures include psychiatrists and other therapists, physicians, lawyers, clergymen, and teachers or mentors. Women are particularly vulnerable to sexual pressures in dealing with such power figures. A therapist, for example, may convince a woman that he can provide her with the kind of sexual experience she needs to work through her problems. A clergyman may convince a woman that there is some kind of divine sanction to their relationship. Although we don't know the number of women exploited in this way, increasing attention is being paid to the problem. Indeed, some professional organizations have explicitly condemned such behavior in their codes of ethics.

Finally, violence is the ultimate assault on the dignity of women. Hundreds of thousands of violent acts are committed against women every year, and about a fifth of all

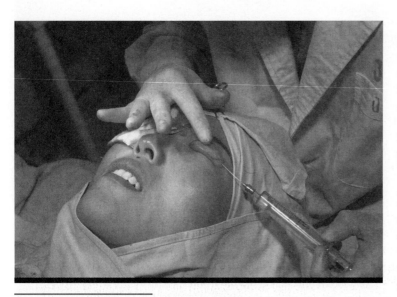

The beauty myth results in a great deal of cosmetic surgery.

violence against women comes from an intimate partner. The problem is worldwide. According to United Nations data, one in every three women in the world has been beaten, abused, or sexually assaulted, usually by someone known to the victim (United Nations Population Fund 2001).

Contributing Factors

As with all social problems, many factors contribute to gender inequality. As we examine these factors, it will be clear that the problem is not simply one of men versus women but of a plexus of factors that together create and maintain this inequality.

Social Structural Factors.   The *normative role of the female* is an important factor in gender inequality because *gender roles specify certain kinds of behavior as appropriate, and other kinds as inappropriate, for men and women.* What, then, is the *traditional role for the American female,* and how does this role contribute to inequality?

In essence, Americans have advocated the *traditional homemaker role of females and the parallel traditional breadwinner role of males.* Certainly, not all females conform to the traditional role. Working-class and African American women, in particular, have been likely to work outside the home. For the bulk of middle- and upper-class whites, however, the wife has been expected to provide a home for her husband and children and to find her fulfillment in caring for her family. The role assumes, then, that a woman will marry and have children and will focus on pleasing her husband and caring for her children.

In the 1960s and 1970s women's attitudes toward this traditional role changed considerably. Yet the traditional view still receives considerable support, particularly with respect to the woman's responsibility for the home. When the Southern Baptist Convention, speaking for the nation's largest Protestant denomination, declared in 1998 that wives should "graciously" submit to the "servant leadership" of their husbands, Fox News polled a national sample of voters, asking whether they agreed or disagreed with the statement. Overall, a third agreed, including 34 percent of men and 32 percent of women (Polling Report 2007).

The traditional role obviously discourages women from pursuing higher education or a career. In a social context in which being female means taking care of a home and family and submitting to one's husband, it may be difficult to secure an advanced degree or to commit oneself to a career.

The research on women's aspirations suggests that if females are treated the same as males, if parents hold similar expectations for their girls and boys and encourage them equally, women will achieve the same levels of education and probably the same levels of work and careers. A great many women would like to work or pursue a career but do not because it conflicts with other role obligations. Only a minority of women prefer either a career without marriage or marriage and children without a career.

The ability to opt for multiple roles is crucial because a *restrictive role for women can lead to illness.* For both men and women, both marriage and employment increase well-being (Burke 1995). Multiple roles not only promote well-being, including physical health, but also tend to lengthen a woman's life (Moen, Dempster-McClain, and Williams 1992; Rose et al. 2004). As a national survey reported, the healthiest women are those who are employed and married, followed by those employed and not married, those married but not in the labor force, and finally those unmarried and not in the labor force (Verbrugge and Madans 1985).

Even though women who go to work have better physical and mental health, working does not solve all their problems. Such women are still likely to have more health problems than their male counterparts. A woman who breaks out of the traditional constraints and goes to work may experience overload. Traditional obligations are not easily cast off even when nontraditional ones are assumed. When women work outside the home, get low pay, and continue to assume the major responsibility for the home, some of the benefits of working are lost (Ross and Mirowsky 1992).

For many women, in other words, having jobs outside the home means "in addition to" rather than "instead of" taking care of their homes. There has been a trend toward greater sharing of household responsibilities, but employed women still spend substantially more hours than their husbands doing housework (Rosenbluth, Steil, and Whitcomb 1998). Using data from a national survey, Shelton and John (1999) found that among married couples where both husband and wife are employed more than 30 hours a week, the wives spend an average of 28.8 hours and the husbands an average of 17.3 hours on household tasks each week. Thus, husbands continue to have more free times than do wives (Mattingly and Bianchi 2003).

Many children are reared in accord with gender stereotypes.

Another problem the working woman faces is the effect her work has on her marital relationship. Husbands of working wives have a tendency to feel less adequate as family breadwinners, and this feeling may lower their satisfaction with their own jobs and with their lives generally (Staines, Pottick, and Fudge 1986). This outcome, of course, is more likely when the husband still clings to traditional notions of male and female roles. However, if both husband and wife prefer her to work, both spouses benefit psychologically from the arrangement, particularly if the husband shares the housework (Ross, Mirowsky, and Huber 1983). When women perceive inequity in the division of household tasks, on the other hand, they are prone to be distressed and depressed (Bird 1999; Frisco and Williams 2003). Thus, working can be a kind of psychological salvation for many women, but only when both spouses have cast off traditional notions about sex roles.

A second important social structural factor in gender inequality is the *socialization that occurs at home, in school, and through the mass media.* In the home, parents tend to treat their sons and daughters differently from the beginning, with the result that children become aware of gender-role differences by as early as two years of age (Witt

1997). The differential treatment continues in the kinds of toys and play activities parents, probably unaware of the effects, provide for their children (Campenni 1999). For example, a Barbie doll can create the desire in young girls for a thinner body (Dittmar, Halliwell, and Ive 2006). And by the time they are in school, they already have a sense of which occupations are appropriate for which sex (Helwig 1998).

Parents also react differently to sons and daughters in the emotional realm. Fathers reward girls but punish boys for expressing sadness and fear (Bayrakdar-Garside and Klimes-Dougan 2002). When children misbehave in ways that could lead to injury, mothers are angry with their sons but disappointed with their daughters, whereas once an injury occurs, mothers attribute their sons' risky misbehavior to factors beyond their control and daughters' risky misbehavior to factors they can influence (Morrongiello and Hogg 2004).

Finally, many parents have lower educational aspirations for their daughters than for their sons, and even believe that their sons are more intelligent than their daughters (Furnham, Reeves, and Budhani 2002). The parents' aspirations are important because *children's aspirations tend to reflect those of their parents* (Marjoribanks 2003).

The school may reinforce the parental pattern. Girls get higher scores than boys on most academic and cognitive tests (Francis and Skelton 2005). Nevertheless, teachers can, like parents, treat boys and girls in terms of traditional gender roles. For example, various studies have found that teachers expect girls to behave better, that they treat boy underachievers as bright but bored and overlook girl underachievers (perhaps they don't consider it as important for girls to achieve academically), and that in physical education boys get more attention and feedback (praise, criticism, technical information) than do girls (Jones and Myhill 2004; Myhill and Jones 2006; Nicaise et al. 2006).

The *mass media are also an important source of gender-role socialization.* Children's picture books, elementary reading books, and the Sunday comics in newspapers are all more egalitarian than in the past, but all still frequently portray males and females in traditional roles (Evans and Davies 2000; Gooden and Gooden 2001; LaRossa et al. 2001; Diekman and Murnen 2004; Hamilton, Anderson, Broaddus, and Young 2006). Some popular magazines and books reinforce the power differences between men and women, portray women as sex objects, and perpetuate the ideal of thinness (Zimmerman, Haddock, and McGeorge 2001; Krassas, Blauwkamp, and Wesselink 2001). Gender stereotyping occurs in television programs and commercials (Ganahl, Prinsen, and Netzley 2003). And an analysis of 100 top-grossing films found that middle-aged men were more likely than their female counterparts to play leadership roles and have occupational power (Lauzen and Dozier 2005).

Such portrayals in the media have an impact. Students exposed to ads in which women are portrayed as sex objects were more likely than others to accept rape myths and less likely to support feminism (MacKay and Covell 1997). Girls and women exposed to the thinness ideal on television and in magazines have an increased likelihood of lowered self-esteem, depression, eating disorders, and approval of cosmetic surgical procedures such as liposuction and breast augmentation (Botta 2003; Vaughan and Fouts 2003; Bessenoff 2006).

fallacy   Another practical consequence of media portrayal of the sexes is that people who engage in the *fallacy of circular reasoning* find support for their arguments. Consider the following exchange we once had with an older man who made the statement: "Everyone knows that men are rational and women are emotional." We asked the man how he knew that. "Everyone knows that. Look around you. Look at television." When the

YOU ARE WHAT YOU READ

Someone has said, "You are what you read." As noted in this chapter, one factor in perpetuating gender-role inequality is the books that you read as a child. Conduct your own research into children's literature. The librarian at a local public library can help you make a selection. Decide on what age level you want to investigate first. Then find five books written for this age level before 1975 and five of the most recent.

Compare the books in terms of the number of male and female characters and the gender roles portrayed. How do the earlier books differ from the more recent ones? To what extent do you believe that the later books overcome gender inequality? Identify two or three aspects of traditional gender roles in the earlier books that are either maintained or eliminated in the later ones.

If the entire class does this project, assign people to cover different age levels (beginning with picture books for preschool children) and see whether there are any differences by age.

man was told that television is fiction, he replied: "But it is based on fact, on what is real about people. And men are really rational and women are really emotional."

A third social structural factor is the economics of gender inequality. Situations that continue in the nation are *likely profitable* for someone, and gender inequality is no exception. The kind of gender inequalities we have discussed are beneficial for men in a variety of ways. They increase men's job opportunities, incomes, and power. It has been said that the hand that rocks the cradle rocks the world (which suggests that real power belongs to women). In most people's experience, however, the hand that holds the biggest purse holds the most power—and this hand typically belongs to a man.

Furthermore, the present amount of income inequality between men and women means that men benefit by having to work less to earn the same amount of money. In essence, a woman might work seven days or more to earn what a man makes in five days (because, as noted earlier, the median income of white women is 77 percent that of white men, and the median income of black and Hispanic women is even less).

Since the end of World War II, women and men have been engaged in an ongoing struggle over the extent of women's participation in the workplace. That the struggle is one for the better positions is illustrated by the relative ease with which women can secure menial and low-paying jobs. Such jobs must be done by someone if other jobs are to be highly paid and employers are to maintain high levels of profit. Who will take such jobs?

Szymanski (1976) showed that **sexism** and *racism* are *functional substitutes* with respect to such jobs. That is, women and racial and ethnic minorities tend to cluster in the low-paying, menial jobs. Where racial or ethnic minorities are available, they provide that labor. Where they are not available, women provide it. We are not saying that where racial or ethnic minorities are available for low-paying jobs, women are equal to men in the labor market. Women are merely next-to-the-lowest group on the hierarchy rather than the lowest.

One other social structural factor in gender inequality is religion. Justification for gender inequality is found in both the teachings and the practices of the world's religions (Deckard 1975). Religious leaders assert or imply that men are superior to women and/or that women should be subservient.

sexism
prejudice or discrimination against someone because of his or her sex

201

In recent decades, a number of Christian theologians, both male and female, have argued that biblical teachings have been misinterpreted by generations of people who used them to justify and maintain patriarchal systems (Meyers 1988; Clifford 2001). Nevertheless, many religious people, but particularly the most conservative ones (known as fundamentalists), justify sexism on religious grounds (Peek, Lowe, and Williams 1991; Bendroth 1994). Religious conservatism and social conservatism tend to go hand in hand. Thus, 85 percent of religious liberals, but only 59.6 percent of religious conservatives, disagree that men are better suited emotionally to politics than are women (McConkey 2001); and 81.2 percent of the liberals, but only 68.1 percent of the conservatives, disagree that it is more important for wives to help their husband's careers than to have careers themselves.

Sexism in religion is also seen in the fact that women generally do not hold the most honored positions—minister, priest, rabbi. An increasing number of groups do ordain women to the most honored position. Even so, women may attain less than men in terms of ecclesiastical position, may have a more difficult time finding a position, and are less likely to have a full-time job (Nesbitt 1997). Lay religious leaders are also likely to be men, even though women may be more numerous and more consistently involved in the activities of the group. In some fundamentalist groups, women are not even allowed to speak before a group or lead public worship.

Social Psychological Factors.   While American attitudes toward gender roles have become more *egalitarian,* some attitudes detrimental to women's continued progress still exist. In particular, some believe that there is no longer any discrimination, that women have opportunities equal to those of men, and that those who continue to complain are troublemakers or "radical feminists."

Such attitudes fly in the face of the realities of women's lives. We have already discussed the amount of sexual harassment with which women must deal. We have also noted the fact that discrimination in the workplace, in spite of the progress made, continues to depress the income of women. And women continue to face *negative attitudes in the workplace* with regard to their competence and commitment to the job.

Many women feel compelled to perform better than men in order to prove themselves and be accepted. For example, there is evidence that women must work harder to prove that they have the ability because men expect women—including women in supervisory and managerial positions—to be less competent than men and this bias enters into the evaluation of women (Biernat and Kobrynowicz 1997; Martell, Parker, and Emrich 1998; Heilman 2001).

As we noted earlier, many women also fear that they will be penalized in their careers if they become mothers. In fact, some employers do place women into two categories: achievers and mothers. A management expert has even proposed that the notion be formalized (Schwartz 1989) by allowing most working mothers to pursue a more moderate career path. Only those women who put aside family considerations would be allowed to pursue the fast lane to executive status. Critics called the moderated career line the "Mommy Track." Again the question arises, why should women be penalized for something that has always been allowed for men?

Ideology is also a factor in gender inequality. Many Americans still believe that a woman's place is in the home and that when she leaves the home to pursue higher education or a career, she leaves her post as one of the guardians of the social order. The ideology that *women's abdication of the home* can only result in *social disorganization* was expressed by those who insisted that women return to their homes after World War II.

Working mothers have children as happy and healthy as do stay-at-home mothers.

They identified working women as a primary cause of delinquency and argued that for women to continue in the labor force would mean instability in the social institutions of the nation. More recently, in the surveys of religious people noted earlier, 81.2 percent of religious liberals, but only 44.2 percent of conservatives, disagreed that everyone is better off if the man is the achiever outside the home and the woman cares for her home and family (McConkey 2001:162).

Many books and magazines also continue to extol the virtues of the stay-at-home mother and to warn mothers of the dangers of going to work while they have children in the home (Johnston and Swanson 2003). Some books portray employed mothers as tired, busy, and guilty, whereas other books laud the bliss of stay-at-home mothers. And although some Americans believe that women's magazines promote a feminist agenda, the image of women that comes from an examination of those magazines is a person who is focused on consumption, is beautiful, and is domestic.

Is it true, as an important part of the ideology asserts, that children are harmed when their mothers work? Many Americans agree with the idea that a mother with small children (and, in some cases, with any children) should remain at home. A review of research conducted throughout the 1990s, however, concluded that there was little relationship between maternal employment and child outcomes (Perry-Jenkins, Repetti, and Crouter 2000). In fact, maternal employment may be beneficial for the children of single mothers and lower-income families.

There are circumstances, however, that might foster negative consequences. For one thing, the effects *depend in part on how family members define the mother's working.* Agreement that it is a good thing for the mother to work minimizes any negative effects and can even have positive outcomes for the children in terms of their educational and career aspirations. Disagreement can create some serious problems.

The consequences of maternal employment also may vary by age of the child. Available research indicates no negative consequences for infants at least two years old. In some cases, day care may even be better than home care, because it offers the children various kinds of enrichment not available in their homes. For infants under the age of two, however, the research is contradictory and not always encouraging for those who prefer to work. In addition to the potential for inadequate care, there may be problems in the mother-child attachment (Meredith 1986). Some research suggests that babies cared for by others are less securely attached to their mothers. Such children may have to cope with problems of insecurity for years or even a lifetime. In addition, there is evidence of some detrimental effects on cognitive development for children whose mothers go to work during the first year of their lives (Baum 2003). Such children score lower on measures of cognitive development than do children whose mothers stayed at home.

In sum, the evidence is that children over the age of two will probably not be harmed by a mother working and may even be helped by it, as long as the family defines the work as appropriate activity and the children have adequate supervision and care. For infants two and under, more research is needed. But it is *a myth that there are inexorable, undesirable consequences for the children when the mother works.*

Public Policy and Private Action

fallacy

Like other social problems, gender inequality is so pervasive and so entrenched that pessimists may commit the *fallacy of retrospective determinism* and argue that the nation will never be rid of it. Whether a perfectly equitable society is achievable may be debatable, but it is clear that progress can be made.

What kind of action can address the problems of women? What kind of public policy is needed, and what other forms of private initiative in addition to consciousness-raising groups can help?

Clearly, the federal government needs to be involved. Federal antidiscriminatory laws have helped American women. But the Council on Contemporary Families (2003) compared American husbands and the American government to their counterparts in Germany, France, Italy, and Japan. The council concluded that American husbands do more housework and child care than do husbands in the other nations, but the U.S. government does the least of all the governments to help employed wives. In France, women workers have a government-mandated and protected benefit of a fully paid leave 6 weeks prior to and 10 weeks after the birth of a child. Both parents can also receive some additional paid leave until the child's third birthday. The United States needs more and better *child care centers* and more extensive *family leave laws* (laws that allow people time off from their jobs without penalty when a child is born, adopted, or seriously ill). The right to parental leave in the United States covers only about half of the private-sector workforce and is generally short and often unpaid. Some other nations offer universal, paid leaves of ten months or more.

The importance of such measures is underscored by the fact that more than 10 million women in the labor force have children under the age of six. The well-being of employed mothers is dependent on adequate child care (Ross and Mirowsky 1988). Employed mothers who have no problems in arranging for child care and whose husbands participate in child care have very low depression levels, whereas those who have difficulties and who have sole responsibility for child care tend to have very high levels of depression.

The children of satisfied mothers are better adjusted whether the mothers stay at home or work away from home. Women who prefer, or who feel the need, to work will not be satisfied to stay at home; but the option of working is closed to many women unless child care centers are available. Such centers are a part of the "bill of rights" of the National Organization for Women (NOW).

As more women become politically involved and are elected to public office, the government is more likely to enact measures that help women. As Swers (2002) has found, women legislators engage in more, and more intense, action in behalf of women's interests than do men. And this finding is true in both political parties.

Changes in education are crucial in order to alter notions of the "proper" roles of the sexes and to attack the ideology that restricts women's sphere of appropriate activity to the home. As presently structured, education affects women's attitudes more than men's and does more to help people recognize gender inequality than to support remedies for that inequality (Kane 1995). Education needs to be restructured to aid people's understanding about the capabilities of women. Educators need to treat males and females equally from kindergarten through graduate training; they need to teach people how to parent so that females are no longer socialized into a subordinate role; and they need to help people develop new norms about women's participation in all sectors of the economy.

The schools themselves should be models of equality. At present, they are not. From the differential treatment of boys and girls in elementary school to the differential treatment of young men and women in college athletic programs, inequality is the norm.

Still another form of action involves changing the policies and practices of organizations. A controversial proposal to eliminate income inequalities is the notion of *comparable worth* (Barko 2000). In essence, the idea is that women should receive equal pay not just for equal work but for work that is judged to be of comparable worth. The basis for such a proposal is the fact that women are overrepresented in such areas as nursing and clerical work, whereas men are overrepresented in such jobs as pilot and truck driver. The occupations in which women are overrepresented tend to pay less than those in which men are overrepresented, even though they may require similar amounts of training. The argument is that when jobs are of comparable worth, they should pay equal salaries. Otherwise gender inequality in income will continue indefinitely.

Why, for example, should beginning engineers (mostly men) earn 30 to 70 percent more than beginning teachers (mostly women) (Barko 2000)? Is a truck driver (probably a man) 45 percent more valuable than a child care worker (a college graduate and probably a woman)? Proponents of comparable worth raise such questions. They argue that experts can examine jobs in terms of their difficulty, responsibility, and education and experience requirements; rate the jobs accordingly; and equalize the pay for equivalent work.

Whatever their feelings on the issue, politicians are taking it seriously. Although there is no national policy, a number of states and corporations have implemented comparable worth programs.

Comparable worth provides women with a powerful weapon. In Santa Clara County, California, a service employees union won nearly $30 million for 4,500 county employees ranging from secretaries to mental health counselors (Barko 2000). A consulting firm studied 150 job titles and found that underpayment was common in those job categories with a high proportion of women. Using the comparable worth principle, the union negotiated successfully for equity raises.

There is still a need for action in the legal sphere, for organizational leaders may change only when they are required by law to change. Unfortunately, *affirmative action programs,* which have helped numerous women gain entry or advancement in various careers, are no longer legal. It is likely that some new form of legal protection and aid will be necessary to combat sex discrimination in the workplace.

Action has been taken to deal with sexual harassment on the job. Victims now have legal redress, and employers are held responsible for harassment that occurs in their places of work. Among other changes, employers have been encouraged to avoid legal problems by making policy statements to employees, setting up grievance procedures for alleged victims, and educating employees on appropriate behavior between the sexes. Such procedures are designed to correct one of the basic reasons for the continuation of harassment: people's ignorance of the problematic nature and consequences of harassment and of the recourse available to victims. Harassment also can be reduced if work organizations assume the responsibility for training all employees to be supportive of women's dignity and intolerant of harassment. Female workers who are surrounded by supportive coworkers and supervisors are less likely to be victimized by sexual harassment (De Coster, Estes, and Mueller 1999).

Legal change can be effective in reducing inequality. Congress passed a number of antidiscrimination laws that resulted in major changes on nearly every college and university campus in the nation (Sandler 1984). Among other changes, discrimination in official policies and practices and admissions quotas have been abolished. Accordingly, students are to be treated equally in terms of rules and services; married women, for instance, are no longer excluded from financial aid because they are married—and sexual harassment is explicitly forbidden. As we noted earlier, covert discrimination still occurs, and the problems of women on the campus are by no means fully resolved; but gains have been made as a result of legal change.

Finally, business and industry can take the important step of *ensuring women equal career opportunities*. In particular, the business world can reject the "Mommy Track" notion and allow women to be mothers without sacrificing a professional career. An example is the "family plan" implemented by Johnson and Johnson to help its employees cope with family responsibilities (Deutsch 1990). Included in the plan are a nationwide resource and referral system for child care and elder care; a year's family care leave, with full benefits for an employee who has to care for a child, a spouse, or a parent; training of supervisors to make them aware of the needs and problems involved in balancing work and family demands; and benefits that pay some of the costs of adopting a child. Some companies offer reduced work hours or other kinds of help for employees with family responsibilities. But such programs are available to only a small minority of women employees.

Follow-Up.   Set up a class debate on this topic: Comparable worth offers the most promising solution for ending gender inequality in the United States.

Homosexuality and Homophobia

heterosexual
having sexual preference for persons of the opposite sex

homosexual
having sexual preference for persons of the same sex; someone who privately or overtly considers himself or herself a homosexual

homophobia
irrational fear of homosexuals

In American society, fulfilling sexual love is often conceived as **heterosexual**—male-female relationships. Yet people gain sexual satisfaction in a variety of ways. In this section we discuss **homosexuals,** those who have a sexual preference for individuals of the same sex. We examine the problems they encounter because of **homophobia,** an irrational fear of homosexuals, and we look at the factors that perpetuate the problems.

Homosexuality: Definitions and Numbers

Not everyone who engages in a homosexual act can be considered a homosexual. Boys commonly engage in homosexual activity during adolescence, but most of them become exclusively heterosexual. We define a homosexual as an individual both who has

Many homosexuals lead well-adjusted lives even when faced with negative social reaction.

a sexual preference for those of the same sex and who also defines himself or herself as homosexual.

Some people are **bisexual,** finding gratification with both sexes and having no strong preference for either, but bisexuals are not as common as those who are exclusively heterosexual or homosexual. The terms *homosexual* and *gay* refer to both males and females. In addition, **lesbian** is used for homosexual females, and *gay men* (or *gay males*) is used for homosexual males. Most studies in the past focused on gay males rather than lesbians.

bisexual
having sexual relations with either sex or both together

lesbian
a female homosexual

Homosexuality is found throughout the world. Research into various societies finds homosexuals in all of them and in roughly the same proportion of the population (Whitam 1983). Moreover, that proportion tends to remain relatively stable over time in each society.

What is the proportion? How many homosexuals are there in America? One of the most comprehensive and most recent studies of sexual behavior was the National Health and Social Life Survey, conducted by researchers at the University of Chicago (Laumann et al. 1994). Using a sample of 3,432 American men and women between the ages of 18 and 59, the researchers found that 2.7 percent of sexually active men and 1.3 percent of sexually active women had a homosexual experience in the past year. Further, they reported that 9.1 percent of men and 4.3 percent of women have had a homosexual experience since puberty, and 7.7 percent of men and 7.4 percent of women said they felt some degree of same-sex *attraction* or interest.

These figures are consistent with those reported by researchers in other nations. For example, researchers reported that 4.5 and 8.5 percent of males, and 2.1 and 3.3 percent of females, in the United Kingdom and France, respectively, have had a homosexual experience in the previous 5 years (Sell, Wells, and Wypij 1995). The figures for homosexual attraction (as opposed to homosexual behavior) were 7.9 and 10.7 percent for males and 8.6 and 11.7 percent for females in the two nations.

It seems safe to conclude that about 3 to 4 percent of American men and 2 to 3 percent of American women prefer to be exclusively homosexual. The proportions are not high, but in absolute terms we are talking about nine million people or more.

Why Are Some People Homosexual?

Enormous pressures exist in American society for people to be heterosexual. Few of you have grown up without hearing the word "homosexual" or another slang term applied to someone in a disparaging way. Moreover, books, television, and observation all reinforce the expectation of heterosexual relations. Why, then, do some people prefer homosexual relations?

Biological Explanations.   A number of observers believe that *homosexuality is genetically programmed into some people.* Both physiological and behavioral evidence support this position, although the evidence so far is sparse and controversial. Physiological evidence is provided by the work of Simon LeVay (1991), who found that an area of the hypothalamus in the homosexual men was more similar to the same region in women than in heterosexual men. Other researchers have found additional differences between homosexuals and heterosexuals, including aspects of brain structure and genetic differences in a region on the X chromosome (Swaab and Hofman 1990; Pool 1993; Harrison, Everall, and Catalan 1994; McCormick and Witelson 1994; Mustanski, Chivers, and Bailey 2002).

The possibility that homosexuality is biological rather than sociocultural is also supported by some behavioral studies. Bell, Weinberg, and Hammersmith (1981) reported finding none of the usual sociocultural factors in their study of 979 homosexuals. Rather, the single most important factor they identified is gender nonconformity at an early age. That is, gay men and lesbians both recall having different preferences and behaviors than most of their peers, suggesting the possibility that they were different from birth. The difference is confirmed in research with parents of gay men, who also recall much atypical gender behavior in their sons, including a lack of interest in sports (Aveline 2006).

Another study, by a psychiatrist (Green 1987), supports the conclusions of Bell, Weinberg, and Hammersmith. Green studied two groups of boys over a 15-year period. One group was composed of boys who had feminine or cross-gender characteristics, and the other group consisted of boys who behaved in a more conventional male fashion. Green administered various tests to the boys and interviewed both them and their parents. Three-fourths of the 44 gender nonconformists grew up to be either homosexual or bisexual, compared to only one of the masculine boys.

Subsequent studies lend further support (Landolt et al. 2004). Studies of lesbians report that, as children, they preferred masculine roles and "boy's games" (Cooper 1990; Palzkill and Fisher 1990; Whitam and Mathy 1991). A study comparing recalled childhood experiences of three groups of men—a heterosexual group, a bisexual group, and a homosexual group—found that the homosexuals had diverse experiences, but more than a third reported few or no gender-conforming behaviors (Phillips and Over 1992).

Additional evidence emerges in studies of twins (Dawood et al. 2000). In a study of male twins in which at least one brother was gay, two researchers found that in 52 percent of 56 sets of identical twins, both brothers were gay, compared to 22 percent of 54 sets of fraternal twins (Bailey and Pillard 1991). They also looked at 57 families in which a gay son had an adoptive brother and found that only 11 percent of the adoptive brothers were also gay.

Similarly, a study of female twins in which at least one of the sisters was a lesbian reported that 48 percent of identical twins are also lesbian, compared to 16 percent of nonidentical twins (Bailey and Benishay 1993). The researchers also included a sample of women who had grown up with adoptive sisters; only 6 percent of the adoptive sisters turned out to be lesbian.

The point is that the chances that both siblings will turn out to be homosexual increases dramatically according to the amount of genes they share. At the same time, as the researchers acknowledge, the fact that not all the identical twins were homosexual suggests that sociocultural factors play a role. Let's look at some of those factors.

Sociocultural Explanations. Some social scientists argue that homosexuality is a *learned pattern of behavior* rather than the natural outgrowth of an innate drive (Minton and McDonald 1984). Because there are strong pressures toward heterosexuality, these social scientists look for factors in family life or in patterns of interaction that differ for homosexuals and heterosexuals.

Some researchers have found that homosexuals have *disturbed relationships with their parents.* Harry (1989) reported that gays were more likely to suffer abuse by their parents, though the abuse may have been a result rather than a cause of the son's sexual preference. Others have found that homosexuals were more likely than heterosexuals to have been the victims of incest (Cameron and Cameron 1995). Note, however, that only a minority of the homosexuals indicated an incestuous experience. Studies of lesbians also report family problems, including physical and sexual abuse (Sang, Warshow, and Smith 1991; Bradford, Ryan, and Rothblum 1994).

The issue of problematic family experiences remains clouded. Most studies rely on the recollections of adults. Earlier ones, conducted from the 1950s through the 1970s, tended to find deficiencies in the family life of homosexuals, whereas subsequent

Gay activists parade to protest the negative societal reaction they must often endure.

studies tend to find no differences between homosexual and heterosexual backgrounds. Thus, we cannot say with certainty whether family experiences contribute to the development of homosexuality.

One family factor that is intriguing but has not so far been convincingly explained either biologically or socioculturally is birth order in a family with two or more sons. There is a correlation between sexual orientation and the number of older brothers (Cantor et al. 2002). Each older brother that a man has raises his odds of being homosexual by about 33 percent. This fraternal birth order effect accounts for the sexual orientation of about one of every seven gay men.

A sociocultural factor that may be important, however, is the *norms of one's peers during adolescence.* Some young males engage in homosexual activities with adults to earn money. It may be a purely financial transaction for the boys that is approved by group norms. The same norms, on the other hand, define the adult homosexuals as "queers." The boys do not regard themselves as homosexuals and do not continue homosexual activity when they become adults.

By contrast, if an adolescent participates in a *homosexual clique,* homosexuality may be defined as preferable, and the individual may accept a homosexual identity as he or she internalizes the norms of the group. Some, perhaps a majority, of young male prostitutes engage in sex with adults not merely for money, but because their own orientation is homosexual (Earls and David 1989).

What can you conclude from all this information? The overall evidence suggests that *there are both genetic and sociocultural factors involved in the development of homosexuality.* The genetic component is strong, but if homosexuality were purely genetic in origin, then all sets of identical twins would be homosexual and all brains of homosexuals would differ from those of heterosexuals. If homosexuality were purely sociocultural in origin, on the other hand, then differences in gender orientation would not be observable from an early age, and the findings of the twin studies could not be explained. However, we do not yet know the precise way in which genetic and sociocultural factors combine to lead to a homosexual identity.

Homosexuality and the Quality of Life

Homosexuality is a pattern of behavior involving social contradictions that both homosexuals and heterosexuals define as incompatible with the desired quality of life. Homosexuals point to two contradictions in particular. One is that the *American ideology of equality contradicts American attitudes and behavior toward homosexuals.* The other is that the stereotyped homosexual role (see the discussion of myths in the following section) contradicts the actual homosexual role. People who condemn homosexuals are frequently condemning the stereotyped rather than the actual role.

In other words, homosexuals argue that their behavior is a problem detracting from quality of life not because something is intrinsically wrong or damaging about it, but because of the *societal reaction.* In the following paragraphs we look at some ways in which the quality of life is diminished for homosexuals because of such aspects as restricted opportunities, ridicule, being labeled sick or perverted, and stress.

Myths about Homosexuality.   A contradiction exists between the ideal of the *dignity of human beings and the prevalent ideology about homosexuals.* This contradiction is manifested in a *number of myths about homosexuality,* myths that involve the *fallacies of personal attack and appeal to prejudice.* Perhaps the most common myth is that homosexuals have characteristics that are normal for the opposite sex—males are "effeminate" and females are "masculine." Actually, as Bell, Weinberg, and Ham-

fallacy

mersmith (1981) reported in their large-scale study, such traits characterize only a minority of homosexuals.

A second myth about homosexuals is that they fear, and are incapable of, having heterosexual relationships. Homosexuality is commonly attributed to unsatisfactory heterosexual experiences that cause fear of relationships with the opposite sex.

Although experiences with people of the opposite sex may be a factor in the development of homosexuality, there does not seem to be any evidence that homosexuals are incapable of relating to the opposite sex. By definition, a homosexual prefers sexual relations with those of his or her own sex exclusively. However, homosexuals do make and maintain good relationships with people of the opposite sex. Research by the Institute for Sex Research, founded by Kinsey, showed that about one-fifth of homosexuals in the sample had been married at one time and about half of them had intercourse from two to four times a week during the first year of marriage (Bell and Weinberg 1978). Bell, Weinberg, and Hammersmith (1981) reported that the lesbians in their sample had early histories of heterosexual experiences that were virtually identical to those of straight women.

A third myth is that people typically become homosexual by being seduced by a homosexual. No evidence supports this myth.

Still another myth is that a homosexual is attracted to, and will make advances to, anyone of his or her own sex, children as well as adults. The homosexual, however, is as selective as a straight person and is unlikely to be a pedophile. A study of erotic age preference reported that gay males who prefer mature partners respond no more to male children than do heterosexual males, who also prefer mature partners to children (Freund, Watson, and Rienzo 1989).

Finally, there is the myth that homosexuals do not form the same kinds of long-term attachments as heterosexuals. When homosexuality was even more of a stigma than it is today, it would have been difficult to maintain such a relationship without rousing suspicions. By the 1980s, however, researchers were reporting long-term, high-quality relationships (Silverstein 1981; McWhirter and Mattison 1984). In fact, long-term homosexual relationships are indistinguishable from their heterosexual counterparts in most respects (Gottman et al. 2003). They want the same kinds of things in a relationship—being able to talk about feelings, being able to laugh together, giving and receiving support, and so on (Peplau 1981). In other words, *homosexual couples have the same hopes, the same needs, the same desires, and, indeed, the same problems as heterosexual couples* (Patterson 2000). The problems include instances of verbal and physical abuse (Lockhart et al. 1994).

Homosexuals may want, like heterosexuals, to be parents and may find great satisfaction in parenting. Of 47 lesbian couples studied by Koepke, Hare, and Moran (1992), 40 percent had children and were more satisfied with their relationship and their sexual relations than were the childless couples. Gay men who are fathers are similar to heterosexual fathers in both parenting style and attitudes (Bigner and Jacobsen 1992).

Independent of desire and satisfaction is the question of the *well-being of children raised in a homosexual family*. Researchers who compared children, ages three to nine, raised in 15 lesbian families with those raised in 15 heterosexual families found no differences in cognitive functioning or behavioral adjustment (Flaks et al. 1995). The lesbian couples, however, appeared to have more parenting awareness skills than did the heterosexual couples. In sum, research indicates that the overall well-being of children raised in a homosexual family is as high as that of children raised in heterosexual families (Patterson 2000; Wainwright and Patterson 2006).

sodomy
intercourse defined as "unnatural"; particularly used to refer to anal intercourse

Equality of Opportunity.   The American ideology of *equality of opportunity contradicts the norms and laws about the hiring of homosexuals.* The homosexual is a criminal wherever there are **sodomy** laws. Legally, the term "sodomy" is ambiguous. Depending on the state, it may refer to anal intercourse, mouth-genital sex, or sex with animals. Sodomy laws were established to prevent what people considered to be "unnatural" kinds of sexual behavior. In practice, however, the laws have been used mainly to prosecute homosexuals. Even where the statutes prohibit oral sex, they are used to prosecute homosexuals, not heterosexuals. The laws have not always been enforced, and some have been successfully challenged in the courts. But homosexuals and lesbians have had to contend with a number of legal barriers to equal opportunity within both the government and the business sectors.

The lack of equal opportunity is not based on any lack of ability or inferior performance by homosexuals. In fact, homosexuals may *suffer discrimination in spite of proven adequate or even superior performance.* They may experience harassment, stalled careers, and even termination if their sexual orientation is known. In 2001, 1,250 gays were dismissed from the military for no other reason than their sexual orientation (Zuckerbrod 2002).

sanctions
mechanisms of social control for enforcing a society's standards

Negative Sanctions.   **Sanctions** are rewards (positive sanctions) or punishments (negative sanctions) designed to influence behavior. Homosexuals are subjected to *numerous negative sanctions,* including ridicule, suppression, physical abuse, and ostracism. Negative sanctions contradict the American ideology that every citizen has a right to life, liberty, and the pursuit of happiness. All the sanctions, of course, are aimed at changing the homosexual into a heterosexual.

The sanctions can come from parents or caretakers, other family members, friends, acquaintances, or strangers (Balsam, Rothblum, and Beauchaine 2005). And few escape the sanctions. One study of 528 gay, lesbian, and bisexual youth found that because of their sexual orientation nearly 80 percent had been verbally abused, 11 percent had been physically abused, and 9 percent had been sexually victimized (D'Augelli, Grossman, and Starks 2006).

The verbal abuse includes such things as being *labeled perverts* or *called mentally ill.* Some young gays who live on the streets and survive by engaging in homosexual prostitution were forced out of their homes because of their sexual orientation (Kruks 1991). The physical abuse may be sufficiently severe to result in injuries or even death (D'Augelli and Grossman 2001).

Fear.   It is little wonder that *homosexuals live with a certain amount of fear,* including the fear of making their sexual identity known to physicians because of possible negative reactions (Lehmann, Lehmann, and Kelly 1998). One of the freedoms cherished by Americans is the freedom from fear. For the homosexual, this ideal is contradicted by the norms and laws that apply to gay people as well as by the experience of being abused.

In other words, the homosexual is subject to fear of exposure if he or she decides to remain secretive and to fear of negative sanctions if he or she decides to come out. Not every homosexual goes around constantly haunted by fear. Nevertheless, all homosexuals must come to terms with realistic fears. These fears are realistic because all homosexuals are familiar with stories of harassment and attacks. For example, imagine what it must be like to be a homosexual and read in a national magazine of a gay man who, because he led a campaign against an antigay resolution passed by the local government in the area where he and his partner lived, received anonymous telephone calls that threatened to "slit your throat and watch your faggot blood run in the street"

(Henry 1994:57). Gays know that such incidents are neither rare nor confined to isolated areas of the nation.

Psychological and Emotional Problems. You might expect that it is difficult for homosexuals to avoid psychological and emotional problems as they wrestle with the contradictions that impinge upon their lives. In fact, a number of studies have identified problems that result from the *stress generated by the societal reaction to an individual's homosexuality* (Radkowsky and Siegel 1997; Hershberger, Pilkington, and D'Augelli 1997). In brief, homosexuals have higher rates than heterosexuals of isolation, depression, low self-esteem, attempted suicide, and alcohol abuse (Grossman and Kerner 1998; Cochran and Mays 2000; Diaz et al. 2001; Mills et al. 2004).

For example, among a sample of middle-aged lesbians, 73 percent had sought counseling for emotional problems and 16 percent had tried to commit suicide (Sang, Warshow, and Smith 1991). In the National Lesbian Health Care Survey, over half the sample acknowledged having had thoughts about suicide at some time and 18 percent had attempted suicide (Bradford, Ryan, and Rothblum 1994). About three-fourths had been in counseling, and half of those had sought counseling for sadness and depression. On the other hand, there are no significant differences between homosexuals and heterosexuals in the incidence of neurotic disorders, and homosexuals generally function adequately in society (Latorre and Wendenburg 1983; Strickland 1995).

What do all these findings mean? First, there is no basis for claiming that a homosexual orientation is associated with clinical symptoms of mental illness. As the American Psychiatric Association has underscored by removing homosexuality from its list of mental disorders, the notion that gays are inherently disturbed individuals who need therapy in order to change their sexual preference is no longer tenable. Second, the stress induced by societal reaction to the individual's homosexuality creates emotional and psychological problems (Meyer 2003). Third, many homosexuals come to terms with the societal reaction, cope with the problems, and lead well-adjusted and productive lives.

Contributing Factors

Without the societal reaction to homosexuality among Americans, we could not speak of homosexual behavior as a social problem. In this section we look at some of the multiple-level factors that account for this societal reaction and that create stress for homosexuals.

Social Structure Factors. In the United States, *normative sexual behavior* is heterosexual. The norms of society define homosexuality as deviant, but such norms do not reflect universal standards or innate biological imperatives. In fact, even when heterosexual relations are dominant, a society may not disapprove of or *punish homosexuality*. In her study of a variety of primitive societies, Brown (1952) found that 14 of 44 of the societies for which data were available did not punish male homosexuality, and 8 of 12 did not punish female homosexuality.

Many modern societies refrain from formally punishing homosexual acts that are conducted in private between consenting adults. These acts, for example, are not considered a crime in Japan, Korea, Mexico, Argentina, Uruguay, Egypt, and the Sudan.

In the United States, the norms that define homosexuality as deviant are supported by various social institutions. For instance, the norms are incorporated into the legal system. Many states still have antisodomy laws that are used to justify the suppression of homosexuality. In the late 1990s, a number of states passed laws banning homosexual marriages.

The United States is the only large Western nation that allows the punishment of adults who privately engage in consensual homosexual acts. This attitude reflects the English heritage of America, particularly the views of the Puritans, who saw homosexuality as one symptom of the moral corruption of England in the 17th century (Mitchell 1969). Changes have since occurred in England. In 1967 the House of Commons reformed the laws on homosexuality and removed private, consensual homosexual acts between adults from the criminal statutes. The United States not only allows communities to retain homosexuality as a criminal act, but allows police to actively harass and apprehend homosexuals as well.

The changes in England were facilitated by the support of prominent Anglican and Catholic clergymen. In the United States, many religious leaders, particularly fundamentalist Christians, stress that homosexuality is a "vice" condemned by various biblical teachings. In general, although most religious people are becoming more tolerant, the more conservative people are in their faith, the more negative their views on homosexuality (Barna Research Online 2001).

Gay Christians and Jews have formed a number of organizations, including Evangelicals Concerned, and Dignity (Roman Catholic), in an effort to win acceptance for themselves (Tivnan 1987). Some religious leaders have spoken out in support of homosexuals; by and large, however, religious groups continue to view homosexuality in negative terms.

The result is that trying to attend church or a synagogue can be a stressful experience for a homosexual. It may only intensify a sense of guilt. At the least, it underscores the fact that official religion is likely to be as much a problem as a comfort.

Social Psychological Factors. The homosexual's stressful environment is maintained by social psychological factors that support and reinforce norms and institutional arrangements. In the first place, a substantial number of Americans hold negative attitudes toward homosexuality (figure 7.3). Attitudes have become much more tolerant since 1990 (Loftus 2001). As figure 7.3 shows, the great majority no longer believe in discriminating against homosexuals in employment. Yet, millions still vigorously oppose homosexual rights in various areas, including marriage and child rearing. For example, national polls in 2004 found the following (Bowman 2004):

- 49 percent say that homosexual relations between consenting adults should not be legal.
- 44 percent would not permit their child to read a book with a story about a same-sex couple.
- 61 percent say that homosexual marriages should not be legal.
- 42 percent oppose civil unions for homosexuals that would give them some of the same legal rights as married couples.
- 47 percent believe that gay spouses should not have the right to adopt children.

Such negative attitudes are clearly based on the presumption that something about homosexuality is "wrong."

In general, negative attitudes are stronger among older age groups, the less educated, men, political conservatives, and fundamentalist Protestants (Whitley and Kite 1995; Wood and Bartkowski 2004). But a considerable amount of homophobia is also found among elementary school children, college students, and highly educated popu-

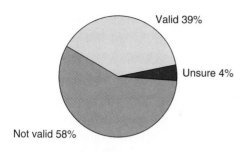

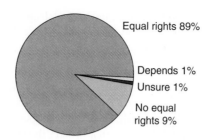

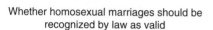

Whether homosexual marriages should be recognized by law as valid

Whether homosexuals should have equal rights in employment

FIGURE 7.3
Attitudes about Homosexuality.
Source: Polling Report 2007.

lations such as medical students and practicing physicians (Baker and Fishbein 1998; Klamen, Grossman, and Kopacz 1999; Horvath and Ryan 2003).

Has the fear of AIDS affected attitudes toward gays? According to polls, most Americans say no. Still, a great many feel that homosexuals should be barred from being food handlers, doctors, or day care nurses, or should be tested for AIDS before taking those jobs. The strong feelings of those with negative attitudes because of AIDS may affect others. A student reported his own experience in disquieting words:

> With the growing fear of AIDS, people are talking more about heterosexuality. And the people I talk to talk about gays as if they are animals. "Kill them all" or a variation of that attitude seems to prevail. It scares me. Not because I'm gay, but because it reminds me of Nazi Germany. Hate is a disease. It spreads.

The negative societal reaction to homosexuality is also legitimated by the ideology that homosexuals are "sick." For the professional, this attitude means that people who prefer homosexual relations suffer from an emotional disorder and need to be treated in the same way as any other emotionally disturbed individual. We heard a therapist analyze homosexuals as people who can never be happy because heterosexual relations are basic to human development and well-being. This view implies that *those who prefer homosexual relations should be identified, treated, and cured.*

Many nonprofessionals view homosexuals as not only sick but also perverse *(the fallacy of personal attack)*. Just as many Americans believe that alcoholics could stop drinking "if they only wanted to," they also believe that homosexuals could change their sexual behavior "if they only wanted to." In other words, many Americans view homosexuality as a personal problem, not a social one. They believe that the norms, institutional arrangements, attitudes, values, and ideology that work together to condemn and oppress homosexuals are legitimate.

fallacy

Public Policy and Private Action

An important way to deal with the oppression and discrimination experienced by homosexuals is to *change the legal status of homosexuals.* In the early 1980s, the gay rights movement began to focus more on national politics and gave priority to three issues (Schneider and Lewis 1984):

> extend the Civil Rights Act to prohibit discrimination based on sexual preference of individuals; end all federal policies that restrict free movement (such as immigration)

and mobility (in terms of job opportunities) for gays; and increase federal investment in research on AIDS, the disease that has sent shock waves of terror through the gay community. . . .

In short, homosexuals are seeking to acquire the status of a recognized and protected minority group in American politics (Schneider and Lewis 1984:16).

As a result of these efforts, considerable progress has been made. A number of states have decriminalized sexual acts between consenting adults, and dozens of cities have passed ordinances that protect the rights of homosexuals in housing and employment. In 1989, San Francisco became the first city in the nation to officially recognize homosexual couples. In 2000, Vermont became the first state in the nation to recognize homosexual unions as "civil unions" and grant them all the state benefits of those couples who are married. An even more significant gain occurred when Massachusetts became the first state to make same-sex marriages legal in 2004. And in 2006, the New Jersey state Supreme Court ruled that same-sex couples have the same constitutional rights to marriage as heterosexual couples.

However, in the face of such gains a number of states enacted constitutional amendments that limit marriage to one man and one woman. And some conservative religious groups led campaigns to boycott businesses that attempted to treat homosexuals and heterosexuals equally in terms of such things as health benefits for employees' families.

Interestingly, an analysis of the efforts to shape public policy between 1974 and 1999 found that opponents of gay rights were more likely to be successful by mobilizing popular support and using ballot initiatives (Werum and Winders 2001). In contrast, proponents were more likely to be successful by working through government channels such as legislatures and the courts.

There is a need for further research and for educational programs for people to understand both the nature of homosexuality and the perspective of homosexuals. There are college seminars on homosexuality as well as gay and lesbian programs. Articles in the print media and television and movie programs are powerful tools for combating antigay attitudes. Such educational efforts help people recognize that prejudice and discrimination achieve nothing but trauma. They also help young homosexuals to receive the social support from friends and family that will enable them to deal with the challenges and stresses in their lives (Anderson 1998). The importance of educational efforts is also seen in the impact that the lesbian and gay rights movement had on American attitudes during the 1990s (Loftus 2001). A growing proportion of Americans agree that homosexuality is an acceptable lifestyle and that homosexuals should have equal opportunities.

Follow-Up. Investigate whether your school has any classes or seminars on homosexuality. Ask the instructors about the content of the classes, the assigned reading materials, and how effective the courses are in developing understanding of and tolerance for homosexual lifestyles.

Summary

Because they have suffered some of the same problems as minorities, women have been called America's "largest minority." In fact, they compose a slight majority of the population. Until recently, much of professional and popular opinion viewed the disadvantages of women as rooted in biology rather than in society. But the bulk of evidence points to sociocultural rather than biological factors for most differences between men and women.

Gender inequality means that women do not have the same opportunities for work and career as do men. Women's income is also less than men's. And women are victimized by the beauty myth and by harassment and violence.

The normative role of the female in American society is an important structural factor perpetuating women's problems. That role is reinforced by socialization at home, at school, and through the mass media. Some religious groups also help maintain women's subordination.

Among social psychological factors in gender inequality are attitudes, such as the belief that women now have equal opportunities with men, and the ideology that asserts that wives and mothers who work outside the home pose a threat to their own families and to the well-being of the entire society.

Homosexuality, the sexual orientation of 2 to 3 percent of American women and 3 to 4 percent of American men, is also associated with inequality. Both biological and social factors are involved in sexual orientation. But some Americans view homosexuality as nothing more than a perverse choice.

The quality of life for homosexuals is diminished by such things as the myths that detract from their human dignity, negative sanctions, fear, and problems resulting from societal rejection and oppression. Social structural factors that tend to perpetuate the problem include societal norms and the legal and religious policies and practices that support those norms. Social psychological factors include a number of attitudes and the ideology that homosexuals are either sick or perverse.

Key Terms

Bisexual
Gender
Gender Role
Heterosexual
Homophobia
Homosexual
Innate
Lesbian
Sanctions
Sex
Sexism
Sexual Harassment
Sodomy

Study Questions

1. What is the evidence for both biological and social factors as the basis for sex differences?
2. To what extent do women have equal economic opportunities with men?
3. How does the "beauty myth" affect the lives of women?
4. How does socialization affect the role of women?
5. Discuss the stance of religion on women's role in society.
6. What are the attitudes and ideologies that tend to perpetuate gender inequality?
7. What steps can be taken to reduce gender inequality?
8. What is meant by homosexuality and homophobia?
9. What is the evidence for biological and sociocultural factors in someone becoming homosexual?
10. What kind of negative sanctions do homosexuals face?
11. What attitudes and ideologies help you understand the problems homosexuals face?

Internet Resources/ Exercises

1. Explore some of the ideas in this chapter on the following sites:

http://www2.asanet.org/sectionsexgend/ The Sex and Gender section of the American Sociological Association, with links to numerous other useful sites.

http://www.gendercenter.org/ The Gender Issues Research Center offers book reviews, public opinion poll results, statistics, and other information.

http://www.glaad.org/ Defends gays and lesbians against defamation; offers publications and other resources as well as ongoing reporting of news about homosexuals from media around the nation.

chapter 7 review

2. Use a search engine to explore "gender equality." Find materials on the problem of equality and inequality between men and women in other nations. How would you compare the United States with those other nations? In what kinds of nations do women seem to have the most equality? the most inequality?

3. Explore the Internet for sites that condemn homosexuality and those that assert that sexual orientation can be changed. How would you respond to these sites using the materials in your text

For Further Reading

Bordo, Susan. *Unbearable Weight: Feminism, Western Culture, and the Body.* Berkeley, CA: University of California Press, 1993. An examination of eating disorders and other aspects of women's care of their bodies in terms of a disorder in American culture. The net result for women, Bordo argues, is an undermining of their ability to achieve their full potential.

Dinnerstein, Myra. *Women between Two Worlds: Midlife Reflections on Work and Family.* Philadelphia: Temple University Press, 1992. An in-depth examination of 22 middle-class women who began their adult lives as mothers but eventually pursued professional careers. Shows the conflicts and adjustments they were required to make.

Flexner, Eleanor. *Century of Struggle: The Woman's Rights Movement in the United States.* New York: Atheneum, 1972. An excellent and thorough history of the struggle of American women—both white and black—from colonial times to 1920.

hooks, bell. *Feminism Is for Everybody: Passionate Politics.* Cambridge, MA: South End Press, 2000. An examination of a range of issues facing women, including the meaning of feminist politics, consciousness raising, education, abortion rights, work, and the beauty myth.

Stiers, Gretchen A. *From This Day Forward: Commitment, Marriage, and Family in Lesbian and Gay Relationships.* New York: St. Martin's Press, 2000. Interviews with 90 gay men and lesbians, who offer their perspectives on making a commitment, getting married, and having a family in a homosexual relationship.

Wharton, Amy S. *The Sociology of Gender.* New York: Blackwell, 2004. An overview of gender issues, including theory and research on gender at the individual, interactional, and institutional levels.

Williams, Joan. *Unbending Gender: Why Family and Work Conflict and What to Do about It.* New York: Oxford University Press, 2000. A discussion of the contradictions between the economy and family life, and policy suggestions for resolving the problems. Williams advocates what she calls "reconstructive feminism."

Race, Ethnic Groups, and Racism

OBJECTIVES

1. Discuss the meanings of the terms *race, ethnic group,* and *racism.*

2. Understand the extent and origin of the problems of minorities.

3. Identify the ways in which the problems of minorities

negatively affect the quality of life for them.

4. Know the social structural and social psychological factors that contribute to the problems of minorities.

5. Show some ways to address the problems of minorities.

Will It Ever End?

Daryl is in his 50s, black, and a college administrator. He was a teenager when the civil rights movement began to have a strong impact. Daryl has lived in two different worlds, because he spent his early years in the segregated South; but, as he recounts, there are some disturbing continuities:

I can remember going into a department store and finding the drinking fountain that said "colored only" on it. We couldn't drink out of the same fountains or go into the same bathrooms as the whites. I've achieved a place in society that neither my grandfather nor my father could have ever dreamed of being.

But it hasn't been easy. I guess I could forget those segregated water fountains if white people didn't keep reminding me that I'm different. I served in the army for a time in Germany. I married a white, German woman. We came back to this country so I could pursue a graduate degree. We took a trip down South in 1969 so I could show my wife where I grew up. We drove around my old neighborhood, then went into a restaurant in the suburbs. It was the last time we tried that. I had come back here to pursue my graduate degree, not to get into conflict with a lot of hostile people. They couldn't tolerate an interracial couple. Their glares made us both extremely uncomfortable during dinner. We wound up eating hurriedly and getting out.

I've had a lot of other incidents to contend with, sometimes with my wife and sometimes just on my own. You'd think it would be over by now, wouldn't you? But recently I attended a conference of black college administrators in a resort area. There was a convention of doctors there at the same time. One morning I came down into the lobby to meet a friend and saw one of our female administrators in a heated argument with a doctor. I stepped in and broke it up. It turned out that she was just standing at the desk when he came up and started making remarks to her about how hostile and arrogant blacks are. He said blacks keep causing trouble because we cry about discrimination when we have just as many opportunities as anyone else.

Instead of going out for a pleasant morning with an old friend, I wound up calling a meeting of our officers and trying to decide what to do about the incident. I don't think white people realize what it's like to be vulnerable to those kinds of things just because of the color of your skin. And I really wonder sometimes if it will ever end.

Introduction

Are people with white skin biologically inferior? Are they inherently less capable, less deserving, or less willing to work to get ahead than others? These questions may sound absurd to some of you, but millions of Americans who are minorities confront such questions about themselves. Throughout American history, minorities have been treated as if they were somehow inferior human beings; but racial inequalities are rooted in sociocultural rather than biological factors. We are all one species—human.

Before discussing the race problem (which is a shorthand phrase for the problem of relationships between people of diverse racial and ethnic backgrounds), we explore the meaning of race. Then we look at the origin and distribution of America's minorities, what the "race problem" means for them, what factors contribute to the problem, and how the problem can be attacked.

The Meaning of Race, Ethnic Groups, and Racism

race
a group of people distinguished from other groups by their origin in a particular part of the world

biological characteristic
an inherited, rather than learned, characteristic

We define **race,** in accord with the U.S. Census Bureau, as a group of people who are distinguished from other groups by their origin in a particular part of the world (Grieco and Cassidy 2001). As such, they tend to share a particular *skin color* (blacks originated in Africa, whites in Europe, the Middle East, or North Africa, etc.). Many people use the single **biological characteristic** of skin color to identify races, but there are so many shades of skin color that classifying someone as a member of one or another race solely on skin color is arbitrary.

In addition, if race were a purely biological phenomenon, a number of other biological characteristics could be used: blood type, the presence or absence of the Rh factor in the blood, or the ability to taste the chemical phenylthiocarbamide. In each case the groups would be composed of different people. For instance, people who can taste the chemical (as opposed to those who cannot taste it) include large numbers of Europeans, Americans, American Indians, and Chinese. The point is that any biological basis for distinguishing among people is arbitrary and results in different groupings, which is why geneticists view race as more of a sociological than a biological phenomenon (Lewis 2002).

All human beings belong to one biological species—*Homo sapiens.* The breakdown of that species into subcategories is arbitrary. A frequently used system of classification, devised by Coon, Garn, and Birdsell (1950), used geographical distributions, **morphological** characteristics, and population size to identify six major "stocks" comprising 30 races. The six stocks are Mongoloid, White, Negroid, Australoid, American Indian, and Polynesian. Each represents a group of races that share certain characteristics. For example, the Mongoloid category includes all races that have adapted to very severe winters and the Negroid category includes all races that have achieved special adaptation to extreme light and heat.

Although this scheme is more elaborate than some others, it is also arbitrary. As Jefferson Fish (1995:55) sums it up: "The short answer to the question 'What is race?' is: There is no such thing. Race is a myth. And our racial classification scheme is loaded with pure fantasy." Nevertheless, people continue to identify different races primarily on the basis of skin color, and the inequalities people experience follow directly from that identification. We follow the categories of the U.S. Bureau of the Census, which uses people's self-identification to place them into one of the following: white or non-Hispanic white, black, Asian/Pacific Islander, American Indian/Eskimo/Aleut, other, and two or more races. In addition, the Census Bureau collects data on one ethnic group—Hispanic origin, which includes people of any race.

The term **ethnic group** refers to people who have a shared historical or cultural background that leads them to identify with each other. Although the Census Bureau routinely gathers data only for Hispanics, numerous ethnic groups have been involved in the growth of the nation. Many, such as the Irish and the Polish, have faced problems of acceptance. At present, Hispanics are the largest ethnic group struggling with integration into American society.

Keep in mind that *all people have more shared than different characteristics, and no group is biologically superior to another.* Nevertheless, **racism,** the belief that some racial groups are inherently inferior to others, has been common and is used to *justify discrimination and inequality.* Essed (1991) has identified three forms of "everyday" racism: *marginalization* is making people of other races feel excluded and unimportant; *problematization* is imputing racial problems to those of other races rather than to one's own race; and *containment* refers to efforts to deny the existence of racism. While racism can exist in any racial group (Elijah Muhammad, a black Muslim leader, taught his followers that the black race was superior to the white), racism in the United States is largely a matter of white beliefs and practices against American Indians and African Americans. We'll explore various forms of such racism throughout this chapter.

morphological
pertaining to form and structure

ethnic group
people who have a shared historical and cultural background that leads them to identify with each other

racism
the belief that some racial groups are inherently inferior to others

Extent and Origin of Races and Racism in America

As table 8.1 and figure 8.1 show, the composition of the American population is changing. In 2005, racial minorities and Hispanics made up a third of the total population. And their proportion continues to grow. By the middle of the 21st century, they will comprise half the population.

TABLE 8.1

U.S. Resident Population, by Race and Hispanic Origin, 1980 and 2005

Race	Number (1,000)		Percent Distribution	
	1980	2005	1980	2005
All races	226,546	296,410	100.0	100.0
White	194,713	237,855	85.9	80.2
Black	26,683	37,909	11.8	12.8
Hispanic origin	14,609	42,082	6.4	14.2
Asian/Pacific Islander	3,729	12,687	1.7	4.3
American Indian, Eskimo, Aleut	1,420	2,863	0.6	1.0

Note: Persons of Hispanic origin may be of any race and are included in the figures for the other races.
SOURCE: U.S. Census Bureau 2007.

FIGURE 8.1

Composition of U.S. Population, 2000–2050.

Source: "Projected population of the United States," U.S. Census Bureau Web site.

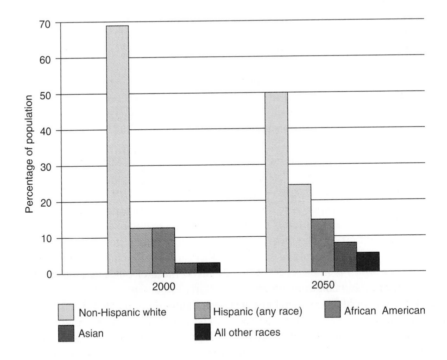

Non-Hispanic white   Hispanic (any race)   African American
Asian   All other races

Both the Hispanic and the Asian American population are growing at much faster rates than the population as a whole (Bernstein 2004). And because of increasing inter-marriage rates and increasing willingness to acknowledge their background, the number of Americans who are identified as multiracial increased tenfold from 1960 to 1990 (Lee and Bean 2003). By 2000, there were 6.8 million Americans, 2.4 percent of the population, who were reported as multiracial.

Both immigration and high birth rates contribute to the rapid growth of the Hispanic population. According to the Census Bureau, between mid-2004 and mid-2005, about one of every two people added to the population were Hispanic. Nearly two-thirds of Hispanics are of Mexican background.

As we discuss the quality of life of the racial and ethnic groups, it is important to keep in mind the diversity within groups. Among Hispanics, for example, the Cubans differ sharply from Mexicans and Puerto Ricans in such matters as economic status, occupational level, immigration status, and ability to speak English (Aponte 1991). Similarly, although Asians as a group are among the more educated and higher-income groups in the nation (including whites), some of the immigrants from Southeast Asia, such as the Vietnamese, have lower education levels and higher unemployment and poverty rates.

Racism in American History

Why do problems exist among the various races and ethnic groups in America, the supposed "melting-pot" nation of the world? In part, the problems stem from historical circumstances. For example, the high rates of poverty and other problems among American Indians cannot be separated from events that began with the European colonization of the Americas. The colonists decimated both the population and the culture of the various Indian groups. Indians were defrauded of, or forced off, their traditional lands. Solemn treaties between tribes and the American government were repeatedly broken by the latter with little or no compensation to the Indians. And granting tribes a certain autonomy on reservations is a mixed bag at best. They are free from much federal law, but they are also isolated to a considerable extent from the mainstream of the nation's economy.

Similarly, the problems of African Americans cannot be separated from their historical experience of slavery and segregation. The first African Americans to arrive, in 1619, were indentured servants, not slaves. However, states soon passed laws that legitimated slavery, and *those brought here as slaves were legally defined as property, not as persons.* Their enslavement was justified by various kinds of "evidence" of the inherent inferiority of the black race.

The system of slavery ultimately gave way to a castelike system. In a caste system, people are categorized into groups according to some characteristic over which they have no control, such as their race or the status of their parents. The groups have differing amounts of power, status, and access to those things that are valued. In America, whites formed one caste and African Americans another, with the whites having the bulk of the power, status, and financial resources. Of course, there were also differences within the two races. But even lower-class whites could be better off than higher-

Minorities continue to use nonviolent protest to strive for equality.

class blacks. That is, the two races were like two separate class systems, with the great majority of African Americans in the lower levels of their class system, and with the black upper class at roughly the same level as the white middle class in terms of material advantages. Segregation in such things as housing, schools, and public accommodations helped maintain the system.

Finally, in the 1950s, black leaders, including Martin Luther King, Jr., led a civil rights movement designed to break down segregation and give African Americans all the rights and privileges enjoyed by whites. They fought the notion of inferiority, rejected discrimination and prejudice, and insisted upon nothing less than full equality of opportunity for all of America's citizens. Their efforts resulted in many significant gains. Nevertheless, severe problems of racial and ethnic inequality continue to tarnish the American dream of freedom and justice for all.

All of this is not to say that racism is a distinctively American problem, nor that apart from the historical events we have briefly noted there would be no race problem in the United States. In point of fact, no nation in the world is able to contain diverse groups without some degree of tension between them. *Dividing people into "us" and "them" occurs routinely.* Combined with competition for jobs, power, and prestige, the potential for intergroup conflict is high. Once groups enter into conflict, the animosity can linger for generations or centuries. Thus, when the former Soviet Union and Yugoslavia broke up in the early 1990s, old ethnic rivalries surfaced again, and vicious wars erupted between groups that had been seemingly united.

In sum, despite our *ideology of equal opportunity for all,* racism or ethnic hostility confronts many people who hope to take advantage of the American dream. The United States is not a melting pot. Someone has suggested that a more apt metaphor is a salad bowl, since the various groups tend to retain their identity even as they mix together in the society.

Even the salad bowl metaphor overstates the case, however. For *racial and ethnic segregation persist* in the nation. There may be less, and different patterns of, segregation in metropolitan areas, but segregation is not disappearing (Clark and Blue 2004; Nelson, Dawkins, and Sanchez 2004; Farley and Squires 2005). The predominant pattern, however, is still segregation. Unfortunately, segregated children who grow up in segregated areas are likely to define that as both normal and desirable and perpetuate the pattern—and segregation works against the American dream of equal opportunity and freedom from discrimination.

Race, Ethnicity, and the Quality of Life

What does it mean to be a minority in America? How does being a minority affect the *quality of life?* We will look at four areas in which all Americans are supposed to have equal rights:

1. Certain rights as citizens.
2. Equal economic opportunities.
3. The right to life, liberty, and the pursuit of happiness.
4. The right to dignity as a human being.

In each of the four areas, being white is a distinct advantage, although the advantage is not as great as it was in the past.

The Rights of Citizenship

The mass media often remind you of the *rights and privileges attached to your citizenship:*

1. This is a nation governed by laws rather than by individuals.
2. As a citizen, you have both the privilege and the responsibility of participating in the political process to ensure that laws reflect the will of the people.
3. The people do not exist to serve the government; the government exists to serve the people, and to serve all equally.

All these statements break down when we consider minority groups.

The Right to Vote.   If you don't like the way things are going, it is said that you can express your disapproval at the polls. Indeed, voting is the responsibility of every citizen because one way that Americans are presumably able to change things is by exercising their right to vote. However, this right and privilege, basic as it is to our notions of government, has often eluded African Americans and was long withheld from American Indians.

When the 15th Amendment to the Constitution was ratified in 1870, all male Americans over age 21 had the right to vote, regardless of their race, creed, color, or prior condition of servitude (Rodgers and Bullock 1972). In the latter part of the century, however, various steps were taken to keep African Americans from voting. The southern states passed laws that effectively **disfranchised** black voters. Some of the laws required literacy and property tests. Others imposed a poll tax. Such laws excluded poor whites as well as African Americans, however, so loopholes were created. One loophole was the "understanding clause," which allowed a registrar to enroll any individual who could give a "reasonable" explanation of a part of the state constitution that was read to him. Similarly, the "grandfather clause" exempted from the literacy test those who descended from pre-1865 voters.

disfranchise
to deprive of the right to vote

Intimidation also was used to keep African Americans from registering and voting. Sometimes the threat of violence or actual violence (including even murder) discouraged African Americans. The pressure of economic intimidation also was applied. They faced the possibility of losing their jobs or of being refused supplies at local stores.

Nor is all of this disfranchisement mere history now. From time to time, a report appears in the news media about efforts to keep various minorities from voting. Rather than intimidation, however, a tactic more likely to be used is drawing voting district lines in a way that neutralizes the power of minority votes (by, for example, splitting areas with heavy concentrations of minorities into separate districts so that whites are in the majority in each of the areas). Various other measures may be used in local situations. In the bitterly contested vote for president in Florida in 2000 (see chapter 9), lawsuits were filed over discriminatory treatment of both black and Hispanic voters (Holland 2002). The allegations are that some minority voters were kept from polls, or their votes were discarded for various reasons, or they were asked for two kinds of identification when only one was required. Even in this most fundamental of rights, the battle for equality is not yet over.

The Rule of Law.   Another right and privilege of citizenship is to live in a land governed by laws rather than by individuals. The laws, however, have failed to fully protect minority rights in the areas of *housing, public accommodations, and school desegregation.*

.   With regard to housing, the laws forbid discrimination in the sale, rental, or financing of any housing. Legally, a home that is for sale should be available to anyone who can afford it. However, some white property owners have "restrictive covenants" in their deeds that bar racial minorities from purchasing their homes (San Francisco Bureau 2001), and a certain amount of *racial steering* (diverting minorities away from predominantly white neighborhoods) still occurs. A study of 20 major metropolitan areas found racial steering of African Americans and discrimination against Hispanics in access to rental housing (Ross and Turner 2005).

Even if minorities don't encounter obstacles in obtaining the kind of housing they prefer, they may find themselves at a disadvantage in the financing process. In the study of 20 major metropolitan areas, the researchers reported that Hispanics got less help in obtaining financing (Ross and Turner 2005). Lending agents may reject minority applicants at a higher rate than that for whites (the rejection rate for high-income minorities is often as high as that for low-income whites), and may require minorities to pay the higher interest rates of subprime lenders (Daniels 2004; Williams and Nesiba 2005). Race, in other words, may be as important as income in getting an approved mortgage.

With regard to public accommodations, segregation was declared unconstitutional in 1964. Prior to that time, segregated facilities prevailed in various degrees throughout the nation. The first "Jim Crow" cars (segregated public conveyances) appeared in Massachusetts in 1841 (Nearing 1969). In the South, restrooms and drinking fountains were also segregated, with signs posted that said "White Only" and "Colored Only." In fact, nearly all government services were offered separately to the races, including hospitals and health centers. Restaurants in both the South and the North often catered to one race or the other, but not both, and theaters had segregated seating.

During the 1960s, segregated facilities were challenged by "sit-ins" at lunch counters. African Americans and their white supporters would sit at a lunch counter and refuse to move until they were served. Ultimately, such protests, combined with federal legislation and the 1964 Supreme Court decision, opened nearly all public accommodations to African Americans as well as whites. Compliance with the law has been widespread in this area, probably because businesspeople find the new situation more profitable than the old.

Finally, *segregated educational facilities* were declared illegal in the now-famous 1954 Supreme Court decision in the *Brown v. Board of Education of Topeka* case. Such facilities were ruled unconstitutional on the grounds that they are *inherently unequal,* but the desegregation process has been agonizingly slow. In recent years, moreover, there has been a tendency toward reversal; that is, the schools are becoming more rather than less segregated (Frankenberg, Lee, and Orfield 2003; Davis 2004). The segregation would be less if all children attended nearby public schools, but a large number go to private, magnet, and charter schools and thereby increase the segregation in local, public schools (Saporito and Sohoni 2006). African Americans and Hispanics tend to be more segregated than Asians, but all minorities still experience segregated schooling to some extent.

Equality before the Law.   All Americans are supposed to stand as *equals before the law.* Most people, of course, quickly recognize that not all Americans are treated equally. The wealthy are rarely accorded the harsh treatment endured by the poor. Probably few people are aware of the extent to which minorities receive unequal treatment in virtually every aspect of civil and criminal proceedings (Butterfield 2000).

For example, police are more likely to be verbally abusive and to use excessive force against Hispanics and African Americans (Shapiro 1997; Weitzer and Tuch 2004). Hispanic and black youth are more likely to be detained by the police and the courts than are white youth (Demuth and Steffensmeier 2004; Leiber and Fox 2005). A study of youths on probation found that the officers consistently described black youths differently from white youths in their written reports, attributing blacks' offenses to negative attitudes and personality traits and whites' offenses to the social environment (Bridges and Steen 1998).

Federal courts mete out harsher penalties for black and Hispanic than for white perpetrators (Steffensmeier and Demuth 2000; Demuth and Steffensmeier 2004). Minorities are more likely than whites to be stopped while driving and to be imprisoned, even for the same offense (Daniels 2004). As a result, there is a disproportionate number of African Americans and Hispanics in jails and prisons. Two researchers estimated that for men born between 1965 and 1969, 3 percent of whites and 20 percent of African Americans served time in prison by their early thirties (Pettit and Western 2004). And the U.S. Department of Justice concluded that about 1 in 3 black males, 1 in 6 Hispanic males, and 1 in 17 white males, over their lifetime, will spend time in prison (Bonczar 2003).

Finally, a disproportionate number of minorities, particularly African Americans, are given the death penalty (Bureau of Justice Statistics 2006a). In 2004, 3,314 prisoners were under the sentence of death, and 42 percent of them were African Americans. In other words, the proportion of African Americans on death row is more than three times their proportion of the population.

The Right to Equal Economic Opportunities

Among other factors, racial and ethnic discrimination means that minorities are more likely to be poor, unemployed, or—if they work—underemployed. Minorities also receive, on the average, less income than whites.

Employment. A group might have *unequal access to employment* in at least four ways. First, the group might have a higher rate of unemployment than other groups. Second, a greater proportion of the group might be *underemployed.* Third, members of the group might be clustered at the lower levels of occupational categories (i.e., even if the proportion of minorities in a category is the same as that of whites, the minorities cluster at the lower levels). Fourth, a disproportionate number of the group might become disillusioned and drop out of the labor market.

All four kinds of inequality apply to minorities in America (Herring 2002; Coleman 2004). And the *inequality is maintained by practices at the job candidate, job entry, and job promotion stages.* At the job candidate stage, many of the better jobs are still discovered through informal methods such as friends as much as through a formal recruitment process. A survey of 185 Chicago firms found that employers focus their efforts on white neighborhoods and avoid recruitment strategies that could bring them a disproportionately inner-city, black labor force (Neckerman and Kirschenman 1991). A study of Asian American professionals concluded that they face a "glass ceiling" similar to the one that women encounter if they aspire to the higher positions (Woo 2000).

Immigrants may be particularly disadvantaged by this process (Vogel 2006). For example, Asian immigrant women wind up in garment sweatshops on the West Coast (Kim et al. 1992). The nature of the jobs is described by Helen Wong, who came with her husband and five children from Hong Kong in 1988 and found work in a small shop (Louie 1992). She worked on women's dresses and pantsuits for piece rates, which means that any breaks and other time off were unpaid. She worked Monday through Saturday, and came in on Sundays when there was a special rush order. The pay was the same regardless of how many hours or days she worked. On the average, she made between $1 and $2 an hour.

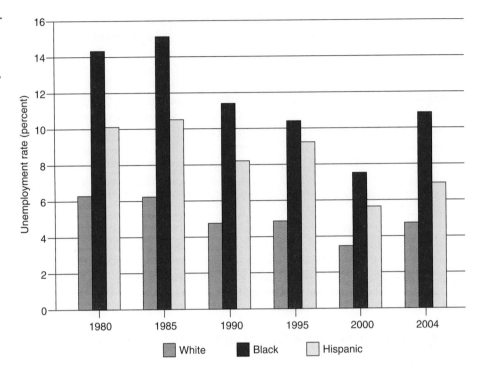

FIGURE 8.2
Unemployment Rates,
1980–2004.

Source: "Unemployed workers,"
U.S. Census Bureau Web site.

Among the most accessible data on inequality in employment are unemployment rates (figure 8.2; in this and other figures and tables in this chapter, all groups are included for which data are available). For the past 50 years, the unemployment rates of African Americans have been double or more those of whites, whereas the rates for Hispanics have been between one and a half and two times those of whites. In 2005, according to the Bureau of Labor Statistics, the black unemployment rate was more than double that of whites: 4.4 for whites and 10.5 for African Americans. Of all minorities, however, American Indians have the highest unemployment rates–about 46 percent in 2004 (Center for Community Change 2005).

Underemployment (working fewer hours than desired or at a job for which the worker is overqualified) is also more common among minorities, and it is detrimental to the well-being of workers (see chapter 10). Jensen and Slack (2003) calculated the underemployment of a variety of racial and ethnic groups and found the proportion of people underemployed was as follows: non-Hispanic whites, 11.3 percent; Asians, 12.7 percent; non-Hispanic African Americans, 19.9 percent; Hispanics, 21.3 percent; and Native Americans, 23.3 percent.

To be a member of a minority group, then, may mean greater difficulty in finding meaningful and rewarding positions. Even *trade unions have been notoriously resistant to including African Americans.* In the past, African Americans were kept out of unions by tests that seemed to have little to do with the work (such as asking applicants for steamfitter apprenticeships about the relationships of Brahms to music and Whitman to poetry). By 1985, minorities held union membership in proportions roughly equal to their proportion of the overall population, but they still tended to cluster in the lower-status, lower-paying kinds of work.

Table 8.2 offers additional evidence on the problem of *discrimination in job opportunities.* Note how minorities are disproportionately represented in various occupational

Occupation	Percent of Total That Is	
	African American	Hispanic
Total	10.8	13.1
Managerial and professional	8.1	6.4
Service occupations	15.8	19.2
Sales and office occupations	11.2	11.1
Natural resources, construction, maintenance	7.1	23.1
Production, transportation, material moving	14.1	19.2

TABLE 8.2
Employed Persons, by Race and Occupation, 2005

SOURCE: "Employed persons by detailed occupation, sex, race, and Hispanic or Latino ethnicity," Bureau of Labor Statistics Web site.

categories (if there were perfect equality, the proportions in the table would be the same as the group's proportion in the labor force: 10.8 percent for African Americans and 13.1 percent for Hispanics). The first category, managerial and professional, offers the highest prestige and highest average income. The next category, service occupations, has some of the lower-paying jobs. African Americans and Hispanics are underrepresented in the first and overrepresented in the second. Furthermore, a detailed inspection of each of the categories shows that minorities tend to cluster in the lower levels of those categories.

For example, in the managerial and professional category, the proportion of African Americans and Hispanics who are chief executives, physicians, and lawyers are less than half the two groups' proportion of the population. On the other hand, their proportion in some of the less prestigious and less rewarding occupations in that category—such as tax examiners, community and social service specialists, and teacher assistants—is greater than their proportion of the total population.

Furthermore, once in a job or a career line, minorities are likely to find advancement more difficult for them than for their white peers. A study of female workers found that African Americans and Hispanics experienced less job mobility than did whites (Alon and Tienda 2005b). And a researcher who investigated promotion experiences reported that, compared to white men, black men had to work longer periods of time after leaving school and Hispanics had to have more years with their current employer before getting a promotion (Smith 2005). And black and Hispanic women, compared to white men, needed more job-specific experience and more overall work experience in order to get a promotion.

Clearly, *race and ethnic background are factors in all aspects of employment.* And that includes the loss of work and change of job or career. Here, again, minorities may suffer more than their white counterparts. For one thing, minorities are more vulnerable to losing their jobs (Wilson 2005). Zwerling and Silver (1992) found that African Americans were more than twice as likely as whites to be fired from jobs in the federal government, even after controlling for such factors as tenure, union protection, absenteeism, and disciplinary actions. For another thing, minorities are less likely than whites to benefit when finding new employment. Among workers displaced from some high-technology industries, African Americans and Hispanics suffered greater earnings losses than did whites, whether their new jobs were within or outside the high-tech sector (Ong 1991).

TABLE 8.3

Money Income of
Households, 2005 (*percent
distribution by income
level, by race, and by
Hispanic origin*)

Income	Percentage of Households			
	White Non-Hispanic	Black	Hispanic	Asian
Under $10,000	6.4	17.1	10.0	7.8
$10,000–$14,999	5.9	8.9	7.4	4.6
$15,000–$24,999	11.3	16.1	16.2	8.5
$25,000–$34,999	10.9	12.6	15.0	7.1
$35,000–$49,999	14.6	15.1	17.1	12.2
$50,000–$74,999	19.1	15.1	17.2	19.2
$75,000–$99,999	12.1	7.3	8.2	13.1
$100,000 and over	19.7	7.8	8.8	27.5

SOURCE: DeNavas-Walt, Proctor, and Lee 2006.

FIGURE 8.3

Median Household Income,
by Race and Hispanic Origin,
1972–2005.

Source: De Navas-Walt,
Proctor, and Lee 2006. (Data
on Asian income only available
after 1986.)

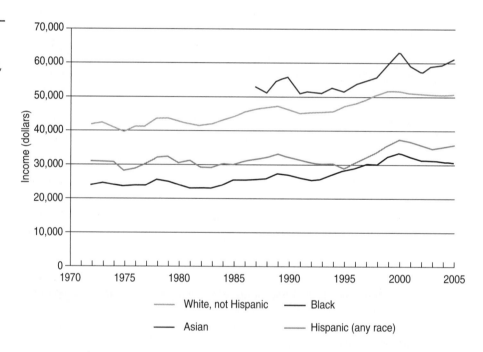

Income and Wealth. Wealth includes all the assets of a family—housing equity, investments, insurance, and so on. Great disparity exists between the races in wealth. Census data show that the median net worth of non-Hispanic white households is 10.6 times that of black households and 8.1 times that of Hispanic households (Orzechowski and Sepielli 2003).

An important component of wealth is income. Table 8.3 shows the extent to which minorities are concentrated more heavily than whites in the lower income brackets. Some people believe that minorities have made significant progress. However, although the income of all racial groups has been increasing, the gap between whites and minorities other than Asian Americans is greater than it was in the 1970s (figure 8.3).

In 2005, black household income was 60.8 percent and Hispanic household income was 70.8 percent of white household income. Among the minorities, only the Asian–Pacific Islanders compare favorably to whites. Their median household income has been consistently higher than that of any other group, including whites (figure 8.3).

In general, income inequality is widespread across occupations and is certainly a consequence of discrimination. Black income is lower than that of whites even for those workers with the same education, occupation, experience, authority, and number of hours worked (Smith 1997; Coleman 2003). The gap actually increases in the higher-income occupational categories (Grodsky and Pager 2001). Moreover, because of the type of assets and pension plans available, the disadvantage of African Americans is even greater in retirement than it was during their working years (Hogan and Perrucci 1998).

The Right to Life and Happiness

The right to "life, liberty, and the pursuit of happiness" was affirmed in the Declaration of Independence. However, those rights are not distributed equally in the United States. Surveys report *less happiness and less satisfaction among African Americans* than among whites (Aldous and Ganey 1999; Saad and Newport 2001). African Americans score lower than whites on life satisfaction, happiness, marital happiness, and perceived health, and they score higher on mistrust.

Like most other minority groups, African Americans have not had ample access to those things important to happiness and life satisfaction: work, recognition and success, financial well-being, health, and good housing. For example, African Americans and Hispanics are far more likely than whites to live in low-quality housing and to report dissatisfaction with that housing (Cook and Bruin 1994; Golant and La Greca 1994). In this section, we look at two other areas crucial to happiness: life chances and freedom from fear.

Life Chances. Insurance companies and government agencies compile large amounts of information on **life chances,** which include probability of divorce, disease, suicide, mental illness, and premature death. The life chances of whites are generally better than those of minorities (McLaughlin and Stokes 2002; Smedley, Stith and Nelson 2002; Williams, Neighbors, and Jackson 2003; Plant and Sachs-Ericsson 2004). For example, compared to whites, minorities tend to have (1) lower levels of physical and mental health; (2) a higher rate of infant deaths and deaths from tuberculosis, AIDS, and homicide; (3) a lower median family income; (4) lower-level jobs; (5) proportionately fewer full-time and white-collar jobs; and (6) fewer people receiving old age and survivor insurance benefits. Many of the differences are striking. Black and Puerto Rican women have particularly high rates of infant mortality (Hummer et al. 1999). A black baby's life expectancy is nearly five years less than that of a white baby, and this gap has changed little in more than half a century (Carr 2005). And the risk of a black youth being murdered is four times that of a white youth (Snyder and Sickmund 2006).

Disadvantages with respect to life chances are rooted in a number of factors. Racism is a major contributor to problems of both physical and mental health (Byrd and Clayton 2001; Dana 2002; Schulz et al. 2006). Minorities are more likely to live near hazardous waste facilities and be exposed to toxic materials (Stretesky and Hogan 1998; Ash and Fetter 2004; Pastor, Sadd, and Morello-Frosch 2004). Because of such factors as pressure to perform and a sense of isolation, being the token minority in a work organization is more likely to lead to depression and anxiety than to a sense of having "made it" (Jackson, Thoits, and Taylor 1995). Finally, minorities are disadvantaged in

life chances
the probability of gaining certain advantages defined as desirable, such as long life and health

Native Americans are the poorest minority group in the United States.

life chances because of their lower economic levels (Meckler 1998; McLaughlin and Stokes 2002). People who live in poverty or who try to survive at low income levels have higher rates of physical and emotional problems. Impoverishment combined with racism takes a dreadful toll on poor African Americans in high rates of cirrhosis of the liver, homicide, accidents, and drug and alcohol abuse.

It is understandable, then, that African Americans are about twice as likely to have high blood pressure as whites. Some observers thought that a genetic factor was involved in the higher rates of African Americans, but research suggests that the *stress of living in a race-conscious society* and possibly some dietary factors are more likely than genetic factors to be responsible (Whittle et al. 1991).

Minorities are also more likely to be victims of both property and violent crimes (Bureau of Justice Statistics 2006b). In 2005, for every 1,000 people in the racial/ethnic group, 27 African Americans, 25 Hispanics, 20 whites, and 14 persons of other races were victims of a violent crime. Part of the difference in the life expectancy of whites and African Americans is the result of the high rate of black murder victims (Potter 2001). For property crimes in 2005, the overall rate was higher for whites than for African Americans because of a higher rate of theft for the former; burglary and auto theft rates were higher among African Americans. For Hispanics, the overall property crime rate was 210 per 1,000 households, compared to 148 for non-Hispanics.

Of all the racial/ethnic groups, American Indians/Alaska Natives are the most deprived in terms of life chances. They are more likely than others to be poor and unemployed (Castor et al. 2006). They have higher rates of criminal victimization than any other group. In fact, the rate of violent victimization of American Indians is more than twice that of African Americans, 2.5 times that of whites, and 4.5 times that of Asian Americans (Bureau of Justice Statistics 2006b). A survey of Indian and Alaska Native women in New York City found that 65 percent had experienced some form of interpersonal violence, including childhood physical abuse (28 percent), rape (48 percent), and domestic violence (40 percent) (Evans-Campbell, Lindhorst, Huang, and Walters 2006). The women reported high levels of emotional trauma resulting from the violence. In addition to abuse, American Indians also have serious problems of neglect, alcoholism, fetal alcohol syndrome, mental and physical disabilities, depression, school problems, and delinquency (Nelson et al. 1992; Grant et al. 2004).

Freedom from Fear.   One of the four basic freedoms proclaimed by President Franklin Roosevelt was freedom from fear. No one should have to live in constant fear of offending someone who claims to be superior. Yet, for decades black mothers and fathers taught their children to fear offending white people. Richard Wright related an incident from his own childhood that illustrates the point (Bernard 1966). A group of white boys threw broken bottles at him and some of his friends, and the two groups fought. Wright was badly cut. He went home and sat on his steps to wait for his mother to come home from work. He felt that she would understand both the pain of the cut and the hurt that was inside him. Rather than sympathy, he received a severe beating. Had a white mother treated her son in this way, you might have questioned her love; but Wright's mother was teaching him what she regarded as a most important lesson—to avoid such encounters at all costs. She was teaching him what it meant to be black in America: that he would always be the loser in battles with whites. Her method was severe, but so was the reality in which she knew he would exist.

Violence and threats of violence against people because of some characteristic of a group to which the people belong are now called *hate crimes* (Harlow 2005). The characteristic may be religion or sexual orientation or being a member of a gang, but the majority of hate crimes are motivated by the victim's race or ethnicity. Such crimes remind minorities that some people despise them and are willing to use violent means to intimidate them. You need only read the daily papers to realize that the victims of hate crimes include African Americans, Hispanics, Jews, Asians, and Indians. The crimes range from verbal abuse to physical violence and even murder. People who survive hate crimes are likely to suffer severe emotional problems (McDevitt et al. 2001). In recent years, the incidents have included chaining a black man to the rear of a truck and dragging him to his death, shooting Jewish children at a day care center, and brutally beating a Hispanic boy with a metal pipe.

Many hate crimes are committed by members of the approximately 400 racist and neo-Nazi groups in the nation (Padilla 1999). The groups have somewhat varied ideologies, but all of them proclaim the superiority of the white race and the threats to whites posed by various racial minorities. Stimulated by such ideology, their members commit thousands of hate crimes every year (Maguire and Pastore 2006).

The cherished rights of Americans to move about as they please, to live according to their means, and to enjoy the use of all public facilities has not yet been fully extended to minorities. Minorities who try to break down old barriers are still subject to threats of violence and efforts at intimidation. Freedom from fear is an unmet promise rather than a reality.

The Right to Dignity as a Human Being

Most of the material already discussed in this chapter illustrates how minorities are directly *deprived of their dignity as human beings.* When African Americans and Hispanics were asked whether they ever felt discriminated against in public life or in employment, only a minority said "never" (Polling Report 2007). Twenty percent of Hispanics and 39 percent of African Americans indicated a frequency of from once a month to daily experiences of discrimination. What kind of discriminatory behavior do they encounter? Much of it is what Eddings (1995) called **stealth racism,** which in-

stealth racism
hidden or subtle acts of prejudice and discrimination that may be apparent only to the victim

volves hidden or subtle acts of prejudice and discrimination, acts that may be apparent only to the victim. Examples of stealth racism include taxis that never stop for minorities; suspicious stares from clerks in stores; the assumption that the minority individual is in a subordinate role (like the couple who came out of an expensive restaurant and asked an African American man to get their car, not realizing he was a senior editor at a national magazine); the sense of being unwelcome (such as when looking for a new home in a well-to-do neighborhood); and the surprise expressed when the minority person is articulate and sophisticated.

Some of the incidents are irritating and demeaning. For instance, a black woman returning a rented video is ignored by the clerks until she speaks up and asks for help (St. Jean and Feagin 1998). Or consider the problem of "dwb"—driving while black. There is evidence that black drivers are far more likely to be stopped by police than are white drivers; they are also more likely to have their cars searched (Stetz 1999). Stealth racism also can be hazardous for the victims, such as when physicians are less likely to order sophisticated cardiac tests for African Americans who complain of chest pains than for whites with the same symptoms (Schulman et al. 1999). At that point, the right to dignity may mean the right to life-saving measures.

The right to dignity also includes the right to truthful representation of one's group. Two often-heard myths violate this right.

The Myth of Success around the Corner.   A common American myth is that *success is "just around the corner" for anyone who is willing to work for it.* The implication is that the minorities can end their impoverishment merely by being willing to work as hard as other people. "If they want to get ahead," it is said, "let them work for it and earn it." The point, of course, is that if they do not get ahead, it is their own fault. The *fallacy of personal attack* is used to defend an unjust social order. The reasoning is that if the minorities have as many opportunities as everyone else and yet remain in the lower levels of society, something is wrong with the minorities.

Unfortunately, many people do believe that minorities have the same opportunities as whites. A Gallup poll asked whether racial minorities in this country have equal job opportunities as whites (Polling Report 2007). While 53 percent of non-Hispanic whites agreed that the minorities do have equal opportunities, 81 percent of African Americans and 62 percent of Hispanics said the minorities do *not* have equal opportunities.

Many whites believe not just that minorities have an equal opportunity, but that minorities now possess an advantage. These whites see themselves as hampered in their access to the best education and the most desirable jobs and careers because of their race (Cohen 2003; Flynn 2003). They believe that they have lost out, or potentially could lose out, to people less qualified than they are simply because the other people are part of a minority. In other words, they see themselves as victims of *reverse discrimination,* with their own opportunities becoming restricted as minority opportunities have opened. They cite cases in which minorities (including women) have been given preference over white males even when the white males have seniority or somewhat better qualifications. According to such beliefs, if minorities do not achieve success, it is clearly their own fault.

Associated with the myth that success is readily available to those willing to work for it is the notion that African Americans prefer welfare to hard work. This notion is also a distortion of the truth. African Americans did not appear on welfare rolls in large numbers until the late 1940s. Furthermore, few able-bodied men of any race are receiving welfare. Poor African Americans are, like anyone else, eager to escape their poverty. There is no evidence that minorities prefer welfare to work or that they are failing to take advantage of work opportunities available to them. Quite simply, the notion that success is just around the corner for anyone willing to work for it is a myth.

The Myth of Inferiority. The insidious myth that minorities are *inherently inferior* is still around. The argument about inferiority takes a number of different forms. One argument is that minorities are, and always have been, biologically inferior. This argument can take the form of the *fallacy of circular reasoning.* An individual argues that African Americans are inferior because their IQs are lower than those of whites. "But," one could reply, "they are only lower for those who live in deprived conditions." "No," is the response, "they are lower because they are inferior people."

fallacy

The theory of biological inferiority has also been claimed in a few scientific circles. The most recent attempt to argue for innate inferiority is *The Bell Curve,* by Herrnstein and Murray (1994). Herrnstein, a psychologist, and Murray, a political scientist, claimed that about 60 percent of IQ is genetic. Differences in achievement, therefore, are both inevitable and unchangeable. The work of Herrnstein and Murray has been criticized and refuted on various grounds. One of the more forceful refutations is that of three psychologists, who pointed out that there is no gene that is conclusively linked to intelligence, so that it is not possible to prove any genetic link of intelligence with race, which itself is a social construction with no scientific basis (Sternberg, Grigorenko, and Kidd 2005).

The argument of a second form of the inferiority myth is that minorities are *culturally inferior.* Whatever may or may not be true biologically, it is argued, the culture of a particular people is obviously inferior and the people therefore are unfit to rise above their low status.

African Americans, Hispanics, and American Indians are all perceived to have cultural characteristics that make them different and less committed to such traditional American values as education and hard work; but most people in America tend to have the same aspirations for themselves and their families. Thus, a study of the life goals of graduating high-school seniors found similar educational and occupational aspirations among the white, black, Hispanic, and Asian youths (Chang et al. 2006). The aspirations were high for all groups. The fact that minorities have not achieved such aims cannot be attributed to cultural inferiority nor to cultural values that differ from those of white America.

Contributing Factors

The problems of minorities in America are well described by the title of Gunnar Myrdal's classic work *An American Dilemma* (Myrdal 1944). The author, a Swedish social economist, came to the United States in 1938 to direct an analysis of the problem. The book that resulted defined the problem as a moral issue and stated that the *dilemma involved a contradiction between the American creed and our racial behavior.* The creed proclaims the primacy of individual dignity, equality, and the right of all citizens to the same justice and the same opportunities, but the racial behavior systematically denies minorities the same rights and benefits accorded to whites.

The problem also involves *contradictory value systems.* Some people define the segregated and deprived state of African Americans as a problem, but others define efforts to "mix" the races as the real problem. The latter vigorously resist efforts of the former to alter the existing structure of segregated relationships. They fear an integrated

BECOMING COLOR BLIND

We were once involved in arranging an exchange of ministers and choirs between a black and a white church. After the black pastor had spoken at the white church, one of the members said to us, "You know, the longer that man preached, the less I thought of him as black." It was her way of saying that the contact had broken down some of the prejudice she had harbored all her life.

Social scientists have long known that interracial contact is one way to deal with prejudice. Arrange for a visit with a group of a race other than your own. It might be a local church, a student organization on campus, or some kind of community organization. Talk with some of the members and explore how they feel about the current racial situation. Ask them about their aspirations for themselves and their children. Discuss their outlook on the future. Do they feel that the situation for their race has improved or worsened in the 2000s? Why?

What insights into the life of the other race did you gain from the visit? Do they have any needs and aspirations that are fundamentally different from your own? How does America's race problem look from their point of view? Can you see the basis for their point of view?

If possible, you might arrange some kind of exchange visit with the group. As the people from the different races mingle with each other, note any changes in prejudicial attitudes and any increases in mutual understanding.

society for various reasons. They argue that such a society will lack the strength and vigor of the present society.

Finally, the problem involves *contradictions in the social structure*. Minorities today are hampered by the changed economy, for our economy has developed to the point where the demand for unskilled and semiskilled labor is relatively small. Unlike the immigrants earlier in our history, therefore, people cannot better their lot today by going to work in vast numbers in the factories, where few or no skills are required.

Social Structural Factors

The tables in this chapter show that minorities occupy a *low position in the stratification system*. This finding raises the question of whether the main problems facing minorities are due to social class, racial or ethnic identity, or both. The answer seems to be both. Minorities share some characteristics with lower-class whites, but, as you have seen, even those who achieve higher socioeconomic levels still face various disadvantages and assaults on their dignity.

institutional racism
policies and practices of social institutions that tend to perpetuate racial discrimination

The disadvantages are not always due to biased individuals. The term **institutional racism** was coined to refer to the fact that established policies and practices of social institutions tend to perpetuate racial discrimination. In other words, whether or not the people involved are prejudiced or deliberate in their discriminatory behavior, the normal practices and policies themselves guarantee that minorities will be short-changed. Policies and practices are set by those in power, and minorities typically have lacked the power necessary to control institutional processes. We examine institutional racism in four important areas: the media, education, the economy, and government.

Mass Media. *The portrayal of minorities in the media has tended to perpetuate various negative stereotypes.* The problem was particularly severe in the past when movies and radio and television programs—such as the *Amos 'n Andy* radio show—portrayed African Americans as lazy, inferior, stupid, and dishonest. After the mid-

1960s, the portrayals changed, and various racial minorities appeared more frequently and in more positive roles.

Racial and ethnic minorities still do not receive equitable treatment in the media, however (Children Now 2004). An examination of television commercials concluded that white men tended to be portrayed as powerful and white women as sex objects, whereas black men were more likely to be aggressive and black women were inconsequential (Coltrane 2000). A study of prime-time television programs for the 2001–2002 season found (Children Now 2004):

- Most white youth interacted with their parents, but only a fourth of Hispanic youth did.
- A homogenous and segregated world was portrayed in the eight P.M. programs.
- The number of Hispanics increased over past seasons, but nearly half were in low-status positions and jobs.
- Virtually all service workers and unskilled laborers were people of color.

Other media also contribute to the problem of negative stereotypes. A study of children's books drew a number of conclusions (Pescosolido, Grauerholz, and Milkie 1997). First, the number of black characters varied over time: The number declined from the late 1930s through the late 1950s, was almost nonexistent through 1964, increased considerably to the early 1970s, then leveled off. Second, there is an absence of intimate, egalitarian interracial relationships. Third, few books have a black adult as a central character. Even college textbooks can be misleading. In her examination of economics textbooks, Clawson (2002) found black faces "overwhelmingly portrayed" among the poor (recall that, in terms of numbers, there are far more poor whites than poor blacks).

In sum, some progress has been made, but the mass media as a whole continue to either neglect minorities or reinforce negative stereotypes.

Education. Four primary and secondary educational practices that perpetuate discrimination are *segregated schools, so-called IQ testing, so-called ability-grouping of children, and differential treatment of children based on racial or ethnic identity.* All these practices discriminate against people in the lower socioeconomic strata, and because most minorities are disproportionately in the lower strata, they suffer disproportionately from such practices.

Schools continue to be more segregated than integrated. In fact, as we indicated earlier, the schools have once again become more segregated. By 2000, the percentage of white classmates of the average black student was lower (less than 31 percent) than at any time since 1970 (Cose 2004). Attending a black segregated school depresses achievement, whereas attending a white segregated school raises test performance (Roscigno 1998). This difference is due, among other reasons, to the fact that segregated schooling provides minorities with a lower-quality education (Maxwell 1994). Segregated minority schools are lower in quality in every way, including fewer resources and less technology (such as multimedia computers) than are available at other schools (Trotter 1997).

IQ testing also works to the disadvantage of minorities. A child may do poorly on an IQ test, for example, because little in his or her home environment has served as preparation for tests constructed by middle-class educators. Then, when placed in a group of lower ability, a child may accept the label of mediocrity or even inferiority.

At the college level, efforts are made to recruit more minority students than have attended in the past. Some of the efforts are successful. But students who begin their educational journey from a deprived, minority base will face many built-in hurdles. For example, Hispanic enrollment in colleges and universities has been hampered by a combination of factors: rising admission standards, decreasing financial aid, and a hostile campus climate (Halcon and Reyes 1991).

Finally, minority students may be treated differently from white students. A researcher who looked at the discipline patterns of 11,000 middle-school students found that black students were more than twice as likely as whites to be sent to the principal's office or suspended, and more than four times as likely as whites to be expelled (Morse 2002). Another researcher studied an urban school intensively and drew a number of conclusions about discipline (Morris 2005). First, teachers and administrators tended to view black girls' behavior as "unladylike," and attempted to discipline them into dress and manners more acceptable to the adults. Second, school officials tended to define the behavior of Hispanic boys as threatening, so that the boys were often disciplined in strict, punitive ways. And third, school officials tended to see the behavior of white and Asian American students as both nonthreatening and gender appropriate; discipline for these students was likely to be less strict and punitive.

It is difficult to learn if your school makes you feel more vulnerable to disciplinary action simply because of your race. It is also difficult to learn if your school's cultural values and teaching methods are contrary to the cultural values of your family and community. Such an incongruity helps explain why 25 to 60 percent of all American Indian students drop out of high school each year (Klug and Whitfield 2002).

The Economy.   Institutional racism has pervaded the economy in at least three ways: **exploitation** *of minority labor, exclusion of minorities from full participation in the economy, and exploitation of minority consumers.* Some gains have been made, of

exploitation
use or manipulation of people for one's own advantage or profit

Segregated schools help perpetuate discrimination.

course. For example, racial/ethnic segregation in employment has declined since the 1960s (Tomaskovic-Devey et al. 2006). Nevertheless, as we noted earlier, minorities tend to secure the lower-paying jobs, a tendency that was reinforced by the shift from an industry- to a service-based economy (Jaret 1991; Woody 1991). And even in the same occupational categories, a gap exists between minority and white income (McCall 2001). Minorities also tend to have the worst jobs in terms of health hazards; a disproportionate number (11.7 percent for African Americans and 18.5 percent for Hispanics) suffer occupational injuries and illnesses (Bureau of Labor Statistics 2006b).

As for participation in the economy, minorities come out best during economic booms and worst when the economy falters. Thus, black-white inequality in employment is greater in those regions of the country where the economy is not as strong (Cohn and Fossett 1995). When restructuring or downsizing occurs, minorities are likely to suffer more job loss than are whites, particularly the black minority (Singh 1991). A study of the recession in the nation in the early 1990s found that whites, Hispanics, and Asians all gained jobs, but African Americans had a net loss of jobs (Sharpe 1993). At one corporation, African Americans were 26.3 percent of the workforce when the recession began, but they lost 43.6 percent of all jobs cut. At some other corporations, African Americans lost jobs at more than twice the rate of the overall reductions.

Minorities also fail to participate fully in the economy as entrepreneurs, a fact that is closely related to credit practices and policies. Lending institutions traditionally demand credit history, some kind of collateral, and some evidence of potential success before they lend money to prospective businesspersons, whether or not they are white. These are standard practices, defined as necessary and practical when giving credit; but applying them to minorities, who may have poor credit records because of exploitation and who may have nothing to use as collateral because of poverty, means that the standard practices only ensure continued white domination of the economy.

Insisting on comparable "sound" business practices when the prospective customers are minorities results in exploitation of the minority consumer. It is true that the poor are greater credit risks and that businesses in ghetto areas must pay higher insurance premiums because of the greater probability of theft and property damage; yet it is also true that these higher costs of doing business exploit the minority consumer, who must then pay more than others for the same quality of goods.

The most serious exploitation may be in housing, however. African Americans are often forced to pay more than whites for the same quality of housing. In fact, ghetto housing is sometimes costlier in terms of square footage and is frequently costlier in terms of quality square footage than is housing in suburban areas. When minorities attempt to find better housing, they may find themselves, as noted earlier, steered into some areas and kept away from other areas by real estate agents. And if they do purchase a home, they may find themselves facing higher costs and mortgage payments. A study of 125 American cities found that African Americans were 2.7 times more likely than whites and Hispanics 1.4 times more likely than whites to receive high-cost loans when refinancing (ACORN 2005).

Economic deprivation of minorities has meant economic gains for whites. When minorities are kept in a subordinate position, whites are able to secure a higher occupational status, lower rates of unemployment, and higher family income (Tomaskovic-Devey and Roscigno 1996). At least some of those who resist equal opportunities are not unaware of such implications.

Government. The government is supposed to protect and help all citizens equally. Yet minorities do not always benefit from the government as much as whites do, and legislation may work strongly against minorities. An example is the legislation passed by Congress in the late 1980s when strong concern developed about the use of crack cocaine (Tonry 1995). Because the lawmakers viewed crack as more dangerous than powdered cocaine, they mandated the same sentence for possession or sale of one ounce of crack cocaine as for 100 ounces of powdered cocaine. Actually, both types of cocaine are potent, but the powdered form is used more by whites whereas the crack is used more and sold more by minorities.

Whether or not the legislation was intentionally racist, it is in effect a racist law, punishing African Americans more severely than whites for an equivalent crime. As of this writing, however, Congress has resisted requests to change the law.

Minorities are not always the victims of government, of course. Some have benefited from government employment practices, particularly at the federal level. Of the 1.81 million civilian, nonpostal employees of the federal executive branch, 17.0 percent are African American (U.S. Census Bureau 2005:322). Hispanics have not fared as well; their 6.9 percent share of the jobs is far less than their proportion in the population.

If minorities are to make headway in their efforts to achieve equality of opportunity, they must be able to secure *political power* and find help in the courts. However, minorities have barely begun to infiltrate positions of political power. By 2003, only 9 percent of U.S. representatives in Congress were African American, and only 5 percent were Hispanic. Although there were no black or Hispanic senators in 2003, there was one African American and two Hispanics in the Senate by 2006, making a total of three African Americans and six Hispanics in the Senate since the latter part of the 19th century. Very few minorities reach the highest levels in politics.

There has been some progress, of course. The numbers of minorities in elected offices have risen dramatically since 1970. The bulk of them are in local and state positions. However, the Reverend Jesse Jackson, a black minister, sought the Democratic nomination for president in 1984. Even a decade earlier, a black candidate for president would have been unthinkable. And two African Americans served as Secretary of State in the early 2000s. Nevertheless, the overall record of minority participation in the political process shows minimal gains over the past half century.

Social Psychological Factors

We said previously that ideology affects social interaction. Why does the ideology of equal opportunity not alter the superior/inferior kind of interaction between whites and minorities that results from the social structure? It might, except for the many ideologies in any society. Some of the ideologies of America have helped shape and sustain the traditional interaction patterns between the races. In fact, some values, attitudes, and ideologies among both whites and minorities tend to perpetuate the race problem. We examine those of the whites first.

Majority Perspectives. The initial low position of minorities in America stems from the circumstances of their arrival—as indentured servants, slaves, or unskilled laborers. The *ideology necessary to legitimate the enslavement or subordination of minorities was already present.* The first white settlers in America believed in their own racial superiority and certainly considered themselves superior to the "savages" who were native to America. Similarly, the English, on first making contact with Africans, considered them very "puzzling" creatures and tried to determine why the people were black. In one explanation, blacks were said to be the descendants of Ham, whom the Bible says God had cursed. Actually, as stated in the ninth chapter of Genesis, the curse was pronounced by Noah, not God, and it was against Ham's son, Canaan. The fact that many people have accepted the argument underscores the power of the *fallacy of the appeal to prejudice,* for those who accepted the argument undoubtedly acted out of prejudice rather than knowledge of the Bible. In any case, Africans were a different kind of people, and the difference was seen to be undesirable.

fallacy

A number of white groups entered the country in low-status, low-power positions (and were to some extent the objects of prejudice), but none of them were so looked down upon as the minorities. A number of additional factors worked against minorities but not against whites: (1) the economy needed less and less unskilled labor, (2) their skin color was a "visible" disability, (3) the political system no longer offered jobs for votes so freely, and (4) their smaller households probably did not have several wage earners.

Prejudice, a "rigid, emotional attitude toward a human group" (Simpson and Yinger 1965:15), is an attitude that is widespread in the white majority (Bonilla-Silva, Goar, and Embrick 2006). Prejudice against any group legitimates different treatment of group members, generates resistance to programs designed to help the group (such as affirmative action programs that increase the number of minorities in higher education and the workplace), and creates the desire to live in areas with few or none of the group members (Torres and Charles 2004; Loury 2005; Iceland and Wilkes 2006). White prejudice, then, helps perpetuate white dominance.

prejudice
a rigid, emotional attitude that legitimates discriminatory behavior toward people in a group

Prejudice is an individual characteristic, but its causes lie outside the individual— no one is born with prejudice. Simpson and Yinger (1965:49–51) identified a number of sources of prejudice. The sources included personality needs; the usefulness of prejudice for certain groups (low-status whites, for instance, who have been better off than African Americans); group tradition (children learn to hate without knowing precisely why); and certain attributes possessed by the minority group. "Group attributes" are questionable as a source, however. They may serve as a useful rationalization for prejudice, but they do not generally cause that prejudice.

Prejudice does not necessarily have so rational a basis as a consistent set of beliefs about or a well-defined image of the target group. Social psychologists have known for a long time that certain groups can be defined as undesirable even when the attributes of those groups are vague. This insight is expressed in an old poem:

> I do not love thee, Dr. Fell,
>> the reason why I cannot tell.
>> But this I know and know quite well,
>> I do not love thee, Dr. Fell.

One consequence of prejudice is that it facilitates fallacious thinking. To the prejudiced person, certain *fallacies of non sequiturs* come easily: They are on welfare, therefore they don't want to work; they have more children than they can properly care for, therefore they show themselves to be immoral; they don't speak proper English, therefore they are intellectually inferior; and so forth. The "they" of course is whichever minority group the speaker wants to castigate. The same arguments have been used about many different groups.

fallacy

Prejudice continues to exist, in spite of decades of efforts to combat it. Most whites believe that minorities have equal opportunities now, but minorities assert that they encounter prejudice frequently or even daily (Polling Report 2007). Studies of interracial

No group is free of prejudice
or of being victims of
prejudice.

behavior in everything from classrooms to stores to street encounters to choice of housing location confirm the existence of a great deal of prejudice (Feagin and Vera 1995;
Emerson, Yancey, and Chai 2001).

Stereotypes that reinforce prejudice and discriminatory behavior also continue
(Jackson et al. 1997; Frederico 2006). Even positive stereotypes can be used to maintain white dominance. For example, Asian Americans are frequently viewed as the
"model minority." In this view, they succeed because of their strong family life, their
hard work, and their high value on education. While the stereotype has some validity,
it has been used to dismiss the need for programs that help minorities by providing
more educational and work opportunities (Yu 2006). The idea is: if Asian Americans
can do it, why can't the other minorities? The argument that if one does it, all can, is
another example of a *non sequitur.*

The insidious nature of prejudice is illustrated by the way it legitimates and helps
perpetuate the interaction patterns occurring in institutions. In the schools, for instance,
a black child may perform poorly because, in part, he or she senses a teacher's hostility,
born of prejudice. The teacher labels the child as having mediocre ability and places him
or her in an appropriate group. The child may accept the teacher's definition of his or her
ability, and that definition may be further reinforced through IQ tests and subsequent
teachers' reactions. Thus, prejudice further reduces the chances of academic success for
a poorly prepared child, and the normal policies and practices of the school, such as IQ
testing and grouping by ability, reinforce an official definition of the child's ability. If a
child rebels against this hostile and repressive environment and becomes a "behavior
problem," the teacher will conclude that his or her initial hostility is fully justified.

Minority Perspectives.   In the face of disparaging attitudes and ideologies, minorities can get trapped in a vicious circle. By experiencing disparagement, deprivation,
and powerlessness, members of a minority group may develop attitudes of alienation
and cynicism about society. We have already noted that far more minorities than whites

PREJUDICE IN EUROPE

Prejudice is found everywhere. It varies from one country to another as well as within countries. In the United States, the fear of economic competition (for jobs and income) has often fanned the flames of prejudice and led to racial tensions and riots. The threat—real or not—of economic competition is also a factor in prejudice in other nations.

Quillian (1995) studied prejudice in a number of European countries. He found that the average prejudice scores varied from one country to another (figure 8.4). He also looked at the extent to which the people in each nation defined the threat from people of other races and nationalities as being due to such things as adding to problems of delinquency and violence, leading to lower educational quality, and creating a drain on social security benefits.

Quillian's analysis showed that perceived threat explained most of the variations in average prejudice scores in the 12 European nations. He found that such individual characteristics as education, age, and social class had little impact on prejudice and explained none of the variations between countries. Rather, the economic conditions in each country and the size of the racial or immigrant group and the more problematic the economy, the more the minorities are perceived to be an economic threat and the higher level of prejudice.

SOURCE:
Quillian 1995

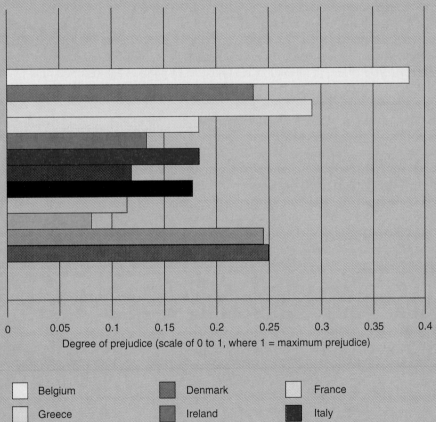

Degree of prejudice (scale of 0 to 1, where 1 = maximum prejudice)

Belgium Denmark France
Greece Ireland Italy
Luxembourg Netherlands Portugal
Spain United Kingdom West Germany

FIGURE 8.4   Racial Prejudice in Europe.
Source: Adapted from Quillian 1995.

agree that minorities suffer from discrimination and do not have equal job opportunities. They are also much less satisfied than whites with the treatment they receive in American society, and many believe that they are disliked by the rest of Americans (Saad and Newport 2001; Polling Report 2007).

Such attitudes can lead minorities to despair of being able to make significant advances in their lives. They may accept their low position rather than to struggle against it. In turn, remaining deprived and powerless confirms their perspective. How does this situation compare with our earlier observation that African Americans place an even higher value on education than whites do? Mickelson (1990) answers the question in her research with nearly 1,200 high school seniors. She, too, found that African Americans believed more strongly than whites that education is essential to mobility, but African Americans were also more skeptical than whites about the value of education to them personally. They were more likely to believe that the education would not pay off for them as it does for whites and that they would be treated unfairly in the workplace regardless of their education. In other words, many minorities who might otherwise aspire to higher education will not go through the struggle to get it because they are convinced that they still live in a racist society in which they face unfair treatment.

Moreover, to the extent that minorities hold negative attitudes about the value of education to them, they will not achieve positions of power in education, which would allow them to alter the structure of the institution. Their attitudes and values minimize their participation and in turn allow continuation of policies and practices that maintain them in subordinate positions.

Finally, for minorities in ghetto areas, there is the additional problem of a *lack of role models* (Wilson 1987). One unfortunate consequence of the exodus of middle- and upper-class African Americans from segregated areas since the 1960s is that ghetto youths no longer see these people. They no longer see people who got a good education, work at good jobs on a regular basis, and thereby become examples of what can be accomplished. They could also be mentors to young, impoverished African Americans. Instead, those who remain in the ghettoes see a pervasive hopelessness, cynicism, and rejection of educational and occupational aspirations. They live in a climate of low expectations, and many social psychologists argue that the expectations are crucial, virtually guaranteeing continued deprivation unless the expectations are somehow changed.

Public Policy and Private Action

Minority groups themselves have launched attacks on the forces that discriminate against them to the detriment of their desired quality of life. The result has been *intergroup conflict* as minorities strive to alter values, attitudes, ideologies, and social structural arrangements.

Resolution of the problem requires more than the actions of the minorities, however. What kind of actions may be taken, keeping in mind that any action will probably involve some conflict (verbal debate at the very least)?

First, attitudes and ideologies can be changed through a policy of persistent education in schools and the mass media. Many efforts have already been initiated, of course, but throughout the country there still are extensive prejudice and adherence to ideologies that disparage minorities. Educational efforts, incidentally, should attack not only the negative attitudes and ideologies about minorities but also the unrealistic ideas that many whites have about the consequences of an integrated society. Many are unaware that school desegregation brings benefits to whites as well as to minorities (Scherer and Slawski 1981; Mickelson 2001). Private initiatives that bring whites and minorities together in social and religious settings also can reduce prejudice (Vora and Vora 2002).

Second, minorities need to continue to mobilize for political action that will shape public policy. It is imperative to exercise expanded influence in the government at all levels. For example, an analysis of black employment in the civil service in 43 American cities showed that not only the size of the black population but also the presence of a black mayor increased the levels of black employment (Eisinger 1980).

Political action is particularly important in the area of employment (Herring 2002). Even though job discrimination is against the law, it continues to occur. New policies and programs are needed to increase workplace equality. Local and state governments could help with the auditing of companies to ferret out instances of discrimination. Funding can be restricted and contracts withheld from firms that repeatedly discriminate against racial and ethnic minorities.

Third, equal educational opportunities must be guaranteed to all minorities. In the late 1980s, Asian Americans protested about discrimination when their numbers were restricted in the California University system. Asian Americans were qualifying in disproportionate numbers for university admission; officials restricted their entry to maintain room for other racial groups. But why should people who are performing well be penalized?

The problem of other groups—notably African Americans and Hispanics—is different. Too few are seeking and gaining entrance to higher education. Programs are needed to keep minorities in school (Hispanics have particularly high dropout rates) and encourage them to seek the highest possible level of attainment. Among other factors, having a higher proportion of faculty and administrators who are minorities and increasing the contact of student affairs officers with minority students help raise the retention rate (Opp 2002). Educators can also recruit those minority students who are in higher education to help analyze the situation and develop strategies for redressing the problem (Hobson-Horton and Owens 2004).

Fourth, legislation must be continually introduced and backed up by the commitment of the federal government to enforce the law. Many beneficial changes have occurred in the wake of such legislation and commitment. Some observers despair of the law having any force, but they often expect too much from law. Laws can change attitudes and alter behavior, but only by increments. A law is passed, people find ways to circumvent it, and a new law is passed to address the contradiction between the intended and the actual results of the first law. Over time the intent of the law is increasingly realized.

Programs must attack institutional racism directly. For example, *affirmative action programs* attempted to increase minority participation in business, industry, education, and service agencies. In essence, affirmative action was a preemptive policy, preventing discrimination before it ever occurred (Reskin 1998). In spite of considerable evidence that such programs can be effective (Fosu 1992; Davidson and Lewis 1997; Button and Rienzo 2003; Alon and Tienda 2005a), they have been dismantled and their legality denied in the courts. Some new programs that achieve the same aims are needed.

One aspect of the race problem that has broad implications is *residential segregation*. The majority of American Indians live on reservations. Most Hispanics live in their own segregated neighborhoods, or "barrios." African Americans are concentrated in the inner cities of metropolitan areas. Residential segregation virtually guarantees segregated social life and education (unless there is busing), and it inhibits the kind of intergroup contact that can break down myths, prejudice, and racist ideologies (Ellison and Powers 1994). It follows that a program designed to achieve residential integration could have a significant influence on the problem. One such effort, the Gautreaux Program, was designed to help low-income black families move into better housing in white suburbs and black inner-city neighborhoods (Rosenbaum et al. 1991). Both the families who moved into the white areas and those who moved into the black areas reported making friends and finding support from their neighbors. Those who moved into the suburbs did report more experiences of harassment, but they were relatively minor and decreased over time. Thus, it is possible to move low-income minorities into middle-class white communities with minimal problems.

Follow-Up. Think about the relationships you have had with people of other racial groups. What factors made some of these relationships more positive than others?

Summary

America's black, American Indian, Asian, Pacific Islander, and Hispanic minorities comprise a substantial and growing proportion of the population. Inequalities between the majority white race and minority races are primarily the result of sociocultural factors. Skin color is a minor biological characteristic, but it is a major sociocultural factor.

The meaning of the problem and the diminished quality of life it imposes on minorities may be summed up in terms of citizenship rights; economic opportunities; the rights of life, liberty, and the pursuit of happiness; and the right to dignity as a human being. In each of these four areas, it is a distinct advantage to be white. Minorities have been deprived of basic citizenship rights, such as the right to vote and the right to be governed by and be equal before the law. Economically, minorities have suffered discrimination in employment opportunities and income. With respect to the value Americans place on life and happiness, minorities have been disadvantaged in terms of life chances. They often have lived in fear and been treated as though their lives were of less value than the lives of whites. Their right to dignity has been violated by the myth of "success around the corner" and the myth of inferiority.

An important social structural factor that contributes to the problem is institutional racism. Minorities are kept clustered in the lower levels of the stratification system and are exploited by the normal policies and practices of institutions, including the mass media, education, the economy, and government. Social psychological factors of attitudes, values, and ideologies of both the white majority and the minorities compound the structural discrimination. Whereas the social structural factors lead to devaluation of minorities, the social psychological factors can lead, in addition, to self-defeating behavior on the part of minorities.

Key Terms

Biological	Life Chances
Characteristic	Morphological
Disfranchise	Prejudice
Ethnic Group	Race
Exploitation	Racism
Institutional Racism	Stealth Racism

Study Questions

1. What do social scientists mean by "race"?
2. Discuss the extent and origin of races, ethnic groups, and racism in America.
3. How do prejudice and discrimination affect minorities' rights of citizenship?
4. Do minorities have equal economic opportunities?
5. In what sense do prejudice and discrimination violate minorities' rights to life and happiness and to dignity as human beings?
6. How is their position in the stratification system a factor in the problems of minorities?
7. Discuss the ways in which social institutions diminish minorities' quality of life.
8. What are the social psychological aspects of the white majority that are involved in the problems of minorities?
9. What kinds of attitudes on the part of minorities exacerbate the race problem in America?
10. Discuss some of the institutional changes that are needed to address the problems of America's minorities.

Internet Resources/ Exercises

1. Explore some of the ideas in this chapter on the following sites:

http://www.naacp.org Site of the National Association for the Advancement of Colored People, with the latest news on racial issues and a variety of other resources.

http://www.census.gov The U.S. Census Bureau site, with special reports and comprehensive statistics on racial and ethnic groups.

http://www.hrw.org Information on race problems throughout the world by the Human Rights Watch.

2. Find a Hispanic site—a Hispanic magazine or journal, or a Hispanic advocacy group, or a Hispanic news site—and make a list of the concerns expressed over the last year or so on the site. To what extent do those concerns reflect and/or address the inequalities identified in the text?

3. Compare the situation of African Americans with that of Asian Americans. Gathering materials from sites for each of the groups, compare both their grievances and their achievements. On the basis of your findings, what kinds of recommendations would you make to each group?

For Further Reading

Bowser, Benjamin P., and Raymond G. Hunt, eds. *Impacts of Racism on White Americans.* 2nd ed. Thousand Oaks, CA: Sage, 2002. Various chapters show that, far from disappearing, racism is still strong in America, and there are both advantages and disadvantages for white Americans in racist practices.

Cafferty, Pastora San Juan, and David W. Engstrom, eds. *Hispanics in the United States: An Agenda for the Twenty-First Century.* New Brunswick, NJ: Transaction, 2002. A comprehensive overview of the quality of life of Hispanics in the United States and their role in various social institutions.

Dobratz, Betty A., and Stephanie L. Shanks-Meile. *"White Power, White Pride!": The White Separatist Movement in the United States.* New York: Twayne Publishers, 1997. A useful review of extremist groups such as the Ku Klux Klan and American Nazis, including their ideologies and political efforts.

Feagin, Joe R. *Racist America: Roots, Current Realities and Future Reparations.* New York: Routledge, 2001. A sociological analysis of racism that shows how it is embedded in the system, including a discussion of the historical roots of racism in our European heritage.

Friedman, Murray, and Nancy Isserman, eds. *The Tribal Basis of American Life: Racial, Religious, and Ethnic Groups in Conflict.* Westport, CT: Praeger, 1998. Various authors explore ways in which America is not a "melting pot" but a mix of increasingly contentious groups.

Graves, Joseph L., Jr. *The Emperor's New Clothes: Biological Theories of Race at the Millennium.* Brunswick, NJ: Rutgers University Press, 2001. A biologist gives a history of the idea of race and shows how race is a social rather than a biological construct.

chapter 8 review

PART 4

Problems
of Social
Institutions

Social institutions exist in every society to solve the problems and meet the needs of people. The government should protect people, secure social order, and maintain an equitable society. The economy should provide the basic necessities of life. Education should fulfill people and train them to function well in society. The family should nurture its members and provide them with emotional stability and security. The health care system should maintain emotional and physical well-being.

Unfortunately, social institutions create as well as solve problems. In this section, you'll learn how the government and the political system fail in some of their functions; how the economy, including work, is detrimental to the quality of life for some people; how education fails to fulfill its functions for some individuals; how family life can detract from, rather than enhance, well-being; and how the health care system does not adequately meet the physical and emotional needs of some Americans.

Society cannot exist without social institutions, but not everyone benefits equally from those institutions. Some even become victims. Institutions need reshaping in order to maximize the well-being of all Americans.

Government and Politics

"Why Isn't There Help for People Like Me?"

Jacquelyn is the single mother of two preschool children. Shortly before her second child was born, her husband, Ed, lost his job. He was unable to find another one. About the time they had exhausted their savings, he announced that he couldn't take it any more and disappeared. Jacquelyn, who only has a high-school education, is struggling to survive:

We lost our home. The kids and I are living in a cheap apartment. We're barely getting by. I don't have enough money to even buy my kids any new toys. And when I go to the grocery store, I see other mothers putting all kinds of good food into their baskets that I can't afford. My parents give us a little, but my dad is on disability and they have a hard time meeting their own bills. I married Ed right out of high school. So I've never worked, and I don't have any skills. I can't even use a computer.

I remember that we were promised the government would give us a safety net. Well, where is it? I'm in a job training program now, but who's going to take care of my kids while I work? And how am I going to pay for someone to take care of my kids? How much do they think I'm going to make from the kinds of jobs they're training me for?

What I'd like to know is, why isn't there some real help for people like me? The government tells me I have to get a job in a couple of years or I won't get any more welfare. Why doesn't the government find Ed and make him help support his kids? For all I know, he's found work somewhere else and has plenty of money. Or why doesn't the government make sure that I get a job that will pay me enough so I can give my kids a decent life? Our country goes all over the world helping people in need, and forgets about people like me. I'd like to see some of those politicians take my place for a while. Maybe then they would realize how some of us die a little bit every day from worrying about what's going to happen to us and our kids and how we're going to survive.

Introduction

What adjectives would you use to describe American government? How about American politics? If you are like many students we have taught, you probably came up with such adjectives as "huge," "inefficient," "corrupt," and "self-serving." However, we have also had students who described government and politics as "effective" and "helpful."

Let's follow up with another question: What role does government play in social problems? Some students see government as a major contributor to social problems. Others see it as the only hope for resolving them. Most students agree that the government should take a leading role in attacking various problems.

Each of these responses has some validity. Throughout this book, we note various ways in which the government and politics enter into both the causes and the resolution of social problems. In this chapter, we concentrate on the ways in which government and politics are themselves problems. We begin by examining the functions of government—what people believe they can legitimately expect from government. We then look at four specific ways in which government and politics are problems, how those problems affect people's quality of life, and various structural and social psychological factors that contribute to the problems. Finally, we explore possible ways to attack the problems of government and politics.

Why Government?

anarchism
the philosophy that advocates the abolition of government in order to secure true freedom for people

Can you imagine a society without any government? Some people can. **Anarchism** is a philosophy that advocates the abolition of government in order to secure true freedom for people. According to anarchists, people are free only when they can cooperate with each other to achieve their ends without the restraints of government and law. To be sure, history provides abundant examples of governments that have deprived people of freedom. Nevertheless, we agree with the student who said: "When I look at the way that governments have exploited and oppressed people throughout history, I am sympathetic to the idea of anarchism. But I still think we need government."

The question is, why do we need government? What do people expect from their government? What functions does it fulfill? We shall discuss four important functions. Keep in mind that government at all levels—federal, state, and local—is involved in fulfilling these functions.

Protect the Citizenry

The first function of government is to protect the citizenry. Americans expect government to protect them from foreign aggressors. This function will be explored in greater detail in chapter 14. They also expect the government to protect them from various threats to their well-being, *threats that come from sources more powerful than any individual* (Sypnowich 2000). For example, people look to government for protection from environmental hazards, unsafe or unfair business practices, and corporate exploitation of consumers. In recent years, many Americans have looked to government to stop the flow of illegal immigrants into the nation. It's estimated that as many as 850,000 people come in illegally each year (Marsh 2006), and some Americans believe that they take away jobs from citizens and use services that increase taxes and costs to citizens. As of this writing, governments at all levels are trying to stem the flow. The federal government is proposing to increase border security, including the building of hundreds of miles of fence along the border with Mexico. Some state and local governments have enacted, or are considering enacting, laws that punish employers who hire illegals and landlords who rent to them.

Protection at the federal level comes in the form not only of laws but of regulatory agencies. A **regulatory agency** is an organization established by the government to enforce statutes that apply to a particular activity. For instance, the Securities and Exchange Commission (SEC) monitors the trading of stocks and bonds, whereas the National Labor Relations Board (NLRB) monitors employer-employee issues. Although many people complain about the irrational and autocratic procedures of the regulatory agencies, they were established mainly in response to demands from citizens who felt the need for protection.

An example of the way the protective function works is seen in the Food and Drug Administration's (FDA's) monitoring of prescription drugs. In the early 1960s, the world

regulatory agency
an organization established by the government to enforce statutes that apply to a particular activity

The police are one way the government performs its function of regulating behavior and maintaining civil order.

was shocked at the news of babies being born without arms or legs. The tragedy took place, for the most part, in Europe and Australia and was linked to mothers' ingestion of the drug thalidomide. Thalidomide had been used as a tranquilizer and to treat nausea in pregnant women (Colborn, Dumanoski, and Myers 1997), but it was eventually shown that the drug also caused terrible deformities in children who were exposed to it while in the womb. Although Americans didn't avoid the tragedy altogether, they did escape the large number of cases that occurred in other nations because a physician at the FDA delayed approval of the drug, insisting on more safety data before the agency would agree to its use. The action of the agency protected a great many children from serious handicaps.

Secure Order

A second function of government is to *secure order*. In contrast to anarchists, many observers argue that government is necessary to control individuals so that society does not degenerate into chaos and violence. By regulating people's behavior in the economy and other areas of social life, government helps prevent the destructive disorder that would result from a situation in which individuals acted to benefit themselves (Durkheim 1933).

Although there may be disagreement about whether government is necessary for social order, there is no disagreement about the importance of that order. Imagine what it would be like to live in a society in which there were no consensual rules about such matters as traffic, education of the young, or the right to private property. *Order is essential to both emotional and physical well-being.*

Distribute Power Equitably

A third function of government is to distribute power equitably so that every citizen has *an equal opportunity for life, liberty, and the pursuit of happiness.* In other words, a person's freedom and aspirations should not be constricted because of his or her sex, race, age, religion, or socioeconomic background. A person should not have more power than others simply because he is male rather than female, white rather than nonwhite, and so on.

We have shown in previous chapters that such factors have and do affect people's life chances. We have also noted the role of the government in redressing these inequities. A good example is the right to vote (Burns, Peterson, and Cronin 1984). In the early years of the nation, the right to vote was limited to white, male adults who were property owners and taxpayers. Thus, in the first election for which a popular vote was recorded (1824), less than 4 percent of the population voted. In response to public demands, federal and state governments took action to broaden voting rights. For example, a number of constitutional amendments assisted in gradually enlarging the franchise. The 15th Amendment, ratified in 1870, gave black males the right to vote, although state and local governments found numerous ways to subvert this right. In 1920 women gained the right as a result of the 19th Amendment. Finally, the 26th Amendment, ratified in 1971, extended the right to vote to 18-year-olds.

Provide a Safety Net

Finally, government functions *to provide a safety net, a minimum standard of living below which it will not allow citizens to fall.* Even if opportunities abound, some people—because of such things as the economy and life circumstances—are not able to achieve what most Americans define as a minimal standard of living. In addition, as Americans discovered in the Great Depression that followed the stock-market crash in 1929, there are times when opportunities are severely limited. It was in response to the hardships of the Depression that, in the 1930s, President Franklin Roosevelt initiated the New Deal, which featured programs like the Social Security system. Since that time, Americans have come to expect government actions to provide a safety net that secures a minimum standard of living (Kryzanek 1999).

Differences exist over what should be included in the safety net. Currently, safety-net benefits include, for example, Social Security and Medicare for the retired, short-term financial aid for the unemployed, subsidized lunches for poor school children, and health insurance for children who otherwise would be uninsured (Long and Marquis 1999; Felland et al. 2003).

Problems of Government and Politics

The problems discussed in this section reflect the fact that *political parties and government bureaucracy play a central role in the way representative democracy functions in the United States.* **Political parties** are organized groups that attempt to control the government through the electoral process. A **bureaucracy** is an organization in which there are specific areas of authority and responsibility, a hierarchy of authority, management based on written documents, worker expertise, management based on rules, and full-time workers. The government bureaucracy includes those government employees whose jobs do not depend on elections or political appointment.

Inequalities in Power

The actual distribution of power in American society contradicts the expectation that the government should ensure equity. But exactly how is power distributed? This question is not easy to answer.

Pluralism or Power Elites?   Who holds the most power in the United States? Many social scientists believe that America is a *pluralistic society* in terms of the distribution of power. **Pluralism** means that power is distributed more or less equally among **interest groups,** which are groups that attempt to influence public opinion and political decisions in accord with the particular interests of their members. Thus, an interest group such as the National Rifle Association (NRA) exercises power in the political sphere to protect its members' insistence on the right to own firearms. The National Organization for Women (NOW) exercises power to protect and advance the rights of women.

In contrast to the pluralist view, the **power elite model** asserts that power is concentrated in a small group of political, economic, and military leaders (Mills 1956). In essence, the top leaders in government, in business, and in the military determine the major policies and programs of the nation—and they do this in a way that furthers their own interests and solidifies their power. A variation, held by Marxists and some others, is that capitalists wield the power, including power over the government (Barry 2002). Most of the people who hold to the power elite view argue that interest groups have some power, but mainly in their capacity to lobby members of Congress, whereas the great bulk of individuals is an unorganized, powerless mass controlled by the power elite.

political party
an organized group that attempts to control the government through the electoral process

bureaucracy
an organization in which there are specific areas of authority and responsibility, a hierarchy of authority, management based on written documents, worker expertise, management based on rules, and full-time workers

pluralism
the more or less equal distribution of power among interest groups

interest group
a group that attempts to influence public opinion and political decisions in accord with the particular interests of its members

power elite model
a model of politics in which power is concentrated in political, economic, and military leaders

Evidence can be gathered in support of both the pluralist and the power elite positions. Domhoff's (1990) analysis of decision making, for example, concludes that the upper class generally rules the nation. Many observers found support for the power elite model in the Bush administration's ties to the oil industry. President Bush owned an oil company. Vice President Cheney was head of Halliburton, an energy and construction firm. And Condoleezza Rice, the national security adviser, had been on the Chevron board of directors for a decade. Critics charged that the U.S. Middle East policy, including the war on Iraq, was shaped by the administration's close ties to the oil industry. Further evidence of the ties was the awarding of billions of dollars of government contracts to Halliburton for various projects in rebuilding Iraq and servicing U.S. troops still in Iraq (Burger and Zagorin 2004).

Power and Inequality.   Although there is some validity to both the pluralist and the power elite positions, neither seems to capture fully the realities of power distribution. *People are not powerless, particularly when they organize.* The National Rifle Association has been able to block much gun-control legislation even in the face of strong public opinion favoring such legislation. Mothers Against Drunk Driving (MADD) has influenced the passage of new legislation on drinking while driving, helping to reduce the number of deaths caused by drunk drivers.

At the same time, *there clearly are power inequities;* otherwise the poor, women, and minorities, among others, would not have had to struggle for so long against their various disadvantages. In spite of its efforts, for example, the National Organization for Women could not get the Equal Rights Amendment (ERA) ratified; and in spite of the work of numerous civil rights organizations, African Americans and other minorities have made only modest headway in their efforts to achieve equity in the economy.

In other words, regardless of which model of power distribution most accurately reflects the realities of social life, the government clearly has not maintained an equitable distribution of power. The longstanding deprivations of certain groups show that Americans have not yet achieved the ideal of liberty and justice for all.

The Failure of Trust

An important part of the task of securing order is the building of trust (Levi 1998). Trust in this context means having confidence that others will fulfill their responsibilities. Citizens need to trust each other and they need to trust the government. Trust is essential if people are to cooperate and work together in maintaining the norms and the laws of society. If citizens distrust their government, they are more apt to resist and even ignore governmental policies and laws.

How much do Americans trust their government? As figure 9.1 shows, the answer is "not very much." In 2005, only the military, police, and organized religion had half or more of Americans express "a great deal" or "quite a lot" of confidence in them. Fewer than half expressed such confidence in the presidency or Supreme Court and only about one out of five Americans expressed such confidence in Congress.

Why do Americans view government with more skepticism than they do other social institutions? Unfortunately, researchers who survey people on their level of confidence do not probe into the reasons for their responses. It is probably true, as Levi (1998) asserts, that such factors as the breaking of campaign promises, incompetence, and the lack of responsiveness to people's interests and needs lead to distrust. Scandals and corruption also contribute to distrust. Scandals and corruption have never been absent

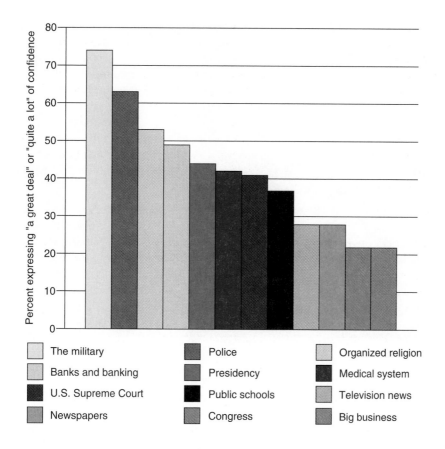

FIGURE 9.1
Public Confidence Levels in Selected Institutions, 2005.

Source: Maguire and Pastore 2006: 113.

from American political life, but the Watergate scandal of the Nixon administration seems to have had a particularly strong impact on people. Public confidence in government began to decline dramatically after the media exposed the break-in at the office of the Democratic National Committee and the attempts to cover up the involvement of President Nixon and officials in his administration (Kryzanek 1999).

Other events in the 1960s and 1970s—including the growing disillusionment with the Vietnam War and with the truth of official reports about the war—also contributed to the decline in confidence. Moreover, Americans have continued to learn about instances in which the government has not been truthful. What are people to think, for example, when they hear that the Central Intelligence Agency (CIA) admitted lying about the nature of unidentified flying objects (UFOs) in order to keep secret its growing fleet of spy planes, or that the Bush administration created an Office of Strategic Influence that would create news items, some of which would be false, in order to gain support for government decisions (Broad 1997; Wilson 2002)? It is not surprising that in response to the question of how much of the time you can trust the federal government to do what is right, 5 percent of Americans in 2002, compared to 16 percent in 1958, said "just about always," whereas 44 percent in 2002, compared to 23 percent in 1958, said only "some of the time" (National Election Studies 2004).

Whatever the reasons for the growing lack of trust, a number of consequences follow from it. We discuss three: lack of citizen participation, altered voting patterns, and political alienation.

Despite efforts by states to make it easier to register to vote, Americans seem reluctant to go to the polls at election time.

Lack of Citizen Participation.   Why participate in the political process if you lack confidence in the government? Why vote if you believe that no matter who is elected the government will not function as it ought?

Although it is not the only reason for not voting, the *failure of trust is certainly one reason* for the relatively low proportion of Americans who vote (Jamieson, Shin, and Day 2002). It is not true, as some people believe, that low voter turnout is a new phenomenon in American politics. Rather, the proportion of people voting has fluctuated over time. Between 1840 and 1908, the proportion who voted in presidential elections varied from about 65 to 82 percent of eligible voters (U.S. Census Bureau 1975:1071–72). The proportion then began to fall. As table 9.1 shows, the proportion continued to vary between 1932 and 2004 but was never more than 62.8 percent for president or 58.5 percent for representatives. Voting proportions for representatives in nonpresidential year elections (these years are not shown in table 9.1) are even lower, ranging from about 33 to 38 percent since 1974 (U.S. Census Bureau 2006). In general, then, *about half or less of the voting-age population participates in national elections, and the proportion is much lower for state and local elections.*

The proportion of people who vote varies considerably by a number of demographic factors. In the 2004 election, for example, the proportion who voted varied by age from 41 percent of those 18 to 20 years to 68.9 percent of those 65 and older; by gender from 56.3 percent of males to 60.1 percent of females; by race/ethnicity from 60.3 percent of whites to 56.3 percent of African Americans to 28 percent of Hispanics; and by education from 32.5 percent of those with 8 years or less to 61.5 percent of those with a high school degree to 78.1 percent of those with four or more years of college (U.S. Census Bureau 2007). Marital status also affects voting patterns of whites, with divorce depressing turnout by nearly 10 percent (Sandell and Plutzer 2005).

At one time, many politicians believed that an important reason for low participation was the *difficulty of registering to vote.* In 1993, therefore, Congress passed the

Percentage of Voting-Age Population Casting Votes For:			Percentage of Voting-Age Population Casting Votes For:		
Year	President	U.S. Representatives	Year	President	U.S. Representatives
1932	52.5	49.7	1968	60.9	55.1
1936	56.9	53.5	1972	55.2	50.7
1940	58.9	55.4	1976	53.5	48.9
1944	56.0	52.7	1980	52.8	47.6
1948	51.1	48.1	1984	53.3	47.8
1952	61.6	57.6	1988	50.3	44.9
1956	59.3	55.9	1992	55.1	50.8
1960	62.8	58.5	1996	49.0	45.8
1964	61.9	57.8	2000	51.2	47.2
			2004	55.5	51.4

TABLE 9.1
Participation in Elections, 1932–2004

SOURCE: U.S. Census Bureau 2007.

National Voter Registration Act, which required states to register voters at driver's license and motor vehicle bureaus, welfare offices, and military recruiting stations. The new law made it easier to register but turned out to have no significant impact on voting participation (Martinez and Hill 1999). Clearly, more than ease of registration is needed to bring more people to the polls.

Altered Voting Patterns. A second consequence of the failure of trust is altered voting patterns. That is, whereas some people neglect to vote, others *change the way they would have voted under conditions of high levels of trust.* In particular, third parties are likely to benefit when people do not trust the government. A study of the third-party nominees of recent decades—George Wallace, John Anderson, and Ross Perot—concluded that lower citizen trust levels strongly predicted a vote for them (Hanenberg and Rojanapithayakorn 1998). The number of votes received by third-party candidates has varied from 33,000 for the Socialist Workers' candidate in 1964 to 19.7 million for Ross Perot in 1992 (U.S. Census Bureau 2007). Some observers believe that the 2.9 million votes cast for Ralph Nader in 2000 were enough to snatch victory away from Al Gore and give the presidency to George Bush. In elections with no third-party candidates, distrustful voters are more likely to vote against the incumbent—whatever the incumbent's party affiliation (Hetherington 1999).

Some political scientists see third parties as a threat because they believe that the two-party system is best for the United States (Bibby and Maisel 1998). Other political scientists disagree, arguing that a responsible three-party system would work well (Lowi and Romance 1998). All agree that government and politics would be different under a three-party system. The three-party system might work better than the present two-party system, or it might create the kind of instability and inaction that have plagued some European nations.

If the failure of trust continues to intensify, Americans may well find out how they will be affected by a three-party system. Whether such a system will restore people's confidence in the government or simply plunge them into even deeper disillusionment is something that no one can say with certainty.

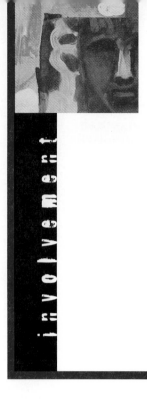

WHY DON'T PEOPLE TRUST THE GOVERNMENT?

As noted in the text, researchers who have surveyed people about their confidence in American institutions have not asked about the reasons for their responses. Why do most people have little confidence in the government, whereas others still have a good deal of confidence?

Conduct your own survey. Ask 10 people how much confidence they have in the federal, state, and local governments. Have them respond to one of four choices: a great deal, quite a lot, some, or very little. Then ask them why they responded as they did. Use follow-up questions until you feel you fully understand their reasoning.

We hope that you found people whose responses fell into each of these four categories. Why did they respond as they did? Can you categorize their responses (e.g., "Politicians are self-serving," "The whole system is flawed," etc.)? How do your respondents' answers differ by level of government? What conclusions would you draw about Americans' views of their government if your respondents are typical?

If the entire class participates in this project, assign different social categories for the interviews. Assign the following kinds of respondents to various class members: males, females, whites, African Americans, Hispanics. Tabulate all the results and note any gender, racial, and ethnic differences.

---

political alienation
a feeling of political disillusionment, powerlessness, and estrangement

Political Alienation. The third consequence of the failure of trust is **political alienation,** *a feeling of political disillusionment, powerlessness, and estrangement.* Alienated people lose interest in political life (Dennis and Owen 2001; Henn, Weinstein, and Forrest 2005). They do not necessarily blame individual politicians for the sorry state of affairs in political life. And they are not merely turned off by the mudslinging and broken promises and endless conflict in the political arena. Rather, they are *disillusioned with the entire system,* including the voting process. For example, just before the 2006 elections, only 49 percent said they were "very confident" that their vote would be accurately counted (Polling Report 2007). The rest were unsure or lacked total confidence that they could vote and have it counted! About the same time, another poll asked Americans how common they believed corruption to be in Washington, D.C. Fifty-eight percent said it is "widespread" and another 39 percent agreed that there is a limited amount (Polling Report 2007).

In short, alienated people believe that the system itself is fundamentally flawed (Scher 1997). For such people, it will take more than appeals to civic duty to involve them once again in the nation's political life.

Waste, Corruption, and Scandals

Americans believe they have a right to expect effectiveness, efficiency, and honesty from the politicians who are running their government. Unfortunately, Americans believe they observe contrary qualities—waste, corruption, and scandals—in those politicians. Moreover, professional assessments of government effectiveness and efficiency do little to change those beliefs. In 2000, for example, various news media reported the results of a study by the Government Performance Review Project of Syracuse University's Maxwell School of Citizenship and Public Affairs (Allen 2000). The researchers looked at the 20 federal agencies that have the most contact with the public and gave them an overall grade of B−. Work done by the agencies includes such activities as cleaning up New York Harbor, administering the national park system, overseeing air traffic, and ensuring that immigrants are in the nation legally. Some agencies did much

The news media frequently report political scandals.

better than others, but all suffered from such problems as reduced funding in the face of expanded work loads and political interference with their tasks.

Some government tasks, in other words, are not being carried out effectively or efficiently because of political decisions. "Government waste," on the other hand, refers to such things as excessive *paperwork, excessive costs, and unnecessary expenditures.* A watchdog group, Citizens Against Government Waste (2006), publishes an annual "pig book" that lists all instances of waste in the annual budget. In the 2006 budget, 9,963 projects were added to various appropriations bills, adding $29 billion to the budget. From 1991 to 2006, such projects cost the taxpayers $241 billion. States with senators on the appropriations committee tend to receive the most benefit from the projects (which included such things as $13.5 million for the International Fund for Ireland, which helped finance the World Toilet Summit, and $500,000 for the Sparta Teapot Museum in Sparta, North Carolina). All the projects met at least one, and most met at least two, of the seven criteria used by the group to identify items for its pig list. The seven are that the project: (1) was requested by only one chamber of Congress; (2) was not specifically authorized; (3) was not submitted for competitive bids; (4) had not been requested by the president; (5) cost significantly more than the amount in the president's budget or the previous year's funding; (6) was not given a congressional hearing; and (7) served only some local or special interest.

You want to beware of the *fallacy of non sequitur* at this point. It does not follow from the fact that a particular project is on the pig list of the Citizens Against Government Waste that the project clearly represents government waste. What one group

fallacy

calls "waste," such as some environmental projects, might be considered important and needed by another group. Nevertheless, no one disputes the fact that waste is a serious problem of government at all levels.

Nor does anyone dispute the *existence of fraud, corruption, and scandals.* A government official estimated that 5 percent of all federal spending in 2005 was lost to fraud, much of it to defense contractors and companies with contracts to rebuild Iraq (Kopecki 2006). In the early 2000s, a number of members of Congress were indicted and jailed or forced out of office by various kinds of corrupt practices and ethics violations, including a sex scandal (homosexual overtures to a Congressional page), bribery, exchanging favorable legislation for campaign contributions, using legislative power to enhance their personal wealth, and using their positions to obtain financial benefits for family members (Sloan 2006). For example, one congressman went to prison for amassing personal wealth by agreeing to get government contracts for various businesses in return for monetary payoffs. Another congressman named his wife as his campaign fund-raiser. She had no other clients and no experience in fund-raising. But she received 15 percent of all funds raised for his campaign.

Such things are not new, of course. There is a long history of corruption and scandals in government at every level. In general, the instances of corruption or scandal involve *a politician acting in terms of self-interest or particular interests to the detriment of the politician's constituency or the general public.* The outcome is not only economic waste but also negative attitudes toward the government and lower levels of trust in government officials (Anderson and Tverdova 2003).

A corrupt practice that is less common today than earlier in the nation's history is **patronage,** giving government jobs to people who are members of the winning party. Recall that one of the fundamental characteristics of a bureaucracy is the expertise of workers. Yet politicians have often hired, or used their influence to obtain employment for, relatives, friends, and party workers no matter their level of expertise. This practice is less common than it once was, because the bulk of government jobs now come under civil service. But the fundamental principle of awarding those who support the winners is still carried out in other ways. Thus, states that support the winning presidential candidate, or that have a governor of the same party as the winning candidate, are likely to receive more federal funds than are other states (Larcinese, Rizzo, and Testa 2006). And a study of contracts awarded to companies to engage in post-war reconstruction in Afghanistan and Iraq found that campaign contributions and political connections were important factors in securing a contract (Hogan, Long, Stretesky, and Lynch 2006).

Corruption may also take the form of "stuffing the ballot box" or other methods of rigging elections. The outcome of the 2000 presidential election was delayed for weeks by disputed votes in Florida (Cannon, Lavelle, and Ragavan 2000; Slevin and Kovaleski 2000). Initially, the news media projected a Democratic victory. Later, they said it was too close to call. After some recounts, the final tally gave George W. Bush an extremely narrow edge over Al Gore. Charges of impropriety quickly surfaced, including flawed ballots, improper instructions, questionable counting methods, and discrimination against nonwhite voters. Democrats took their case to the Florida Supreme Court and, eventually, to the U.S. Supreme Court, whose ruling ensured a narrow victory for George W. Bush. Florida subsequently changed its voting system and abolished the use of punch-card ballots. Americans may never know for certain which candidate was actually preferred by a majority of the Florida voters.

What we do know is that many people were illegally purged from voters rolls (a list sent to election officials included the names of 8,000 Florida residents who had

patronage
giving government jobs to people who are members of the winning party

committed misdemeanors rather than the felonies for which they could legitimately be purged) (American Civil Liberties Union 2004). There were also efforts to intimidate black and Hispanic voters (Miller 2005).

Finally, a number of state governments have approved the requirement of a government-issued identification card before an individual can register and vote (Cohen 2006). Proponents argue that such cards will reduce voting fraud. Opponents point out that those most likely to be affected (discouraged from trying to vote) are the poor, the uneducated, and minorities for whom English is not the first language.

Gridlock

Frequently, the government seems *mired in inaction,* unable to legislate new policies because of ideological conflict, party differences, or a standoff between the executive and legislative branches of the government. Such a situation is known as **gridlock** (Brady and Volden 1998). Gridlock may reflect the fact that politicians are taking stands in accord with contradictory values and are unable to reach a compromise. However, gridlock also occurs when politicians are engaged in power struggles in which who is in control is more important than what gets done (Chiou and Rothenberg 2003).

gridlock
the inability of the government to legislate significant new policies

Gridlock can occur at any level of government. In the late 1990s, a number of states experienced gridlock because they had an increased number of decisions to make after the federal government deferred certain issues to the state level (Levy 1999). For example, in New York the 1999 gridlock prevented passage of the state budget, which was three months late. This delay hampered planning by schools and other nonprofit groups, and important health care proposals languished in political limbo.

Gridlock is likely to maintain or even intensify the failure of trust. A government mired in inaction appears weak to the public it supposedly serves.

Government, Politics, and the Quality of Life

As with all the problems we are examining, government and politics affect the quality of life of great numbers of people. We consider here the way government action or inaction leads to three problem areas that affect quality of life: unequal opportunities for a high quality of life, inadequate protection of freedoms and rights, and the lack of responsiveness to needs.

Unequal Opportunities for a High Quality of Life

Today, Americans generally expect government to maintain an equitable distribution of power so that they have an equal opportunity to secure a high quality of life. Politicians themselves acknowledge their role in this quest for a high quality of life. As we wrote this chapter, we searched the Internet for "quality of life and government." The following are among the tens of thousands of items we found:

- The New York City site encouraged citizens to record complaints related to, and point out problems that detract from, their quality of life.
- A Los Angeles news item discussed local government's role in the city's quality-of-life goals.

- A Kansas City report discussed local elections and their consequences for the area's quality of life.
- A Jacksonville, Florida, annual report considered the quality of life in the community.
- An item from Chicago talked about the county government's role in the area's quality of life.
- A report from Philadelphia noted receipt of a grant to combat crimes that depress the city's quality of life.

Clearly, *politicians and citizens alike expect government at all levels to have a role in those matters that affect the quality of life.* Yet government has not measured up to these expectations and maintained a system in which all Americans have an equal opportunity to reap the benefits deemed necessary for a high quality of life. We noted in the previous three chapters various ways in which some groups benefit to the detriment of others: how, for instance, the wealthy benefit more than the poor from tax laws and other government policies and practices and how white males have more opportunities than do women or people of either sex from racial and ethnic minorities.

These disadvantages mean a lower quality of life for whole groups of people. For example, African Americans, Hispanics, and people in the lower socioeconomic strata have higher rates of negative mood, such as feelings of sadness, than do whites and people in the higher strata (Blackwell, Collins, and Coles 2002).

The relationship between advantages and quality of life holds true in other nations as well. Surveys of people's sense of their well-being in 55 nations, representing three-fourths of the earth's population, found that the higher the income and the greater the amount of equality in the nation, the higher the people's sense of well-being (Diener, Diener, and Diener 1995).

In essence, then, *the government has failed to maintain a social system in which all individuals, regardless of their social origins, have equal opportunities.* People do not expect equal outcomes. The nation's ideology is that anyone can succeed, but no one expects the government to ensure that every individual achieves the highest quality of life. However, Americans do expect the government to ensure a system in which no one's quality of life is diminished automatically because of his or her sex or social origins.

Inadequate Protection of Individual Rights

There is also *a contradiction between the value of individual rights and the way government functions to protect them.* As we noted in the last two chapters, government has not always protected the rights of women and of racial and ethnic minorities. In addition, government has threatened or violated certain basic rights that every citizen ideally possesses. For example, for many years the FBI secretly gathered information and kept files on thousands of Americans who openly opposed certain government programs and policies. Some of this information was secured by illegal means, such as breaking and entering or unauthorized taps of telephone lines. Among those under surveillance by the bureau were Martin Luther King, Jr., and others in the civil rights movement.

It is important to acknowledge that at least a part of the problem of inadequate protection of individual rights lies in the *dilemma faced by government—how can individual rights and social order both be preserved?* A classic instance of the dilemma is the clash between individual rights and national security. During World War II, the clash was decided in favor of national security, resulting in the internment of around 100,000 Japanese Americans. Even though they were American citizens, they were viewed as a threat because of the war with Japan. Some observers still believe that the internment was the appropriate course of action (Rehnquist 1998). Others, however, have concluded that Japanese American citizens were deprived of their rights; in fact, lawsuits were instituted in the 1990s to obtain reparations for the injustice.

Individual rights versus national security remains a prominent issue. In the 1990s, various right-wing militias, fringe groups, and Islamic militants engaged in acts of violence against the government. These acts increased the pressure for measures that are likely to violate individual rights such as more covert domestic spying and information gathering by the government. We explore this issue in more detail in chapter 14.

Additional areas in which individual rights may be threatened or suppressed by government include the criminal justice system, free speech on—and use of—the Internet, drug policies, the rights of immigrants, the rights of homosexuals, police practices, the right to privacy, and religious freedom (American Civil Liberties Union 1999). Consider, for example, the situation of some immigrants. The Immigration and Naturalization Service (INS) uses secret evidence in a small number of cases to deport people considered potential threats (American Civil Liberties Union 1999). Most of the cases involve Arabs or Muslims who cannot fight the deportation order because they do not have access to the "evidence."

Immigrant's rights have also been suppressed by the 1996 Personal Responsibility and Work Opportunity Reconciliation Act, which resulted from perceptions in Congress that immigrants and refugees abuse the welfare system (Hing 1998). The act effectively curbs benefits available to immigrants and refugees. It ignores the fact that immigrant labor serves an important economic function and that second-generation immigrants have significantly lower rates of welfare use than did the first generation.

The Freedom of Information Act of 1966 addressed at least some of the problems of individual rights (Unsworth 1999). The act gave the public access to government records and documents. Access is limited to records of the executive branch and only to those materials that have been "declassified" (i.e., that are not a threat to national security). The number of documents declassified has varied depending on the president. Presidents Nixon and Carter expanded declassification, whereas President Reagan restricted it. President Clinton tried to expand it once again. Unfortunately, even if material is declassified, there is no penalty imposed on an agency that refuses to comply with a citizen's request. The issue of the protection of individual rights continues to be a nettlesome one.

Lack of Responsiveness to Needs

Any satisfying relationship, including the relationship individuals have with organizations, *requires give and take*. If you find school a satisfying experience, for example, it is because you have given your time, money, and energy to complying with the school's requirements and have gained from your classes the knowledge and credentials needed to pursue your goals. People expect the same sort of give and take from government. Yet some Americans perceive the government to be all "take"—in the form of taxes and the demand for compliance with laws and regulations—and no "give"—in the sense of being unresponsive to the needs of the citizenry (see "Why Isn't There Help for People Like Me?" at the beginning of the chapter). Many people perceive the government to be more "take" than is legitimate and less "give" than is responsible.

In the computer age, people expect government service to be as speedy and efficient as the service they may encounter in the private sector (Dawes et al. 1999). In many cases, government service seems torturously slow; in some cases, it never occurs.

Skilled politicians often give the appearance of responsiveness without constraining their own preferences. In responding to people's policy preferences, Cohen (1997) has argued, presidents limit their responses to ideological assertions and expressions of sympathy. A president, for example, will publicly affirm the need for an improved health care system or express dismay at the plight of people struggling in poverty. Yet little will be done to bring about the kind of changes that people have in mind.

Or, as happened in 2005 when Hurricane Katrina devastated the city of New Orleans, officials at all levels, from the president to the governor to the mayor, will promise full and rapid aid to victims. Yet the aid may be minimal and slow in coming. When President Bush visited New Orleans shortly after the hurricane struck, he promised "one of the largest reconstruction efforts the world has ever seen" (Krugman 2006). The governor of Louisiana and the mayor of New Orleans also issued statements promising aid. But a year later, nearly a third of the debris remained in the city. Congress had allocated $17 billion to the Department of Housing and Urban Development, mainly to give cash assistance to homeowners; only $100 million was spent within the first year. Local governments in affected areas in Louisiana and Mississippi struggled to get money from the federal government to rebuild facilities like fire stations and sewer systems. And 13 months after the hurricane, more than half the population of New Orleans had not returned to the still-devastated city (Nossiter 2006).

Although government at all levels shared some blame for the inadequate response to the disaster, attention focused in particular on the federal government and the Federal Emergency Management Agency (FEMA). FEMA was set up to deal with such crises, but the agency's response was so inept that its leader (a political appointee) and a number of others had to resign. Perhaps some of the best help received by the people of New Orleans and other hard-hit areas in the region came not from government but from the hundreds of thousands of volunteers from across the nation who contributed (and continue to contribute) money and their time to assist in the rebuilding efforts (Schwartz 2006).

When government responds so slowly and inadequately, or fails to respond at all, people understandably become cynical. They begin to view *government not as their protector and safety net, but as their competitor for the good things of life, or even as their enemy.* The citizens lose an important source of security and confidence, and the government loses a substantial amount of commitment to civic duty as people ignore or subvert laws and regulations whenever they feel they can do so with impunity.

Contributing Factors

Although many Americans blame inept or self-serving politicians, the problems of government cannot be reduced to defects in elected officials. You don't want to engage in the *fallacy of personal attack* and claim that the problems of government will be solved when present officials are replaced with better ones. Rather, you must recognize and deal with the varied social structural and social psychological factors that create and help perpetuate the problems of government.

fallacy

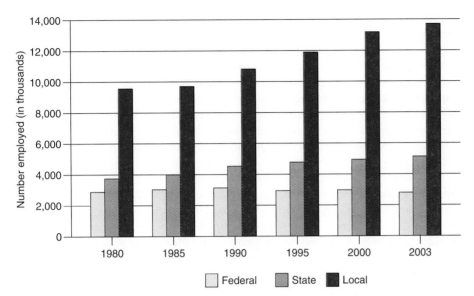

FIGURE 9.2
Government Employees, 1980–2003.

Source: U.S. Census Bureau Web site.

Social Structural Factors

Size. "There is no country in the world today where the entire government establishment of 1910 could not comfortably be housed in the smallest of the new government buildings now going up, with room to spare for a grand-opera house and a skating rink" (Drucker 1968:172). This assessment, now four decades old, dramatizes the growth of government. Figure 9.2 illustrates that growth. Note that, contrary to the beliefs of many Americans, the federal government has not been growing (at least, in terms of the number of people employed). There are fewer people working for the federal government now than there were in the 1990s. Employment by state and local governments, on the other hand, has increased considerably over the past few decades. In 1950, the number of federal, state, and local government employees amounted to 4.2 percent of the total population; by 2005, the proportion was 6.6 percent.

Of course, the number of people employed is not the only way to measure size. In addition to those directly employed, there are those who provide goods and services under contracts, grants, and mandates (Light 1999). If these are added, the size grows by tens of millions of people.

The growth of government reflects both a growing population and a growing number of functions and services assumed by government. Government was smaller and simpler in the early years of the nation. There were far fewer people and a more homogeneous population. There were also no income taxes to collect, no services to the poor to regulate, no monitoring and regulating of the conduct of businesses, no governmental health care obligations, no elaborate defense system to support, and so on. Whether the size of government today is necessary may be debatable; but a substantial amount of the growth was either inevitable because of the growing population or a response to public demand for protection or assistance.

Still, *size—both the size of government and size of the population—has consequences for functioning.* Consider the size of government. It is more difficult for large organizations to be efficient and responsive to the needs of people. Questions must be addressed and procedures must be followed that are not necessary when individuals help each other or small community organizations help people locally. When an individual seeks assistance from the federal government, for example, such questions as the following arise: What agency is responsible for helping? Who in the agency should handle the situation? What procedures (including filling out necessary paperwork) must be followed to meet the requirement of accountability? Who in the agency and/or other government organizations must approve the assistance? And so on. In the case of entire groups who need help (the poor, those suffering discrimination, those without health insurance, etc.), the questions and answers become even more complicated and demanding.

The size of the governed population also affects function. It is more difficult to gain compliance and enforce rules when regulating a large number of people. For instance, Ehrenhalt (1997) reported that there were nearly 3.1 million outstanding violations of the New York City housing code in 1996. However, the city's 200 inspectors can make only about 160,000 inspections per year. Most of the violations will never be addressed. As Ehrenhalt noted, the city government's failure to respond to these violations is rooted in neither indifference nor ineptness. Rather, there are simply more citizens violating the law "than even the most efficient government can possibly keep track of." It may be that the difficulties of effectively governing large cities is one reason why two researchers found in a study of 55 American cities that the larger the size of the city, the less trust the citizens had in their local government (Rahn and Rudolph 2005).

The Structure of Government.   Two aspects of the structure of government contribute to the problems. The first is the extent to which a government is a political democracy. Frey and Al-Roumi (1999), who define democracy as the extent to which a nation maintains political rights and civil liberties for the citizenry, gathered data on the quality of life from 87 countries of the world. Quality of life was measured by infant mortality rate, literacy rate, and life expectancy. They found *a strong relationship between the level of political democracy and the quality of life in the nations.* It seems that such advantages as competitive elections, the opportunity for all citizens to participate in the political process, and a free press contribute to the government's being more responsive to people's needs and implementing policies that enhance their well-being. To the extent that political democracy is maintained, the government is more of a solution than a problem.

The other aspect of structure is *the way the government is organized to fulfill its functions.* In the United States, the federal system provides a constitutional separation of powers between the national and state governments. In addition, there are county, municipal, and township governments. All have direct authority over individuals. This arrangement creates unity without enforcing uniformity, encourages experimentation, and keeps government close to the people (Burns, Peterson, and Cronin 1984).

However, there are disadvantages as well. What level of government is best equipped to provide efficient and effective service? What level of government is responsible for dealing with various social problems? Consider, for example, the following questions: Is a safety net for the poor the primary responsibility of the federal government or of state and local governments? Who is going to handle problems of discrimination based on race/ethnicity, gender, age, or sexual orientation? Should there be national standards for education, or should education be completely under the control of local school boards?

An ongoing struggle among various levels of government over responsibility, or the efforts of government at one level to shift responsibility for a problem to government at another level, can result in an inadequate response to people's needs. As we discussed in chapter 6, the current transfer of major responsibility for poverty from the federal to the state and local level in the form of workfare is having a negative impact on the quality of life of many of America's poor.

Finally, *the government is organized along bureaucratic lines in order to fulfill its various functions.* Look back at the characteristics of a bureaucracy that we discussed earlier, and you will see that it should be a highly efficient and effective form of large-scale administration. If people in a bureaucracy function according to the criteria we listed, the organization should help people expertly and impartially.

In practice, however, bureaucracies never measure up to the ideal. As a result, and in spite of many positive achievements, the very term "bureaucrat" has become a term of disparagement, and a wide variety of government problems are blamed on the bureaucrats. To blame bureaucrats, however, is to substitute the *fallacy of personal attack* for a realistic appraisal.

fallacy

There are various reasons for the disparity between the ideal and the reality. Middle-class bureaucrats may not treat lower-class citizens with the same respect and concern that they do citizens in higher classes. Bureaucrats who try to be impartial in their dealings with people face severe pressure and potential reprisals from individuals who want special consideration. Some government bureaucrats may be in positions for which they have not been properly trained and for which they lack needed expertise.

Other bureaucrats may rigidly follow the rules of the organization even if the rules don't apply well to particular cases. Two business writers call such bureaucrats the "white-collar gestapo," arguing that they mindlessly enforce a growing number of arbitrary rules and regulations (McMenamin and Novack 1999). Indeed, even though the bureaucratic rules and regulations are supposed to cover all circumstances, you can raise the question of whether this is possible when dealing with a large, heterogeneous population. Perhaps bureaucrats need the flexibility to exercise more discretion.

Furthermore, in spite of the highly bureaucratic nature of government, *the government is not organized in a way to deal effectively with waste and corruption.* One way to stop waste and corruption would be to encourage employees to act as internal watchdogs and report such practices (to be "whistleblowers" in contemporary terminology). From time to time, this happens; but in spite of the Whistleblower Protection Act of 1989, most government employees fear reprisals if they blow the whistle on corrupt or wasteful practices (Maier 1998). Their fears are realistic, because the most likely outcome for whistleblowers is demotion or loss of job. Even the U.S. Department of Justice was sued in 2004 by a number of prosecutors and investigators who worked for the department (Fleischer-Black 2004). The employees claimed that the department retaliated against them when they tried to report wrongdoing, including, in one case, firing a lawyer and then investigating her for possible criminal charges.

The Economics of Campaigning. How much would it cost you to become a U.S. senator? It would depend on the state in which you ran, of course, but you could count on a minimum of $3 million and as much as $20 to $30 million (Center for Communication and Civic Engagement 2005). If you started your campaign early, running it for four years, you would need to raise anywhere from $19,000 to $120,000 or more every week! Political advisors can put a price tag on every race from the presidency to local offices, and the total spent on campaigns is staggering.

Campaigning for elective office is expensive, and critics argue that the wealthy are at an advantage when they have millions of dollars of their own money to spend in their efforts to be elected.

The cost of political office is not only high but continually rising (Cantor 2006). In 1976, all elections (at every level) cost approximately $540 million; by 2004, the cost had risen to nearly $4 billion. On the average, a winning House seat cost $87,000 in 1976 and $1 million in 2004, while a winning Senate seat went from $609,000 in 1976 to $7 million in 2004. Figure 9.3 illustrates the rising costs for Congressional campaigns. Note that the costs over the 20-year period covered nearly tripled for Senate campaigns and more than tripled for House campaigns.

In light of the costs of running a campaign, *it is evident that people without access to considerable sums of money or money-raising skills are unlikely to win an election.* In recent decades, some very wealthy individuals have invested millions from their own fortunes as they sought political office. Such a use of personal wealth raises the concern that the nation may be entering a time when only the rich can successfully run for office.

In order to gain and remain in office, whether they are personally rich or not, politicians need massive amounts of money. This need makes politicians beholden to the wealthy and to various interest groups. A politician may be able to vote against the interests and preferences of those who support him or her only at the cost of continuing in office. The fact that poor people in a politician's district have pressing needs for various kinds of aid is not likely to take priority over the interests of the wealthy individuals and interest groups that provide the money that keeps the politician in office.

Some measures have been taken to *reform campaign financing,* which became a hotly debated issue in the late 1990s. In the 1970s, Congress set up the Federal Election Commission and limited the amount that individuals can contribute to a campaign. However, wealthy individuals and interest groups circumvent the intent of the law by giving so-called soft money, contributions directly to the party instead of to an individual candidate.

In 2002, new legislation was enacted that banned national parties from raising soft money (they raised $500 million in 2000) (Woellert 2002). Politicians and their advisors began immediately to find ways to circumvent the law, aided by the Federal Election Commission's interpretation of the new law. One way to circumvent the law is through the so-called *527 political organizations.* These are political interest groups (discussed later) that are tax-exempt under Section 527 of the Internal Revenue Code and that have not been regulated by the Federal Election Commission. In 2004, they spent nearly $425 million on elections (Cantor 2006). Clearly, campaign financing is still problematic.

The Media.   In the first of the televised presidential debates in 1960, Richard Nixon looked unkempt and nervous in contrast to John F. Kennedy, who appeared crisp and confident. Although Nixon won the debate among radio listeners, Kennedy came out ahead among television watchers. This event began a new era in the relationship between media coverage and election results.

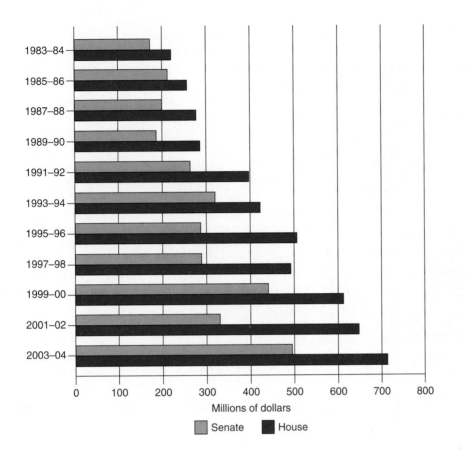

FIGURE 9.3
Cost of Congressional Campaigns.
Source: U.S. Census Bureau Web site.

The media have always played a role in American politics, of course—but *both the nature of the coverage and the influence of the media have changed as radio, network television, cable television, and now the Internet have been added to the print media as factors in the political process.* Let's explore the impact of the media on three aspects of political life: elections; political agendas and action; and public trust.

First, the media are important in political campaigns. For one thing, advertising by candidates accounts for a substantial proportion of the enormous costs of campaigns. Television advertising is particularly expensive, but it is necessary because *69 percent of Americans rely on television for their political news* and television ads affect the outcome of elections (Kryzanek 1999; Drew and Weaver 2006). Yet relying on television means that voters get far less information than is provided by the print media or even by radio. Voters depend heavily on "sound bites"—those brief excerpts from the campaign trail that, in the opinion of television editors, capture something informative about the candidate's position or newsworthy and sensational about the candidate's activities. Interestingly, the length of sound bites decreased from 42.3 seconds in the Nixon-Humphrey campaign of 1968 to 7.3 seconds in the Clinton-Bush campaign of 1992 (Kryzanek 1999:95). How much accurate information can a 7.3-second excerpt from a speech give about a candidate's position?

The point is, voters' knowledge of candidates and their positions are derived from decisions by the people who control the media. What appears in the media, therefore, affects how people vote. The way that the media interpret an incumbent president's

BUREAUCRACY IN INDONESIA

As noted in the text, bureaucrats are supposed to have expertise and act impartially in accord with written rules—but they do not always function that way. In some areas of Indonesia, for example, people are able to purchase positions in the government bureaucracy; they need money, not expertise, to secure the position (Kristiansen and Ramli 2006). Dwight King (1998a, 1998b) made an intensive study of the Indonesian civil service and found a number of additional reasons why the bureaucracy falls short of the ideal.

The Indonesian civil service is organized in 17 ranks. Each employee has a grade and a step ranking within the grade that is based on education and seniority. Employees who perform their duties well advance one step every four years and eventually can qualify for a higher grade. At a certain level, however, the employees must acquire additional education or pass a test in order to continue their advancement.

In spite of this apparently well-organized arrangement, there is often a disparity between an individual's qualifications and the requirements of the position that he or she holds. For instance, an individual who has a graduate degree in liberal arts might be promoted to the head of the agency on public works because no one with an engineering degree is in as high a grade at the time as is the liberal arts graduate. Bureaucrats' educational attainment and civil service grade are more important in determining where they work in the government than is their educational specialization.

In addition, a substantial number of civil servants are promoted even when they have not reached the required grade. Two practices are at work here. One is to promote someone to an "acting" position. The other is to utilize an exception clause in the regulations that allows individuals who have performed in an "extraordinary" way for two years to be promoted even when they are not in the necessary grade.

For some functions, the Indonesian government bureaucracy is also hampered

---

performance, for example, strongly influences his or her chances for reelection (Dover 1998). Similarly, a study of House elections and the media concluded that incumbents have an advantage, particularly among less educated voters, because they have had more television coverage and much of that coverage is positive (Prior 2006). In fact, the more television stations in a district, the greater the advantage of the incumbent.

Cable television may be making the sound bites and comments of television reporters even more important. In earlier decades, presidents could schedule speeches or important news conferences for prime time. Because all the networks carried the event, the president spoke to a considerable segment of the American population. With the growth of cable television, however, a smaller proportion of Americans listen to such speeches and press conferences, opting instead for programs on cable channels (Baum and Kernell 1999).

The Internet offers another outlet for campaigning with as yet unknown consequences for the electoral process. By October 1998, more than two-thirds of congressional candidates had Web sites (Dulio, Goff, and Thurber 1999). The Web sites are used to solicit financial support as well as to provide information about the candidate's qualifications and positions on various issues. In 2004, President Bush's campaign had an e-mail list of six million addresses (Barone 2004). And although television and newspapers still remain the main source of political news, increasing numbers of people are surfing the Web to get their political information (Nelson 2004).

The second impact of the media is on political agendas and government actions. The influence of the media is not limited to elections. As Cook (1998) has argued, *the media are an integral part of the governing of the nation*. Government officials use the by the lack of clearly defined areas of responsibility. For example, three different agencies have responsibility for education: the Ministry of Education and Culture (MOEC), the Ministry of Home Affairs (MOHA), and the Ministry of Religious Affairs (MORA). MOEC is responsible for secondary and higher education, but shares responsibility for primary education with MOHA. MORA is responsible for the Islamic schools, which are mainly at the post-primary level.

This dispersion of responsibility has negative consequences for Indonesian education. First, little effort is made to improve primary education because neither MOEC nor MOHA seeks the resources needed. MOHA secures funding for primary education, but has not sought additional funds because it is responsible for funding, not for quality. MOEC is aware of the need for improvement, but funding is not part of its responsibility.

Second, some schools do not receive the resources they need. For example, MOEC publishes textbooks and sends them to regional warehouses. From there, the regional government is supposed to distribute them to the schools. But the regional governments complain that they do not have the necessary funds to distribute books. Thus, some schools, particularly those in relatively isolated areas, may not receive needed texts and materials.

Third, career advancement for primary school teachers occurs in the context of the contrary decisions of MOEC and regional governments. MOEC evaluates the teachers' performance. Regional governments, however, make promotion and transfer decisions—often independently of MOEC evaluations.

In sum, government bureaucracy in Indonesia is similar to that in other nations: It falls short of the bureaucratic ideal. Yet it does no good to simply complain of "bureaucrats." A different set of people in the same system would make little or no difference in the outcome. It is the way the bureaucracy is organized, not the kind of people in it, that is primarily responsible for the problems.

---

media to shape public opinion and gain support for decisions and programs. In turn, officials are influenced in their decision-making process by the information they glean from the media (Edwards and Wood 1999). To a considerable extent, the media help decide what are the issues, problems, and crises to which political leaders must respond (Dye 1995).

If the media were impartial and accurate, their influence would not be a cause for concern. *However, control of the media lies in the hands of a small group of corporations* (Dye 1995). Four corporations account for the bulk of news coverage on television, and 15 newspaper conglomerates are responsible for over half the newspaper circulation in the nation.

The way in which owners can influence the news coverage is illustrated by an investigation into Fox News (Coyle 2004). The television network is owned by Rupert Murdoch, a wealthy conservative. But Common Cause, a nonpartisan watchdog group, and a liberal political advocacy group filed a petition with the Federal Trade Commission arguing that Fox should stop using its slogan of being "fair and balanced" in the news. In fact, the groups maintained, the news on Fox is consistently biased in favor of the Republican Party and right-wing perspectives. That such a biased perspective affects voters is shown in an analysis by two economists, who found that when Fox News becomes available in a town, Republicans gain votes (DellaVigna and Kaplan 2006).

This point does not mean that media information is always biased or distorted. It does mean, however, that people must be careful not to engage in the *fallacy of authority* and assume that what comes to them through the media is *ipso facto* accurate and impartial. It also means that serious problems, affecting considerable numbers of citizens, may be largely invisible because they are ignored by the media.

Finally, the media have contributed to the failure of trust. Is government more corrupt, unreliable, and unresponsive now than it was in the past? On the one hand, such factors as the civil service, term limits, and extension of the right to vote are evidence that government and political life are more democratic and more effective now than in the past. On the other hand, all too frequent scandals and deceptions at the various levels of government raise questions about the integrity of government and undoubtedly contribute to the failure of trust. Still, such scandals are not new.

What is new is *the way in which the media give so much coverage to scandals, including matters that would have been glossed over as private affairs in past decades.* The mainline media play up stories of scandals and potential scandals in ways similar to those of the tabloids. During the Clinton administration, for example, the media gave enormous attention to the president's sexual improprieties. The media also provided extensive coverage when a number of members of Congress resigned because of sexual or other scandals.

Many Americans indicated a weariness with this extensive coverage, noting its negative impact on their trust in government. At the same time, many Americans admitted to an almost *insatiable curiosity about the scandals* (Ricchiardi 1998). As long as this public demand exists, the media will continue to provide in-depth reports that may expose problems in politics but may also contribute to the growing distrust in government.

Interest Groups.   The most effective way to influence a massive organization like government is through other organizations. The lone individual has little chance of bringing about change, but an organization can put considerable pressure on politicians. For that reason, *interest groups have become an increasingly important factor in American political life.*

There are at least 30,000 interest groups in the United States. Many have political action committees (PACs) that are registered with the government and legally entitled to raise funds and make contributions to election campaigns and political parties (table 9.2). The number of political action committees grew considerably after 1980. In the 2004 election, they contributed $842.9 million to various candidates (U.S. Census Bureau 2006).

lobbyist
an individual who tries to influence legislation in accord with the preferences of an interest group

Interest groups also hire **lobbyists,** individuals who try to influence legislation in accord with the preferences of the interest groups. *Lobbyists use various means to influence politicians.* They may provide a politician with information that supports the interest group's position on a given issue. They may try to cultivate personal friendships with particular politicians. They may treat a politician to expensive dinners and trips. In addition, there is always the promise of support through votes and contributions by members of the interest group.

There are now about 35,000 registered lobbyists in Washington, D.C. (not all lobbyists register, because the rules are unclear and the penalty for not registering is slight). In the first half of 2005 alone, corporations and other interest groups spent $1.16 billion in lobbying (Mullins 2006). The money is not merely to pay the salaries of the lobbyists. One of the lures the lobbyist uses is a substantial contribution to a politician's campaign. The money is also used to wine and dine politicians, provide them with tickets to sporting events and concerts, offer them free trips, and provide them with gifts of various kinds.

TABLE 9.2
Number and Type of Political
Action Committees

Type	Number 1980	Number 1990	Number 2004
Corporate	1,206	1,795	1,756
Labor	297	388	328
Trade, membership, and health	576	695	986
Nonconnected	374	1,062	1,650
Cooperative	42	59	38
Corporation without stock	56	136	110
Total	2,551	4,172	4,867

SOURCE: U.S. Census Bureau Web site.

The abuses of the practice were dramatized in 2006 when a powerful lobbyist, Jack Abramoff, pleaded guilty to fraud, tax evasion, and conspiring to bribe public officials (Stone 2006). Abramoff gained enormous personal wealth while funneling money and other perks to lawmakers in return for favorable legislation. Linkages with Abramoff cost a number of politicians their positions either through resignation or through defeat at the polls.

Another aspect of lobbying that most Americans find troublesome is the fact that many lobbyists are relatives of lawmakers or members of their staff (Eisler and Kelley 2006). In a poll, 80 percent of Americans agreed that it's wrong for relatives to lobby lawmakers. Nevertheless, an investigation reported 53 cases in one year in which members of the House or Senate appropriations committee or their top aides had relatives who were lobbyists. And of those relatives who attempted to get money in appropriations bills for their clients, 22 were successful.

Social Psychological Factors

Public Attitudes. The American ideal is that government is of the people, by the people, and for the people. This statement means that government originates in the people, involves the people, and effectively represents them. Government is meant to be the people's ally, not their opponent. But consider the following (Polling Report 2007):

- 39 percent say that corruption in Congress is "a very serious problem";
- 59 percent have little or no confidence in Congress enforcing high ethical standards;
- 46 percent are very concerned and another 29 percent somewhat concerned about the influence of lobbyists and special interest groups in Washington; and
- 81 percent believe that lobbyists' bribing of members of Congress is common rather than an isolated problem.

Such attitudes reflect the failure of trust. They also help perpetuate the failure of trust. Instead of stimulating people to get involved in government and make necessary reforms, *negative attitudes lead to alienation and withdrawal from political life* (Plane and Gershtenson 2004).

The irony here is that people who believe that the government does not help them become alienated and do not bother to vote. But research shows that members of

Congress not only strive to direct resources into their districts but also try to put those resources where they appear to pay off in terms of votes (Martin 2003). In other words, *alienation becomes a self-fulfilling prophecy,* because negative attitudes lead to non-participation and nonparticipation results in fewer benefits.

In addition to negative attitudes about government and politics, a set of *contrary attitudes* contribute to the problem. Cronin and Genovese (1998) have identified a number of these contrary attitudes in their discussion of the "nine paradoxes" of the American presidency:

> Americans want strong leaders, but they also fear the abuse of power that a strong leader might bring to the office.

> Americans have favorable attitudes toward ordinary people holding political office (thus, the traditional appeal of the candidate who was born in a log cabin), but they also value charisma in their leaders.

> Americans want leaders who will unify the people, but they do not want to compromise their own positions in order to forge the unity.

> Americans admire leaders with vision, but they also believe that leaders should be responsive to public opinion.

Moreover, Americans tend to approve of such items as lower taxes, reduced government spending, and less government interference in daily life. Yet Americans also resist proposals to reduce government or government spending in those areas from which they benefit or which they support for ideological reasons (Young 1998). For example, about half of Americans believe that, in general, the government has too much power and does too much. Yet, when asked about specific programs, a majority believes that the government should do as much or more than it is doing now (Cantril and Cantril 1999). Fewer than 10 percent of the people interviewed wanted the government to do less than it now does on such specific programs as job training, medical research, subsidizing teachers, college student aid, clean air standards, and Head Start.

Such contrary attitudes pose *a dilemma for politicians.* In essence, no matter what a politician does, some segment of the population will be disappointed and frustrated. The easiest course of action is to follow his or her conscience when possible and, at other times, follow the desires of those who contribute the funds necessary to stay in office.

Ideologies.   Americans, for the most part, are suspicious of extreme ideologues and value compromise in resolving political conflicts. Indeed, when politicians of opposing ideologies work together, the result is usually compromise; but under some circumstances, the result may be gridlock. Brady and Volden (1998) studied legislative gridlock in the U.S. Congress. They concluded that members of Congress fall at various points on a liberal-conservative continuum. The median ideology of Congress is also somewhere on this continuum. Recall that the median is the point at which half the cases are above and half are below. For example, if you use -10 as the extreme conservative position, and $+10$ as the extreme liberal position, then calculate the average of all the members of Congress, you might find that the median position of a particular Congress is -2 (slightly conservative).

Let's say that a new policy is proposed, and that it can be placed at $+1$ (slightly liberal). It has a good chance of passing, because it is not that far from the median. It has an even better chance of passing if the existing policy is more liberal than the proposed one. It has less chance if the existing policy is -2, that is, right at the median.

The situation is compounded by Senate filibusters and presidential vetoes. Taken together, these factors indicate a "gridlock region," an area on the continuum that results in gridlock if a proposed new policy falls in this region. The gridlock reflects the fact that there is a sufficient number of politicians on both sides of opposing ideologies so that the issue cannot be resolved.

Public Policy and Private Action

Many of the factors that contribute to the problems of government pose an ongoing dilemma. For example, you cannot reduce the size of the population served. It is doubtful that the overall size of government can be reduced (the number of federal employees declined in the 1990s, but government employees at other levels increased, so that there was a net increase in the total).

Although selected restructuring might be helpful, it is always a trial-and-error process. For example, some people believe that term limits will enable politicians to function more effectively because they will not be hampered by catering to special interests or their own ambitions to pursue long-term careers. However, in states that have instituted term limits for legislators, the tendency is for more power to go to the governor (Mahtesian 1999). With little time to gain political savvy, legislators are likely to have far less influence than the executive branch of state government. At this point, therefore, it is not clear whether term limits for state legislators make state governments more or less responsive to people's needs.

Campaign finance reform is one of the most needed areas for addressing the problems of government. Individuals and groups with money have the most power in government because politicians are dependent on them to gain, and remain in, office. In recent elections, the candidate who raised the most money was also most likely to win. In spite of reforms in recent years, such as certain limits on contributions to specific candidates, huge amounts of money flow from individuals and interest groups into the political coffers as corporations and rich donors find ways to *circumvent the laws on contribution limits* (Rosen 2000).

A number of states have implemented campaign financing reforms that could serve as a model for the federal government. Maine and Arizona became the first states to have a completely subsidized public finance system for legislative candidates (Francia and Hernson 2003). A number of other states offer partial funding. Candidates who accepted the full funding spent less of their time raising money than did other candidates, including those who had partial public funding. Many European nations also have publicly financed elections (Kryzanek 1999). If the United States adopted such a system, it would mean that campaigns would be shorter, less expensive (fewer television ads, etc.), and more likely to focus on issues rather than on personal attacks and extravagant events. To enact such a change, Congress will have to overcome the resistance of interest groups, wealthy individuals, television executives, and others. Without a change, however, politicians will continue to be captive to their sources of money.

Greater citizen participation is another step needed to address the problems of government. When large numbers of people get involved and vote, they can overcome some of the shortcomings of politicians. For example, publicity about the absentee rates of senators and representatives in votes on legislation led voters in many areas to reject at the polls those politicians with high rates of absenteeism (Mintz 1998). As a result, participation in voting on congressional legislation rose steadily over the last 30 years of the 20th century.

At the state and local levels, a number of cases of citizen participation in the governing process illustrate the value of the practice (Kramer 1999). For example, officials in a county in Florida wanted to attack several social problems, including juvenile crime in a poor community composed mostly of racial and ethnic minorities. At first, they made no progress. But when they worked with citizens of the community and included representatives of the racial and ethnic groups in the discussions, the project was not only successful but became a model for other communities. Only when the people became involved were the government officials able to fully understand the situation and become responsive to the people's needs.

The problem is, given the political alienation of so many citizens, how do you secure more participation? One way you can change attitudes is to encourage citizens to become part of a group that engages in political discussions. The National Issues Forum (NIF) sponsors deliberative forums and study groups on national issues. A study of people who participated in NIF discussions found that, at the end of their participation, they had a much more coherent understanding of issues and much less attitudinal uncertainty about political issues (Gastil and Dillard 1999).

Certainly, politically alienated people have little motivation to join such a group. Thus, to increase citizen participation in the governing process, it is necessary to educate people about the effectiveness of such groups and to publicize efforts at various levels of government that have brought about change.

Other measures that increase citizen participation include easing the registration process and allowing citizen-initiated ballot measures at the state level. Increased numbers of people vote in those states that now permit registration on election day (Brians and Grofman 2001). A comparison of states that allow citizen-initiated ballot measures with those that do not showed considerably higher turnout in the former (as much as 35 to 45 percent higher in presidential elections) (Tolbert, Grummel, and Smith 2001).

Finally, *face-to-face canvassing increases the number who vote* (Michelson 2003). Voters who are contacted are significantly more likely to vote than those who are not. And this contact may have a long-term payoff. In a field experiment with 25,200 registered voters, researchers found that those people who were urged to vote either through direct mail or face-to-face canvassing not only voted in significantly higher proportions but also were more likely to vote in subsequent elections (Gerber, Green, and Shachar 2003).

Follow-Up.   What recommendations would you make to government and school officials to increase voter participation?

Summary

Government is necessary because it fulfills a number of important social functions, functions that reflect people's expectations of their government. First, government is expected to protect the citizenry from foreign aggressors and from threats to individual well-being. Regulatory agencies were established to protect citizens from threats to their well-being. Second, government is expected to secure social order. Third, government is expected to distribute power equitably so that citizens have an equal opportunity for life, liberty, and the pursuit of happiness. Fourth, government is expected to provide a safety net, a minimum standard of living below which it will not allow citizens to fall.

A number of problems of government and politics exist in the United States. There are inequalities in the distribution of power. Social scientists disagree about whether power is distributed in accord with a pluralistic or a power elite model. The failure of trust is a second problem. Americans trust most other institutions far more than they trust the government. This distrust has a number of consequences: it leads to a lack of citizen participation in the political process; it alters people's voting patterns; and it leads to political alienation, a feeling of political disillusionment, powerlessness, and estrangement.

A third problem involves waste, corruption, and scandals in government. Waste refers to such problems as excessive paperwork, excessive costs, and unnecessary expenditures. Corruption and scandals usually involve a politician acting in terms of self-interest or particular interest to the detriment of the politician's constituency or the general public.

Gridlock is a fourth problem. Gridlock means that the government is mired in inaction, unable to legislate significant new policies because of ideological conflict, party differences, or a standoff between the executive and legislative branches. Gridlock is likely to intensify the failure of trust.

Problems in government and politics affect the quality of life in a number of ways. Such problems mean that people have unequal opportunities for a high quality of life. They mean that the freedoms and rights of citizens are not always adequately protected and that the government is not adequately responsive to people's needs.

Various factors contribute to the problems of government and politics. The size of the population served and the size of the government itself both affect how well the government can function. The way the government is organized to fulfill its functions—the separation of powers between the national and state governments and the bureaucratic nature of government agencies—also creates some difficulties in effective functioning. On the other hand, the government is *not* organized so as to deal effectively with waste and corruption.

The costs and financing methods of campaigning have particularly adverse effects. Many social scientists believe that campaign finance issues threaten the democratic process itself and virtually ensure politicians' unresponsiveness to people's needs.

The media also contribute to the problems. They are a substantial part of the cost of campaigns, and they determine the information and perspectives that voters receive about the candidates. The media affect political agendas and actions of those in office, which gives them an integral part of the governing of the nation. They also contribute to the failure of trust.

Interest groups have become an increasingly important part of American political life through contributions, lobbyists, and influence on voting blocs. Interest groups can affect legislation in a way that protects particular interests to the detriment of the general well-being.

Social psychological factors that contribute to the problems include the attitudes of the public and the ideologies of politicians. Negative attitudes of the public lead to alienation and withdrawal from political life; contrary attitudes pose a dilemma for politicians. Ideological positions of politicians can lead to gridlock.

Key Terms

Anarchism	Pluralism
Bureaucracy	Political Alienation
Gridlock	Political Party
Interest Group	Power Elite Model
Lobbyist	Regulatory Agency
Patronage	

Study Questions

1. What is meant by anarchism, and why does it appeal to some people?
2. What are the functions of government?
3. Explain the different views on the distribution of power in the United States.

chapter 9 review

4. What is meant by the "failure of trust," and what are the consequences of this failure?

5. Give some examples of waste, corruption, and scandals in government.

6. How can legislative gridlock occur?

7. In what ways do problems of government and politics affect Americans' quality of life?

8. What social structural factors contribute to the problems of government and politics?

9. How do public attitudes affect the political life of the nation?

10. Explain how political ideologies can lead to gridlock in the government.

11. What are some of the important steps to be taken in order to deal with the problems of government and politics?

Internet Resources/ Exercises

1. Explore some of the ideas in this chapter on the following sites:

http://www.gao.gov   Access reports of the General Accounting Office, the congressional watchdog of federal spending.

http://www.uspirg.org   Reports plus access to information and programs of state organizations associated with the Public Interest Research Group.

http://www.fedstats.gov   The gateway site to all the statistical data published by the federal government, including data on government at all levels.

2. Go to the PIRG site listed above. Select one of the state PIRGs. Then read their materials on an area of interest to you (higher education, health care reform, government reform, etc.). If you live in the state, write a letter to your representative advocating one or more of the changes or programs in the PIRG materials. If you live in a different state, try to locate materials on the same topic and compare them with the state PIRG materials.

3. Find information on corruption, scandals, or waste in one or more other countries. How does the information you get compare with materials in the text on such problems in America? Do other nations have the same or different kinds of problems? Which nation seems to have the most serious problems?

For Further Reading

Cook, Timothy E. *Governing with the News: The News Media as a Political Institution.* Chicago: University of Chicago Press, 1998. Examination of the relationship between the media and political life both historically and in the present, showing how the news sets political agendas and stimulates action.

Katz, Richard S. *Democracy and Elections.* New York: Oxford University Press, 1997. Discusses various matters related to elections in a democratic society, including a history of voting and elections and how tensions develop in a democratic society.

Lakoff, George. *Moral Politics: How Liberals and Conservatives Think.* 2nd ed. Chicago: University of Chicago Press, 2002. An examination of the worldviews and ways of thinking of liberals and conservatives, including their differing views of morality and their diverse approaches to such issues as taxes, crime, the death penalty, and the environment.

Lipset, Seymour Martin. *American Exceptionalism: A Double-Edged Sword.* New York: W. W. Norton, 1996. An analysis of the American political system and how it functions in the light of systems in other cultures.

Terry, Janice J. *U.S. Foreign Policy in the Middle East: The Role of Lobbies and Special Interest Groups.* London: Pluto Press, 2005. A case study of the pro-Israel lobby and the way it affects foreign policy, illustrating the power of special interests and lobbyists on the U.S. government.

Wiesberg, Herb F., and Samuel C. Patterson. *Great Theater: The American Congress in the 1990s.* New York: Cambridge University Press, 1998. An analysis of the U.S. Congress in the 1990s, showing the consequences of the ideological conflict and the partisan divisions.

Wilensky, Harold L. *Rich Democracies: Political Economy, Public Policy, and Performance.* Berkeley: University of California Press, 2002. Uses a variety of data, including hundreds of interviews, to analyze differing styles of conflict resolution and the common social, economic, and labor problems of modern governments.

CHAPTER

Work and the Economy

OBJECTIVES

1. Identify various ways in which the economy is changing.

2. Know how work and the workforce are changing, and how problems of work detract from people's quality of life.

3. Understand the ways in which the economic system is detrimental to the well-being of many Americans.

4. Identify the ways in which the government and social roles contribute to the problems of work.

5. Discuss attitudes toward work and workers, including the ideology of the work ethic, as aspects of the work problem in America.

6. Suggest steps that can be taken to reduce the problems and make work more meaningful.

"I'm Not a Worrier, But . . ."

Some people are optimistic by nature. They tend not to worry even when they are struggling with problems. But, as Ted points out, unemployment can strain even the most optimistic of outlooks. Ted is in his late 40s. He has been out of work for more than a year, a situation that was inconceivable to him only a few months before he lost his job:

I'm an engineer. I've never been out of work before. In fact, only a few months before I was laid off, I was planning to stay in my job until I retired. A group of us were laid off at the same time. We were all completely taken by surprise. We knew things were slack, but there was no talk of any layoffs. They just called us each in one day and told us they didn't have a job for us any more.

At first, I was kind of cocky about it. I was hurt, because I really liked working there. But I was also sure that I would have another job in a few weeks. Probably even with better pay. I fantasized about writing them a letter and thanking them for giving me the opportunity to advance myself. You know, rub it in, and make them sorry.

That was over a year ago. It was about a hundred résumés and applications ago. I'm not a worrier. But I'm really worried now. And every month when the mortgage comes due, I worry a little more. My wife's job keeps us afloat, but we've about exhausted our savings, and we're now thinking about selling our house and moving into an apartment.

But you know what the worst part of it is? Just waiting and waiting and not hearing, and feeling more and more useless and more and more helpless. I've lost the chance at jobs for which I'm a perfect fit because they could hire someone younger and cheaper. It's really depressing. I'll keep trying, but it gets harder all the time to make yourself go through the application process, and it gets harder all the time to feel hopeful, to really believe that this could be the place that will finally hire me.

Introduction

Many Americans fantasize about becoming independently wealthy so that they can do whatever they please. Moreover, they believe that the American economy offers that possibility. Think about this fantasy for a moment. Do you believe that the American economy offers you the possibility of becoming independently wealthy? If so, what are your chances? If it happens, what will you do? Will you continue to work?

When we pose such questions to social problems classes, virtually everyone agrees that he or she could become independently wealthy. Many do not think the chances of this are very good, however, and nearly all the students say they would continue to work.

In general, the students believe that the American economy is the best economy, and they are committed to it and to the work ethic. The **work ethic** involves the notion that *your sense of worth and the satisfaction of your needs are intricately related to the kind of work you do.*

In this chapter we explore evidence related to these beliefs about work and the economy. We look at the changing nature of the economy, work, and the workforce as well as the diverse meanings people attach to their work. We consider the kinds of problems associated with work, discuss how they affect the quality of life, and note the factors that contribute to and help to perpetuate those problems. Finally, we outline a few approaches to resolving the problems.

work ethic
the notion that your sense of worth and the satisfaction of your needs are intricately related to the kind of work you do

The Economy, Work, and the Workforce in America

All things change. The American economy, the nature of work, and the nature of the workforce are vastly different today from what they were at various times in the past.

The Changing Economy

Initially, the United States was *an agrarian society,* that is, a society in which agriculture is the dominant form of work and people and animals are the major sources of energy. It has been estimated that as late as 1850, 65 percent of the energy used in American work was supplied by people and animals (Lenski 1966). After the middle of the 19th century, the nation industrialized rapidly. In simple terms, *industrialization is economic development through a transformation of the sources and quantities of energy employed.*

Many American workers have lost their jobs as their companies have shifted production to other countries where wages are significantly lower.

American industrialization, like that of most nations, occurred in the context of **capitalism,** an economic system in which there is private, rather than state, ownership of wealth and control of the production and distribution of goods. In a capitalist system, people are motivated by profit and they compete with each other to maximize their share of the profits. The premise is that the combination of private ownership and the pursuit of profit benefits everyone, because it motivates capitalists to be efficient and to provide the best goods and services at the lowest possible prices.

In a pure capitalist system, government involvement in the economy is minimal. In the United States, the government role in the economy has grown over the past century. In addition, our economy is affected by various other factors such as the global economy, weather, wars, and so on. *The global economy has become particularly important.* In simplest terms, globalization of the economy means a significant increase in the amount of international trade and investment (Weisbrot 2000). In the United States, for example, trade as a percentage of the gross domestic product is now nearly double what it was in the early 1970s. As an economist has put it: "the business enterprise is now the major actor on the world stage and the global marketplace is a key driver of the U.S. economy" (Weidenbaum 1999:506). Supermarkets have become more important than superpowers for key economic decisions. When governments try to impose restrictions to protect or enhance the national economy, enterprises simply shift the work to another setting. For instance, when Japan raised postage rates, direct mailers sent their mailings to Hong Kong, which mailed them back to Japan at considerably less cost to the mailers; and when the United States put limits on the number of work permits given to foreign computer programmers, some companies changed the work location to other nations.

Technology has driven down the cost of international communication and travel. Thus, there has been a growth in trade, the flow of capital across national borders, foreign investment, shared research and development, and movement of personnel

capitalism
an economic system in which there is private, rather than state, ownership of wealth and control of the production and distribution of goods; people are motivated by profit and compete with each other for maximum shares of profit

(including students attending universities in foreign countries). Business enterprises maximize their profits by locating the best markets and the least expensive places for operations. As a result, a particular product may have components made in various parts of the world.

In other words, the economy is now truly global. According to Weidenbaum (1999), about $1 trillion moves across national borders every hour! Many large U.S. firms, including Exxon, Colgate-Palmolive, and Coca-Cola, obtain the majority of their income from overseas markets.

The consequences of globalization are controversial. On the one hand, researchers have identified positive consequences such as a reduction in occupational sex segregation and gender inequality (Meyer 2003). On the other hand, many observers argue that globalization has led to a growing gap between the world's rich and poor (Amin 2004). Whatever the consequences for the world as a whole, globalization and new technologies combine to present the U.S. economy and the American worker with new challenges. *Globalization means that businesses shift their operations to other nations where the employees work for lower pay than Americans and other business expenses are less, thus lowering the costs of products and services.* The results of this process, called *outsourcing,* are debatable. For example, two studies (both at Duke University) of outsourcing among engineering firms came to different conclusions (Engardio 2006). One study reported that the companies resort to outsourcing because they need more talent and they shift some of their more complex work to countries such as India and China because they can decrease the time it takes to get their products to market. The other study, however, argued that the outsourcing reflects no shortage of talent in the United States; rather, the only motivation is to reduce costs.

In any case, it is undeniable that one outcome of outsourcing is that well-paid, lower-skilled jobs in the United States are increasingly difficult to find. In fact, there has been a growing gap in the earnings between the top and the bottom wage earners, with the top 10 percent of full-time workers averaging nearly 4.4 times as much per week as the bottom 10 percent. Although, as you shall see, unemployment is down considerably, many American workers have experienced job loss or less job security. From 1997 to 1998, 1.9 million workers permanently lost jobs they had held at least three years because their company or plant closed or moved (Helwig 2001). Moreover, unions lose their bargaining power when companies can simply shift operations to a different nation.

In the competitive context of the global economy, then, *a number of changes have occurred that are detrimental to the well-being of many American workers* (Caskey 1994; Harrison 1994; U.S. Department of Labor 2000):

downsizing
reduction of the labor force in a company or corporation

- Businesses and corporations have used both outsourcing and **downsizing** (reduction of the labor force) to reduce costs and maximize profits.
- An increasing number of jobs are temporary or part-time, with no fringe benefits such as health insurance.
- Unions continue to decline in membership and power.
- Corporate tax obligations have been reduced, cutting back on revenues necessary to support social programs.
- When corrected for inflation, the income of many American families has declined.

As a result of such changes, many Americans are not only unable to better their lot in comparison to their parents, but are finding themselves worse off than their parents.

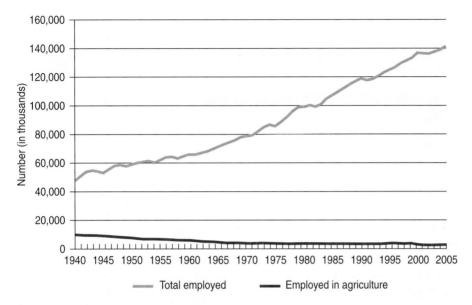

FIGURE 10.1
Civilian Employment, 1940–2005.

Source: "Employment status of the civilian noninstitutional population," Bureau of Labor Statistics Web site.

In sum, the nature of the changes in the economy means that many American families are worse off financially in the early 2000s than they were in the 1970s. For many, the American dream seems more remote than ever.

The Changing Workforce

The **labor force** (defined as all civilians who are employed or unemployed but able and wanting to work) has increased enormously since the founding of the nation. The number of those actually employed has also risen steadily (figure 10.1). It was the rapid increase since the beginning of the 19th century that made the nation's swift industrial growth possible. The workforce was low in 1800 because all but a small proportion of Americans lived on farms, and the family farmer along with his wife and children are not counted—only those who work for pay outside the home are included in the workforce. Since 1940 the labor force has been growing faster than the population.

The *occupational structure* also has changed with an increasing **division of labor,** or *specialization*. There are now more than 30,000 different occupations. This change is not due to growth in all job categories, however. If you look at the categories of occupations used by the Census Bureau, you will find that since the beginning of the 20th century the proportion of workers in professional, technical, managerial, clerical, and service jobs has increased greatly. The proportion of workers classified as farm workers, on the other hand, has declined dramatically. In 1900, 17.7 percent of all employees worked on farms (U.S. Census Bureau 1975:144). As figure 10.1 shows, the number of agricultural employees continues to decline, comprising only 1.5 percent of all employees in 2005.

Jobs requiring more skill and training have tended to increase at a faster rate than others. In other words, there has been a general upgrading of the occupational structure. With increased industrialization and technological development, the need for farmers and unskilled workers has diminished and the need for skilled workers and clerical and other white-collar workers has increased. The United States has moved into a service and, some would argue, an informational society, in which growing

labor force
all civilians who are employed or unemployed but able and desiring to work

division of labor
the separation of work into specialized tasks

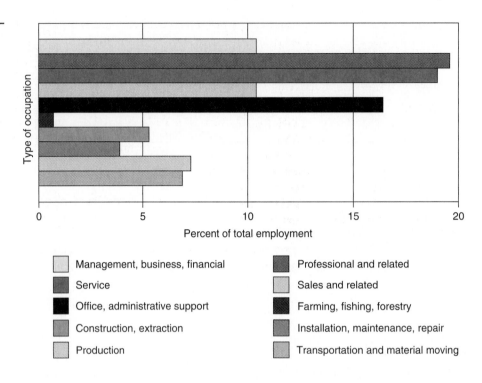

FIGURE 10.2
Distribution of Occupations.
Source: Hecker 2005:71.

numbers of workers are needed outside the manufacturing areas (figure 10.2). It is increasingly likely that workers will engage in tasks involving *substantive complexity* such as verbal and math skills and abstract thinking rather than motor skills such as lifting, stooping, coordination, or finger dexterity. Unfortunately, many new jobs, particularly those in the service area, do not pay well. Many workers—7.86 million of them, or 5.4 percent of all employed workers in the fall of 2006, according to the Bureau of Labor Statistics—supplement their income with second jobs. Thus, many American workers either work longer hours or face a lower standard of living.

The Changing Composition of the Labor Force

As the general skill level increases, *the educational level of the workforce also increases.* In 1970, 38.7 percent of the labor force had less than four years of high school, whereas 12.0 percent had four or more years of college. By 2005, the comparable figures were 9.6 percent with less than four years of high school and 33.1 percent with four or more years of college (U.S. Census Bureau 2007).

Another substantial change in the labor force involves the *proportion of workers who are female.* From 1950 to 2005, the participation rate of men fell from 82.4 to 73.3 percent, whereas that of women rose from 32.0 to 59.3 percent (U.S. Census Bureau 2007). Census Bureau projections estimate that women will constitute 47.4 percent of the civilian labor force by 2012.

A third change is the increasing number of illegal immigrants in the workforce. *Nearly 5 percent of all workers are illegal immigrants* (Broder 2006). The majority come in from Mexico and other Latin American nations. They are generally concentrated in the lower-paying occupations, such as farming, cleaning, construction, and food preparation.

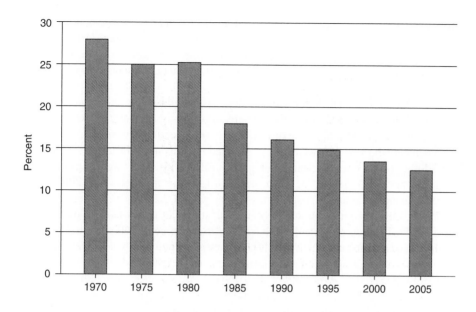

FIGURE 10.3
Membership in Labor Unions as a Proportion of the Labor Force, 1970–2005.
Source: U.S. Census Bureau Web site.

Finally, the labor force also became more *unionized* until the 1960s. Since then, however, the proportion of workers who are union members has declined (figure 10.3). By 2005, only 12.5 percent of wage and salary workers were union members (U.S. Department of Labor 2006a). The type of workers who are unionized has changed as well. Unions no longer involve mainly blue-collar workers. Federal, state, and local government workers comprise a substantial proportion of all union workers. In 2005, nearly four in ten government workers were in unions, compared to fewer than one in ten private-sector employees. Among occupational groups, the unionization rate is highest among workers in protective services, such as police officers and firefighters. In private industry, the highest union membership rates are found in communications, public utilities, and transportation.

The Changing Meaning of Work

When we try to determine the *meaning of work* for Americans, we find ourselves in a morass of contradictions. Some people argue that work is one of the most important activities in an individual's life. They maintain that those who do not have a satisfying job do not have a fully satisfying life. Others insist that work is purely instrumental, a way to attain the goal of *maximum consumption*. There is also disagreement about whether Americans enjoy their work, with some observers claiming that most Americans hate their jobs and others asserting that there is a high rate of *job satisfaction*.

What about the *work ethic,* the notion that work is intrinsically good and useful and that people should therefore continue to work even if they are financially independent? Do Americans still believe this? Or would they gladly abandon work for leisure pursuits if they had the means to do so?

Although it is difficult to resolve these contradictions, surveys taken over the last three decades do indicate something of Americans' feelings about their work. For example, these surveys show that the work ethic has remained strong among both males and females, the various racial groups, and differing occupational categories (Weaver 1997). In a survey that asked people how important it is to teach children that "with hard work and perseverance, anyone can succeed in America," 83 percent of the respondents agreed that the theme is essential or very important.[1] Similarly, a British study showed that people have a high level of commitment to work, which is one reason that unemployment (as discussed later) has a negative effect on mental health (Ingmar-Paul and Moser 2006).

With regard to work satisfaction, the evidence is not consistent. Polls taken from the 1970s through the 1990s showed that 80 percent or more of Americans were satisfied with their jobs. In 1999, 89 percent of workers surveyed said they were satisfied, including 55 percent who said they were "very" satisfied (Harrison and Dautrich 1999). In the early 2000s, polls of various groups had mixed results, with some indicating continuing high levels and others indicating lower levels of satisfaction. However, a 2005 survey of a representative sample of 5,000 households reported that only 14 percent said they were "very satisfied" with their jobs, while about half are less than satisfied (Conference Board 2005). This represents a decline from 1995, when nearly 60 percent of workers said they were satisfied with their jobs. The most dissatisfied group of workers are those in the 45 to 54 age group, and those earning between $25,000 and $35,000 a year. The study also reported that 40 percent of workers feel disconnected from their employers. At this point, we have no explanation for these varied, incompatible survey results.

In any case, an increasing number of Americans no longer accept the notion that their self-worth is tied in with their work or that they have a moral duty to work. On the contrary, Americans increasingly expect their work to have *meaning,* be emotionally and intellectually *stimulating,* and offer an opportunity to feel *good about themselves and the products of their labor* (Hudson 2001). Income is no longer the most important facet of an individual's work.

In evaluating job quality, an individual is likely to consider not just income, but such nonincome factors as job duties and working conditions, job satisfaction, period of work, job status, and job security (Rosenthal 1989; Moen and Yu 2000). *Job duties and working conditions* refers to such matters as whether the job is hazardous, repetitious, stressful, closely supervised, and isolated (versus working with a team). *Job satisfaction* increases when the worker engages in problem solving, has the opportunity to be creative, gains recognition, can fully utilize skills and learn new skills, and has the chance for advancement.

Period of work is the extent to which the job involves weekend or shift work, overtime, or flexible work hours. *Job status* includes both social status (being recognized by outsiders as having a more prestigious or less prestigious job) and status within the organization. *Job security* is closely related to how positively workers evaluate their job; workers are less comfortable with seasonal jobs and with those that have a high risk of layoff.

fallacy

Americans, then, are not rejecting work. They are rejecting meaningless work and low-quality jobs. To say, as we have heard from some students and employers, that Americans today "just don't want to work anymore" is the *fallacy of personal attack.* In a national survey, only 5.1 percent of those not working said it was because they were "not interested in working" (Weismantle 2001). The great majority wants work, but work that is important and that fosters a sense of achievement.

underemployment
working full time for poverty wages, working part time when full-time work is desired, or working at a job below the worker's skill level

Work as a Social Problem

Because most Americans want to work and expect their work to provide some degree of personal fulfillment, there are three basic problems associated with work in America today. First, there is the problem of *unemployment and* **underemployment.** People are underemployed if they work full time for poverty wages, work part time when they desire full-time work, or work at jobs that are temporary or below their skill levels. Second, there is the problem of *dissatisfaction and alienation*. Finally, there is the problem of various kinds of *work hazards*.

Unemployment and Underemployment

Underemployment is perhaps as serious as unemployment for people who look to work for meaningful activity. Underemployment results in frustration, financial worry, and stress. Two researchers have estimated that 13.1 percent of American workers are underemployed (Jensen and Slack 2003). The proportion varies by various demographic factors, with the highest rates occurring among the 18- to 24-year-old workers (29.1 percent) and workers with less than a high school education (29.0 percent). Rates are also higher for women than for men and for racial and ethnic minorities than for non-Hispanic whites.

A substantial number of the underemployed are working part time, which means that they have no benefits (including health insurance). Lacking the kind of social benefits available in countries such as Sweden, such workers *cannot achieve their desired quality of life without working full time* (Reynolds 2004). Another large group of the underemployed are those in temporary jobs. And professionals—lawyers, accountants, engineers, and so on—make up an increasing proportion of the temporary market (Thottam 2004). Businesspeople claim that temporary work serves the interests of those people who want something other than a permanent work situation. However, *temporary workers are underemployed because most of them are looking for full-time permanent employment* and most dislike the lack of stability and the degradation of being a temporary worker (Parker 1994).

With regard to those out of work, reliable data exist on the **unemployment rate.** The rate fluctuates considerably (table 10.1). By 2005, the overall rate was 5.1 percent, or 7.59 million workers. This statistic does not mean, however, that only 7.59 million Americans were affected by unemployment in that year. Many people are unemployed for only a portion of the year. The median duration of unemployment is about

unemployment rate
the proportion of the labor force that is not working but is available for work and has made specific efforts to find work

TABLE 10.1
Unemployment Rates, 1950–2005

Year	Total	White	Black	Hispanic	Asian
1950	5.3	4.9	9.0		
1955	4.4	3.9	8.7		
1960	5.5	4.9	10.2		
1965	4.5	4.1	8.1		
1970	4.9	4.5	8.2		
1975	8.5	7.8	14.8		
1980	7.1	6.3	14.3	10.1	
1985	7.2	6.2	15.1	10.5	
1990	5.5	4.7	11.3	8.0	4.2
1995	5.6	4.9	10.4	9.3	5.0
2000	4.0	2.6	5.4	4.4	2.7
2005	5.1	4.4	10.0	6.0	4.0

SOURCE: Bureau of Labor Statistics and U.S. Census Bureau Web sites.

2.4 months (Gottschalck 2006). Women tend to be unemployed for a shorter time than men, and white, non-Hispanics are unemployed for a shorter time than Hispanics, African Americans, and Asian Americans.

In addition, a good many Americans who want to work are not counted as part of the labor force or the unemployment rate because they are not actively looking for work. In mid-2006, 1.6 million Americans wanted to work and had looked for a job in the prior 12 months, but were not counted as unemployed or part of the labor force because they had not looked for work in the four weeks preceding the survey (Bureau of Labor Statistics 2006c). Various reasons are given for not being in the labor force, including discouragement after unsuccessfully looking for work for a year or more or being an unmarried mother on welfare. Millions, particularly men, have dropped out because they could not find a job that paid near what they once earned (Leonhard 2002). People who want work but are not actively looking are not counted in the unemployment rate. When you take into account those unemployed for a part of the year and those not in the labor force, the number of people affected by unemployment is far higher than the official figures.

As table 10.1 shows, *unemployment does not strike all groups the same.* Typically, the rates are higher for minorities than for whites and are higher for younger than for older workers. In some years, the unemployment rate for workers 16 to 19 years of age is double, triple, or more the rate for the workforce as a whole. In 2005, the overall unemployment rate was 5.1 percent, but the rate for workers 16 to 19 years of age was 16.6 percent (Bureau of Labor Statistics Web site).

Unemployment also varies by occupational category with rates tending to be higher among blue-collar and service workers. In 2005, for example, with an overall unemployment rate of 5.1 percent of the workforce, the rates for occupational categories

Unemployment rates tend to be highest among blue-collar workers.

were: managerial and professional occupations, 2.3 percent; service occupations, 6.4 percent; sales occupations, 4.8 percent; and occupations in the areas of natural resources, construction, maintenance, production, transportation, and material moving, 6.5 percent (Bureau of Labor Statistics Web site).

Dissatisfaction and Alienation

In chapter 4, we defined *alienation* as a sense of estrangement that is usually measured by an individual's feelings of powerlessness, normlessness, isolation, and meaninglessness. This definition is a subjective approach to alienation. Alienation is an objective phenomenon, according to Karl Marx. In a capitalist society the worker is *estranged from his or her own labor* (because work is something that is coerced and external to the worker rather than a fulfillment of the worker's needs), from other people, and from his or her own humanity. The worker sinks to the level of a commodity and becomes the most wretched of commodities. Because capitalism wrenches the means of production from the control of those intimately involved in production, workers are necessarily alienated whether or not they feel any sense of alienation.

The amount of alienation in the workplace, therefore, depends on whether you take a Marxist or a social psychological approach to the question. For Marxists, all workers in a capitalist society are alienated by definition. For social psychologists, workers are alienated to the extent that they perceive themselves as powerless and isolated. Social psychological studies indicate that some American workers, but by no means the majority, are alienated. In fact, some researchers have found that many workers say they would rather continue their jobs than to get the same wages for not working.

Nevertheless, indications are that dissatisfaction is still a problem. First, no matter which polls are used to measure job dissatisfaction, the results translate into tens of millions of dissatisfied American workers. Second, there is evidence of various troublesome issues among workers who say they are satisfied. People who work in companies that have cut the workforce tend to rate their employer lower on everything from management practices to ethics (Stoneman 1999), and workers in demanding, fast-paced jobs in the high-tech world experience family and personal problems that lead to unscheduled absences from work (Stone 1999).

Work Hazards and Stress

In 2005, 4.2 million injuries and illnesses occurred in private industry workplaces— 4.6 cases per 100 full-time workers (Bureau of Labor Statistics 2006d). This figure represents a continuing decline in the number and rate of injuries and illnesses. Among the various occupational categories, workplace injury rates varied from 0.5 percent in mining to 15.7 percent in health care and social assistance. Workplace illnesses (skin diseases, respiratory conditions, poisonings, hearing loss, and other illnesses arising from workplace conditions) varied from 0.3 percent in mining to 38.8 percent in manufacturing.

Many of the illnesses and injuries are serious, resulting in lost days at work and *temporary or permanent disability*. In addition, 5,702 workers were killed on the job in 2005. Because these figures are based on reports from business and industry, it is likely that the actual numbers are higher. Moreover, a multitude of minor accidents and work-related illnesses are not included in the figures.

UNEMPLOYMENT RATES IN INDUSTRIAL NATIONS

Unemployment is a huge and ongoing problem in many underdeveloped nations. For one thing, economic growth lags behind population growth, so that even a robust economy cannot absorb all the new workers coming into the labor force each year. In the developed nations, unemployment tends to be smaller but is still an enduring problem. The unemployment rate varies considerably, however, depending on how the economy is structured. Note in table 10.2 that some nations have lower rates than the United States, and others have higher rates.

Although the rates are strikingly low in some cases, every nation confronts the problem in which a segment of its population wants but is unable to obtain employment—and in every nation, unemployed people face some of the same problems of stress and self-worth as do Americans. One major difference is that in countries such as Sweden and Japan, more benefits are available for the unemployed, so that unemployment is not as likely to be associated with abject poverty.

Country	1985	1995	2005
United States	7.2	5.6	5.1
Canada	10.2	8.6	6.0
Australia	8.3	8.2	5.1
Japan	2.7	3.2	4.5
France	10.5	11.3	9.7
Germany	7.2	8.2	11.2
Italy	6.0	11.3	7.8
Netherlands	9.6	6.6	4.7
Sweden	2.8	9.1	7.7
United Kingdom	11.4	8.7	4.8

TABLE 10.2
Unemployment Rates, by Country, 1985–2005
SOURCE: Bureau of Labor Statistics Web site.

We use the term "work hazards" broadly to include *work-induced stress* as well as *work-related injuries and illnesses*. For example, a spot welder on an auto assembly line told about some of the daily hazards to which he is exposed.

> I pulled a muscle in my neck, straining. This gun, when you grab this thing from the ceiling, cable, weight, I mean you're pulling everything. . . . This whole edge here is sharp. I go through a shirt every two weeks, it just goes right through. My overalls catch on fire. I've had gloves catch on fire. (Indicates arms.) See them little holes? That's what sparks do. I've got burns across here from last night. (Terkel 1972:224)

Psychological as well as physical hazards occur in the workplace. Some occupations are particularly likely to expose workers to stress. For instance, many taxi drivers work under the continual threat of robbery. Salespeople often endure harassment from customers. Many high-tech workers feel ongoing pressure to produce and to make their work the consuming focus of their lives. Psychiatrists and psychotherapists often find their work to be emotionally draining. In other jobs, stress is associated with such conditions as lack of communication and delegation of authority by management, fast-paced work in poor environmental conditions, frequent overtime, conflict between workers, recent reduction of employee benefits, and downsizing (Koretz 1997; Grunberg, Anderson-Connolly, and Greenberg 2000).

Work and the Quality of Life

Many people thoroughly enjoy their work. They find it meaningful and satisfying, thus providing them with a higher quality of life. They are more likely to enjoy their work when they perceive themselves to be included in the information network and the decision-making processes of their workplace (Barak and Levin 2002).

There are also many people for whom the effect of working is a kind of *emotional and spiritual malaise*. They do not despise their work, but neither are they excited by it. At best, they are apathetic or resigned. At worst, they sense an uneasiness or mild but chronic frustration. One important area that work affects is the mental and physical health of the worker.

Work, Unemployment, and Health

Ironically, both working and not working can adversely affect your health. What are the risks?

Work and Health.   Work can have a *negative impact on both the emotional and the physical well-being of workers* (Spector 2002; Guimont et al. 2006). Feelings of alienation or high levels of job dissatisfaction may lead to heavy drinking in an effort to cope (Greenberg and Grunberg 1995; Martin and Roman 1996) or to burnout (Powell 1994). People whose work provides relatively low rewards (including low job security or advancement possibilities) for high levels of effort may increase their risk of cardiovascular disease three to fourfold (Siegrist 1995). Regardless of the level of effort, job insecurity puts workers under continual stress and can produce various kinds of health problems (Heaney, Israel, and House 1994; Bernhard-Oettel, Sverke, and De Witte 2006). In some high-stress occupations, such as physicians and law enforcement, suicide rates are high (Boxer, Burnett, and Swanson 1995). A study of death rates across various occupations found that high-risk occupations (those associated with higher death rates at earlier ages) include taxi drivers, cooks, longshoremen, and transportation operatives (Johnson, Sorlie, and Backlund 1999). Finally, people who work overtime have more health problems than other workers do (Rau and Triemer 2004).

Underemployment also poses health risks. People who are underemployed, in the sense of being overeducated and overqualified for their jobs, are likely to lack job satisfaction and to leave their jobs sooner than other workers (Tsang, Rumberger, and Levin 1991). Further, they are more likely than adequately employed workers are to report lower levels of health and well-being and exhibit symptoms of depression (Dooley, Ham-Rowbottom, and Prause 2001; Friedland and Price 2003).

To what extent, then, do Americans find the job satisfaction that adds to their well-being? In a survey of 1,300 workers, 40 percent reported their jobs to be extremely stressful, resulting in frequent problems of anxiety, anger, fatigue, or exhaustion (Brecher 1993). A study by the National Safe Workplace Institute concluded that more than 71,000 Americans died in one year from diseases such as cancer and from cardiovascular and neurological problems induced by work conditions (Scott 1990a). The study called job-related illnesses "America's invisible killer." A national study of workers reported that, although Americans generally like their jobs, the majority of them admit to one or more problems that reflect stress (Bond, Galinsky, and Swanberg 1998). Finally, another national study found that a third of all workers feel chronically overworked (Galinsky et al. 2005). The study also reported that the overworked have higher levels of stress, a higher proportion with depression and more reports of poor health than do other workers.

There is, in sum, a strong relationship between stressful working conditions and physical and emotional illness. And the stress occurs in all kinds of work. A Protestant minister described his own health problems caused by stress at work. The stresses he experienced could occur in virtually any kind of job, and his story shows that no one is immune.[2]

> I arrived at my new church with an intense anticipation of a rewarding and fruitful ministry. I brought the enthusiasm and recklessness of youth to a job that demanded the caution and wisdom of age. For about a year, the enthusiasm was sufficient. It carried me through some discouragements and minimized any overt criticism. Then I made the mistake of criticizing an older member of the church. The criticism was neither harsh nor malicious, but the member was quite sensitive and quite influential. I also plunged ahead and pushed programs and began projects without first consulting the officers. At the beginning of my second year, criticism erupted and quickly mushroomed.
>
> For about the next five years, I had problems with various people in the church. And I had a series of things go wrong with myself, both emotionally and physically. At one point, it seemed that everything was coming to a head and there would be a final all-out struggle to see whose way would prevail—mine or those that felt I was taking the church down the wrong road. Just before this culminating battle, I lost about 20 pounds from my slender physique. One week I broke out in a rash. I had severe sinus problems. Worst of all, I nearly developed a phobia about being in an enclosed area with a lot of people. I found it torturous to go to a crowded restaurant. One day I had to leave a church conference because my heart was pounding and I felt intense panic. Sometimes I even felt serious anxiety when I led the worship service.
>
> As it turned out, the "final" battle was not really the final one after all. It had only served to trigger the various physical and mental ailments that I endured for the next few years. Ultimately, we were able to work out the differences we had. I think I gained some in wisdom and lost some of my recklessness. The church began to stabilize and then grow, and some of those with whom I had fought became my best friends. After about eight years or so, I finally lost my fear of crowded places. In a way, I suppose you could say it all had a happy ending. But I wouldn't go through that again for anything. It was the only time of my life when the thought of suicide entered my mind as an appealing option.

Unemployment and Health.   The stress of being forcibly unemployed can be as serious as the stress of working in undesirable conditions or in an unfulfilling job. For most people, *unemployment* is a traumatic experience. Millions of Americans are affected by unemployment every year. Two researchers looked at work in the early 2000s and called it the era of the "disposable worker" (Dixon and Van Horn 2003). They pointed out that nearly a fifth of American workers lost their jobs and that the great majority of these workers had no advance notice, no severance pay, and no career counseling from their employers. Some workers who lose their jobs are unemployed for only a portion of the year. Some find employment, but the work is not meaningful to them. Some have dropped out of the labor force, discouraged by their inability to find employment in their line of work. Some are the victims of downsizing that eliminated their jobs (Uchitelle and Kleinfield 1996).

Stress Indicator	Percent Increase
Suicide	4.1
State mental hospital admissions	3.4
State prison admissions	4.0
Cirrhosis of the liver mortality	1.9
Cardiovascular-renal disease mortality	1.9

TABLE 10.3
Impact of a Sustained
1 Percent Rise in
Unemployment

SOURCE: M. Harvey Brenner. *Estimating the Social Costs of National Economic Policy: Implications for Mental and Physical Health and Criminal Aggression.* (A study prepared for the Joint Economic Committee of Congress.) Washington, DC: Government Printing Office, October 26, 1976.

Whatever the reason for being out of work, *unemployment is detrimental to both physical and emotional well-being* (Reine, Novo, and Hammarstrom 2004). Unemployment is associated with high levels of stress and lowered life satisfaction (Fenwick and Tausig 1994). It can lead to such problems as depression, lowered self-esteem, anger and resentment, shame and embarrassment, social isolation, serious mental illness, physical health problems, alcohol abuse, criminal behavior, and suicide (Crutchfield, Glusker, and Bridges 1999; Fergusson, Horwood, and Woodward 2001; Voss et al. 2004; Ingmar-Paul and Moser 2006). The negative consequences are likely to be more severe for workers who experience a second job loss (or who lose three or more jobs) than for those who experience their first loss (Chen, Marks, and Bersani 1994).

Brenner (1978) calculated the impact for a sustained 1 percent rise in unemployment in the United States from about 1940 to the early 1970s. The corresponding increases in various physical and emotional ills are shown in table 10.3.

The detrimental physical and emotional consequences of unemployment also are seen in other nations. In Canada and England, researchers found an association between unemployment and rates of illness (including cardiovascular disease), mortality, and suicide (Jin, Shah, and Svoboda 1995; Bartley, Sacker, and Clarke 2004). A Swedish study reported higher tobacco and drug use, increased crime rates, and higher mortality rates (especially by suicide and accidents) among unemployed youth (Hammarstrom 1994). In Australia, researchers found youth unemployment to be associated with such psychological symptoms as depression and loss of confidence, and with suicide (Morrell, Taylor, and Kerr 1998). A comparison of unemployed with employed people in Spain reported that the unemployed had higher rates of respiratory illness (Kogevinas et al. 1998).

Interpersonal Relationships

A number of studies support the notion that both work-related stress and unemployment *can adversely affect interpersonal relationships*. Work in stressful conditions can lead to marital tension and conflict at home (Menaghan 1991; Story and Repetti 2006). The stress can be rooted in multiple factors, including the general conditions under which the work is performed. A particularly stressful condition is shift work, which may *create both personal stress and interpersonal problems* (Grosswald 2003; Presser 2004). Researchers have found that shift work tends to increase conflict in the family, depress marital happiness and interaction, and increase various problems such as sexual and child-rearing disagreements (White and Keith 1990; Demerouti, Geurts, Bakker, and Euwema 2004).

Underemployment is also stressful, and people who are underemployed may be less satisfied than others with their marriages (Zvonkovic 1988). The strains and frustrations of stressful work conditions or of underemployment often carry over into family life, increasing tension and conflict and decreasing satisfaction.

Unemployment tends to place even more strain on an individual's relationships, including relationships within the family. During the Great Depression, when the unemployment rate went as high as one-fourth of the labor force, many workers blamed themselves for their unemployment, became disillusioned with themselves, and began to have trouble within their homes (Komarovsky 1940). Even in less serious economic recessions, workers are embarrassed by being unemployed, may begin to withdraw from social contacts, and may direct some of their hostility toward members of their families. It is, of course, not merely the embarrassment and stress of being unemployed but also the strain of trying to meet the expenses of food, clothing, housing, and health care that contributes to the conflict between spouses and between parents and children (Dail 1988).

Not all the problems are due to either unemployment or job dissatisfaction. Some situations are simply a *conflict between work and family life* (Hugick and Leonard 1991; Voydanoff 2004). For men, the conflict generally focuses on excessive work time—they are spending too much of their time and energy on their work. For women, the conflict is more likely to be one of scheduling problems or fatigue and irritability. In any case, the outcome is a certain amount of conflict between family members.

Contributing Factors

The factors that contribute to unemployment are generally different from the factors involved in work dissatisfaction, alienation, and work hazards. Although we focus on the latter factors, we also examine the political economy of unemployment.

Social Structural Factors

The Capitalist Economy.   We noted earlier that people in a capitalist economy are motivated by profit. *In business and corporations, profit tends to be the "bottom line."* That is, the goal is profit, and managers do whatever is necessary to maximize profits. This bottom-line approach has led owners, executives, and managers to act in ways that have adverse consequences for large numbers of people. One type of action is longstanding: the subservience of workers' needs to organizational needs. Three other actions changed in nature or increased greatly after 1980: union busting, downsizing, and the use of temporary workers.

The *subservience of workers' needs to organizational needs* is illustrated by the other three actions. Workers need well-paying and meaningful jobs, but union busting, downsizing, and the use of temporary workers are ways to meet the organization's need for profits at the expense of the workers' needs. In addition, workers may be abused and exploited by tyrannical managers and supervisors who focus on efficiency and productivity rather than the workers' needs for self-esteem, encouragement, and fulfillment (Ashforth 1994).

Union busting has been going on since the unions were first formed, but a change occurred in the 1980s (Rosenblum 1995). In 1981, the Reagan administration fired and permanently replaced more than 1,200 striking air-traffic controllers. Thereafter, an increasing number of companies dealt with strikes by hiring permanent replacements rather than by negotiating with the union.

The power of labor unions has been weakened in recent years by antilabor government policies.

Downsizing and outsourcing also reflect the drive to maximize profits. Downsizing, however, has taken on a different character—because it increases profits it now occurs independently of whether a company is doing well or poorly and of whether the economy is booming or in recession (Simone and Kleiner 2004). Ironically, executives are rewarded for downsizing, because to the extent that profits increase as a result of the lower costs of a smaller workforce, executive bonuses go up. Similarly, outsourcing has economic benefits not only to the company but to the economy as a whole (Smith 2006). There is, therefore, little incentive on the part of either business or government to regulate the practice.

Finally, *there is increasing use of temporary and part-time workers.* Temporary employment grew rapidly during the 1990s. It declined in 2000 and 2001, but began increasing again, so that at the end of 2005 temporary help accounted for nearly 2 percent of all nonfarm payroll employment (U.S. Department of Labor 2006a). Interviews with managers of temporary employment firms show that the higher demand for temporaries does not reflect workers' preference but rather employers' desire for flexibility and lower costs (Parker 1994). Some temporary workers are former employees who return as "rentals" to the company for which they formerly worked (Uchitelle 1996). Not surprisingly, they often struggle with resentment over now doing the same work at lower pay and with few or no fringe benefits.

About 17 percent of all workers worked part time (less than 35 hours per week) in 2005 (U.S. Department of Labor 2006a). Most preferred their part-time status, but 3.1 million worked part time because of such things as slack work or business conditions, and the inability to find full-time employment.

The Political Economy of Work. The traditional notion of man as the breadwinner assumed that a man's work would allow him to support his family. One of the problems of work today is that *a large number of jobs provide inadequate support and benefits to enable a family to live well.* A substantial number of Americans have to work longer hours or hold more than one job in order to provide sufficient income for their families. In 2005, 7.4 million workers, representing 5.1 percent of the workforce, held two or more jobs (Bureau of Labor Statistics 2006c). Nearly 300,000 worked two full-time jobs.

Many workers also struggle with wages that have not kept pace with inflation, or they contend with reduced employee benefits. When corrected for inflation, median household income reached a peak in 1999, then declined through 2004 (U.S. Census Bureau 2007). And even during the growing levels of the 1990s, hourly earnings for many production workers either declined or remained stagnant. At the same time, many workers have experienced no increase or even a decrease in benefits (such as reduced health coverage and pension plans). By early 2006, 29 percent of workers in private industry had no access to medical care plans and 40 percent had no access to employer-sponsored retirement plans (U.S. Department of Labor 2006b). Most of those in medical care plans had to contribute to both their own coverage and that of their families–an average of $296.88 per month for family coverage and $76.05 per month for single coverage.

The result of these various trends is that about one of seven U.S. jobs offers workers low pay and no health insurance or pension benefits (Kalleberg, Reskin, and Hudson 2000). The notion of a single breadwinner in a family—one person who has one job and provides for all the family's needs—is increasingly unrealistic.

The Political Economy of Unemployment.   It is important to distinguish between *structural and discriminatory unemployment.* Discriminatory unemployment involves high unemployment rates for particular groups, such as women and minorities, and is discussed in the chapters that deal with those groups. Structural unemployment is the result of the *functioning of the political-economic system itself.*

Structural unemployment takes various forms. Since the Great Depression, the American economy has been regulated basically in accord with the theories of the English economist John Maynard Keynes. In Keynes's view, governments can *control the swings of the economy,* greatly moderating the inflationary and deflationary trends, programs, and taxation. There is *an inverse relationship between unemployment and inflation.* When the rate of inflation is high, the government may take steps that will result in an increase in unemployment. Some unemployment is necessary, and some fluctuations are inevitable. Yet because of the moderating impact of government intervention, fluctuations need not be as severe as they were earlier in U.S. history.

The unemployment rates shown in table 10.1 reflect in large part the government's efforts to regulate the economy. There will always be some unemployment in a capitalist economy. The amount can be controlled and perhaps lessened by government intervention, but unemployment cannot be eliminated.

In addition to the overall rate of unemployment, the functioning of the political-economic system contributes to the high rates of unemployment in particular areas or in particular occupations at certain times. *Government spending* can create many jobs and then eliminate those jobs when the priorities change. For example, massive federal funding of the space program in the 1960s created many jobs, some of which vanished when the priorities changed in the 1970s.

Technological changes such as automation or the introduction of computers into a business can displace workers and lessen the need for them in the future. Old industries in the United States are in serious trouble. Numerous workers in the auto and steel industries have lost their jobs or have been indefinitely laid off. The problem may worsen as humans are replaced by robots in basic industries. Pioneered by the Japanese, robots are effective mechanisms of production in such industries as automobile manufacturing.

The Organizational Context of Work: Unions. The union movement has been instrumental in bringing about higher wages, fringe benefits, and safer conditions for workers (Doyle 2002; U.S. Department of Labor 2003). For example, in 2005 full-time wage and salary workers who were union members had median weekly earnings of $801, compared with a median of $622 for those not represented by unions (U.S. Department of Labor 2006c). However, as we noted earlier in this chapter, a smaller proportion of workers are now unionized. Various factors have brought about the decline of unions. Some losses occurred as a result of layoffs in manufacturing. In addition, unions have faced adverse rulings by conservative federal judges and the National Labor Relations Board (NLRB) regarding the right of unions to organize and strike. Meanwhile, management often has been supported by the legal system in efforts to keep unions out or to break existing unions. The globalization of the economy also has weakened the bargaining power of unions by allowing employers to opt for foreign locations for a part or all of the work. Finally, some unions have failed to engage in vigorous recruiting efforts.

The obstacles faced by unions are illustrated by a study of an Arizona miners' strike (Rosenblum 1995). The miners, who were largely Mexican Americans, went on strike against one of the world's largest copper producers. The strike was a reaction to the company's demand that cost-of-living adjustments and some other benefits be eliminated. The company replaced all the workers, and the replacements voted to decertify the union. The National Labor Relations Board ruled in favor of the company when the union protested.

Union membership has declined, then, not because workers have become disillusioned with their unions but because of various social factors and processes. If the unions continue to decline, there may be an increase in the kinds of work problems we have discussed.

Contemporary Work Roles and Environments. Job dissatisfaction and alienation reflect the *nature of work roles and work environments* in contemporary society. Workers suffer when they lack such benefits as positive relationships at the workplace, clear definitions of their work, and physical comfort in the work environment (Turnipseed 1992). They particularly suffer when they feel they have no control over their work lives and no security in their jobs, a situation that is exacerbated by a growing tendency to use part-time and temporary workers.

Work roles in American society result from a combination of factors, including *technological developments, efforts to maximize profits, and the bureaucratization of work*. The disposable worker is one consequence of the effort to maximize profits. At least three consequences of the technological developments bear upon the meaningfulness of work. First, technology brought with it *highly specialized tasks*, with the result that many workers focus on a narrow range of tasks and may have little or no sense of the overall project.

Second, and associated with the intense specialization, many jobs are stressful. A survey of American workers found that 5 percent reported being "extremely" stressed at work, 14 percent said they were stressed "quite a bit," and 33 percent regarded themselves as "somewhat" stressed (Yung 2004). The other 47 percent reported their stress level at work as "a little or not at all." Reasons for the stress include too much responsibility, too many demands, too much pressure, and jobs that involve *extremely repetitious, routine tasks.* Quite a few workers must *come to terms with the boredom of their work.* The tactics they use include such activities as daydreaming, playing, singing, and talking.

Barbara Garson (1975) described the *coping mechanisms* utilized by people who work in routine jobs ranging from typists, to keypunchers, to workers who stack Ping-Pong paddles all day, to tuna cleaners in a seafood plant. The deadly routine of many jobs is portrayed in the account of Cindy, a girl who worked for a time in the Ping-Pong factory.

> My job was stacking the Ping-Pong paddles into piles of fifty. Actually I didn't have to count all the way up to fifty. To make it a little easier they told me to stack them in circles of four with the first handle facing me. When there got to be thirteen handles on the second one from the front, then I'd know I had fifty. . . . As soon as I'd stack 'em, they'd unstack 'em. Maybe it wouldn't have been so bad if I could have seen all the piles I stacked at the end of the day. But they were taking them down as fast as I was piling them up. That was the worst part of the job. (Garson 1975:1–2)

Such jobs are stressful. They may also be physically and emotionally harmful. Interviews with 52 women with *repetition strain injury,* the result of work in either a telecommunications organization or a chicken processing factory, found the women to report reduced capacity for housework, troubled family relationships, mental distress, and lowered self-esteem (Ewan, Lowy, and Reid 1991).

Third, technological developments are associated with *depersonalization* within the workplace. Workers tend to be *isolated* in certain kinds of jobs. For instance, isolation may occur when the work is computerized or automated. In such cases, the workers may have to pay closer attention to their work, have less interaction with people, and engage in fewer tasks that require teamwork.

Work roles also are affected by *bureaucratization of work.* Perhaps the majority of Americans work in bureaucratic organizations, which tend to be *authoritarian.* A defining characteristic of a bureaucracy is the hierarchy of authority. Workers in an authoritarian organization are likely to experience negative emotions and attitudes ranging from job dissatisfaction to alienation. People prefer to be *involved in decisions that affect them and their work.* Their satisfaction with their work, their motivation, and their effectiveness all can be enhanced by participation in the decision-making process (Schnake, Bushardt, and Spottswood 1984; Barak and Levin 2002).

Participation gives the worker some control over his or her work. The more control that workers have, the more likely they are to be satisfied and the more likely the work is to enhance their health, while less control means less satisfaction and more physical and emotional problems are likely (Spector 2002; Gelsema et al. 2006; Brand, Warren, Carayon, and Hoonakker 2007).

Unfortunately, workers are unlikely to have the opportunity for participation and a sense of control in many bureaucratic organizations. Lacking that opportunity, they are likely to have lower levels of job satisfaction, lower morale, and lower levels of motivation.

In addition to the frustrations of working in an authoritarian organization, workers must deal with a certain amount of *built-in conflict* that bureaucracies tend to generate. In theory, such conflict is unnecessary because the chain of command is clear: All workers are experts in their own jobs, and there are rules to cover all tasks and any problems. In reality, a certain amount of conflict is invariably found in work roles. There may be *role ambiguity* (a lack of clear information about a particular work role) that results in lower job satisfaction and higher stress levels (Revicki and May 1989; McCleese and Eby 2006). There may be *role conflict* because different groups in the workplace have different expectations for a particular work role or because the role expectations are excessive. Role conflict, like role ambiguity, leads to lower satisfaction and higher stress levels. The important point is that these problems are not the result of the individual worker's cantankerous nature but of contradictions that are part of the work role itself. The individual falls victim to the role and suffers the consequences of lowered satisfaction and higher stress levels.

The Political Economy of Work Hazards.   Some jobs necessarily entail more risk than others, and others entail more risk than necessary. Many work-related illnesses and injuries could be prevented or at least minimized if the health and well-being of workers took priority over profit. Historically, untold numbers of American workers have died in the name of profit and with the approval or apathy of the government.

The government has not yet engaged in the vigorous efforts needed to maintain a safe work environment. Both the federal and state governments have been lax in the criminal prosecution of companies in which workers die because of inadequate safety measures. Further, the federal government tends to prosecute employers on civil rather than criminal grounds.

One government program that has been effective is the Occupational Safety and Health Administration (OSHA). OSHA (1996) was established in 1970 to protect the health and lives of workers. Around 1,120 inspectors work with other professionals such as investigators, engineers, and physicians to establish and enforce safety standards. Overall, the workplace death rate has been cut by more than half since 1970; more than 100,000 workers could have died on the job but did not because of the improved safety and health conditions required by OSHA.

Although the results of OSHA are impressive, accidents and deaths in the workplace continue to be a problem. As long as the issue remains a civil rather than a criminal matter, work hazards probably will continue to put many workers at risk.

Despite the efforts of OSHA to protect the health and lives of workers, on-the-job accidents and deaths continue to be a problem, especially in high-risk occupations.

FUN AND GAMES AT WORK

As various studies in this chapter indicate, many Americans find little pleasure in their jobs, though most expect their work to be enjoyable and fulfilling. By young adulthood, most people have worked at some job. Consider how much enjoyment and fulfillment you have received from your own work experiences. With respect to any job (or jobs) you have had, think about your feelings toward the work, the impact that the work had on your life, and the problems and satisfactions connected to the work. Imagine that someone is interviewing you about your experiences. Write out your answers to the following questions about a job you have had or now have.

What did you most like about the job?
What did you most dislike about the job?

How would you feel about working at the job for all or the major portion of your life? Why?

How were you treated by others in your work role?

Did the job make any difference in the way you feel about yourself? Why or why not?

How could the job be made more meaningful to workers?

Gather with other class members working on this project and summarize the results. What do the results say about the amount of worker dissatisfaction and alienation in America? If the only jobs available were the kinds discussed by the class, would most Americans prefer not to work? Could all the jobs be made into meaningful and fulfilling experiences?

Social Psychological Factors

Attitudes. Attitudes toward unions hurt many workers. We noted that union power may be diminishing along with declining membership. In addition, public opinion about unions and union leaders is not strongly positive. In a national survey, 29 percent of Americans said they disapprove of labor unions (Polling Report 2007). Another 12 percent offered no opinion. Less than two-thirds of Americans, therefore, approve of unions. When asked about whether they would like unions to have more influence than they now have, 30 percent said yes; but 36 percent preferred for unions to retain the same influence they now have, and 32 percent would like to see them have less influence.

The negative attitudes that many Americans have about unions sometimes lead them into the *fallacy of circular reasoning,* as exemplified by the following exchange between two students in a social problems class:

"Unions hurt the economy and they hurt the workers."
"But the workers are much better off than they were in the past, before they had unions."
"They're not better off than they would be without the unions."
"How do you know? How can you say that?"
"Because unions hurt people. They keep workers from getting the best deal for themselves in the free market."

Negative thinking about unions is interesting in view of the union movement's achievements. The power of labor unions, along with government intervention, has helped eliminate many lethal work situations and has greatly improved the conditions of labor. Without the support of the public, labor unions will find themselves increasingly unable to gain further benefits for their members and for labor as a whole. Public opinion vacillates, of course, and may shift again in a more favorable direction. However, the decline in public approval of labor unions is an unwelcome sign to people who strive to improve the lot of workers.

Another attitude that enters into work problems is the sense of superiority that people might have toward certain workers. The attitudes of many Americans toward service workers, manual laborers, and clerical workers range from patronizing to contemptuous. If some workers are dissatisfied or alienated, it is in part because others *treat them with little or no respect because of their jobs*. For example, we have seen many instances of secretaries and clerks being treated with contempt by their superiors or by customers who feel they should quickly respond to demands from those who "pay your salary."

Socialization. One of the more important reasons that Americans desire interesting work that makes full use of their skills and abilities is that they have been socialized to expect it. *The socialization process in America involves an emphasis on achievement,* and that achievement involves a job that will enable you to do better than your parents and to fulfill yourselves (Chang et al. 2006). Work—the right kind of work—is an integral part of the American dream. That is why parents will forgo some of their own pleasure in order to send their children through college, and why professionals frequently prefer for their children to follow them in some kind of professional career.

In other words, you learn at an early age that if you are going to engage seriously in the pursuit of happiness that is your right, you must secure the kind of work that is conducive to the pursuit. As long as work is an integral part of individual fulfillment, and as long as the economy does not yield sufficient numbers of jobs that facilitate fulfillment, Americans will continue to have the quality of their lives diminished by the contradiction between socialized expectations and the realities of society.

The Ideology and Reality of Work

A final factor in work problems is the incongruity between the ideology about work and the reality of work. One line of thought, which dates back to the first Protestants, insists on the *value of all work*. The classic devotional writer William Law (1906:32) said, "Worldly business is to be made holy unto the Lord, by being done as a service to Him, and in conformity to His Divine will." This ideology regards work as a sacred obligation and implies that all work is equally good.

Although American ideology emphasizes the value of work and the equal value of all work, in practice not all work is given equal value. As we noted in the previous section, some kinds of work are disparaged by people who have jobs with higher prestige. Many Americans accept the ideology that work of any kind is intrinsically superior to nonwork, only to find themselves disparaged by other Americans who have "better" jobs. This ideology compounds the problems of the unemployed, who tend to define a social problem as personal and blame themselves for their plight. In addition, the work ideology may make the unemployed feel guilty about not working, even though they are the victims of a political-economic system rather than blame-worthy violators of the American way.

Public Policy and Private Action

The problems of work can be attacked in a number of different ways. First, with regard to unemployment, it is unlikely that the rate can go much lower than it was from the late 1990s through 2001. The challenge is not to bring the unemployment rate down to zero; this won't happen (even economists do not mean zero unemployment when they use the term "full employment"). The challenge is to keep the rate low by maintaining a strong economy while supporting those who are unemployed.

Government programs to train, or retool, and find jobs for the unemployed are one form of support. Although such programs often benefit people, they also are usually controversial in terms of cost and effectiveness. Finding an effective job-training program is as much a political as a technical matter and, thus, requires a strong commitment from politicians.

Unemployment benefits are another form of support. Such benefits depend on action by both federal and state governments. Contrary to what some people believe, unemployment benefits are not automatically available to anyone who loses a job. As many as half or more of the unemployed are not covered by unemployment insurance (U.S. Census Bureau 2006).

The government could also require other kinds of benefits for workers. Only six of ten American workers in private industry have access to medical care and retirement benefits (U.S. Department of Labor 2006b). Health care coverage is a particular concern of the unemployed. A national health plan could provide such coverage both for them and for the workers who do not now receive such a benefit. Time off from work is another benefit that is important to the well-being of workers (Etzion 2003). But American workers have fewer days of paid vacation than workers in many other nations. After a year on the job, blue-collar workers tend to receive an annual paid vacation of five days, and white-collar workers receive ten days. Longer paid vacations come only after years on the job. By contrast, all the European Union nations have a statutory minimum vacation of at least 20 days a year after one year on the job (Worklife Report 2003). Public holidays add another 10.8 days per year to the average time off.

Various measures can alleviate the problem of work-family conflict. These measures can be voluntarily undertaken by firms or mandated by the government. Work-family conflict can be minimized, for example, among those people who are able to work from their homes (e.g., via computer), those parents who are able to work part-time for a few years without jeopardizing their careers, and those workers who have more control over their hours and work conditions (Work and Family Newsbrief 2003; Hill, Martinson, and Ferris 2004).

Regarding the problem of work hazards, governmental and union actions have significantly reduced the incidence of occupational injuries and illnesses. The Occupational Safety and Health Administration of the Department of Labor acts as a watchdog group to enforce safety regulations. As a result of OSHA's activity, the number of injuries per 100 workers fell from 10.6 in 1973 to 4.6 in 2005, and the number of workers killed on the job fell from 13,800 in 1970 to 5,702 in 2005 (U.S. Department of Labor 2006d; Bureau of Labor Statistics Web site). Some employers resent the OSHA regulations and complain about government intervention in their business. Yet the data on diminishing injuries and deaths support the continuing efforts of OSHA to provide workers with a safe working environment.

Various measures can help address the problems of job dissatisfaction and alienation. From this chapter's discussion about the causes of the problems, you can see that more challenging work, greater worker participation and control, and more worker autonomy are needed. In addition, the quality of the relationship between bosses and coworkers is closely related to job satisfaction. Workers who are on good terms with and feel supported by others at the workplace have higher levels of satisfaction than do other workers (Ting 1997; El-Bassel et al. 1998). Thus, programs that engage in team-building and conflict resolution skills can enhance the quality of workplace relationships.

Job enrichment efforts also can reduce dissatisfaction and alienation. Job enrichment involves such changes as more worker responsibility and less direct control over the worker. It also includes the upgrading of skills required for a job and enlargement of the job so that the worker is not confined to a single, highly specialized task. Some job enrichment programs have resulted in higher job satisfaction, higher levels of worker morale, fewer grievances, and less absenteeism and turnover.

Still another measure for dealing with dissatisfaction and alienation is *flextime,* which made its debut in America in 1970 after being used successfully in Europe. There are at least three different types of flextime systems, varying by the amount of choice given to the worker. In one type, the employer lets the workers choose from a range of times to start their eight-hour workdays. A second type allows employees to choose their own schedules. Once chosen and approved, the schedules must be followed for a specified length of time. In a third type, employees can vary their own schedules on a daily basis without prior approval of supervisors. All types have limits within which employees must function. Millions of Americans now work under flextime, and the results include greater satisfaction, higher morale, increased productivity, and less stress driving to work (Kelloway and Gottlieb 1998; Lucas and Heady 2002).

Dissatisfaction and alienation also can be addressed through *participatory management or organizational democracy, which involves worker participation in the decision-making process.* Marshall Sashkin (1984) has called this measure an "ethical imperative." He notes that employees may participate in the decision-making process in four areas: setting organizational goals, solving problems, selecting from alternative courses of action, and making changes in the organization. In more extreme forms of involvement, employees participate in decisions about hiring and firing and about their own wages and benefits.

Employees may participate in the decisions as individuals, as part of manager-employee pairs, or as members of a group of managers and employees. Such participation fulfills the needs of employees for some degree of control over their lives, for more meaningful work, and for the kind of involvement that attacks the problem of alienation. Participation programs can be costly to implement and conflict with the traditional management-worker relationship. However, they can improve productivity, quality control, and a company's market share of the product (Levin 2006).

A final measure is *employee ownership,* including the more radical form of *employee takeover of a company.* Thousands of companies now offer workers an employee stock ownership plan (ESOP). There are three types of employee ownership plans in the United States (Tucker, Nock, and Toscano 1989). In *direct ownership,* employees simply own shares in the company. This is the most common form of employee ownership in the United States (Blasi and Kruse 2006). In *trust ownership,* employees acquire some portion of shares over time as stock is transferred to them as a part of their benefits. In *cooperative ownership,* employees get votes in accord with the number of shares they hold; this type of ESOP gives the employees some control of the enterprise. These plans generally lead to increased job satisfaction and worker performance (Yates 2006).

In a few cases, employees have assumed ownership and full responsibility for a company or have been allowed to work without supervisory personnel. The results tend to be uniformly positive: higher productivity, lower costs, and greater worker satisfaction and morale.

Follow-Up.   Some critics say that Americans expect too much from their work. They not only want good pay, they also want their jobs to be fulfilling. What do you think? Should people just be grateful that they have paying jobs, and find their fulfillment in after-work activities?

chapter 10 review

Summary

The American economy, the nature of work, and the nature of the workforce all have changed over time in America. Some recent changes in the economy that are detrimental to many Americans are corporate downsizing, increased use of temporary workers, declining union strength, reduced corporate tax obligations, and decline in income for some families. The labor force and the division of labor have increased substantially. The educational level and the proportion of females in the labor force are also increasing. The work ethic remains strong, but workers now insist that their jobs be a source of fulfillment and not solely a source of income.

Work is a social problem because of unemployment and underemployment, work hazards, and dissatisfaction and alienation. Each year millions of Americans are unemployed, though the rate varies for different groups and different occupations. Many Americans are not deeply dissatisfied with or alienated from work, but many also desire a job different from the one they have. Among the hazards of work are work-induced stress and work-related injuries and illnesses.

Work is intimately related to the quality of life because it involves the worker's health. Work-induced stress, injuries and illnesses, and job dissatisfaction can all adversely affect the worker's health. Unemployment tends to be a traumatic, stressful experience that adversely affects the worker's interpersonal relationships and health.

Capitalism with its emphasis on profit is one of the factors that contributes to problems in the American economy. Subservience of workers' needs to organizational needs, union-busting, downsizing, and increased numbers of temporary jobs all reflect the drive for profit. Structural unemployment is also a product of the capitalistic system, which includes the natural swings of the economy, technological change, government spending priorities, and the growth of multinational corporations. The nature of work roles in the American technological, bureaucratic society produces much dissatisfaction, stress, and conflict. Work hazards are frequently more common than necessary because companies give priority to profit, not to worker health and safety.

Among social psychological factors that add to the problems of work are the attitudes of Americans toward unions and toward other Americans whose jobs they regard as inferior to their own. The contradiction between the ideology and reality of work is another contributing factor. The ideology glorifies work and working and places an equal value on all work. The reality is disparagement of some work and a political-economic system that guarantees a certain amount of unemployment.

Key Terms

Capitalism	Underemployment
Division of Labor	Unemployment Rate
Downsizing	Work Ethic
Labor Force	

Study Questions

1. How have the economy, work, and the workforce been changing in America?
2. What are some consequences for workers of the globalization of the economy?
3. Discuss whether the meaning of work is changing.
4. How much and what kinds of unemployment are there in the United States?
5. How serious are the problems of work dissatisfaction and of hazards at work?
6. How do work problems affect people's health and interpersonal relationships?
7. How does the political-economic system affect the problems related to the American economy and work?
8. In what ways do contemporary work roles increase job dissatisfaction and alienation?
9. What kinds of attitudes toward work, workers, and unions contribute to the problems of work?
10. Discuss the contradiction between the ideology and the reality of work in America.
11. What can Americans do to reduce unemployment, job hazards, and job dissatisfaction?

Internet Resources/ Exercises

1. Explore some of the ideas in this chapter on the following sites:

http://www.dol.gov   The U.S. Department of Labor site has the latest numbers from the Bureau of Labor

Statistics plus reports on every aspect of work in the United States.

http://www.bls.gov/opub/mlr/mlrhome.htm The Monthly Labor Review site provides abstracts of all articles from 1988 to the present.

http://www.aflcio.org/home.htm News and information about various aspects of work, including safety, from the AFL-CIO.

2. The text points out that studies are inconclusive about the degree of worker satisfaction. Use a search engine to research the topic "worker satisfaction." What would you conclude about the topic on the basis of the text materials and the materials you found?

3. Use the government sites listed above to explore work and working conditions in other nations. What kinds of problems exist in other nations that are largely or totally absent in the United States? What kinds of benefits do workers have in other nations that are lacking in the United States? On the whole, which nations do you believe have the best working conditions?

For Further Reading

Heckscher, Charles, and Paul Adler. *The Corporation as a Collaborative Community.* New York, Oxford University Press, 2006. An examination of the way the vital quality of "community" (in the form of loyalty)—both within and between businesses—has been eroded through such things as downsizing and restructuring and a description of the new form of community that is emerging.

Lipset, Seymour Martin, Noah M. Meltz, Rafael Gomez, and Ivan Katchanovski. *The Paradox of American Unionism.* Ithaca, NY: ILR Press, 2004. Compares unionism in Canada and the United States, showing how the emphasis on individual freedom and the workings of government affect labor legislation.

Milkman, Ruth. *Farewell to the Factory: Auto Workers in the Late Twentieth Century.* Berkeley: University of California Press, 1997. A case study of an automobile plant that experienced downsizing and transformation. Describes in detail the experience of workers both before and after the change.

Roediger, David R., and Philip S. Foner. *Our Own Time: A History of American Labor and the Working Day.* Westport, CT: Greenwood Press, 1990. Two historians, one a distinguished historian of the labor movement, examine the struggle of organized labor to win the 40-hour workweek. They argue that the labor movement's decline is a result of a drift away from its original European philosophy.

Rogers, Jackie Krasas. *Temps: The Many Faces of the Changing Workplace.* Ithaca, NY: Cornell University Press, 2000. A critique of the temporary worker trend, dispelling some of the myths about why people work part time and showing the stress experienced by those unwillingly caught up in temp work.

Rubery, Jill, and Damian Grimshaw. *The Organisation of Employment: An International Perspective.* New York: Palgrave Macmillan, 2003. A readable introduction to the way that employment and labor markets are organized in advanced capitalist countries. Compares such things as trends in labor market participation, vocational training systems, the regulation of the labor market, and the ways that firms deal with work and employment.

Zlolniski, Christian. *Janitors, Street Vendors, and Activists: The Lives of Mexican Immigrants in Silicon Valley.* Berkeley, CA: University of California Press, 2006. An exploration of the use of Mexican immigrants for low-wage jobs in the high-tech industry, showing both how the workers are exploited and how they are affecting such things as the political process and union activity.

Endnotes

1. Reported in *The Public Perspective,* April–May 1999, p. 16.

2. The minister supplied us with this account.

CHAPTER

11

Education

"I Kept My Mouth Shut"

In theory, all Americans have an equal chance to prove themselves in school. In practice, you are disadvantaged if you come from a poor or minority-group family. Marcia is an undergraduate student who comes from a middle-class family. She remembers with some regret about the time she learned how others are disadvantaged:

I was in the first grade when I learned that we weren't all really equal at school. It was recess and I was playing on the monkey bars. One of my classmates was playing beside me. Her name was Ramona. She came from a poor family. I didn't think about it at the time, but she was very ill-kept. Neither she nor her clothes were very clean. But I liked her. I enjoyed playing with her at recess.

As we were playing, and Ramona was turning around on the bars, some of the other girls began to make fun of her and talk about her dirty underwear. I felt sorry for her and mad at the other girls for saying such mean things to her. I hollered to them: "She can't help it if her underwear is dirty." No sooner had I said it than the strong voice of our teacher came booming at us: "Yes, she can."

I could see the embarrassment on Ramona's face. She got off the monkey bars and went over and sat by herself on a bench for the rest of the recess. I'm ashamed to say that the teacher really intimidated me. I felt really bad about Ramona, but I was very careful to keep my mouth shut about

313

it after that. I didn't want to incur the teacher's wrath, and I didn't want all the other girls to reject me.

I think it was about the fourth grade when I no longer saw Ramona. I don't know if she dropped out or her family moved or what. I do know that she never did well in school. But I don't think it was because she wasn't smart. Ramona just never had much of a chance.

Introduction

Historically, Americans have viewed education as an answer to many social ills; but a national poll found that 47 percent of Americans would give the nation's public schools a grade of C for the quality of their work, and 19 percent would grade the schools as D or F. When asked about the schools in their own community, slightly less than half graded the schools as A or B, 35 percent gave a grade of C, and 11 percent assigned grades of D or F (Polling Report 2007).

Americans apparently have a sense that education is a problem as well as a solution to other problems. When education is in trouble, it is a very serious matter because education is the foundation of American life.

In what sense has education become a problem? In this chapter we first look at the functions of education and the high value typically placed on education. We also show how the high value is reflected in the continually "higher" amount of education attained by Americans.

In the light of the functions and value of education, we look at how certain problems such as unequal opportunities bear upon the quality of life of Americans. We then examine some structural and social psychological factors that contribute to the problems and conclude with some examples of efforts to resolve the problems.

Why Education?

What do Americans expect their educational system to achieve for them personally and for their society? In 1787 the Northwest Ordinance included a provision for the encouragement of education on the grounds that "religion, morality, and knowledge" are "necessary to good government and the happiness of mankind." The significance of this, as Parker (1975:29) pointed out, is that "a people, not yet formed into a nation, declare education to be an essential support of free government and set aside western lands for schools and education."

Thus, one function of education is to create *good and effective citizens* (Tyack 2003). There is some dispute about what it means to be a good citizen, however. Some people believe that education should produce citizens who will accept traditional values and protect the "American way of life" (which obviously means different things to different people). Education achieves this function when it transmits the **culture** from one generation to the next, that is, when it *socializes the young into the basic values, beliefs, and customs of the society.* Others believe that education should equip the citizenry to

culture
the way of life of a people, including both material products (such as technology) and nonmaterial characteristics (such as values, norms, language, and beliefs)

reshape their society so that the flaws and inequities are eliminated. In any case, education has been held to be essential in the process of creating effective citizens in the republic.

A second function of education is to provide the individual with the *possibility for upward mobility*. For a long time Americans have associated education with good jobs. Most students in colleges and universities are there to prepare for the better-paying and more prestigious jobs, not for the love of learning. Education achieves this function when it *instructs the young in knowledge and skills*.

The third function of education is personal development. Education *liberates people from the bonds of ignorance and prepares them to maximize their intellectual, emotional, and social development*. This function is important to educators, but few people set educational goals with personal development in mind.

Whatever their views of the primary aim of education, most Americans would probably agree that all three functions are legitimate. The schools should produce good citizens. They should help the individual to better himself or herself, and they should prepare the individual to maximize his or her own development. Because all three functions are related to the *quality of life* of the individual, if any person or group is not given the opportunity to secure an education that fulfills the functions, education becomes a social problem. Quality of life is diminished when the individual lacks the tools necessary to participate effectively in political processes, to achieve some measure of success in work or a career, or to develop his or her potential to its fullest.

Educational Attainment and Payoff

Because of its importance to quality of life, you would expect Americans to secure an increasing amount of education over time. Most do aspire to a high level, but what about the **attainment?** Once attained, does education yield the expected payoff? Is the high value on education reflected in concrete results?

Levels of Attainment

In 1870, 57 percent of youths 5 to 17 years old were enrolled in school, and 1.2 percent were in high schools. By 2004, 95.4 percent of 5- and 6-year-olds, 98.4 percent of 7- to 13-year-olds, and 96.5 percent of 14- to 17-year-olds were enrolled in school (National Center for Education Statistics 2006b).

A few generations ago, completion of elementary school was considered a good *level of attainment*. Today, completion of high school is the minimal level considered appropriate. As figure 11.1 shows, an increasing proportion of the population has been reaching that level. In fact, as the figure illustrates, an increasing proportion of the population is attaining a college degree. And many students find they need or desire an advanced degree—between 1976 and 2004, enrollment in graduate programs increased 61.8 percent to 2.2 million students (U.S. Department of Education 2006). The increasing amount of education is reflected in the data on different age groups in table 11.1. Compare, for example, the rates for people aged 65 and older with those in the 25 to 34 age group.

Another way to look at the increasing education attainment is to note the diminishing *dropout rate*. Students begin to drop out of school after the fifth grade. Since the 1920s, the proportion dropping out, especially before completing elementary school,

attainment
as distinguished from educational "achievement," the number of years of education completed by a student

FIGURE 11.1
Educational Attainment of
Adults (25 years and older).

Source: U.S. Census Bureau
2007.

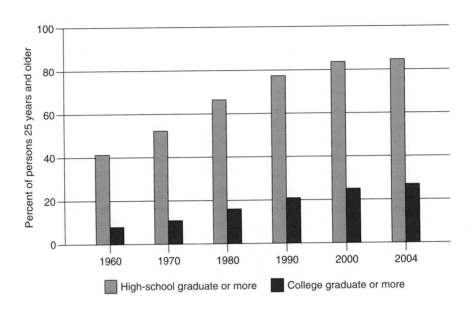

Percent of persons 25 years and older

■ High-school graduate or more   ■ College graduate or more

	Percent of Population					
	Not a High School Graduate	High School Graduate	Some College, but No Degree	Associate's Degree	Bachelor's Degree	Advanced Degree
Total	14.8	32.0	17.0	8.4	18.1	9.6
Age:						
25–34 years	12.9	28.7	19.3	8.8	22.3	7.9
35–44 years	12.0	31.5	17.0	9.9	20.2	9.3
45–54 years	10.3	31.4	17.6	10.1	19.1	11.5
55–64 years	13.6	33.3	17.0	7.9	16.1	12.2
65–74 years	23.6	36.3	14.6	5.0	11.6	8.8
75 years or over	30.6	35.7	12.8	4.2	10.2	6.5
Sex:						
Male	15.2	31.1	16.8	7.5	18.6	10.8
Female	14.6	32.8	17.3	9.3	17.6	8.5
Race:						
White	14.2	32.2	17.0	8.5	18.4	9.8
Black	19.4	36.0	19.2	7.8	12.3	5.3
Other races	15.6	23.0	14.0	8.2	24.2	15.1
Hispanic	41.6	27.7	13.2	5.4	8.8	3.3

SOURCE: National Center for Education Statistics 2006b.

TABLE 11.1
Years of School Completed,
by Age, Sex, Race, and
Hispanic Origin, 2004
(persons 25 years old and
older)

has decreased greatly. The likelihood of dropping out varies among different groups.
Males are more likely to drop out than are females. Students in the lower socioeconomic strata are more likely than those in higher strata to drop out. And except for
Asian Americans, minority groups have higher dropout rates than do whites. The rate
is particularly high among Hispanics. In 2003, the proportions of those in the 16 to

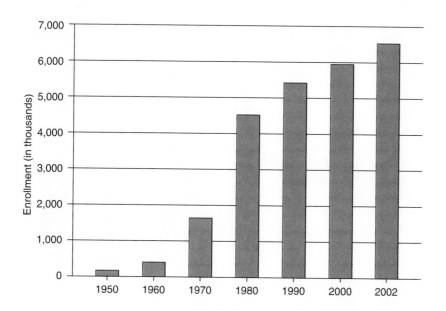

FIGURE 11.2
Enrollment in Community (two-year) Colleges, 1950–2002.

Source: U.S. Census Bureau Web site.

24 age group who dropped out of school were: 6.8 percent of whites, 11.8 percent of African Americans, and 23.8 percent of Hispanics (National Center for Education Statistics 2006b).

One factor that has aided educational attainment is the proliferation of two-year colleges. Their enrollment increased fivefold from 1960 to 1970 and more than doubled from 1970 to 1980 (figure 11.2). After 1980, enrollment continued to rise, but much more slowly. The community colleges offer both preparation for four-year colleges and universities and numerous terminal programs. Many students use the community college experience to decide on their educational and career goals.

Overall, then, the level of educational attainment has been steadily increasing in the United States, a reflection in part of the changing occupational structure and the consequent need for increased education (Walters 1984). The minimum amount of education considered appropriate today is completion of high school, and the majority of Americans have reached that level. The dropout rate, which once increased steadily from the fifth grade on, now tends to remain minimal until after the eighth grade. Americans are getting more and more education. Is it yielding the expected payoff?

Attainment and Payoff

In some ways you cannot talk about the *payoff of education*. You cannot, for instance, measure the personal development of individuals and correlate that with education. However, there is a positive relationship between happiness and educational level; that is, the higher the level of education, the higher the reported happiness and satisfaction with life (Jonas and Wilson 1997). Of course, happiness and life satisfaction are not measures of personal development—the fulfillment of an individual's potential. At best, you can say that the greater happiness and satisfaction reported by the better educated may reflect a tendency toward greater fulfillment of potential.

Similarly, there is only minimal evidence that education creates an effective citizenry. We know, for instance, that there is a *direct correlation between level of education and voter participation*. For example, in the 2004 election, the percentage

EDUCATIONAL ATTAINMENT, BY COUNTRY

A nation cannot successfully modernize or implement a political democracy without an educated populace. People must be educated in order to function effectively in the kinds of jobs associated with an industrial economy, and they must be educated in order to participate meaningfully in a democratic political process.

An economist argued that economic growth cannot begin in a country until at least 6 percent of the population is enrolled in primary school (Peaslee 1969). As the country continues to modernize, increasing educational levels are required. Thus, nations like the United States that are the most economically and technologically developed typically have the highest average levels of educational attainment.

Political leaders are aware of the crucial importance of education and in most nations are attempting to provide expanded educational opportunities. There are still some dramatic disparities, however. While the great majority of nations enroll most of their children at the elementary level—grades one through six—some nations fall far short. In 2002, for example, the proportion of children enrolled in elementary education was 90 percent or more in the majority of countries for which information was available, but it was 68 percent in Pakistan, 67 percent in Saudi Arabia, 60 percent in Sudan, and 44 percent in Niger (National Center for Education Statistics 2006b).

Enrollment in higher education has also expanded greatly throughout the world. In fact, enrollment rates in developing countries are now higher than the rates were in Europe a few decades ago (Schofer and Meyer 2005). Table 11.2 shows the proportions of the population enrolled in secondary and postsecondary institutions in a number of countries. As with many things, the United States is neither the most nor the least educated nation in the world. Unfortunately, data are not available for most of the developing nations. But their educational opportunities are more limited

of people voting was 23.6 percent for those with eight years or less of education, 52.4 percent for those who completed high school, and 74.2 percent for those who had four or more years of college (U.S. Census Bureau 2007).

More educated people are also more likely to hold democratic values and to support democratic practices. Although such relationships indicate positive contributions of education to citizenship, they do not tell us whether education helps people to detect and reject demagoguery and to participate meaningfully in the defense of freedom and the shaping of a just social order. Education does increase political participation and understanding. However, the more educated people usually are the political and corporate heads who accept and maintain the institutional policies and practices that can contribute to the various social problems of the nation.

There is more evidence with respect to the third function of education—providing a means of upward mobility. A strong relationship exists between levels of education and income. As table 11.3 shows, in 2004 people with a bachelor's degree averaged 2.5 times as much annual income as those with eight years or less of education and 1.6 times as much as those with a high school education. In fact, the median income goes up with each higher level of education.

Do these numbers mean that an individual can maximize his or her income by maximizing education? In general, yes. But to assume that *anyone* can reach the highest levels of income by maximizing education is the *fallacy of non sequitur.* Your background, including your racial or ethnic identity, and the economy are among the factors than those in the developed countries. As long as such disparities exist, it is unlikely that the inequalities between nations in such factors as income, employment, and standard of living will diminish.

Country	Percent of Specific Age Groups Enrolled In			
	Secondary Schools (17-year-olds)	Postsecondary Institutions		
		(18–21 years)	(22–25 years)	(24–29 years)
Australia	80	35	20	10
Belgium	100	42	18	5
Czech Republic	98	20	16	5
Finland	94	21	39	19
Germany	93	12	20	12
Greece	70	46	24	11
Italy	79	24	21	8
Mexico	34	15	7	3
Norway	93	17	27	13
Spain	82	35	24	8
Switzerland	85	10	18	9
United Kingdom	74	30	12	6
United States	79	46	25	11

TABLE 11.2
Educational Attainment, by Country
SOURCE: National Center for Education Statistics 2006b.

TABLE 11.3
Median Income of Persons 25 Years and Older, by Educational Attainment, 2004

Educational Attainment	Median Income
Less than ninth grade	$ 17,017
9th to 12th grade (no diploma)	18,874
High school graduate	26,104
Some college, no degree	30,610
Associate's degree	32,383
Bachelor's degree	42,087
Master's degree	81,319
Professional degree	71,146
Doctorate degree	100,000

SOURCE: National Center for Education Statistics 2006b.

that affect your chances. We discuss this situation in some detail later in this chapter, but our point here is that the high correlation between education and income does not mean that education is the open road to success. People who attain high levels of education are likely to be those whose parents had a relatively high level of education. There is mobility in the United States, but education is more useful to the privileged as

a means of passing on their privileges to their children than as a means for the under-
dog to be upwardly mobile.

Some people have argued that education is of no use in reducing inequality in America, that schools do virtually nothing to help the poor be upwardly mobile, and that
education has little effect on the future incomes of people. Rather, they feel that economic opportunities depend upon the state of the economy; one's family background;
and various other noneducational factors, such as the contacts one is able to make.

It is true that education alone is not sufficient to deal with economic inequality in
America, and it is true that the best way to "get ahead" in America is to start from a
high socioeconomic position (obviously something over which the individual has no
control). This argument overstates the case, however. The advantaged child will not
maintain his or her advantage without an education, and at least some people gain new
advantages through education. Education is not a cure-all, but it is not useless in the
struggle for new advantages. Thus, in their study of how people achieve positions in
top corporate management, Useem and Karabel (1986) found that

1. Those who achieve such positions tend to have a bachelor's degree from a top-
   ranked college or university, an MBA from a prestigious program, or a law degree
   from a top-ranked university.
2. Given the same amount of education, an upper-class background improves one's
   chances of reaching the top.

You may conclude, then, that although many people are upwardly mobile through
educational attainment, those most likely to benefit from education are already in the
middle and upper strata. In terms of mobility, the payoff from education is not equally
likely for all groups.

Education and the Quality of Life

Ideally, as we have shown, education performs a number of valued functions that enhance the quality of life for Americans. It prepares you to be a good, effective citizen.
It is the pathway to your social and economic betterment. It is the tool by which you develop your full potential as an individual. To perform such functions, education would
have to be of high quality, be equally available to all, and consistently yield the expected payoff. Education is a problem because there are inequalities and the expected
payoff does not always occur.

Inequality of Opportunity and Attainment

Besides the inequality of attainment we have touched on, there is *inequality of opportunity*— a debatable and ambiguous notion, as you will see. Such inequalities contradict *the American value of education and the ideology of equal opportunities* for all.
Ideally, every American ought to have equal opportunity to maximize his or her education. However, minorities and the poor do not attain the same educational levels as
white males. Is this inequality of attainment a reflection of unequal opportunities or of
some characteristics of the groups themselves? You have seen in previous chapters that
the answer is both but that the characteristics of the groups do not include an inferior
level of intelligence. Part of the reason a son of a poor white farmer does not go to college may be his own lack of motivation, but even that lack must be seen as a social phe-

nomenon that is rooted in a complex situation in which multiple factors work together. In other words, unequal educational attainment does not mean that those groups with lower levels of attainment are incapable of extending their education. It is important to keep this aspect in mind as we explore the ways in which educational opportunities and attainment are distributed in society.

The Meaning of Unequal Opportunities.   There is debate over the meaning of inequality of opportunity. Most Americans, including most social scientists, would affirm the *ideal of equal educational opportunity* for all. But what does that ideal mean? Does it mean that a child should have the opportunity to attend a nonsegregated school? Does it mean that all children should be schooled with equal amounts of money? Does it mean that the proportion of people of various kinds (minorities and those from different socioeconomic strata) in the differing educational levels should be the same as their proportion in the total population? Does it mean that each child should have access to the same quality and the same amount of education? Does it mean that the same amount of education should yield the same payoff in terms of income or personal development?

Or are all these matters important? If, for instance, you define equality as all children attending nonsegregated schools, there may still be considerable inequality of funding among various schools. If you define equality as equal funds per student, children could still attend segregated schools or be less likely to attend college if they are black or poor.

Because the meaning of unequal opportunities is debated, it is unlikely that we can settle on a definition that will be acceptable to everyone. Nevertheless, it is important to select a meaning so that we can explore the extent of inequality in America. For our purposes, equality of educational opportunity means that every child has access to quality education and is not deterred from maximizing that education by social background or economic factors. Social background factors include race, ethnic origin, sex, and socioeconomic status. Economic factors include the funding of education and the cost to the student. In brief, equality means that all Americans, whatever their background, have the opportunity to attain fairly equal amounts of education. It also means that students attend schools that are equally funded and that the cost of education (college or graduate school) does not force some students to drop out before they have reached their goal. In these terms, how much inequality is there?

Inequality of Attainment.   We have given figures in previous chapters on *differences in educational attainment.* A measure of inequality may be the proportion of various groups that has attained different levels of education. In 2004, for example, the proportion of adults 25 years and older who had completed high school were: whites, 85.2 percent; African Americans, 80.6 percent; Asian Americans, 86.8 percent; and Hispanics, 58.4 percent (U.S. Census Bureau 2007). The proportions completing a bachelor's degree or more were: whites, 28.2 percent; African Americans, 17.6 percent; Asian Americans, 49.4 percent; and Hispanics, 12.1 percent.

There are variations among Hispanics in the extent to which educational attainment is low (U.S. Census Bureau 2007). Thus, the proportions in 2005 with a high school degree were: Mexican-origin, 52.2 percent; Puerto Rican–origin, 72.3 percent; and Cuban-origin, 73.5 percent. For a bachelor's degree or more, the proportions were: Mexican-origin, 8.3 percent; Puerto Rican–origin, 13.8 percent; and Cuban-origin, 24.7 percent. The reasons for these variations are unclear, but they do caution us against the assumption that ethnicity per se is the only important variable in understanding attainment levels of America's minorities.

Funding and Costs.   The second aspect of unequal opportunities is the *funding and cost of education.* Children do not have equal educational opportunities if they attend schools with unequal resources or if they are forced to drop out at some point because they cannot pay for the cost of their education.

There are considerable inequalities of resources, both among the states and among school districts within a state. In 2004, the average expenditure per pupil ranged from $5,556 in Utah and $5,595 in Arizona to $12,394 in Connecticut and $12,408 in New York (U.S. Census Bureau 2007). The school expenditures in a state, of course, tend to reflect such things as the overall wealth of the state, the cost of living in the state, and the personal income of the residents of the state. The expenditures also reflect the ideology of the people and the state government. Although Utah and Arizona spend less than any other state per pupil on education, there are many other states with a lower median household income. In any case, the amount spent on a child's education varies enormously between the states.

We are cautious about our conclusions. A particular school in a state with lower-than-average funding may offer an immeasurably better education than a ghetto school in New York, but to conclude from this example that the lower-than-average state offers a better education is the *fallacy of dramatic instance.* The point is not that every school in the better-funded state is better than every school in the more poorly funded state. Rather, overall, the schools in the better-funded state have an advantage in resources for educating students, so that the typical student is likely to experience an education backed by greater resources.

Funding also varies considerably within states. Schools have been funded by the property tax (discussed in more detail later in this chapter). Property tax funding means that a school district populated largely by people from lower-income groups who live in cheaper homes will have a low tax base. School districts that encompass affluent areas, on the other hand, may actually have a lower rate of taxation (number of dollars of school tax per assessed value of the property) but a much higher per-pupil income. An affluent school district may have double, triple, or quadruple the funds per pupil than an adjacent poor school district has. Should the funds available for a child's schooling be considerably less because of the neighborhood in which he or she happens to be born?

Similarly, you may ask whether an individual should drop out of college because of inadequate financial resources even though he or she is quite capable of doing the work. There is not sufficient money to provide scholarships and loans for all students who would like to go to college, and the cost of attending college has risen rapidly. In fact, the cost of attending college has risen more rapidly than most other costs. In the 2004–2005 school year, the average annual cost (including tuition, fees, room, and board) was $34,698 at a private four-year university, and $12,604 at a public four-year university (National Center for Education Statistics 2006b). These figures are more than double the amounts for 1990–1991. This increase means that millions of American families have annual incomes less than the cost of room, board, and tuition at an average private university. Obviously, many Americans are priced out of the better colleges and universities in the nation. Moreover, the disparity between those who can and those who cannot afford college is expected to grow. There are no signs yet that the spiraling costs of higher education will stop.

In sum, the quality of life for many Americans is depressed because of unequal opportunities at all levels of education. Many children cannot afford to go to a better college or even to any college. Their level of attainment will be less than their abilities warrant and often less than they desire. Those same children probably attended elementary and secondary schools that spent less on them than other schools could spend. Inequality in education exists from kindergarten to the university.

The Atmosphere: Learning or Surviving?

Another kind of inequality that contradicts the American ideology of equal opportunity involves the **atmosphere** of the school. Some atmospheres are conducive to learning, some inhibit learning, and some require the student to focus on surviving, on merely getting through the institution with body and sanity intact.

atmosphere
the general mood and social influences in a situation or place

Education as Boring. One frequently heard criticism is that education is boring (Babbage 1998; Wurdinger 2005). For example, boredom often results when students are required to memorize large amounts of data that are not integrated with each other and not linked to important principles or ideas. Thus, history students may be required to memorize names, dates, and events without discussing their significance for understanding the processes of social life.

Boredom can afflict students at any level. The slowest students may be bored because they cannot grasp the materials. Others may be bored because they see no point to what they are doing. Gifted children may also suffer from boredom. Gifted elementary students typically master from a third to a half of the curriculum in five basic subjects before they even begin the school year (U.S. Department of Education 1993). Boredom leads to a variety of negative consequences. Students may behave as if they lack interest or the ability to focus their attention (Webb 2000). Or they may cut classes or even drop out of school (Fallis and Opotow 2003).

The Atmosphere of Fear. Perhaps worse even than boredom is the *atmosphere of fear* in which some students must function. Without a safe environment, teachers find it difficult to teach and students find it difficult to learn. Unfortunately, a considerable amount of crime and violence exists in the schools.

To keep the situation in perspective, it is important to note two facts. First, *students are safer at school than away from school* (DeVoe et al. 2003). That is, they are more likely to be victimized while away from the school than in the school building itself. Second, the amount of crime and violence has decreased from the early 1990s. For students age 12 through 18 who were victimized, violent crimes decreased from 48 per 1,000 students in 1992 to 28 per 1,000 students in 2001

Education doesn't yield a high payoff when students are bored.

(DeVoe et al. 2003). However, such a decline does not erase the fear that students experience in school, because a considerable amount of crime and violence still takes place. Consider the following results from a national survey of 9th- through 12th-grade students (DeVoe et al. 2003):

13 percent reported being in a fight on school property.

7 to 9 percent reported being threatened or injured with a weapon such as a gun, knife, or club on school property during the preceding 12 months.

6 percent admitted carrying a weapon on school property within the previous 30 days.

8 percent reported being bullied at school in the last 6 months.

9 percent of teachers were threatened with injury by a student, and 4 percent were physically attacked by a student.

12 percent of students said that someone at school had used hate-related words against them (such as racial slurs).

All these problems are more severe in poor, inner-city schools in which many students are affected by the crab bucket syndrome. The *crab bucket syndrome* refers to the fact that inner-city students who try to free themselves from the culture of gangs, drugs, and violence and do good work face enormous pressure, harassment, and even violence as others try to pull them back into the bucket (Shanker 1994). In one inner-city school prior to an awards ceremony, names of outstanding students were kept secret lest the honorees would refuse to show up out of fear. One recipient had to be ordered to the stage to receive his reward; he walked up amid the sneering catcalls of others.

Ritualized Deprivation.   Another condition that exists in many American classrooms is described as **ritualized deprivation.** The teacher performs in a substandard fashion and may be with the children for only a short period of time. The building and facilities are substandard and contain little if anything to stimulate curiosity or motivate the intellect. The school offers a daily ritual—some of the motions of teaching and learning are present. However, the ritual occurs in such a deprived context that the student is more concerned about surviving the process than learning.

ritualized deprivation

a school atmosphere in which the motions of teaching and learning continue, while the students are more concerned about surviving than learning

The kind of school that has an atmosphere of ritualized deprivation is most likely to be found in the urban ghetto or other dominantly low-income area. Kozol (1992) describes such a school in Chicago. It is a high school with no campus and no schoolyard, though it does have a track and playing field. Forty percent of its 1,600 students are chronic truants. Only a fourth who enter ever graduate. It has some good teachers, but others who the principal admits "don't belong in education." He is not allowed to fire them, so they continue teaching.

Kozol sat in on a 12th-grade English class. The students were learning to pronounce a randomly selected list of words that are difficult, for example, "fastidious," "auspicious," and "egregious." He asked a boy who was having difficulty pronouncing "egregious" if he knew what the word meant. The boy had no idea. The teacher never asked the students to define the words or to use them in a sentence, only to try to pronounce them.

Thus, the ritual goes on. The students in the school struggle not only with fear, threats, and drugs, but with teachers who take them through pointless exercises. There seems to be little learning, just survival.

The Payoff: A Great Training Robbery?

One of the American expectations about education is that it will pay off in terms of upward mobility (Grubb and Lazerson 2004). Historically, the correlation between education and income has been strong, but in the early 1970s a *contradiction developed between education and the economy.* Educational attainment outstripped the capacity of the economy to absorb the graduates into jobs commensurate with their training. Even when the unemployment rate is very low, many workers cannot find employment that utilizes the skills and training they have (Livingston 1998). *The disparity between educational attainment and the skill demands of the workplace means that some workers are underemployed.*

Another part of the problem is the assumption that greater educational attainment guarantees career advancement. In fact, employers do not routinely reward educational attainment; rather, they reward it only when they believe it will contribute to the employee's productivity (Spilerman and Lunde 1991).

However, keep in mind the strong correlation between education, occupation, and income (table 11.3). Over a lifetime, average income will range from $1.2 million for high school graduates, to $2.1 million for those with a bachelor's degree, to $3.4 million for those with a doctoral degree, to $4.4 million for those with professional degrees (Bergman 2002). It is a minority of workers who are affected by a contradiction between their training and the economy.

You also should keep in mind that the diminished payoff refers strictly to employment and income. Unfortunately, Americans have focused so strongly on the economic payoff that many consider their college education useless if it does not yield a desirable, well-paying job. Only in this sense can we speak of an "oversupply" of college graduates. We could argue that all or at least the majority of Americans would profit by some college because higher education can enable the individual to think more deeply, explore more widely, and enjoy a greater range of experiences; but as long as education

Some teachers are assigned to classes that they are not prepared to teach; lack of discipline can create chaos in the classroom.

is valued only for its economic payoff, any failure to yield that payoff will depress the quality of life of those involved.

American Education: A Tide of Mediocrity?

Periodically, there are severe criticisms of American education. Over the past two decades, a series of reports criticized education at every level, and all the reports suggested that the educational system is marred by mediocrity. This mediocrity means a *contradiction between the American value of and expectations about education,* on the one hand, and *the functioning of the educational system,* on the other hand.

For example, a 1993 study of higher education concluded that a "dangerous mismatch" exists between what students need and what they get in colleges (Wingspread Group of Higher Education 1993). The study noted that too many college graduates cannot perform simple reading, writing, and mathematical tasks. It also criticized colleges and universities for giving priority to graduate education and research over undergraduate teaching.

A 1997 report by *Education Week*—a journal that regularly evaluates and grades various aspects of American education—graded the 50 states on achievement (fourth-grade reading scores and eighth-grade math scores), standards and assessments (what students are expected to know and how they are evaluated), quality of teaching, school climate, and resources (*Education Week* 1997). Among the grades were: B for standards and assessments; C for quality of teaching; C− for school climate; and C+ for spending sufficient funds. No grade was given for achievement, but the report called the evidence "discouraging." The report noted, for example, that Iowa led the nation on a national math test, but 69 percent of its eighth-grade students fell below the proficient level.

A report on the condition of education in 1999 looked at the quality of teaching (*Education Week* 2000). The report concluded that millions of American students have teachers who lack the minimum requirements set by the states to teach in public schools. Various loopholes and waivers are used (probably under the pressure of obtaining sufficient numbers of teachers) to put teachers into classes for which they are inadequately prepared. A follow-up study (*Education Week* 2003) described efforts to recruit and retain competent teachers, but also pointed out that the efforts were not directed toward the problem in high-poverty, high-minority, or low-achieving schools. Students in those schools were still far more likely than others to have incompetent, inexperienced, or inadequately trained teachers.

Finally, a report by the U.S. Department of Education stated that more than a third of high school seniors lack a basic competency in mathematics and nearly a fourth lack good reading skills (National Center for Education Statistics 2001). Thus, a substantial number of students graduate from high school without the skills necessary for well-paying jobs in today's economy.

Is the American system as mediocre as these dismal results suggest? On the one hand, Americans need to acknowledge that the United States has achieved an impressive level of education among the citizenry. On the other hand, they need to face up to the fact that serious deficiencies exist in the educational process. Progress has been made in response to the various studies we have noted, but deficiencies still exist. Consider the following points made in evaluations by the National Center for Education Statistics (2000a, 2004, 2006a) of changes since the 1980s:

Student performance has improved in math and science but not in reading.

Students have been taking more courses in core academic subjects, and the difficulty of the courses has increased. Greater percentages of high school students are completing algebra and higher-level math, biology, chemistry, and physics.

Although scores have increased, 12th-grade students still do not fare as well on math and science tests as do students in many other nations.

More than half the faculty at two-year colleges are part time.

More than half of colleges offer remedial courses, and nearly a third of college freshmen are required to enroll in at least one of them.

A substantial number of Americans see yet another deficiency in the schools—the lack of a religious perspective. A poll reported that 60 percent of Americans disagree that school prayer violates the separation of church and state (Walsh 2001). In response to the perception that the schools are spiritually deficient, there is a growing number of Christian schools. In the 2003–2004 school year, there were 2.4 million students in Catholic schools and 1.8 million in other religious schools (National Center for Education Statistics 2006b). Included in the latter were 774,000 students in conservative Christian schools. What is the quality of education in these schools?

The nation, of course, has always had religiously based schools. *The parochial school tradition has been strong among Roman Catholics and Lutherans.* Some people believe that such private schools offer a better education. However, a study that compared achievement in grades four and eight between public and private schools found little difference in reading and math scores (Braun, Jenkins, and Grigg 2006). Eighth-grade students in private schools did score higher on reading. Otherwise, when taking into account characteristics of the students (such as gender and race/ethnicity), the differences in reading and math scores were insignificant.

Such scores are not, of course, the only measure of effectiveness. We need to raise the question of how religious schools, and conservative Christian schools in particular, teach the various disciplines, including the sciences. Since the schools teach pupils to think and behave in accord with particular religious doctrines (Wagner 1990), religious ideology enters into every facet of the curriculum. Such schools may teach creationism instead of (not along with) evolution and Darwinism.

In short, religious ideology is pervasive throughout the educational process, and for that reason critics charge that the Christian schools not only fail to address the issue of mediocrity, but also increase the amount of miseducation in the nation. They say the schools promote racial segregation (some began in the 1960s in the face of court-required integration), use outmoded methods of teaching (discipline is often strict), and give students distorted views of human knowledge (everything is filtered through religious doctrine).

To some extent, one's evaluation of the conservative Christian schools depends on one's values. It seems clear, however, that the schools do violate some of the basic principles of education, including free inquiry. The emphasis is not on raising questions and learning to think creatively, but on accepting answers and learning to think narrowly in accord with a particular religious doctrine.

Contributing Factors

Why are there inequalities in educational opportunities and attainment? Why hasn't education yielded the expected payoff for some people? As you will see, part of the answer does lie in the structure and processes of the educational system. A greater part of the answer lies in nonschool factors. The problems of education are only partially a problem of the schools.

Social Structural Factors

Social Class, Family Background, and Educational Inequality.   In our discussion of poverty, we pointed out that *families in the lower strata* of society are different in a number of respects from those in the middle and upper strata. Certain characteristics of the lower-strata family tend to depress **cognitive development.** Children who come from such families enter school with an intellectual disadvantage that tends to depress their performance and academic achievement (Guo 1998; Petrill, Pike, Price, and Plomin 2004; Noble, Farah, and McCandliss 2006). Their school work is further hurt by the fact that they come to school with a background that includes poor health care, parents who are minimally involved with them, few preschool opportunities, unsafe neighborhoods, and some degree of malnourishment (Chira 1991). As a result, a third or more of the students who come to kindergarten are *not prepared to learn;* they lack the vocabulary and sentence structure skills necessary for success in school. Even if they attend equally good schools and receive equal treatment from teachers, children from such a disadvantaged background cannot have educational opportunity equal to that of others.

Thus, *the position of the family in the stratification system has a close relationship to the educational attainment of the children.* Parental educational attainment and parental influence and expectations for children strongly affect children's educational aspirations and achievement (Bourque and Cosand 1989; Goyette and Xie 1999). In turn, the parental behavior is related to social class; the higher the social class, the more likely parents are to have high attainment, hold high expectations, and positively influence the child to attain a high degree of education. The greater the parental income and the fewer children in the family (both of which tend to characterize the higher strata), the more willing the parents are to pay for higher education (Steelman and Powell 1991).

Socioeconomic background affects a child at every point in his or her academic career. Students from low-income backgrounds are less likely to graduate from high school, less likely to go to college even if they do graduate (in part because they are more likely to marry at an early age), less likely to complete college if they enroll, and less likely to go to a prestigious school regardless of their ability or aspirations (Hearn 1991; Davies and Guppy 1997; Roscigno, Tomaskovic-Devey, and Crowley 2006).

Socioeconomic status is also one of the prime factors in unequal educational **achievement** at all levels of education, from elementary school through college (Betts and Morell 1999; Hossler, Schmit, and Vesper 1999; Lee and Burkham 2002). We are not saying that students from a lower socioeconomic background can never succeed. Some poor youths who have had strong parenting and sufficient opportunities have risen above their circumstances and carved out a better life for themselves (Furstenberg et al. 1999).

Yet the poor will always have a greater struggle. The struggle begins at the "starting gate" of kindergarten. The children enter a lower-quality school with less well-prepared and less-experienced teachers, less positive attitudes on the part of those teachers, and little in the home or neighborhood to nurture whatever motivation and aspirations they have (Lee and Burkham 2002). For such children, the school may be an alien setting. They and their teachers from the middle strata of society may be totally unprepared

cognitive development
growth in the ability to perform increasingly complex intellectual activities, particularly abstract relationships

achievement
as distinguished from educational "attainment," the level the student has reached as measured by scores on various verbal and nonverbal tests

WHAT IS THE PURPOSE OF EDUCATION?

In recent decades, the proportion of majors in such disciplines as English, philosophy, history, and modern languages has dropped considerably. In many American colleges and universities, students can graduate without studying such subjects as European history, American literature, or the civilizations of ancient Greece and Rome. What do these facts say about the purpose of education? To what extent do colleges and universities help Americans fulfill the functions of education noted at the beginning of this chapter?

Interview a number of students and faculty members at your school. Ask them what they believe to be the purposes of education. Then ask them to what extent your school has goals that fulfill those purposes. Ask them to identify both their personal educational goals (in the case of faculty, their goals in teaching) and what they believe to be the true goals of the school. If your school promotes the disciplines noted in the previous paragraph, ask your respondents how they feel about the place of history, literature, and philosophy in the education of people.

What is education for, according to your respondents? Do you agree or disagree? Would you affirm or modify the three purposes of education discussed in this chapter?

involvement

---

to deal with each other. The teachers may react to the children's range of experiences with astonishment and perplexity. The children may not even be able to distinguish the various colors when they enter school, and they may appear to have little grasp of abstract qualities such as shape and length. They may be unfamiliar with such cultural phenomena as Frosty the Snowman and *Green Eggs and Ham,* which teachers may take for granted are known to all students. Most teachers' training does not prepare them for these kinds of students.

As these children progress through school, their academic problems become more rather than less serious. Learning depends increasingly on the ability to deal with abstractions. What is a society? What is a nation? What happened in the past? Children from a deprived background may even have difficulty with such fundamental distinctions as bigger and smaller, higher and lower, round and square.

Such children could be looked upon as a challenge, but teachers may be more likely to react to them with despair or contempt. Indeed, one of the reasons that children from poor families do not achieve in school is that their *teachers may not like them.* Poor children have, if anything, a greater need for acceptance and warmth but are less likely to receive it than are middle-class children.

In addition to socioeconomic level, a number of other family background factors are important in achievement. One is the extent to which parents are involved in the process of education (e.g., meeting with teachers, volunteering at school, monitoring their children's progress, ensuring that homework is done, etc.). Children whose parents are highly involved tend to show high levels of achievement, whereas dropouts are more likely to have parents who are uninvolved (Marcon 1999; Jimerson et al. 2000).

Finally, *living with both biological parents* is associated with higher levels of achievement than those living with a stepparent or a single parent (Cavanagh, Schiller, and Riegle-Crumb 2006; Jeynes 2006). Children who live with a single parent or a stepparent during adolescence receive less encouragement and less help with schoolwork and achieve less than children living with both birth parents (Astone and McLanahan 1991; Hanson 1999). Among those in single-parent households, grades are lower than for those living with both parents, and grades are lowered even more by father absence than by mother absence (Mulkey, Crain, and Harrington 1992; Coley 1998).

329

The Organization of Education.   The gap between children from the lower socioeconomic strata and those from the middle and upper strata tends to increase with the level
of school. This finding suggests that the schools *may somehow contribute to educational inequality—children who are disadvantaged by their social background when
they enter school become even more disadvantaged as they progress through school.*

At least two factors contribute to the disadvantage. One is the quality of teaching.
Many instructors are teaching subjects for which they are not trained (*Education Week*
2000). Tens of thousands of teachers have been hired with emergency or substandard
certification (Applebome 1996). These teachers are more likely to be in schools serving
the lower strata. Schools with a larger proportion of pupils in the lower strata also tend
to have a greater number of teachers with three or fewer years of teaching experience
(National Center for Education Statistics 2006a). And even if the teachers are competent, they are likely to come from middle-class backgrounds and find it difficult to
understand, relate to, and help children from disadvantaged backgrounds (Potterfield
and Pace 1992).

A second factor is the *evaluation and labeling of ability.* This grouping by ability, or *tracking,* of students has been common in public schools, beginning in the first
grade. It is a controversial practice. Proponents point out that tracking is necessary for
dealing with the boredom and lack of adequate progress among bright students when
course work proceeds too slowly in order to accommodate slower students. Tracking
allows students to proceed at their own pace. "Detracking," they argue, not only hurts
the brighter students but also can harm the self-confidence of low achievers when they
are forced to compete with the bright students (Loveless 1999).

Opponents of tracking argue that high achievers do not benefit that much, while low
achievers are stigmatized and deprived of opportunities for success (Kershaw 1992;
Romo 1999; Oakes 2005). Tracking also hurts minorities, a disproportionate number
of whom are placed in the low-achieving tracks. Once in a low-achievement track, it is
difficult for students to escape it. Among other things, they take the kind of classes that
ensure that they will remain in the same track, and their teachers tend to label them as
low achievers and to expect them to perform accordingly.

Tracking, then, helps perpetuate the status quo. Because the students from a disadvantaged background are more likely to come to school unprepared to learn, they will
be placed in a slower track. Once in the slow track, everything works to maintain the
situation, including the fact that slower students cannot benefit from the stimulation of
interacting with more advanced students.

As Shanker (1993) has noted, then, both the advocates and the critics of tracking
make valid claims, so that the question should not be one of tracking or not tracking.
Rather, the real question is how to organize schools and classrooms in light of the fact
that children learn differently and at different rates. The important point to keep in
mind is that inequality of achievement during the first years of school does not mean
that the low achievers lack the capacity to attain high educational levels. Low achievement, as we have shown, tends to follow from a particular kind of social and family
background. We also have shown, in previous chapters, the effects of labeling. If the
low achiever is labeled as one with a low capacity, both the reaction of the teacher and
the self-expectations of the child are negatively affected. In effect, labeling becomes a
form of the *fallacy of personal attack,* blaming the students rather than the system for
their lack of achievement.

fallacy

The effects of labeling on children's achievement are dramatized in an elementary
school experiment that showed that teachers' expectations about the intellectual abilities of their students were reflected in the students' IQ scores (Rosenthal and Jacobson

1968). A student whom the teacher expected to do poorly tended to get lower scores, and a student whom the teacher expected to do well got higher scores. The performance of people, whether children or adults, can be significantly influenced by the expectations of others and can reflect those expectations more than any innate abilities.

Thus, labels can become *self-fulfilling prophecies,* retarding or stifling the achievement of able students. Is there any evidence that the labels are inaccurate? Can't teachers detect and encourage children who are bright but who perform poorly on achievement tests? No doubt some teachers can and do. However, children from lower socioeconomic backgrounds may have a capacity that is masked by their initial disadvantage and by their subsequent experiences and performance in the school. The evidence is scattered and, in some cases, indirect. We will furnish some evidence when we discuss the effects of desegregation in the last section of this chapter.

The Politics of School Financing. We have noted the large differences in the money allocated per child among various school districts. Although money per se is not the answer to all the problems of education, the funding per child makes a difference in the quality of teachers hired and the physical conditions of the school. These factors, in turn, raise attendance rates and student achievement (Condron and Roscigno 2003; Pinkerton 2003).

One way, then, to deal with inequality is to *equalize the money available* to various districts. Such equalization cannot occur because public education is financed largely by the property tax. As a result, pupils in wealthier districts with more expensive homes have more money available for their education. Throughout the nation, children in more advantaged areas are likely to have clean, well-staffed schools with good facilities and up-to-date books and technological aids, whereas children in more disadvantaged areas are likely to attend class in dilapidated school buildings staffed by less than fully qualified teachers and supplied with outdated textbooks and few, if any, technological aids. The differences in resources are illustrated by the availability of computers. A child today whose early education is devoid of computer use lacks an important resource and has a serious deficiency in his or her education. Yet schools in poorer areas are likely to have far fewer computers available to the students than are schools in more advantaged districts. The point is that *even if the student in a lower socioeconomic area overcomes the handicaps of a disadvantaged family, he or she faces obstacles to educational attainment in the school itself.*

In principle, many Americans support the idea of equalizing the funds available to school districts—but how would that be done? Some have argued that it can be accomplished only by eliminating the property tax as the basis for funding. They point out that no child should be denied a quality education simply because his or her parents happen to live in a poorer area.

Such arguments finally have begun to effect change in a number of states. In the late 1980s and early 1990s, a number of state courts ruled that existing methods of financing schools were unconstitutional. Montana, Kentucky, Michigan, and Texas were the first

Poorer school districts cannot provide the resources enjoyed by wealthier districts.

states to construct alternative financing systems. In Kentucky, the court decision led to a comprehensive school-reform effort that included channeling more money into poorer schools and restructuring the state education department so that its primary task is to assist local school districts rather than issue directives to them. An assessment of the situation a few years later concluded that more financial resources were available to districts but that patterns of resource allocation had not changed (Adams 1997). Clearly, the process of gaining equity in funding will be a slow and difficult one.

There is another aspect to the politics of financing—the extent to which political leaders give high priority to education. School districts get revenues from local, state, and federal sources. Of all revenues received by the public schools, states provide 48.7 percent, local governments contribute 42.8 percent, and the federal government provides 8.5 percent (National Center for Education Statistics 2006a). When support at one of the levels declines for whatever reason, education is likely to suffer.

The Economics of Education.   The politics of school financing interact closely with the economics of education. As with so many important areas of American life, *education is affected by the ups and downs of the economy,* and political and economic factors are intertwined as they affect the educational process. Educational decisions may be made on the basis of economic considerations. For example, a Texas survey found that 68 percent of the elementary teachers had students who were promoted to the next grade even though they had failed the class, and 61 percent of middle school and junior high teachers had students who moved on without repeating a course they had failed (Shanker 1996). In part, the practice was justified by the social stigma attached to being held back, but another part of the justification was economic: It costs a good deal to fail students and add a year or more to their schooling.

Economic factors can become even more powerful in times of recessions, when political leaders look with jaundiced eyes at the costs of education and resist any changes that involve more money. Inflation also can be troublesome. Inflation may rapidly outstrip the fiscal resources of schools and result in problems regarding salaries and the purchase of supplies.

As we pointed out in the previous section, *economic problems are also political problems.* Not everyone and not everything suffers equally in times of economic difficulty—political leaders make decisions that bear upon the resources available. The governor of a state must decide whether education, mental health, highway maintenance, or a number of other areas will receive priority consideration when budgets must be cut.

Obviously, the problems of education cannot be separated from other problems in a time of national economic difficulty. When resources are scarce, the decision to more fully fund one area—such as education—is a decision not to adequately fund another area—such as health programs. A faltering economy, therefore, inevitably means an intensification of at least some social problems.

Social Psychological Factors

Attitudes.   We have already noted some *attitudes that contribute to educational problems.* Parental attitudes are particularly important, because parental expectations are one of the stronger factors in a child's educational achievement (Jacobs and Harvey 2005). The child's attitudes are also important, and children from the lower strata are less likely to aspire to higher levels of attainment. Even if they do have the desire for higher attainment, they may not expect to be able to realize those aspirations (Hanson 1994). Their attitudes reflect those of their parents, who neither expect high educational attainment from their children nor behave in ways to encourage such attainment (Crosnoe, Mistry, and Elder 2002). When the lower expectations of the parents and children are combined with the low expectations and negative attitudes of their teachers, the impediments to achievement are enormous.

The attitudes of students toward school and schoolwork also affect their achievement. Three researchers who did an extensive study of 20,000 high school students and hundreds of parents in California and Wisconsin reported *widespread student apathy toward learning* (Steinberg, Brown, and Dornbusch 1997). About 40 percent of the students indicated that they were simply "going through the motions" in school and had little interest in what happens in the classroom. These attitudes are reinforced by a teen culture that disparages academic success. Large numbers of students strive to be a part of some social clique, such as the "populars" or "jocks" or "partyers," each of which tends to scorn high academic achievement. Nearly 20 percent of students admitted that they don't try as hard as they could because they are concerned about what their friends would think if they got good grades.

The attitudes of teachers also contribute to educational problems. The attitudes of teachers are rooted in the conditions under which they must work. Low salaries, inadequate resources, and other poor working conditions may lead teachers to change professions. Others remain in teaching, but they develop jaded attitudes about their work and education generally; and sinking teacher morale usually is accompanied by lower student achievement (Black 2001).

Values. Many educational problems, such as segregation and school financing, are difficult to resolve because they involve a conflict of values. In essence, Americans have tried to address educational issues in the context of a *clash between the value on individualism and the value on egalitarianism* (Hochschild and Scovronick 2003). "Individualism" means that Americans expect their schools to be the means to individual advancement, and this belief translates into such attitudes as "I should be able to choose the kind of school—public or private—that my children attend without being penalized by the tax system" and "I should be able to veto any policies or practices that I deem harmful to my child's education." "Egalitarianism," on the other hand, means that Americans expect their schools to help equalize opportunities for all students, and this belief translates into such attitudes as "Poor schools should get as much money as rich schools" and "No child should be denied entrance into any school because of the child's color or social standing."

Resolving the issues that are caught up in the matrix of clashing values will never be easy. Rather, such clashing values illustrate why efforts to deal with social problems are typically accompanied by intergroup conflict.

A Concluding Note on Inequality in Education

We have suggested that if the various factors we identified are all taken into account, then children of different racial, ethnic, and socioeconomic backgrounds should be able to show about the same levels of achievement. Earlier research by the Office of Education supports this conclusion. Figure 11.3 shows the achievement scores for sixth graders when various factors in their backgrounds are taken into account. If we look only at the scores of unequalized whites, Asian Americans, American Indians, African Americans, Mexicans, and Puerto Ricans in the United States, we see considerable differences in their achievement. The Puerto Rican students had the lowest average score and the white students the highest, about 50 percent higher.

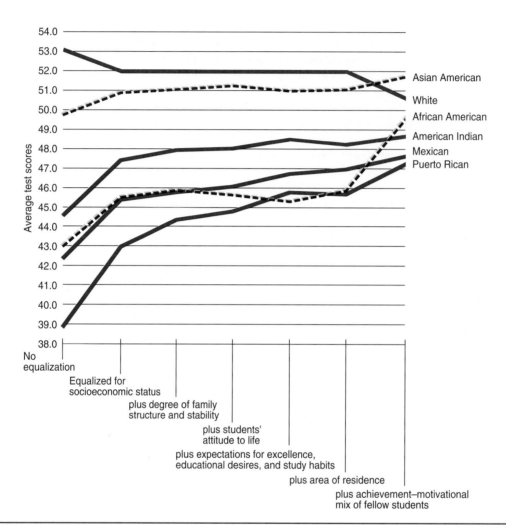

FIGURE 11.3 Racial and Ethnic Group Achievement Means of Sixth-Grade Pupils, Adjusted for Social Background Conditions.

Source: Adapted from George W. Mayeske et al., *A Study of Achievement of Our Nation's Schools* (Washington, DC: Government Printing Office, 1973), p. 137.

Suppose we control for socioeconomic background. What will the differences be for children of different racial and ethnic groups but the same socioeconomic level? The answer is in the second set of points in figure 11.3, labeled "Equalized for socioeconomic status." The spread narrows considerably, showing that a good part of the differences that were observed among the groups was really rooted in different socioeconomic backgrounds. As we continue to move to the right in the figure, each set of points takes progressively more background factors into account, and the differences in scores diminish correspondingly. The third set of points adjusts the scores to equalize for socioeconomic status *plus* degree of family structure and stability. The next set of points adds the students' attitude to life (as described in this chapter). The fifth set of points takes in the students' expectations for excellence, educational desires, and study habits. The sixth adds to those factors the area of residence. The last set includes the achievement-motivational mix of fellow students, which means if the students were to come from the same socioeconomic background, have the same family experiences, and exhibit the same social psychological processes, the differences between the scores of the various racial and ethnic groups, as shown in figure 11.3, is about 1 percent.

Thus, unequal educational achievement in the United States is a sociocultural matter, not a racial-genetic one (Myerson et al. 1998; Farkas 2004). Since efforts to enhance the performance of poor and minority students began, they have made considerable gains in SAT scores and narrowed the gap between their scores and those of whites (Huang and Hauser 1998). Gaps in reading and math and science scores also narrowed in response to programs designed to aid minorities (National Center for Education Statistics 2006a). Such results underscore both the social nature of the problem and the importance of social action for addressing it.

Public Policy and Private Action

Our analysis suggests a variety of ways to attack the various problems of education. Clearly, it must be a multifaceted attack. Undoubtedly, parental involvement is one of the crucial factors in children's educational attainment. Among other parental factors, having high expectations for the children's education, creating an educationally rich environment in the home, and helping with homework will make a difference in how much children achieve academically (Okagaki and Frensch 1998).

Another obvious need is *reform of school financing*. The inequities between school districts must be addressed. Action taken by the state of Vermont suggests one possible way. In 1997, the Vermont legislature passed the Equal Education Opportunity Act, which drastically increased the proportion of state money designated for public education and altered the taxation system (Proulx and Jimerson 1998). A statewide property tax now provides a general state support grant to school districts.

In addition, a variety of other efforts and proposals exist that hold promise: vouchers, quality enhancement measures, efforts to reduce racial and ethnic inequality, and compensatory and other innovative programs. Some are quite controversial.

Use of Vouchers

A good deal of controversy exists over the *use of school vouchers* (Medler 2002). A **voucher system** enables parents to use tax funds to send their children to private as well as public schools. Proponents argue that a voucher system will result in higher academic achievement, increased parental involvement in children's education, better use of tax monies, and pressure on the public schools to improve the quality of education. Opponents argue that vouchers will mainly subsidize parents who can already afford to send their children to private schools, violate the separation of church and state (because most private schools are religious), and ultimately destroy the public school system. Whatever the merits or problems in theory, states that have tried to implement a voucher system have encountered problems of administration and of courts that have declared it unconstitutional (Balona 2004; Sarche 2004; Dillon 2006).

voucher system
a system that allows parents to use tax money to send their children to a school, private or public, of their choice

Quality Enhancement Measures

A variety of suggestions exist for enhancing the quality of education. Lengthening the number of days in the school year could help poor children, who lose ground in the summer when they lack the intellectual demands of the classroom (Entwisle and Alexander 1992). Establishing standards-based education, which includes testing and account-

Some parents have sought to maximize their children's education by removing them from traditional schools opting instead to home school

ability for meeting minimum standards in subject areas, has yielded gains in student achievement in a number of states (Editorial Projects in Education Research Center 2006). Improving the school atmosphere by ensuring student safety and making schools drug- and gun-free could facilitate learning (Ingersoll and LeBoeuf 1997). Providing all children with the opportunity to attend preschool can enhance both their emotional and intellectual well-being, and can be particularly helpful to those from disadvantaged backgrounds (Scott and Delgado 2005; Arnold et al. 2006). Finally, placing all children in small classes can improve performance, because from kindergarten on those in small classes do better academically than those in large classes (Finn et al. 2001).

Some analysts believe that all such efforts are only "tinkering" with the system, and that *what is needed is a complete restructuring of the schools and even the community itself* (Shanker 1990; Emery 2006). There are varied ideas on what restructuring would involve, but most advocates agree that it requires decentralization (whether in the form of school-site management, a choice plan, or some variation on privatization).

Restructuring through decentralization gives parents and local schools greater control over the educational process. At first glance, this step sounds like a positive one. Why should all schools have to conform to a uniform set of policies and procedures? Who knows the needs of a particular school and its students better than the principal and teachers?

However, the evidence so far is mixed on the value of restructuring. In some cases, restructured schools showed greater gains in achievement than those in the same area that had not been restructured (Fouts 1999). In other cases, restructuring failed to yield any positive results (Shanker 1997). Thus, even if restructuring is useful, there is no single form of restructuring that will work well everywhere.

A different way to enhance quality is to start from scratch with a school—namely, establish a **charter school.** *Charter schools are nonreligious public schools that are approved by the local school district but are free of many regulations and policies*

charter school
a nonreligious public school approved by the local school district but free of many regulations and policies that apply to other public schools

that apply to other public schools. Charter schools can be converted public schools or entirely new facilities. They are operated by educators, parents, and/or community members. In essence, the district and the school negotiate a contract or "charter" that covers a specified number of years and that spells out the school's mission, program, goals, type of student body, and method of accountability.

The first state charter-school law was passed in Minnesota in 1991 (National Study of Charter Schools 2000). By 1999, there were 1,484 charter schools in 36 states, with more than 250,000 students. Most of the schools were small (the median enrollment was 137, compared to 475 for all public schools in the charter states).

Some charter schools are successful, as measured by improved scores on standardized tests, whereas others do no better or even worse than the traditional public schools (Bowman 2000; American Federation of Teachers 2002). An analysis of 2003 test scores found that students at charter schools had lower scores in both reading and mathematics than did students in regular public schools (Robelen 2006).

One quality-enhancement measure that seemed promising was the "No Child Left Behind Act" of 2002, which requires all schools receiving federal money to meet certain standards and to educate low-income students to improve student test scores every year (Moran 2002). Students in a school in which scores do not improve for two consecutive years can receive free transportation to a school that does meet the standards. Unfortunately, the federal government has failed to adequately fund the program, and the program has also had problems of legality and of mixed results when states have attempted to implement it (Dillon 2005; Ripley and Steptoe 2005; Rudalevige 2005).

Reducing Racial and Ethnic Inequality

Racial and ethnic inequalities in education must be reduced in order to create a society of equal opportunity. One crucial step is desegregation of schools. In the 1954 case *Brown v. Board of Education of Topeka, Kansas,* the U.S. Supreme Court ruled that segregated education imposed by governments was not legal. This ruling reversed a 19th-century decision that argued that "separate but equal" facilities may be provided by the states. The 1954 decision, which declared that separate facilities were inherently unequal and thus unconstitutional, furnished momentum for the movement to desegregate the nation's public schools.

Does desegregation help disadvantaged students? There is evidence that achievement levels of black children are raised by attending desegregated schools (Entwisle and Alexander 1994; Mickelson 2001). Moreover, those who attend desegregated schools are more likely to secure jobs in desegregated workplaces (Braddock, Dawkins, and Trent 1994).

Unfortunately, after some small and slow gains in the 1960s and 1970s, the desegregation process went into reverse. *Segregated housing patterns, white flight to the suburbs, resistance to busing children from their neighborhoods in order to integrate schools, and the establishment of private schools all helped subvert the desegregation effort* (Jacobs 1998; Saporito and Sohoni 2006).

Some efforts have been made to bring white children to black schools rather than the reverse, but those efforts were stopped by the courts. Court decisions also dismantled affirmative action programs, decreasing the enrollment of minorities in higher education. The result is a pattern of resegregation over the past two decades (Cohen 2004). On the average, white students attend schools that are 78 percent white, black students attend schools that are only 30 percent white, and Hispanic students attend schools that are only 28 percent white (Orfield and Lee 2005).

State and local governments need to devise plans to reverse the resegregation process. In the area of higher education, for example, the state of Texas initiated a plan that brought more minorities to colleges and universities (Yardley 2002). In essence, the plan guarantees slots in state universities to the top 10 percent of graduates in each high school without regard to SAT scores or grade-point averages. A student in the top 10 percent of a disadvantaged school may have a lower SAT score and/or grade-point average than a student who ranks at the 75th percentile of another high school. However, the student from the disadvantaged school will still be guaranteed a place in a public college or university.

Compensatory and Other Innovative Programs

compensatory programs
programs designed to give intensive help to disadvantaged pupils and increase their academic skills

Compensatory programs are aimed at *disadvantaged pupils.* They focus on skills such as reading and speech and attempt to offer an intensive program of help so that the disadvantaged pupil can approach the level of others in the school. Some compensatory programs are remedial. They attempt, among other benefits, to reduce the number of students per teacher, to provide the student with extra help (including after-school hours), and to use special teaching materials. The Head Start program stimulates learning of verbal and social skills among preschool disadvantaged children.

Another program aimed at disadvantaged children is called CIS, or Communities in Schools (Cantelon and LeBoeuf 1997). The program uses resources from the local, state, and national levels to provide at-risk youths with four items basic to the child's well-being and academic performance:

A personal one-on-one relationship with a caring adult.

A safe place to learn and grow.

A marketable skill.

An opportunity to give something back to peers and the community.

Evaluations of the CIS program find that a majority of students with high absenteeism and low grades prior to their participation improved both their attendance records and their grades.

The Deschooling Movement

The *deschooling movement* aims at providing students with a situation in which they will maximize their learning. The movement emphasizes the necessity of a break with the existing educational structure and the creation of new schools where the children can be free to learn.

The most common manifestation of deschooling today is *home schooling.* People decide for various reasons to teach their children at home rather than send them to the schools (Stevens 2001). Initially, most home schooling was done by conservative Christians who felt that their children were not given sufficient moral guidance in the schools (Hawkins 1996). As a five-year-old girl explained to the author, she would not go to public school because "they don't teach about God there." The second wave of home schoolers, however, includes more people who are either dissatisfied with the quality of teaching in the schools or with the potential for emotional or physical harm to their children in the schools (Cloud and Morse 2001).

Estimates of the number of children home schooled from kindergarten through high school vary. The number is probably around 1.1 million and growing (Princiotta, Bielick, and Chapman 2005). How well are these children educated? There is not a great deal of evidence, but what we have suggests that home-schooled children do well on the whole. They score well on standardized tests of achievement, and they appear to be as socially and emotionally adjusted as children in public or private schools (Ray 1999; Rudner 1999; Collom 2005).

Undoubtedly, some children receive an inadequate education through home schooling; but, on average, those who are home schooled appear to be benefiting. Parents who opt for it, however, need to recognize the extent to which they are committing themselves to their children's lives. Parenting is a consuming task as it is; when home schooling is added, parenting becomes more than a full-time job.

Follow-Up.   In what ways were your parents involved in your elementary and high school education? Which of these ways were helpful? Were any harmful? What will you do differently to enhance your own children's education?

chapter 11 review

Summary

Education is a problem when it fails to fulfill its expected functions: creating good and effective citizens, providing the possibility for upward mobility, and facilitating individual development. For these purposes education is highly valued by Americans. Lack of education is frequently associated with failure to achieve one's ambitions in life.

America has become an increasingly educated society. Whether this education has yielded the expected payoffs is not always clear. The greater degree of happiness reported by the highly educated may reflect a tendency toward greater fulfillment of individual potential. Education increases political participation and understanding. There is a strong relationship between education and income, but those most likely to benefit from education are already in the middle and upper strata.

Education is a problem because there are inequalities, and the expected payoff does not always occur. Educational attainment is unequally distributed among various groups. Educational funding is unequally distributed among states and school districts within states. The cost of education prices many Americans out of the better colleges and universities. The learning atmosphere of some schools (critics would say nearly all schools) is rigid and joyless and precludes individual schedules of learning; sometimes students suffer an atmosphere of fear and threat or ritualized deprivation.

A series of reports have charged that American education is in danger of being overwhelmed by mediocrity. The mediocrity affects education at every level and applies to student performance, faculty performance, administrative functioning, and academic programs. Many Americans believe that a particular kind of deficiency afflicts the schools—a non- or anti-Christian bias—and they have opted to send their children to Christian schools.

Among the social structural factors that contribute to the problems of education, social class and family background are particularly important. The organization of education also makes a difference in students' achievement and attainment. Particularly important are the distribution of funds, the assignment of teachers, the socioeconomic composition of the student body, and the evaluation and labeling of ability. The inequitable distribution of funds is a political issue that must be resolved by political action. Finally, the quality of education varies with the economy. Both recessions and inflation drain the resources available to schools.

Attitudes of parents, students, and teachers are important social psychological factors that contribute to the problems of education. The attitudes of parents and students toward school and intellectual activities, and toward the educational potential of the students are strongly related to achievement. Teacher attitudes can inhibit or facilitate student achievement.

Our analysis implies that when the various contributing factors are taken into account, children of different social backgrounds have the same capacity for achievement. The Office of Education survey supports this position. Given the same socioeconomic background, family background, attitudes, and the like, there is only about a 1 percent difference in the achievement scores of the various racial and ethnic groups.

Key Terms

Achievement	Compensatory
Atmosphere	Programs
Attainment	Culture
Charter School	Ritualized
Cognitive	Deprivation
Development	Voucher System

Study Questions

1. What are three functions of education?
2. Discuss the levels of educational attainment in America and the varied payoffs from that attainment.
3. How much inequality of opportunity is there in America, and how does it affect attainment?
4. What kinds of school atmosphere contribute to the problems of education?
5. Is education a "great training robbery"? Why or why not?
6. Explain the meaning of "a tide of mediocrity."
7. In what ways is family background important for education?
8. What aspects of the organization of education contribute to the education problem?

9. What are the political and economic factors involved in educational problems?

10. Discuss attitudes and values involved in education problems.

11. What are ways to resolve educational problems?

Internet Resources/ Exercises

1. Explore some of the ideas in this chapter on the following sites:

http://nces.ed.gov Site of the National Center for Education Statistics, a government effort to collect and analyze data about education in the United States and other nations.

http://www.eric.ed.gov Access to ERIC, the comprehensive collection of research and ideas about all facets of education.

http://www.edweek.org Site of Education Week on the Web, a weekly journal with news, evaluation, and analyses of various aspects of education.

2. Select an educational level that interests you, from preschool through graduate school, and research it on the Internet. Find five things that are fitting or useful at that level and five things that are troublesome or problematic. Comparing your two lists, how would you evaluate the educational level you have researched?

3. The text points out that American elementary and high school students do not score as high on tests of math and science as do students in many other nations. Find information on math and/or science education in Japan or one of the European nations. What are they doing that can help explain the higher scores? What recommendations would you make for American schools in order to close the gap in the scores?

For Further Reading

Banks, James A., ed. *Diversity and Citizenship Education: Global Perspectives.* New York: Jossey-Bass, 2007. Case studies and examples of successful programs and practices from 12 nations in which there are schools that have addressed the problems of education of a diverse population for living and working together as citizens of one nation.

Gittell, Marilyn J. *Strategies for School Equity: Creating Productive Schools in a Just Society.* New Haven, CT: Yale University Press, 1998. A discussion of how school financing creates inequities and a suggested way for the federal government to resolve the inequities and create a just system of education.

Graham, Patricia Albjerg. *Schooling America: How the Public Schools Meet the Nation's Changing Needs.* New York: Oxford University Press, 2006. An examination of the way in which public education, from kindergarten through college, changed in the United States over the 20th century in order to meet changing expectations; includes accounts of both failure and success in the process.

Kozol, Jonathan. *Savage Inequalities: Children in America's Schools.* New York: Crown Publishers, 1992. A comparison of schools in some poor areas in the nation with others in well-to-do districts, dramatizing the way in which students who come from a disadvantaged background continue to struggle in a deprived educational setting.

Pope, Denise Clark. *Doing School: How We Are Creating a Generation of Stressed Out, Materialistic, and Miseducated Students.* New Haven, CT: Yale University Press, 2001. An in-depth study of five high school students who represent the "best and brightest" and who illustrate the shortcomings and problems of education today.

Sexton, Robert. *Mobilizing Citizens for Better Schools.* New York: Teachers College Press, 2004. An in-depth analysis of the changes in Kentucky schools after the state's Supreme Court declared the school system unconstitutional. Includes lessons learned that can be used in other states.

Smith, Mary Lee. *Political Spectacle and the Fate of American Schools.* New York: Routledge/Falmer, 2003. Case studies that illustrate the ways in which educational policies and practices have been shaped by political considerations as much as by reasoning, research, and discussion.

CHAPTER

12

Family Problems

"I Survived the Abuse"

Patricia is a self-confident, middle-aged, professional woman. Yet she could have turned out quite differently, because she grew up in a home in which she suffered ongoing verbal abuse from her mother. To most people, Patricia's mother was a genteel southern lady. Patricia knew a different side of her mother:

My mother was beautiful. She looked like a movie star. I grew up with her and my grandparents after she divorced my father when I was an infant. And I remember the verbal abuse vividly. She never shouted. She never sneered. In her pleasant, soft voice, she simply said things that were gut-wrenching to me. Like the time she took me to buy some shoes, and told the clerk in a giggly voice that he should just bring a shoe box because he probably didn't have shoes that were big enough to fit my feet. Do you know what that does to an adolescent girl?

When I was a teenager, my mother and I were about the same size. She would buy dresses for herself, then try them on me. I didn't say, "Let me try them on," because I never volunteered nor wanted to do it. I knew what her reaction would be. It was always the same—she would look at me in her dress, sigh, and shake her head as though it were hopeless. It was her way of letting me know how ugly I was compared to her. She also let me know this once when we were looking at a picture of us together when I was younger. She said it was too bad I was smiling and showing my big, ugly teeth.

One thing that saved me was my schoolwork. I was always good in school. I loved to read. I studied hard. My mother acknowledged my intelligence, but said it was a good thing I was smart because I would never be pretty. So I grew up thinking I was the world's best example of the ugly duckling. Except I expected to stay ugly. And in my mother's book, it was looks, not brains, that were a woman's most important asset. But at least I knew I was not a total loss.

The other thing that saved me was my husband. It took me a long time to accept his compliments as sincere. I still remember the first time he told me I was beautiful. I thought he was just trying to con me into something. Eventually, I began to see myself in a different light. And now when I look at pictures of myself as a child, my first thought is: "That's no ugly duckling. You were a lovely child. How could your mother have done that to you?"

A lot of my childhood pictures show a girl who is unsmiling and unhappy. That's the way I was. In some ways, I feel that I lost a good deal of my childhood. But I feel good about myself now. Most of the time, anyway. I still have occasional doubts. But I have a man in my life who keeps telling me I am beautiful. And I have a career that is going well. I only wish I had a mother whom I felt really loved me. But I guess you can't have everything.

Introduction

Is the family a dying institution? Some observers say yes, arguing that the family is doomed. Others go further, maintaining that the family *should* be doomed because it no longer functions in a useful way. The family, according to this argument, contributes more misery than benefit because it is ill adapted to modern social life.

Still others argue that the family is essential and ineradicable. What is needed, they argue, is help for troubled families, not radical changes or the abolition of family life. In this chapter we consider the argument that the family is doomed. Then, taking the position that it is not doomed, we look at the family as a problem. In previous chapters we asked how the family contributed to other problems. Now we examine the nature and extent of family problems. We also describe how those problems affect the quality of life. Finally, we identify the structural and social psychological factors that contribute to family problems and inquire into ways to resolve the problems.

Is the Family Doomed?

A **family** is a group united by marriage, blood, and/or adoption in order to satisfy intimacy needs and/or bear and socialize children. The family, thus, is a crucial factor in both individual well-being and social life. Nevertheless, if prophecies could kill, the family would have died long ago. The popular and the professional literature continues to forecast the *death of the family,* at least the death of the **nuclear family** consisting of a husband, a wife, and their children, if any. The evidence used to support the notion that the nuclear family is dying typically includes factors such as **divorce rates,** birthrates, runaway children, people who abandon their spouses and/or children, and **cohabitation** (by 2004, over 5.8 million couples were cohabiting). The high rate of family disruption, combined with various other changes going on, makes family life appear to be in peril to some observers. At the same time, the fact that alternative forms of family life, including cohabitation, have proliferated suggests that *intimate relationships* must and will continue. Some people are merely finding alternate ways to express their intimacy needs.

family
a group united by marriage, blood, and/or adoption in order to satisfy intimacy needs and/or to bear and socialize children

nuclear family
husband, wife, and children, if any

divorce rate
typically, the number of divorces per 1,000 marriages

cohabitation
living together without getting married

Alternative Forms of the Family

Many alternatives to the traditional nuclear family have been explored by Americans (Lauer and Lauer 1983). One alternative is group marriage, which has been tried in some communes. In this arrangement, all males and females have access to each other for sex and companionship. Other proposed alternatives include trial marriages with renewable contracts for specified periods of time, and "open marriages" in which each partner has the right to sexual and companionate relationships with someone other than the spouse.

Another arrangement, which has increased enormously since the 1970s, is cohabitation. As we just noted, over 5.8 million unmarried couples are living together. The *reasons for cohabiting* are varied: as an alternative to marriage, as a preparation for marriage and family living, or as a way to deal with loneliness (Popenoe and Whitehead 1999). Those who view cohabitation as a preparation for marriage may be cautious because of the high divorce rate or because they have been previously married and divorced. A substantial number of cohabiting couples have children in the home. In fact, it is estimated that a fourth of all children will live in a family headed by a cohabiting couple sometime during their childhood (Graefe and Lichter 1999).

Generally, cohabitation tends to end fairly quickly in either disruption of the relationship or marriage, but contrary to expectations, cohabitation does not enhance the chances for a successful marriage in either stability or satisfaction (Stets 1993; Popenoe and Whitehead 1999; Heaton 2002). Compared to couples who are married, cohabitors have higher rates of violence and abuse, lower rates of relationship happiness and fairness, higher rates of depression, less commitment to the relationship, and a greater chance of breaking up even if the relationship is relatively satisfying (Nock 1995; Skinner et al. 2002; Stanley, Whitton, and Markham 2004; Shackelford and Mouzos 2005; Bouchard 2006). Children living with cohabitors have less family stability and lower levels of emotional and behavioral well-being than those living with married parents (Brown 2004; Manning, Smock, and Majumdar 2004).

Moreover, those who cohabit before marriage report less satisfying relationships after marriage, are more likely to have an extramarital affair, are more likely to perceive the possibility of divorce than those who do not cohabit, and actually have higher rates

FIGURE 12.1
Composition of American
Households, 1970–2005.

Source: U.S. Census Bureau
2007.

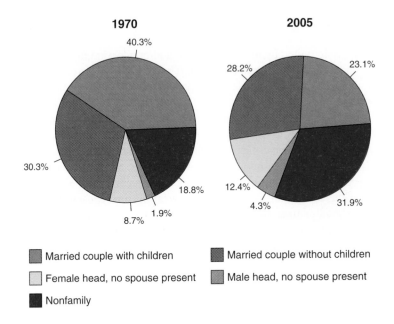

1970 / 2005

Married couple with children
Married couple without children
Female head, no spouse present
Male head, no spouse present
Nonfamily

of divorce (Thomson and Colella 1992; Treas and Giesen 2000). The higher rate of breakup among those who cohabited also was found in earlier studies among Canadians (White 1987, 1989) and Swedes (Bennett, Blanc, and Bloom 1988).

To return to the initial question: Is the family doomed? Clearly, the American family is changing in important ways. Yet, as we discuss later in this chapter, most Americans retain some traditional values about the family. We take the position that, despite the critics and the changes, the family remains strong and crucial to the well-being of people. At the same time, it is clear that fewer people opt for the traditional form of the family in which there is a breadwinner husband, a housewife, and children. Precisely how, then, is the American family changing?

The Changing American Family

Among the important changes in American families in recent times are *increases* in (1) age at first marriage, (2) proportion of young adults remaining single, (3) divorced adults, (4) adults living alone, (5) unmarried couples, (6) families maintained by adults with no spouse present, (7) children living with only one parent, (8) wives and mothers working, and (9) dual-career families (in which both husband and wife pursue careers, with minimal, if any, interruption of the wife's career for childbearing). At the same time, there has been a *decrease* in the number of children couples have. One effect of the various changes has been to dramatically alter the typical composition of American households over the past decades. As figure 12.1 shows, the proportion of households with married couples has declined significantly, while the proportions of other kinds of families and of nonfamily households (such as people living alone, friends living together, and homosexual couples) have increased significantly. Consider some specific data (U.S. Census Bureau 2007):

> From 1970 to 2005, the proportion of people who were never married increased from 18.9 percent to 28.2 percent of adult males and from 13.7 percent to 21.6 percent of adult females.

From 1970 to 2005, the proportion of Americans who were married dropped from 71.1 percent to 53.9 percent.

From 1970 to 2004, the birthrate per 1,000 women decreased from 87.9 to 66.3; the average size of families is smaller than it has ever been.

Since 1970, the proportion of all births that occur out of wedlock has more than tripled: 35.8 percent of all births are to unmarried women.

The divorce rate rose dramatically after 1965; it has declined from a high of 5.2 per 1,000 people in 1980 to 3.7 per 1,000 people in 2004, but is still far higher than the rate of 2.5 per 1,000 people in 1965.

Among married women, 59.8 percent of those with children under age 6 and 75.0 percent of those with children between ages 6 and 17 are in the labor force.

In 2005, only 67.4 percent of children under the age of 18 lived with both parents.

Although such changes may be interpreted as threatening to the traditional nuclear family, you also must consider other evidence. First, many of the statistics that we just cited reflect a reversal rather than a continuation of a trend. For example, the divorce rate has tended to decrease since 1980. Second, most Americans marry at some time in their lives. Only a minority of those who are single are so by choice. Third, the bulk of Americans rate a good marriage and family life as extremely important to them (Whitehead and Popenoe 2001). Fourth, most Americans are satisfied with their own family life. A 2001 Harris poll of adults reported that 96 percent felt good about relations with their family and 61 percent felt good about their marriage (Polling Report 2007).

Indeed, married people generally are happier and healthier than the nonmarried. More than 130 studies have reported that both married men and married women are happier and less stressed (as measured by such factors as alcoholism rates, suicide rates, and physical and emotional health) than are the unmarried (Lauer and Lauer 1986, 2007).

Clearly, then, Americans still value the traditional nuclear family. Just as clearly, there is an increasing tendency to prefer nontraditional roles, particularly an egalitarian arrangement (in which husband and wife both work and share responsibility for home and children).

Functions of the Family

Whether Americans opt for a traditional or a nontraditional family arrangement, they face certain problems. The problems reflect not only the expectations and values about family life but also the *functions of the family*. Those functions, like other aspects of the family, have changed over time. At one time the family was primarily responsible for matters such as education, religious training, recreation, and providing the necessities of life. Those functions have been largely assumed by other institutions. However, the family continues to be an important factor in *regulating sexual behavior, reproduction, and rearing of children*.

Another important function of the family is to provide a *primary group* for individuals. The **primary group,** consisting of the people with whom you have intimate, face-to-face interaction on a recurring basis, is of enormous importance. In a classic study, a children's home created "artificial" families after it was noted that the children were having developmental problems (Stanton and Schwartz 1961). Previously, all the children had been cared for by all the attendants, who carefully avoided too much

primary group
the people with whom one has intimate, face-to-face interaction on a recurring basis, such as parents, spouse, children, and close friends

involvement with any one child so as not to appear to have favorites. However, when this arrangement was abandoned and the home was divided into family groups of about four children and a "mother," the results were "astonishing."

> The need for individual attachment for the feelings which had been lying dormant came out in a rush. In the course of the one week all six families were completely and firmly established . . . the children began to develop in leaps and bounds. The most gratifying effect was that several children who had seemed hopeless as far as the training for cleanliness was concerned suddenly started to use the pot regularly and effectively. (Stanton and Schwartz 1961:236)

Primary groups are important for adults as well as children. You have a personal status in primary groups. You gain an understanding of the kind of person you are and learn the kind of norms by which you are to live. Primary groups, in other words, are crucial to your well-being as a functioning human. For most Americans, the family is a primary group *par excellence.*

When problems arise in the family, they arise in the group that is important to your well-being, that provides you with important emotional support, and that is of central importance to your life satisfaction and happiness (Lauer and Lauer 2007). The family is not always a solution; it is also a problem, as we will explain later in this chapter. The point is that the family is a central aspect of your well-being; thus, when family life becomes problematic, you are threatened at the very foundation of the quality of your life.

The Extent of Family Problems

The family becomes a problem when it does not fulfill its purposes, particularly its purpose as a primary group. The American ideal is that the family should be *structurally complete.* Children should have both a father and a mother in the home. The family should be a *supportive group,* providing emotional support for each member. "Ideal" in this context does not mean "perfect" (and therefore unrealistic). Rather, the ideal is defined as realistic and expected. When the actual situation falls short of the ideal, the *quality of life* is diminished. Expectations are thwarted, the most important primary group is disrupted, and family members experience stress.

For many people today, the expectations are thwarted more than once. In your lifetime, you might live in five, six, or more different families, each of which could fail in some way to fulfill your needs for structure and support. If your parents were divorced when you were young, and you lived with one parent for a while, then a stepparent for some years, you would have three different family experiences before adulthood. As an adult, if you cohabited, married, divorced, and remarried one or more times your family experiences would rise to six or more.

Consider next the extent of structural and supportive problems. *Structural problems* relate to the breaking up of husband and wife and/or parent and child. *Supportive problems* involve the lack of emotional support.

Disrupted and Reconstituted Families

Divorce rates, one measure of structural problems, have fluctuated in the United States, but the *general trend has been upward.* The rates are affected by business cycles and special circumstances such as war. Since 1860 there has been a general increase in the

Divorces	1960	1965	1970	1975	1980	1985	1990	1995	2000	2004
Total (1,000)	393	479	708	1,026	1,189	1,190	1,182	1,169	n.a.	n.a.
Rate per 1,000 population	2.2	2.5	3.5	4.8	5.2	5.0	4.7	4.4	4.1	3.7
Rate per 1,000 married women, 15 years and over	9.2	10.6	14.9	20.3	22.6	21.7	20.9	19.8	n.a.	n.a.
Percent divorced, 18 years and over:										
Male	2.0	2.5	2.5	3.7	5.2	7.6	7.2	8.0	8.8	8.8*
Female	2.9	3.3	3.9	5.3	7.1	10.1	9.3	10.3	10.8	11.5*

TABLE 12.1
Divorces, 1960–2004
n.a. = not available.
* = Figures for 2005.
SOURCE: U.S. Census Bureau 2007.

number of divorces per 1,000 population. There was a surge after World War II, and another surge began after 1965 (table 12.1). By the mid-1970s the United States had the highest divorce rate in the Western world.

After 1980, divorce rates tended to decline. The 2004 figure of 3.7 was lower than any since the early 1970s. Even so, millions of Americans continue to be affected by divorce. Children as well as adults are affected. In 1970, 85 percent of children lived with both parents. By 2005, 67.4 percent of all children lived with both parents (U.S. Census Bureau 2007).

During the 1960s and 1970s, divorce was the major cause of single-parent families. Since then, however, delayed marriage and out-of-wedlock births are responsible for more mother-child families than is divorce (Bianchi 1995). As we noted earlier, 3 out of 10 children are born to unmarried mothers. A parent also may be lost through death, separation, and abandonment. The combination of all these factors has meant a dramatic increase in the number of single-parent families since 1970. Table 12.2 shows the proportion of children living in various arrangements. The proportion living with both parents has decreased for all groups but is particularly low for African Americans and, to a lesser degree, Hispanics. We show later in this chapter some of the consequences of living in a single-parent family.

About three-fourths of people who divorce eventually remarry. If the remarriage includes children from a previous marriage of one or both partners, a **stepfamily** is formed. We do not know exactly how many stepfamilies there are in the nation, because the government does not gather that information. However, by the late 1990s estimates were that more than one of five families with two parents in the home were stepfamilies, involving between seven and eight million children under the age of 18 (Lauer and Lauer 1999). At some point in the future, according to demographers, the stepfamily could become the main type of American family.

stepfamily
a family formed by marriage that includes one or more children from a previous marriage

Strain and conflict with or about stepchildren is common in such families (Stoll, Arriaut, Fromme, and Felker-Thayer 2005). As a result, the marital relationship is stressed, and the divorce rate among second marriages is even higher than that among first marriages. White and Booth (1985) found that the percentage who divorced over a four-year period was slightly higher for remarried (8 percent) than for first-married (6 percent) couples if one of the partners in the remarriage was previously unmarried. The chances of divorce went up (to 10 percent) if both partners were previously

TABLE 12.2

Living Arrangements of
Children under 18 Years, by
Race and Hispanic Origin
(numbers in thousands)

SOURCE: U.S. Census Bureau
2007.

Living Arrangement	Number	Percent Distribution
White Non-Hispanic		
Children under 18 years	43,122	100.0
Living with		
Two parents	32,754	76.0
Mother only	7,066	16.4
Father only	2,050	4.8
Neither parent	1,252	2.9
Black		
Children under 18 years	11,295	100.0
Living with		
Two parents	3,970	35.1
Mother only	5,657	50.1
Father only	559	4.9
Neither parent	1,110	9.8
Asian and Pacific Islanders		
Children under 18 years	2,860	100.0
Living with		
Two parents	2,394	83.7
Mother only	292	10.2
Father only	102	3.6
Neither parent	72	2.5
Hispanic		
Children under 18 years	14,248	100.0
Living with		
Two parents	9,225	64.7
Mother only	3,612	25.4
Father only	678	4.8
Neither parent	733	5.1

married (with no children) and went up considerably (to 17 percent) if both were previously married and one or both brought stepchildren into the marriage.

Family Violence

Information on the amount of *violence in families* shows that it is not a rare phenomenon. Violence, of course, represents an alarming example of the failure of supportiveness. It is found in every kind of family and can reach extreme levels. For example, family fights are one of the most frequent reasons for police calls. Almost a fourth of murders are against a family member, and aggravated assaults by family members comprise about 10 percent of all aggravated assaults (Durose et al. 2005). *The likelihood of being a victim of family violence varies by a number of demographic characteristics.* Nearly three-fourths of the victims are females. Whites and African

MARITAL QUALITY AND WELL-BEING OF CHILDREN

As noted in the text, the family is a central element for individual well-being. In nations throughout the world, the more stable and harmonious family life, the higher the life satisfaction of family members. Four researchers surveyed 2,625 male and 4,118 female college students from 39 nations on six continents (Gohm et al. 1998). They categorized the nations by whether they have a collectivist or individualist culture. In individualist cultures (such as the United States, Germany, Australia, Japan, and Spain), people perceive their lives as depending largely on their own actions. They see society as a collection of individuals rather than as a highly integrated group. They believe that the course of their individual lives has no necessary relationship to the course of social life. Thus, they see possibilities for individual success and happiness even if the society as a whole is deteriorating.

In collectivist cultures (such as China, Brazil, India, and Tanzania), people perceive their lives as inextricably bound up with what happens in groups and in the nation as a whole. They cannot conceive of individual success that is independent of the groups to which they belong. Individual happiness, for them, is not as important as group well-being.

The researchers thought that the well-being of the college students in their survey might vary not only by the kind of family in which they grew up but also by the kind of culture in which they lived. Some of their results are shown in figure 12.2.

Clearly, there were both cultural and state-of-marriage differences in student well-being. Generally, students in individualist cultures scored higher on a life satisfaction test than did students in collectivist cultures. But regardless of the type of culture, students from intact homes (with two natural parents or a remarriage) in which there was low interparental conflict tended to score higher than those from homes with a single parent or with high interparental conflict. The highest scores of all were those in homes headed by a married couple with low conflict.

In sum, for people everywhere, the family is important for individual well-being. If the family is functioning well, the well-being of each member is maximized. If the family is functioning poorly, all members are adversely affected.

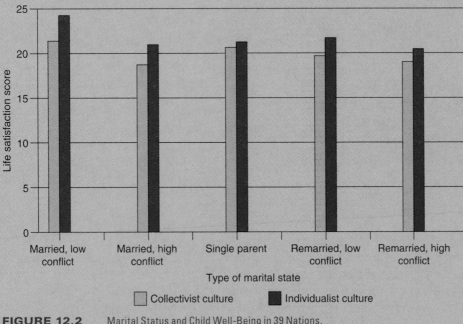

FIGURE 12.2 Marital Status and Child Well-Being in 39 Nations.
Source: Gohm et al. 1998.

Severe violence occurs in some families.

Americans have higher rates of victimization than do Hispanics and those of other races. And those in the 35- to 54-year-old age group have higher rates than do other age groups.

Studies of *spouse abuse* and *child abuse* were rare until the 1960s. Since then, numerous studies, including some national surveys, have been undertaken. The first national survey of family violence occurred in 1975, and the second took place in 1985 (Gelles and Straus 1988). The researchers found that the overall rates declined during this 10-year period, perhaps because of such factors as an increase in the average age at marriage (violence is more common among younger couples), a more prosperous economy (financial stress increases violence), and less willingness to tolerate violence in the family (shelters for battered women rose from 4 to more than 1,000).

Still, there is a *high level of violence in intimate relationships generally and in families in particular.* Over the course of a year, more than 600,000 Americans age 12 and over experience violence from a current or former spouse, boyfriend, or girlfriend (Catalano 2006b). And a third of American women will be raped or sexually coerced by a husband or intimate partner during their lifetime (Basile 2002). Children who witness violence between parents are also victims, for it is a traumatizing experience to see one's parents in a violent confrontation. It is estimated that more than 15 million American children have witnessed such violence at least once and 7 million live in homes in which severe partner violence has occurred (McDonald et al. 2006).

Of course, family violence is not an exclusively American problem. In Canada, for example, a survey of women in Quebec found that 6.1 percent had suffered physical violence and 6.8 percent had experienced sexual violence perpetrated by their male partners (Rinfret-Raynor et al. 2004). For many people, then, "intimate" means threat and harm as much as it means fulfillment.

Family violence may take the form of spouse abuse, child abuse, or abuse of parents (including the abuse of elderly parents by adult children). Abuse of parents is probably less common than the others. Still, in a survey of 469 university students, Browne and Hamilton (1998) found that 14.5 percent acknowledged using violent tactics with a mother and/or father, and 3.8 percent admitted that they were severely violent. A substantial number of the violent students, it should be noted, also reported being maltreated by their parents in earlier years.

Spouse abuse involves wives beating husbands as well as husbands beating wives. In fact, more incidents of husband abuse than of wife abuse are reported. In the 1985 survey, the rate (per 1,000) of husband abuse was 44, while that of wife abuse was 31 (Gelles and Straus 1988:109).

The violence of women against their husbands is frequently a case of self-defense or, at least, a response to prior abuse by the husband. The probability of being injured is also greater for the woman than for the man (Bookwala, Sobin, and Zdaniuk 2005). However, interviews with 90 women and 10 men who filed assault charges against an intimate partner found that the adverse emotional effects on the victimized women and men were about the same (McFarlane et al. 2000).

Child abuse, another form of family violence, is more likely when one of the natural parents is missing. Children in a single-parent home, or those with a stepparent, are much more likely to be victims of abuse (Snyder and Sickmund 1999). Estimates of the amount of child abuse in the nation vary widely. One problem in getting reliable figures is that mandatory reporting laws were not passed in the states until the 1960s. In 2004, there were 872,088 substantiated cases of maltreatment (including neglect, physical and sexual abuse, and emotional maltreatment) (U.S. Census Bureau 2007). Of these, 16.7 percent involved infants a year old or younger, and another 47 percent involved children between two and nine years of age. Females were slightly more likely to be victims than were males.

These numbers are undoubtedly conservative. How many cases go unreported? One way to obtain more accurate information is to ask the victims themselves. For child abuse, this means asking them when they are older whether they have ever been abused. Some still will not remember or will have repressed the memory, so even the results from victimization research will underestimate the amount. A national study of adolescent health asked American youth, among other things, about their experiences of maltreatment (Hussey, Chang, and Kotch 2006). Being left home alone as a child (a possible case of neglect) was named by 41.5 percent. It was the most common kind of maltreatment. In addition, 28.4 percent reported experiencing physical assault, 11.8 percent said they had been physically neglected, and 4.5 percent reported sexual abuse. Clearly, maltreatment is more prevalent than the number of cases officially substantiated by state agencies.

Incest, which we discussed briefly in chapter 5, is likely to be an extremely traumatizing experience for a child (Sheinberg and Fraenkel 2001). The effects tend to be long lasting. A study of 17 incest survivors who became mothers found that the women had poorer relations with their own mothers and lower psychological adjustment than a comparable set of mothers who had not been sexually victimized (Fitzgerald et al. 2005). In addition, although the incest survivors appeared to be mothering as well as the others, they did not see themselves as being very effective mothers.

Girls are more likely than boys to be victims (Russell 1986), but we do not know how many victims there are in the United States. A survey of 1,672 male and female adolescents in Korea, however, reported that 3.7 percent had been victimized (Kim and Kim 2005). The families of the victims had high levels of other kinds of problems, such as mental illness, criminal behavior, and alcoholism. The victims, compared to adolescents not so victimized, had higher rates of emotional and social problems.

Besides the observable and measurable supportive problems in family violence, a considerable amount of supportive failure cannot be measured—intense conflict or alienation within families. In addition is the problem of neglect, which affects over a half million children each year (U.S. Census Bureau 2007). Neglectful parents abuse their children psychologically through lack of feeling and caring. They are emotionally distant from their children. They may be struggling to retain their own sanity or totally absorbed in their own pleasures. For whatever reason, they provide none of the support that parents typically give. Neglected children may never learn to trust adults. They may suffer various physical ailments because of inadequate nutrition, clothing, and sleep. They are likely to have retarded intellectual development and be insecure, withdrawn, and unable to express emotions.

Family Problems and the Quality of Life

The effect of family problems on the *quality of life* is sometimes obvious and sometimes not. Physical violence against a person by someone in his or her primary group produces emotional trauma as well as physical pain. *Alienation from those in one's primary group is emotionally traumatic.*

Less obvious is the effect of a broken home on children and their parents. Parenting is demanding and stressful even when there are two parents in the home. Not surprisingly, both single parents and their children face a broad range of stresses, including feelings of responsibility, task, and emotional overload on the part of the parent; and emotional, interpersonal, and school problems on the part of the children (Goldberg et al. 1992; McLanahan and Sandefur 1994; Gringlas and Weinraub 1995; Dunifon and Kowaleski-Jones 2002).

Supportive problems mean, by definition, that family members endure some degree of stress. But the consequences of structural problems are less clear. Consequently, much of this section will be an examination of structural problems. You will discover that supportive problems also have some not-so-obvious consequences for the quality of life.

Most of the effects that we discuss later in this section involve a *contradiction between interaction patterns and American values.* Supportive problems mean that interaction patterns within the family contradict the value of emotional and physical health. Structural problems result in interaction patterns that contradict the value of social adjustment. Because children who grow up in broken homes lack experience with either a mother or a father, they often have various problems of adjustment and have to cope with such problems as illness, poverty, and deviant behavior more than others do.

The structural characteristics peculiar to the stepfamily, on the other hand, can lead to different types of problems (Lauer and Lauer 1999). Each member of a stepfamily may have lost an important primary relationship. Children may be angry about the loss and focus that anger on the stepparent. The noncustodial parent may interfere with the stepfamily's adjustment. The children and the stepparent also might compete for the custodial parent's attention and affection; the stepparent, after all, is entering an ongoing relationship as an "extra" member. The stepparent and children may even have difficulty because the role of stepparent is still somewhat ambiguous. Is the stepparent to be like a parent, a friend, or a teacher? Finally, the children may try to work their natural parents one against the other to gain various ends. Thus, both in single-parent and stepfamilies, interaction patterns may diminish the quality of life.

Physical and Emotional Difficulties

Physical and mental illnesses are rooted, in part, in family arrangements. National data show that children growing up with both biological parents receive more social, emotional, and material support than children in any other kind of family (Marks 1995). In contrast, broken homes (structural failure) and homes in which parents frequently quarrel (supportive failure) have been linked to stress in children, often resulting in physical or emotional illness (Vandervalk et al. 2004).

Divorce. For adults, adjustment to divorce has *striking similarities to the bereavement process.* Contrary to a popular notion that divorce may be an avenue to freedom and therefore an exhilarating experience (at least once the legal procedure has been completed), divorced people typically face a painful process of adjustment not unlike that which occurs after a death in the family. In both death and divorce, a *primary relationship has been disrupted,* and the disruption of a primary relationship is always traumatic. The consequences include a sense of loss and bewilderment, various kinds of deprivation (including financial and emotional support), and susceptibility to emotional problems such as depression (Hilton and Kopera-Frye 2006).

Particularly in the first months, divorce is more likely to bring emotional and physical disturbances than a sense of freedom. In fact, various studies report that divorced people have higher rates of suicide, accidents, death from various causes, physical and mental ailments, and alcoholism (Kurdek 1990; Richards, Hardy, and Wadsworth 1997; Yip and Thorburn 2004; Lorenz, Wickrama, Conger, and Elder 2006). Of course, these problems are not always the result of a divorce. In some cases, they existed prior to, and helped bring about, the divorce, but they also can result from the divorce (Wade and Prevalin 2004). In addition, there can be long-lasting as well as short-term consequences. A study of divorced women found that anger, loneliness, and depression can continue for 10 years or more after a divorce (Wallerstein 1986). Although some people can turn a divorce into a positive experience of growth, even they suffer short-term negative consequences (Lauer and Lauer 1988). Unfortunately, others experience long-term trauma.

These consequences together with its high rate make divorce a major health problem in the nation. The problem is likely to become more severe as fathers play a more nurturing role in the family and thereby suffer greater loss if the relationships with their children change (Jacobs 1982). Incidentally, in assessing the amount of trauma involved in divorce, do not overlook the larger family group, such as the parents of the divorcing couple. They may be sufficiently distressed by the divorce to require supportive help (Johnson and Vinick 1981).

Although parents, grandparents, and other relatives may endure varying degrees of distress, children suffer the most in divorce. The negative consequences for young children and adolescents whose families are disrupted by divorce include the following problems:

Children in divorced families are more likely to be anxious, depressed, and withdrawn than those in intact families, and their mental health problems tend to persist when they become adults (Peterson and Zill 1986; Dawson 1991; Amato 2001).

Children in divorced families are more likely to have eating problems and disorders (Wynn and Bowering 1990).

Young women from divorced families rate themselves as less attractive and report more dissatisfaction with their bodies than do women from intact families (Billingham and Abrahams 1998).

An increasing number of Americans struggle in their role of single parent.

Children in divorced families tend to receive less maternal warmth and empathy (the conflict and pain of most divorces leave little energy for nurturance of children), which contributes to various emotional and behavior problems (Kline, Johnston, and Tschann 1991).

Children in divorced families rate themselves lower in social competence, and, in fact, are likely to be less sociable and less responsive at home, school, and play (Peretti and di Vitorrio 1993).

Children in divorced families tend to have lower levels of educational attainment and achievement and more problems in school than children from intact families (Center for Marriage and Families 2005).

Children in divorced families have lower levels of emotional well-being when they become adults (Amato and Sobolewski 2001; Wauterickx, Gouwy, and Bracke 2006).

Children in divorced families have a higher probability of divorce themselves when they become adults and marry (Wolfinger 2005).

Children also face *problems of adjustment*. They confront questions from peers, particularly when they are in elementary school, about why they have only one parent at home. They have to adjust to a change in primary relationships and possibly to restricted interaction with one of the parents (generally the father). They may have to cope with parental conflict, which often continues after the divorce, and with attempts by each parent to gain the child's loyalty and affection at the expense of the other. It is not surprising, then, that children whose parents are divorced are prone to both emotional and physical problems.

In general, the effects of divorce are greater for children who are very young at the time of dissolution (Allison and Furstenberg 1989). However, as we noted earlier in this chapter, negative effects can occur at any age. People whose parents divorce when they are young adults tend to find the experience painful and disillusioning, and they have a difficult time adjusting to the dissolution (Cain 1989; Bonkowski 1989).

Nevertheless, the discord that leads to divorce is probably more stressful for the child than is divorce itself. Parents who stay together "for the children's sake" may actually harm the children more than if they were to separate. A home with continual conflict or emotional coldness can be more damaging to the children than a home that is broken. Children from divorce-disrupted families have higher rates of depression and withdrawal than others, but the rates are even higher for those who live in a home with persistent conflict than for those who live in a single-parent home (Peterson and Zill 1986). A study of college students concluded that being in a conflicted home as a child significantly increased the chances of subsequent distress and emotional disorders such as depression and alcohol abuse (Turner and Kopiec 2006). Consequently, if the family is a severely dysfunctional one, the children may actually benefit by a divorce (Strohschein 2005b).

Thus, the intact home may have supportive problems that are far more damaging to the child or to the spouses than a structural problem would be. In other words, structural problems of broken homes are associated with various kinds of physical and emotional problems, but the intact home is not free of such problems.

What about the stepfamily? Does remarriage mitigate the negative health effects of divorce? As noted earlier, the stepfamily has its own peculiar set of problems. In the long run, stepchildren seem to do as well as those who grow up with both biological and adoptive parents. However, in the short run, children in stepfamilies do exhibit more behavior problems of various kinds (Hetherington 1993; Thomson, Hanson, and McLanahan 1994); but they are not lower than those in intact families in self-esteem, psychological functioning, or academic achievement—although the outcome may vary by type of stepfamily. One study found that sixth- and seventh-grade students living with stepfathers had higher self-esteem and reported fewer problems than those living with stepmothers (Fine and Kurdek 1992).

Abuse. The effects of abuse tend to lead to both *short-term and long-term trauma.* Abused children may become withdrawn and isolated; feel shame, guilt, or unworthiness; and become anxious and depressed (Cole 1995). They are likely to exhibit, to a greater degree than nonabused children, a variety of problem behaviors, such as quick anger, frequent fighting, resisting of parental authority, school problems, and violence (Markward 1997). Abuse at an early age can also lead to impaired brain functioning (Teicher 2002).

The problems of abused children tend to persist into adulthood. Physical or sexual abuse during childhood is associated with a wide assortment of problems among adults: physical ailments, emotional problems, substance abuse, posttraumatic stress disorder, and attempted suicide (McGruder-Johnson et al. 2000; Dube et al. 2001; Feerick and Snow 2005; Downs, Capshew, and Rindels 2006). These problems can also appear in children who witness violence between their parents and/or who try to intervene in the adult violence (Jarvis, Gordon, and Novaco 2005). When they grow up and marry, abused children tend to have lower marital satisfaction and a higher probability of marital disruption (Whisman 2006).

Adults as well as children suffer physical and emotional harm from both psychological and physical abuse (Taft et al. 2006). Abused adults have higher rates of impaired mental health, impaired physical functioning and health, and problems in social functioning (Laffaye, Kennedy, and Stein 2003; Loxton, Schofield, and Hussain 2006). A study of Hispanic women in the southeastern part of the United States asserted that so many of the women are victims of domestic violence that the abuse is a "major health problem" for them (Murdaugh et al. 2004).

Thus, the damage from abuse can be severe. The physical harm ranges from bruises and broken bones to permanent brain damage and even death. The emotional harm is more difficult to measure. Yet some indication may be seen in the high rates of both mental disorders and attempted suicide (deWilde et al. 1992).

Poverty

We previously noted that *female-headed families* are more likely to experience *poverty* than male-headed families. Because most single-parent families have a female head, they have a higher probability of being in poverty than do other households. Moreover, the never-married single mother is even more likely than the divorced, single mother to be in poverty. Because of low welfare payments and low wages in available jobs, the single mother may be caught in a bind: Whether she works or stays home and receives welfare, she may find herself and her family living in poverty (Tilly and Albelda 1994). In recent years, the rate of poverty among families headed by a female with no husband present has been more than twice that of the general population. About half of the millions of children living in poverty are in female-headed families.

Because of the correlation between the *absence of the father and lower academic achievement* (recall that education is vital to upward mobility), poverty tends to be perpetuated by the absence of the father from the home. Children in single-parent homes tend to have lower academic self-concepts. Compared with teenagers who grow up with both natural parents, teenagers who spend part of their childhood apart from their natural father are twice as likely to drop out of high school (McLanahan and Sandefur 1994). They are, therefore, less likely to achieve higher levels of education, occupation, and income (Caspi et al. 1998). They are more likely than teenagers who grew up with both natural parents to be both out of school and out of work into their early 20s (McLanahan and Sandefur 1994; Caspi et al. 1998).

Deviant Behavior

Sexual variance, drug and alcohol abuse, and juvenile delinquency have been associated with disturbed family life (Bjarnason et al. 2003; Fagan 2003). We pointed out in earlier chapters that prostitutes and drug and alcohol abusers often have a background of disturbed relationships with their parents. There is also a higher rate of deviant behavior among children in single-parent homes (Pfiffner, McBurnett, and Rathouz 2001). Using a representative national sample of adolescents, Dornbusch et al. (1985) found that children in mother-only homes are more likely than those in two-parent homes to have two or more contacts with the law, to have been arrested, to be truants, to have problems at school, to be runaways, and to smoke regularly (see also Thornberry et al. 1999).

Additional research underscores the negative impact of disturbed family life. Thus, intact-family children have fewer absences at school; higher popularity ratings; higher IQ, reading, spelling, and math scores; and fewer behavioral problems at school than do children from divorced families (Guidubaldi, Perry, and Nastasi 1987; Dawson 1991). Adolescents from divorced families tend to have higher rates of drug use (including alcohol) and premarital sexual activity, poorer academic performance, and higher rates of dropout from school (Flewelling and Bauman 1990; Needle, Su, and Doherty 1990; Zimiles and Lee 1991; McLanahan and Sandefur 1994). Even when the child in a single-parent home is strongly attached to the custodial parent, the child is still more likely to engage in delinquent activity than are children in an intact home who are strongly attached to both parents (Rankin and Kern 1994).

The deviant behavior is likely to continue into adulthood. Researchers examined the records of a group of 1,575 children over a period of years. The children had all been physically or sexually abused or neglected in their early years. By the time they were in their mid- to late-20s, 49 percent had been arrested, and 18 percent had been arrested for a violent crime, compared to 38 percent of those in a control group of the same age, gender, race, and social class (National Institute of Justice 1996b).

Maladjustment

People who come from disturbed families tend to have various difficulties that we subsume under the category of **maladjustment:** antisocial behavior (such as aggression and bullying), insecurity, overconformity to one's peers, a tendency to withdraw from relationships, difficulties in relating to others, problems with one's personal identity, and various problems as adults. For example, people who grow up in a single-parent home are, as adults, more likely to be fitfully employed and more likely to have marital problems, including divorce (McLanahan and Sandefur 1994).

maladjustment
poor adjustment to one's social environment

The maladjustment affects all areas of a child's life. Divorce, severe parental conflict, and abuse all are associated with higher rates of conduct disorder and problems with both adults and peers (Fendrich, Warner, and Weissman 1990; Gringlas and Weinraub 1995; Flisher et al. 1997). Such children have problems with trusting others, and therefore it is difficult for them to establish effective relationships.

The problems of maladjustment continue to afflict the children as they grow into adulthood. Adults who were physically punished during childhood tend to have more physical and verbal aggression with their spouses, to be more controlling of their spouses, and to be less able to see things from the spouse's perspective (Cast, Schweingruber, and Berns 2006). And a significant number of abused children will become abusers, including the abuse of their own children.

From the point of view of the child, *abuse is a form of rejection.* It is, however, not the only way in which parents can reject and distress a child. Parental hostility is a form of supportive failure that can result in maladjustment as the child attempts to relate to others. Inconsistency—including inconsistency in discipline—in how the parent treats the child is another form of supportive failure. Inconsistency means the child lives in a capricious environment, and no one functions well with chronic uncertainty. Consequently, parents who are inconsistent in the way in which they relate to and discipline their children foster various kinds of maladjustment, including hostility and difficulties in relating to peers and to adults (Gross, Sambrook, and Fogg 1999).

The *child's sense of self-esteem,* so important in his or her social functioning, is crucially related to family experiences. Self-esteem tends to be high when a child has nurturing parents and a harmonious family environment (Scott, Scott, and McCabe 1991). Parents build self-esteem through such actions as affirming and supporting their children, showing their children how to constructively express their feelings, taking an interest in their children's activities, showing respect for their children's point of view, and teaching their children how to exercise self-control and handle responsibility. In contrast, supportive failure, including abuse, is related to low self-esteem (Gelles and Straus 1988), and low self-esteem tends to lead to emotional and interpersonal problems.

Contributing Factors

The factors we examine in this section contribute to both structural and supportive problems. Some families suffer from both types of problems. The two types can be independent, but more often are interdependent. Structural problems, for instance, may either make supportive failure more likely or reflect supportive failure in the past.

Social Structural Factors

Social Norms.   An important factor in the divorce rate is that divorce is more "respectable" now than it was in the past. In other words, the *norms about divorce have changed.* In the past, religion and the law both said, in effect, "You should not get a divorce. You should make every effort to work it out and stay together." Today the norms about divorce reflect a loosening of the laws ("no-fault" divorce) and greater tolerance among religious groups. In contrast to the *stigma* formerly attached to divorce and to divorced people, most Americans now agree that divorce is an acceptable option if the marriage isn't working out. This new attitude is based on the norm of happiness, the notion that each individual has the right, if not the obligation, to be happy. The *fallacy of non sequitur* may be involved in the process: "I have a right to be happy; therefore, I must get a divorce." Even if you agree to the individual's right to happiness, it doesn't follow that divorce is necessary. All marriages have troubled times. Couples who have achieved long-term, satisfying marriages point out that happiness comes by working through problems, not by avoiding or leaving them (Lauer and Lauer 1986). Of course, some marriages may be hopeless, but many break up too quickly because people believe the marriage is infringing on their right to happiness.

Divorce is more likely if people marry at a young age and have a short or no engagement period. In particular, people who marry as adolescents have higher rates of divorce than those who marry as adults (Amato and Rogers 1997). Age at marriage is one of the more important factors in marital instability. One study reported that 59 percent of women who married when they were younger than 18 years, compared to 36 percent of those who married when they were 20 years or more, either separated or divorced within 15 years (Bramlett and Mosher 2001).

Both structural and supportive problems are more common among the very young. In fact, adolescent marriage and parenthood has been called a case of "children raising children." Not only is the marriage more likely to break up, but problems of childrearing are likely to be serious, including a greater probability of child abuse. A study of infanticide reported that whereas young women under the age of 17 have 2 percent of all births, their babies are 7 percent of all infant homicide victims (Overpeck et al. 1998). The study also reported that having more than one child before the age of 19 involves a ninefold increase in the risk of an infant homicide compared to having children after the age of 25.

Why do adolescents marry at a young age? Social norms define the appropriate time for marriage. For most Americans, that time has been soon after high school graduation or, at the latest, soon after college. In the 1950s, people lowered the ideal age for getting married. Females who were not married by the time they were 20 could develop a sense of panic that they would become old maids. Males who waited until their late

fallacy

20s or after to get married might be suspected of having homosexual tendencies or an inadequate sex drive (which was an affront to their manhood). Subsequently, however, the norm about marital age has reverted to earlier notions. It is now acceptable for an individual to be and to remain single. Yet the average age for marriage is still relatively young, and the single individual may not be wholly acceptable to many businesses and corporations who still prefer their young executives to be married. As long as these attitudes persist, structural and supportive problems due to marriage at a young age will continue.

Norms also contribute to the amount of family violence in the nation. A common norm in families is that it is proper to hit someone who is misbehaving and who does not respond to reason. Many Americans consider the use of physical punishment in the rearing of children as virtually an obligation (Gelles and Straus 1988). Recall the old saying "Spare the rod and spoil the child." In some cases it is applied with a vengeance.

Divorce rates are higher among those who marry at a young age.

Role Problems. A number of *role problems* contribute to both structural and supportive problems. Indeed, whatever else may be true of modern marital roles, they place an *emotional burden on people that is probably unprecedented in human history.* Modern couples often do not have the proximate interpersonal resources available to those in extended families or to those in small, preindustrial communities. Instead, they rely heavily on each other for advice, intimacy, and emotional support in times of difficulty or crisis.

Moreover, the marital role is ambiguous as well as demanding. *Role obligations* in a changing society are not as clear-cut as those in more traditional settings. Couples who disagree on role obligations of husband and wife are more prone to divorce than are those who agree. The nature of these obligations is not as important as whether the couple agrees on them and on whether each feels that the other is fulfilling them. A gap between expectations and perceived behavior increases dissatisfaction.

The majority of American couples are willing to participate in activities once regarded as the domain of the opposite sex, but they do not want to give up their own traditional gender roles (Robinson and Godbey 1997). A husband's expectations still carry more weight than a wife's in determining the division of labor. Wives are more accepting of noncompliance with expectations than husbands are. Again, however, the crucial factor is not whether the couple is traditional or nontraditional, but whether they agree on their arrangement of role obligations.

For women, *role flexibility* is important for well-being. That is, women need to be free to choose whether to work outside the home. The number who make that choice will probably continue to increase inasmuch as women who work full time outside the home have greater work satisfaction than women engaged in full-time housekeeping (Weaver and Matthews 1990).

The divorce rate is higher among women who work outside the home (South 2001). Financial independence allows women to escape from unhappy unions, such as those in which they perceive severe inequity in the relationship. When wives work outside the home, then, negotiation over role obligations may be required to effect a more equal sharing of both responsibilities and privileges. A study of 42 dual-career couples found that those most satisfied with their marriages perceived equality and reciprocity in the sense that each spouse both gave support to and received support from the other, the partners were involved in each other's careers and had equal commitment to their relationship, and they were equally involved in making decisions about work and home (Ray 1990).

Finally, role problems can be critical in the reconstituted family. Exactly what is the relationship between stepparent and stepchild? People often bring unrealistic expectations to stepfamilies. Women who become stepmothers, for example, tend to expect themselves to:

Somehow compensate the children for the distress caused by the death or divorce.

Create a happy and close-knit family unit.

Maintain happiness and contentedness in all family members.

Demonstrate through appropriate behavior that the notion of the wicked stepmother is just a myth.

Love, and be loved by, the stepchildren almost immediately as if the stepchildren were her own natural children. (Lauer and Lauer 1999)

People who impose such role obligations on themselves, or who have them imposed by others, are certain to encounter problems.

Family Continuity.   People who are reared in problem families tend to perpetuate the problems in their own families. Those who come from families in which one or more parents died tend to have rates of disruption similar to those who come from intact families. But people who come from families in which the parents were divorced or separated have higher marital disruption rates than do those coming from intact families (Amato and DeBoer 2001).

Similarly, family violence tends to be continued from one generation to the next (Stith et al. 2000; Coohey 2004). Parents who abuse their children were often abused by their own parents. The battered child of today is likely to become the battering parent of tomorrow, perpetuating the problem of family violence. Marital abuse also is transmitted from one generation to another. The husband who abuses his wife is likely to be a man predisposed to violence because he learned such behavior from his parents. He may have been abused, or he simply may have witnessed violence between his parents (Kalmuss 1984; Carlson 1990). Unfortunately, some children learn from watching their parents that those who love you also hit you, and that this action is an appropriate means to get your own way and deal with stress. Such children are *modeling their behavior* after that of their parents, although that behavior may be considered undesirable or immoral by most others.

Even if the child does not grow up to be an abuser, *the mere fact of witnessing violence between one's parents tends to lead to problems of adjustment*—problems that can continue into adulthood (Henning et al. 1996). Witnessing violence in the home is associated with such maladies as depression and other emotional ills, delinquency, and behavior problems (O'Keefe 1994; Graham-Bermann and Levendosky 1998).

A family can perpetuate its problems into the next generation simply because it is such an important factor in the *socialization* of the child. The family is an important place for learning what it means to be a male or a female, how to function as a parent, and generally how to relate to others. Thus, there is some continuity in parent-child relationships and husband-wife relationships from generation to generation.

Stratification and Family Problems.   Families in different social classes exhibit different problems. For one, *divorce is more common in the lower strata than in the middle and upper strata.* A government survey found that the proportion of women whose marriage broke up within 10 years was 44 percent in the low-income group, 33 percent in the middle-income group, and 23 percent in the high-income group (Bramlett and Mosher 2002). Because of the relationship between racial and ethnic background and income, variations exist in the probability of divorce among racial and ethnic groups. The same government study reported that the proportion of marriages that broke up within 10 years was 32 percent for white women, 47 percent for black women, 20 percent for Asian women, and 34 percent for Hispanic women.

The relationship between income and divorce may seem contrary to common sense, the well-to-do can afford the costs of divorce more easily than the poor; but financial problems put enormous strains on marital and family relationships. In fact, income is one of the best predictors of family stability. The increasing rates of structural failure as you go down the socioeconomic ladder reflect the greater potential for financial difficulties, which, in turn, produce interpersonal problems that lead to marital disruption.

Another factor that bears on the divorce rate is jointly owned property and financial investments, both of which are more likely to be held by people in the middle- and upper-income levels. Divorce is more difficult and expensive when it involves a division of assets. Middle- and upper-income people are also more likely to have a network of friends and relations who will resist their divorce and who may support them as they try to work through their problems.

Finally, the combination of the higher rates of unmarried mothers and higher divorce rates means that fewer children in the lower socioeconomic strata live with both parents (table 12.3). Thus, the undesirable consequences of living in a disrupted or single-parent home are more prevalent in the lower socioeconomic strata.

Supportive failure is suggested by data on abuse and neglect. A certain amount of abuse occurs in middle- and upper-class families, but both neglect and abuse seem to be more prevalent in the lower than in the middle or upper strata (Gelles and Straus 1988; Whipple and Webster-Stratton 1991; Kruttschnitt, McLeod, and Dornfeld 1994).

The Family in a Changing Structure.   Rapid change of the social structure creates its own problems, including problems for families. Certain kinds of change can affect the divorce rate. If roles are in a state of flux, the potential for conflict within the family is increased and the probability of divorce becomes greater. Rapid change may

Income Level	Percentage with Both Parents
Under $5,000	18.5
$5,000–$9,999	17.4
$10,000–$14,999	38.6
$15,000–$24,999	51.8
$25,000–$39,999	63.5
$40,000–$49,999	83.9
$50,000 and over	91.6

TABLE 12.3
Proportion of Children under 18 Living with Both Parents, by Income, 1998

SOURCE: U.S. Census Bureau Web site.

involve confusion and ambiguity about what it means to be a husband, a wife, or a parent, which leads to more stress, more conflict, and more structural and supportive problems.

Most observers agree that the current society is a time of rapid change. Any family can put down an anchor somewhere and suddenly find that there is nothing solid to hold it in place. A family moves into a neighborhood in the hope of having a better life, only to find the neighborhood deteriorating. A family moves to a new city because the father or mother is offered a better job, only to face unemployment when an economic reversal occurs. To compound the problem, the family has no roots in the area and the family members are wholly dependent on each other for emotional support. Moreover, even if the new job opportunity works out well, the family still may be strained by the lack of a social support system. Thus, the divorce rate in America is positively related to urbanity, population change, and lack of church membership (Breault and Kposowa 1987; Amato and Rogers 1997), all of which are indicators of a lack of integration into a local community.

Social Psychological Factors

Attitudes.   Generally, Americans have negative attitudes toward the single-parent family. These attitudes contribute to the problems of the single-parent family. For example, female-headed households are found in many different societies, but they are not viewed as inherently inferior or pathological, nor do their children suffer disproportionately from economic or psychological deprivation (Bilge and Kaufman 1983). Even in American society, children in single-parent, female-headed families tend to be emotionally well adjusted as long as they are not impoverished or hampered by being socially stigmatized (Olson and Haynes 1993).

Attitudes are also a factor in problems of abuse. Men who sexually abuse their children come up with a variety of rationales that minimize or even justify the incest (Hartley 1998). In situations in which there is no intercourse, they may dismiss the seriousness of the relationship on the grounds that it "wasn't really sex." In situations in which intercourse occurs, they may define it as an adult-to-adult rather than an adult-to-child relationship or maintain that the child was a willing participant who gave permission for the incest.

Some Americans agree that violence in intimate relationships is acceptable or even necessary at times (Simon et al. 2001). While few Americans believe that women are the *cause* of their own abuse, a fourth still believe that at least some women *want* to be abused, and most are convinced that women can end abusive relationships (Worden and Carlson 2005). Abusive husbands maintain their spouses deserve the beatings for some reason (Eisikovitz et al. 1991). *Blaming the victim is one of the more common characteristics of husbands who abuse their wives.* A small proportion of abused women agree that they deserved to be beaten.

How could a woman justify wife beating? Unfortunately, many victims have attitudes that lead them to remain in a violent relationship (Marano 1996; Barnett 2001). Some of these attitudes are understandable: The women may fear that they will lose their children (courts have been known to award custody to the father when a battered woman leaves the home), or be unable to protect their children, or risk their own lives. The risk to their own lives is a real one: Abusers threaten to kill their wives if they try to leave, and in fact, more abuse victims are killed when trying to leave their abusers than at any other time.

Battered women may have rationales that are difficult to counteract. Ferraro and Johnson (1983) interviewed more than 100 battered women. The women who opted to remain in their relationships justified the decision in six ways, many of which involve fallacious modes of thinking. Some of the women had a "salvation ethic"; they viewed their husbands as troubled or "sick" individuals who needed them in order to survive. Some said that the problem was beyond the control of either the women or their husbands; the violence was caused by some external factor or factors such as work pressure or loss of a job. Of course, this is the *fallacy of non sequitur.* It does not follow that a man will necessarily abuse his wife when he has problems with his work. A third explanation involved a denial of injury; some women insisted that the beatings were tolerable and even normal. Fourth, some of the women used the *fallacy of personal attack against themselves,* blaming themselves for the abuse. They said that the violence could have been averted if they had been more passive and conciliatory. A fifth reason was the women's insistence that they had no other options; some of the women believed that they were too dependent on their husbands either financially or emotionally. Finally, some of the women used the *fallacy of an appeal to authority,* claiming that a "higher loyalty"—such as a religious faith or a commitment to a stable family—motivated them. Such attitudes may be rationalizations that disguise a deeper reason for maintaining an abusive relationship, or they may be potent factors in their own right. In any case, they are used by the victims to justify and perpetuate the violence.

fallacy

fallacy

fallacy

Finally, *attitudes toward the self* are important factors in abuse. Mothers who abuse their children tend to have lower levels of self-esteem than other mothers do (Zuravin and Greif 1989; Wolfner and Gelles 1993). Husbands who abuse their wives tend to be dissatisfied with their lives, believe that the man should be the head of the family, and lack the resources to be dominant in the family (Gelles and Straus 1988)

Values and Homogamy. When you marry, you undoubtedly hope that the relationship will last and be rewarding to both you and your spouse. Is marital happiness more likely to happen if you and your spouse have similar or dissimilar backgrounds? The answer to this question has been debated by social scientists. Some have argued that couples with *dissimilar backgrounds* (**heterogamy**) will be attracted to each other and will *complement* each other so that the marriage is more rewarding and successful. Others have argued that *similar backgrounds and shared rather than different values* (**homogamy**) are more likely to produce a rewarding and lasting marriage.

heterogamy
marriage between partners with diverse values and backgrounds

homogamy
marriage between partners with similar values and backgrounds

Research generally supports the view that homogamy is more conducive to a lasting marriage. Although homogamy does not mean that the couple must have similar backgrounds in every respect, it appears that the greater the similarity, the greater the likelihood of a satisfactory marriage (Whyte 1990; Mullins et al. 2004). This kind of relationship is more likely to result when there is similarity in family background, socioeconomic background, cultural background, personality traits, and religion. Homogamy tends to correlate with marital happiness. Perhaps the more similarity between spouses, the fewer areas of conflict. In any case, shared rather than dissimilar values are important in securing a satisfactory marriage. Structural and supportive problems are more likely to occur when the couple come from dissimilar backgrounds and hold diverse values.

The Value of Success. The American *value of success* can lead to supportive failure in the family. Merton (1957:136) showed how the "goal of monetary success" pervades society so that Americans "are bombarded on every side by precepts which affirm the right or, often, the duty of retaining the goal even in the face of repeated frustration."

ONE BIG HAPPY FAMILY

Some utopian communities that have arisen in the United States have considered traditional family arrangements detrimental to human well-being. The 19th-century Oneida community, for instance, was founded on the notion of "Bible communism." Private property was abolished, including the private property of a spouse or child. The entire community was a family. Every adult was expected to have sex relations with a great variety of others. Women who bore children cared for them for the first 15 months and then placed them in the children's house where they were raised communally and taught to regard all adults in the community as their parents.

Obtain literature about utopian communities of the present or past (see Lauer and Lauer 1983). For example, you might investigate Bethel, Brook Farm, Oneida, Ephrata, the Icarians, the Rappites, the Shakers, or any one of numerous contemporary communes. Consider what kinds of family arrangements they have created. Do any of these arrangements solve the kinds of problems discussed in this chapter? Why or why not? Do the utopian arrangements appear to create other kinds of problems? Would the utopian arrangement be practical for an entire society? What is your own ideal after reading about the utopians and the alternatives mentioned earlier in this chapter?

In families, schools, and the mass media, Americans are urged to pursue the goal with unrelenting diligence. Most Americans share this value of success. Even in the lower socioeconomic strata, where people often do not *expect* success, they still *wish* for it.

Monetary success often requires long hours at work and minimal contact with family. What are the consequences? A survey of employees in a Fortune 500 company found that the more time an individual spent at work, the greater was the interference with family life and the higher was the level of distress (Major, Klein, and Ehrhart 2002). In addition, family members may feel neglected by the person who is working the long hours. Clearly, then, a strong emphasis on success that leads to spending long hours at work can result in supportive failure in the family. Individuals who are attaining such success may be neglecting their families. Individuals who are severely frustrated in their attempts to attain success may react with violence in the family setting. In either case, the family members are the victims of a value that is deeply ingrained in American society.

Ideology of the Family.   Unfulfilled or conflicting expectations about role obligations can lead to marital dissatisfaction and dissolution (Pasley, Kerpelman, and Guilbert 2001). *The American ideology of the "good" family generates a set of expectations* that may create problems if the expectations are not met. Two versions of this ideology exist, each of which can give rise to unrealistic or conflicting expectations.

One version asserts that *a good family is a happy family* and that *happy families are harmonious* and free of conflict. Further, the family is a kind of miniature society in which all important human relationships and feelings can be experienced. Each person can find within the family a complete range of experiences in the context of harmony and happiness. This view of family life is unrealistic, and the result is a higher rate of emotional stress when conflict is suppressed because of the ideology.

A different version of the ideology of the good family stresses the need to express feelings and engage in creative conflict. This ideology has grown out of small-group work and says, in effect, that the good family maintains *healthy relationships* and that healthy relations can be obtained only when people give *free expression to their feelings*. People should "level" with each other and accept each other.

Many Americans believe that lack of time together is the family's greatest threat.

If the first ideology errs by condemning conflict in the family, the second one errs by encouraging too much *anger and aggression* in the home. Giving free expression to feelings may provide you with a sense of release and relief, but it does not enhance the quality of your interpersonal relationships. The free expression of anger is likely to lead to verbal and even physical aggression. In marriage, the higher and more severe the level of aggression, the lower your satisfaction and the more likely you are to experience disruption (Rogge and Bradbury 1999).

Finally, two ideologies worsen the problem of abuse within the family. One is the *ideology that the man should be the breadwinner.* Men who accept this ideology and equate breadwinning with masculinity may resort to violence if their wives earn a significant part of the family income (Atkinson, Greenstein, and Lang 2005). In such cases, the violence is an attempt to reassert male dominance in the relationship and in the family.

The other is the *ideology of nonintervention,* which asserts that outsiders should not interfere in family affairs. People who might aid a woman being beaten by a man would not interfere if that same man were beating his wife. People who might stop a woman from abusing a child would not intervene if that child were her own.

The ideology of nonintervention affects the police as well. As Ferraro (1989) found, the police may use their ideologies about battered women and family fights to evaluate specific incidents. The police officers with whom Ferraro worked believed that if battered women opted to stay in their situations, it was not the responsibility of the police to control the violent behavior. One male officer even insisted that because a man's home is his castle, he should be able to do whatever he wants there. Furthermore, the officer asserted, most wife abuse is provoked by the woman herself. Thus, in spite of a presumptive arrest policy (arrests are required when there is probable cause and the offender is present), the police frequently did not arrest the offender. Rather, they would reassure the woman and tell her to call them if anything further happened.

We should note that educational efforts are changing the ideology, so that most victims have positive and helpful experiences with the police now (Apsler, Cummins, and Carl 2003). But negative experiences still exist and lead some women to be hesitant about trying to get help from the police. Research with victims who came to a battered women's shelter found that two-thirds of the women had contact with the police some time during the previous six months, but most did not have as much contact as they had needed (Fleury et al. 1998). The women gave various reasons for not calling the police, including *fear of even greater violence* and *previous negative experiences with the police themselves.*

Public Policy and Private Action

As with all problems, *both therapeutic and preventive measures* can be applied to family problems. Therapeutic measures include the more traditional counseling services as well as newer efforts involving discussion and interaction in small-group settings. Public policy could require intervention, counseling, and needed protection in cases of abuse and divorce. Such measures, of course, attempt to resolve problems after they have already begun.

What kind of preventive measures could be taken? That is, what measures might minimize the number of family problems in the nation? Consider, first, what government and business can do. Much has been said about "family values" in the political arena in recent years. The question is, what are political and business leaders doing to strengthen American families?

We pointed out in the chapters on poverty and work some of the ways in which government and business can help families that are poor (some of the problems of family life are intertwined with the problem of poverty) and can address the problems created by work conditions (e.g., too much time at work and too stressful work both have negative impacts on family life). Some other nations do far better than America on these and other matters; some countries offer day care for workers' children and paid time off for new parents (Remery, van Doorne-Huiskes, and Schippers 2003). If businesses do not adopt such family-friendly policies on their own, they may need to do so by government mandate (Gray and Tudball 2003). Single-mother families are particularly in need of help, because most have already suffered the pain of disruption and because they have the highest poverty rate of any group in the nation. America desperately needs policies and programs that support and help single working mothers through such benefits as child care and flexible work hours (Albelda, Himmelweit, and Humphries 2004).

The arguments against government-mandated policies include the resistance to any expansion of government into the private sector and the claim that the additional costs will harm business. The answer to the first argument is simply that if the government does not require these changes, they will not happen. With a few exceptions, business leaders are not known for voluntarily taking steps to enhance the well-being of workers when those steps involve additional costs. With regard to the second argument, a survey of 120 employers in New York found that the employers who offered flexible sick leave and child care assistance had significant reductions in turnover, offsetting some of the costs involved in the benefits (Baughman, DiNardi, and Holtz-Eakin 2003).

Numerous other courses of action also fall into the category of preventive measures. For example, states could experiment with a legalized system of trial marriage. Couples would contract to marry for a specific period of time and then have the option of renewing the contract. However, you need to be aware of the nature of experiments. They are searches—often blind gropings—for answers, and not firm guidelines. Some experiments may work, but others may not (and perhaps may even make a problem worse).

A contrary approach would be to make it harder to divorce. Some states presently allow *covenant marriages,* in which spouses sign a legal contract that they will not seek divorce except for abuse or adultery. If they want to divorce for any other reason, they agree to first undergo counseling and wait two years before finalizing the decision. A researcher tracking 600 newly wed couples, half of whom were in covenant marriages, reported that after the first two years the rate of divorce was much lower among those in the covenant marriages (Perina 2002).

Beneficial *family life education* at all stages of the life cycle, through the schools and the mass media, could change negative attitudes about single-parent families and the legitimacy of violent behavior as well as break down harmful ideologies about the "good" family. Family life education might change some norms. The way in which changed norms could affect family well-being is illustrated by the norm of family size. As Blake (1989) has shown, children from small families do better than those from large families in numerous ways, including educational attainment and social and cultural activities. Of course, the norms for family size have changed over time. Many families are reaping the advantages of fewer children, but people in the lower socioeconomic strata are likely to have larger families than are those in the middle and upper strata, thus perpetuating their disadvantaged situation.

The point is that changing norms is not a trivial matter. New norms can affect family life in crucial ways. Norms needing to be changed include those about young marriages (again, this change applies mostly to families in the lower socioeconomic strata) and those about roles and the division of labor in the home. Husbands today are more willing than in the past to agree with greater role freedom for their wives. Yet even women who have careers still tend to take major responsibility for home and children. Americans are egalitarian in theory but not yet in practice.

A great many false or counterproductive ideas can be attacked through educational programs. *Marriage enrichment programs* can help couples confront and work through the common issues in marriage and family life. Such programs teach couples, for example, how to create and maintain good communication patterns, handle conflict constructively, work out an equitable division of labor in the home, and manage their finances.

The problem of family violence needs to be addressed through the law, education, and practical aids like shelters for battered women. These efforts need to be buttressed by bringing about ideological changes in the culture. Religious groups can help in these efforts, because a lower amount of domestic violence occurs among families who report regular attendance at religious services than among those who are not regular or who are nonattenders (Ellison, Bartkowski, and Anderson 1999; Cunradi, Caetano, and Schafer 2002).

Ideologies of the family in which authorities and others (such as neighbors or relatives) regard domestic violence as a private matter need to be changed. If domestic violence is a private matter, then people will be hesitant to intervene and offer help to the victim, particularly when the ideology is combined with the *fallacy of personal attack.* **fallacy** The fallacy of personal attack is the argument that the woman has done something to deserve the violence. A former victim of abuse told us that she stayed in her marriage for many years because everyone she knew, including her priest and her own family, kept telling her that she must be doing something wrong to make her husband act so violently! Education through schools and the mass media can change people's understanding of family violence, get rid of the old ideologies, and lead to an open confrontation of the problem. Spouse and child abuse must be seen for what they are: crimes of violence and not justifiable acts within the confines of a group—the family—that is off limits to outsiders.

Finally, shelters for battered women also address the problem of violence. They provide many services, including emergency shelter, crisis counseling, support groups, child care, and assistance with housing, employment, and education. These shelters help reduce the amount of domestic violence. The very existence of shelters warns batterers that their wives have an alternative to remaining in an abusive relationship. Although the number of shelters has increased over the past few decades, there are still too few to meet the demand (Goodyear 2001). Even when the shelters have room, they may require women to find alternative housing within weeks; and the waiting lists for public or subsidized housing can be anywhere from seven months to years. The lack of alternatives ultimately forces many of the women to return to the men who battered them. Additional shelters would allow more women to escape abusive relationships, and the shelters also would stand as a visible reminder to men that violence against women is no longer tolerable.

Follow-Up.   Set up a debate in your class on the topic "Divorce is too easily attained and too readily accepted in the United States today."

Summary

Family problems are so common that some observers have argued that the family is doomed. Those who predict the end of the present type of family suggest a number of alternatives, such as group marriages, trial marriages, open marriages, or cohabitation. But most Americans continue to marry and establish homes, and to prefer that option over alternatives.

The problems of the family stem from the fact that it is one of the most important primary groups. Americans believe the family to be the cornerstone of society and that an ideal family provides stability, support, and continuity for American values. We identify two basic types of problems: structural (disruption and reconstitution of families) and supportive (lack of emotional support).

Several kinds of data suggest the extent and seriousness of family problems. Structural problems may be measured by the divorce rate, by the number of single-parent families, and by the number of reconstituted families that contain a stepparent-stepchild relationship. Supportive problems are evident in the amount of family violence, including child abuse.

All family problems diminish the quality of life. Physical and emotional difficulties may result from family conflict. Additional problems of adjusting to a broken home result from separation or divorce. And problems of adjustment to new and ambiguous roles must be confronted in the stepfamily. Poverty is more frequently associated with a female-headed than with a two-parent family, and the poverty tends to be perpetuated because the child from a single-headed family does not perform as well academically as other children do. Several kinds of deviant behavior have been associated with disturbed family life: sexual deviance, drug and alcohol abuse, and juvenile delinquency. People who come from families with problems tend to develop various kinds of maladjustment: antisocial behavior, interpersonal problems, and low self-esteem.

Norms that are permissive about divorce and that encourage young marriages are two social structural factors that contribute to family problems. Role problems contribute to marital dissatisfaction and thereby lead to both structural and supportive failure. Family problems are especially likely to occur when there is disagreement on role obligations and when expectations are in conflict and unfulfilled for one or both spouses. The stepfamily has its own peculiar set of problems, stemming from the difficulties of the stepparent-stepchild relationship. The family itself also contributes to future family problems. Because parents act as role models for their children, the children may learn patterns of behavior that will create future problems.

Family problems are generally more prevalent in the lower social strata, partly because of financial strains and partly because of different norms and roles. Rapid social change is yet another structural cause of family problems.

Among the social psychological factors, attitudes are important. A number of attitudes contribute to family problems, including negative attitudes about single-parent families and attitudes that justify abuse. Values are also a significant factor in family problems. A couple with similar values based on similar backgrounds is more likely to have a satisfactory marriage. The value of success in American culture, on the other hand, puts a strain on marriages and family life because certain occupations can consume family members who are striving for that success.

Two "good family" ideologies generate expectations and behavior that strain marriage and family relationships. One says the good family is happy and free of conflict, which can lead to a suppression of conflict and guilt. The other claims that in the good family, people can freely express their feelings, including aggression; this ideology can perpetuate debilitating conflict. Both ideologies tend to result in supportive problems. Families need a balance between excessive openness and free expression of feelings, on the one hand, and suppression and guilt, on the other hand. Finally, the ideologies that the man should be the breadwinner and that outsiders should not intervene in family affairs both worsen the problem of abuse within the family.

Key Terms

Cohabitation	Maladjustment
Divorce Rate	Nuclear Family
Family	Primary Group
Heterogamy	Stepfamily
Homogamy	

Study Questions

1. What are some alternative forms of the family?
2. In what ways is the American family changing?
3. What are the important functions of the modern family?

4. What are the various kinds of problems that afflict families, and how extensive are those problems?

5. How does family disruption affect the physical and emotional well-being of people?

6. How do family problems relate to deviant behavior and maladjustment in families?

7. What norms contribute to family problems?

8. Explain the role problems that can result in both structural and supportive difficulties in families.

9. What are the relationships between the stratification system and family problems?

10. Name and explain the kinds of attitudes, values, and ideologies that contribute to family problems.

11. What are the therapeutic and preventive measures that can address family problems in the United States?

Internet Resources/ Exercises

1. Explore some of the ideas in this chapter on the following sites:

http://marriage.rutgers.edu   Publications and links from the National Marriage Project at Rutgers University.

http://www.childtrends.org   Site offering publications and links to information that helps strengthen families and increases the well-being of children.

http://www.divorcemag.com   News, information, and links about all aspects of divorce.

2. Most of the information in this chapter involves what can go wrong in a family. Search the Internet for information about healthy family life. What are the characteristics and qualities of such families? Design a one-day "healthy family" seminar based on your findings.

3. Choose one or more nations other than the United States and find information about divorce laws and/or divorce statistics. How do your findings compare with information in this chapter on divorce in the United States? How would you explain any differences and similarities between nations?

For Further Reading

Booth, Alan, and Ann C. Crouter, eds. *Just Living To-gether: Implications of Cohabitation on Families,*
Children, and Social Policy. Mahwah, NJ: Lawrence Erlbaum Associates, 2002. An exploration, by a variety of experts, of individual, familial, and social causes and consequences of cohabitation.

Casper, Lynne M., and Suzanne M. Bianchi. *Continuity and Change in the American Family.* Thousand Oaks, CA: Sage, 2002. An examination of various facets of change and continuity in family life in America in the last half of the 20th century, including cohabitation, work, parenting, and single-mother families.

Daniels, Cynthia R., ed. *Lost Fathers: The Politics of Fatherlessness in America.* New York: St. Martin's Press, 2000. A collection of diverse perspectives on how the lack of a father in the home intersects with such issues as welfare, poverty, sexuality, family values, children's well-being, and the race problem.

Hertz, Rosanna. *Single by Choice: How Women Are Choosing Parenthood Without Marriage and Creating the New American Family.* New York: Oxford University Press, 2006. Based on in-depth interviews with 65 middle-class, single women who chose to be single mothers, Hertz explores different ways to become a mother and how the women balance parenthood with work.

Holyfield, Lori. *Moving Up and Out: Poverty, Education, and the Single Parent Family.* Philadelphia, PA: Temple University Press, 2002. The author, a high-school dropout mother who later managed to secure her PhD and become a university professor, examines a program in Arkansas that helped her and other single parents and that could be a model for other states.

Lauer, Robert H., and Jeanette C. Lauer. *'Til Death Do Us Part: How Couples Stay Together.* New York: Haworth Press, 1986. A study of 362 couples who have been married 15 years or more, showing how they keep their marriage intact. Compares happy, long-term marriages to those in which one or both partners are unhappy.

Wolfinger, Nicholas H. *Understanding the Divorce Cycle: The Children of Divorce in Their Own Marriages.* New York: Cambridge University Press, 2005. Explores the ways in which the divorce of one's parents affects every facet of one's intimate relationships; includes a discussion about the effects of no-fault divorce laws.

Health Care and Illness

Physical and Mental

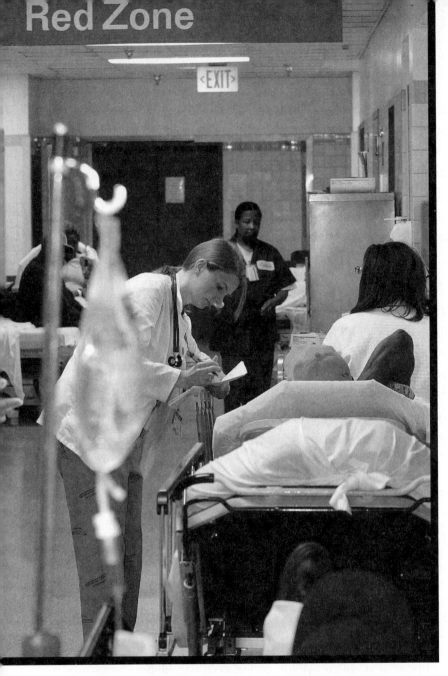

Red Zone

"If You Want to Live a Long Life"

Tami, in her 40s, has what she calls a "bizarre, cruel disease." She also says the disease may be helping her live a long life: "If you want to live a long life, get a chronic disease and take care of it." Tami's story illustrates both the trauma of chronic illness and the ability of some people to triumph over the trauma and live a reasonably normal life:

I have lupus. It is intermittent and recurrent, and I know it can destroy my life, my will to live, and my ability to cope. In lupus, your body and soul are enmeshed in a web of pain and desperation. When the symptoms first appeared, people thought I was a hypochondriac. Doctors said nothing was wrong with me. They labeled me a neurotic, and I began to think of myself that way. Friends and family saw me looking well one moment and distressed the next. My internist finally turned me over to a psychiatrist. Nothing helped.

Then I got a new physician, and I had the shock of learning that I had a complicated, chronic illness that would alter all my plans and dreams for my life. I was both relieved and in panic. It was a relief to finally identify the problem. It was panic to know what the problem was. I suddenly had to confront the possibility of my own death. A feeling of emptiness spread throughout my body.

Before I got sick, I was full of life. Now I was physically, emotionally, and spiritually exhausted. At times, I could barely raise my arms to attend to personal needs. My husband remained optimistic. My daughter was angry. But as time passed, I was forced to make a decision: I had to try to take charge of my life, or waste away into nothing. I began a program of educating myself. Slowly, I got stronger. I went into remission. No one knows if it was the treatment or my changed attitudes or just a natural process.

I harbor no false hopes. I know I'm not cured. Sometimes, when the sun is shining I feel sad. I want to go out and bask in it. I want to forget that the sun is my enemy, that it can kill someone with lupus. But I get over the sadness. I can't make the lupus disappear by an act of my will, but I can refuse to let it destroy my spirit. I don't know what the future holds. For now, I just focus my energy on what I can control, and live moment to moment.

Introduction

If you were living before 1910, were sick, and randomly chose a doctor, your chances of benefiting from that doctor's ministrations were less than 50 percent. Your chances today are much better, but they vary according to such factors as whether you are physically or mentally ill, live in the city or a rural area, and are poor or well-to-do. The unequal probabilities of all Americans having good health and good health care contradict the *value of equality*. Inequality of care, then, is one reason why health care is a social problem.

Another reason why health care and illness are social problems is that both physical and mental illness may be induced by social factors. For instance, poverty may force an individual to live in an unhealthy physical environment. Rapid social change may generate anxiety, depression, or other mental disorders.

prevalence
the number of cases of an illness that exist at any particular time

incidence
the number of new cases of an illness that occur during a particular period of time

epidemiology
the study of factors that affect the incidence, prevalence, and distribution of illnesses

Adverse effects on health are serious because Americans place a *high value on good health*. Indeed, good health is one of the most important factors in happiness and life satisfaction (Michalos, Zumbo, and Hubley 2000; Pew Research Center 2006a). And health and health care are used as measures of the quality of life in communities.

In this chapter, we examine health care and illness by first drawing the distinction between physical and mental illnesses and then discussing their **prevalence** in American society. (Prevalence is the number of cases of a disease that exist at any particular time, while **incidence** is the number of new cases that occur during a particular period of time.) Next, we show how the problem affects the quality of life. Then we consider the **epidemiology** of physical and mental illness—the factors that affect the incidence, prevalence, and distribution of illnesses. Finally, we discuss ways to deal with the problem.

Nature of the Problem: Health Care and Illness

Are Americans unnecessarily concerned about their health and health care system? After all, we spend more on health care (measured either on a per capita basis or as a proportion of the gross domestic product) than any other industrial nation (Mishel, Bernstein, and Allegretto 2006). And people come from other nations to some of our famed health care centers. Nevertheless, Americans express *deep concerns about health care in this country.* A Gallup poll found that 46 percent rated the quality of health care as only fair or poor, while 16 percent said the health care system is in a state of crisis and 55 percent said it has major problems (Polling Report 2007).

As we examine the nature and extent of physical and mental illness, keep in mind that the two are not really separable (Jacobsen et al. 2002; Whooley 2006). Physical illness can cause emotional problems. Mental illness can be manifested in physical distress (Ruo et al. 2003). Both physical and mental illness have social causes. However, the methods used to assess the extent of physical and mental illnesses are different and must be discussed separately.

Physical Illness

Important indicators show that Americans have made significant advances in health matters. For instance, **life expectancy,** the average number of years a person can expect to live, has increased dramatically (table 13.1). In 1900, life expectancy was less than two-thirds of the present figure. In large part, this increase in life expectancy *reflects reduced infant mortality and lower rates of infectious diseases.* It isn't that the majority of people only lived until their late 40s in the early 1900s. Rather, the large number of infant deaths combined with the high rate of infectious diseases among the middle-aged severely depressed the average length of life. Sanitation, better diet, reduced fertility, and advancing medical knowledge and technology greatly reduced both

life expectancy
the average number of years a newborn can expect to live

TABLE 13.1
Expectation of Life at Birth, 1900–2004

Year	Total	Male	Female
1900	47.3	46.3	48.3
1910	50.0	48.4	51.8
1920	54.1	53.6	54.6
1930	59.7	58.1	61.6
1940	62.9	60.8	65.2
1950	68.2	65.6	71.1
1960	69.7	66.6	73.1
1970	70.9	67.1	74.8
1980	73.7	70.0	77.5
1990	75.4	72.0	78.8
2000	77.0	74.3	79.7
2004	77.9	75.2	80.4

SOURCE: *Historical Statistics of the United States, Part I* (Washington, DC: Government Printing Office, 1975), p. 55, and U.S. Census Bureau (2007).

Cause	Sex		Race or Ethnic Origin			
	Male	Female	White	Black	Asian	Hispanic
Diseases of the heart	286.6	190.3	230.9	300.2	134.6	173.2
Malignant neoplasms (cancer)	233.3	160.9	192.4	233.3	113.5	126.6
Cerebrovascular diseases	54.1	52.3	51.7	74.3	45.2	40.5
Chronic lower respiratory diseases	52.3	37.8	47.0	30.1	16.2	20.2
Accidents	51.8	24.1	38.8	36.1	18.0	30.6
Diabetes mellitus	28.9	22.5	22.1	49.2	17.3	35.0
Influenza and pneumonia	26.1	19.4	22.0	23.3	17.3	18.4
Suicide	18.0	4.2	12.7	5.2	5.6	5.6
Chronic liver disease and cirrhosis	13.0	6.0	9.0	8.4	3.0	14.7
AIDS	7.1	2.4	2.0	21.3	0.7	5.9

TABLE 13.2
Death Rates, by Sex and Race or Ethnicity (age-adjusted death rate per 100,000)

SOURCE: National Center for Health Statistics 2006.

the prevalence and the seriousness of infectious diseases. Despite the progress, physical illness is a major problem. It is even a problem for the young, with as many as one of every five adolescents having at least one serious health problem (Cimons 1991).

Table 13.2 shows the diseases primarily responsible for death. Cardiovascular diseases, including high blood pressure, coronary heart disease, rheumatic heart disease, and strokes, afflict millions of Americans and have been at the top of the list since the beginning of the 20th century.

Chronic diseases are the major cause of death in the United States (table 13.2). Chronic diseases are those of long duration. They may be classified along a number of dimensions (Rolland 1987). They may be *progressive* (worsening over time) or *constant*. Lung cancer is progressive, whereas stroke is constant. Their onset may be *acute* (short-term) or *gradual* (occurring over an extended period of time). Stroke is acute, whereas lung cancer is gradual. They may be *fatal* (lung cancer), *possibly fatal or life-shortening* (stroke), or *nonfatal* (kidney stones). Although heart disease and cancer are the leading causes of death, the most common chronic conditions are arthritis and sinusitis. Dementia, including Alzheimer's disease, afflicts a third or more of those people who live to age 85 (St. George–Hyslop 2000). Increasing concern has developed over health problems created by obesity (32.2 percent of adults and 17.1 percent of children are obese) and diabetes (10.3 percent of the population has diabetes) (National Center for Health Statistics 2006; Ogden et al. 2006).

There is also concern about a *resurgence of infectious diseases*. Infectious disease mortality declined during the first eight decades of the 20th century from 797 deaths per 100,000 to 36 deaths per 100,000 (Armstrong, Conn, and Pinner 1999). However, the rates began to increase in the 1980s and 1990s. Today, infectious diseases are a serious problem throughout the world (see the *Global Comparisons* box in this chapter). Infectious diseases cause more deaths worldwide than heart disease and cancer combined. In addition to increasing rates of such diseases as tuberculosis, at least 30 previously unknown diseases have emerged in recent decades, including Lyme disease (caused by a tick bite), AIDS (discussed next), Legionnaires' disease (caused by air-conditioning systems), toxic shock syndrome (caused by ultra-absorbent tampons), and SARS (severe acute respiratory syndrome, caused by a virus). New infections whose source may be obscure and for which there is no known treatment continue to appear.

Infections are caused by bacteria, including bacteria that mutate, and by new strains of diseases like tuberculosis that are resistant to antibiotics and other drugs now available (Reichman and Tanne 2001; Simon 2006).

As table 13.2 shows, *the health problems you are likely to face vary according to your gender.* In general, women have higher rates of acute diseases (such as respiratory ailments and viral infections), short-term disabilities, and nonfatal chronic diseases. Men have more injuries, more visual and hearing problems, and higher rates of life-threatening chronic diseases such as emphysema and the major cardiovascular diseases.

Health problems also vary according to racial or ethnic origin. This may be due as much to socioeconomic differences as to racial factors per se (Haywood et al. 2000). For example, strokes (which may be related to diet) are a leading cause of death, but the mortality rates are higher among African Americans, American Indians, and Asian Americans than among whites (Centers for Disease Control 2000). Rates also vary within ethnic groups. According to the National Center for Health Statistics (2000), Puerto Ricans have more health problems than other Hispanics. For instance, more Puerto Ricans report limiting activities, having fair or poor health, and spending time in a hospital.

Finally, *health problems vary by age and tend to intensify with age.* Older people are more likely than those in other age groups to define their health as only "fair" or "poor" (Haug and Folmar 1986). The fact that people are living longer does not mean that they all have a better quality of life.

AIDS
acquired immune deficiency syndrome, a disease in which a viral infection causes the immune system to stop functioning, inevitably resulting in death

AIDS. **AIDS** is caused by a virus that attacks certain white blood cells, eventually *causing the individual's immune system to stop functioning.* The individual then falls prey to one infection after another. Even normally mild diseases can prove fatal. Many AIDS patients develop rare cancers or suffer serious brain damage.

There is no cure for AIDS. Drugs can prolong the lives of some AIDS victims, but each infection takes its toll, and the immune system continues to collapse. In the advanced stages of HIV infection, 15 to 20 percent of patients develop a type of dementia that involves slow mental functioning (Portegies and Rosenberg 1998). Eventually, the individual succumbs and dies.

How does AIDS spread? The two primary ways are through sex (oral, anal, or vaginal) with someone infected with the AIDS virus and by sharing drug needles and syringes with an infected person. Some people were infected through blood transfusions before blood was tested for the virus. Infected mothers can transmit the disease to their babies before or during birth or while breast feeding (Schwarez and Rutherford 1989). Primarily, then, the *virus is spread through blood or semen.* Females who get the disease are either intravenous drug users or sex partners of an infected male (Cohen, Hauer, and Wofsy 1989). In fact, a woman is 12 times as likely as a man to be infected with the AIDS virus during heterosexual intercourse and, once infected, is likely to die more quickly (Ickovics and Rodin 1992).

Who is most likely to be infected? In sub-Saharan Africa, where more than half of all AIDS victims reside, the infection is spread mainly by heterosexual intercourse (Sills 1994). In other nations, including the United States, the main causes are homosexual relationships and intravenous drug use. Worldwide, about 40 million people

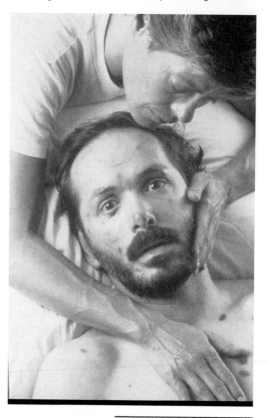

Compounding the personal devastation wrought by AIDS is the impact on society when almost half of the people infected in the United States are only 35 to 44 years old.

THE WORLDWIDE CHALLENGE OF INFECTIOUS DISEASES

Most research money in the United States is devoted to the study of chronic diseases, the primary cause of death for Americans. In many of the developing nations, particularly in Africa, infectious diseases are more prevalent and far more likely to be the cause of death. Worldwide, about 11 million people a year die from infectious disease (figure 13.1). Some of these diseases are relatively rare in the United States and other Western nations. Many, not shown in figure 13.1 because they afflict fewer numbers (such as tropical diseases), are unknown in the United States. Nevertheless, the developed nations are vulnerable to these diseases because of such things as international travel and bioterrorism (Becker, Hu, and Biller-Andorno 2006).

Both new and re-emerging infectious diseases afflict both the developed and the developing nations (Peleman 2004). Their spread is rapid because of such factors as pathogens that are resistant to antibiotics and disease-carrying insects that are resistant to insecticides.

The problems of dealing with these diseases is illustrated by efforts to stop malaria in Africa. For a number of years, mosquito-killing insecticide reduced the number of deaths from malaria. But the insects could not be effectively controlled in the long run, and the incidence of malaria increased again in the 1990s. As figure 13.1 shows, malaria once again is a serious health problem, causing about a million deaths a year. Children account for a majority of the deaths.

An increasingly more deadly infection worldwide is tuberculosis (Ducati, Ruffino-Netto, Basso, and Santos 2006). Scientists estimate that a third of the world's population is infected with tubercle bacilli, and that there are 8 to 10 million new cases of tuberculosis each year. The great majority of the new cases and the deaths occur in the developing nations. Tuberculosis is difficult to treat because bacterial mutations make it resistant to any single drug, and drugs that are effective at one point in time eventually become ineffective as the bacilli become resistant.

Although the U.S. death rate from tuberculosis is now quite low, the disease presents a challenge to Americans as well as

are infected with the AIDS virus, 63 percent of them in sub-Saharan Africa (Engeler 2006). Since the first reported case in 1981, more than 25 million people have died of AIDS, making it one of the most destructive illnesses in the history of humankind.

In the United States, the number of new AIDS cases peaked in the early 1990s, then declined. The total number of cases by 2004 was 908,905 (U.S. Census Bureau 2007). Rates vary considerably by race and ethnicity. Of those Americans living with AIDS, 35.1 percent are non-Hispanic whites, 42.9 percent are non-Hispanic blacks, 20.2 percent are Hispanics, 1.0 percent are Asian Americans, and 0.4 percent are American Indians. Nearly 45 percent of them contracted the disease through homosexual activity. The age group with the largest number of cases was 35 to 44 years. Thousands of children under the age of 13 also were infected.

The reaction to AIDS has varied from skepticism about its importance to near-panic. Some researchers have warned of an AIDS epidemic sweeping over the nation and over the world. The extent to which Americans are concerned is seen in a number of ways. There has been some increase in bias against homosexuals because of their role in spreading the disease. New dating services have appeared that test people regularly and issue them cards showing that they are free of sexually transmitted diseases. Many people are afraid even to be around individuals with AIDS.

Some people believe that the concern over AIDS is overdrawn. Certainly, it seems an exaggeration to say that AIDS is an *epidemic*. The incidence is low compared to to other nations because of the new strains that are resistant to formerly effective drugs. Tuberculosis is also more likely to develop in people who are infected with HIV (the virus that causes AIDS). As a result, tuberculosis could once again become a leading cause of death in the world (as it was in the early years of the 20th century). In any case, it is clear that, looking at the world as a whole, infectious diseases are still a major (and increasingly serious) health problem.

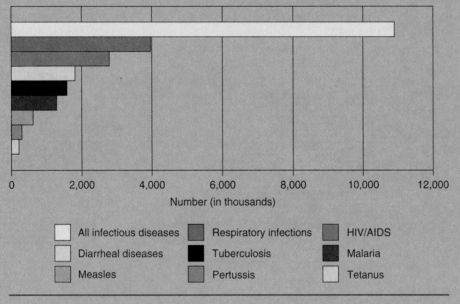

Number (in thousands)

- ☐ All infectious diseases
- ☐ Diarrheal diseases
- ☐ Measles
- ☐ Respiratory infections
- ■ Tuberculosis
- ☐ Pertussis
- ☐ HIV/AIDS
- ☐ Malaria
- ☐ Tetanus

FIGURE 13.1   Worldwide Deaths, by Selected Infectious Diseases.
Source: World Health Organization Web site 2007.

other diseases. Death rates are down. Moreover, there are ways to minimize the risks. Health experts advise the use of condoms as one of the best preventive measures (condoms are not foolproof, however). Others argue that the disease can be eliminated only if people change their sexual and drug-use behavior. Unfortunately, too many people ignore the preventive measures. People continue to share drug needles and to have unprotected sex (in some cases, even those who know they are HIV positive) (Diaz et al. 2002; Semple, Patterson, and Grant 2002). It is likely that AIDS will be a matter of great concern for some time to come.

Mental Illness

Types of Mental Illness.   Some sociologists prefer the term "mental disorder" to mental illness. "Illness" suggests to them a medical model, a problem deeply rooted in an individual that may also have an organic basis. "Disorder" suggests to them a problem that is more social in its origin and resolution. We believe that both perspectives are valid in part. A particular individual's problem may be a biologically based illness, or it may be behavior that results from the actions and reactions of others (see the discussion of labeling at the end of this chapter). Or it may be a combination of both. Thus, we use the terms "mental illness" and "mental disorder" interchangeably to avoid any simplistic assumptions about the problems.

381

psychosis
a disorder in which the individual fails to distinguish between internal and external stimuli

Before 1980, mental disorders were separated into three broad categories: psychoses, neuroses, and psychosomatic disorders. This breakdown is still a useful way to get a general sense of the kinds of disorders that afflict people. In a **psychosis,** the individual is unable to distinguish between internal and external stimuli. The individual's thinking and perceptions are disordered. In everyday terms, he or she has "lost touch with reality." The individual may have hallucinations or fantasize in a way that has no relationship to the real world. The individual may experience chronic perplexity and uncertainty. Emotions may vacillate between extreme elation and depression, and behavior may involve either hyperactivity or extreme inactivity.

neurosis
a mental disorder involving anxiety that impairs functioning

Neurosis refers to a disorder with symptoms that are distressing, and are defined as unacceptable or alien. Neuroses involve anxiety sufficiently intense to impair the individual's functioning in some way.

psychosomatic disorder
an impairment in physiological functioning that results from the individual's emotional state

Psychosomatic disorders are *impairments in physiological functioning that result from the individual's emotional state.* Certain phrases express the reality of psychosomatic disorders, such as he "is a pain in the neck" or she "gives me a headache." Such expressions can be literally true. *Your emotional reactions to others* can result in aches and pains of various kinds.

Rather than a simple division of mental illness into psychoses, neuroses, and psychosomatic disorders, multiple categories are now used (American Psychiatric Association 1994). The major categories (with some illustrative, specific disorders) are:

Disorders usually first evident in infancy, childhood, or adolescence (mental retardation, conduct disorders, eating disorders).

Organic mental disorders (alcohol-induced amnesia).

Substance use disorders (alcohol or drug abuse).

schizophrenia
a psychosis that involves a thinking disorder, particularly hallucinations and fantasies

Schizophrenic disorders (various forms of **schizophrenia,** a psychosis that involves a thinking disorder, particularly hallucinations and fantasies).

Paranoid disorders (various forms of paranoia).

Affective disorders (**manic-depressive reaction,** in which the individual fluctuates between emotional extremes).

manic-depressive reaction
a disorder involving fluctuation between emotional extremes

Mood disorders (phobias, obsessive-compulsive disorder).

Somatoform disorders (the conversion of emotional into physical problems, as in hysteria).

Dissociative disorders (multiple personality).

Psychosexual disorders (transsexualism).

Disorders of impulse control (pathological gambling, kleptomania).

Personality disorders (narcissism, an absorbing preoccupation with one's own needs, desires, and image).

Extent of Mental Illness.   *Mental illness is a problem in all societies.* It is found among preindustrial people and in small, relatively isolated communities as well as in modernized societies. How many Americans suffer from mental disorders? There are two ways to estimate. We can examine the data on *hospitalization rates,* or we can research communities to get estimates of *"true" prevalence* ("true" because only a minority of people with mental disorders are hospitalized).

deinstitutionalization
a movement to change the setting of treatment of mental disorders from hospitals to the community through rapid discharge of patients

Rates of hospitalization must be interpreted cautiously because they reflect changing styles of treatment as well as changing levels of prevalence. Therapy with new drugs became common in the late 1950s. In the 1960s, **deinstitutionalization**—a movement

EXCEPT ME AND THEE?

There is an old saying that all the world is crazy except "me and thee, and sometimes I am not too sure of thee." As we pointed out in this chapter, it is probable that only a minority of the population is free of any psychiatric symptoms. To say that someone has symptoms, of course, does not mean that the individual requires psychiatric care or has problems functioning in his or her responsibilities. Nevertheless, the ideal for Americans would be the very best health—freedom from all symptoms.

How do you stack up? You can test yourself on a set of symptoms suggested by Walter Gove and Michael Geerken (1977). For the symptoms listed, write "often," "sometimes," or "never" beside each to indicate how often you have experienced them during the past few weeks.

1. I felt anxious about something or someone.
2. I was bothered by special fears.
3. I felt that people were saying things behind my back.
4. I felt it was safer not to trust anyone.
5. I couldn't take care of things because I couldn't get going.
6. I was so blue or depressed that it interfered with my daily activities.
7. I was bothered by nervousness.
8. I was in low spirits.
9. I was bothered by special thoughts.
10. I was so restless I couldn't sit for long in a chair.
11. I felt that nothing turned out the way I wanted it to.
12. I felt alone even when I was among friends.
13. I felt that personal worries were getting me down, making me physically ill.
14. I felt that nothing was worthwhile anymore.

Give yourself two points for each "often," one point for each "sometimes," and no points for each "never."

Your total score can range between 0 and 28. A score of 0 would mean that you are completely free of psychiatric symptoms. A score of 28 would mean that you have serious levels of those symptoms. If the entire class participates in this exercise, each score can be given anonymously to the instructor, who can give you the range and compute the average for the entire class. What do you think the results say about the prevalence of psychiatric symptoms in the population? Do you think students' scores would be higher or lower than those of the population at large? Why?

---

to change the setting of treatment from the state mental hospital to the community—began. (We discuss deinstitutionalization later in this chapter.) Thereafter, the number of patients in hospitals decreased, although the number of admissions increased until the 1970s. Since the mid-1980s, the proportion of Americans admitted to mental hospitals has fluctuated a little but remained around 2.6 per 1,000 population (U.S. Census Bureau 2007). Even some chronically mentally ill people are not hospitalized, and those who are admitted are staying a shorter time. Thus, the total population in hospitals is less than it was from 1965 to 1975.

Surveys are a better way to estimate prevalence. A national survey (Substance Abuse and Mental Health Services Administration 2003) reported the following statistics about the United States in 2002:

About 17.5 million adults age 18 or older had some kind of serious mental illness.

The rates of illness were highest for people age 18 to 25 (13.2 percent) and lowest for those age 50 or older (4.9 percent).

Rates were higher for women (10.5 percent) than for men (6.0 percent).

Rates varied considerably by racial and ethnic group: People reporting two or more races, 13.6 percent; American Indian and Alaska Native, 12.5 percent; African American, 8.8 percent; white, 8.4 percent; Asian, 7.5 percent; Hispanic, 6.9 percent; Native Hawaiian or other Pacific Islander, 5.4 percent.

The different types of mental illness vary in their prevalence. A national survey reported that anxiety disorders were the most prevalent in a 12-month period, afflicting 18.1 percent of Americans (Kessler, Chiu, Demler, and Walters 2005). Mood disorders were the next most common (9.5 percent). Lifetime prevalence estimates (as opposed to the rates for a particular year) show that 46.4 percent of Americans will have a mental disorder at some time in their life (Kessler et al. 2005). And the disorders are likely to appear early in life: half of all lifetime cases appear by the age of 14 and three-fourths by age 24.

Thus, *variations exist in both the prevalence of the different disorders and in the at-risk background factors*. Women have more anxiety disorders, including depression; men have more problems with substance abuse and higher rates of antisocial personality disorder.

The prevalence of the various disorders does not necessarily remain stable over time. In fact, the rates of some disorders are going up. Anxiety disorders have increased among children and young adults in recent decades (Twenge 2000). *The problem of depression is particularly serious among people born after World War II* (Klerman 1986). Rates of depression among baby boomers and following generations increased about tenfold over those of previous generations. Depression affects twice as many women as men and is particularly high among African American women aged 35 to 44 (Blazer et al. 1994). A higher rate of depression among women, incidentally, also has been found in Canada, Puerto Rico, France, Germany, Italy, Lebanon, Taiwan, Korea, New Zealand, and other nations (Weissman et al. 1996; Klose and Jacobi 2004).

Health Care, Illness, and the Quality of Life

One effect that illness has on the quality of life is this: People must endure considerable stress and suffering because of illness, which is a contradiction to Americans' value of good health. In addition, illness impacts interpersonal relationships, involves people in inadequate health care, interferes with individual freedom, and costs the individual and the nation economically.

Stress and Suffering

The obvious impact of illness on the quality of life is the *stress and suffering* that illness imposes on people. Consider Anton Boisen's (1936:3) account of his psychotic episode:

> [T]here came surging in upon me with overpowering force a terrifying idea about a coming world catastrophe. Although I had never before given serious thought to such a subject, there came flashing into my mind, as though from a source without myself, the idea that this little planet of ours, which has existed for we know not how many millions of years, was about to undergo some sort of metamorphosis. It was like a seed or an egg. In it were stored up a quantity of food materials, represented by our natural resources. But now we were like a seed in the process of germinating or an egg that had just been fertilized. We were starting to grow. Just within the short space of a hundred years we

had begun to draw upon our resources to such an extent that the timber and the gas and the oil were likely soon to be exhausted. In the wake of this idea followed others. I myself was more important than I had ever dreamed of being; I was also a zero quantity. Strange and mysterious forces of evil of which before I had not had the slightest suspicion were also revealed. I was terrified beyond measure and in terror I talked. . . . I soon found myself in a psychopathic hospital. There followed three weeks of violent delirium which remain indelibly burned into my memory. . . . It seemed as if I were living thousands of years within that time. Then I came out of it much as one awakens out of a bad dream.

Physical illness also involves *stressful disruptions* in a person's life. If the person's work is disrupted, he or she may experience economic anxiety. If the illness is chronic, the individual may struggle with his or her identity (what kind of person am I?) and with alterations in lifestyle (Charmaz 1995). Protracted or chronic illness also affects the rest of the family (Lundwall 2002). Taking care of a chronically ill individual is demanding and stressful (Adams et al. 2002). The marital relationship may suffer (Woods and Lewis 1995). Family patterns may be altered and highly constrained by the sick member.

Because physical and mental health are intertwined, physical health problems can generate *long-term fears* and even *serious emotional problems*. A substantial number of people experience high levels of psychological distress before or after surgery (Glosser et al. 2000). People diagnosed with serious diseases such as AIDS may develop high levels of anxiety and depression, problems with their work and social lives, and thoughts of suicide (Griffin et al. 1998).

Heart attack victims and cancer patients may have problems readjusting to normal routines. They often experience depression and anxiety even when the prognosis for the future is good, and they may have serious reservations about returning to a normal routine (Peleg-Oren and Sherer 2001). Patients with arthritis report a *significantly lower quality of life* than those without chronic disease (Anderson, Kaplan, and Ake 2004).

Serious *emotional problems* often are involved in cases of *organ transplants* (Dew et al. 2001). Severe depression and even psychosis have been reported. Men who receive organs from women may fear that their characters will be altered or that they will be feminized. Some patients develop fantasies about the transplanted organ and think of it almost in human terms as a living being within them. Some develop an image of the organ as a malevolent or hostile being; others conceive of it as life-giving. Not every patient has such serious problems, of course, but some long-term fears are probably common.

The *disabled* also endure stress and suffering because they are often *socially disvalued*. Social devaluation is particularly acute when the disability is visible. The visibly disabled individual may be treated as inferior and may be subject to serious disadvantages in job opportunities. Such experiences result in insecurity and anxiety.

The close relationship of physical and mental illness works both ways, because emotional problems can lead to physical illness. A physician has shown how high levels of cynicism and hostility cause bodily responses that lead to heart attacks (Williams 1989). To some extent, the problem can become a vicious circle for the individual, who may become entangled in the interaction between physical and mental disorders.

Interpersonal Relationships

There is a contradiction between the *sick role* and Americans' attitudes and values about desirable behavior; this contradiction can result in disrupted interpersonal relationships. Although people realize that illness is inevitable, they are reluctant to allow illnesses of others to disturb their routines. Furthermore, some illnesses, such as cancer and various kinds of mental illness, carry a social **stigma** (Mechanic et al. 1994; Angermeyer et al. 2004; Sandelowski, Lambe, and Barroso 2004). A national study of cancer survivors found discriminatory treatment at the workplace and a lower likelihood of marriage than for people without cancer (Christian 1991). A survey of parents and spouses of 156 first-admission psychiatric patients found that half of them concealed the hospitalization to some degree (Phelan, Bromet, and Link 1998). They did not want people to know that someone in their immediate family had a mental disorder.

The *strain on interpersonal relationships* when one of the interactants is ill is also seen in patterns of family relationships. Both physical and mental illness can lead to disruption in the family. In families with a chronically ill member, the ill member can become a focal point of family life. If the mother is ill, the husband and children may experience an emotional void in their lives. If the father is ill, there is a likelihood of economic problems and a lowered standard of living. Moreover, the father may tend to monopolize the attention of his wife, leaving the children feeling neglected. If the family develops a subculture of illness, they withdraw into themselves, isolated from outsiders.

Not all families respond to serious illness in this way, of course. Some families become more integrated, and the members experience a greater richness of family life. Others experience a temporary breakdown but recover and return to normal. Still others disintegrate in the face of the challenge, especially if the family was already weakly integrated. In every case, however, illness presents a serious challenge to the family.

One reason serious illness tends to disrupt family life is that it *precludes proper role functioning.* The physically or emotionally ill may be incapable of adequately fulfilling the role of spouse, parent, or breadwinner (Peleg-Oren and Sherer 2001). The normal functioning of family life may give way to a focus on the ill person. In extreme cases, most activities of family members reflect the ill person's needs and limitations.

As with the interplay between mental and physical illness, the relationship between interpersonal relations and illness can become a vicious circle. Poor interpersonal relationships can be a factor in the onset of a mental disorder, and mental disorders adversely affect interpersonal relationships. On the other hand, *good interpersonal relationships are associated with better health* (Berkman 2000). Two psychologists found, in a national sample, that people with a strong desire and ability to engage in intimate relations have better mental health than others (McAdams and Bryant 1987). Women who scored high said they are generally happy and satisfied with work, family, and leisure. Men who scored high reported fewer problems of mental and physical health, less drug and alcohol abuse, and less uncertainty about the future.

In sum, there is a relationship between patterns of interaction and health. Illness, whether physical or mental, tends to be associated with disturbed interpersonal relationships. The relation between interaction and illness may be a vicious circle: bad interpersonal relationships being a factor in the onset of illness, and illness being a factor in causing disturbed relationships.

Inadequate Care

The value of good health is contradicted by the *inadequate care* that many Americans receive for both physical and mental illnesses (a national study about the latter concluded that *most* people with mental disorders are either untreated or poorly treated) (Wang et al. 2005). Inadequate care may result from a variety of factors. One impor-

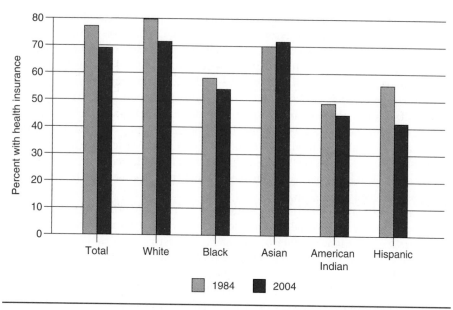

FIGURE 13.2   Percent Health Insurance Coverage, by Race/Ethnicity.
Source: National Center for Health Statistics 2006.

tant factor is *the lack of health insurance,* including 41.9 percent of all children (National Center for Health Statistics 2006). Figure 13.2 shows two additional disturbing facts about health insurance coverage. First, while a majority of Americans have some coverage, the proportion covered has been decreasing and was lower in 2004 than in 1984 (for all groups except Asian Americans). More than 100 million Americans now have no coverage at all. Second, there are clear racial/ethnic disparities in coverage. White Americans are most likely to have insurance, while American Indians are least likely. Fewer than half of American Indians and Hispanics and only a little more than half of African Americans have health insurance. Lack of insurance can lead people to delay or avoid necessary treatment or to find affordable but questionable or useless kinds of treatment (e.g., the use of a copper bracelet to treat arthritis).

Errors by the medical establishment are another factor in inadequate care. Errors include **iatrogenic** problems, those caused by the physician in the course of a patient's treatment. Physicians may misdiagnose a case, prescribe the wrong medication, and even order unnecessary surgery (Weinberg and Stason 1998; Pilippo et al. 1999; Shojania 2003). In their study of one hospital's admissions over a 14-month period, Weinberg and Stason (1998) found problems in 6 percent of all admissions, including missed or delayed diagnoses, inappropriate treatments, and complications caused by physicians. The behavior of physicians was central to three-fourths of the problems.

Women seem to be particularly prone to iatrogenic problems. One study concluded that 81.2 percent of the caesarean sections performed in four hospitals were unjustified (Gomez and Carrasquilla 1999). Another study drew the same conclusion about 70 percent of the hysterectomies performed on 497 California women (Broder et al. 2000).

Hospital personnel, including medical lab technicians, also make mistakes. A study of medication in 36 hospitals reported that nearly one of five doses were in error—given at the wrong time, not given, given in the wrong amount, or were an unauthorized

iatrogenic
caused by the physician in the course of his or her treatment of a patient

drug (Barker et al. 2002). A national study concluded that on average a hospital patient suffers at least one medication error each day, and that such errors harm 1.5 million patients and kill thousands each year in the United States (Aspden, Wolcott, Bootman, and Cronenwett 2007). And a survey of 134 Wisconsin hospitals found that 3.4 percent of the children discharged had one or more medical injuries, injuries resulting from medications, procedures, devices, implants, or grafts (Meurer et al. 2006).

Overall, medical errors probably cause more deaths than car accidents, breast cancer, suicide, homicide, or AIDS. A study by HealthGrades, an organization that rates doctors and hospitals, reported that 195,000 patients die in hospitals each year from preventable errors (Allen 2004). "Preventable errors" include such problems as overdoses, postsurgical infections, and slow medical staff responses to signs of infection or other life-threatening problems.

The value of good health is also contradicted by the actual state of the science of medicine. Contrary to the expectations and attitudes of many Americans, *medicine is an inexact science*. Many symptoms, such as extreme fatigue or a pain in the back, are difficult to diagnose. Diagnosing mental disorders is even more problematic. Psychiatry is a field of *competing ideologies* rather than a science of mental therapy. There are various schools of therapy with different ideologies of health and illness and different views about diagnostic categories. A psychiatrist's diagnosis of a case will depend partly on *which school of therapy* he or she follows, but even within a particular ideology, diagnosis of mental disorders is difficult.

fallacy

A psychiatric diagnosis also may be influenced by stereotyped thinking. That is, the diagnosis may be a perfect illustration of the *fallacy of non sequitur:* "because this is a woman, her symptoms show her to be hysterical," and so forth. It isn't that the therapist consciously thinks in those terms, of course, but the diagnosis does reflect stereotypes, whether the stereotype involves gender, race, or social class (Dixon, Gordon, and Khomusi 1995; Wang, Demler, and Kessler, 2002).

For example, 209 psychiatrists evaluated two cases of patients with a schizophrenic disorder (Loring and Powell 1988). All the symptoms were presented, but the researchers varied the race and gender of the patients. Some of the psychiatrists thought they were evaluating two white males, whereas others evaluated two white females, two black males, two black females, or two clients with unnamed sex and race. A majority correctly identified the disorder as schizophrenia when no sex or race was listed. For the other cases, less than a majority made the correct diagnosis. Only 21 percent diagnosed the white females correctly. The race and gender of both the psychiatrist and the patient tended to affect the diagnosis. In general, when the race and sex of psychiatrist and patient were the same, the diagnosis tended to be the same as if there were no information about the patient's sex and race. In other cases, however, the psychiatrists were affected by stereotypical thinking.

In addition to incompetence, errors, and the fact that medicine is an art as well as a science, many Americans do not receive the quality of care they desire because of the *maldistribution of medical care*. Both economic and geographic factors enter into the maldistribution. *Maldistribution of doctors* means that people in certain areas have less access to doctors than those in other areas. There are a disproportionate number of doctors and nurses in cities and in the more well-to-do areas of the cities, leaving many rural areas and impoverished urban neighborhoods with inadequate care. For example, in 2004 the number of physicians per 100,000 population varied among the states from a low of 169 in Idaho to a high of 450 in Massachusetts (the highest was Washington, D.C., with 798 physicians per 100,000) (U.S. Census Bureau 2007).

Deinstitutionalization

The inadequate care of the mentally ill has been compounded by the deinstitutionalization movement that began in the mid-1950s (Lamb 1998). Partly because of newly available drugs, state and county hospitals began discharging a great many patients, including some with serious mental disorders and some who could not be effectively treated without 24-hour care. The goal was to provide a more humane, more effective, and less costly method of treating the disorders by using a community setting rather than a mental hospital. The drugs would keep the patients from harming others or themselves and enable them to function relatively well while they recovered. Their recovery would be facilitated by more normal living conditions. Further, their civil rights would be respected. In other words, the movement seemed to offer a new and enlightened approach that would transform the care of the mentally ill. Unfortunately, the reality diverged sharply from the ideal, adding to the problem of inadequate care.

One goal was met: A great many patients were released from hospitals. Patients who now go into hospitals are likely to stay only a short time compared to those who were institutionalized before 1960. As a result, the hospitals are treating more people than formerly, but they also have fewer patients in residence at any one time. The number of occupied state hospital beds has decreased from 339 to 29 per 100,000 population (Lamb 1998).

Nevertheless, deinstitutionalization has not only failed to solve many problems, it has also created new ones. In fact, many observers regard the movement as a total failure because it has basically taken the mentally ill out of the hospitals and put them on the streets or in the jails (Isaac and Armat 1990; Gilligan 2001).

Studies of the homeless illustrate the way in which deinstitutionalization has failed. A majority of the homeless have serious problems of mental illness, including drug addiction (Sleegers 2000; National Coalition for the Homeless 2006d). Homeless shelters are available, but they are hardly adequate to provide treatment for the mentally ill

As a result of deinstitutionalization, many severely mentally ill patients have become homeless.

even if the staff had the time. Thus, large numbers of the deinstitutionalized mentally ill are lost and homeless or in jails. The problem is compounded by laws that make it difficult to involuntarily hospitalize the mentally ill. Thus, the legal basis for the deinstitutionalization movement—the rights of patients—keeps some mentally ill individuals at liberty until they act violently toward themselves or others (Isaac and Armat 1990). Unfortunately, most individuals with severe mental disorders require medication, and the disorders are likely to impair their judgment and make it unlikely that they will voluntarily submit to treatment.

Other problems created by deinstitutionalization include economic strain on Medicare and Medicaid budgets, adverse citizen reactions to the presence of patients in their communities, citizen fears about the dangers and lowered property values that might result if a small group home for mental patients is set up in their communities, and increased stress on individuals who must care for a chronically mentally ill family member (Wright, Avirappattu, and Lafuze 1999).

Individual Freedom

Americans are an individualistic people. They cherish the *freedom of the individual* and tend to react strongly to anything that threatens that freedom. However, there is sometimes a contradiction between the value of individual freedom and the value of good health. Some religious groups, for example, resist medical procedures such as blood transfusions and vaccinations on the grounds that these procedures violate their religious beliefs. If they are forced to undergo such medical treatment, their religious convictions and freedom of choice are violated. However, a counterargument is made that they may jeopardize the health or the lives of others by their refusal; thus, their freedom cannot extend to the point at which it affects the well-being of others. The same issue of individual freedom versus public well-being arises in such issues as providing a health identification number for every individual, mandatory notification of the parents of adolescents who use health care services, and the right of noncompliance with treatment of tuberculosis and other infectious diseases (Netter 2003; Adams 2004; Senanayake and Ferson 2004).

The issue of freedom is also raised by advances in biological engineering. The 1972 National Sickle Cell Anemia Control Act required people to submit to a screening blood test to determine the likelihood of their producing children with sickle cell anemia. Many people felt that this law was a clear invasion of privacy. Many more would probably consider it an invasion of privacy if the next step were taken: preventing people with certain genetic deficiencies from having children or even from marrying. Certain genetic diseases can be controlled only by forbidding certain couples to have children. Which, then, is more important: individual freedom or public health and welfare?

The history of medicine is marked by ongoing conflict between the advocates of medical advance and those who defend the freedom of the individual. Greater advances in medicine will intensify the conflict and compound the problems.

Economic Costs

An increasing amount of the nation's *economic resources* is channeled into the effort to combat illness and promote good health. From 1960 to 2005, national health expenditures rose from $26.9 billion to over $2 trillion and are projected to reach more than $4 trillion by 2015 (U.S. Census Bureau 2007). Thus, illness involves *a societal cost* as well as a personal cost.

The personal cost can be massive. About a fifth of Americans live in families in which health care costs more than 10 percent of family income (Banthin and Bernard 2006). And 7.3 percent are living in families in which the costs are 20 percent or more of family income. Such burdensome costs often result from long-term chronic diseases and from diseases requiring the use of *sophisticated medical technology.* Even with health insurance, an individual or a family may *find the cost of illness oppressive.* Why the dramatic increase in costs? Three factors can account for the increase in expenditures on medical care since 1950: inflation, population growth, and technological advances and the increasing use of medical services involving these expensive advances (Callahan 1998).

Thus, an increasing portion of the economic resources of individuals, families, and the nation are consumed by medical care (Toner and Stolberg 2002). The national cost of mental disorders exceeds $150 billion and may increase rapidly (National Institute of Mental Health 2004). A part of this cost is the value of goods and services not produced because of illness. For example, workers with depression cost employers an estimated $44 billion per year in lost productive time (Stewart et al. 2003). Physical illness also results in lost productive time; in a national study, 13 percent of the workforce experienced a loss in productive time during a two-week period because of a common pain condition (headaches, back pain, arthritis pain, etc.) (Stewart et al. 2003). With the costs of both physical and mental health care continuing to rise each year, an interesting question arises. Despite the high value placed on good health, is there a point at which Americans will forgo some measure of health care in order to retain more of their economic resources?

Contributing Factors

We have pointed out that there are sociocultural factors in illness. In this section we examine some of those factors in detail. We show that sociocultural factors are involved not only in the **etiology** (causes of diseases) but also in inadequate care and the maldistribution of care.

etiology
the causes of a disease

Social Structural Factors

Roles. Many studies have shown that *stress* leads to a variety of physical and mental health problems, including cardiovascular disease, digestive problems, heightened susceptibility to infection, problems of the skeletal-muscular system, and mental disorders (Mayer, Craske, and Naliboff 2001; House 2002). Stress can be a product of roles that are excessively demanding, contradictory, or overly restrictive. Not everyone who occupies a particular role will experience the same amount of stress, nor will everyone who occupies a particular role get sick. Nonetheless, *certain roles are considered stress-inducing* because they have been associated with a disproportionate amount of illness, particularly the female role and certain occupational roles in American society.

Women seem to have more health problems than men. Health statistics consistently show that women in the United States and other Western nations have higher rates of **morbidity,** health service usage, and certain mental disorders (Ladwig et al. 2000; Kendler, Thornton, and Prescott 2001; National Center for Health Statistics 2006). In part, these health problems reflect the fact that women generally suffer more distress

morbidity
the prevalence of a specified illness in a specified area

(sadness, anger, anxiety, aches, etc.) than men (Mirowsky and Ross 1995)—and this, in turn, may be rooted in the female role.

One characteristic of the female role is that *women are more emotionally involved than are men in the lives of the people around them* (Kessler and McLeod 1984). Women are more likely than men to be stressed by "network" events (events in the lives of loved ones) such as the death of a spouse, divorce, and illness of a family member. The cost of this caring is greater vulnerability to stress and illness.

The *traditional role of married women* is another reason for higher rates of illness (DeStafano and Colasanto 1990). Married women have higher rates of mental disorders than married men, but single or widowed women tend to have lower rates than their male counterparts. (Among both sexes, married people have lower rates than unmarried [Robins and Regier 1991].)

We have noted that the majority of married women now work outside the home. Is it, then, a problem of overload? Interestingly, working tends to enhance rather than diminish the health of women (Hibbard and Pope 1991). In other words, *multiple roles are associated with better health* (Hong and Seltzer 1995; Ahrens and Ryff 2006). The point is, the restrictions of the traditional role—staying at home and taking care of the house and children—are more stressful for many women than taking on additional responsibilities. To be sure, some women find the traditional role fulfilling, but others do not. Women who are confined to, but dissatisfied with, the traditional role of housewife exhibit the higher rates of illness (Shehan, Burg, and Rexroat 1986). This conclusion is supported by research showing that when men and women have equivalent gender roles, the gender differences in health tend to disappear (Bird and Fremont 1991; Gutierrez-Lobos 2000). In sum, for both men and women, role satisfaction is associated with better health (Wickrama et al. 1995).

We noted in chapter 10 that certain occupational roles generate considerable physical and/or mental risks. In some cases, the occupational role may carry intrinsic risks—for example, mining occupations or high-pressure sales jobs. In other cases, the risks reflect the particular shape the role is given by the people in the workplace. For example, an engineer told us:

> I love my work. But I hate this job. My boss terrorizes everyone. If it was just the work I do, I would love going in. But I get a feeling of dread when I go through the gates every morning because I never know from one day to the next what new craziness we'll all have to endure from the boss. His demands are unreasonable, and you can't sit down and discuss things with him. He has managed to turn enjoyable work into a daily grind.

The Family Context of Illness.   Among the institutional arrangements that contribute to illness are family patterns of interaction and **socialization** (the process by which an individual learns to participate in a group). We noted in the previous section that married people of both sexes have lower rates of mental illness than the unmarried. The mental health of the married couple depends on the quality of the marriage, however. When the intimate relationship between a man and a woman is defined by both as basically rewarding, the pair is more likely to enjoy positive mental and physical health (Lee and Bulanda 2005; Kaplan and Kronick 2006; Tower and Krasner 2006). Infidelity or a conflicted relationship, in contrast, is associated with major depression (Cano and O'Leary 2000).

For children, both physical and mental health are crucially related to the *quality of the relationship between the child and parents* (Feeney 2000). Children who have a good relationship with their parents and who feel themselves to be an integral part of

socialization
the process by which an individual learns to participate in a group

Many workers are exposed to carcinogenic materials in their workplace.

family life are less likely to engage in various kinds of health risk behavior, including the use of alcohol, tobacco, and other drugs (Resnick et al. 1997).

Family disruption is stressful for children and typically leads to higher rates of physical and emotional problems. A study of two-year-olds, for example, reported a higher proportion of accidents and higher rates of treatment for physical illnesses among those in single-parent and stepfamilies than those in intact homes (Dunn et al. 2000).

The adverse effects of a troubled family life may continue into adulthood. A long-term study of physicians reported that those who developed cancer or mental illness or who committed suicide had scored significantly lower on tests of family relationships taken when they were medical students (Locke and Colligan 1986). They felt less close to their parents and less emotionally attached to their families than did other physicians.

Siblings as well as parents are important to a child's well-being. Thus, in a community study, researchers found that children who had siblings with a substance abuse problem were more likely both to use drugs themselves and to suffer from depression (Reinherz et al. 2000). They also found more depression among children whose parents were depressed.

The Industrial Economy. Certain aspects of the American economy, and indeed of the world economy, are involved in the onset of illness. In an increasingly industrial, technological world, people and materials move around the globe in great numbers. An infectious virus can now travel around the world in a few hours.

In the modern economy, both agricultural workers (because of the use of artificial fertilizers, herbicides, and pesticides) and other workers are exposed to materials that are **carcinogenic** (cancer-causing). Some common carcinogens in nonagricultural occupations are shown in table 13.3. People who work in industries using carcinogenic materials are more likely to get cancer than are others.

carcinogenic
causing cancer

An industrial economy also exposes the citizenry to illness through *different kinds of pollution*. Lead poisoning can have disastrous effects on children: mental retardation, behavioral difficulties, perceptual problems, and emotional instability. Lead poisoning is most common among ghetto children, who ingest chips of paint from flaking

Agent	Organ Affected	Occupation
Wood	Nasal cavity and sinuses	Woodworkers
Leather	Nasal cavity and sinuses; urinary bladder	Leather and shoe workers
Iron oxide	Lung; larynx	Iron ore miners; metal grinders and polishers; silver finishers; iron foundry workers
Nickel	Nasal sinuses; lung	Nickel smelters, mixers, and roasters; electrolysis workers
Arsenic	Skin; lung; liver	Miners; smelters; insecticide makers and sprayers; tanners: chemical workers; oil refiners; vintners
Chromium	Nasal cavity and sinuses; lung; larynx	Chromium producers, processors, and users; acetylene and aniline workers; bleachers; glass, pottery, and linoleum workers; battery makers
Asbestos	Lung (pleural and peritoneal mesothelioma)	Miners; millers; textile and shipyard workers
Petroleum, petroleum coke, wax, creosote, shale, and mineral oils	Nasal cavity; larynx; lung; skin; scrotum	Workers in contact with lubricating oils, cooling oils, paraffin or wax fuel oils or coke; rubber fillers; retort workers: textile weavers, diesel jet testers
Mustard gas	Larynx; lung; trachea; bronchi	Mustard gas workers
Vinyl chloride	Liver; brain	Plastic workers
Bis-chloromethyl ether, chloromethyl methyl ether	Lung	Chemical workers
Isopropyl oil	Nasal cavity	Isopropyl oil producers
Coal soot, coal tar, other products of coal combustion	Lung; larynx; skin; scrotum; urinary bladder	Gashouse workers, stokers, and producers; asphalt, coal tar, and pitch workers; coke oven workers; miners; still cleaners
Benzene	Bone marrow	Explosives, benzene, or rubber cement workers; distillers; dye users; painters; shoemakers
Auramine, benzidine, alpha-naphthylamine, magenta, 4-aminodiphenyl, 4-nitrodiphenyl	Urinary bladder	Dyestuffs manufacturers and users; rubber workers (pressmen, filtermen, laborers); textile dyers; paint manufacturers

TABLE 13.3
Common Occupational Carcinogens

SOURCE: American Public Health Association; *Health and Work in America* (Washington, DC: Government Printing Office, 1975).

walls or other substances containing lead (Richardson 2002). Use of lead in paint was discontinued for the most part by 1950, but leaded paint still exists in older buildings. Craving for such unnatural substances—a condition called **pica**—is frequently associated with impoverished living. In rural areas, pica may lead to eating dirt and clay, which is not healthful but is probably less damaging than leaded paint.

The most familiar pollutant to many Americans is automobile exhaust, which contains carbon monoxide. Carbon monoxide poisoning can lead to apathy, headaches, perceptual problems, retardation, and even psychosis. However, the precise effects of carbon monoxide poisoning are unclear. The amount of carbon monoxide released into the air from automobile exhaust varies considerably from one area to another. We discuss chemical pollutants further in chapter 15.

Noise is another kind of pollution linked to the industrial economy that can have deleterious effects. The noise level endured by some workers can create mental stress, as can road traffic noise and the noise associated with living near an airport (Stansfeld and Matheson 2003). Children appear to be particularly vulnerable to noise pollution. Environmental noise can impair reading comprehension, long-term memory, and motivation and may also be associated with elevated blood pressure (Haines et al. 2003; Stansfeld and Matheson 2003). A study of German children concluded that high exposure to traffic noise, especially at nighttime, stimulates bodily processes that increase the problem of bronchitis (Ising et al. 2004).

As we noted in chapter 10, *fluctuations in the state of the economy* also have been identified as having adverse effects on people's health. Unemployment is associated with health problems in all societies (Rodriguez 2001). In fact, a study of 42 nations showed that unemployment lowers well-being even in those countries with high levels of social security (Ouweneel 2002).

The Politics of Illness.   Usually people do not think of illness as a political issue, but *government policy* is a crucial factor in health care. We noted earlier the large number of Americans without health insurance. Many other nations have national health insurance, but efforts to enact such a program in the United States have failed. As Quadagno (2005) has shown, the resistance by physicians, business, and insurers has effectively prevented a national plan. In effect, the *government has yielded to special, powerful interests to the detriment of millions of Americans' well-being.*

Political factors also enter into the struggle against various health problems and diseases. American infant mortality rates, for example, are higher than the rates of many other nations, and the rate for African Americans is nearly 2.5 times that for whites (U.S. Census Bureau 2007). Yet the African Americans most at risk—those in impoverished areas—are least likely to have the political influence necessary to secure federal funds for infant health programs.

Funding for research into causes and cures of diseases also reflects political as well as scientific and humanitarian considerations, as exemplified by the current controversy over *stem cell research* (Rosenberg 2002). Stem cells are obtained from human embryos, which are destroyed in the process. The medical value of embryonic stem cells lies in the fact that they can become any type of cell in a child or adult, which means that they have the potential to cure a variety of diseases that result from particular cells in the body being disabled or destroyed (diabetes, Parkinson's disease, cirrhosis of the liver, etc.).

But because the embryos are destroyed in the process, the Bush administration limited federal funding of research to existing stem cell lines in 2001. Many researchers

pica
a craving for unnatural substances, such as dirt or clay

consider these lines to be inadequate in number and of poor quality (Hampton 2006). But under the law, no new lines could be created by researchers who are federally funded. The scientific community claimed that the restrictions would severely hamper research that could lead to cures for many debilitating diseases. A few researchers considered moving to another nation, such as England, where the research can be freely pursued.

The decision to ban new lines was political and religious, not scientific (Dickens and Cook 2006). Roman Catholics and fundamentalist Protestants argue that human life begins at conception. Therefore, even though the stem cells may be harvested from a small cluster of cells rather than a viable human life, the destruction of the embryo is considered an act of murder. The Bush administration shared this perspective and imposed the ban in the name of respect for human life.

Responding to the promise of cures and the needs of researchers, some states have begun to fund the research. In 2004, California established a stem cell research institute that would provide $3 billion for research at state universities and research institutions (Hall 2007). Other states have approved the research and/or have begun the search for ways to fund it. Of course, if the political climate in the federal government changes, the research could be approved. In any case, it is clear that political decisions are at least as important as scientific ones in research that bears upon the health of Americans.

Finally, there is the issue of governmental regulations that can reduce exposure to a number of known health threats. Fagin and Lavelle (1999) ask why no regulations exist on such actions as the use of certain toxic weed killers that have been linked with cancer and birth defects in farming communities, the use by dry cleaners of a chemical that pollutes homes, and "dry clean only" labels in clothing that can now be cleaned by cheaper and safer water-based alternatives. Of course, the answer to these and the other examples they cite is that political considerations outweigh public health needs.

The Stratification of Illness.   When we speak of the stratification of illness, we are referring to the *different patterns of illness* and *variations in health care among the socioeconomic strata.* People in the lower strata have more physical health problems (including more chronic diseases) than people in the middle and upper strata; have more mental health problems; suffer more days of restricted activity due to illness; are less knowledgeable about and less likely to use health care services (including fewer visits to physicians and dentists); are less knowledgeable about and less likely to engage in good health practices (nonsmoking, proper diet, etc.); are less likely to have basic preventive health measures like vaccinations; and are far less likely to have health insurance (only about one in five of those in poverty are insured) (Strohschein 2005a; Lawlor et al. 2006; National Center for Health Statistics 2006; Shishehbor, Litaker, Pothier, and Lauer 2006). They are also likely to die at an earlier age even when their health risk behavior is no different from the behavior of people in higher strata (Lantz et al. 1998; Steenland, Hu, and Walker 2004).

Ironically, then, poor and uneducated Americans have the fewest resources to meet medical expenses and the greatest likelihood of discovering that they have a serious, chronic, disabling, or even fatal illness. The pattern of physical illness in American society—more problems and less help as people descend the socioeconomic ladder—is likely to continue because of both the lack of information and resources among the poor and the concentration of medical services outside the areas where they live.

The pattern for mental illness is similar. In general, the rates of psychiatric disorders are higher in the lower strata (Wheaton and Clarke 2003; Williams, Takeuchi, and Adair 1992; Turner and Lloyd 1999; Gilman et al. 2002).

The higher rates of illness in the lower strata reflect in part their lower likelihood of having health insurance and regular health care. They also reflect, however, the greater number and intensity of stressors in their lives: more role problems, more family disorganization, more financial stress, and a greater number of stressful life events (Grzywacz et al. 2004; Lantz, House, Mero, and Williams 2005).

Changing Structure: The Future Shock Thesis. Both the nature of the social structure and the *structure's rate of change* influence health and illness. When norms, roles, institutional arrangements, and the stratification system are in rapid flux, the individual may endure considerable stress, which can result in illness. The individual may be so overwhelmed by the lack of stability in the world that he or she may succumb to *"future shock"* (Toffler 1970).

One effort to determine the effects of change on illness involves the use of the Social Readjustment Rating Scale. A respondent indicates which of the 43 events composing the scale have occurred to him or her within the last year. The events include role changes (such as death of spouse, divorce or marriage, beginning or stopping work) and changes in institutional participation (school, church activities, financial status). Each event is rated in terms of how much adjustment it requires. Scores range from 100 for the most stressful event (death of a spouse) to 11 for the least stressful (a minor violation of the law). The total score reflects the number and kinds of events that have occurred in an individual's life during the previous year. In one study, 79 percent of people scoring 300 or above, 51 percent of those scoring between 200 and 299, and 37 percent of those scoring between 150 and 199 had changes in their health in the following year (Holmes and Masuda 1974).

Considerable research since the early 1970s supports the thesis. For example, a high rate of change in life events can result in more injuries (Lee et al. 1989), panic attacks (Pollard, Pollard, and Corn 1989), a lessening of the body's ability to ward off disease (Zautra et al. 1989), and various other physical and emotional disorders (Turner and Lloyd 1995; McQuaid et al. 2000; Tiet et al. 2001).

Note, however, that although a rapid rate of change does increase stress, the stress may be moderated if the people perceive the changes as desirable (Lauer 1974; Vinokur and Selzer 1975). It is *undesirable life events,* rather than change per se, that are likely to cause illness (Seivewright 1987). People may function in a context of rapid change with minimal effects on their physical and mental health as long as they desire the changes that are occurring (and, perhaps, as long as they have areas of stability in the midst of the change).

Social Psychological Factors

Attitudes and Values. Certain attitudes and values of individuals who are ill, of the public, and of medical personnel affect rates of illness and the nature of health care. Negative attitudes toward one's work can increase the risk of illness. An individual's work is a focal point of his or her existence as well as one of the most time-consuming areas of life. If it is defined in negative terms, the risk of illness is increased (Spector 2002).

A particular personality type, identified by a cluster of attitudes and values, has an increased probability of coronary heart disease (Eaker et al. 2004). Men who are ambitious, highly competitive, and self-driving and who impose frequent deadlines on themselves have a higher incidence of coronary heart disease than do men with opposite characteristics (Ganster 1986; Rosenman 1990). All these characteristics are admired in American society; they are long-standing American values. Unfortunately, when accepted and followed diligently, they are also the precursors of illness.

The sick person's attitudes about his or her illness and prospects for recovery are another important factor. Some people are skeptical about the ability of medical care to affect their health (Fiscella, Franks, and Clancy 1998). Such skepticism is stronger among young, white males in the lower socioeconomic strata. In contrast, other people believe that their prospects for recovery from illness are very good. They rely confidently on medical help and, in some cases, also believe that God is at work to bring about healing. Positive attitudes, especially ones that are grounded in spirituality, are associated with shorter and fewer illnesses, improved immune functioning, better mental health, and longer life (Phillips, Ruth, and Wagner 1993; Oxman, Freeman, and Manheimer 1995; Braam et al. 2004; Kliewer 2004).

The attitudes of other people may be as important as the ill person's own attitudes. We have noted the stigma that is associated with certain kinds of physical and mental illness, a stigma that creates adverse reactions in individuals who are ill. For example, people with Parkinson's disease tend to feel ashamed and want to withdraw from public situations because, among other difficulties, they are unable to control their saliva and have difficulty speaking (Nijhof 1995). They are aware of the embarrassment and unease created in people with whom they interact.

fallacy

Mental illness tends to be even more of a stigma, so much so that many Americans who would benefit from therapy either refuse to seek help or drop out before the therapy is complete (Corrigan 2004). The stigma of mental illness is fueled by a number of myths (Socall and Holtgraves 1992; Wahl 2003). The myths are a form of the *fallacy of personal attack,* because they stigmatize current and past mental patients. The following are some of the common myths:

A person who has been mentally ill can never be normal.

Persons with mental illness are unpredictable.

Mentally ill persons are dangerous.

Anyone who has had shock treatment must be in a really bad way.

When you learn that a person has been mentally ill, you have learned the most important thing about his or her personality.

A former mental patient will make a second-rate employee (National Institute of Mental Health 1988).

These statements are myths. Note, however, that although the vast majority of people with serious mental illness are no more dangerous than those in the general population, there is a subgroup of the mentally ill that does pose a risk of acting violently (Torrey 1994; Swanson et al. 2002). People with a history of violent behavior, those who do not take their medication, and those with a problem of substance abuse are more likely than other people to engage in violent behavior. Yet for the great majority of the mentally ill, all the statements just listed, including the statement that they are dangerous, are myths.

The myths illustrate the way in which people who are troubled or different tend to be labeled. Thomas Scheff (1966) made the most thorough use of labeling theory to analyze mental illness. According to Scheff, the mentally ill are *rule breakers,* though

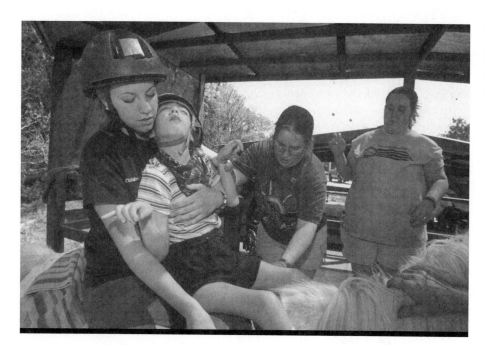

Some mental and physical illnesses are more difficult to cope with because of public stigma.

the rules they break are different from the rules criminals break. The mentally ill break rules that govern normal social interaction, rules that define "common decency" and indicate an acceptance of social reality as defined by the group. Everyone occasionally breaks such rules with impunity. You may, for example, overreact to an insult, refuse to talk to someone who has angered you, or talk too loudly or too softly. The person who consistently breaks the rules of conventional interaction runs the risk of being labeled mentally ill.

Yet not everyone who breaks the rules is labeled mentally ill. In fact, most rule breaking is "denied and is of transitory significance" (Scheff 1966:51). A certain amount of rule breaking always goes unnoticed or unpunished. The response of other people varies in accord with the kinds of rules that are broken. Loud speech, for example, is less likely to be negatively sanctioned than the refusal to speak at all.

How do people know when to label someone as mentally ill when there are various kinds of behavior that break rules? Scheff points out that *stereotyped imagery of mental illness* is learned early in life and that these stereotypes are reinforced in normal interaction. People avoid behavior that is a stereotype of mental illness and thereby reinforce the image of that behavior as a symptom of mental illness. Furthermore, they evaluate others according to the stereotype.

If an individual behaves in accord with the stereotype, he or she may be labeled mentally ill and rewarded for playing out the stereotyped role. Moreover, the individual may be punished for any attempt to abandon the role and adopt more conventional behavior. This objection occurs because people desire a *predictable social order,* that is, they expect to know how a mentally ill person behaves even if they do not define that behavior as desirable. Just as criminals who avow they are beginning new, law-abiding lives are likely to be treated with some suspicion (their behavior is no longer predictable), the mentally ill who seem to be recovering may be told that they are not as well as they think. In other words, once an individual is labeled as ill, the responses of other people tend to perpetuate the behavior involved.

Scheff denied that his is a complete explanation of mental illness. His aim was not to supplant psychiatric approaches but to supplement them and to stimulate new thinking about mental illness.

Evidence shows that labels do have a significant impact (Markham 2003). In an important study, Link (1987) found that people who were labeled (former patients and repeat patients), compared to people who were not labeled (first-treatment patients, untreated cases in the community, and people with no severe psychopathology), were more likely to believe that they would be devalued and discriminated against by most people. The results of these beliefs were higher rates of demoralization, unemployment, and income loss. Moreover, patients and former patients may become secretive and withdrawn because of their fears of rejection, weakening the social support system that is important to their well-being (Link et al. 1989). Unfortunately, various strategies (like avoidance-withdrawal, secretiveness, and attempts to educate others) for trying to cope with the stigma are ineffective and may do more harm than good (Link, Mirotznik, and Cullen 1991). Labeling is a powerful social factor, and even if it does not directly lead to mental illness, it clearly seems to have negative outcomes (Rosenfield 1997).

Attitudes and values also affect medical care of physical illness. The *distribution of physicians* in the United States does not reflect medical need. Physicians, of course, are attracted to places that have desirable resources, abundant professional opportunities, and an active medical community. They also cluster in areas where they are likely to maximize their income. This pattern has been characteristic for some time, and it implicitly means that many Americans are receiving inadequate medical care. Apparently, physicians' attitudes toward working with the less affluent and the value physicians place on income outweigh their commitment to good medical care for all.

The attitudes and values of physicians have inhibited development of governmental programs that would reduce the maldistribution of medical care. Although most physicians now accept and even support Medicare, the American Medical Association (AMA) vigorously opposed the program when it was first proposed. Earlier, organized medicine had opposed Blue Cross plans for many of the same reasons. In both cases the financial benefits to physicians have been enormous. The programs also have provided more Americans with better medical care. Yet this result has often been in spite of, rather than because of, the attitudes and values of physicians.

Public Policy and Private Action

As in the case of drug and alcohol abuse, more money and effort have been expended on the treatment of ill health than on its prevention. In order to change this focus, there needs to be an expansion or improvement of existing programs and the development of new, innovative programs. An example of an existing program that can be expanded is the neighborhood health center, which addresses the maldistribution of care by bringing medical services to previously neglected groups. Poor people, minority groups, and residents of rural areas have benefited from these federally funded centers (Wright et al. 2000). However, the centers have faced difficulties in maintaining a stable professional staff and receiving adequate funding from the federal government.

Innovations in the Delivery of Health Care

There is a need for ongoing innovations that effectively deliver health care. For example, an innovation that has emerged in the face of escalating costs is the *managed-care plan, which includes health maintenance organizations (HMOs), point-of-service (POS) plans, and preferred provider organizations (PPOs).* The original idea of the HMO was to offer people a comprehensive, prepaid health care plan. The individual pays an annual fee and receives total medical care, including necessary hospitalization and/or surgery. There are different kinds of HMOs, but one of the important distinctions for the quality of care is that of the not-for-profit versus the investor-owned HMO. An analysis of 248 investor-owned and 81 not-for-profit HMOs concluded that the investor-owned delivered lower quality of health care on every measure used (Himmelstein et al. 1999), and a national survey found that patients in the not-for-profit HMOs were more likely to be very satisfied with their care than were patients in the investor-owned groups (Tu and Reschovsky 2002).

There are problems with care by an HMO. One is that administrators who are not physicians or therapists are making decisions about the kind and the length of treatment that will be allowed. Their decisions may be based on keeping costs at a minimum rather than on doing what the physician or therapist considers best for the patient.

Another problem is *capitation,* which means that the doctor receives a fixed monthly amount for each patient (Kuttner 1998). Any additional costs incurred in the treatment of patients must be absorbed by the physician or group of physicians involved. Therapists face the same dilemma in treating mental disorders.

HMOs, in sum, may not provide the solution that some Americans hoped. On the one hand, many people are satisfied with the health care they receive under their HMO, and HMOs do increase physician visits and the use of such preventive services as mammography screening and flu shots (Tu, Kemper, and Wong 2000). On the other hand, people in HMOs get less care from specialists and are less likely than those in non-HMOs to be satisfied with their care and to trust their physicians (Kemper, Reschovsky, and Tu 2000).

Dissatisfaction with HMOs has led to a growth in the use of the point-of-service (POS) and preferred provider organization (PPO) plans. The *point-of-service* plan allows a patient to go to a health care provider outside the HMO, but the patient must bear the additional cost. The *preferred provider organization* is composed of a network of physicians and hospitals that offer care at discounted rates. A particular PPO may contract with HMOs to treat their patients. The difference is that the physicians remain in their own offices and have patients other than those who come from the HMO.

Clearly, managed-care plans face a dilemma: how to give adequate care while maximizing profits or without entailing exorbitant costs. At the heart of the issue of costs is this question: Who will pay for health insurance—the individual, employers, the government, or some combination of the three?

Employers have been increasingly reluctant to pay for such insurance, leaving tens of millions of Americans without any health insurance. Without some kind of intervention from the federal government, it is unlikely that this problem can be effectively resolved.

Innovations in Treatment

Innovations in treatment are also needed. There are, of course, continuing technological innovations that facilitate diagnosis and treatment of various physical illnesses; but there is a need for innovations that consider the close relationships between physical and mental health and between mind and body. The mind plays a key role in health, a fact that needs further exploration and exploitation (Jacobs 2001).

Innovations in the treatment of mental disorders also have been developed in an effort to achieve quicker, more effective results. One approach is the *community support system* (Stroul 1989; Roskes et al. 1999). In essence, a variety of services, supports, and opportunities are set up within communities to enable mental patients to function. Among other benefits, the support system can include therapy, health and dental care, a crisis-response service, housing, income maintenance, family and community support, and protection and advocacy services. Community support systems can be more effective than hospitalization in dealing with mental illness (Chinman et al. 2001).

Another program offers support to the patient's family when the family is the primary caretaker of the chronically ill person (Ferris and Marshall 1987; Bull and McShane 2002). Family care, which is an alternative to hospitalization, generates various kinds of stress. Groups of families entrusted with the care of a chronically ill member meet for support, skill training, and information. With the aid of a mental health professional, the families are able to form a support group that enables each of them to cope with the difficult task. Some professionals believe that a family-oriented approach offers the highest probability of a positive outcome for mentally ill individuals (Schmidt 1989).

Prevention

It is usually much less costly and always more beneficial to people to *prevent illnesses* than to treat them once they have emerged. Preventive medical care includes such things as the neighborhood or community health centers that provide checkups for early detection or prevention of physical illness. Similarly, "preventive psychiatry" has emerged as an effort at early detection of mental disorders. Any realistic effort at prevention has to address the sources of stress in society. Stress-inducing roles must be changed. Help must be provided for troubled families. Economic deprivation must be eliminated. Government policy and its agencies must be responsive to health needs rather than to business interests.

One program of prevention that gained momentum in the 1980s is aimed at minimizing or eliminating smoking. Spurred by reports from the surgeon general and antismoking groups, the federal government has banned or restricted smoking in all federal facilities. Many states have done the same, or have gone even further. California, for example, forbids smoking in all public buildings, including restaurants. Such measures, along with increased education and higher taxes on cigarettes, have resulted in a substantial decline in the number of Americans who smoke.

Finally, *a crucial aspect of prevention is lifestyle.* In fact, the three leading causes of death in America are all related to lifestyle. In 2000, the leading causes of death were tobacco (18.1 percent of all deaths), poor diet and physical inactivity (16.6 percent of all deaths), and alcohol consumption (3.5 percent of all deaths) (Mokdad et al. 2004). Nevertheless, in spite of considerable information about the value of a healthy lifestyle, *the lifestyle of Americans is becoming less rather than more healthy.* Less than half of American adults engage in an adequate amount of leisure-time physical activity (where "adequate" means enough to maintain optimum health (U.S. Census Bureau 2007). The annual per capita consumption of fats and oils increased from 56.9 pounds in 1980 to 87.5 pounds in 2004 (U.S. Census Bureau 2007). And as noted earlier, nearly a third of adults and 17.1 percent of children are obese. Obesity makes people more vulnerable to disability and various diseases, including arthritis, diabetes, and cancer (Ferraro and Kelley-Moore 2003; Calle et al. 2003; Leveille, Wee, and Iezzoni 2005). Researchers estimate that obesity causes more than 100,000 excess deaths in the United States each year, and is the seventh leading cause of death (Flegal, Graubard, Williamson, and Gail 2005; Johnson 2005). Obesity is a problem in other nations as well; the World Health Organization estimates that more than half of the deaths in the world are caused by obesity-related illnesses such as heart disease and type 2 diabetes (Okie 2005).

The point is, you have a good deal of control over your own health, and you choose to ignore that control at your own peril. A healthy lifestyle is essential for both physical and mental health.

Follow-Up.   In what ways do you try to manage your lifestyle in an attempt to prevent illness? What more could you do?

Summary

Good health is a primary value of Americans. Some advances have been made, as indicated by the increasing life expectancy. The main problem of physical health today is chronic diseases rather than the infectious diseases that plagued society in earlier times. Millions of Americans are limited in their activities because of chronic conditions. There is general agreement about the classification of mental disorders, which are found in all societies.

Illness affects the quality of life in many ways. The illness itself and the inadequate care that many Americans receive cause stress and suffering. Interpersonal relationships are adversely affected. Individual freedom is threatened by certain medical advances. Often, heavy economic costs are involved for the nation and for individuals. Both physical and mental illnesses cause fears and anxiety. There is, in fact, a close relationship between physical and mental illness; each can be a factor in bringing about the other, so the individual can be caught in a vicious circle.

Structural factors contribute to the problem. Certain stress-inducing roles have been associated with illness, especially the female role and certain occupational roles. Patterns of interaction and socialization in the family can promote or inhibit good physical and mental health. The industrial economy exposes people to carcinogenic materials and to various pollutants. Fluctuations in the economy generate stress. Political decisions reflect economic interests rather than health needs.

Health care problems are more serious for individuals in the lower than the higher socioeconomic strata. People in the lower strata suffer higher rates of mental and physical illness and receive less adequate care for both. Also, different kinds of illness characterize the various socioeconomic strata.

One other important structural factor is the rate of change of the structure itself. There is evidence that rapid change may result in illness. A crucial factor in the effects of a changing structure is whether the people define the changes as desirable.

Among social psychological factors, attitudes and values are related to illness. The ill person's attitudes about the illness and his or her prospects for recovery are important. Negative attitudes toward work and certain attitudes rooted in traditional American values increase the probability of illness. Once a person is ill, negative attitudes of other people can inhibit recovery—a problem stressed by labeling theory. The attitudes and values of physicians have contributed to the maldistribution of care and have delayed federal programs designed to correct that maldistribution. These attitudes and values are supported by the ideology of free enterprise, which stresses governmental noninterference in medical care.

Key Terms

AIDS	Morbidity
Carcinogenic	Neurosis
Deinstitution-	Pica
alization	Prevalence
Epidemiology	Psychosis
Etiology	Psychosomatic
Iatrogenic	Disorder
Incidence	Schizophrenia
Life Expectancy	Socialization
Manic-Depressive	Stigma
Reaction	

Study Questions

1. What are the various kinds of physical and mental illness, and how prevalent are they?
2. What kinds of suffering are associated with illness?
3. How does problematic health affect interpersonal relationships?
4. In what sense can it be said that Americans have inadequate health care? How has deinstitutionalization contributed to this problem?
5. How does illness affect individual freedom?
6. What are the economic costs of health and illness?
7. How do gender and occupational roles contribute to health and illness?
8. In what ways is the health problem affected by the family, the economy, and the polity?
9. What kinds of attitudes and values on the part of those who are ill, the public, and health personnel affect rates of illness and the nature of health care?
10. What innovations could help ameliorate the health problem?

Internet Resources/ Exercises

1. Explore some of the ideas in this chapter on the following sites:

http://www.cdc.gov/nchs The National Center for Health Statistics site has the most comprehensive collection of health data available.

http://www.mentalhealth.org The site of the U.S. Substance Abuse and Mental Health Services Administration, with full coverage of news and data about mental health.

http://medlineplus.gov The National Library of Medicine site, which has information about all health topics.

2. Many nations have national health coverage. Search the Internet for programs in at least two industrialized nations. Compare information about coverage and health conditions in those nations with the United States. What facts could you use to support or to reject a national health program in this country?

3. There is an ongoing struggle in the United States. between consumer advocate groups, big business, and politicians over government regulations or potential regulations that bear upon health. Research a recent controversial issue. What were the arguments pro and con for federal regulation? What measures were taken by various groups to get acceptance for their position? Did the outcome, in your judgment, benefit or harm public well-being? Report your findings to the class.

For Further Reading

Blanc, Pul D. *How Everyday Products Make People Sick*. Berkeley, CA: University of California Press, 2007. A discussion of the kinds of everyday products, such as glue, bleach, a rayon scarf, or the wood in a patio deck, that can be hazardous to your health, including the difficulty of getting controls or alerting the public to the dangers.

Budrys, Grace. *Unequal Health: How Inequality Contributes to Health and Illness*. Lanham, MD: Rowman and Littlefield, 2003. Illustrates the various ways in which differing kinds of inequality, separately and in combination with each other, significantly affect health and illness throughout an individual's lifetime.

Charmaz, Kathleen C. *Good Days, Bad Days: The Self in Chronic Illness and Time*. New Brunswick, NJ: Rutgers University Press, 1991. Uses in-depth interviews to show how coping with a chronic illness affects people's lives, including their self-concepts.

Goodman, John C., Gerald L. Musgrave, and Devon M. Herrick. *Lives at Risk: Single-Payer National Health Insurance in Countries around the World*. Lanham, MD: Rowman and Littlefield, 2004. Examines the national health insurance systems of various countries and the problems that typically arise with such systems, particularly the way in which the problems intersect with politics.

Himmelstein, David, Steffie Woolhandler, and Ida Hellender. *Bleeding the Patient: The Consequences of Corporate Health Care*. Monroe, ME: Common Courage Press, 2001. A critique of profit-driven health care, showing the varied ways in which patients are victimized by the system.

Kearney, Margaret H. *Understanding Women's Recovery from Illness and Trauma*. Thousand Oaks, CA: Sage, 1999. Explores how women deal with health problems ranging from eating disorders to chronic illnesses of various kinds. Points out how the health and illness of women involve social and political factors.

Kreider, Katherine. *The Big Fix: How the Pharmaceutical Industry Rips Off American Consumers*. New York: Public Affairs, 2003. A detailed study of the prescription drug industry, including the methods used to market the drugs and the reasons that prices are so high.

Shorter, Edward. *From the Mind into the Body: The Cultural Origins of Psychosomatic Symptoms*. New York: Free Press, 1994. Argues that at least some illnesses reflect the fact that a certain number of people are born with a biological predisposition to develop physical symptoms in response to stressful situations. The symptoms, in turn, reflect what is currently fashionable in the way of ill health.

Whitaker, Robert. *Mad in America: Bad Science, Bad Medicine, and the Enduring Mistreatment of the Mentally Ill*. Cambridge, MA: Perseus Publishing, 2002. A history of how psychiatrists have treated schizophrenics, underscoring the fact that treatment is a trial-and-error process that changes from generation to generation.

PART

Global
Social
Problems

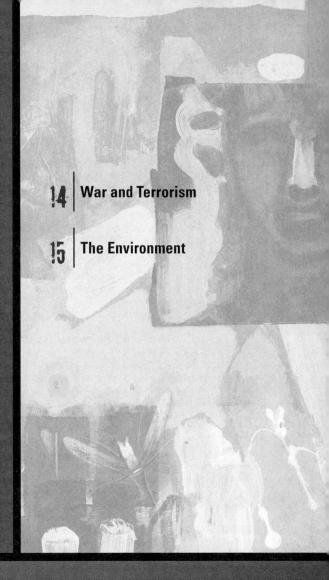

Is there hope for civilization? Ever since the invention of gunpowder, pessimists have been predicting that humans will destroy themselves with their own technology. Their pessimism doesn't seem all that far-fetched, particularly because war, terrorism, and environmental problems all pose serious threats to the quality of human life, if not to the very existence of the human race.

In this final part, we examine these problems. We cannot discuss them meaningfully without seeing them in their global context. The threat they pose goes beyond any particular nation and inevitably includes all nations. We examine war and terrorism first. Then we explore the vexing environmental problems that are not only threatening but also involve painful dilemmas.

War and Terrorism

1 Distinguish between war, civil war, and terrorism, and know the extent of each.

2 Discuss the varied ways in which war and terrorism detract from the quality of life.

3 Identify the political and economic factors that contribute to the problems of war and terrorism.

4 Explain the kinds of attitudes and ideologies that legitimate war and terrorism.

5 Suggest steps that can be taken to address the problems of war and terrorism.

"I Didn't Want to See It"

Steve is 22. He is a veteran of the 1991 war against Iraq. In many ways, Steve is fortunate. He was not wounded, and he has not suffered from posttraumatic stress syndrome. He returned home to a wife and baby girl with minimal problems of adjustment. But in another way, Steve also suffers from the war. His suffering is the memory of things he wished he had never seen:

When we chased the elite Iraqi forces back into their own country and literally overwhelmed them, we all felt a sense of pride and exultation. It was the sweet taste of victory. A victory that cost us very little in terms of lives. I wish I had come home immediately after that. But we were stationed for a time within the borders of Iraq, guarding against any return of their forces. That's when I saw the real costs of the war. I didn't want to see it. But I couldn't avoid it.

Every day we would face Iraqi children begging for food. We saw hundreds of refugees camped out in the desert, living in burned-out cars and trucks. When I came through one of the refugee camps, I nearly got ill.

But it was the children that really got to me. I have my own little girl. I couldn't help but think about her when I saw those Iraqi kids. Some of them would look at our guns and start crying. And then there were the mothers holding crying babies who needed food or medicine. And there was nothing at all we could do.

One day an Iraqi professor came up to us. She spoke English, and she went on and on about how miserable their lives were. They had no food, she said, and nothing but dirty water to drink. They had no drugs, no hospitals, and no way to treat people who were wounded or sick.

I tell you, the combat was frightening at times. But it was far easier than dealing with those hurting people. I don't think I'll ever be able to forget the children begging for food. I'm home. I'm safe. I guess the war is still going on for some of them.

Introduction

On September 11, 2001, four American passenger jets were hijacked by terrorists. Two of the planes crashed into the Twin Towers of the World Trade Center and a third slammed into the Pentagon. A fourth plane, headed for the White House, went down in Pennsylvania after passengers tried to stop the hijackers. With more than 3,000 deaths from this terrorist attack, "war" took on a new meaning for Americans.

The next month, the United States launched an attack on Afghanistan, where the perpetrators of the September 11 attack were believed to be in hiding. And in March 2003, the United States and Great Britain invaded Iraq, calling it Operation Iraqi Freedom and justifying the action on the grounds that the Iraqi government had ties with the terrorists and also had weapons of mass destruction that were threatening our two nations. Over the next few years, opposition to the war grew dramatically. In January 2007, when a CBS News poll asked Americans an open-ended question: "Of all the problems facing the country today, which one do you want the new Congress to concentrate on first?" 45 percent said the war in Iraq (The Polling Report 2007). The next most frequent response was the economy and jobs, named by only 7 percent. Terrorism was seventh on the list, named by 2 percent. Clearly, the war in Iraq had become an overriding concern, and terrorism was of greater concern than many other issues.

In this chapter, we begin by looking at the nature and extent of the problem. We show the ways that war and terrorism detract from the quality of life. We identify the sociocultural factors that contribute to the problem. Finally, we discuss some proposals for minimizing or eliminating war and terrorism.

War, Civil War, and Terrorism

When you hear the word "war," your first thought may be of armies from two opposing nations clashing with each other. However, this definition doesn't best describe present-day wars, which are more likely to be civil wars or wars of terrorism.

The New Face of War

Modern warfare is no longer confined to opposing armies facing each other on the battlefield. Nor is it merely a matter of nuclear powers confronting each other with the threat of mass destruction. Rather, the small armaments that have flooded the world can be used by dissidents to destroy a nation's infrastructure. And:

Civilians are targets as much as combatants, often more so. . . . Children fight alongside
adults. The front line may be someone's bedroom. Hospitals and libraries are fair game.
Even humanitarian aid workers become pawns. (Musser and Nemecek 2000:47)

Not only have the struggles spread from the battlefield to the bedroom, but increasingly they have involved civil wars and terrorism. *Civil war* is rebellion by dissident groups within a nation. If the groups are small, they may simply engage in acts of domestic terrorism (discussed in chapter 5). **International terrorism** is politically motivated violence against citizens of political entities different from those of the perpetrators in order to coerce and intimidate others into accepting the perpetrators' goals. Terrorism is not new, but the September 11, 2001, attacks made Americans painfully aware both of its destructive potential and of their vulnerability to it.

The Extent of the Problem

Wars and Civil Wars.   When the United States is not involved in war, Americans tend to think that the era is one of relative peace. Yet at any point in time the world experiences a large number of armed conflicts, including both wars and minor armed conflicts. A **war** is defined as a major armed conflict between nations or between organized groups within a nation in which 1,000 or more people are killed (Renner 1997). Minor armed conflicts may involve the same kind of weaponry and fighting, but they result in fewer deaths. The number of wars in the world has tended to decline since the early 1990s, but by 2005 there were still 28 wars in the world as well as sporadic armed conflicts (Renner 2006a).

Most wars in recent decades involve the developing nations of the world, but the United States and other developed nations can be drawn into the conflicts under certain circumstances. One such circumstance occurred in late 1990, when Iraq invaded and took over Kuwait. When Iraq refused to respond to U.N. demands to withdraw, a multinational force began a massive air bombardment in January 1991, thus starting the Gulf War.

Although the war was brief, the damage was massive and it should serve as a reminder that war is always possible. In fact, current events threaten future wars. As of this writing, the United States occupies Iraq and is caught in the midst of unstable and often chaotic conditions that most observers define as a civil war (Hashim 2007). Pakistan and India continue to struggle over Kashmir. Palestinians and Israelis continue to kill each other. Islamic terrorists in various parts of the world are calling on all Muslims to engage in a holy war against Israel and the United States. And the list goes on. The point is that *you live in a world that is never free of war or the threat of war.*

The bloodiest wars in recent years have been civil wars and wars involving just two nations (Renner 1999). More than 1.5 million died in the civil war in the Sudan (97 percent of them civilians), more than 1 million died in the Mozambican civil war from 1981 to 1994, nearly 4 million died in the war that broke out in the Democratic Republic of the Congo in 1998 (and continues in the northeastern region), and about 1.5 million died in the Soviet intervention in Afghanistan between 1978 and 1992. The incidence of civil wars has been increasing since the end of World War II (Fearon and Laitin 2002). They tend to involve ethnic minorities who want political autonomy or insurgents who want to take control of the government. Millions have died in these often-protracted wars.

Terrorism.   For most Americans prior to September 11, 2001, terrorism was something that was a problem elsewhere. Little was made in our news media about terrorism other than the acts of various leftist movements, the Irish Republican Army, and the

international terrorism
politically motivated violence against citizens of political entities different from those of the perpetrators in order to coerce and intimidate others into accepting the perpetrators' goals

war
a major armed conflict between nations or between organized groups within a nation in which a thousand or more people are killed

attacks on U.S. embassies in Kenya and Tanzania in 1998 that killed 301 people. Since the end of the Cold War, attacks by leftist groups have declined, while those by Islamist groups have increased dramatically (Robison, Crenshaw, and Jenkins 2006). The September 11 attack was the worst terrorist attack ever in terms of the number killed.

Nevertheless, Americans have suffered far fewer attacks and far fewer casualties than the rest of the world. According to the U.S. Department of State (2006), the known acts of terrorism against U.S. citizens in 2005 resulted in 56 deaths, 17 injuries, and 11 kidnappings. But for the world as a whole in 2005, about 40,000 individuals were wounded or killed in 11,111 terrorist attacks. These figures include Iraq, and therefore represent a sharp increase over previous years. Taking the incidents in Iraq out of the figures, the number of incidents and casualties remained fairly stable in the early 2000s.

Of course, the main purpose of terrorism is not merely to kill people. It is to use the killings and the destruction to dramatize a condition that the terrorists find unacceptable (Northern Ireland remaining under British control; Israel's domination of Palestinians; American troops in Muslim countries; etc.), and to warn people that none of them is safe as long as the condition persists. Thus, terrorist attacks in the past few years have included: a school in Russia in which 323 people, half of them children, were killed; suicide bombings in Egyptian resorts; the bombing of four commuter trains during morning rush hour in Madrid, Spain; the bombing of the Australian embassy in Jakarta, Indonesia; subway bombings in London, England; and more than 400 small bombs exploding in cities and towns in Bangladesh.

It is unlikely that terrorist attacks will decline significantly in the near future. An important reason is that there is no single group or cause involved. The State Department claims that some progress was made against the radical Islamist group, al-Qaida, by 2005, with the killing of a number of its key leaders and the disruption of its base operations in Afghanistan. But by that same year, al-Qaida had stepped up its propaganda campaign, thereby enlisting the cooperation of a variety of other groups throughout the world. Also, a number of smaller, loosely organized terrorist groups emerged. And the number of suicide bombers increased (the suicide bombing in London in 2005 was the first such attack in Europe). Thus, the report of the U.S. Department of State (2006) concludes that "we are still in the first phase of a potentially long war."

Although bombings have been the most common form of terrorism, there is concern that other, possibly even more destructive, forms will emerge, including biological terrorism (Kuhr and Hauer 2001). A vast number of biological, chemical, and radioactive materials are capable of causing mass illness and death, and terrorists are capable of securing many if not most of these materials.

War, Terrorism, and the Quality of Life

Like the impact of violence at the interpersonal and intergroup levels, it is not possible to fully capture in writing the impact of war and terrorism. To give you a sense of what people are doing to each other through such violence, consider a few reported experiences. You will see that war and terrorism destroy and dehumanize.

Human Destruction and Injury

Human destruction reaches a peak in war. The 20th century was the bloodiest in human history. More than 100 million deaths occurred, compared to 19.4 million in the 19th century and 3.7 million from the 1st to the 15th centuries (Renner 1999:10). The

TABLE 14.1
War Casualties of American Military Personnel (in thousands)

War	Battle Deaths	Nonbattle Deaths	Wounded
Civil War*	140	224	282
World War I	53	63	204
World War II	292	114	671
Korean War	34	3	103
Vietnam War	47	11	153
Persian Gulf War	**	**	1
War on Iraq***	2.4	0.6	23

*Union troops only.
**Fewer than 500.
***As of January 6, 2007.
SOURCES: U.S. Census Bureau and U.S. Department of Defense Web sites.

figures for American casualties in various wars are shown in table 14.1. From the Civil War (including Union troops only) to the present, nearly 1 million American military personnel have died as a result of wars. And nearly 1.5 million more have been wounded.

Increasingly, civilians are the main victims of war through a combination of direct injuries, starvation, and disease. Civilians accounted for half of all war-related deaths in the 1950s, three-fourths of deaths in the 1980s, and nearly 90 percent of deaths in 1990 (Renner 1993a:9). In the current war in Iraq, American military deaths toward the end of 2006 were just under 3,000. Estimates of Iraqi civilian deaths, in contrast, varied greatly but ranged from 150,000 to 600,000 (Hurst 2006; Tavernise and McNeil 2006). In addition, more than a million Iraqi citizens fled their homes and their country to escape the violence.

Similarly, an analysis of death in the Congo's civil war reported that for every combat death there were 62 nonviolent deaths, 34 of them children (Lacey 2005). These deaths result from such things as malnutrition and various diseases resulting from the chaos and deprivation.

Civilians are also the main victims in terrorist attacks. The great majority of Americans killed by terrorists have been civilians. The thousands of Palestinians and Israeli casualties in the ongoing terrorist attack-retaliation cycle in Israel and the occupied territories also have been mainly civilians.

In addition, *children are increasingly the likely victims of war and terrorism.* Children are victims in a number of ways. First, they are often among those killed. Second, they suffer severe and sometimes permanent injuries, are left without parents and/or homes, or fall prey to hunger and disease. Third, children are recruited for, or forced into, being combatants in wars and terrorist activities. Hundreds of thousands of children, some as young as seven years old, have fought in armed conflicts or participated in terrorist attacks around the world. Palestinian children, for example, are taught the virtue of self-sacrifice, are encouraged to throw stones at Israeli soldiers and to become suicide bombers, and are assured that if they die they will receive the reward of martyrs (Burdman 2003). Finally, children may be victimized when women who participate in war have babies with birth defects. Women who served in Vietnam, for example, were far more likely to have children with birth defects than were other women (Brooks 1999).

A United Nations report summarized the current situation with regard to children and war and terrorist activities as follows (United Nations General Assembly 2006:4):

> Today, in over 30 situations of concern around the globe, children are being brutalized and callously used to advance the agendas of adults. It has been estimated that over 2 million children have been killed in situations of armed conflict; another 6 million have been rendered permanently disabled; and, more than 250,000 children continue to be exploited as child soldiers. Increasingly, children and women are the casualties of war, with the fatalities of civilians disproportionately higher than ever before in the history of warfare.

The report also notes that thousands of girls are raped and sexually exploited, and both boys and girls are being seized and taken away from their homes and communities in large numbers. Such suffering and death of children are among the most agonizing effects of war (see "I Didn't Want to See It" at the beginning of this chapter).

Various factors account for the human destruction in war. The obvious factor, of course, is the use of weaponry, including bombs. Even when bombs are aimed at military targets, a certain number will hit civilians. For instance, the 1991 war against Iraq, with its "smart" bombs and missiles that hit military targets with pinpoint accuracy, was heralded as an example of the wonders of modern military technology. However, many hospitals also were hit, including the only hospital in the nation that performed kidney transplants and advanced heart surgery (Burleigh 1991). In addition, the destruction of power plants prevented some hospitals from operating even basic equipment like incubators and refrigerators.

Land mines are also responsible for many civilian deaths and injuries (Renner 1997). At present, an estimated 120 million land mines are planted in more than 70 countries—most of which are the poorer nations of the world. These mines, along with unexploded bombs, can remain lethal for decades (Lovering 2001), and millions more are planted every year. Land mines kill or maim at least one person every hour (Wil-

Each year, land mines kill or maim more than 25,000 people, many of them children like this young Afghan girl.

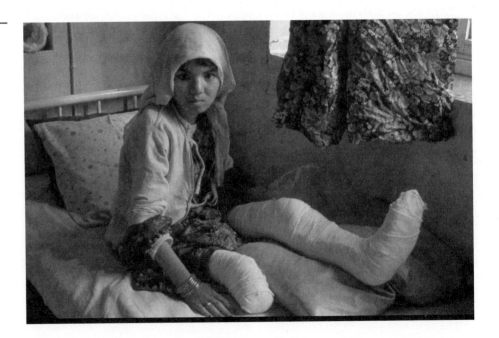

liams 2004). One in every 236 people in Cambodia is an amputee because of land mines. Yet, although 134 countries have signed a mine ban treaty and 18 countries have destroyed their stockpiles, 47 other countries (including the United States, China, and Russia) have not signed the treaty and have stockpiled as many as 200 million mines.

The more recent version of land mines is the *improvised explosive device,* or IED (Bryce 2006). IEDs are homemade bombs designed to kill or incapacitate the opposition. They can be hidden and camouflaged so effectively that they are extremely difficult to detect. They are usually triggered by the victims, but can also be triggered remotely. They have emerged as major weapons in the war in Iraq. About 3 percent of American combat deaths in World War II were due to mines or booby traps. The figure for the Vietnam War was 9 percent. But in Iraq, through the end of 2005, IEDs accounted for fully 65 percent of U.S. combat deaths and about half of all nonfatal injuries.

Another reason for the destructiveness of war is that, throughout human history, conquering armies have considered the vanquished to be undeserving of humane treatment. Girls and women experience a higher probability of being raped. Rape occurs in all wars, including civil wars. A survey of households in Sierra Leone reported that 94 percent contained at least one person who had suffered abuse in the previous 10 years of the nation's civil war, and one of eight of the households contained someone who had been victimized by some kind of war-related sexual violence (Physicians for Human Rights 2002).

Finally, war is destructive because, in their quest for military power or military victory, governments may act in ways that harm their own people. In 1993 the Department of Energy acknowledged that the United States had conducted about 800 radiation tests on humans between 1945 and 1970—and some of these people were unaware of the risks (Wheeler 1994). Part of the justification for the research, which was often supported financially by the Department of Defense or the Atomic Energy Commission, was the presumed threat of nuclear war and, thereby, the need to know the effects of radiation on the human body as well as ways to counter those effects.

Wars always have been destructive, but they are more destructive now than they were in the past. Clearly, one reason for the increasing number of people killed, as well as the increasing proportion of civilians among those killed, is the *changed nature of war,* which now involves the total population of nations rather than military personnel only.

Another reason for the increased destructiveness of war is the *increasingly sophisticated nature of military technology* compared to past weaponry. It is now possible to kill people in numbers that are staggering. In World War I, fewer than three people per 100,000 were killed by bombs in England and Germany. In World War II, nearly 300 people per 100,000 were killed by bombs (Hart 1957:44). World War II also saw the introduction of atomic weapons. Two Japanese cities, Hiroshima and Nagasaki, were each decimated by a single bomb. About 140,000 people in Hiroshima and 70,000 in Nagasaki died immediately or within a few weeks, and another 130,000 died within five years after the attack (Committee for the Compilation of Materials on Damage Caused by the Atomic Bombs in Hiroshima and Nagasaki 1981). It is sobering to realize that whereas the Hiroshima bomber delivered 25,800 tons of TNT-equivalent explosives, a bomber today can deliver *literally hundreds of times more destructive power,* and that the missiles carried by just one Russian Delta 4 submarine could kill 6.7 million people in the first 30 minutes after detonation, and an additional 6 to 12 million would die of radiation sickness in the following weeks (Helfand 1999).

In addition to the destruction of bombs and bullets, there is the horror of biological and chemical warfare. During the Iran-Iraq war from 1980 to 1988, the Iraqis used mustard gas, breaking a 63-year-old international agreement that forbids the use of any chemical weapons.[1] The gas initially causes sneezing and coughing and sometimes nausea and vomiting. Within hours, the victim suffers tightness in the chest and shortness of breath as a result of respiratory inflammation. Painful blisters appear on the body, causing patches of skin to fall off. Some victims recover, but some die and others suffer bone marrow or gastrointestinal problems for years.

The destruction can continue even after a war has officially ended. An examination of 50 nation-wars showed *increased homicide rates in the postwar years.* The increases occurred in both the victorious and the defeated nations and in those with improved as well as those with worsened economic conditions (Archer and Gartner 1979). An analysis of U.S. violence during the 1980s, when the nation conducted four major foreign military operations, showed that yearly rates of murder, rape, and aggravated assault rose dramatically (Bebber 1994). However, *the increase in the rate of criminal violence occurred only in the years immediately after the four military operations.* The legitimation of violence that occurs during war apparently carries over into the postwar years.

A different kind of carryover involves the increased rates of physical problems among veterans. Veterans of the Vietnam War face a 50 percent greater risk of cancer of the lymph nodes than do men who were not in Vietnam.[2] Veterans of the Gulf War developed a number of persistent physical symptoms: chronic fatigue, skin rashes, muscle and joint pain, shortness of breath, headaches, and diarrhea (Clark 1994; Gray et al. 2002). And Gulf War veterans who may have been exposed to nerve agents during a 1991 demolition of weapons in Khamisiyah, Iraq, have elevated rates of death from brain cancer (Bullman, Mahan, Kang, and Page 2005). The causes of long-term consequences are disputed, ranging from exposure to toxic war materials to the intense stress and anxiety of combat.

Finally, the destruction of human life and well-being is affected by the threat of war as well as by war itself. *The production and storage of weapons of war are hazardous even if the weapons are never used.* Radioactive wastes from the production of nuclear weapons contaminate water and soil. A news magazine called the production of nuclear weapons in this country a long "record of neglect."[3] For example, arms plants in Ohio and Washington routinely released large amounts of radioactive particles into the air. Some government nuclear-production facilities disposed of radioactive waste as though it were harmless; the result was the contamination of some water supplies. Even apart from carelessness, however, no nation has yet solved the problem of safely disposing of the wastes. The result is an increased risk of cancer, leukemia, and genetic damage.

Psychological and Interpersonal Disruption and Dehumanization

Psychological and interpersonal disruption and dehumanization occur during and after war and terrorist attacks—both of which are disruptive for military and civilian personnel. No one escapes the trauma.

The Trauma for Civilians.   Civilian trauma of the severest kind followed the atomic bombings of the Japanese cities of Hiroshima and Nagasaki during World War II. Hiroshima was a city accustomed to crises, having experienced periodic disastrous floods.

Civilians are the emotional and physical victims of war in massive numbers.

Nevertheless, the social order of the city collapsed after the atomic bomb was dropped. The city was rebuilt mainly through the work of migrants from the hinterland rather than through the efforts of the surviving residents. The survivors

> suffered from extreme shock and fatigue that lingered for a year. . . . Demoralization was so extreme that industrial alcohol was sold as a substitute for saki; many citizens died or went blind from drinking it. (Dentler and Cutright 1965:420)

Drugs were used to escape reality. Children who survived developed a fear of becoming attached to others and of having their own children when they became adults. Crimes of violence and thefts of precious water and other scarce goods were common. Four months after the bomb had been dropped, the number of reported crimes for one month was as high as all reported crime throughout the entire war. Years later, the survivors were still not capable of leading normal, happy lives. Most of them carried a *deep sense of guilt,* including the guilt of surviving when so many had died.

Hiroshima became a city of chaos, pain, crime, anxiety, and deep-rooted fear. So many people continued to feel sick a month after the bomb fell that a rumor spread that the bomb had left a poison that would give off deadly fumes for seven years (Hersey 1946:94). Such rumors, of course, intensified the already pervasive anxiety and fear of the people and contributed to an atmosphere that drained people of the necessary psychological strength to function normally and proceed with the work of rebuilding.

The suffering need not be on the scale of Hiroshima for people to experience the emotional trauma of war. Civilians in war zones suffer emotional problems in large numbers (Cardozo et al. 2000), and the problems may continue even after they are out of the war zone. Increased depression and posttraumatic stress disorder were found in a study of 124 Cambodian refugees living in Utah (Blair 2000). A team of researchers interviewed nearly a thousand Cambodians living in a refugee camp on the Thailand-Cambodia border. Many of them had witnessed the murder of a family member, had been raped, or had been physically assaulted during the civil war in their country. More than 80 percent felt depressed (with 55 percent meeting the criteria for clinical depression) and 15 percent had symptoms of posttraumatic stress syndrome (Mollica et al. 1994). Similarly, a survey of Guatemalan refugees living in Mexico 20 years after a long civil conflict in Guatemala found that the refugees had high rates of mental problems, including anxiety, depression, and posttraumatic stress disorder (Sabin et al. 2003). Widespread mental health problems not only exist among civilians who endured the war in Bosnia, but in some cases have been getting worse as the survivors age (Carballo et al. 2004). Finally, a team of researchers made a long-term assessment of the psychological impact on Iranian Kurds of being exposed to chemical weapons during the Iran-Iraq war of the 1980s. They found high rates of major anxiety, severe depression, and posttraumatic stress syndrome (Hashemian et al. 2006).

Children as well as adults are traumatized by war. Consider, for example, what it must have been like to have been a Jewish child in a Nazi concentration camp during World War II. In Czechoslovakia, the camp at Terezin had 15,000 children. Only 100 of the 15,000 survived, but some of their drawings and writings also survived. Following is part of a poem written by a 15-year-old boy:

> I was once a little child
> Three years ago.
> That child who longed for other worlds.
> But now I am no more a child
> For I have learned to hate.
> I am a grown-up person now,
> I have known fear.
>
> Somewhere, far away out there, childhood sweetly sleeps,
> Along that path among the trees,
> There o'er that house
> Which was once my pride and joy.
> There my mother gave me birth into this world
> So I could weep. . . .[4]

Or consider what life is like for Lebanese children who have grown up in a land wracked by war and civil war. Those children who experienced the death of a family member or the forced displacement of their family, or who saw their home destroyed or someone killed, were about 1.7 times more likely than other children to be nervous or depressed and to exhibit aggressive behavior (Chimienti, Nasr, and Khalifeh 1989). Continued shelling and killing were also responsible for depression among Lebanese mothers, and their depression, in turn, was associated with the illness of their children (Bryce et al. 1989). Among young people injured by shelling in 1996, half suffered some kind of impairment and 29 percent who had been enrolled in school did not continue their education (Mehio Sibai, Shaar Sameer, and el Yassir 2000).

Many children and young people in the Middle East have never experienced an extended time of peace. It is little wonder, then, that children in the Gaza Strip who have been exposed to war conflict have a high rate of emotional and behavioral problems (Thabet and Vostanis 2000). Studies of children in other war situations yield similar results (Ajdukovic 1998; Brajs-Zganec 2005; Hoge et al. 2007).

The Trauma for Combatants. During the latter days of World War II, the American Air Force launched a massive air attack on German positions near Saint Lo, France. The famous war correspondent Ernie Pyle was there to record his reaction as the planes began to come:

> [T]hey came in a constant procession and I thought it would never end. . . . I've never known a storm, or a machine, or any resolve of man that had about it the aura of such a ghastly relentlessness. . . . It seems incredible to me that any German could have come out of the bombardment with his sanity. When it was over I was grateful, in a chastened way that I had never before experienced, for just being alive. (Commager 1945:441,444)

In part, because of the horror of battle, there is *a high rate of posttraumatic stress disorder among veterans* (Prigerson, Maciejewski, and Rosenheck 2002; Dohrenwend et al. 2006). They may reexperience the war trauma in dreams, have recurring images and thoughts related to the trauma, feel a lack of involvement in life, experience guilt about having survived in situations in which others died, and struggle with sleep disturbances. The rates are higher among veterans who experience combat and veterans who are taken as prisoners of war (Stuart and Bliese 1998; Ford 1999; Neria et al. 2000; Wallis 2004).

It is possible that the rate of traumatization among combatants is increasing. Hayman and Scaturo (1993) reported higher rates of posttraumatic stress disorder among Vietnam veterans than those reported by studies of veterans of other wars. A study of Gulf War veterans also noted rates of disability compensation two to three times higher than those of World War II, the Korean Conflict, or the Vietnam War (Haley, Maddrey, and Gershenfeld 2002). There is as yet no explanation for these increasing rates.

The psychological problems vary in their severity but affect a substantial number of veterans. They tend to generate not only personal distress, but also interpersonal problems, including depressed satisfaction with intimate relationships, troubled marital relationships, increased sexual dissatisfaction, and higher rates of divorce (Prigerson, Maciejewski, and Rosenheck 2002; Cook et al. 2004; Cohan, Cole, and Davila 2005; Dekel and Solomon 2006). Younger soldiers may be more likely than older ones to develop serious problems. A study of 57 veterans of the Vietnam War found that those who were adolescents (17 to 19 years old) at the time of their tour of duty were more likely than older soldiers to have problems of adjustment (Harmless 1990). The younger soldiers experienced later on a greater number of conflicted relationships and work problems.

As we noted in chapter 13, there is an integral relationship between physical and emotional health. Continued emotional problems will adversely affect physical health. Thus, an examination of 605 male combat veterans of World War II and the Korean War found that posttraumatic stress symptoms were associated with increased onset of various physical problems, including arterial, gastrointestinal, skin, and musculoskeletal disorders (Schnurr, Spiro, and Paris 2000).

Combatant trauma stems from more than battle conditions, however. Military personnel may be traumatized and dehumanized by their own acts. Consider, for example, some of the acts that took place during World War II, such as mass extermination of and "medical" experiments on Jews. Some of the worst acts of the war were committed in the infamous *concentration camps,* especially Dachau (Gellhorn 1959:235–42). For example, Nazi Germans wanted to know how long their pilots could survive without oxygen. At Dachau they put prisoners into a car and pumped out the oxygen. Some prisoners survived for as long as 15 minutes. Nazi Germans also wanted to see how long pilots could survive in cold water if they were shot down over the English Channel or some other body of water. Thus, prisoners were placed in vats of ice water that reached to their necks. Some subjects survived for two and a half hours. Both experiments resulted in painful deaths for all the subjects.

Inhuman punishments were meted out to prisoners at Dachau who violated such rules as standing at attention with their hats off when an SS trooper passed within six feet. Prisoners were lashed with a bullwhip, hung by bound hands from a hook, or placed in a box that prevented them from sitting, kneeling, or lying down.

Perhaps the most disquieting aspect of all was the crematorium. A reporter who was in Dachau after it had been captured by the Allies wrote her reaction on seeing piles of dead bodies:

> They were everywhere. There were piles of them inside the oven room, but the SS had
> not had time to burn them . . . the bodies were dumped like garbage, rotting in the sun,
> yellow and nothing but bones, bones grown huge because there was no flesh to cover
> them, hideous, terrible, agonizing bones, and the unendurable smell of death. . . .
> Nothing about war was ever as insanely wicked as these starved and outraged, naked,
> nameless dead. (Gellhorn 1959:240)

Dehumanizing acts are not confined to any one people. Americans learned during the Vietnam War that they too are capable of atrocities. That war was particularly vicious for soldiers because there were no "lines" in the usual sense of the word. The enemy was everywhere and could not be distinguished from allies. Americans and some Vietnamese were fighting other Vietnamese. As we heard a Vietnam veteran put it: "After a while you get so sick of the trouble that you start killing everyone. It gets so you don't feel so bad about shooting at a six-year-old kid because the kids are throwing grenades at you." The South Koreans who fought with the Americans and South Vietnamese reportedly wiped out entire villages, including men, women, and children, when they suspected that enemy forces were present. In Iraq, American guards at Abu Ghraib prison subjected Iraqi prisoners to abuse and humiliation of a kind that enraged people throughout the Arab world and led President Bush to express a "deep disgust" and a promise to bring to justice the guards who were responsible (Roston and McAllister 2004).

Soldiers who perform such acts may have *serious psychological problems* once they reflect on what they have done. They have treated other human beings as objects, dehumanizing them, and they are appalled at their own actions. Even soldiers who do not participate in such actions may be traumatized. Just being in combat seems to bring some individuals to the point of irrationality, if not insanity. Since the time of the ancient Greeks, soldiers have succumbed to madness as a result of the horrors of combat (Gabriel 1987). Anything from fatigue to hysterical paralysis to psychosis may afflict them.

Terrorism and Trauma.   *Terrorist acts* also generate emotional trauma (Pfefferbaum 2001, 2002; Verger et al. 2004). A number of studies of Americans after the September 11, 2001, attacks reported an increase in emotional distress, including depression (Stein et al. 2004; Knudsen, Roman, Johnson, and Ducharme 2005). Telephone interviews with 1,008 Manhattan residents between one and two months after the attacks found that 7.5 percent reported symptoms consistent with posttraumatic stress syndrome and 9.7 percent reported symptoms of depression (Galea et al. 2002). Some of these symptoms existed prior to the attacks, but the researchers were able to determine that the rate of posttraumatic stress syndrome tripled in the weeks following the attacks.

Other research showed an increase in smoking and in alcohol and marijuana use after the attacks (Vlahov et al. 2004), and a survey of adolescents reported a sharply increased sense of vulnerability to dying than was found among adolescents prior to the attacks (Halpern-Felsher and Millstein 2002). Finally, a national survey reported that 11 percent of Americans said they were "very worried" and another 34 percent said that they were "somewhat worried" that they or a family member might become a victim of terrorism (Maguire and Pastore 2006:126).

Studies of other nations also find various kinds of trauma resulting from exposure to terrorist acts. A survey of Jewish and Palestinian citizens in Israel found that those exposed to terrorist acts had higher rates of depression and of posttraumatic stress disorder (Hobfoll, Canetti-Nisim, and Johnson 2006). And a study of Israeli adolescents found that being exposed to terrorism significantly increased the level of violent behavior by the youth (Even-Chen and Itzhaky 2007).

Environmental Destruction

As you will see in the next chapter, a precarious balance exists between natural resources and the growing demand for energy. *Conservation of natural resources throughout the world is essential; but there is a contradiction between this need and the willingness of people to engage in war,* because war always involves a certain amount of **environmental destruction.** Increasing sophistication in weaponry and increasing power of destructiveness have made wars more disastrous for the land.

Before the war, Vietnam was the "rice bowl of Asia," but the land was so decimated by bombing that the nation had to import rice after the war. The military also sprayed millions of gallons of herbicides on fields and forests in an effort to flush out guerrillas. We do not yet know the long-term effects on the environment, but the short-term effects included serious disruption of agriculture.

The Gulf War also turned into an environmental disaster when the Iraqis dumped hundreds of millions of gallons of crude oil into the Persian Gulf and set fire to hundreds of wellheads in Kuwait. At one point, Kuwaiti officials estimated that the fires were burning six million gallons of oil a day, about 9 percent of the total world consumption of petroleum (Renner 1991:28). The smoke caused daytime April temperatures to drop as much as 27 degrees below normal and created severe smog as far as 1,000 miles away. Black rain (soot washed out of the air) coated people, animals, buildings, and crops with a black, oily film (Renner 1991:28).

The longer the warfare lasts, the more severe the environmental consequences. In 2001, the United States and other nations launched an attack on Afghanistan to unseat the ruling Taliban because they had harbored terrorists. The Taliban were defeated and a new government was installed within a matter of months, but the nation had already endured 23 years of wars and the warfare of opposing factions. The resulting environmental destruction has been severe (Garcia 2002). Irrigation canals were destroyed, dense forests were decimated, and a number of species of birds and mammals are close to extinction. Without the trees, the ground has eroded. Dust often hangs in the air, blocking sunlight and causing respiratory problems and other diseases.

environmental destruction
alterations in the environment that make it less habitable or useful for people or other living things

Although much of the environmental destruction is the result of intensive bombing, the evidence suggests that such bombing contributes little to winning a war. A study of the strategic bombing of Germany during World War II concluded that at least 300,000 Germans were killed (including adults and children) and 780,000 injured; 155,546 British and American airmen also died in the assaults. Nevertheless, "the slaughter made little contribution to victory" (Wilensky 1967:25); and although the United States dropped more bombs in Vietnam than all the Allied forces dropped in World War II, the United States did not win in Vietnam.

As with other effects, it is not only wartime itself that results in environmental destruction; the years of preparation and the years following a war also have deadly consequences for the environment. Thus, it may take decades to repair the damage in nations such as Vietnam and Afghanistan. A 2002 report noted that more than half a century after the naval battles of World War II, the oil, chemicals, and unexploded ammunition on sunken ships in the Pacific still pose a serious peril to people and fisheries.[5] Land also continues to be contaminated by materials from World War II, including land on which armaments were made. Each new war adds to the peril.

You will see in chapter 15 that one of the serious environmental problems is that of toxic waste dumps. One of the worst polluters is the U.S. government's various weapons laboratories and assembly plants (Morain 1990). Experts estimate that it will require as many as 30 years and cost up to $200 billion to clean up toxic wastes at federal facilities throughout the nation. At other sites, including military bases, a range of toxic wastes such as pesticides, asbestos, old fuel, chemicals, and even radioactive materials threaten the environment and pose hazards to human health and life. In fact, the hazards may be far greater than those created by bombings.

The Economic Costs

War is *one of the greatest devourers of economic resources.* The total cost to the United States, in 2002 dollars, of World War I, World War II, the Korean War, the Vietnam War, and the Persian Gulf War was $6.33 trillion (Ericson and Hossain 2003). In late 2006, it was estimated that the Iraq War was consuming more than $1.4 billion each week, and that the total cost would be somewhere between $1 and 2 trillion (Coopersmith 2006; Kristof 2006)! The waging of war is increasingly expensive.

Consider also the cost of stockpiling weaponry and preparing for possible wars. The lengthy arms race between the United States and the Soviet Union that lasted until 1996 cost Americans a staggering $5.5 trillion (Newman 1998). A look at military spending throughout the world (see "Global Comparison") makes it clear that an enormous amount of the world's resources is being channeled into paying for past wars and preparing for future wars.

Military spending in many nations, including the United States, declined for a time. But in the 2006 budget U.S. defense spending ($535.9 billion) accounted for 19.8 percent of all spending and 4.1 percent of the gross domestic product (U.S. Census Bureau 2007). Veterans' benefits added another $69.6 billion to the budget, including $24.5 billion compensation for service-connected disabilities. And the Department of Homeland Security, formed to combat terrorist activities in the United States, added yet another $54.9 billion (U.S. Census Bureau 2007).

One reason for the *high cost of preparedness* as represented by the defense budget is the technological advances made in weaponry, which cost considerably more than weapons of the past (Wood 2004). Still, it is sobering to realize that the world's per-

Some people argue that military spending increases the number of jobs. Others point out that the same expenditure of funds in other sectors would create far more jobs.

capita military spending is larger than the per-capita gross domestic national product of some of the poorest nations of the world. Some nations allocate more to their military than they do to health and/or education. It's all part of a frantic effort by most of the nations of the world to gain **military parity** if not military superiority.

The economic costs are more than the money spent, of course. Indirect economic costs include the money spent to combat the emotional and physical problems resulting from war and preparations for war. Indirect costs also result from so much money being funneled into the military. For example, although military contracts produce jobs, they are one of the least cost-effective ways to create jobs: "Government programs for virtually any other purpose produce more jobs, and more less-specialized jobs, than nuclear weapons modernization outlays" (Marullo 1987:138). Military research has yielded many technological advances, but some of the technology does not get to the civilian sector because of secrecy requirements. Finally, the growth of some industries has been retarded because of the heavy investment in defense-related industries.

military parity
equality or equivalence in military strength

What if the United States invested the billions spent on military preparedness in electronics, education, health, and other sectors that benefit human beings? What if those nations in which substantial numbers of adults are illiterate and chronically hungry invested their resources in health, education, and industrial development? What could be accomplished?

Consider first what needs to be accomplished. Each year:

- Hundreds of thousands of children become partially or totally blind because of vitamin A deficiency.
- Millions of children die of diseases that could have been prevented by relatively inexpensive immunization.
- Millions of children die before they reach the age of five.
- Millions of children are deprived of a primary education.

- Hundreds of millions of women are illiterate.
- Hundreds of millions of people are chronically malnourished.
- More than a billion people lack access to safe drinking water.

If only a relatively small part of the billions of dollars expended every year on the military were diverted to social programs, many of these needs could be addressed.

Ironically, you live in a world in which there are more soldiers than physicians per capita, a world in which military technology makes the distance between western Europe and Russia a matter of minutes while poor women in Africa must walk for hours each day just to get the family's water supply. A military mentality results in an enormous waste of resources that could be channeled into the enhancement of the quality of life of people throughout the world.

Terrorism also has economic costs, and it has become particularly costly since September 11, 2001. The most dramatic economic loss was the World Trade Center—about $40 billion (Friedman 2002). But the costs of terrorism involve far more than the facilities damaged or destroyed. Since September 11, 2001, governments and businesses have invested huge sums of money to increase security (Moritsugu 2001). Businesses also must bear the costs of such things as reduced revenues (because of decreased activity of consumers who may fear leaving their homes), higher insurance rates, and impeded international trade because of tighter security at borders. A survey that looked at the cost of terrorism estimated that for Standard and Poor's 500 companies alone, the direct and indirect costs are $107 billion a year for the United States (Byrnes 2006).

There is also the additional cost to the government. As noted earlier, the Department of Homeland Security's budget for 2006 was $54.9 billion (U.S. Census Bureau 2007). The money is used for a wide variety of purposes, including better screening of baggage and people at airports, more vaccines and bioterrorism antidotes, tighter border security, new bomb-detection machines, and more FBI agents. Clearly, the threat of terrorist activity has made the world as a whole, including the United States, a much different economic environment.

War, Terrorism, and Civil Liberties

The right of free speech is a long-standing American value. However, there *is a contradiction between this value and the perceived need for consensus during a war.* Davenport (1995) examined events in 57 nations over a 34-year period and found that "increasing the resources given to the army enhanced the likelihood that censorship and political restrictions would be applied by governments." These restrictions occurred in nations with democratic as well as autocratic governments.

In the United States, both citizens and government officials have participated in the suppression of civil liberties during wartime. During World War I there was mob violence against dissenters and numerous prosecutions of people who spoke out against American involvement. In the later years of the Vietnam War, there were cases of mass protests against the war, mob violence against war protestors, massive arrests of demonstrators, and resultant court cases in which the issue of civil liberties was fought.

Violations of civil liberties were less severe for most Americans during World War II, but some German Americans were imprisoned in the early days of the war, and Japanese Americans were almost totally deprived of their civil rights. In 1942, more than 100,000 Japanese Americans were relocated from their homes into detention camps in isolated areas. They had committed no crimes. There was no evidence that they supported Japan rather than America in the war, but they were defined as potential sources of subversion. Long-standing prejudice against the Japanese Americans and jealousy of their landholdings, especially on the West Coast, played into this decision. The relocations caused serious economic and psychological problems for many of the victims. The wholesale deprivation of civil liberties was upheld as legal by the U.S. Supreme Court, which ruled that the government did not have to respect traditional rights during a national emergency.

Unfortunately, if a war is considered legitimate by the masses of people, they may passively accept restrictions on their civil liberties. Furthermore, their institutions, including religion and the mass media, may actively help build consensus. During the Gulf War, the mass media facilitated consensus by not informing the public of Middle Eastern history, by "the jingoistic behavior of American reporters and anchorpersons," and by biased reporting (Stires 1991). For example, just before the bombing began in January 1991, polls showed that the American public was evenly divided between using military and economic sanctions against Iraq to try and force it out of Kuwait; but a content analysis of network news programs between August 8, 1990, and January 3, 1991, reported that of 2,855 minutes of coverage of the Gulf crisis, only a little over 1 percent noted grassroots dissents from presidential policies, only one of 878 news sources was a peace organization, and more professional football players than peace activists were asked about their attitudes toward the war (Stires 1991:141–42).

Terrorism poses as severe a threat to civil liberties as does war (Lacayo 2003). Government actions following the September 11, 2001, attacks alarmed civil libertarians (Liptak, Lewis, and Weiser 2002). More than 1,200 people suspected of violating immigration laws or of being material witnesses to terrorism were detained for weeks or months without being charged. The attorney general altered federal rules to allow the monitoring of communications between inmates and their lawyers if the government believed there was a reasonable suspicion of terrorist information. The government considered trying suspected terrorists by military tribunals rather than in the courts.

Within weeks of the attack, Congress passed what the attorney general called the "Patriot Act," which gave officials nearly unprecedented peacetime authority to "nullify the constitutional rights of individual citizens" (Van Deerlin 2003). And the administration created the Department of Homeland Security, which is responsible for preventing terrorist attacks and reducing the nation's vulnerability to terrorism. The department must gather information on citizens to fulfill its mandate. Invasive surveillance measures by government agents increased immediately after September 11 (Gould 2002). They have continued under the Patriot Act and the department. And the fears of civil libertarians seem to be justified because the Patriot Act has already been used by prosecutors to deal with people charged with common crimes (Caruso 2003).

In 2005, news broke that President Bush had authorized domestic spying by the National Security Agency without court approval (Condon 2005). The president defended the need for such spying (including such things as eavesdropping on telephone calls and e-mail between the United States and other nations) and called the leaking of the program a "shameful act." Had the news not leaked out, the spying would have probably continued. But after resisting the critics for some time the president relented and declared in early 2007 that the government would disband the warrantless surveillance program and that future spying would be overseen by the secret court that governs clandestine spying in the nation.

Not everyone is concerned about the violations of civil liberties that have occurred since 2001. In fact, some observers argue that Americans face a trade-off. As one

MILITARISM: "A WORLD GONE INSANE"

We were discussing the problem of war in a social problems class, focusing on the militarism of American society. A student objected: "Let's not make this an American problem. It's a *world* problem. Even the poorest nations are spending their resources on the military. We live in a world gone insane with arms."

He was right. Militarism is not a problem of any single nation but of the entire world. From the poorest to the richest of nations, military expenditures are consuming resources that could be used to enhance the quality of life of the citizenry.

To assess the impact of military spending on a nation, it is necessary to know not only the total amount, but the per capita amount and the proportion of the GDP represented by the expenditures. In 2005, for example, the United States spent $1,604 per capita on the military, which was double the next highest of $809 by the United Kingdom (Stockholm International Peace Research Institute 2007). In fact, the United States accounted for *nearly half of the total world military expenditures*

in 2005. Other nations with a high per-capita expenditure were France, Japan, and China.

As a proportion of the GDP (the most recent figures available as of this writing were for 2003), we noted that the U.S. spending represented 4.1 percent, which is actually lower than many other nations (including some of the poorer nations). For example, military expenditures in Eritrea accounted for 19.4 percent of the GDP, the highest of any nation (Stockholm International Peace Research Institute 2007). Other nations high in spending as a proportion of the GDP were Oman (12.2 percent), Israel (9.1 percent), Kuwait (9.0 percent), Jordan (8.9 percent), and Saudi Arabia (8.7 percent). In addition to Eritrea, the poorer nations of Angola, Burundi, Pakistan, and Syria, among others, invested a greater proportion of their resources in the military than did the United States.

Of course, whether a nation can "afford" its military expenditures is a matter of values. But one measure of well-being in a nation is the infant mortality rate (number of deaths of children under one year of age per 1,000 live births in a given year). Higher rates typically reflect poverty and inadequate health care. For 2006, the infant mortality rate in the

jurist put it, "it stands to reason that our civil liberties will be curtailed. They *should* be curtailed to the extent that the benefits in greater security outweigh the costs in reduced liberty" (Posner 2001:46). And, in fact, many Americans agree. The greater the perceived threat of terrorism, the more people are willing to give up civil liberties in order to gain more security (Davis and Silver 2004).

For civil libertarians, this argument is the *fallacy of non sequitur.* To say that Americans need increased security does not mean that the government must necessarily curb traditional civil liberties. As the American Civil Liberties Union (2002) argued, without civil rights and privacy protections, "What's to stop the Department [of Homeland Security] from abusing the very citizens it is responsible for protecting?"

Undoubtedly the debate will continue. The extent to which civil liberties are curtailed by the effort to deal with terrorism remains to be seen.

fallacy

Contributing Factors

War and terrorism are complex phenomena. Some thinkers have tried to make them, like violence, a simple outgrowth of a *human need for aggression.* Yet, like aggression and violence, they are linked with *cultural values and patterns.* Some societies, for example, have no notions of organized warfare. The Hopi Indians traditionally had no

United States was 6.17 (U.S. Census Bureau 2007). Compare that with the rates in the poorer nations mentioned: Eritrea, 46.3; Angola, 186.6; Burundi, 63.1; Pakistan, 70.5, and Syria, 28.6. Improvements in infant mortality rates and other health matters, in educational opportunities, and in other economic benefits cannot be implemented when military spending consumes so much of a nation's resources, a situation that one of our students called "a world gone insane with arms."

Not to be overlooked in this is the fact that the United States is also one of the world's leading supplier of arms. As table 14.2 shows, the total amount of arms sales to other nations has fluctuated since 1995, but generally has remained in excess of $1 trillion.

Year	Total Amount (millions of dollars)
1995	$12,100
1996	11,710
1997	15,663
1998	13,179
1999	16,888
2000	10,436
2001	12,001
2002	10,240
2003	9,315
2004	10,681

TABLE 14.2
U.S. Military Sales Deliveries to Other Countries

SOURCE: U.S. Census Bureau 2007.

place for offensive warfare and did not idealize the warrior as did other tribes. Furthermore, the Hopi conceived of the universe as a harmonious whole, with gods, nature, people, animals, and plants all working together for their common well-being.

Why do people support wars? In particular, why do they support wars in view of the consequences we have described? Why do people support terrorism? What makes a terrorist willing to commit suicide in order to hurt or kill civilians? In the following sections, we examine various factors that help answer these vexing questions.

Social Structural Factors

The Economics of War and Terrorism.   The idea that wars have an *economic cause* is an ancient one. The Greek philosophers Plato and Aristotle both argued that economic factors are fundamental in the outbreak of war. Plato believed that the quest for unlimited wealth brings on not only war but a number of other human problems. Aristotle saw economic competition as the root of wars. In particular, poverty is the "parent" of both revolution and crime. The same economic inequality that leads to revolution within a nation results in wars between nations.

Marxists also argue that war has an economic basis. The **Marxist** view is that war is a *mechanism for maintaining inequalities* in a struggle for control of raw materials and markets. The inequalities are necessary because capitalism requires an ever-expanding

Marxist
pertaining to the system of thought developed by Karl Marx and Friedrich Engels, particularly emphasizing materialism, class struggle, and the progress of humanity toward communism

market to endure. Warfare is one way to ensure that a nation will have control over adequate resources and an expanding market. Consequently, war is an inevitable outcome of capitalism.

Although the Marxist explanation of war is debatable, economic factors are probably always at work in war and in preparations for war (Renner 1999). High military budgets mean considerable profits to a number of industries. In 2005, the U.S. government awarded businesses $269.2 billion in military prime contracts (U.S. Census Bureau 2007). With such funds at stake, it is not surprising that there are intense lobbying efforts in Congress to maintain and even increase military expenditures. One way that members of Congress can pump money into their districts or states is to maintain a military presence (in the form of a base) or secure military contracts for local industries. The military presence may no longer be needed and the military contracts may be wasteful, but the economic benefits to the district or state outweigh such considerations.

Economic factors are also at work in civil wars and terrorism. Some nations experience sharp economic inequality between racial, ethnic, or religious groups. *These racial, ethnic, or religious divisions may form the basis for civil war or terrorist activities* (Bonneuil and Auriat 2000; Reynal-Querol 2002).

A prime example is the Palestinian suicide bombers in Israel (Ratnesar 2002). Between 2000 and 2002, more than 70 bomb attacks or suicide bombings killed or injured hundreds of civilians. Although even some top leaders of the Palestinians have condemned the bombings, the majority of Palestinians defend the killing of Israeli citizens on the grounds that Palestinians are killed by Israeli troops.

Why do the majority of Palestinians defend what many people in the world community denounce as terrorism? Because these terrorist activities have developed in a context of what a U.N. human rights official has called daily experiences of discrimination, inequality, and powerlessness. Palestinians have lost land, work opportunities, freedom of movement, and access to water. In 2000, at least a fourth of Palestinians were living in poverty. The ongoing cycle of violence and retaliation between Palestinians and Israelis has greatly increased their poverty. By 2002, Palestinian unemployment soared to more than one out of two workers, and a survey reported that 4.3 percent of Palestinians in the West Bank and 13.2 percent of those in the Gaza Strip were suffering from severe malnutrition (Brilliant 2002). The cycle of violence and the cycle of increasing inequality have fed on each other.

The Politics of War: Militarism.   From a political point of view, there are advantages to both militarism and war (Marullo 1987). The presence of a foreign threat, whether real or fabricated by politicians, can create cohesion within a society, including support for both domestic and foreign policies that might otherwise be resisted. One important source of unity in American foreign policy has been the support of both Republicans and Democrats for anticommunist policies.

In the international arena, a strong military gives a nation higher status and more power. The nuclear arsenal of the United States, for example, is a "big stick" that can be used to facilitate the nation's diplomatic efforts and economic trade relations with its allies as well as its enemies. Some observers see this as necessary and proper in order to spread democracy in the world. Others see American foreign policy over the last century or so (including the 2003 war on Iraq) as an expression of imperialism. Chalmers Johnson (2004) argued that the nation has been on a steady path to imperialism, building an empire not through colonies but by establishing military bases

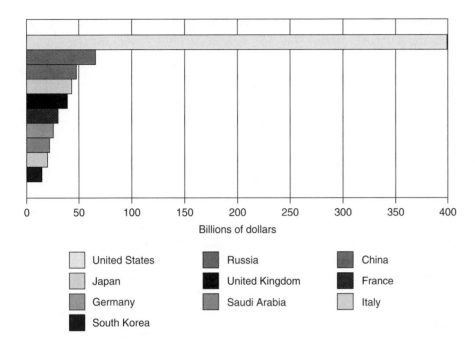

FIGURE 14.1
Military Budgets, by
Country.
Source: U.S. Census Bureau
2004/2005.

throughout the world—at least 725 bases outside the nation's borders. Imperialism is manifest in such things as the justification of interference in the affairs of other nations (including the overthrow of governments that are said to be hostile to our interests) and of preemptive war (Walt 2005). President Bush publicly stated that we have a unilateral right to overthrow any government that poses a threat to us.

Militarism is seen not only in foreign policy, but also in the resources allocated to defense. Some defend the defense budget on the basis that it has consumed an increasingly smaller proportion of the total federal budget. That was true before the war on Iraq, but it is also true that the total amount has continued to rise (U.S. Census Bureau 2007). In fact, as shown in figure 14.1, the U.S. military budget is vastly higher than that of any other nation (the amounts in figure 14.1 are for 2002, prior to the war on Iraq). Moreover, through arms sales, the United States, along with Britain, France, Russia, and China, is contributing to the high level of weaponry throughout the world. Two-thirds of arms sales are to developing nations, which desperately need their resources for social, educational, and health programs (Grimmett 2006).

Why is an arms buildup, or the maintenance of high levels of arms, in other nations of concern? When the communist governments in Eastern Europe fell during the 1990s and the United States and Russia engaged in an arms limitation agreement in 1990, a new era of peace appeared to be at hand. Wars and civil conflicts continued in various parts of the world, but there seemed little likelihood of a world war breaking out. Since 2001, however, peace once again appears to be precarious. The U.S. wars against Afghanistan and Iraq have angered many Muslims throughout the world. Anti-American sentiment worldwide is at a high level (Goode 2004).

In addition, a number of nations continue to build up their weaponry. Iran and North Korea, neither of which is friendly to the United States or the West in general are working hard to build new biological, chemical, and nuclear weapons along with long-range missiles. In short, as of this writing, militarism is flourishing throughout the world.

The Politics of Terrorism: Autonomy.   Throughout the world are groups who both desire and lack political autonomy—the right of people to govern their own affairs. Generally, when people press for autonomy, they believe that their interests are not adequately represented (or are even ignored) by the current government. Indeed, the United States became a nation under such circumstances.

The lack of political autonomy is a major factor in terrorism. For example, much bloodshed occurred in the struggle by East Timor to gain independence from Indonesia and the attempt by Yugoslavia to suppress the political autonomy of Kosovo. East Timor was finally granted the right to govern itself, and the Yugoslav Republic broke apart when U.N. forces took military action to stop the political oppression of minorities.

The early years of the 21st century are rife with examples of the struggle for political autonomy, including:

- Terrorist acts arising from the dispute between India and Pakistan over Kashmir, and the desire of Kashmir to be independent.
- The Chechnyan revolt against Russia.
- Terrorist acts by Palestinians who want to be free of Israeli control.
- Terrorist acts by the Irish who want Northern Ireland to be free of English control.
- Basque separatists' terrorist acts against Spain.
- Terrorist acts by Islamic extremists who want the Muslim world to be free of all influence and control by the West.

A careful analysis of every suicide terrorist attack in the world from 1980 through the early 2000s concludes that suicide bombers are not primarily the result of Islamic fundamentalism (Pape 2005). (In fact, the Tamil Tigers of Sri Lanka, who are secular and Marxist, have been the most frequent users of suicide terrorism.) The great bulk of suicide bombings take place in the context of campaigns that strive to get rid of foreign military forces from territory that the terrorists regard as their own. Moreover, contrary to assumptions, suicide bombers are not impoverished, uneducated religious fanatics, but more often are educated, middle-class political activists.

In support of these conclusions, Pape notes such things as the fact that prior to Israel's invasion of Lebanon in 1982 there was no Hezbollah suicide campaign against Israel. Nor were there any suicide attacks in Iraq until after the American invasion in 2003. Nor did the Tamil Tigers engage in suicide attacks before the Sri Lankan military moved into Tamil areas of the island in 1987.

Sometimes governments get involved in helping terrorists—providing such things as sanctuary, personnel, weapons, and economic aid—with whose cause they sympathize. In particular, the U.S. Department of State's 2006 terror report identified Cuba, Iran, North Korea, Sudan, and Syria as being *state sponsors of terrorism* (Perl 2006). However, the same report noted that state sponsorship is declining, so that only Iran, and to some extent Syria, continue to be strong, active supporters. The major thrust of terrorism currently is a cluster of independent, cell-based units that do not rely on particular states for their support (Benjamin and Simon 2005). Instead, terrorist groups use various methods to gain financial support for their activities, including "charities" and illegal enterprises such as drugs, extortion, and kidnapping (Perl 2006).

Social Psychological Factors

Attitudes.   Militarism and war are legitimated by a number of attitudes. The concept of a "just war" has a long history in the West. A just war is one that meets a number of tests, such as whether it has a just cause and whether all peaceful alternatives have been exhausted. If the war is just, the people are expected to support it fully. Shortly before the 1991 war against Iraq, some religious leaders questioned whether the notion of a just war is still valid in the face of the awful destructiveness of modern weapons (Day 1991). Indeed, Stires (1991) called the subsequent war against Iraq a "sanctioned massacre" because of the way in which the U.S. military technology overwhelmed the Iraqi forces. In spite of disparities in the military technology of nations and the incredible destructiveness of modern weapons, most people accept the notion that at least some wars are just.

The attitude that the United States has a mission to be "number one" in the world helps the country justify militarism. "We feel a collective strength and confidence that comes from being 'number one' in military power" (Marullo 1987:143). National pride is involved in attaining a place of military superiority. Gibson (1994) has argued that this need for being a "winner" facilitated U.S. involvement in Grenada, Panama, and the Persian Gulf. These military actions reflected the American dream of "redeeming Vietnam and recovering from all the other disappointments and traumas of the late 1960s and 1970s" (Gibson 1994:269). After the Gulf War in particular, Americans purchased a spate of military-type items: commemorative handguns, rifles, knives, and T-shirts and uniforms. Many of those who made the purchases were celebrating the restoration of the nation as the supreme military power of the world.

International misperception is a set of attitudes that legitimate both militarism and war. In a classic analysis, White (1966) identified six forms of misperceptions that recur in cases of international wars:

1. The *diabolical-enemy image* imputes flagrant evil to the enemy, who is conceived to be thoroughly criminal in behavior. Prior to the 1991 war against Iraq, the nation's political leaders "indulged in personal name-calling, false analogies to past wars and demonic leaders of earlier times" (Mack and Rubin 1991). In 2002, when President Bush urged new action against Iraq, he said that the Iraqi regime not only raped women to intimidate them but also tortured dissenters and their children and that President Saddam Hussein was a "dangerous and brutal man" who sought to acquire the destructive technologies that matched his hatred (Kozaryn 2002). Ironically, portraying the enemy as diabolically cruel can justify using the same behavior against the enemy (Dutton, Boyanowsky, and Bond 2005).

2. The *virile self-image* implies preoccupation with one's strength and courage and the need to avoid humiliation by determined fighting.

3. The *moral self-image* affirms the nation's goodness; Americans are the people of God and the enemy is of the devil. This attitude is the *fallacy of personal attack* and ignores the fact that among the enemy are many innocent, decent people who also are victims of the struggle between the nations.

   fallacy

4. *Selective inattention* means that only the worst aspects of the enemy are noticed; at the same time Americans attend to the best aspects of themselves, reinforcing the idea of the war as a conflict between black and white, good and evil.

"WHAT A GREAT WAR THAT WAS"

A friend of ours served as a navigator in the Air Force during World War II. "Those," he says "were some of the best days of my life." He recalls his days in the military as a time of adventure. He does not desire war, but neither does he think of it in terms of the detrimental consequences discussed in this chapter.

Interview a number of armed forces veterans. If possible, find veterans who served in different wars, and include some who did have combat experience as well as some who did not. How do they describe the experience of war? Do they mention any of the consequences discussed in this chapter? Would they be willing to serve in another war or to have their children serve? Note any differences based on service in different wars or on combat versus noncombat experience. If everyone felt as your respondents did, would the probability of future wars be greater or less?

5. *Absence of empathy* means the inability to understand how the situation looks from the other's viewpoint. An American might wonder, for example, how any German could fight on behalf of Hitler, or how any South Vietnamese could not welcome the American effort to save Vietnam from communism. People on both sides of a war fail to understand how the war could be justified by those on the other side. In the 1991 war against Iraq, Americans denied their contribution to the problem (later reports indicated that the United States had assured the Iraqis it would not interfere if they invaded Kuwait, and it had built up the Iraqi forces during the 1980s) and placed the blame totally on Iraq's shoulders (Mack and Rubin 1991).

6. *Military overconfidence* refers to the conviction that our side can win. In the case of the 1991 war against Iraq, the Iraqi leaders boasted (and no doubt believed to some extent) that the enemy would be soundly and humiliatingly defeated.

These attitudes can be found on both sides of a conflict and are encouraged by the opposing leaders. For decades, American leaders portrayed the Soviet Union as an evil empire that threatened the nation's fundamental (and righteous) values. On the other hand, *Pravda,* the Soviet Communist Party's daily newspaper, discussed attempts at arms control with the United States in terms of dealing with "militaristic ambitions," "hotheads in the Pentagon," and "insane anti-logic" (Lichter et al. 1987:12).

Misperceptions were also at work in the 2003 war against Iraq (Kull, Ramsay, and Lewis 2003). Many Americans accepted the notion that Iraq was involved in the September 11, 2001, terrorist attacks, that Iraq had developed and was prepared to use weapons of mass destruction, and that a good part, if not most, of world opinion favored the American position. The news media, particularly Fox News, helped shape these misperceptions. People who watched Fox network were three times more likely to hold those misperceptions than were people who watched other networks. Misperceptions were also fostered among the Iraqi people. They were told that America was the "Satan" of the world and that American forces would be soundly defeated if they invaded Iraqi soil.

In any confrontation between nations, the perceptions on both sides are remarkably similar, and people will support war to the extent that they accept such attitudes. Because both sides have the same attitudes, the attitudes obviously cannot be realistic. Nevertheless, they have typically been defined as valid and have served to legitimate international violence.

We noted earlier in this chapter that the majority of Palestinians support the suicide bombers and other acts of terror against Israel. Even though most Muslim leaders (both religious and political) condemn terrorism, the people take the attitude that the terrorists are only acting in defense of the Palestinian people and are doing nothing worse than what is being done to them.

Other terrorists also justify their actions on the grounds that they are really defending rights and seeking the well-being of the oppressed. They may also believe that change is nonexistent or too slow and that attention needs to be called to their cause (Jacobs 2001).

War, Terrorism, and Ideology. *Ideologies* support militarism and the attitudes discussed. There is, for example, the ideology that asserts that Americans are the *police officers of the world*. This ideology says that America maintains the kind of democratic society that is best for all people and has a duty to protect and extend that kind of society. It may be necessary (even though many would prefer to avoid it) to engage in small wars wherever the American way of life is suppressed or threatened. The nation is, thereby, protecting people from evil systems, according to this ideology.

This ideology was a part of the rationale for initiating the war against Iraq in 1991. It was necessary, Americans were told, for the United States to take steps to protect the world against dictators like Saddam Hussein. Of course, the ideology is used selectively. In other situations in which dictators and totalitarian governments have initiated action against another country or against a segment of their own country, America has responded only with moral support or arms. In Iraq, however, the ideology was used to justify a massive assault.

The Islamic extremists who resort to terrorism use a fundamentalist interpretation of the Koran to help motivate their followers (Del Castillo 2001; Hassan 2001). They represent what one researcher called "political Islam" rather than "personal religiosity" (Haddad 2003). For them, religion and politics are intertwined and inseparable. Their ideology includes a rejection of Western culture, a belief in Islamic law as a basis for the state, and the assertion that believers who are martyred in the cause of pursuing those aims are ensured entrance to eternal paradise. Many of the extremists received their education in fundamentalist religious schools, where they learned only a particular interpretation of the Koran and little that was modern except for the use of armaments.

Public Policy and Private Action

Inequalities of wealth and power among nations and between groups within nations, political and ideological conflicts, and economic factors all contribute to the likelihood of war and terrorism. An important step toward solving the problem would be to negotiate treaties that reduced the weaponry and armaments in the world. Current stockpiles, which are more than sufficient to eradicate life on the earth, need to be cut back. Military spending must be reduced. The sale of weapons of mass destruction is not an acceptable way to boost the supplier nation's economy. The massive number of weapons in the world also aids the cause of terrorists, who are able to secure sufficient arms to carry out their attacks.

Nations that thwart the effort to reduce arms or that abet terrorism can be subjected to economic sanctions through the United Nations. Such sanctions should be used judiciously. They eventually worked against Libya, which seems to have withdrawn from the ranks of those countries that sponsor terrorism (Collins 2004). Sanctions did not work to overthrow the Iraqi regime of Saddam Hussein, however. The main outcome of the sanctions was "enormous human suffering, including massive increases of child mortality and widespread epidemics" (Gordon 2002:44).

One problem with fighting terrorism is the sophisticated and strong financial infrastructure of some groups (Basile 2004). Terrorists have the economic resources they need to train their people, purchase arms, and pay the expenses needed to carry out their missions. International cooperation will be necessary to break up the financial base of terrorism because it is rooted in both legitimate and illegitimate businesses and charities and it transfers money around the world through poorly regulated banking networks.

Although the United States has tried to take the lead in committing the world's nations to a concerted fight against terrorism, cooperation will be difficult because of unilateral actions the country has taken in the name of its own interests (Cameron 2002). The 1989 Convention on the Rights of the Child was ratified by every nation except Somalia and the United States. The Comprehensive Test Ban Treaty of 1996 to halt nuclear testing and the development of new nuclear weapons was ratified by all the NATO nations and Russia but rejected by the United States. The United States rejected the Ottawa Treaty to Ban Landmines, while 142 other countries approved it. In 2002, the Bush administration gave notice that the United States was pulling out of the 1972 Anti-Ballistic Missile Treaty, which limited the testing and deployment of antimissile weapons. A day later, Russia announced that it was no longer bound by the 1993 START II agreement, which outlawed multiple-warhead missiles and other weapons in the strategic arsenals of the two nations.

In essence, U.S. foreign policy in recent decades reflects more a determination to protect what political leaders define as the nation's self-interest (defined, in part at least, in terms of the international misperceptions described earlier) than a desire to be a leader in the construction of world peace. It is questionable how long the nation can continue to press for cooperation in fighting terrorism while asserting its right to take unilateral action on other issues whenever it pleases.

The United States also needs to stop the ongoing sale of arms to nations throughout the world. As Renner (1993a) has argued, armaments may simply be a symptom of deep conflicts between people, but curbing the availability of arms is still crucial for three reasons. First, arms proliferation tends to gain a momentum of its own, because no nation is satisfied with just being equal to others but wants an advantage over its enemies or potential enemies.

Second, if arms are readily available, nations will more likely rely on them than on diplomacy and negotiations to settle their disputes (recall that in chapter 5 we noted that the availability of a weapon makes it more likely that it will be used). Third, when arms are readily available, the ensuing hostilities are likely to be far more devastating than they would be otherwise. For instance, the United States and the Soviet Union both shipped large amounts of arms to Somalia during the Cold War, each trying to lure the country into its sphere of influence. After the Cold War ended, a civil war broke out in Somalia in 1991, decimating the country and turning it into a nightmare of heavily armed, competing factions.

Of course, it is risky for any nation to demilitarize unless its potential adversary does the same, but there is some evidence to suggest that the risk is minimal. In the process called *Graduated Reciprocation in Tension-Reduction* (GRIT), one nation initiates an action that visibly reduces the way it threatens the other nation without at the same time endangering its own security. The action is an invitation to the other side to reciprocate (Elms 1972). Will such reciprocation occur? Following the 1962 Cuban missile crisis, President John F. Kennedy announced that the United States would stop atmospheric nuclear tests and would resume them only if another country's action compelled it to do so. The next day the Soviet Union agreed to a Western-backed proposal in the United Nations to send observers to Yemen (a proposal the Soviets had been blocking). America reciprocated by agreeing to restore the Hungarian delegation to full status in the United Nations. A few days later Khrushchev announced that Russia would stop producing strategic bombers. Shortly thereafter the "hot line" between the White House and the Kremlin was installed. This series of concessions was the result of each side taking a step that led the other to reciprocate.

Subsequently, Soviet President Gorbachev initiated a number of efforts to reduce tensions and to engage in arms reductions. The United States responded to each effort positively. Neither nation used concessions by the other as an opportunity to attack or even to gain an advantage by further buildup.

In contrast, the reverse process occurred in the Israeli-Palestinian conflict. Each side believed it had the right to—indeed, that it *must*—retaliate against the other after each attack. Clearly, such a process has no end (Brym and Araj 2006). There can be a graduated reciprocation in tension building as well as in tension reduction.

In addition to a halt to unilateral action and the breaking of international agreements, and to actively working to reduce arms and demilitarize the world, there is a need in the United States for changed attitudes and ideologies. More contact between peoples—cultural, educational, and political contact—could alter some of the misperceptions that abound in the world. Education should include an international perspective, so that Americans become increasingly aware of the smallness of the world and of the similarities among human beings everywhere. Instead of viewing other countries as adversaries or as problems, Americans should view them as partners working together on common problems. If the United States strives to be a world leader, let it be a leader in peace and in promoting the well-being of people rather than a leader who uses strength for pursuing self-interest.

The effort to avoid war and terrorism and to reduce the costs of preparing for war entails a great deal of work and frustration; but the alternatives to making the effort are grim. A noted man of peace, Martin Luther King Jr., put it this way:

> In a day when sputniks dash through outer space and guided ballistic missiles are carving highways of death through the stratosphere, nobody can win a war. The choice today is no longer between violence and nonviolence. It is either nonviolence or nonexistence. (quoted in Weinberg and Weinberg 1963:74)

Follow-Up.   What kind of measures would you like to see become a matter of public policy to maximize your own protection from terrorist attacks?

Summary

Americans are greatly concerned about war and terrorism. Warfare is no longer just a matter of opposing armies on the battlefield, but increasingly involves civil wars and terrorist activities.

War diminishes the quality of life of people and destroys the lives of many. From the Civil War to the present, nearly a million American military personnel have died as a result of wars. And nearly 1.5 million more have been wounded. During the 20th century, the bloodiest of all centuries, wars killed more than a hundred million people. War and terrorism cause psychological disruption and dehumanization of everyone involved. As illustrated by posttraumatic stress disorder, the effects last after the war or terrorist act is over. Much environmental destruction is involved. The economic costs of war, of preparation for possible wars, and of terrorism are staggering. The costs of fighting war and stopping terrorism inevitably mean that certain social needs will be neglected. War and terrorism always pose a threat to civil liberties, as illustrated by sanctions against dissenters and the detention of Japanese Americans in isolated camps during World War II and measures taken by the government after the September 11, 2001, attacks.

Social structural and social psychological factors help bring about war and terrorist activities and motivate people to support them. Economic factors are involved in wars and terrorism. Military spending is highly profitable to some industries, and people who profit from such spending tend to exercise considerable power in the government. Severe economic inequality between racial, ethnic, or religious groups within nations can give rise to civil war or terrorism.

Militarism is a political factor that can lead to war. The military influence in America is strong. The military, the government, and the corporations have some shared interests. This military-industrial-governmental linkage tends to maintain high levels of defense spending. Arms races tend to be self-perpetuating because each side views developments of the other with alarm and responds with its own efforts, which then become the stimuli to the other side to make further advances.

The desire for autonomy is a political factor in terrorism. People everywhere want the right to govern themselves and may assert that right through civil war or terrorist activities when they believe their interests are not represented in the government.

A number of attitudes justify war and terrorism, including the notion of a just war, the idea that Americans have a mission to be number one in the world, the set of attitudes called "international misperception" held by people on both sides of a potential conflict, and the belief that terrorist acts are a necessary form of self-defense. Finally, the ideology that Americans must be the police officers of the world supports militarism and war, and Islamic extremists use a religion-based ideology to justify terrorist acts.

Key Terms

Environmental Destruction	Marxist
International Terrorism	Military Parity
	War

Study Questions

1. How extensive is the problem of war and terrorism?
2. How has the amount of human destruction and injury during war changed over time?
3. What is meant by "psychological and interpersonal disruption and dehumanization" as a consequence of war and terrorism?
4. What effects does the problem have on the environment?
5. What are the economic costs?
6. How do war and terrorism affect civil liberties?
7. How do economic factors enter into war and terrorism?
8. What kinds of political factors contribute to the problem?
9. What attitudes and ideologies legitimate wars and terrorism?
10. What steps could be taken to diminish the possibility of war and terrorist acts?

Internet Resources/ Exercises

1. Explore some of the ideas in this chapter on the following sites:

http://www.terrorism.com The Terrorism Research Center site has essays, thought pieces, and links to other sites that deal with terrorism throughout the world.

http://www.fbi.gov The FBI site features the latest news and information about terrorist activities.

http://www.iwpr.net The Institute for War and Peace Reporting site has news about conflicts throughout the world.

2. Go to the site of the Institute for War and Peace Reporting. Summarize the various wars and armed conflicts currently reported there. Where are the trouble spots in the world? What are the more common kinds of conflicts—wars between nations or civil wars? What materials in the text could you use to help understand the reasons for the conflicts?

3. Search the Internet for a particular aspect of terrorism, such as the history of terrorism, terrorism in the United States, the war on terrorism, terrorist groups, etc. Make a report to the class, showing how your findings fit in with, or modify, the text materials.

For Further Reading

Cole, David, and James X. Dempsey. *Terrorism and the Constitution: Sacrificing Civil Liberties in the Name of National Security.* 2nd ed. Washington, DC: First Amendment Foundation, 2002. Two constitutional scholars show how civil liberties are threatened by the government's response to real or perceived threats, from the communists of the 1950s to the Islamic terrorists of the 21st century.

Grynberg, Michal, ed. *Words to Outlive Us: Eyewitness Accounts from the Warsaw Ghetto.* New York: Henry Holt, 2002. Detailed accounts from individual diaries, journals, and other writings show life in the Jewish community from the first bombardments of the capital to the razing of the Jewish ghetto. The struggles, deprivations, and suffering are graphically portrayed in these previously unpublished accounts.

Harwayne, Shelley. *Messages to Ground Zero: Children Respond to September 11, 2001.* Portsmouth, NH: Heinemann, 2002. A compilation of poems, drawings, and essays that illustrate children's reactions to the terrorist attacks, ranging from admiration for the heroic rescuers to personal feelings of anxiety and grief.

Hiro, Dilip. *The Longest War: The Iran-Iraq Military Conflict.* New York: Routledge, 1991. An examination of the war between two Middle Eastern nations from 1980 to 1988, showing the enormous destruction and, from an external point of view, the total pointlessness of some wars.

Howard, Michael, George J. Andreapoulos, and Mark R. Shulman, eds. *The Laws of War: Constraints on Warfare in the Western World.* New Haven, CT: Yale University Press, 1995. An examination of the formal constraints on war from ancient times to the present, including the role of Christian ethics as set forth by Catholic theologians in the Middle Ages.

Howard, Russell, and Reid Sawyer, eds. *Terrorism and Counterterrorism: Understanding the New Security Environment.* Guilford, CT: McGraw-Hill/Dushkin, 2002. A collection of articles by terrorism experts analyzing terrorism from many perspectives, including suggestions on how to deal with the current terrorist groups.

Margulies, Joseph. *Guantanamo and the Abuse of Presidential Power.* New York: Simon & Schuster, 2006. A close examination of a major point of contention over civil liberties—the American prison at Guantanamo Bay, Cuba, including abuses at the prison and the efforts of the president to defend the situation by extending the bounds of presidential authority.

Endnotes

1. *Time,* August 22, 1988, p. 46.

2. *Science News,* April 14, 1990, p. 236.

3. *Newsweek,* October 31, 1988, p. 29.

4. *I Never Saw Another Butterfly: Children's Drawings and Poems from Terezin Concentration Camp, 1942–1944.* New York: McGraw-Hill, n.d.

5. *Oil Spill Intelligence Report,* April 11, 2002, pp. 1–3.

CHAPTER

15

The Environment

"We're Not Safe Here Anymore"

Karl is a civilian employee on an air force base in a western state. Karl lives in a home that was occupied by his great-grandparents—built long before the air force base. Yet Karl isn't sure whether his children or his grandchildren will live in this place.

I can't imagine living anywhere else. But I can't imagine my children or grandchildren living here. I don't even want them to. We're not safe here anymore. The hazardous wastes from the base have contaminated our water supply. We can't grow our gardens anymore. We can't drink the water. We don't even feel safe taking a bath in it.

And it's not just the water. When you know that stuff is all around you, you feel like you're living in poison. Of course, I try not to think about it most of the time. But you can't keep it out of your mind altogether. And whenever I do think about it, I can feel myself getting nervous. Or sometimes I just get depressed.

I love this place. It's my home. But sometimes I hate it. At least, I hate what's happened to it. I don't know yet what we're going to do. But I do know that even if my wife and I don't leave, our kids will. And that will be the end of generations of my family on this land.

Introduction

In 2004, the Nobel Peace Prize was awarded to an environmentalist activist, Wangari Maathai of Kenya. She founded and led a movement to plant millions of trees to replenish the dwindling forests that provide Africans with cooking fuel. To many observers, declaring an environmentalist the winner of the Peace Prize seemed strange. But Christopher Flavin, president of Worldwatch Institute, declared it a most fitting award, because "the insecurity the world struggles with today is inextricably linked to the ecological and social problems" that Maathai strives to address (Flavin 2005:xix). In other words, although Americans tend not to consider them as serious as other matters we have addressed in this book, the problems we deal with in this chapter are crucial to the security and general well-being of people everywhere.

We look first at the ecosystem to set the stage for an understanding of environmental problems. Then we examine various kinds of environmental problems and how extensive they are. We show how these problems affect the quality of life and what structural and social psychological factors contribute to them. Finally, we consider several proposed as well as actual efforts to resolve these problems.

The Ecosystem

ecosystem
a set of living things, their environment, and the interrelationships among and between them

The **ecosystem** refers to the interrelationships between all living things and the environment. The emphasis is on the interdependence of all things: people, land, animals, vegetation, atmosphere, and social processes. Commoner (1971:16–17) called the ecosystem of the earth a "machine" and described some of the crucial interrelationships:

> Without the photosynthetic activity of green plants, there would be no oxygen for our engines, smelters, and furnaces, let alone support for human and animal life. Without the action of the plants, animals, and microorganisms that live in them, we could have no pure water in our lakes and rivers. Without the biological processes that have gone on in the soil for thousands of years, we would have neither food crops, oil, nor coal. This machine is our biological capital, the basic apparatus on which our total productivity depends. If we destroy it, our most advanced technology will become useless and any economic and political system that depends on it will founder. The environmental crisis is a signal of this approaching catastrophe.

Nature is not "out there" to be conquered for human benefit. Rather, people, nature, and the earth form a delicately balanced system. What is done at one place can have serious consequences for the system at other places. Consider, for example, the problems of acid rain and the threat to the ozone layer. The problem of acid rain is caused by sulfur dioxide emissions from coal-burning plants and factories and by nitrogen oxides from automobile exhaust and some industries. These chemicals, as they rise, mix with water vapor to form sulfuric and nitric acids that then fall to the earth as rain or snow. Acid rain threatens lakes and forests, kills fish and birds, reduces crop yields, contributes to health problems, and damages buildings and monuments (Lenssen 1993; Bright 2000; Leslie 2003; Youth 2003). Moreover, the damage may occur hundreds or thousands of miles away from where the sulfur dioxide emissions occurred.

In recent decades, tougher air pollution regulations have significantly reduced sulfur dioxide emissions. Some damaged lakes and forests are beginning to recover. However, researchers point out that the effects of acid rain are long term and that cutting power plant sulfur dioxide emissions by an additional 80 percent may still only bring partial recovery from the damage by 2050 (Krajick 2001).

The threat to the ozone layer is another example of current environmental problems. Ozone is a rare form of oxygen that is poisonous to human beings at ground level but is necessary in the upper atmosphere to absorb the deadly ultraviolet radiation of the sun. There is a natural balance of ozone distribution from ground level to the stratosphere. However, human activity disturbs that natural balance. High-voltage electrical equipment, including electrostatic air cleaners used to reduce other kinds of air pollution, create ground level ozone, and higher than normal concentrations at ground level pose health problems to the eyes, throat, and lungs.

The ozone in the upper atmosphere is reduced as a result of a number of human activities, including the use of nitrogen fertilizers, supersonic airplanes, fluorocarbons from aerosol spray cans (now banned in most nations), and nuclear explosions in the atmosphere. The effects of a depleted ozone layer are far reaching, involving changes in the earth's climate, destruction of some plant and animal life, reduced crop yields, increased incidence of skin cancer, possible genetic damage to plants and humans, and an impact on the food chain of the oceans (McGinn 1999).

Environmental problems dramatize the interdependence in the ecosystem. A poet once wrote that one cannot stir a flower without troubling a star. It is imperative that individuals make every effort to evaluate all the implications of human action for their delicately balanced ecosystem.

Types of Environmental Problems

Environmental problems can be divided into two types: **environmental pollution** and **environmental depletion.** "Pollution" refers to degradation of air, land, water, climate (global warming), aesthetic environment (eye pollution), and sound environment (noise pollution). "Depletion" refers to the diminishing supply of natural resources, illustrated well by the challenge of meeting the ever-increasing demand for energy.

Environmental Pollution

"Pollution is the harmful alteration of our environment by our own actions. **Pollutants** are either unwanted by-products of our activities or the obnoxious residues of things we have made, used, and thrown away" (Revelle 1971:382). In this chapter, we discuss numerous kinds of pollution and pollutants. It is important to keep in mind that in an ecosystem the overall impact of pollutants is greater than the impact of particular pollutants in particular places.

Pollution can occur in two ways: through catastrophes and through the slower, more insidious poisoning that occurs as a result of various processes and activities. The catastrophes dramatize the problem. In 1984, vapors from a deadly chemical used to manufacture pesticides escaped through a faulty valve into the air in Bhopal, India. Within a few hours, more than 2,500 people were dead, and thousands were critically ill. It was one of the worst industrial disasters in history. The accident underscored the horrendous consequences of exposure to toxic substances. Yet even more important than the catastrophes are the countless ways in which industries are exposing millions of people to high levels of toxic materials. Many of the victims in Bhopal died quickly. Others will die more slowly or suffer long-term health problems, the result of regular

environmental pollution
harmful alterations in the environment, including air, land, and water

environmental depletion
increasing scarcity of natural resources, including those used for generating energy

pollutant
anything that causes environmental pollution

exposure to toxic materials in the air, water, and land. The people were so traumatized by the disaster that 20 years later, in 2004, survivors and their supporters demonstrated in front of the gates of the former plant, demanding justice for those still suffering ill effects (*The San Diego Union-Tribune,* December 4, 2004).

Air Pollution.   Millions of tons of pollutants are released into the air every year in the United States and are visible in the smog that darkens urban areas. Much other pollution is not visible to the naked eye because it results from the discharge of gases and tiny particulate matter into the air. In some areas, atmospheric conditions tend to concentrate pollutants in the air. Even when winds blow the pollutants away from the populated area in which they are generated, damage still occurs.

Major air pollutants include suspended particulates (dust, pollen, ash, soot, chemicals, etc.), sulfur dioxide (from industrial processes), carbon monoxide (from motor vehicle exhaust, forest fires, decomposition of organic matter, etc.), and nitrogen dioxide (from motor vehicle exhaust, atmospheric reactions, etc.). The burning of fossil fuels—oil, natural gas, and coal—is the primary source of air pollution (Flavin and Dunn 1999).

While many people think of air pollution in terms of outside air, *a major problem throughout the world is indoor air pollution* (World Health Organization 2005). In developing countries, the indoor smoke resulting from burning solid fuels pollutes indoor air and is responsible for much illness and early death. In the United States and other developed nations, there are numerous sources of indoor pollution, including the polluted outdoor air but also including numerous everyday products found in all buildings, from offices to homes (figure 15.1). For example, formaldehyde, which emits toxic vapors that can lead to respiratory ailments and cancer, is used in a great many products, including bed sheets, permanent press shirts, fingernail hardeners and polishes, latex paints, plywood and particle-board cabinets, and plastic-laminated kitchen counters (Horowitz 1999; Raloff 1999). The vapors emitted by many of these products is small and sometimes temporary (while they are new), but they add to the total amount of indoor air pollution.

Water Pollution.   There are eight different kinds of water pollution (Revelle 1971; Sampat 2000). First is organic sewage, which requires dissolved oxygen in order to be transformed into carbon dioxide, water, phosphates, nitrates, and certain plant nutrients. Less oxygen is needed if the sewage is treated, but the amount of treatment varies and in some places there is no treatment at all.

eutrophication
overfertilization of water due to excess nutrients, leading to algae growth and oxygen depletion

Eutrophication, a second kind of water pollution, is overfertilization of water from excess nutrients, leading to algae growth and oxygen depletion. Eutrophication threatens aquatic life. It has already killed great numbers of fish in the United States and in other nations.

A third type of water pollution results from infectious agents. Many water-borne bacteria that cause disease have been eliminated in the United States, but there is still danger from infectious viruses such as hepatitis. Organic chemicals such as insecticides, pesticides, and detergents cause a fourth kind of water pollution. These chemicals may also be highly toxic to aquatic life.

Inorganic and miscellaneous chemicals constitute a fifth category of water pollutants. These chemicals can alter the life of a body of water, kill fish, and create unpleasant tastes when the water is used as a drinking supply. Sixth, sediments from land erosion may cause pollution. These sediments can diminish the water's capacity to assimilate oxygen-demanding wastes and block the sunlight needed by aquatic plants.

OUTDOOR SOURCES	BUILDING EQUIPMENT	COMPONENTS/ FURNISHINGS	OTHER POTENTIAL INDOOR SOURCES
Polluted Outdoor Air • Pollen, dust, mold spores • Industrial emissions • Vehicle and nonroad engine emissions (cars, buses, trucks, lawn and garden equipment) **Nearby Sources** • Loading docks • Odors from dumpsters • Unsanitary debris or building exhausts near outdoor air intakes **Underground Sources** • Radon • Pesticides • Leakage from underground storage tanks	**HVAC Equipment** • Mold growth in drip pans, ductwork, coils, and humidifiers • Improper venting of combustion products • Dust or debris in ductwork **Other Equipment** • Emissions from office equipment (volatile organic compounds [VOCs], ozone) • Emissions from shop, lab, and cleaning equipment	**Components** • Mold growth on or in soiled or water-damaged materials • Dry drain traps that allow the passage of sewer gas • Materials containing VOCs, inorganic compounds, or damaged asbestos • Materials that produce particles (dust) **Furnishings** • Emissions from new furnishings and floorings • Mold growth on or in soiled or water-damaged furnishings	• Science laboratory supplies • Vocational art supplies • Copy/print areas • Food prep areas • Smoking lounges • Cleaning materials • Emissions from trash • Pesticides • Odors and VOCs from paint, caulk, adhesives • Occupants with communicable diseases • Dry-erase markers and similar pens • Insects and other pests • Personal care products • Stored gasoline and lawn and garden equipment

FIGURE 15.1 Typical Sources of Indoor Air Pollutants.

Source: U.S. Environmental Protection Agency Web site.

Radioactive substances, a seventh kind of pollutant, are likely to become more serious if nuclear power plants to generate electricity become more common. The eighth kind of water pollution is waste heat from power plants and industry. Overheated water holds less oxygen, and fish and other aquatic life are generally very sensitive to temperature changes.

Not only are lakes and rivers being polluted, but the oceans are as well. Oil spills and the dumping of waste into the oceans have made many beaches unsafe for swimming. Millions of barrels of oil are poured into the ocean each year from the cleaning of the bilges of tankers. In addition, thousands of oil-polluting incidents occur every year from such problems as tanker accidents. Incidents in and around U.S. waters result in various amounts of spillage. In 2001, the spillage was 854,520 gallons, but the worst year was 1990 when 7.9 million gallons were spilled (U.S. Census Bureau 2007).

pesticide
a chemical used to kill insects defined as pests

herbicide
a chemical used to kill plant life, particularly weeds

Land Pollution.   **Pesticides, herbicides,** chemical wastes, radioactive fallout, acid rain, and garbage all infect the soil. Some chemicals used in pesticides, herbicides, and a number of manufactured products are hazardous to human health and are highly stable, remaining in the soil for decades (McGinn 2000).

The pesticide DDT, for example, was banned in the United States (Postel 1987). DDT was found to interfere with the formation of normal eggshells in certain birds, adding to the potential extinction of some species. It is incredibly stable, having been detected in Antarctic penguins, in the blood and fat of most Americans, and in carrots and spinach sold in supermarkets more than a decade after being banned.

Nor is the threat posed only by the "active" ingredients in pesticides. The so-called inert ingredients can constitute up to 99 percent of the contents, and many of those ingredients are biochemically active. For example, an unlisted ingredient in Dibrom, a mosquito pesticide, is naphthalene, which may cause cancer and developmental problems in children (Epstein 2003).

The problem of pesticides is compounded by the fact that the pests tend to develop a resistance to them; thus, increasing quantities are required over time. And if the natural enemies of a particular pest disappear, a pest control program may require monstrous increases in dosage of the pesticide.

Global Warming.   Air pollution from gases such as carbon dioxide is a major factor in the so-called greenhouse effect (Dunn 2002). The gases trap solar energy in the atmosphere, which, in turn, leads to global warming. Without appropriate action, a warming of 10 degrees or more could occur. This increase would melt the polar ice caps, raise sea levels, flood low-lying lands, alter the earth's climate, and cause economic and political chaos as people attempt to deal with the severe disruptions (Fisher 1990).

Global warming is a controversial issue. Critics argue that the world may simply be in a warm phase of long-term cyclic temperature variations. Most scientists, however, accept the greenhouse effect as a process demanding action. One scientist puts it bluntly: "The debate on global warming is over. Present levels of carbon dioxide . . . are higher than they have been at any time in the past 650,000 years" (Stix 2006). Moreover, since the late 1800s, average global surface temperature has increased about 0.75 degrees Celsius, and most of the warming has occurred since 1950 (Hansen 2004). Glaciers around the world are retreating, and the ice has thinned in both the Arctic and Antarctic. When figures were released on the amount of melting ice, many scientists were surprised and now believe that the rise in sea level will occur sooner and will be more catastrophic than previously predicted (Overpeck et al. 2006).

Noise Pollution.   Prolonged exposure to noise of sufficient intensity can not only damage hearing, but can also increase stress and lead to harmful physiological changes such as an increased heart rate (Vera, Vila, and Godoy 1994). At lower levels, noise can increase irritability, prevent sleep, and impair performance on tasks (Persson et al. 2001). Many things—from traffic to industrial processes to vacuum cleaners—contribute to noise pollution. You may find the noise level in a particular situation as anything from annoying to painful. For most people, the noise environment is worsening. Indeed, hundreds of millions of people throughout the world are exposed to unacceptable noise levels at work and at home (Skanberg and Ohrstrom 2002).

Aesthetic Damage.   An aesthetically pleasing environment is one component of a high quality of life (Sirgy et al. 2001). An attractive environment can affect mood and influence health-promoting behavior like exercise (Craig et al. 2002). It is no minor point, then, that pollution involves *deterioration of the beauty of the environment* as well as actual physical damage.

Air pollution, for instance, leads to the deterioration of buildings, statues, and paintings. It can inhibit visibility, obscure scenic views, and produce noxious odors. This kind of aesthetic damage—whether from air and water pollution or from litter—is the effect on the environment that most people first recognize. Whatever the source, aesthetic damage signals that the environment is less pleasing, that the beauty of the natural world has been scarred by human activity.

Environmental Depletion

The Dwindling Natural Resources.   Air, water, and land can be restored, but the problem of dwindling resources is another matter. If the air is cleaned, it may become just as useful as before it was polluted. But once a mine has been exhausted, an oil well pumped dry, or a patch of soil ruined for farming, you have lost a resource that cannot be reclaimed easily or quickly, if at all.

For a long time Americans tended to think that the nation had virtually unlimited natural resources. In 1973 a group of oil-producing nations temporarily suspended the sale of oil to other nations, and Americans confronted the fact that no nation in the modern world can be self-sufficient by virtue of its own natural resources. The United States does not have sufficient oil in its own reserves to meet its needs. Nor does it have sufficient supplies of various other natural resources. In 2005, the United States imported 100 percent of seven minerals and metals used in various manufacturing processes: bauxite, columbium, fluorspar, manganese, sheet mica, strontium, and vanadium (U.S. Census Bureau 2007). Imports of other minerals and metals were also substantial, ranging from 15 percent of iron and steel to 91 percent of platinum and 93 percent of tin. No nation in the modern world, including the United States, is self-sufficient in terms of natural resources.

Energy consumption per capita is higher in the United States than it is in any other country in the world.

TABLE 15.1
Energy Production and
Consumption, 1950–2005

Year	Total Production (quad. Btu)	Total Consumption (quad. Btu)	Consumption/ Production Ratio
1950	35.5	34.6	0.97
1960	42.8	45.1	1.05
1970	63.5	67.9	1.07
1975	61.4	72.0	1.17
1980	67.2	78.4	1.17
1985	67.7	76.7	1.13
1990	70.7	84.6	1.20
1995	71.2	91.5	1.29
2000	71.3	100.0	1.40
2005	69.2	99.9	1.44

SOURCE: U.S. Census Bureau 2007.

Energy Production and Consumption.   An integral part of the pollution problem and the dwindling of resources is the production and consumption of energy. As table 15.1 shows, energy consumption has risen rapidly in the United States. Although the United States does not have the highest per capita usage of energy, our usage is nearly five times the world average (U.S. Census Bureau 2007). With about 4.6 percent of the world's population, we account for 22 percent of the world's energy consumption.

Moreover, consumption is growing more rapidly than production (table 15.1). And the problem is compounded by the fact that *per capita consumption is increasing.* From 1950 to 2005, per capita consumption of energy in the United States increased by 50 percent (Glover and Behrens 2006).

How Big Are These Environmental Problems?

How serious are the environmental problems of this country? Using the same two categories of environmental pollution and environmental depletion, consider what the data reveal.

Environmental Pollution

The federal Environmental Protection Agency (EPA) has established standards for six "criteria" air pollutants: sulfur dioxide, particulate matter, carbon monoxide, ozone, lead, and nitrogen dioxide. Many states and cities have adopted the Pollutant Standards Index (PSI), which indicates when any of the six criteria pollutants are at a level considered to be adverse to human health. These six criteria pollutants are not the only sources of the problem but are the ones used by the federal government to evaluate air quality.

In general, enforcement of *air pollution standards* has been reducing the amount of the pollutants released into the air (U.S. Census Bureau 2007). In spite of the decline, the problems of air pollution in the United States remain severe. A study of pollution in various states reported that Vermont, which was the lowest polluter among the 50 states, still emitted more greenhouse gases than did 33 developing countries combined (National Environmental Trust 2002). In 2002, 34.3 percent of children under the age of 18 lived in an area that did not meet one or more of the air quality standards (Federal Interagency Forum on Child and Family Statistics 2004). This figure was an increase from 1990, when 28 percent of children lived in such an environment.

Air quality has improved in the rest of the industrialized world as well, but in many places—particularly the developing nations—it is a more serious problem than in the United States. Nearly half of the world's population now lives in urban areas. Urban air pollution accounts for 800,000 premature deaths each year, about 65 percent of them in the developing nations of Asia (United Nations Environment Programme 2006).

As noted earlier, *indoor air pollution* is also a serious problem. It is the eighth most important risk factor in illness, accounting for 2.7 percent of diseases and 1.6 million deaths in the world (World Health Organization 2005). In some developing nations, only malnutrition, unsafe sex, and lack of safe water and sanitation account for more deaths than does indoor smoke.

In the United States and other developed nations, indoor air pollution can cause the *"sick building syndrome."* In a sick building, the workers suffer from acute physical and/or psychological discomfort that is eased when they leave the building (Thorne et al. 2001). The sick building syndrome includes a variety of symptoms: mucous membrane irritation, eye irritation, headaches, nausea, feelings of lethargy, fatigue, the inability to concentrate, breathing difficulties, and fainting (Soine 1995; Mann 1998). The syndrome is due to such factors as inadequately maintained air conditioning and heating systems; pests (e.g., cockroaches and dust mites); moisture and mold in ceiling tiles, carpet, insulation, and furnishings; improper ventilation; and toxic vapors from copy-machine liquids, paint, flooring, and cleaning agents (Mann 1998; Mendell et al. 2006).

In severe cases, the air quality inside the building may be far worse than the urban air outside the building. It is not known how many buildings are sick, but a number of surveys indicate that from 40 to 55 percent of office occupants will experience one or more sick building symptoms each week (Hood 2005).

Nor are people's homes necessarily safe. We have noted that formaldehyde is toxic and that a wide range of materials and products used in homes contain formaldehyde. In the 1970s, about half a million homes were insulated with urea formaldehyde. In addition, there are other toxic chemicals in virtually all homes, making them one of the more hazardous places to be. Some of the chemicals in the home may not be toxic in themselves but can combine with common kinds of air pollution to cause health problems (Hughes 2004).

Another problem in homes and other buildings is the *presence of radon gas, which can cause lung cancer after long periods of exposure* (Barros-Dios et al., 2002; Pawel and Puskin 2004). The Environmental Protection Agency claims that millions of homes and buildings contain high levels of the gas (Environmental Protection Agency 1996). The gas is odorless and colorless and can be detected only by appropriate testing. Radon is produced by the decay of uranium in rocks and soil.

Electromagnetic radiation is another possible form of air pollution. We say "possible" because the issue is controversial. Some scientists argue that such items as power lines, computer terminals, cell phones, and even electric blankets are hazardous to health, causing everything from cancer to miscarriages (Brodeur 1989). However, it is not certain what levels, if any, are unsafe for humans. Researchers have reported

Per capita, Americans discard almost twice as much garbage as do people in Western Europe or Japan; much of it ends up in landfills.

such problems as increased rates of cancer and increased risk for Alzheimer's disease among people exposed to sustained, high levels of radiation (Gorman 1992; Sobel et al. 1995; Miller et al. 1996). On the other hand, a 16-member committee of the National Research Council examined more than 500 studies and concluded that there is no convincing evidence that such exposure is related to health problems (Leary 1996). At most, there may be a very weak connection between exposure and illness, but the issue is still unresolved (Brodsky et al. 2003; Moulder, Foster, Erdreich, and McNamee 2005; Kheifets, Afifi, and Shimkhada 2006).

With regard to global warming, we noted earlier that both temperature rise and melting ice are strong evidence that warming is not only occurring but is doing so at a faster rate than scientists previously believed. If the trend continues, a number of adverse consequences are likely (Dunn and Flavin 2002). They include reduced crop yields, less availability of water in the subtropics, increased exposure to water-borne diseases (e.g., cholera and malaria), and increased flooding.

Some advances have been made in *water pollution control*. The volume of pollutants discharged into the nation's waterways has decreased, and thousands of acres of lakes and thousands of miles of rivers and streams have been restored and made safe for swimming and fishing. The problem remains serious, however. We have already noted the problem of oil spills. In addition, serious pollution occurs from various toxic materials dumped into the oceans and waterways and from nitrogen and phosphorus from agricultural runoff. The greenhouse gases that fuel the warming are also a threat to the ecosystem of the oceans (Lieberman 2004). Oceans contain increasing concentrations of carbon dioxide, which can hamper the efforts of many marine animals to form shells. In 2000, 39 percent of rivers and streams; 45 percent of lakes, reservoirs, and ponds; 78 percent of the Great Lakes shoreline; and 14 percent of ocean shoreline were polluted (U.S. Census Bureau 2007).

Pollution by hazardous wastes has also declined, but the problem is still severe. In 2004, 3.74 billion pounds of toxic chemicals were released into the environment, compared to 6.73 billion pounds in 1998 (U.S. Census Bureau 2007). This form of pollution intersects with the problems of racial or ethnic origin and poverty because chemical plants and toxic wastes tend to be in areas where the poor and minorities live (Krieg 1998; Pine, Marx, and Lakshmanan 2002).

Finally, there is the staggering amount of trash and garbage discarded each year. Americans discard hundreds of millions of tons of trash and garbage every year, and the amount is increasing. As figure 15.2 shows, the amount of waste that is recovered (recycled) is also growing. But recovery has not kept pace with generation, so that the net amount of waste dumped into the environment continues to increase. On the average, people in the industrialized nations throw out around 1,235 pounds of trash and garbage per person per year, and Americans produce 51 percent more waste than the average resident of any other nation (Gardner, Assadourian, and Sarin 2004). Put in

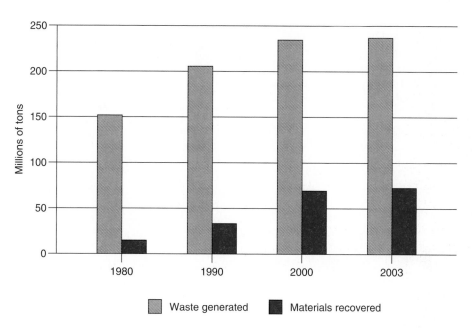

FIGURE 15.2
Municipal Solid Waste
Generation and Recovery.

Source: U.S Census Bureau
2007.

other terms, the *ecological footprint refers to the amount of productive land needed to produce the resources and absorb the waste for a particular economy.* The world as a whole contains 1.9 hectares of productive land per person, but the average American requires 9.7 hectares!

Trash illustrates the dilemmas of environmental problems. To help clean the air, incinerators, which once burned a good part of the trash, were phased out and "sanitary" landfills became the main method of disposal. Because a good part of the trash is paper, much that is thrown away is supposedly biodegradable. That is, it will eventually break down, decompose, and become a part of the earth.

Unfortunately, biodegradation doesn't happen in landfills. Archaeologists have discovered that so-called biodegradable trash and garbage are preserved rather than destroyed in landfills, probably because the materials are tightly packed and covered, with little exposure to light or moisture (Grossman and Shulman 1990). Most of the trash remains essentially unchanged in weight, volume, and form for at least four decades.

It is difficult to estimate the seriousness of all kinds of pollution, partly because measurement techniques have not been developed and partly because the potential hazards involved have been recognized only recently. Some forms of pollution, such as noise pollution and aesthetic damage, are undesirable or annoying rather than hazardous. How can their seriousness be assessed? In spite of such problems, it is clear that pollution in general is one of the serious problems confronting the nation, and it is a problem for which there are no easy answers.

Environmental Depletion

Many experts believe that the astounding pace at which people are consuming natural resources threatens the resource capacity of the earth (Gardner and Sampat 1999). We mentioned earlier that Americans now import a major proportion of many important minerals and will import even more in the future as they continue to devour their own resources at a high rate.

WORLD ENERGY PRODUCTION AND CONSUMPTION

As noted in the text, energy production and consumption are an integral part of the problems of pollution and dwindling resources. They also play an integral part in the quality of people's lives. For example, try to imagine a world without electricity and the internal combustion engine. It would still be a livable world, but as Flavin and Dunn (1999:23) put it:

> Homo sapiens has relied for most of its existence on a virtually limitless flow of renewable energy resources—muscles, plants, sun, wind, and water—to meet its basic needs for shelter, heat, cooking, lighting, and movement. The relatively recent transition to coal that began in Europe in the seventeenth century marked a major shift to dependence on a finite stock of fossilized fuels.

This shift affected every aspect of life—health care, education, leisure activities, and so on. People throughout the world desire the standard of living produced by the shift. As developing nations strive to achieve the standard of living now enjoyed by the developed nations, questions of practicality arise. Does the earth have enough resources for all nations to achieve such a standard? Energy use per capita varies enormously around the world (table 15.2) Note the difference between a developing nation such as India and the developed nations such as the United States.

Notice that even among the developed nations there is a considerable difference in the amount of energy consumed per capita. Some of these differences reflect varying climates (e.g., heating and air conditioning are needed far more in some nations than in others). Yet the figures raise the question of how much energy per capita is needed for a decent standard of living. Is life in the United States, where energy consumed per capita is double or more that of the United Kingdom, Austria, Germany, and Japan, far superior to that of other developed nations? Or is there a good deal of unnecessary energy use in the United States? Could Americans cut down on their energy use without seriously or even moderately diminishing the quality of their lives?

Look also at the figures on the production of major sources of energy. The figures underscore the interdependence of the nations of the world, with some nations clearly far more dependent than others on outside resources.

The problem of depletion, of course, is international. For example, a major concern for the well-being of the earth is deforestation. Between 2000 and 2005, Africa lost 3.2 percent of its forested area, and South America lost 2.5 percent (Gardner 2006). Over the course of human history, nearly half of the earth's forests have been depleted, most of which has occurred since 1970. Tropical forests may contain as many as half of the world's plant and animal species, including many plants used for medicine. In addition, they are a major impediment to the buildup of carbon dioxide and, thereby, to global warming. Yet millions of acres are cut down each year to provide fuel and land for development and agriculture.

Increasing energy use is another major concern. Energy use per capita is increasing in most of the developing nations (U.S. Census Bureau 2007). The United States uses more energy than most other countries both because of the size of its population and because energy use per person is higher than that of most other nations (table 15.2). Industry accounts for 32.0 percent of this use, residential and commercial purposes account for 39.9 percent, and transportation accounts for 28.1 percent (U.S. Census Bureau 2007).

The amount of energy Americans consume driving their vehicles is staggering, and the number of miles traveled continues to increase in spite of rising gas prices and efforts to encourage car pools. In 1970, Americans drove their cars, vans, pickups, and

Country	Primary Energy Consumed per Capita (million Btu)	Natural Gas Production (quad. Btu)	Crude Petroleum (1,000 bbl per day)	Coal Production (million short tons)
World	66	90.7	68,057	5,266
United States	342	19.4	5,801	1,121
Austria	176	0.1	19	1
Brazil	51	0.2	1,295	5
China	31	1.1	3,300	1,459
Germany	174	0.8	65	226
India	13	0.8	642	339
Japan	172	0.1	6	4
Mexico	59	1.3	3,157	13
Nigeria	8	0.6	2,256	*
Russia	195	20.5	7,049	300
Saudi Arabia	233	1.9	8,031	n.a.
United Kingdom	165	3.7	2,282	35

TABLE 15.2
Energy Production and Consumption of Selected Nations

n.a. not available.
*Less than 500,000 short tons.
SOURCE: U.S. Bureau of the Census 2003:866.

SUVs 1.043 trillion miles; by 2004, the number rose to 2.72 trillion miles (U.S. Census Bureau 2007). The population increased by 44 percent during that period, but miles driven increased 261 percent! Americans account for 44 percent of all motor gasoline consumed in the world (Renner 2006b).

How can Americans keep up with their voracious appetite for energy? Some experts believe that nuclear sources are the only hope, but reliance on nuclear power plants poses serious problems. Total reliance on nuclear power is not even feasible because of the number of plants that would have to be built and the problem of storing radioactive wastes. In addition, there is the ever-present possibility of accidents and disasters. This possibility became a reality in April 1986 when two large explosions occurred at the Chernobyl plant in the Soviet Union, "a blast heard round the world" (Flavin 1987). Within days, much of Europe reported the highest levels of radioactive fallout ever. Within two weeks, elevated levels of radioactivity were detected throughout the Northern Hemisphere. For weeks afterward, fresh vegetables in many areas of Europe were contaminated. Cows that grazed on contaminated grass soon produced milk with unhealthy levels of radioactivity. For a number of months, as many as 100 million people had to alter their diets.

The Soviet Union, of course, suffered the worst consequences. Thirty-one people were killed and 1,000 were injured immediately. Another 135,000 were evacuated from their homes. Of the 25,000 workers under the age of 35 who participated in the cleanup, 5,000 to 7,000 died (Chernousenko 1991). As many as 4 million people in the region are at high risk for cancer and other illnesses. The incidence of these illnesses began to increase within a few years after the accident (Parks 1991). Ten years after the disaster, researchers found a variety of psychosomatic symptoms and high levels of fear and stress (Specter 1996). And nearly 20 years later, other researchers linked the disaster to increasing rates of thyroid cancer in the Czech Republic, which had received only a moderate amount of radioactive fallout (Murbeth et al. 2004).

The Chernobyl disaster, along with subsequent accidents and near-disasters, has intensified concerns about the utility of nuclear power for generating energy. As a result, several nations—including the United States, Great Britain, and Germany—have cut back on the number of reactors in operation.

Environmental Problems and the Quality of Life

Environmental problems confront Americans with *a number of inherent contradictions:* the value of growth and progress versus the value of freedom to choose the size of one's family; the desire for abundant energy versus the value of a clean environment; the preference for reasonably low energy prices versus the value of independence in the world arena. It is impossible to have all these options, so Americans must engage in *trade-offs* between such choices as cost and abundance, national independence and abundance, and abundance and quality of the environment.

The Environmental Threat to Life and Health

The *environmental threat to both physical and emotional well-being* occurs from all the environmental problems named thus far.

The Physical Threat.   The physical threat is summarized by the U.S. Public Health Service (1995:80):

> Among the numerous diseases and dysfunctions that have a known or suspected environmental component are cancer, reproductive disorders such as infertility and low birthweight, neurological and immune system impairments, and respiratory conditions such as asthma. Exposure to environmental hazards can be through air, food, or water and covers a broad range of factors such as pesticides, toxic chemicals, and radiation.

An even more dramatic statement of the threat is offered by the World Resources Institute (1999), which asserted that in the poorest regions of the world, environmentally related diseases will kill as many as one in five children under the age of five. This is equivalent to 11 million childhood deaths in the world, equal to the combined populations of Australia and New Zealand.

You are surrounded by hazards of all kinds. Consider some of the illnesses that severe air pollution can cause or contribute to:

Permanent lung damage in children (Roan 1990)

Fetal deaths (Pereira et al. 1998)

Infant mortality, including sudden infant death syndrome (Penna and Duchiade 1991; Dales et al. 2004)

Respiratory illness and death from respiratory infections (Spix et al. 1998; Samet et al. 2000)

Cardiovascular disease (Samet et al. 2000)

Skin problems, ulcers, and liver and kidney damage (Organization for Economic Cooperation and Development 1991)

Premature deaths (Revkin 2001)

Asthma attacks (Sarafino, Paterson, and Murphy 1998; Schwartz 2004)

Lung cancer (Moore 1999; Parent et al. 2007)

These adverse consequences may be caused by either outdoor or indoor air pollution. We pointed out earlier in this chapter that many products and materials in the home give off toxic vapors. A similar situation exists in workplaces. Workers in particular kinds of jobs may be exposed to, or may work with, one of the chemicals known to be a factor in respiratory problems, cancer, and other illnesses.

For example, a study of 125 pregnant women who were exposed to organic solvents in their jobs found an increased risk of major fetal malformations; they were thus more likely than nonexposed women to give birth to babies with major defects (Khattak et al. 1999). The researchers also found an increased risk of miscarriage among the exposed women.

Some of the chemicals to which workers are exposed are known to be neurotoxic, causing damage to the nervous system, with resulting behavioral and emotional disorders. The problem of neurotoxins came to public attention in the 1970s when workers at a fabrics plant suffered various degrees of nerve damage. The workers had been exposed to a solvent used as an ink thinner and machine cleaner. As a result, they experienced weakness in their hands and feet (so much so that some could barely turn a key or use a screwdriver), loss of weight, and problems with walking (Anderson 1982).

Exposure to toxic materials can also lead to sterility. Male sperm counts have been declining for many decades (Lemonick 1996). The decline may reflect the fact that industries use a number of chemicals that can result in infertility. In Costa Rica, 1,500 banana plantation workers developed permanent sterilization from exposure to a toxic pesticide (Thrupp 1991). In the United States, children born to women who live within a quarter mile of a toxic waste dump have higher rates of birth and heart defects (Roosevelt 2004).

The depleted ozone layer raises the risk of skin cancer, whereas high ozone levels at ground level are harmful to both humans and plant life. In fact, high ozone levels are associated with increases in the number of cardiovascular and respiratory deaths (Gryparis et al. 2004). In rural areas, high ozone levels reduce crop yields (Monastersky 1999).

Acid rain is a threat to forests and lakes. Eutrophication in waterways can kill massive numbers of fish, which means less food available for a world in which millions of people are starving. Ironically, some of the eutrophication problems arise from efforts to produce an adequate food supply. More than half the phosphorus that overfertilizes water comes from municipal wastes, but a substantial minority is due to urban and rural runoff. As farmers continue to apply fertilizer in increasing quantities to improve the yield of needed agricultural products, they also increase the likelihood of eutrophication of waterways and the consequent destruction of needed fish.

Routinely used pesticides and herbicides produce yet another hazard (Alarcon et al. 2005). The consequences of exposure to pesticides and herbicides include increased risk for stillbirth, birth defects, children's asthma, injury to the nervous system and reproductive organs, lung damage, problems with the immune and endocrine systems, and cancer (Savitz, Whelan, and Kleckner 1989; Mansour 2004; Salam et al. 2004).

A number of adverse consequences of global warming have already surfaced (Epstein 2000). Disease-causing bacteria, viruses, and fungi are spreading more widely; malaria and other mosquito-associated diseases have begun to appear in areas of the world where they were once absent. The problem will only intensify as the warming continues.

Finally, noise pollution is at best a nuisance and at worst a hazard to personal well-being. Excessive noise levels can result in hearing damage, high blood pressure, increased risk of cardiovascular disorders, sleep disturbance, lower work productivity, and problems in relating to others (Blanchard 1998; Niskar et al. 1998; Haines et al. 2003).

The Emotional Threat.   The emotional threat is illustrated by the fact that people who work around hazardous materials may suffer from increased anxiety and depression (Roberts 1993). They experience stress over potential health problems—from uncertainty about the seriousness of the exposure and from a sense of powerlessness over the situation (what can an individual do to change the situation?) (Hallman and Wandersman 1992; Matthies, Hoger, and Guski 2000).

Edelstein (1988) interviewed a number of New Jersey residents whose water supply had been contaminated by a municipal landfill. He found that knowledge of the contamination brought with it a radical change in the way the people viewed the world. They began to fear for their own and their families' health. They felt a loss of control over their lives. They viewed their homes as places of danger rather than havens of security. They lost trust in the government.

Another study of psychological consequences involved a survey of 421 people living near a toxic waste landfill in California (Stefanko and Horowitz 1989). The people expressed both negative beliefs and negative feelings. They had little trust in the authorities, and their feelings about their quality of life were fairly low. Those people who lived nearest the landfill and/or who had small children expressed the most negative attitudes.

Noise also detracts from emotional well-being. People in New York City identify noise pollution as the worst infringement on their quality of life (Tierney 1998).

Threat to the Ecological Balance

Many of the examples given in this chapter show that human actions can result in a whole chain of consequences for the environment. One consequence can be an upsetting of the ecological balance. Paul Ehrlich argued that lust for more affluence and unrestrained population growth are ravaging the environment. But don't be deceived, he wrote,

> the imbalance will be redressed. . . . Man is not only running out of food, he is also destroying the life support systems of the Spaceship Earth. The situation was recently summarized very succinctly: "It is the top of the ninth inning. Man, always a threat at the plate, has been hitting Nature hard. It is important to remember, however, that NATURE BATS LAST." (Ehrlich 1971:364)

One way that the ecological system has been altered is through the *disappearance of a number of species of animals and plants* as a result of human activity. Hundreds of animals and plants have become extinct. Hundreds more are endangered (in danger of becoming extinct) or threatened (likely to become endangered). The endangered species list includes 324 mammals, 252 birds, 347 other kinds of animal life, and 600 plants (U.S. Census Bureau 2007). A declining number of species means less diversity, represents a vast biological loss, and poses a direct threat to the quality of human life. As Tuxill (1999:7-8) writes:

> In addition to providing the genetic underpinnings of our food supply, plant diversity keeps us healthy—one in every four drugs prescribed in the United States is based on a chemical compound originally discovered in plants. Plants also furnish oils, latexes, gums, fibers, timbers, dyes, essences, and other products that we use to clean, clothe, shelter, and refresh ourselves and that have many industrial uses as well. Health assemblages of native plants renew and enrich soils, regulate our freshwater supplies, prevent soil erosion, and provide the habitat needed by animals and other creatures.

Finally, a diminishing diversity increases the likelihood of pest infestations and outbreaks of disease.

Clearly, *people depend on biological diversity for the quality of their lives* (MacDonald and Nierenberg 2003). Still, caution needs to be exercised about the loss of species. Ecosystems are dynamic, not static. Some species would disappear regardless of human activity. On the other hand, humans need to be careful not to fall into the *fallacy of circular reasoning* by arguing that only those species disappear for which there is no use or importance. Therefore, the argument would run, those species that have become extinct are not needed anyway; humans are doing just fine without them. This line of reasoning ignores the fact that some species became extinct because of human activity rather than the natural workings of nature. People need to be concerned that the ecological balance is not upset, that they do not start a chain of consequences that will be detrimental to human life.

Perhaps more important than the balance among the species is the possibility that humans will somehow intrude into the major processes of the ecosystem and cause irreversible damage that could threaten life—for the continuation of life demands certain processes, including reproduction, **photosynthesis,** and the recycling of minerals. The reproduction of some species has been affected by certain pollutants. For instance, the use of DDT caused the eggshells of some birds to become thinner and to crack before the young hatched, thus threatening the birds' reproductive capacity. DDT also has affected the reproductive capacity of some fish. Other pesticides and herbicides also may impair reproduction.

Photosynthesis may be adversely affected by air pollution, by pesticides and herbicides, and above all, by the spread of the human population, which destroys the habitat of other species. Air pollution inhibits the plant life in which photosynthesis occurs, whereas human activity such as **urbanization** destroys plants by destroying their habitat. It is also possible that the pesticides and herbicides accumulating in the oceans will disrupt the process there as well. Photosynthesis is essential in the production of oxygen; it helps maintain the carbon dioxide balance in the atmosphere and is of fundamental importance in producing the organic material needed for supporting life. It is difficult to imagine that photosynthesis would halt completely. If it did, it would be a catastrophe. But whether or not the process could totally stop, it is clearly adversely affected by certain human activities.

fallacy

photosynthesis
a natural process essential to life, resulting in the production of oxygen and organic materials

urbanization
the increasing concentration of people living in cities

The Economic Costs

It is difficult to place a price tag on ecological problems. To fully assess the cost, we would have to include an enormous number of items: damage to livestock, trees, and crops; the death of wildlife; the expense of pollution-control measures; the cost of

Pollution results in damage to health, property, and vegetation.

medical care for those whose health is adversely affected; the lost work time due to ill health; the expense of maintaining and refurbishing buildings and other structures that deteriorate because of pollution; and the cost of restoring the quality of the air and of waterways. The public is barely aware of the *innumerable ways in which economic resources are consumed by ecological problems.*

Consider the factors involved in analyzing and estimating these economic costs. First, the pollutants are emitted at a particular time and place. Second, they affect the environmental quality. (For example, the amount of sulfur dioxide in the air at a particular time and place may increase and may cause an increase in the number of people with respiratory problems.) Finally, a dollar cost must be assigned to the damages.

Every factor in this process is marked by uncertainty. We are not yet aware of all the amounts and kinds of pollutants being emitted. Nor do we yet know how all the pollutants act and interact in the environment. Thus, identifying actual damages is problematic. It is relatively easy to assign a dollar value to some damages, but extremely difficult for others. We can estimate the cost of painting a building marred by air pollution or the cost of replacing damaged crops, but what is the dollar value of a human life; a clear sky; a place for recreation; or a species that contributes to the diversity, complexity, and stability of the ecosystem?

Keeping these difficulties in mind, we can still estimate some of the economic costs of pollution. The costs, in terms of damage to property, materials, health, and vegetation, run into many billions of dollars each year for air pollution alone. An analysis of the air pollution just from ships engaged in international trade put the cost at $126 million per year from sulfur dioxide and $412 million per year from nitrous oxide (Gallagher and Taylor 2003). It is estimated that cleaning up just a small proportion of the hazardous waste sites in the nation—those on the Environmental Protection Agency's priority list—will cost $31 billion (Gardner and Sampat 1999). In other words, eliminating the hazards of pollution will be extremely costly. Environmentalists argue, however, that on balance the economic benefits will be greater than the costs. They point out that although the economic costs of addressing environmental problems are considerable, they are not as great as the cost of allowing the environment to deteriorate.

Threat to World Peace

The contradictions between the demand for energy, the desire for a clean environment, the desire for reasonably low prices for energy, the struggle for natural resources, and the value on political independence are manifested on the international level in the form of a *threat to world peace.* A number of armed conflicts in the world can be traced to the struggle for control of various natural resources (Renner 2002).

In addition, the developing nations of the world are demanding to share in the affluence enjoyed by the West and Japan. Inequality among nations has become a matter of international concern. On May 1, 1974, the General Assembly of the United Nations adopted the "Declaration on the Establishment of a New International Order," which asserted a determination to work for a new and more equitable international economic order. If the widening gap between the developed and the developing nations is not eliminated, many observers fear that the result will be a world war between the relatively few rich nations and the far more numerous poor nations.

Questions arise about whether the earth's resources are sufficient and whether the environmental damage can be adequately contained if the developing nations are to achieve the same standard of living as the developed nations. On the one hand, if the gap between the rich and the poor nations is not narrowed, peace is threatened by those nations or groups of nations that would resort to violence to achieve a higher economic status (Renner 1999). On the other hand, if rich nations help poor nations achieve a higher standard of living, depleted resources and a damaged environment may drastically lower the quality of life for the entire world. It appears that the contradictions inherent in these ecological problems will continue to plague us in the future.

Contributing Factors

Before looking at the sociocultural factors that contribute to environmental problems, you should note that some of the problems are caused by *ignorance and accidents.* Ignorance is involved because people often do not know and generally cannot anticipate the environmental consequences of their behavior. DDT, for instance, seemed beneficial because it controlled many pests, including the carriers of malaria. What was not known at the time was that DDT would impair the reproductive capacity of some fish and birds and would remain in the food chain with such persistence.

Accidents also contribute to environmental problems. It is not possible, for example, to avoid all oil spills. Weather conditions cannot be controlled. Human error cannot be totally eliminated. Thus, it was human error that led to a nuclear reaction in a uranium-reprocessing facility in Tokaimura, Japan, in 1999. The reaction lasted nearly 20 hours and had the potential for creating a Chernobyl-type disaster.

In addition to ignorance and accidents, however, a number of sociocultural factors contribute to environmental problems. As with other social problems, both social structural and social psychological factors are involved.

Social Structural Factors

Population Growth.   *A growing population poses a threat to the environment* (Gardner, Assadourian, and Sarin 2004). Population growth accelerates the consumption of the earth's natural resources to the point that oil, natural gas, and certain minerals may eventually be exhausted. The population could even reach a number at which it would be impossible to produce enough food. The point is, any given area on the earth has a *limited carrying capacity,* that is, a limit to the number of people who can live there without causing a collapse of the biological system. If the biological system collapses, the inhabitants must either be supported by outside resources, move from the area, or face massive deaths.

Fortunately, the rate of population growth has slowed. Nevertheless, the 6.4 billion people who inhabited the earth in 2005 were twice as many as there were in 1950, and the number increases by millions each year (Nierenberg 2006). Moreover, nations with the highest growth rates are among the poorer nations of the world, and their rapidly growing populations severely impede their efforts at improving their economic and social well-being.

With rapidly increasing populations, what are the prospects for raising the standard of living in the poorer nations and for maintaining a high standard for those in the developed nations? Brown and Flavin (1999) address the question in their discussion of what is required for 10 billion people to live at the standard now enjoyed by Americans. They estimate that it would require 360 million barrels of oil a day, more than five times the current production; and it would demand nine billion tons of grain a year, more than four times the current output. These estimates provide an answer to questions about whether the poor nations can achieve the same standard of living as the rich nations. The answer is no, if the population continues to grow as expected in the next half-century.

The problems of population growth are compounded by the fact that the effects of increased population are more than additive. We noted earlier in this chapter that people generally, and Americans in particular, are consuming increased amounts of energy and other resources *per capita*. In other words, the impact per person on the environment is far greater today than it was in past years.

A second reason that a growing population has more than an additive impact on the environment is the *threshold effect*. Vegetation in an area may be able to survive a certain size of population and the air pollution created by that population. But further increase in the population might create just enough additional pollution to kill the vegetation. It becomes "the straw that breaks the camel's back."

The threshold effect can occur in all kinds of pollution. A number of cases illustrate this problem (Brown and Postel 1987). For example, in 1982, about 8 percent of the trees in West Germany were damaged from pollution. The figure jumped to 34 percent one year later, and then to 50 percent by 1984. Something had tipped the balance and caused a sudden surge in deterioration. Several Canadian scientists showed the effects of acid rain by deliberately acidifying a small lake. Over an eight-year period, they gradually increased the concentration of acids in the lake and found a particular point at which a dramatic change occurred in the ability of the various species of fish to reproduce and survive. The effects of population may be additive to a point, and beyond that point *the increasing quantitative changes become a qualitative change*.

The Industrial Economy.   Both pollution and depletion of the environment are rooted in the industrial economy. This finding is dramatically illustrated by the fact that the United States, with about 4.6 percent of the world's population, accounts for 22 percent of the world's carbon dioxide emissions (U.S. Census Bureau 2007). Various industrial processes, from the generation of electricity to the production of goods, are responsible for a considerable part of the air pollution problem.

Water pollution is also a by-product of industrial processes. This problem includes thermal pollution, which occurs when water is taken from a waterway in large quantities and used for cooling. In the cooling process, the water absorbs heat. When this heated water is dumped back into the river or lake, it can then raise the temperature to a point that is dangerous for aquatic life.

A major cause of air pollution in the United States is the *extensive use of the automobile*. The automobile also bears heavy responsibility for the rapid depletion of the world's oil reserves. America is involved in a love affair with the automobile. More than a fourth of all cars in the world are on U.S. roads; automobiles and light trucks are responsible for 40 percent of U.S. oil consumption and have an effect on climate change equal to that of all economic activity in Japan (Sawin 2004). As noted earlier, Americans use 44 percent of all automobile gasoline consumed in the world, a figure that reflects, in part, the fact that fuel economy standards for automobiles were no higher in 2005 than they were in 1985 (Renner 2006b).

The burgeoning number and use of automobiles creates increasing pollution. Despite the fact that emissions per automobile have been greatly reduced over the past few decades, overall air quality has worsened in many cities because of the increased number of cars. Yet to drastically reduce the use of the automobile not only would be contrary to the American value of freedom and mobility, it also would cause serious economic problems. The automobile, a prime factor in environmental pollution and depletion, is an integral part of our affluent economy. Significant numbers of workers depend on the manufacture, distribution, service, and use of motor vehicles. An attack on the automobile is clearly an attack on the economy. Thus, a way must be found to deal with the environmental problem without ignoring the economic consequences.

As the automobile illustrates, the industrial economy operates at a pace that outstrips the ability to counteract the environmental problems it creates. Consider the chemical industry. Cancer is largely an environmental problem often *caused by carcinogenic chemicals* (Napoli 1998; McGinn 2002). There are approximately two million known chemical compounds, and thousands more are discovered each year. Some of these new compounds will be carcinogenic, but there are insufficient facilities to properly test them all.

These chemical compounds are one example of useful new products. Unfortunately, useful products can have undesirable environmental side effects. Because industrial technology can produce enormous quantities of any single product and an enormous range of products, and because the economy is set up to maximize growth, the whole

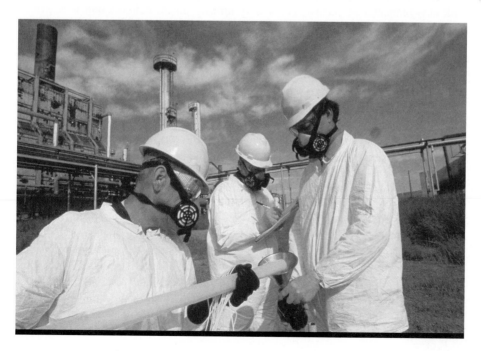

Many industrial workers are directly exposed to a variety of hazards to their health.

situation is self-sustaining. Continual expansion is the goal. That goal is facilitated by (1) massive advertising; (2) the proliferation of products, many competing for the same market; (3) the planned obsolescence of products; and (4) lobbying at various levels of government to ensure that governmental decisions will be favorable to business and industry. "Planned obsolescence" refers to the fact that many products are specifically designed to last only a limited time. In fact, some are designed and advertised as throwaway products: clothing, pots and pans, and safety razors are to be used once or twice and then discarded. The consequences of planned obsolescence are the production of more trash that must be disposed of, the use of more resources, and the creation of more pollutants from industries that make such products.

Business and industry not only lobby for industrial growth, they also vigorously oppose pollution-control proposals and, in some cases, have managed to defeat those proposals either by lobbying or by influencing public opinion. Thus, the industrial economy intersects with the polity in environmental problems.

The Politics of the Environment.   Environmental problems have generally not been high-priority items with politicians. This lack of attention is unfortunate, because one way to get something done about environmental problems is to create positions that have specific responsibility for those problems. For environmental problems, this solution means governmental positions. Although Americans dislike the creation of new governmental positions, without them little may be done. There is little incentive for private industry to take the lead in addressing ecological problems.

Pollution is a national problem that requires federal action. In the past, the federal government either ignored the problem or delegated responsibility to the states. This attitude changed with the creation of the Environmental Protection Agency. Today, most politicians express interest and concern for environmental issues. Unfortunately, the rhetoric is not always matched by effective action.

The current status of forest areas graphically illustrates the political failure to deal with environmental problems. As we have already noted, deforestation is a serious problem. Yet even if a government controls a significant proportion of its nation's forests, it may sell the forested land at prices below what the timber is worth (Abramovitz 1998). It also may sell the timber for far less than it is worth. In effect, governments pay private enterprise to take public timber. In the United States, for example, most sales of National Forest trees resulted in less money to the treasury than the Forest Service spent preparing for the sales! Between 1992 and 1994, the timber sales program lost $1 billion, a figure that does not include the costs of reforesting, erosion of streams, and lost fisheries. Overall, timber sales from federally owned land have been profitable in only three years during the last century.

Thus, the stance of the administration on environmental issues is crucial. Consider what happened when President George W. Bush took office. Some gains in protection had occurred during the Clinton presidency; but within months after he took office, Bush "scuttled new standards for arsenic in drinking water, pulled out of the Kyoto treaty on global warming, and rejected stricter fuel-efficiency standards" (Kolbert 2002). Davidson (2003) claimed that no previous president has attacked environmental laws "with the same fury" as President Bush. Among other issues, by 2020 an additional 42 million tons of air pollutants will be permitted under Bush's "Clear Skies" plan, leading to an additional 100,000 premature deaths. The Bush administration also set up a 63-person energy advisory team and only appointed one member who lacked any ties to corporate energy interests, reneged on a campaign promise to regulate car-

NATURE BATS LAST

"Of all the problems I've studied," said one student, "the environmental problem is the most frustrating and frightening to me. It seems that no matter what you do, you're trapped. I see what it means to say that nature bats last." In spite of the seriousness of the problems and the dilemmas (such as a new technology that addresses one problem only to create another), this chapter shows that people have made some progress in dealing with environmental problems. Where does your community stand? Make a survey of the environmental problems. Check your newspaper, your library, and local officials to get information about pollution levels. Tour your area and observe the number and, if possible, kinds of pollutants that are daily being released into the atmosphere, the waterways, and the land. Use the materials in this chapter and the data you get from your survey to write an article or a letter to the editor for your local newspaper and/or your school newspaper. Even though nature always bats last, is it possible that both human beings and nature can be winners in the long run?

bon dioxide emissions from power plants, and opened up 220 million acres of public land to logging, road building, and mining.

Another example of politics affecting environmental problems involves the destruction wrought by Hurricane Katrina (Mayer 2005). The state of Mississippi wanted casinos built on the wetlands of the Gulf coast. They wanted the revenue from the casinos, but didn't want them built on dry land because of objections from local conservative moralists. The Environmental Protection Agency argued against the casinos, because the wetlands are the home of aquatic life, are an important mechanism for drainage, and act as a buffer against storm damage. A U.S. senator from Mississippi was influential in having an EPA employee who was holding up the casino permits transferred. The permits were granted, the casinos were built, and the damage both to the casinos and the coast was far more severe than it would otherwise have been. In this case, politics triumphed over environmental needs. But the victory turned bitter with Katrina.

Social Psychological Factors

Attitudes and the Environment. Many people see the earth as a resource to be mined rather than as a trust to be cared for. "Skyrocketing consumption is the hallmark of our era" (Durning 1991:154). The measure of success is the amount of goods that can be consumed. People are admonished that they could be just as happy with less and warned that they are engaged in a process of self-destruction as they abuse the earth for their own excessive gratification, but these warnings largely seem to fall on deaf ears. Environmentalism is honored more in theory than in practice. The prevailing attitude is "I must get all that I can out of this life," rather than "I must cherish and sustain the earth that gives us life."

Existing attitudes about the importance of environmental problems are detrimental to helpful action. A national survey revealed that 42 percent of Americans thought the government was doing about the right amount or too much to protect the environment, 22 percent believed we should *not* abide by the Kyoto agreement on global warming, and another 36 percent had no opinion on the matter (Polling Report 2007). In another survey, 41 percent agreed that global warming is a "very serious" problem, but 42 percent

463

of those also thought that it is due to natural causes or that we can't be sure of the causes (Pew Research Center 2006b). In other words, only a little over a fourth of the respondents agreed that global warming is a very serious problem that is caused by human activity and, therefore, amenable to resolution by the appropriate action. It is not surprising that there is little public pressure for the federal government to be more aggressive in compelling business and industry to be environmentally responsible. Such attitudes will not spur politicians to take actions necessary to deal effectively with environmental problems.

In addition, many people believe that stricter environmental regulations will force business closings and bring about a loss of jobs, a belief unsupported by evidence. There may be an occasional closing or the loss of certain jobs, but to generalize from a few cases is to commit the *fallacy of dramatic instance*. In the nation as a whole, there is no conflict between jobs and the environment (Obach 2002).

fallacy

Racist attitudes contribute to a problem noted earlier: the greater exposure of minorities to hazardous materials both at work and in their homes. *Environmental racism means that the worst of the toxic waste sites are in African American and Hispanic communities* (Maher 1998). It also means that the minorities are more likely to work near such materials. In addition to racial and ethnic minorities, the poor of all races are also more likely to suffer detrimental consequences from environmental problems. The well-to-do, who have more political power than others, have the NIMBY (not-in-my-backyard) attitude that leads them to take action to minimize environmental hazards in their own places of work and housing. Thus, attitudes contribute to the greater exposure of both racial and ethnic minorities and the poor to environmental problems.

Values and the Environment.   The value of growth, "the more the better," has been a theme of American life. Sorokin (1942:255) called this aspect of American culture "quantitative colossalism." It leads to continual expansion of the perception of the "good life," which means ever-increasing goods and services and a concomitant ever-intensifying of environmental problems.

The American value of individualism also contributes to political inaction and thus to the ecological problems. As Hardin (1971) put it, our individualism involves us in the "*tragedy of the commons.*" In the Middle Ages the "commons" was the pastureland of a village. It was owned by no one person because it was available for use by all the people of the village. The "commons" today are the world's resources, and the "tragedy" is that it is advantageous for individuals to exploit those resources but disadvantageous to all when too many individuals pursue their own advantage. Yet, with our value on individualism (rather than on group well-being), we are, said Hardin (1971:247), "locked into a system of 'fouling our own nest,'" by behaving "only as independent, rational, free-enterprisers." The value of individualism also makes Americans reluctant to yield power to government. For many Americans, political inaction is the soul of good government, but in the realm of ecology, political inaction is the harbinger of disaster.

Public Policy and Private Action

At the outset, we need to acknowledge that environmental problems pose numerous dilemmas. There are no easy answers. Some of the "solutions" create new problems. For instance, with the surge in population growth in the 19th century, farmers began looking for ways to increase food production. One way was through the development of nitrogen-based fertilizers, which led to enormously increased food production. But those same fertilizers were, and continue to be, responsible, for "poisoning ecosystems, destroying fisheries, and sickening and killing children throughout the world" (Fisher and Fisher 2001). Thus, the needed additional food is had at the expense of air and water quality.

Still, there are many ways to alleviate the problems. In fact, substantial progress has already been made in a number of areas (U.S. Public Health Service 1995). Blood lead levels among children have been reduced by such measures as converting to unleaded gasoline, reducing the number of food and soft-drink cans with lead solder, and banning the use of leaded paint in homes. Many lakes and waterways that were once unusable for fishing or swimming are once again usable. After the Clean Air Act of 1990, the proportion of people living in counties that meet EPA standards for clean air rose from 49.7 percent to 76.3 percent in just three years. And increasing numbers of people have curbside recycling programs available to them. Yet the problems are still numerous as well as serious. Action is needed by individuals, by business and industry, and by the various levels of government.

What Can Individuals Do?

Knowledgeable people need to educate others about the seriousness of environmental pollution and depletion in order to change attitudes, values, and behavior. When people understand what they can do and the benefits of their efforts, they are more likely to engage in the appropriate behavior (Scott 1999; O'Connor et al. 2002).

Such education helps individuals recognize how much each one can do to alleviate the environmental problems. For example, you could stop using throwaway items such as cameras and razors. You could refuse to buy cheese that is sliced and individually wrapped in plastic. Or parents could use cloth instead of disposable diapers. MacEachern (1990) offers 750 suggestions for individuals to alleviate environmental problems. In addition, each individual can become a role model and an open advocate of environmental protection. Role modeling (such as picking up your trash at a campsite) and verbal appeals do influence others to behave responsibly (Wagstaff and Wilson 1988).

There are many ways in which you can conserve energy. Only minor changes in lifestyle can add up to substantial savings. When millions of people use automobiles that get more miles to the gallon than older models, when millions participate in recycling efforts, when millions use energy-saving appliances and methods that cut back on electricity, the savings are enormous. People could easily save a million or more barrels of crude oil every day without detracting from their standard of living.

What Can Business and Industry Do?

Business and industry must cooperate with governmental efforts to clean up the environment, but must also strive to balance growth with ecological considerations and search for *alternative, clean sources of energy* upon which to base the economy. A number of alternatives are already being studied. Some people advocate nuclear power, but a total conversion to nuclear power is not feasible. Furthermore, nuclear power confronts people with the very difficult questions of how to dispose of radioactive waste and how to ensure against leaks and accidents that can release radioactivity into the atmosphere. Other possible alternatives include solar energy (the light and heat from the sun), geothermal energy (the water and hot rock beneath the earth's surface), and the use of wind-driven generators. The advantages and disadvantages of each of these alternatives must be explored carefully but quickly for the supply of fossil fuels is being rapidly depleted while the demand for energy is increasing throughout the world.

What Can the Government Do?

Government action at every level is crucial in dealing with environmental problems. The federal government could mandate higher gas mileage for all new cars. The government could effect savings in resources and simultaneously help the pollution problem by supporting the development of mass transit. Mass transit can carry 70 times the number of people as a highway, generate only 1 percent of the hydrocarbons, and cost one-tenth as much to build per mile as does a highway (Hagerman 1990). The government could follow through with a Congressional mandate in the early 1990s to set standards for the distribution transformers that convert the high-voltage current transmitted over grids into lower-voltage current for home and business use (Kolbert 2006). More efficient transformers are available, and installing them in place of the less efficient ones now in use could save the nation about 12 billion kilowatt hours of electricity usage a year—enough to power all the households in Iowa for one year.

The federal government could also diminish or eliminate pollution caused by its own operations and by those supported by federal funds. It could provide direct funding and tax incentives for research into pollution control and alternative energy sources. It could impose tax penalties on businesses and corporations that damage the environment, a measure that has proven to reduce problems in the United States and other nations (Roodman 1999). It could approve the Kyoto treaty, which has been signed by 181 nations who have agreed to cut emissions of greenhouse gases by 5 percent in order to avert the problem of global warming. It could reduce the production of greenhouse gases like methane, which is the second largest contributor to global warming, by requiring the use of technology that captures the gas at landfills and waste management facilities and during the mining of fossil fuels (Hansen 2004; Jorgenson 2006).

State and local governments also can play a significant role in addressing environmental problems by establishing recycling laws and policies. Consider the advantages:

> Recycling offers communities everywhere the opportunity to trim their waste disposal needs, and thereby reduce disposal costs, while simultaneously combating global environmental problems. Recycling metals, paper, glass, plastics, and organic wastes would lessen the demand for energy and materials. Producing aluminum from scrap instead of bauxite cuts energy usage and air pollution by 95 percent. Making paper from discards instead of virgin timber not only saves valuable forests, it reduces the energy used per ton by up to three quarters and requires less than half as much water. (Pollock 1987:101–102)

The first advantage listed, trimming waste disposal needs, gets into an area that has almost reached crisis proportions in some cities. The volume of discarded material is surpassing the capacity to manage it. In addition, electronic waste has become the main contributor to high levels of lead in landfills (Saphores, Nixon, Ogunseitan, and Shapiro 2006). Recycling, which can address such problems to a considerable extent, may need to be mandatory. Will people cooperate? Unfortunately, some people will not. But most will, particularly when measures such as curbside pickup of materials are instituted (Domina and Koch 2002).

Follow-Up.   Make a list of the actions you have personally taken to alleviate environmental problems. Which of these, or other actions, would you make a matter of law and which would you make purely voluntary?

Summary

Environmental problems arise out of the need to maintain a balanced ecosystem—a balance between people and their natural environment. Human activity can disrupt this ecosystem to the point of destruction.

Environmental problems may be broadly classified as environmental pollution and environmental depletion. Pollution includes air pollution, water pollution, land pollution, global warming, noise pollution, and aesthetic damage. Depletion refers to dwindling natural resources, including energy.

It is difficult to measure the extent of these environmental problems. Some progress has been made but the problems remain serious.

Environmental problems involve inherent contradictions among a number of American values. We do not fully understand how these contradictions are being manifested in social life, but we know that they diminish the quality of life in a number of ways. Pollutants threaten the health and life of humans, animals, and plants. The ecological balance is threatened by the potential destruction of certain processes that are necessary to sustain life on earth. The economic costs of both pollution damage and pollution control are enormous, and the contradictions between the demand for energy, the need for a clean environment, and the aspirations of the developing world pose a threat to world peace.

Rapid population growth is one of the important threats to the environment. The effects of population growth are more than additive, as evidenced by diminishing returns and the threshold effect. In addition to population growth, the industrial economy is at the root of environmental problems. The products, by-products, and continuing growth in the industrial economy create serious environmental problems. The problems are intensified by the tendency of the government to ignore them or to set up ineffective programs and policies. Federal action is imperative if Americans are to seriously attack the problems of the environment.

Among social psychological factors, attitudes that view the earth simply as a resource to be exploited and that give minimal importance to environmental problems inhibit action. Racist attitudes intensify the problem for minorities by exposing them to more hazards at work and home. The American values of growth and individualism have supported the economic and political arrangements that contribute to the problems.

Key Terms

Ecosystem	Herbicide
Environmental	Pesticide
Depletion	Photosynthesis
Environmental	Pollutant
Pollution	Urbanization
Eutrophication	

Study Questions

1. What is the ecosystem? Why is it important to us?
2. Name and explain the three types of environmental problems people face.
3. How extensive are the environmental problems?
4. In what ways do environmental problems pose a threat to life, health, and the ecological balance?
5. Discuss the economic costs of environmental problems.
6. How do environmental problems threaten world peace?
7. What are some of the undesirable effects of population growth?
8. How does the economy and polity affect environmental problems?
9. What kinds of social psychological factors contribute to environmental problems?
10. What might be done to deal with the problems of environmental pollution and environmental depletion?

Internet Resources/ Exercises

1. Explore some of the ideas in this chapter on the following sites:

http://www.epa.gov The U.S. Environmental Protection Agency has materials on all the environmental problems we have discussed.

http://www.envirolink.org The Envirolink Network offers links to thousands of resources on every environmental issue.

http://ewg.org Site of the Environmental Working Group, whose research is designed to improve health and protect the environment.

chapter 15 review

2. Most scientists agree that global warming is a severe and urgent problem. Some people still disagree. Search the Internet for arguments both for and against global warming as a serious problem. Summarize the points and the supporting data made by both sides. Identify any fallacies of thinking you find in the arguments.

3. Political action is imperative if environmental problems are to be effectively attacked. Use a search engine to explore the relationship between government or politics and environmental problems. Find information on government at all levels. Make a list of the 10 most helpful and 10 most harmful actions (or lack of action) taken by governments in recent years. Use the information to write a letter to your local paper urging governmental action on some environmental problem about which you are concerned.

For Further Reading

Athanasiou, Tom. *Divided Planet: The Ecology of Rich and Poor.* Athens, GA: University of Georgia Press, 1998. A discussion of global environmental problems that stresses the significance of the gap between the developing and the developed nations for the future of the environment.

Dasgupta, Partha. *Human Well-Being and the Natural Environment.* New York: Oxford University Press, 2001. An economist argues that human well-being depends on the natural environment, including places of beauty, as well as on material goods and knowledge.

Harrison, Paul, and Fred Pearce. *AAAS Atlas of Population and Environment.* Berkeley, CA: University of California Press, 2001. Shows how, throughout the world, population growth and density, along with technology, affects the ecosystem. Notes both short-term and long-term effects.

MacEachern, Diane. *Save Our Planet: 750 Everyday Ways You Can Help Clean Up the Earth.* New York: Dell, 1990. Shows how individuals can act to alleviate environmental problems, including what you can do around your home or apartment.

Rischard, Jean-Francois. *High Noon: 20 Global Problems, 20 Years to Solve Them.* New York: Basic Books, 2003. Examines the environmental problems that threaten the planet—global warming, biodiversity losses, depletion of fisheries, deforestation, water deficits, and maritime pollution—as well as the issues related to those problems and ways in which nations must work together to resolve the problems.

Speth, James Gustave. *Red Sky at Morning: America and the Crisis of the Global Environment.* New Haven: Yale University Press, 2004. Speth, a university dean and adviser to two presidents, reviews the dismal lack of progress in dealing with environmental problems, shows the urgency and global nature of the problems, and suggests actions that both individuals and groups (including governments) must take to avert disaster.

Werbach, Adam. *Act Now, Apologize Later.* New York: HarperCollins, 1997. A call to action, and the rationale for such action, by the president of the Sierra Club. Includes some stories of successful activism.

Withgott, Jay H., and Scott R. Brennan. *Environment: The Science Behind the Stories.* 2nd ed. Upper Saddle River, NJ: Prentice-Hall, 2006. Case studies are used to illustrate and discuss every kind of environmental problem in a way that is scientifically sound yet accessible to those not scientifically trained.

abuse improper use of drugs or alcohol to the degree that the consequences are defined as detrimental to the user or society

achievement as distinguished from educational "attainment," the level the student has reached as measured by scores on various verbal and nonverbal tests

addiction repeated use of a drug or alcohol to the point of periodic or chronic intoxication that is detrimental to the user or society

adjudication making a judgment; settling a judicial matter

aggression forceful, offensive, or hostile behavior toward another person or society

AIDS acquired immune deficiency syndrome, a disease in which a viral infection causes the immune system to stop functioning, inevitably resulting in death

alienation a sense of estrangement from one's social environment, typically measured by one's feelings of powerlessness, normlessness, isolation, meaninglessness, and self-estrangement

anarchism the philosophy that advocates the abolition of government in order to secure true freedom for people

atmosphere the general mood and social influences in a situation or place

attainment as distinguished from educational "achievement," the number of years of education completed by a student

attitude a predisposition about something in one's environment

autonomy the ability or opportunity to govern oneself

biological characteristic an inherited, rather than learned, characteristic

bisexual having sexual relations with either sex or both together

bureaucracy an organization in which there are specific areas of authority and responsibility, a hierarchy of authority, management based on written documents, worker expertise, management based on rules, and full-time workers

capitalism an economic system in which there is private, rather than state, ownership of wealth and control of the production and distribution of goods; people are motivated by profit and compete with each other for maximum shares of profit

carcinogenic causing cancer

catharsis discharge of socially unacceptable emotions in a socially acceptable way

charter school a nonreligious public school approved by the local school district but free of many regulations and policies that apply to other public schools

cognitive development growth in the ability to perform increasingly complex intellectual activities, particularly abstract relationships

cohabitation living together without getting married

compensatory programs programs designed to give intensive help to disadvantaged pupils and increase their academic skills

conflict theory a theory that focuses on contradictory interests, inequalities between social groups, and the resulting conflict and change

consumer price index a measure of the average change in prices of all types of consumer goods and services purchased by urban wage earners and clerical workers

contradiction opposing phenomena within the same social system

corporate welfare governmental benefits given to corporations that are unavailable to other groups or to individuals

critical thinking the analysis and evaluation of information

culture the way of life of a people, including both material products (such as technology) and nonmaterial characteristics (such as values, norms, language, and beliefs)

cunnilingus oral stimulation of the female genitalia

cybersex sexual activity conducted via the Internet

dehumanization the process by which an individual is deprived of the qualities or traits of a human being

deinstitutionalization a movement to change the setting of treatment of mental disorders from hospitals to the community through rapid discharge of patients

dependent variable the variable in an experiment that is influenced by an independent variable

detoxification supervised withdrawal from dependence on a drug

differential association theory the theory that illegal behavior is due to preponderance of definitions favorable to such behavior

discrimination arbitrary, unfavorable treatment of the members of some social group

disfranchise to deprive of the right to vote

division of labor the separation of work into specialized tasks

divorce rate typically, the number of divorces per 1,000 marriages

domestic terrorism the use, or threatened use, of violence by people operating entirely within the United States to intimidate or coerce the government and/or citizens in order to reach certain social or political aims

downsizing reduction of the labor force in a company or corporation

ecosystem a set of living things, their environment, and the interrelationships among and between them

environmental depletion increasing scarcity of natural resources, including those used for generating energy

environmental destruction alterations in the environment that make it less habitable or useful for people or other living things

environmental pollution harmful alterations in the environment, including air, land, and water

epidemiology the study of factors that affect the incidence, prevalence, and distribution of illnesses

erotica sexually arousing materials that are not degrading or demeaning to adults or children

ethnic group people who have a shared historical and cultural background that leads them to identify with each other

etiology the causes of a disease

eutrophication overfertilization of water due to excess nutrients, leading to algae growth and oxygen depletion

exploitation use or manipulation of people for one's own advantage or profit

fallacy of appeal to prejudice argument by appealing to popular prejudices or passions

fallacy of authority argument by an illegitimate appeal to authority

fallacy of circular reasoning use of conclusions to support the assumptions that were necessary to make the conclusions

fallacy of composition the assertion that what is true of the part is necessarily true of the whole

fallacy of dramatic instance overgeneralizing

fallacy of misplaced concreteness making something abstract into something concrete

fallacy of non sequitur something that does not follow logically from what has preceded it

fallacy of personal attack argument by attacking the opponent personally rather than dealing with the issue

fallacy of retrospective determinism the argument that things could not have worked out any other way than they did

family a group united by marriage, blood, and/or adoption in order to satisfy intimacy needs and/or to bear and socialize children

fellatio oral stimulation of the male genitalia

forcible rape the carnal knowledge of a female forcibly and against her will

frequency distribution the organization of data to show the number of times each item occurs

gender the meaning of being male or female in a particular society

gender role the attitudes and behavior that are expected of men and women in a society

ghetto an area in which a certain group is segregated from the rest of society; often used today to refer to the impoverished area of the inner city

gridlock the inability of the government to legislate significant new policies

gross national product (GNP) the total value, usually in dollars, of all goods and services produced by a nation during a year

herbicide a chemical used to kill plant life, particularly weeds

heterogamy marriage between partners with diverse values and backgrounds

heterosexual having sexual preference for persons of the opposite sex

homogamy marriage between partners with similar values and backgrounds

homophobia irrational fear of homosexuals

homosexual having sexual preference for persons of the same sex; someone who privately or overtly considers himself or herself a homosexual

iatrogenic caused by the physician in the course of his or her treatment of a patient

ideology a set of ideas that explain or justify some aspect of social reality

incest exploitative sexual contact between relatives in which the victim is under the age of 18

incidence the number of new cases of an illness that occurs during a particular period of time

independent variable the variable in an experiment that is manipulated to see how it affects changes in the dependent variable

innate existing in a person from birth

institution a collective pattern of dealing with a basic social function; typical institutions identified by sociologists are the government, economy, education, family and marriage, religion, and the media

institutional racism policies and practices of social institutions that tend to perpetuate racial discrimination

interaction reciprocally influenced behavior on the part of two or more people

interest group a group that attempts to influence public opinion and political decisions in accord with the particular interests of its members

international terrorism politically motivated violence against citizens of political entities different from those of the perpetrators in order to coerce and intimidate others into accepting the perpetrators' goals

labor force all civilians who are employed or unemployed but able and desiring to work

lesbian a female homosexual

life chances the probability of gaining certain advantages defined as desirable, such as long life and health

life expectancy the average number of years a newborn can expect to live

lobbyist an individual who tries to influence legislation in accord with the preferences of an interest group

maladjustment poor adjustment to one's social environment

malnutrition inadequate food, in amount or type

manic-depressive reaction a disorder involving fluctuation between emotional extremes

Marxist pertaining to the system of thought developed by Karl Marx and Friedrich Engels, particularly emphasizing materialism, class struggle, and the progress of humanity toward communism

mean the average

median the score below which are half of the scores and above which are the other half

military parity equality or equivalence in military strength

morbidity the prevalence of a specified illness in a specified area

morphological pertaining to form and structure

neurosis a mental disorder involving anxiety that impairs functioning

norm shared expectations about behavior

nuclear family husband, wife, and children, if any

obscenity materials that are offensive by generally accepted standards of decency

organized crime an ongoing organization of people who provide illegal services and goods and who maintain their activities by the aid of political corruption

paraphilia the need for a socially unacceptable stimulus in order to be sexually aroused and satisfied

participant observation a method of research in which one directly participates and observes the social reality being studied

patronage giving government jobs to people who are members of the winning party

pedophile an adult who depends on children for sexual stimulation

personal problem a problem that can be explained in terms of the qualities of the individual

pesticide a chemical used to kill insects defined as pests

photosynthesis a natural process essential to life, resulting in the production of oxygen and organic materials

pica a craving for unnatural substances, such as dirt or clay

pimp one who earns all or part of his or her living by acting as a manager or procurer for a prostitute

placebo any substance having no physiological effect that is given to a subject who believes it to be a drug that does have an effect

pluralism   the more or less equal distribution of power among interest groups

political alienation   a feeling of political disillusionment, powerlessness, and estrangement

political party   an organized group that attempts to control the government through the electoral process

pollutant   anything that causes environmental pollution

pornography   literature, art, or films that are sexually arousing

posttraumatic stress disorder   an anxiety disorder associated with serious traumatic events, involving such symptoms as nightmares, recurring thoughts about the trauma, a lack of involvement with life, and guilt

poverty   a state in which income is insufficient to provide the basic necessities of food, shelter, clothing, and medical care

poverty level   the minimum income level that Americans should have to live on, based on the Department of Agriculture's calculations of the cost of a basic diet called "the economy food plan"

power elite model   a model of politics in which power is concentrated in political, economic, and military leaders

predatory crimes   acts that have victims who suffer loss of property or some kind of physical harm

prejudice   a rigid, emotional attitude that legitimates discriminatory behavior toward people in a group

prevalence   the number of cases of an illness that exist at any particular time

primary group   the people with whom one has intimate, face-to-face interaction on a recurring basis, such as parents, spouse, children, and close friends

promiscuity   undiscriminating, casual sexual relationships with many people

prostitution   having sexual relations for remuneration, usually to provide part or all of one's livelihood

psychosis   a disorder in which the individual fails to distinguish between internal and external stimuli

psychosomatic disorder   an impairment in physiological functioning that results from the individual's emotional state

race   a group of people distinguished from other groups by their origin in a particular part of the world.

racism   the belief that some racial groups are inherently inferior to others

recidivism   repeated criminal activity and incarceration

regulatory agency   an organization established by the government to enforce statutes that apply to a particular activity

rehabilitation   resocializing a criminal and returning him or her to full participation in society

reification   defining what is abstract as something concrete

relative deprivation   a sense of deprivation based on some standard used by the individual who feels deprived

retributiveness   paying people back for their socially unacceptable behavior

ritualized deprivation   a school atmosphere in which the motions of teaching and learning continue, while the students are more concerned about surviving than learning

role   the behavior associated with a particular position in the social structure

role conflict   a person's perception that two or more of his or her roles are contradictory, or that the same role has contradictory expectations, or that the expectations of the role are unacceptable or excessive

sadomasochism   the practice of deriving sexual pleasure from the infliction of pain

sanctions   mechanisms of social control for enforcing a society's standards

schizophrenia   a psychosis that involves a thinking disorder, particularly hallucinations and fantasies

self-fulfilling prophecy   a belief that has consequences (and may become true) simply because it is believed

sex   an individual's identity as male or female

sexism   prejudice or discrimination against someone because of his or her sex

sexual harassment   unwelcome sexual advances, requests for sexual favors, and other sexual behavior that either results in punishment when the victim resists or creates a hostile environment or both

socialization   the process by which an individual learns to participate in a group

social problem   a condition or pattern of behavior that contradicts some other condition or pattern of behavior; is defined as incompatible with the desired quality of life; is caused, facilitated, or prolonged by social factors; involves intergroup conflict; and requires social action for resolution

socioeconomic status position in the social system based on economic resources, power, education, prestige, and lifestyle

sodomy intercourse defined as "unnatural"; particularly used to refer to anal intercourse

statutory rape sexual intercourse with a female who is below the legal age for consenting

stealth racism hidden or subtle acts of prejudice and discrimination that may be apparent only to the victim

stepfamily a family formed by marriage that includes one or more children from a previous marriage

stereotype an image of members of a group that standardizes them and exaggerates certain qualities

stigma that which symbolizes disrepute or disgrace

stratification system arrangement of society into groups that are unequal with regard to such valued resources as wealth, power, and prestige

structural functionalism a sociological theory that focuses on social systems and how their interdependent parts maintain order

subsidy a government grant to a private person or company to assist an enterprise deemed advantageous to the public

survey a method of research in which a sample of people are interviewed or given questionnaires in order to get data on some phenomenon

symbolic interactionism a sociological theory that focuses on the interaction between individuals, the individual's perception of situations, and the ways in which social life is constructed through interaction

test of significance a statistical method for determining the probability that research findings occurred by chance

total institution a place in which the totality of the individual's existence is controlled by external forces

trauma physical or emotional injury

underemployment working full time for poverty wages, working part time when full-time work is desired, or working at a job below the worker's skill level

unemployment rate the proportion of the labor force that is not working but is available for work and has made specific efforts to find work

urbanization the increasing concentration of people living in cities

values things preferred because they are defined as having worth

variable any trait or characteristic that varies in value or magnitude

violence the use of force to kill, injure, or abuse others

voucher system a system that allows parents to use tax money to send their children to a school, private or public, of their choice

war a major armed conflict between nations or between organized groups within a nation in which a thousand or more people are killed

white-collar crime crimes committed by respectable citizens in the course of their work

work ethic the notion that your sense of worth and the satisfaction of your needs are intricately related to the kind of work you do

references

Abbott, S. 1987. "A new look at treatment trends." *Alcoholism and Addiction* (March–April):44–48.

ACORN. 2005. *The High Cost of Credit.* Association of Community Organizations for Reform Web site.

Adams, B., M. P. Aranda, B. Kemp, and K. Takagi. 2002. "Ethnic and gender differences in distress among Anglo American, African American, Japanese American, and Mexican American spousal caregivers of persons with dementia." *Journal of Clinical Geropsychology* 8:279–301.

Adams, J. B., et al. 2003. "Relationships between personality and preferred substance and motivations for use among adolescent substance abusers." *American Journal of Drug and Alcohol Abuse* 29:691–712.

Adams, J. E., Jr. 1997. "Organizational context and district resource allocation." *Journal of Education Finance* 23 (Fall):234–58.

Adams, K. E. 2004. "Mandatory parental notification: The importance of confidential health care for adolescents." *Journal of the American Medical Women's Association* 59:87–90.

Agnew, R., and D. M. Petersen. 1989. "Leisure and delinquency." *Social Problems* 36 (October):332–50.

Ahrens, C. J., and C. D. Ryff. 2006. "Multiple roles and well-being." *Sex Roles* 55:801–15.

Ajdukovic, M. 1998. "Displaced adolescents in Croatia." *Adolescence* 33 (Spring):209–17.

Akerlind, I., and J. O. Hornquist. 1992. "Loneliness and alcohol abuse: A review of evidences of an interplay." *Social Science and Medicine* 34 (February):405–14.

Alaimo, K., C. M. Olson, and E. A. Frongillo, Jr. 2000. "Food insufficiency and American school-aged children's cognitive, academic, and psychosocial development." *Pediatrics* 108:44–53.

———. 2002. "Family food insufficiency, but not low family income, is positively associated with dysthymia and suicide symptoms in adolescents." *Journal of Nutrition* 132:719–25.

Alaimo, K., C. M. Olson, E. A. Frongillo, Jr., and R. R. Briefel. 2001. "Food insufficiency, family income, and health in U.S. preschool and school-aged children." *American Journal of Public Health* 91:781–86.

Alarcon, W. A., et al. 2005. "Acute illnesses associated with pesticide exposure at schools." *Journal of the American Medical Association* 294:455–65.

Albelda, R., S. Himmelweit, and J. Humphries. 2004. "The dilemmas of lone motherhood." *Feminist Economics* 10:1–7.

Aldous, J., and R. F. Ganey. 1999. "Family life and the pursuit of happiness." *Journal of Family Issues* 20 (March):155–80.

Alexander, P. C., et al. 1998. "Adult attachment and long-term effects in survivors of incest." *Child Abuse and Neglect* 22 (January):45–61.

Allen, J. T. 2000. "Making the grade, or not." *U.S. News and World Report,* March 13, p. 24.

Allen, S. 2004. "Report puts hospital deaths from preventable errors at 195,000." *San Diego Union-Tribune,* July 27.

Allender, D. M., and F. Marcell. 2003. "Career criminals, security threat groups, and prison gangs." *FBI Law Enforcement Bulletin* 72:8–12.

Allison, P. D., and F. F. Furstenberg. 1989. "How marital dissolution affects children: Variations by age and sex." *Developmental Psychology* 25 (July):540–49.

Alon, S., and M. Tienda. 2005a. "Assessing the 'mismatch' hypothesis: Differences in college graduation rates by institutional selectivity." *Sociology of Education* 78:294–325.

———. 2005b. "Job mobility and early career wage growth of white, African-American, and Hispanic women." *Social Science Quarterly* 86:1196–1217.

Alonso, J., et al. 2004. "Health-related quality of life associated with chronic conditions in eight countries." *Quality of Life Research* 13:283–98.

Amato, P. R. 2001. "Children of divorce in the 1990s." *Journal of Family Psychology* 15:355–70.

Amato, P. R., and D. D. DeBoer. 2001. "The transmission of marital instability across generations." *Journal of Marriage and Family* 63:1038–51.

Amato, P. R., and S. J. Rogers. 1997. "A longitudinal study of marital problems and subsequent divorce." *Journal of Marriage and the Family* 59 (August):612–24.

Amato, P. R., and J. M. Sobolewski. 2001. "The effects of divorce and marital discord on adult children's psychological well-being." *American Sociological Review* 66:900–21.

American Academy of Pediatrics. 2001. "Media violence." *Pediatrics* 108:1222–26.

American Association of University Women. 2006. "Drawing the line survey." AAUW Web site.

American Civil Liberties Union. 1999. *Freedom Network.* American Civil Liberties Union Web site.

———. 2002. "ACLU says Homeland Security Bill step backward." Press release. American Civil Liberties Union Web site.

———. 2004. *Purged! How a Patchwork of Flawed and Inconsistent Voting Systems Could Deprive Millions of Americans the Right to Vote.* American Civil Liberties Union Web site.

American Federation of Teachers. 2002. *Do Charter Schools Measure Up?* Washington, DC: American Federation of Teachers.

American Psychiatric Association. 1994. *Diagnostic and Statistical Manual of Mental Disorders,* 4th ed. Washington, DC: American Psychiatric Association.

Ames, G. M., J. W. Grube, and R. S. Moore. 2000. "Social control and workplace drinking norms." *Journal of Studies on Alcohol* 61:203–19.

Amin, A. 2004. "Regulating economic globalization." *Transactions of the Institute of British Geographers* 29:217–33.

Anderson, A. 1982. "Neurotoxic follies." *Psychology Today* (July):30–42.

———. 1998. "Strengths of gay male youth." *Child and Adolescent Social Work Journal* 15 (February):55–71.

Anderson, C. A. 2004. "An update on the effects of playing violent video games." *Journal of Adolescence* 17:113–22.

Anderson, C. A., and N. L. Carnagey. 2003. "Exposure to violence media." *Journal of Personality and Social Psychology* 84:960–71.

Anderson, C. J., and Y. V. Tverdova. 2003. "Corruption, political allegiances, and attitudes toward government in contemporary democracies." *American Journal of Political Science* 47:91–109.

Anderson, J. P., R. M. Kaplan, and C. F. Ake. 2004. "Arthritis impact on U.S. life quality." *Social Indicators Research* 69:67–91.

Anderson, K. B., C. Harris, and L. Okamura. 1997. "Individual differences and attitudes toward rape: A meta-analytic review." *Personality and Social Psychology Bulletin* 23 (March):295–315.

Angermeyer, M. C., M. Beck, S. Dietrich, and A. Holzinger. 2004. "The stigma of mental illness." *International Journal of Social Psychiatry* 50:153–62.

Annest, J. L., J. A. Mercy, D. R. Gibson, and G. W. Ryan. 1995. "National estimates of nonfatal firearm-related injuries." *Journal of the American Medical Association* 273 (June 14):1749–54.

Antecol, H., and D. Cobb-Clark. 2001. "Men, women, and sexual harassment in the U.S. military." *Gender Issues* 19:3–18.

Applebome, P. 1996. "Many new teachers are unprepared, study says." *The New York Times,* September 13.

Aponte, R. 1991. "Urban Hispanic poverty: Disaggregations and explanations." *Social Problems* 38 (November):516–28.

Apsler, R., M. R. Cummins, and S. Carl. 2003. "Perceptions of the police by female victims of domestic partner violence." *Violence against Women* 9:1318–35.

Archer, D., and R. Gartner. 1979. "Violent acts and violent times: A comparative approach to postwar homicide rates." *American Sociological Review* 41 (December):937–62.

Armstrong, G. L., L. A. Conn, and R. W. Pinner. 1999. "Trends in infectious disease mortality in the United States during the 20th century." *Journal of the American Medical Association* 281 (January 6):61–66.

Arnold, D. H., et al. 2006. "Preschool-based programs for externalizing problems." *Education and Treatment of Children* 29:311–39.

Aronson, M., and B. Hagberg. 1998. "Neuropsychological disorders in children exposed to alcohol during pregnancy." *Alcoholism: Clinical and Experimental Research* 22 (April):321–24.

Arrington, C. 1990. "A generation of men grows up." *Men's Life* (Fall):64–70.

Ash, M., and T. R. Fetter. 2004. "Who lives on the wrong side of the environmental tracks?" *Social Science Quarterly* 85:441–62.

Asher, R. M. 1992. *Women with alcoholic husbands: Ambivalence and the trap of codependency.* Chapel Hill: University of North Carolina Press.

Ashforth, B. 1994. "Petty tyranny in organizations." *Human Relations* 47 (July):755–78.

Aspden, P., J. Wolcott, J. L. Bootman, and L. R. Cronenwett, eds. 2007. *Preventing Medication Errors.* Washington, DC: National Academies Press.

Astone, N. M., and S. S. McLanahan. 1991. "Family structure, parental practices, and high school completion." *American Sociological Review* 56 (June):309–20.

Atkinson, M. P., T. N. Greenstein, and M. M. Lang. 2005. "For women, breadwinning can be dangerous." *Journal of Marriage and Family* 67:1137–48.

Aveline, D. 2006. "Did I have blinders on or what?" *Journal of Family Issues* 27:777–802.

Ayanian, J. Z., and P. D. Cleary. 1999. "Perceived risks of heart disease and cancer among cigarette smokers." *Journal of the American Medical Association* 281 (April 28):1019–21.

Babbage, K. J. 1998. *High-Impact Teaching: Overcoming Student Apathy.* Lancaster, PA: Technomic Publishing.

Bacon, O., et al. 2006. "Commercial sex work and risk of HIV infection among young drug-injecting men who have sex with men in San Francisco." *Sexually Transmitted Diseases* 33:228–34.

Bahr, S. J., S. L. Maughan, A. C. Marcos, and B. Li. 1998. "Family, religiosity, and the risk of adolescent drug use." *Journal of Marriage and the Family* 60 (November):979–92.

Bailey, J. M., and D. S. Benishay. 1993. "Familial aggregation of female sexual orientation." *American Journal of Psychiatry* 150 (February):272–77.

Bailey, J. M., and R. C. Pillard. 1991. "A genetic study of male sexual orientation." *Archives of General Psychiatry* 48 (December):1089–98.

Bailey, W. C. 1990. "Murder, capital punishment, and television: Execution publicity and homicide rates." *American Sociological Review* 55 (October):628–33.

Balona, D. 2004. "State pitches school choice." *Orlando Sentinel,* July 8.

Balsam, K. F., E. D. Rothblum, and T. P. Beauchaine. 2005. "Victimization over the life span." *Journal of Consulting and Clinical Psychology* 73:477–87.

Banthin, J. S., and D. M. Bernard. 2006. "Changes in financial burdens for health care." *Journal of the American Medical Association* 296:2712–19.

Barak, M. E. M., and A. Levin. 2002. "Outside of the corporate mainstream and excluded from the work community: A study of diversity, job satisfaction, and well-being." *Community, Work and Family* 5:133–57.

Barbeau, E. M., N. Krieger, and M. Soobader. 2004. "Working-class matters: Socioeconomic disadvantage, race/ethnicity, gender, and smoking in NHIS 2000." *American Journal of Public Health* 94:269–78.

Barker, K. N., E. A. Flynn, G. A. Pepper, D. W. Bates, and R. L. Mikeal. 2002. "Medication errors observed in 36 health care facilities." *Archives of Internal Medicine* 162:1897–903.

Barko, N. 2000. "The other gender gap." *American Prospect,* June 19, pp. 61–67.

Barna Research Online. 2001. "Born again adults remain firm in opposition to abortion and gay marriage." Barna Research Online Web site.

Barnes, S. L. 2005. *The Cost of Being Poor.* New York: State University of New York Press.

Barnett, O. W. 2001. "Why battered women do not leave." *Trauma, Violence, and Abuse* 2:3–35.

Barnett, W. S. 1998. "Long-term cognitive and academic effects of early childhood education of children in poverty." *Preventive Medicine* 27 (March–April):204–07.

Barone, M. 2004. "The new shoe-leather politics." *U.S. News and World Report,* January 19, p. 36.

Barron, M., and M. Kimmel. 2000. "Sexual violence in three pornographic media." *Journal of Sex Research* 37:161–68.

Barros-Dios, J. M., M. A. Barreiro, A. Ruano-Ravina, and A. Figueiras. 2002. "Exposure to residential radon and lung cancer in Spain." *American Journal of Epidemiology* 15: 548–55.

Barry, B. 2002. "Capitalists rule OK? Some puzzles about power." *Politics, Philosophy and Economics* 1:155–84.

Bartley, M., A. Sacker, and P. Clarke. 2004. "Employment status, employment conditions, and limiting illness." *Journal of Epidemiology and Community Health* 58:501–6.

Basile, K. C. 2002. "Prevalence of wife rape and other intimate partner sexual coercion in a nationally representative sample of women." *Violence and Victims* 17:511–24.

Basile, M. 2004. "Going to the source: Why Al Qaeda's financial network is likely to withstand the current war on terrorist financing." *Studies in Conflict and Terrorism* 27:169–85.

Bauer, J. E., et al. 2005. "Longitudinal assessment of the impact of smoke-free worksite policies on tobacco use." *American Journal of Public Health* 95:1024–29.

Baughman, R., D. DiNardi, and D. Holtz-Eakin. 2003. "Productivity and wage effects of 'family-friendly' fringe benefits." *International Journal of Manpower* 24:247–59.

Baum, C. L., II. 2003. "Does early maternal employment harm child development?" *Journal of Labor Economics* 21:409–48.

Baum, K. 2006. "Identity theft, 2004." *Bureau of Justice Statistics Bulletin,* April.

Baum, K., and P. Klaus. 2005. "Violent victimization of college students, 1995–2002." *Bureau of Justice Statistics Special Report,* January.

Baum, M. A., and S. Kernell. 1999. "Has cable ended the golden age of presidential television?" *American Political Science Review* 93 (March):99–112.

Bauman, K. 1999. "One in five people had difficulty satisfying basic needs in 1995." *Press Release.* U.S. Census Bureau Web site.

Bayrakdar-Garside, R., and B. Klimes-Dougan. 2002. "Socialization of discrete negative emotions." *Sex Roles* 47:115–28.

Bebber, C. C. 1994. "Increases in U.S. violent crime during the 1980s following four American military actions." *Journal of Interpersonal Violence* 9 (March):109–16.

Beck, A. J., and P. M. Harrison. 2006. "Sexual violence reported by correctional authorities." *Bureau of Justice Statistics Special Bulletin,* July.

Beck, E. M., and S. E. Tolnay. 1990. "The killing fields of the deep south: The market for cotton and the lynching of blacks, 1882–1930." *American Sociological Review* 55 (August):526–39.

Becker, H. S. 1952. "Social-class variations in the teacher-pupil relationship." *Journal of Educational Sociology* 25 (April):451–65.

———. 1953. "Becoming a marijuana user." *American Journal of Sociology* 59 (November):235–42.

Becker, J. V., L. J. Skinner, G. G. Agel, J. Howell, and K. Bruce. 1982. "The effects of sexual assault on rape and attempted rape victims." *Victimology: An International Journal* 7 (1–4):106–13.

Becker, J. V., and R. M. Stein. 1991. "Is sexual erotica associated with sexual deviance in adolescent males?" *International Journal of Law and Psychiatry* 14 (1–2):85–95.

Becker, K., Y. Hu, and N. Biller-Andorno. 2006. "Infectious diseases—a global challenge." *International Journal of Medical Microbiology* 296:179–85.

Beitchman, J. H., K. J. Zucker, J. E. Hood, G. A. deCosta, and D. Akman. 1991. "A review of the short-term effects of child sexual abuse." *Child Abuse and Neglect* 15 (4):537–56.

Bell, A., M. Weinberg, and S. Hammersmith. 1981. *Sexual Preference.* Bloomington: Indiana University Press.

Bell, A. P., and M. S. Weinberg. 1978. *Homosexualities: A Study of Diversity among Men and Women.* New York: Simon and Schuster.

Bell, D., 1960. *The End of Ideology.* New York: Free Press.

Bellah, R. N. 1993. "Outrageous thoughts on war and peace." *New Oxford Review* (March):15–20.

Belle, D. 2003. "Poverty, inequality, and discrimination as sources of depression among U.S. women." *Psychology of Women Quarterly* 27:101–13.

Belluck, P. 2003. "Methadone, once the way out, suddenly grows as a killer drug." *The New York Times,* February 9.

Bendroth, M. L. 1994. *Fundamentalism and Gender: 1875 to the Present.* New Haven, CT: Yale University Press.

Benedek, E. P., and C. F. Brown. 1999. "No excuses: Televised pornography harms children." *Harvard Review of Psychiatry* 7 (November–December):236–40.

Benjamin, D., and S. Simon. 2005. *The Next Attack: The Failure of the War on Terror and a Strategy for Getting It Right.* New York: Times Books.

Bennett, N. G., A. K. Blanc, and D. E. Bloom. 1988. "Commitment and the modern union: Assessing the link between premarital cohabitation and subsequent marital stability." *American Sociological Review* 53 (February):127–38.

Bennett, R. R. 1991. "Routine activities: A cross-national assessment of a criminological perspective." *Social Forces* 70 (September):147–63.

Benson, M. L., G. L. Fox, A. DeMaris, and J. Van Wyk. 2003. "Neighborhood disadvantage, individual economic distress, and violence against women in intimate relationships." *Journal of Quantitative Criminology* 19:207–35.

Bergen, R. K., and K. A. Bogle. 2000. "Exploring the connection between pornography and sexual violence." *Violence and Victims* 15:227–34.

Berger, J. 1999. "Panel is proposed to fight corruption in trash industry." *The New York Times,* March 16.

Bergman, M. 2002. "Census bureau report shows 'big payoff' from educational degrees." Press release. U.S. Census Bureau Web site.

Bergner, R. M., and A. J. Bridges. 2002. "The significance of heavy pornography involvement for romantic partners." *Journal of Sex and Marital Therapy* 28:193–206.

Berkman, L. F. 2000. "From social integration to health." *Social Science and Medicine* 51:843–58.

Berkowitz, L. 1981. "How guns control us." *Psychology Today* (June):12–13.

Bernard, J. 1966. *Marriage and Family among Negroes.* Englewood Cliffs, NJ: Prentice-Hall.

Bernhard-Oettel, C., M. Sverke, and H. De Witte. 2006. "Comparing three alternative types of employment with permanent full-time work." *Work and Stress* 19:301–18.

Bernstein, R. 2004. "Hispanic and Asian Americans increasing faster than overall population." Press release, U.S. Census Bureau.

Bessenoff, G. R. 2006. "Can the media affect us? Social comparison, self-discrepancy, and the thin ideal." *Psychology of Women Quarterly* 30:239–51.

Bethke, T. M., and D. M. DeJoy. 1993. "An experimental study of factors influencing the acceptability of dating violence." *Journal of Interpersonal Violence* 8 (March):36–51.

Betts, J. R., and D. Morell. 1999. "The determinants of undergraduate grade point average." *Journal of Human Resources* 34 (Spring):268–93.

Bhattacharya, J., T. DeLeire, S. Haider, and J. Currie. 2003. "Heat or eat? Cold-weather shocks and nutrition in poor American families." *American Journal of Public Health* 93:1149–54.

Bianchi, S. M. 1995. "The changing demographic and socioeconomic characteristics of single parent families." *Marriage and Family Review* 20 (1–2):71–97.

Bibby, J. F., and L. S. Maisel. 1998. *Two Parties—Or More? The American Party System.* Boulder, CO.: Westview.

Bickel, J. 2000. "Women in academic medicine." *Journal of the American Medical Women's Association* 55 (Winter):10–20.

Biden, J. R., Jr. 1990. "They're out there crying for help." *Los Angeles Times,* March 14.

Biernat, M., and D. Kobrynowicz. 1997. "Gender-and race-based standards of competence." *Journal of Personality and Social Psychology* 72 (3):544–57.

Biever, C. 2006. "The irresistible rise of cybersex." *New Scientist* 190:67.

Bigner, J. J., and R. B. Jacobsen. 1992. "Adult responses to child behavior and attitudes toward fathering: Gay and nongay fathers." *Journal of Homosexuality* 23 (3):99–112.

Bilge, B., and G. Kaufman. 1983. "Children of divorce and one-parent families: Cross-cultural perspectives." *Family Relations* 32 (January):59–71.

Billingham, R., and T. Abrahams. 1998. "Parental divorce, body dissatisfaction, and physical attractiveness ratings of self and others among college women." *College Student Journal* 32 (March):148–52.

Bird, C. E. 1999. "Gender, household labor, and psychological distress." *Journal of Health and Social Behavior* 40:32–45.

Bird, C. E., and A. M. Fremont. 1991. "Gender, time use, and health." *Journal of Health and Social Behavior* 32 (June):114–29.

Bitler, M. P., J. B. Gelbach, and H. W. Hoynes. 2004. "Has welfare reform affected children's living arrangements?" *Focus* 23:14–20.

Bjarnason, T., et al. 2003. "Alcohol culture, family structure, and adolescent alcohol use." *Journal of Studies on Alcohol* 64:200–208.

———. 2005. "Familial and religious influences on adolescent alcohol use." *Social Forces* 84:375–90.

Black, S. 2001. "Morale matters." *American School Board Journal* 188:40–43.

Blackwell, D. L., J. G. Collins, and R. Coles. 2002. *Summary Health Statistics for U.S. Adults.* Washington, DC: Government Printing Office.

Blair, R. G. 2000. "Risk factors associated with PTSD and major depression among Cambodian refugees in Utah." *Health and Social Work* 25 (February): 23–30.

Blake, J. 1989. *Family Size and Achievement.* Berkeley: University of California Press.

Blalock, L., V. R. Tiller, and P. A. Monroe. 2004. " 'They get you out of courage': Persistent deep poverty among former welfare-reliant women." *Family Relations* 53:127–37.

Blanchard, N. 1998. "The quietest war." *E,* March–April, pp. 17–22.

Blasi, J., and D. Kruse. 2006. "The political economy of employee ownership in the United States." *International Review of Sociology* 16:127–47.

Blau, G., and D. Tatum. 2000. "Correlates of perceived gender discrimination for female versus male medical technologists." *Sex Roles* 43:105–18.

Blazer, D. G., R. C. Kessler, K. A. McGonagle, and M. S. Swartz. 1994. "The prevalence and distribution of major depression in a national community sample." *American Journal of Psychiatry* 151 (July):979–86.

Bletzer, K. V. 2005. "Sex workers in agricultural areas." *Culture, Health and Sexuality.* 6:543–55.

Blizzard, L., A. Ponsonby, T. Dwyer, A. Venn, and J. A. Cochrane. 2003. "Parental smoking and infant respiratory infection." *American Journal of Public Health* 93:482–88.

Block, F., A. C. Korteweg, and K. Woodward. 2006. "The compassion gap in American poverty policy." *Contexts* 5:14–20.

Blumstein, A., and R. Rosenfeld. 1998. "Assessing the recent ups and downs in U.S. homicide rates." *National Institute of Justice Journal* (October): 9–11.

Blumstein, P., and P. Schwartz. 1983. *American Couples: Money, Work, Sex.* New York: William Morrow.

Boeringer, S. B. 1994. "Pornography and sexual aggression: Associations of violent and nonviolent depictions with rape and rape proclivity." *Deviant Behavior* 15 (3):289–304.

Boisen, A. T. 1936. *The Exploration of the Inner World.* New York: Harper and Bros.

Bombard, J., A. Trosclair, M. Schooley, and C. Husten. 2004. "State-specific prevalence of current cigarette smoking among adults—United States, 2002." *MMWR Weekly* 52:1277–80.

Bonczar, T. P. 2003. *Prevalence of Imprisonment in the U.S. Population, 1974–2001.* Washington, DC: Government Printing Office.

Bond, J. T., E. Galinsky, and J. E. Swanberg. 1998. *The 1997 National Study of the Changing Workforce.* New York: Families and Work Institute.

Bonilla-Silva, E., C. Goar, and D. G. Embrick. 2006. "When whites flock together." *Critical Sociology* 32:229–53.

Bonkowski, S. E. 1989. "Lingering madness: Young adults' response to parental divorce." *Social Casework* 70 (April):219–23.

Bonner, R., and F. Fessenden. 2000. "States with no death penalty share lower homicide rates." *The New York Times,* September 22.

Bonneuil, N., and N. Auriat. 2000. "Fifty years of ethnic conflict and cohesion: 1945–94." *Journal of Peace Research* 37:563–81.

Bookwala, J., J. Sobin, and B. Zdaniuk. 2005. "Gender and aggression in marital relationships." *Sex Roles* 52:797–806.

Botta, R. A. 2003. "For your health? The relationship between magazine reading and adolescents' body image and eating disturbances." *Sex Roles* 48:389–99.

Bouchard, G. 2006. "Cohabitation versus marriage." *Journal of Divorce & Remarriage* 46:107–17.

Bourque, L. B., D. P. Tashkin, V. A. Clark, and R. Schuler. 1991 "Demographic and health characteristics of heavy marijuana smokers in Los Angeles county." *International Journal of the Addictions* 26 (July):739–55.

Bower, B. 2005. "Childhood's end." *Science News* 168:200–01.

Bowker, A., and M. Gray. 2005. "The cybersex offender and children." *FBI Law Enforcement Bulletin* 74:12–17.

Bowles, S., S. N. Durlauf, and K. Hoff, eds. 2006. *Poverty Traps.* Princeton, NJ: Princeton University Press.

Bowman, D. H. 2000. "Charters, vouchers earning mixed report card." *Education Week on the Web,* May 3.

Bowman, K. H. 2004. *Attitudes about Homosexuality.* American Enterprise Institute Web site.

Boxer, P. A., C. Burnett, and N. Swanson. 1995. "Suicide and occupation: A review of the literature." *Journal of Occupational and Environmental Medicine* 37 (April):442–52.

Boyer, D., and D. Fine. 1992. "Sexual abuse as a factor in adolescent pregnancy and child maltreatment." *Family Planning Perspectives* 24 (January–February):4–11.

Braam, A. W., et al. 2004. "Religious involvement and 6-year course of depressive symptoms in older Dutch citizens." *Journal of Aging and Health* 16:467–89.

Braddock, J. H., II, M. P. Dawkins, and W. Trent. 1994. "Why desegregate? The effect of school desegregation on adult occupational desegregation of African Americans, whites, and Hispanics." *International Journal of Contemporary Sociology* 31 (October):273–83.

Bradford, J., C. Ryan, and E. D. Rothblum. 1994. "National lesbian health care survey: Implications for mental health care." *Journal of Consulting and Clinical Psychology* 62 (April):228–42.

Brady, D. W., and C. Volden. 1998. *Resolving Gridlock: Politics and Policy from Carter to Clinton.* Boulder, CO: Westview.

Braga, A. A. 2003. "Serious youth gun offenders and the epidemic of youth violence in Boston." *Journal of Quantitative Criminology* 19:33–54.

Brajs-Zganec, A. 2005. "The long-term effects of war experiences on children's depression in the Republic of Croatia." *Child Abuse & Neglect* 29:31–43.

Bramlett, M. D., and W. D. Mosher. 2001. "First marriage dissolution, divorce, and remarriage: United States." *Advance Data, May 31.* Washington, DC: Department of Health and Human Services.

———. 2002. *Cohabitation, Marriage, Divorce, and Remarriage in the United States.* Washington, DC: Government Printing Office.

Brand, J. E., J. R. Warren, P. Carayon, and P. Hoonakker. 2007. "Do job characteristics mediate the relationship between SES and health?" *Social Science Research* 36:222–53.

Braun, H., F. Jenkins, and W. Grigg. 2006. *Comparing Private Schools and Public Schools Using Hierarchical Linear Modeling.* Washington, DC: Government Printing Office.

Breault, K. D., and A. J. Kposowa. 1987. "Explaining divorce in the United States: A study of 3,111 counties, 1980." *Journal of Marriage and the Family* 49 (August):549–58.

Brecher, E. J. 1993. "Work Stress." *San Diego Union-Tribune,* April 15.

Brenner, M. H. 1978. "The social costs of economic distress." In *Consultation on the Social Impact of Economic Distress,* pp. 3–6. New York: American Jewish Committee, Institute of Human Relations.

Brents, B. G., and K. Hausbeck. 2005. "Violence and legalized brothel prostitution in Nevada." *Journal of Interpersonal Violence* 20:270–95.

Brians, C. L., and B. Grofman. 2001. "Election day registration's effect on U.S. voter turnout." *Social Science Quarterly* 82:170–83.

Bridges, G. S., and S. Steen. 1998. "Racial disparities in official assessments of juvenile offenders." *American Sociological Review* 63 (August):554–70.

Brilliant, J. 2002. "Palestinians suffer malnutrition, poverty." Washington Times Web site.

Brizendine, L. 2006. *The Female Brain.* New York: Morgan Road Books.

Broad, W. J. 1997. "C.I.A. admits government lied about U.F.O. sightings." *The New York Times,* August 3.

Broder, J. M. 2006. "Immigrants and the economics of hard work." *The New York Times,* April 2.

Broder, M. S., D. E. Kanouse, B. S. Mittman, and S. J. Bernstein. 2000. "The appropriateness of recommendations for hysterectomy." *Obstetrics and Gynecology* 95 (February):199–205.

Brodeur, P. 1989. *Currents of Death: Power Lines, Computer Terminals, and the Attempt to Cover Up Their Threat to Your Health.* New York: Simon and Schuster.

Brodsky, L. M., R. W. Habash, W. Leiss, D. Krewski, and M. Rapacholi. 2003. "Health risks of electromagnetic fields." *Critical Review of Biomedical Engineering* 31:333–54.

Brody, G. H., et al. 2001. "The influence of neighborhood disadvantage, collective socialization, and parenting on African American children's affiliation with deviant peers." *Child Development* 72:1231–46.

Bronner, G., C. Peretz, and M. Ehrenfeld. 2003. "Sexual harassment of nurses and nursing students." *Journal of Advanced Nursing* 42:637–44.

Bronte-Tinkew, J., K. A. Moore, and J. Carrano. 2006. "The father-child relationship, parenting styles, and adolescent risk behaviors in intact families." *Journal of Family Issues* 27:850–81.

Brookings Institution Metropolitan Policy Program. 2005. *The Price Is Wrong.* Brookings Institution Web site.

Brooks, C. 1999. "Study prompts VA to help ill kids of female Vietnam vets." *San Diego Union-Tribune,* September 4.

Brown, J. S. 1952. "A comparative study of deviations from sexual mores." *American Sociological Review* 17 (April):135–46.

Brown, L. R. 2000. "Challenges of the new century." In *State of the World 2000,* ed. Lester R. Brown et al., pp. 3–21. New York: W. W. Norton.

Brown, L. R., and C. Flavin. 1999. "A new economy for a new century." In *State of the World 1999,* ed. Lester R. Brown et al., pp. 3–21. New York: W. W. Norton.

Brown, L. R., and S. Postel. 1987. "Thresholds of change." In *State of the World 1987,* ed. Lester R. Brown, pp. 3–19. New York: W. W. Norton.

Brown, S. A., B. A. Stetson, and P. A. Beatty. 1989. "Cognitive and behavioral features of adolescent coping in high-risk drinking situations." *Addictive Behaviors* 14 (1):43–52.

Brown, S. I. 2004. "Family structure and child well-being." *Journal of Marriage and Family* 66:351–67.

Brown, T. L., G. S. Parks, R. S. Zimmerman, and C. M. Phillips. 2001. "The role of religion in predicting adolescent alcohol use and problem drinking." *Journal of Studies on Alcohol* 62:696–705.

Browne, K. D., and C. E. Hamilton. 1998. "Physical violence between young adults and their parents." *Journal of Family Violence* 13 (March):59–79.

Brownfield, D. 1987. "Father-son relationships and violent behavior." *Deviant Behavior* 8 (1):65–78.

Browning, K., and R. Loeber. 1999. "Highlights of findings from the Pittsburgh youth study." *OJJDP Fact Sheet #95.* Washington, DC: Government Printing Office.

Bryant-Davis, T. 2004. "Rape is: A media review for sexual assault psychoeducation." *Trauma Violence and Abuse* 5:194–95.

Bryce, J. W., N. Walker, F. Ghorayeb, and M. Kanj. 1989. "Life experiences, response styles, and mental health among mothers and children in Beirut, Lebanon." *Social Science and Medicine* 28 (7):685–95.

Bryce, R. 2006. "Man versus mine." *The Atlantic Monthly* (January/February):44–46.

Bryjak, G. J. 1999. "Multiple reasons for lower crime rates." *San Diego Union-Tribune,* March 28.

Brym, R. J., and B. Araj. 2006. "Suicide bombing as strategy and interaction." *Social Forces* 84:1969–86.

Bull, M. J., and R. E. McShane. 2002. "Needs and supports for family caregivers of chronically ill elders." *Home Health Care Management and Practice* 14:92–98.

Bullman, T. A., C. M. Mahan, H. K. Kang, and W. F. Page. 2005. "Mortality in U.S. Army Gulf War veterans exposed to 1991 Khamisiyah chemical munitions destruction." *American Journal of Public Health* 95:1382–88.

Burd, L., T. M. Cotsonas-Hassler, J. T. Martsolf, and J. Kerbeshian. 2003. "Recognition and management of fetal alcohol syndrome." *Neurotoxicology and Teratology* 25:681–88.

Burdman, D. 2003. "Education, indoctrination, and incitement: Palestinian children on their way to martyrdom." *Terrorism and Political Violence* 15:96–123.

Bureau of Justice Statistics. 2001. *Sourcebook of Criminal Justice Statistics.* Bureau of Justice Statistics Web site.

———. 2006a. "Capital punishment statistics." BJS Web site.

———. 2006b. "Victim characteristics." BJS Web site.

Bureau of Labor Statistics. 2006a. "Characteristics of minimum wage workers: 2005." BLS Web site.

———. 2006b. "Number of nonfatal occupational injuries and illnesses involving days away from work." BLS Web site.

———. 2006c. "The employment situation: June 2006." BLS Web site.

———. 2006d. "Workplace injuries and illnesses in 2005." BLS Web site.

Burger, T. J., and A. Zagorin. 2004. "Did Cheney okay a deal?" *Time,* June 7, p. 42.

Burgess, A. W. 1984. *Child Pornography and Sex Rings.* Lexington, MA: Lexington Books.

Burgess, A. W., and L. L. Holmstrom. 1974. "Rape trauma syndrome." *American Journal of Psychiatry* 131 (September):981–86.

———. 1979. "Rape: Sexual disruption and recovery." *American Journal of Orthopsychiatry* 49 (4):648–57.

Burke, R. J. 1995. "Work and career experiences and emotional well-being of managerial and professional women." *Stress Medicine* ll (January):51–60.

Burns, J. M., J. W. Peterson, and T. E. Cronin. 1984. *Government by the People,* 12th ed. Englewood Cliffs, NJ: Prentice-Hall.

Bush, P. J., K. P. Weinfurt, and R. J. Iannotti. 1994. "Families versus peers: Developmental influences on drug use from grade 4–5 to grade 7–8." *Journal of Applied Developmental Psychology* 15 (July–September):437–56.

Butterfield, F. 2000. "Report indicates 'juvenile injustice.'" *San Diego Union-Tribune,* April 26.

———. 2004. "Cost of fighting crime zooms in U.S." *San Diego Union-Tribune,* May 3.

Butterfield, H. 1949. *Christianity and History.* London: Fontana Books.

Button, J. W., and B. A. Rienzo. 2003. "The impact of affirmative action: Black employment in six Southern cities." *Social Science Quarterly* 84:1–14.

Byrd, W. M., and L. A. Clayton. 2001. *An American Health Dilemma: Race, Medicine, and Health Care in the United States 1900–2000.* New York: Routledge.

Byrnes, N. 2006. "The high cost of fear." *Business Week,* November 6, p. 16.

Cain, B. S. 1989. "Parental divorce during the college years." *Psychiatry* 52 (May):135–46.

Callahan, D. 1998. *False Hopes: Why America's Quest for Perfect Health Is a Recipe for Failure.* Berkeley: University of California Press.

Calle, E. E., C. Rodriquez, K. Walker-Thurmond, and M. J. Thun. 2003. "Overweight, obesity, and mortality from cancer in a prospectively studied cohort of U.S. adults." *New England Journal of Medicine* 348:1625–38.

Cameron, F. 2002. "Utilitarian multilateralism." *Politics* 22:68–75.

Cameron, P., and K. Cameron. 1995. "Does incest cause homosexuality?" *Psychological Reports* 76 (April):611–21.

Campbell, C. A. 1991. "Prostitution, AIDS, and preventive health behavior." *Social Science and Medicine* 32 (12):1367–78.

Campbell, J. C., et al. 2003. "Risk factors for femicide in abusive relationships." *American Journal of Public Health* 93:1089–97.

Campbell, R. 2006. "Rape survivors' experiences with the legal and medical systems." *Violence against Women* 12:30–45.

Campbell, R., S. M. Wasco, C. E. Ahrens, T. Sefl, and H. E. Barnes. 2001. "Preventing the 'second rape.'" *Journal of Interpersonal Violence* 16:1236–59.

Campenni, C. E. 1999. "Gender stereotyping of children's toys." *Sex Roles* 40:212–38.

Cancian, M., et al. 2003. "Income and program participation among early TANF recipients." *Focus* 22:2–10.

Cannon, A., M. Lavelle, and C. Ragavan. 2000. "In the court of last resort." *U.S. News and World Report,* November 27, p. 33.

Cano, A., and K. D. O'Leary. 2000. "Infidelity and separations precipitate major depressive episodes and symptoms of nonspecific depression and anxiety." *Journal of Consulting and Clinical Psychology* 68:774–81.

Cantelon, S., and D. LeBoeuf. 1997. "Keeping young people in school: Community programs that work." *Juvenile Justice Bulletin,* June.

Cantor, J. E. 2006. "Campaign finance: an overview." *CRS Report for Congress.* Congressional Research Service Web site.

Cantor, J. M., R. Blanchard, A. D. Paterson, and A. F. Bogaert. 2002. "How many gay men owe their sexual orientation to fraternal birth order?" *Archives of Sexual Behavior* 31:63–71.

Cantril, A. H., and S. D. Cantril. 1999. *Reading Mixed Signals: Ambivalence in American Public Opinion about Government.* Baltimore, MD: Johns Hopkins University Press.

Carael, M., E. Slaymaker, R. Lyerla, and S. Sarkar. 2006. "Clients of sex workers in different regions of the world." *Sexually Transmitted Infections* 82:26–33.

Carballo, M., et al. 2004. "Mental health and coping in a war situation." *Journal of Biosocial Science* 36:463–77.

Cardozo, B. L., A. Vergara, F. Agani, and C. A. Golway. 2000. "Mental health, social functioning, and attitudes of Kosovar Albanians following the war in Kosovo." *Journal of the American Medical Association* 284:569–77.

Carlson, B. E. 1990. "Adolescent observers of marital violence." *Journal of Family Violence* 5:285–99.

Carmody, D. C., and L. M. Washington. 2001. "Rape myth acceptance among college women." *Journal of Interpersonal Violence* 16:424–36.

Carr, D. 2005. "Black death, white death." *Contexts* 4:43.

Caruso, D. B. 2003. "Patriot Act reach now extends beyond terrorism." *San Diego Union-Tribune,* September 15.

Caskey, J. P. 1994. *Fringe Banking: Check-Cashing Outlets, Pawnshops, and the Poor.* New York: Sage.

Caspi, A., B. R. Entner Wright, T. E. Moffitt, and P. A. Silva. 1998. "Early failure in the labor market: Childhood and adolescent predictors of unemployment in the transition to adulthood." *American Sociological Review* 63 (June):424–51.

Cast, A. D., D. Schweingruber, and N. Berns. 2006. "Childhood physical punishment and problem solving in marriage." *Journal of Interpersonal Violence* 21:244–61.

Castor, M. L., et al. 2006. "A nationwide population-based study identifying health disparities between American Indians/Alaska Natives and the general populations living in select urban counties." *American Journal of Public Health* 96:1478–84.

Catalano, S. M. 2006a. "Criminal victimization, 2005." *Bureau of Justice Statistics Bulletin,* September.

———. 2006b. "Intimate partner violence in the United States." Bureau of Justice Statistics Web site.

Caton, C. L. M., et al. 2005. "Risk factors for long-term homelessness." *American Journal of Public Health* 95:1753–59.

Cavanagh, S. E., K. S. Schiller, and C. Riegle-Crumb. 2006. "Marital transitions, parenting, and schooling." *Sociology of Education* 79:329–54.

Ceballo, R., T. A. Dahl, M. T. Aretakis, and C. Ramirez. 2001. "Inner-city children's exposure to community violence." *Journal of Marriage and the Family* 63:927–40.

Cebula, R. J., and W. J. Belton. 1994. "Voting with one's feet: An empirical analysis of public welfare and migration of the American Indian, 1985–1990." *American Journal of Economics and Sociology* 53 (July):273–80.

Center for Communication and Civil Engagement. 2005. *Assessment of U.S. Senate Campaign Expenditures in 2000, 2002, and 2004, with Predictions for 2006.* Center for Communication and Civic Engagement Web site.

Center for Community Change. 2005. *"Issues: The Native American project."* CCC Web site.

Center for Marriage and Families. 2005. "Family structure and children's educational outcomes." Institute for American Values Web site.

Centers for Disease Control. 1995a. "First 500,000 AIDS cases—United States, 1995." *Morbidity and Mortality Weekly Report,* 44 (November 24).

———. 1995b. "Health-care provider advice on tobacco use to persons aged 10–22 years—United States, 1993." *Morbidity and Mortality Weekly Report,* 44 (November 10).

———. 1996. "Mortality patterns—United States, 1993." *Morbidity and Mortality Weekly Report,* 45 (March 1).

———. 1998. "Incidence of cigarette smoking among U.S. teens." *Morbidity and Morality Weekly Report,* 47 (October 9).

———. 2000. "Age-specific excess deaths associated with stroke among racial/ethnic minority populations—United States, 1997." *Morbidity and Mortality Weekly Report,* 49 (February 11).

———. 2006a. "Reducing tobacco use." CDC Web site.

———. 2006b. "Youth exposure to alcohol advertising on radio." *Morbidity and Mortality Weekly Report* 55 (September 1).

Chang, E., C. Chen, E. Greenberger, D. Dooley, and J. Heckhausen. 2006. "What do they want in life? The life goals of a multi-ethnic, multi-generational sample of high school seniors." *Journal of Youth & Adolescence* 35:302–13.

Chang, M. L. 2004. "Growing pains: Cross-national variation in sex segregation in sixteen developing countries." *American Sociological Review* 69:114–37.

Chapple, C. L. 1997. "Dow Corning and the silicone breast implant debacle: A case of corporate crime against women." In *Masculinities and Violence,* ed. Lee H. Bowker, pp. 179–96. Newbury Park, CA: Sage.

Charmaz, K. 1995. "The body, identity, and self: Adapting to impairment." *Sociological Quarterly* 36 (4):657–80.

Chen, E., K. A. Matthews, and W. T. Boyce. 2002. "Socioeconomic differences in children's health." *Psychological Bulletin* 128:295–329.

Chen, H., M. R. Marks, and C. A. Bersani. 1994. "Unemployment classifications and subjective well-being." *Sociological Review* 42 (February):62–78.

Chen, M. J., B. A. Miller, J. W. Grube, and E. D. Waiters. 2006. "Music, substance use, and aggression." *Journal of Studies on Alcohol* 67:373–81.

Chen, R. 1996. "Risk factors of sexual abuse among college students in Taiwan." *Journal of Interpersonal Violence* 11 (March):79–93.

Chermack, S. T., S. F. Stoltenberg, B. E. Fuller, and F. C. Blow. 2000. "Gender differences in the development of substance-related problems." *Journal of Studies on Alcohol* 61:845–52.

Chernousenko, V. M. 1991. *Chernobyl: Insight from the Inside.* New York: Springer-Verlag.

Children Now. 2004. "Study finds more Latinos, fewer Asians on prime-time TV." Children Now Web site.

Chimienti, G., J. A. Nasr, and I. Khalifeh. 1989. "Children's reactions to war-related stress." *Social Psychiatry and Psychiatric Epidemiology* 24 (6):282–87.

Chinman, M. J., R. Weingarten, D. Stayner, and L. Davidson. 2001. "Chronicity reconsidered: Improving person-environment fit through a consumer-run service." *Community Mental Health Journal* 37:215–29.

Chiou, F. Y., and L. S. Rothenberg. 2003. "When pivotal policies meets partisan politics." *American Journal of Political Science* 47:503–22.

Chira, S. 1991. "Report says too many aren't ready for school." *The New York Times,* December 8.

Chiroro, P., G. Bohner, G. T. Viki, and C. I. Jarvis. 2004. "Rape myth acceptance and rape proclivity." *Journal of Interpersonal Violence* 19:427–42.

Christian, S. 1991. "Cancer's long shadow." *Los Angeles Times,* August 20.

Cimons, M. 1991. "Serious health problem seen for 1 in 5 U.S. teen-agers." *Los Angeles Times,* April 23.

Citizens Against Government Waste. 2006. *Introduction to the Pig Book*. Citizens Against Government Waste Web site.

Clark, C. 1994. "VA secretary vows to find cause of Gulf War syndrome." *San Diego Union-Tribune,* March 30.

Clark, W. A. V., and S. A. Blue. 2004. "Race, class, and segregation patterns in U.S. immigrant gateway cities." *Urban Affairs Review* 39:667–88.

Clawson, R. A. 2002. "Poor people, black faces." *Journal of Black Studies* 32:352–61.

Clifford, A. M. 2001. *Introducing Feminist Theology*. Maryknoll, NY: Orbis Books.

Cloud, J., and J. Morse. 2001. "Home sweet school." *Time,* August 27, pp. 47–54.

Cochran, S. D., and V. M. Mays. 2000. "Relation between psychiatric syndromes and behaviorally defined sexual orientation in a sample of the U.S. population." *American Journal of Epidemiology* 151:516–23.

Cohan, C. L., S. Cole, and J. Davila. 2005. "Marital transitions among Vietnam-era repatriated prisoners of war." *Journal of Social and Personal Relationships* 22:777–95.

Cohen, A. 2004. "The supreme struggle." *The New York Times,* January 18.

———. 2006. "American elections and the grand old tradition of disenfranchisement." *The New York Times,* October 8.

Cohen, C. 2003. "Winks, nods, disguises—and racial preference." *Commentary* 116:34–39.

Cohen, J. B., L. B. Hauer, and C. B. Wofsy. 1989. "Women and IV drugs: Parental and heterosexual transmission of human immunodeficiency virus." *Journal of Drug Issues* 19 (Winter):39–56.

Cohen, J. E. 1997. *Presidential Responsiveness and Public Policy-Making.* Ann Arbor: University of Michigan Press.

Cohen, L. E., and M. Felson. 1979. "Social change and crime rate trends." *American Sociological Review* 44 (August):588–607.

Cohen, M. A., and T. R. Miller. 1998. "The cost of mental health care for victims of crime." *Journal of Interpersonal Violence* 13 (February):93–110.

Cohen, P. N., and M. L. Huffman. 2003. "Occupational segregation and the devaluation of women's work across U.S. labor markets." *Social Forces* 81:881–908.

Cohen, S. 1984. "Cocaine Anonymous." *Drug Abuse and Alcoholism Newsletter* 13 (3).

Cohn, S., and M. Fossett. 1995. "Why racial employment inequality is greater in northern labor markets: Regional differences in white-black employment differentials." *Social Forces* 74 (December):511–42.

Colborn, T., D. Dumanoski, and J. Peterson Myers. 1997. *Our Stolen Future.* New York: Plume.

Cole, C. V. 1995. "Sexual abuse of middle school students." *School Counselor* 42 (January):239–45.

Coleman, M. G. 2003. "Job skill and black male wage discrimination." *Social Science Quarterly* 84:892–906.

———. 2004. "Racial discrimination in the workplace." *Industrial Relations* 43:660–89.

Coley, R. L. 1998. "Children's socialization experiences and functioning in single-mother households." *Child Development* 69 (February):219–30.

Collins, M. D., and J. H. Frey. 1992. "Drunken driving and informal social control: The case of peer intervention." *Deviant Behavior* 13 (January–March):73–87.

Collins, S. D. 2004. "Dissuading state support of terrorism." *Studies in Conflict and Terrorism* 27:1–18.

Collom, E. 2005. "The ins and outs of homeschooling." *Education and Urban Society* 37:307–335.

Commager, H. S., ed. 1945. *The Pocket History of the Second World War.* New York: Pocket Books.

Committee for the Compilation of Materials on Damage Caused by the Atomic Bombs in Hiroshima and Nagasaki. 1981. *The Physical, Medical, and Social Effects of the Atomic Bombings,* trans. Eisei Ishikawa and David L. Swain. New York: Basic Books.

Commoner, B. 1971. *The Closing Circle.* New York: Alfred A. Knopf.

Compton, W. M., B. F. Grant, J. D. Colliver, M. D. Glantz, and F. S. Stinson. 2004. "Prevalence of marijuana use disorders in the United States." *Journal of the American Medical Association* 291:2114–2121.

Condon, G. E. 2005. "Bush says spying is needed to guard U.S." The San Diego Union-Tribune, December 20.

Condron, D. J., and V. J. Roscigno. 2003. "Disparities within: Spending inequality and achievement in an urban school district." *Sociology of Education* 76:18–36.

Conference Board. 2005. "U.S. job satisfaction keeps falling." The Conference Board Web site.

Conger, R. D., F. O. Lorenz, G. H. Elder, Jr., J. N. Melby, R. L. Simons, and K. J. Conger. 1991. "A process model of family economic pressure and early adolescent alcohol use." *Journal of Early Adolescence* 11 (November):430–49.

Conly, C. H., and J. T. McEwen. 1990. "Computer Crime." *NIJ Reports,* January–February, pp. 2–7.

Connors, G. J., J. S. Tonigan, and W. R. Miller. 2001. "A longitudinal model of intake symptomatology, AA participation, and outcome." *Journal of Studies on Alcohol* 62:817–25.

Coohey, C. 2004. "Battered mothers who physically abuse their children." *Journal of Interpersonal Violence* 19:943–52.

Cook, C. C., and M. J. Bruin. 1994. "Determinants of housing quality: A comparison of white, African-American, and Hispanic single-parent women." *Journal of Family and Economic Issues* 15 (Winter):329–47.

Cook, J. M., D. S. Riggs, R. Thompson, J. C. Coyne, and J. I. Sheikh. 2004. "Posttraumatic stress disorder and current relationship functioning among World War II ex-prisoners of war." *Journal of Family Psychology* 18:36–45.

Cook, P. J., and J. Ludwig. 2000. *Gun Violence: The Real Costs.* New York: Oxford University Press.

Cook, T. E. 1998. *Governing with the News: The News Media as a Political Institution.* Chicago: University of Chicago Press.

Coolbaugh, K., and C. J. Hansel. 2000. "The comprehensive strategy: Lessons learned from pilot sites." *Juvenile Justice Bulletin.* Washington, DC: Government Printing Office.

Coon, C. S., S. M. Garn, and J. B. Birdsell. 1950. *Races.* Springfield, IL: Charles C Thomas.

Cooper, M. 1990. "Rejecting 'femininity': Some research notes on gender identity development in lesbians." *Deviant Behavior* 11 (October–December): 371–80.

Coopersmith, J. 2006. "Who will pay for Iraq and when?" *The San Diego Union-Tribune,* November 6.

Corrigan, P. 2004. "How stigma interferes with mental health care." *American Psychologist* 59:614–25.

Cose, E. 2004. "Brown v. Board: A dream deferred." Newsweek, May 17, pp. 53–59.

Costello, R. M. 2006. "Long-term mortality from alcoholism." *Journal of Studies on Alcohol* 67:694–99.

Cotter, D. A., J. M. Hermsen, S. Ovadia, and R. Vanneman. 2001. "The glass ceiling effect." *Social Forces* 80:655–82.

Council on Contemporary Families. 2003. "U.S. husbands first, U.S. government last in support for working wives." *Work and Family Newsbrief,* June, p. 4.

Coyle, J. "Fox News' use of 'fair and balanced' challenged legally." *The America's Intelligence Wire,* July 20.

Cozzarelli, C., A. V. Wilkinson, and M. J. Tagler. 2001. "Attitudes toward the poor and attributions for poverty." *Journal of Social Issues* 57:207–27.

Craig, C. L., R. C. Brownson, S. E. Cragg, and A. L. Dunn. 2002. "Exploring the effect of the environment on physical activity." *American Journal of Preventive Medicine* 23:36–43.

Crawford, T., and M. Naditch. 1970. "Relative deprivation, powerlessness, and militancy: The psychology of social protest." *Psychiatry* 33 (May):208–23.

Crockenberg, S. 1983. "Early mother and infant antecedents of Bayley scale performance at 21 months." *Developmental Psychology* 19 (5):727–30.

Croghan, I. T., et al. 2006. "Is smoking related to body image satisfaction, stress, and self-esteem in young adults?" *American Journal of Health Behavior* 30:322–33.

Cronin, T. E., and M. A. Genovese. 1998. *The Paradoxes of the American Presidency.* New York: Oxford University Press.

Crosnoe, R. 2006. "The connection between academic failure and adolescent drinking in secondary school." *Sociology of Education* 79:44–60.

Crosnoe, R., R. S. Mistry, and G. H. Elder, Jr. 2002. "Economic disadvantage, family dynamics, and adolescent enrollment in higher education." *Journal of Marriage and Family* 64:690–702.

Crutchfield, R. D., A. Glusker, and G. S. Bridges. 1999. "A tale of three cities: Labor markets and homicide." *Sociological Focus* 32 (February):65–83.

Cummings, P., D. C. Grossman, F. P. Rivara, and T. D. Koepsell. 1997. "State gun safe storage laws and child mortality due to firearms." *Journal of the American Medical Association* 278 (October 1):1084–86.

Cunradi, C. B., R. Caetano, and J. Schafer. 2002. "Religious affiliation, denominational homogamy, and intimate partner violence among U.S. couples." *Journal for the Scientific Study of Religion* 41:139–51.

Curry, T. J. 1991. "Fraternal bonding in the locker room: A profeminist analysis of talk about competition and women." *Sociology of Sport Journal* 8 (June):119–35.

Dail, P. W. 1988. "Unemployment and family stress." *Public Welfare* 46 (Winter):30–34.

Dalaker, J. 2001. *Poverty in the United States: 1998.* Washington, DC: Government Printing Office.

Dales, R., et al. 2004. "Air pollution and sudden infant death syndrome." *Pediatrics* 113:628–31.

Dalla, R. L. 2000. "Exposing the 'Pretty Woman' myth: A qualitative examination of the lives of female streetwalking prostitutes." *Journal of Sex Research* 37:333–43.

———. 2001. "Et tu Brute? A qualitative analysis of streetwalking prostitutes' interpersonal support networks." *Journal of Family Issues* 22:1066–85.

Dana, R. H. 2002. "Mental health services for African Americans." *Cultural Diversity and Ethnic Minority Psychology* 8:3–18.

Daneback, K., A. Cooper, and S. Manisson. 2005. "An internet study of cybersex participants." *Archives of Sexual Behavior* 34:321–28.

Daniels, L. A., ed. 2004. *The State of Black America 2004.* New York: National Urban League.

D'Augelli, A. R., and A. H. Grossman. 2001. "Disclosure of sexual orientation, victimization, and mental health among lesbian, gay, and bisexual older adults." *Journal of Interpersonal Violence* 16:1008–28.

D'Augelli, A. R., A. H. Grossman, and M. T. Starks. 2006. "Childhood gender atypicality, victimization, and PTSD among lesbian, gay, and bisexual youth." *Journal of Interpersonal Violence* 21:1462–82.

Davenport, C. 1995. "Assessing the military's influence on political repression." *Journal of Political and Military Sociology* 23 (Summer):119–44.

Davidson, O. G. 2003. "Dirty secrets." *Mother Jones,* September/October, pp. 49–53.

Davidson, R. C., and E. L. Lewis. 1997. "Affirmative action and other special consideration admissions at the University of California, Davis, School of Medicine." *Journal of the American Medical Association* 278 (October 8):1153–58.

Davies, J. C. 1962. "Toward a theory of revolution." *American Sociological Review* 27 (February):5–19.

Davies, S., and N. Guppy. 1997. "Fields of study, college selectivity, and student inequalities in higher education." *Social Forces* 75 (June): 1417–38.

Davies, S., and J. Tanner. 2003. "The long arm of the law." *The Sociological Quarterly* 44:385–404.

Davis, A. J., et al. 1995. "Home care for the urban chronically ill elderly in the People's Republic of China." *International Journal of Aging and Human Development* 41 (4):345–58.

Davis, D. M. 2004. "Merry-go-round: A return to segregation and the implications for creating democratic schools." *Urban Education* 39:394–407.

Davis, D. W., and B. D. Silver. 2004. "Civil liberties vs. security: Public opinion in the context of the terrorist attacks on America." *American Journal of Political Science* 48:28–46.

Davis, N. J., ed. 1993. *Prostitution: An International Handbook on Trends, Problems, and Policies.* Westport, CT: Greenwood.

Davison, T. E., and M. P. McCabe. 2005. "Relationships between men's and women's body image and their psychological, social, and sexual functioning." *Sex Roles* 52:463–75.

Dawes, S. S., P. A. Bloniarz, D. R. Connelly, K. L. Kelly, and T. A. Pardo. 1999. "Four realities of IT innovation in government." *The Public Manager* 28 (Spring):27–32.

Dawood, K., R. C. Pillard, C. Horvath, W. Revelle, and J. M. Bailey. 2000. "Familial aspects of male homosexuality." *Archives of Sexual Behavior* 29:155–64.

Dawson, D. A. 1991. "Family structure and children's health and well-being: Data from the 1988 national health interview survey on child health." *Journal of Marriage and the Family* 53 (August):573–84.

Day, A. 1991. "Morality, war: Do they mix?" *Los Angeles Times,* January 15.

De Coster, S., S. B. Estes, and C. W. Mueller. 1999. "Routine activities and sexual harassment in the workplace." *Work and Occupations* 26 (February):21–49.

Degenhardt, L., C. Day, E. Conroy, and S. Gilmour. 2006. "Examining links between cocaine use and street-based sex work in New South Wales, Australia." *Journal of Sex Research* 43:107–14.

Dekel, R., and Z. Solomon. 2006. "Marital relations among former prisoners of war." *Journal of Family Psychology* 20:709–12.

Delattre, E. J. 1990. "New faces of organized crime." *American Enterprise* (May–June):38–45.

Del Castillo, D. 2001. "Pakistan's Islamic colleges provide the Taliban's spiritual fire." *Chronicle of Higher Education* 48:A19–21.

DellaVigna, S., and E. Kaplan. 2006. "The Fox news effect: Media bias and voting." NBER Working Paper No. 12169. NBER Web site.

Demarest, J., and R. Allen. 2000. "Body image: Gender, ethnic, and age differences." *Journal of Social Psychology* 140:465–72.

Demerouti, E., S. Geurts, A. Bakker, and M. Euwema. 2004. "The impact of shiftwork on work-home conflict, job attitudes, and health." *Ergonomics* 47:987–1002.

De Micheli, D., and M. L. Formigoni. 2002. "Are reasons for the first use of drugs and family circumstances predictors of future use patterns?" *Addictive Behaviors* 27:87–100.

DeMuth, S., and S. L. Brown. 2004. "Family structure, family processes, and adolescent delinquency." *Journal of Research in Crime and Delinquency* 41:58–81.

DeMuth, S., and D. Steffensmeier. 2004. "The impact of gender and race-ethnicity in the pretrial release process." *Social Problems* 51:222–42.

DeNavas-Walt, C., R. W. Cleveland, and M. I. Roemer. 2001. "Money income in the United States: 2000." *Current Population Reports*. Washington, DC: Government Printing Office.

DeNavas-Walt, C., B. D. Proctor, and C. H. Lee. 2006. "Income, poverty, and health insurance in the United States: 2005." *Current Population Reports*. Washington, DC: Government Printing Office.

Dennis, J., and D. Owen. 2001. "Popular satisfaction with the party system and representative democracy in the United States." *International Political Science Review* 22:399–415.

Dentler, R. A., and P. Cutright. 1965. "Social effects of nuclear war." In *The New Sociology,* ed. I. L. Horowitz, pp. 409–26. New York: Oxford University Press.

DeStafano, L., and D. Colasanto. 1990. "Unlike 1975, today most Americans think men have it better." *Gallup Poll Monthly,* February, 293.

de Tocqueville, A. 1955. *The Old Regime and the French Revolution*. New York: Anchor Books.

Deutsch, C. H. 1990. "Saying no to the 'mommy track.'" *The New York Times,* January 28.

Devine, J. A., M. Plunkett, and J. D. Wright. 1992. "The chronicity of poverty: Evidence from the PSID, 1968–1987." *Social Forces* 70 (March):787–812.

DeVoe, J. F., et al. 2003. *Indicators of School Crime and Safety: 2003*. Washington, DC: Government Printing Office.

Dew, M. A., et al. 2001. "Prevalence and risk of depression and anxiety-related disorders during the first three years after heart transplantation." *Psychosomatics* 42:300–13.

Dew-Becker, I., and R. J. Gordon. 2005. "Where did the productivity growth go?" Paper presented at the 81st meeting of the Brookings Panel on Economic Activity.

deWilde, E. J., I. C. W. M. Kienhorst, R. F. W. Diekstra, and W. H. G. Wolters. 1992. "The relationship between adolescent suicide behavior and life events in childhood and adolescence." *American Journal of Psychiatry* 149 (January):45–51.

Diaz, R. M., G. Ayala, E. Bein, J. Henne, and B. V. Marin. 2001. "The impact of homophobia, poverty, and racism on the mental health of gay and bisexual Latino men." *American Journal of Public Health* 91:927–32.

Diaz, T., D. Viahov, V. Edwards, S. Conover, and E. Monterroso. 2002. "Sex-specific differences in circumstances of initiation into injecting-drug use among young adult Latinos in Harlem, New York City." *AIDS and Behavior* 6:117–22.

Dickens, B. M., and R. J. Cook. 2006. "Acquiring human embryos for stem-cell research." *International Journal of Gynaecology and Obstetrics,* December 20.

Diekman, A. B., and S. K. Murnen. 2004. "Learning to be little women and little men: The inequitable gender equality of nonsexist children's literature." *Sex Roles* 50:373–85.

Diener, E., M. Diener, and C. Diener. 1995. "Factors predicting the subjective well-being of nations." *Journal of Personality and Social Psychology* 69 (November):851–64.

Dillon, S. 2005. "Education law's payoff mixed, new test shows." *The San Diego Union-Tribune,* October 20.

———. 2006. "Florida high court ruling eliminates school vouchers." *The San Diego Union-Tribune,* January 6.

DiMaio, V. J. 2000. "Homicidal asphyxia." *American Journal of Forensic and Medical Pathology* 21 (March):1–4.

Distefan, J. M., J. P. Pierce, and E. A. Gilpin. 2004. "Do favorite movie stars influence adolescent smoking initiation?" *American Journal of Public Health* 94:1239–44.

Dittmar, H., E. Halliwell, and S. Ive. 2006. "Does Barbie make girls want to be thin? The effect of experimental exposure to images of dolls on the body image of 5- to 8-year-old girls." *Developmental Psychology* 42:283–92.

Dixon, J., C. Gordon, and T. Khomusi. 1995. "Sexual symmetry in psychiatric diagnosis." *Social Problems* 42 (August):429–49.

Dixon, K. A., and C. E. Van Horn. 2003. "The disposable worker: Living in a job-loss economy." *Heldrich Work Trends Survey* 6, no. 2.

Dohnt, H., and M. Tiggemann. 2006. "Body image concerns in young girls." *Journal of Youth and Adolescence* 35:135–45.

Dohrenwend, B. P., et al. 2006. "The psychological risks of Vietnam for U.S. veterans." *Science* 313:979–82.

Domhoff, G. W. 1990. *The Power Elite and the State: How Policy Is Made in America*. New York: Aldine de Gruyter.

Domina, T., and K. Koch. 2002. "Convenience and frequency of recycling." *Environment and Behavior* 34:216–38.

Donchin, Y., et al. 1995. "A look into the nature and causes of human errors in the intensive care unit." *Critical Care Medicine* 23 (February):294–300.

Donnerstein, E. 1980. "Pornography and violence against women: Experimental studies." *Annals of the New York Academy of Sciences* 347:227–88.

———. 1984. "Pornography: Its effect on violence against women." In *Pornography and Sexual Aggression,* ed. Neil M. Malamuth and Edward Donnerstein. New York: Academic Press.

Donnerstein, E., and D. Linz. 1984. "Sexual violence in the media: A warning." *Psychology Today* (January):14–15.

Dooley, D., K. A. Ham-Rowbottom, and J. Prause. 2001. "Underemployment and depression." *Journal of Health and Social Behavior* 41:421–36.

Dordick, G. A. 2002. "Recovering from homelessness: Determining the 'quality of sobriety' in a transitional housing program." *Qualitative Sociology* 25:7–32.

Dorius, C. J., S. J. Bahr, J. P. Hoffman, and E. L. Harmon. 2004. "Parenting practices as moderators of the relationship between peers and adolescent marijuana use." *Journal of Marriage and Family* 66:163–78.

Dornbusch, S. M., et al. 1985. "Single parents, extended households, and the control of adolescents." *Child Development* 56 (April):326–41.

Dover, E. D. 1998. *The Presidential Election of 1996: Clinton's Incumbency and Television.* Westport, CT: Praeger.

Downs, W. R., T. Capshew, and B. Rindels. 2006. "Relationships between adult women's mental health problems and their childhood experiences of parental violence and psychological aggression." *Journal of Family Violence* 21:439–47.

Downs, W. R., and S. R. Rose. 1991. "The relationship of adolescent peer groups to the incidence of psychosocial problems." *Adolescence* 26 (Summer):473–92.

Doyle, R. 2000. "The roots of homicide." *Scientific American,* October, p. 22.

———. 2002. "Bad things happen." *Scientific American,* June, p. 26.

Drew, D., and D. Weaver. 2006. "Voter learning in the 2004 presidential election." *Journalism and Mass Communication Quarterly* 83:25–42.

Drucker, P. F. 1968. *The Age of Discontinuity.* New York: Harper and Row.

Drug Enforcement Administration. 2002. "Flunitrazepam (Rohypnol)." DE Web site.

Dube, S. R., et al. 2001. "Childhood abuse, household dysfunction, and the risk of attempted suicide throughout the life span." *Journal of the American Medical Association* 286:3089–96.

Ducati, R. G., A. Ruffino-Netto, L. A. Basso, and D. S. Santos. 2006. "The resumption of consumption—a review on tuberculosis." *Memorias Do Instituto Oswaldo Cruz* 101:697–714.

Duhart, D. T. 2001. *Violence in the Workplace,* 1993–99. Washington, DC: U.S. Department of Justice.

Dukes, R. L., and B. D. Lorch. 1989. "Concept of self, mediating factors, and adolescent deviance." *Sociological Spectrum* 9 (Fall):301–19.

Dulio, D. A., D. L. Goff, and J. A. Thurber. 1999. "Untangled web: Internet use during the 1998 election." *PSOnline,* March. PSOnline Web site.

Duncan, D. F. 1991. "Violence and degradation as themes in 'adult' videos." *Psychological Reports* 69 (1):239–40.

Dunifon, R., A. Kalil, and A. Bajracharya. 2005. "Maternal working conditions and child well-being in welfare-leaving families." *Developmental Psychology* 41:851–59.

Dunn, J., J. Golding, L. Davies, and T. G. O'Connor. 2000. "Distribution of accidents, injuries, and illnesses by family type." *Pediatrics* 106:68–72.

Dunn, S. 2002. *Reading the Weathervane.* Washington, DC: Worldwatch Institute.

Dunn, S., and C. Flavin. 2002. "Moving the climate agenda forward." In *State of the World 2002,* ed. Christopher Flavin et al., pp. 24–50. New York: W. W. Norton.

Durkheim, E. 1933. *The Division of Labor in Society,* trans. George Simpson. New York: Free Press.

Durning, A., 1991. "Asking how much is enough." In *State of the World 1991,* ed. L. R. Brown, pp. 153–69. New York: W. W. Norton.

Durose, M. R., et al. 2005. *Family Violence Statistics.* Washington, DC: Government Printing Office.

Dutton, D. G., E. O. Boyanowsky, and M. H. Bond. 2005. "Extreme mass homicide: From military massacre to genocide." *Aggression and Violent Behavior* 10:437–73.

Dutton, M. A., S. Kaltman, L. A. Goodman, K. Weinfurt, and N. Vankos. 2005. "Patterns of intimate partner violence." *Violence and Victims* 20:483–97.

Dwyer, J., and J. Wilgoren. 2002. "The system dances with death." *The New York Times,* April 21.

Dye, T. R. 1995. *Who's Running America?* Englewood Cliffs, NJ: Prentice-Hall.

Dyer, C. B., V. N. Pavlik, K. P. Murphy, and D. J. Hyman. 2000. "The high prevalence of depression and dementia in elder abuse or neglect." *Journal of the American Geriatric Society* 48 (February):205–08.

Eaker, E. D., L. M. Sullivan, M. Kelly-Hayes, R. B. D'Agostino, and E. J. Benjamin. 2004. "Anger and hostility predict the development of atrial fibrillation in men in the Framingham Offspring Study." *Circulation* 109:1267–71.

Earls, C. M., and H. David. 1989. "A psychological study of male prostitution." *Archives of Sexual Behavior* 18 (5):401–20.

Eddings, J. 1995. "A persistent stealth racism is poisoning black-white relations." *U.S. News and World Report,* October 23.

Edelhertz, H. 1983. "White-collar and professional crime." *American Behavioral Scientist* 27 (October–November): 109–28.

Edelstein, M. E. 1988. *Contaminated Communities: The Social and Psychological Impacts of Residential Toxic Exposure.* Boulder, CO.: Westview.

Edin, K. J. 1995. "The myths of dependence and self-sufficiency: Women, welfare, and low-wage work." *Focus* 17 (Fall–Winter):1–9.

Editorial Projects in Education Research Center. 2006. "State policies on standards-based education over the past decade found to have a positive relationship with gains in student achievement." *Education Week* Web site.

Edlin, B. R., et al. 1994. "Intersecting epidemics—Crack cocaine use and HIV infection among inner-city young adults." *New England Journal of Medicine* 331 (November 24):1422–27.

Education Week. 1997. "Quality Counts: A Report Card on the Condition of Public Education in the 50 States." Education Week Web site.

———. 2000. *Quality Counts 2000: Who Should Teach?* Education Week Web site.

———. 2003. "To close the gap, quality counts." Educational Week Web site.

Edwards, G. C., III, and B. D. Wood. 1999. "Who influences whom? The president, Congress, and the media." *American Political Science Review* 93 (June):327–44.

Egley, A., Jr., and A. K. Major. 2003. "Highlights of the 2001 national youth gang survey." *OJJDP Fact Sheet.* Washington, DC: Government Printing Office.

———. 2004. "Highlights of the 2002 national youth gang survey." *OJJDP Fact Sheet.* Washington, DC: Government Printing Office.

Ehrenhalt, A. 1997. "Big numbers that haunt the government." *Governing Magazine,* January, pp. 7–12.

Ehrenreich, B. 1999. "Nickel-and-dimed: On (not) getting by in America." *Harper's Magazine,* January, pp. 37–52.

Ehrlich, P. R. 1971. "Eco-catastrophe!" In *The Survival Equation,* ed. R. Revelle, A. Khosla, and M. Vinovskis, pp. 352–64. Boston: Houghton Mifflin.

Eichenwald, K. 2002. "White-collar defense stance: The criminal-less crime." *The New York Times,* March 3.

Eisikovitz, Z. C., J. L. Edleson, E. Guttmann, and M. Sela-Amit. 1991. "Cognitive styles and socialized attitudes of men who batter." *Family Relations* 40 (January):72–77.

Eisinger, P. K. 1980. "Affirmative action in municipal employment: The impact of black political power." *Institute for Research on Poverty* (December):621–80.

Eisler, P., and M. Kelley. 2006. "Public wary of links with lobbyists." *USA Today,* October 18.

Eitle, D., S. J. D'Alessio, and L. Stolzenberg. 2006. "Economic segregation, race, and homicide." *Social Science Quarterly* 87:638–57.

El-Bassel, N., N. Guterman, D. Bargal, and K.-H. Su. 1998. "Main and buffering effects of emotional support on job- and health-related strains." *Employee Assistance Quarterly* 13 (3):1–18.

Ellison, C. G., J. P. Bartkowski, and K. L. Anderson. 1999. "Are there religious variations in domestic violence?" *Journal of Family Issues* 20 (January):87–113.

Ellison, C. G., and D. A. Powers. 1994. "The contact hypothesis and racial attitudes among black Americans." *Social Science Quarterly* 75 (June):385–400.

Elmer-Dewitt, P. 1992. "Rich vs. poor." *Time* (June 1): 42–58.

Elms, A. C. 1972. *Social Psychology and Social Relevance.* Boston: Little, Brown.

Emerson, M. O., G. Yancey, and K. J. Chai. 2001. "Does race matter in residential segregation?" *American Sociological Review* 66:922–35.

Emery, M. 2006. *The Future of Schools: How Communities and Staff Can Transform Their School Districts.* New York: Rowman & Littlefield.

Engardio, P. 2006. "Outsourcing: Job killer or innovation boost?" *Business Week Online,* November 9.

Engel, J. 1989. *Addicted: Kids Talking about Drugs in Their Own Words.* New York: Tom Doherty.

Engeler, E. 2006. "'Global epidemic' of the AIDS virus grows, U.N. says." *The San Diego Union-Tribune,* November 22.

Entwisle, D. R., and K. L. Alexander. 1992. "Summer setback: Race, poverty, school composition, and mathematics achievement in the first two years of school." *American Sociological Review* 57 (February):72–84.

———. 1994. "Winter setback: The racial composition of schools and learning to read." *American Sociological Review* 59 (June):446–60.

Environmental Protection Agency. 1996. *Radon.* EPA Web site.

Epstein, D. J. 2003. "Secret ingredients." *Scientific American,* August, pp. 22–23.

Epstein, J. F., and J. C. Groerer. 1997. "Heroin abuse in the United States." *OAS Working Paper.* Rockville, Md.: SAMHSA.

Epstein, P. R. 2000. "Is global warming harmful to health?" *Scientific American,* August, pp. 50–57.

Ericksen, K. P., and K. F. Trocki. l994. "Sex, alcohol and sexually transmitted diseases: A national survey." *Family Planning Perspectives* 26 (November– December): 257–63.

Ericson, M., and F. Hossain. 2003. "In perspective: America's conflicts." *The New York Times,* April 20.

Erlanger, S. 1999. "The guesses that turned out wrong." *New York Times,* March 28.

Eron, L. D. 1987. "The development of aggressive behavior from the perspective of a developing behaviorism." *American Psychologist* 42 (March):435–42.

Esbensen, F., and D. Huizinga. l993. "Gangs, drugs, and delinquency in a survey of urban youth." *Criminology* 31 (4):565–90.

Essed, P. 1991. *Understanding Everyday Racism: An Interdisciplinary Theory.* Newbury Park, CA: Sage.

Etzion, D. 2003. "Annual vacation: Duration of relief from job stressors and burnout." *Anxiety, Stress, and Coping* 16:213–26.

Evans, G. W. 2004. "The environment of childhood poverty." *American Psychologist* 59:77–92.

Evans, L., and K. Davies. 2000. "No sissy boys here: A content analysis of the representation of masculinity in elementary school reading textbooks." *Sex Roles* 42: 255–70.

Evans, N., A. Farkas, E. Gilpin, C. Berry, and J. P. Pierce. l995. "Influence of tobacco marketing and exposure to smokers on adolescent susceptibility to smoking." *Journal of the National Cancer Institute* 87 (October): l538–45.

Evans-Campbell, T., T. Lindhorst, B. Huang, and K. L. Walters. 2006. "Interpersonal violence in the lives of urban American Indian and Alaska Native women." *American Journal of Public Health* 96:1416–22.

Even-Chen, M. S., and H. Itzhaky. 2007. "Exposure to terrorism and violent behavior among adolescents in Israel." *Journal of Community Psychology* 35:43–55.

Ewan, C., E. Lowy, and J. Reid. 1991. "Falling out of culture: The effects of repetition strain injury on sufferers' roles and identity." *Sociology of Health and Illness* 13 (June):168–92.

Fagan, A. A. 2003. "Short- and long-term effects of adolescent violent victimization experienced within the family and community." *Violence and Victims* 18:445–59.

———. 2005. "The relationship between adolescent physical abuse and criminal offending." *Journal of Family Violence* 20:279–90.

Fagan, J. 1990. "Social processes of delinquency and drug use among urban gangs." In *Gangs in America,* ed. C. R. Huff. Newbury Park, CA: Sage.

Fagin, D., and M. Lavelle. 1999. *Toxic Deception: How the Chemical Industry Manipulates Science, Bends the Law, and Endangers Your Health.* Monroe, ME: Common Courage Press.

Faller, K. C. 1989. "Characteristics of a clinical sample of sexually abused children: How boy and girl victims differ." *Child Abuse and Neglect* 13 (2):281–91.

Fallis, R. K., and S. Opotow. 2003. "Are students failing in school or are schools failing students? *Journal of Social Issues* 59:103–20.

Falsani, C. 1996. "Churches, clergy split on capital punishment." *Chicago Tribune,* May 24.

Farhi, P. 1996. "Harmful violence found to fill TV." *Washington Post,* February 6.

———. 1999. "In networks' new programs, a startling lack of racial diversity." *Washington Post,* July 13.

Farkas, G. 2004. "The black-white test score gap." *Contexts* 3:12–19.

Farley, J. E., and G. D. Squires. 2005. "Fences and neighbors: Segregation in 21st-century America." *Contexts* 4:33–39.

Farley, M., and H. Barkan. 1998. "Prostitution, violence, and posttraumatic stress disorder." *Women's Health* 27 (3):37–49.

Fausto-Sterling, A. 1985. *Myths of Gender: Biological Theories about Women and Men.* New York: Basic Books.

Feagin, J. R., and H. Vera. 1995. *White Racism: The Basics.* New York: Routledge.

Fearon, J., and D. Laitin. 2002. "A world at war." *Harper's Magazine,* March, p. 84.

Feder, B. J. 1991. "In the clutches of the superfund mess." *The New York Times,* June 16.

Federal Bureau of Investigation. 2002. *Crime in the United States: 2002.* FBI Web site.

———. 2006. "Arrests." FBI Web site.

Federal Interagency Forum on Child and Family Statistics. 2004. *America's Children.* Washington, DC: Government Printing Office.

———. 2004. "Children's environments." FIFCFS Web site.

Feeney, J. A. 2000. "Implications of attachment style for patterns of health and illness." *Child: Care, Health, and Development* 26:277–88.

Feerick, M. M., and K. L. Snow. 2005. "The relationships between childhood sexual abuse, social anxiety, and symptoms of posttraumatic stress disorder in women." *Journal of Family Violence* 20:409–19.

Feingold, A., and R. Mazzella. 1998. "Gender differences in body image are increasing." *Psychological Science* 9 (May):190–95.

Felland, L. E., et al. 2003. "The resilience of the health care safety net, 1996–2001." *Health Services Research* 38:489–502.

Fellows, J. L., A. Trosclair, E. K. Adams, and C. C. Rivera. 2002. "Annual smoking-attributable mortality, years of potential life lost, and economic costs—United States, 1995–1999." *Morbidity and Mortality Weekly Report* 51:300–03.

Fendrich, M., V. Warner, and M. M. Weissman. 1990. "Family risk factors, parental depression, and psychopathology in offspring." *Developmental Psychology* 26 (January):40–50.

Fenwick, R., and M. Tausig. 1994. "The macroeconomic context of job stress." *Journal of Health and Social Behavior* 35 (September):266–82.

Ferber, A. L. 2000. "Racial warriors and the weekend warriors: The construction of masculinity in mythopoetic and white supremacist discourse." *Men and Masculinities* 3:30–56.

Fergusson, D. M., L. J. Horwood, and E. M. Ridder. 2005. "Partner violence and mental health outcomes in a New Zealand birth cohort." *Journal of Marriage and Family* 67:1103–19.

Fergusson, D. M., L. J. Horwood, and L. J. Woodward. 2001. "Unemployment and psychosocial adjustment in young adults." *Social Science and Medicine* 53:305–20.

Ferraro, K., and J. M. Johnson. 1983. "How women experience battering: The process of victimization." *Social Problems* 30 (3):325–39.

Ferraro, K. F., and J. A. Kelley-Moore. 2003. "Cumulative disadvantage and health: Long-term consequences of obesity?" *American Sociological Review* 68:707–29.

Ferraro, K. J. 1989. "Policing woman battering." *Social Problems* 36 (February):61–74.

Ferris, P. A., and C. A. Marshall. 1987. "A model project for families of the chronically mentally ill." *Social Work* 32 (March–April):110–14.

Ferriss, A. L. 2000. "The quality of life among U.S. states." *Social Indicators Research* 49 (January):1–23.

Field, K. 2004. "Fighting trafficking in the United States." *CQ Researcher* 14:284–85.

Fields, J. 2001a. "America's families and living arrangements." *Current Population Reports.* Washington, DC: Government Printing Office.

———. 2001b. "Living arrangements of children." *Current Population Reports.* Washington, DC: Government Printing Office.

Filipas, H. H., and S. E. Ullman. 2006. "Child sexual abuse, coping responses, self-blame, posttraumatic stress disorder, and adult sexual revictimization." *Journal of Interpersonal Violence* 21:652–72.

Fine, G. A. 2000. "Games and truths: Learning to construct social problems in high school debate." *Sociological Quarterly* 41 (Winter):103–23.

———. 2006. "The chaining of social problems: Solutions and unintended consequences in the age of betrayal." *Social Problems* 53:3–17.

Fine, M. A., and L. A. Kurdek. 1992. "The adjustment of adolescents in stepfather and stepmother families." *Journal of Marriage and the Family* 54 (November):725–36.

Finkelhor, D., G. T. Hotaling, L. A. Lewis, and C. Smith. 1989. "Sexual abuse and its relationship to later sexual satisfaction, marital status, religion, and attitudes." *Journal of Interpersonal Violence* 4 (December):379–99.

Finn, J. 2004. "A survey of online harassment at a university campus." *Journal of Interpersonal Violence* 19:468–83.

Finn, J. D., S. B. Gerber, C. M. Achilles, and J. Boyd-Zaharias. 2001. "The enduring effects of small classes." *Teachers College Record* 103:145–83.

Fiscella, K., P. Franks, and C. M. Clancy. 1998. "Skepticism toward medical care and health care utilization." *Medical Care* 36 (February): 180–89.

Fischer, M., and B. Geiger. 1996. "Resocializing young offenders in the kibbutz." *International Journal of Offender Therapy and Comparative Criminology* 40 (1):44–53.

Fish, J. M. 1995. "Mixed blood." *Psychology Today,* November–December, pp. 55–61.

Fisher, D. E. 1990. *Fire and Ice: The Greenhouse Effect, Ozone Depletion, and Nuclear Winter.* New York: Harper and Row.

Fisher, D. E., and M. J. Fisher. 2001. "N: The nitrogen bomb." *Discover,* April, pp. 50–57.

Fitzgerald, L. F. 1993. "Sexual harassment: Violence against women in the workplace." *American Psychologist* 48 (October):1070–76.

Fitzgerald, M. M., et al. 2005. "Perceptions of parenting versus parent-child interactions among incest survivors." *Child Abuse and Neglect* 29:661–81.

Flaks, D. K., I. Ficher, F. Masterpasqua, and G. Joseph. 1995. "Lesbians choosing motherhood: A comparative study of lesbian and heterosexual parents and their children." *Developmental Psychology* 31 (January):105–14.

Flavin, C. 1987. "Reassessing nuclear power." In *State of the World 1987,* ed. Lester R. Brown, pp. 57–80. New York: W. W. Norton.

———. 2005. "Preface." Pp. xix–xxi in L. Starke, ed., *State of the World: 2005.* New York: W. W. Norton.

Flavin, C., and S. Dunn. 1999. "Reinventing the energy system." In *State of the World 1999,* ed. Lester R. Brown et al., pp. 22–40. New York: W. W. Norton.

Flegal, K. M., B. I. Graubard, D. F. Williamson, and M. H. Gail. 2005. "Excess deaths associated with underweight, overweight, and obesity." *Journal of the American Medical Association* 293:1861–67.

Fleischer-Black, M. 2004. "A season for whistle-blowers." *American Lawyer* 26, n.p.

Fleury, R. E., C. M. Sullivan, D. I. Bybee, and W. S. Davidson, 2d. 1998. " 'Why don't they just call the cops?' Reasons for differential police contact among women with abusive partners." *Violence and Victims* 13 (Winter):333–46.

Flewelling, R. L., and K. E. Bauman. 1990. "Family structure as a predictor of initial substance use and sexual intercourse in early adolescence." *Journal of Marriage and the Family* 52 (February):171–81.

Flisher, A. J., et al. 1997. "Psychosocial characteristics of physically abused children and adolescents." *Journal of the American Academy of Child and Adolescent Psychiatry* 36 (no. 1):123–31.

Flynn, C. A., and W. E. Brown. 1991. "The effects of a mandatory alcohol education program on college student problem drinkers." *Journal of Alcohol and Drug Education* 37 (1):15–24.

Flynn, G. 2003. "The reverse-discrimination trap." *Workforce* 82:106–7.

Fonow, M. M., L. Richardson, and V. A. Wemmerus. 1992. "Feminist rape education: Does it work?" *Gender and Society* 6 (March):108–21.

Ford, C. S., and F. A. Beach. 1951. *Patterns of Sexual Behavior.* New York: Harper and Row.

Ford, J. D. 1999. "Disorders of extreme stress following war-zone military trauma." *Journal of Consulting and Clinical Psychology* 67 (February): 3–12.

Ford, M. E., and J. A. Linney. 1995. "Comparative analysis of juvenile sexual offenders, violent nonsexual offenders, and status offenders." *Journal of Interpersonal Violence* 10 (March):56–70.

Forge, K. L. S., and S. Phemister. 1987. "The effect of prosocial cartoons on preschool children." *Child Study Journal* 17 (2):83–88.

Fosu, A. K. 1992. "Occupational mobility of black women, 1958–1981: The impact of post-1964 antidiscrimination measures." *Industrial and Labor Relations Review* 45 (January):281–94.

Fouts, J. T. 1999. "School restructuring and student achievement in Washington State." *ERIC/CUE Digest* (December):38.

France, M. 2004. "Close the lawyer loophole: Their ability to reduce legal liability for executives is fueling white-collar crime." *BusinessWeek,* February 2, p. 70.

Francia, P. L., and P. S. Hernson. 2003. "The impact of public finance laws on fundraising in state legislative elections." *American Politics Research* 31:520–39.

Francis, B., and C. Skelton. 2005. *Reassessing Gender and Achievement.* London: Routledge & Kegal Paul.

Francoeur, R. T. 1991. *Becoming a Sexual Person.* 2d ed. New York: Macmillan.

Frank, K. 2003. " 'Just trying to relax': Masculinity, masculinizing practices, and strip club regulars." *Journal of Sex Research* 40:61–75.

———. 2005. "Exploring the motivations and fantasies of strip club customers in relation to legal regulations." *Archives of Sexual Behavior* 34:487–504.

Frankenberg, E., C. Lee, and G. Orfield. 2003. *A Multiracial Society with Segregated Schools.* Cambridge, MA: The Civil Rights Project of Harvard University.

Frazier, J. A., and F. J. Morrison. 1998. "The influence of extended-year schooling on growth of achievement and perceived competence in early elementary school." *Child Development* 69 (April): 495–517.

Frederico, C. M. 2006. "Ideology and the affective structure of whites' racial perceptions." *Public Opinion Quarterly* 70:327–53.

Freud, S. 1949. *Three Essays on the Theory of Sexuality.* London: Imago Publishing.

Freudenberg, N., J. Daniels, M. Crum, T. Perkins, and B. E. Richie. 2005. "Coming home from jail." *American Journal of Public Health* 95:1725–36.

Freund, K., R. Watson, and D. Rienzo. 1989. "Heterosexuality, homosexuality, and erotic age preference." *Journal of Sex Research* 26 (1):107–17.

Freund, M., N. Lee, and T. Leonard. 1991. "Sexual behavior of clients with street prostitutes in Camden, NJ." *Journal of Sex Research* 28 (November):579–91.

Freund, M., T. L. Leonard, and N. Lee. 1989. "Sexual behavior of resident street prostitutes with their clients in Camden, New Jersey." *Journal of Sex Research* 26 (4):460–78.

Frey, R. S., and A. Al-Roumi. 1999. "Political democracy and the physical quality of life." *Social Indicators Research* 47 (May):73–97.

Frieden, T. R., et al. 2005. "Adult tobacco use levels after intensive tobacco control measures." *American Journal of Public Health* 95:1016–23.

Friedenberg, E. Z. 1972. "The revolt against democracy." In *The Prospect of Youth,* ed. T. J. Cottle, pp. 147–56. Boston: Little, Brown.

Friedland, D. S., and R. H. Price. 2003. "Underemployment: Consequences for the health and well-being of workers." *American Journal of Community Psychology* 32:33–45.

Friedman, S. 2002. "9/11 boosts focus on interruption risks." *National Underwriter Property and Casualty— Risk and Benefits Management* 106:17.

Frisco, M. L., and K. Williams. 2003. "Perceived housework equity, marital happiness, and divorce in dual-earner households." *Journal of Family Issues* 24:51–73.

Fritz, G. K. 2003. "Inhalant abuse among children and adolescents." *The Brown University Child and Adolescent Behavior Letter* 19:8.

Frone, M. R. 2006. "Prevalence and distribution of alcohol use and impairment in the workplace." *Journal of Studies on Alcohol* 67:147–56.

Furnas, J. C. 1965. *The Life and Times of the Late Demon Rum.* New York: Capricorn.

Furnham, A., E. Reeves, and S. Budhani. 2002. "Parents think their sons are brighter than their daughters." *Journal of Genetic Psychology* 163:24–39.

Furstenberg, F. F., Jr., T. D. Cook, J. Eccles, G. H. Elder, Jr., and A. Sameroff. 1999. *Managing to Make It: Urban Families and Adolescent Success.* Chicago: University of Chicago Press.

Gabriel, R. A. 1987. *No More Heroes: Madness and Psychiatry in War.* New York: Farrar, Straus, and Giroux.

Galea, S., et al. 2002. "Psychological sequelae of the September 11 terrorist attacks in New York City." *New England Journal of Medicine* 346:982–87.

Gallagher, K. P., and R. Taylor. 2003. *International Trade and Air Pollution.* Global Development and Environment Institute Working Paper No. 03-08. Medford, MA: Tufts University.

Galler, J. R., and F. Ramsey. 1989. "A follow-up study of the influence of early malnutrition on development: Behavior at home and at school." *Journal of the American Academy of Child and Adolescent Psychiatry* 28 (March):254–61.

Galliano, G., L. M. Noble, L. A. Travis, and C. Puechl. 1993. "Victim reactions during rape/sexual assault." *Journal of Interpersonal Violence* 8 (March):109–14.

Gallinsky, E., et al. 2005. *Overwork in America.* New York: Families and Work Institute.

Gallup, A., and F. Newport. 1991. "Death penalty support remains strong." *Gallup Poll Monthly,* no. 309 (June):40–45.

Ganahl, D. J., T. J. Prinsen, and S. B. Netzley. 2003. "A content analysis of prime time commercials." *Sex Roles* 49:545–51.

Ganster, D. C. 1986. "Type A behavior and occupational stress." *Journal of Organizational Behavior Management* 8 (Fall–Winter):61–84.

Garcia, M. 2002. "War-stripped, barren Afghan environment will take years to recover." Knight Ridder/Tribune News Service, February 11. Knight Ridder/Tribune Web site.

Gardner, G. 2006. "Deforestation continues." Pp. 102–103 in L. Starke, ed., *Vital Signs: 2006–2007.* New York: W. W. Norton.

Gardner, G., E. Assadourian, and R. Sarin. 2004. "The state of consumption today." In *State of the World 2004,* ed. L. Starke, pp. 3–23. New York: W. W. Norton.

Gardner, G., and B. Halweil. 2000. *Underfed and Overfed: The Global Epidemic of Malnutrition.* Washington, DC: Worldwatch Institute.

Gardner, G., and P. Sampat. 1999. "Forging a sustainable materials economy." In *State of the World 1999,* ed. Lester R. Brown et al., pp. 41–59. New York: W. W. Norton.

Garson, B. 1975. *All the Livelong Day: The Meaning and Demeaning of Routine Work.* New York: Penguin.

Gastil, J., and J. P. Dillard. 1999. "Increasing political sophistication through public deliberation." *Political Communication* 16 (1):3–23.

Gavaler, J. S. 1991. "Effects of alcohol on female endocrine function." *Alcohol Health and Research World* 15 (12):104–109.

Gegax, T. T., and L. Clemetson. 1998. "The abortion wars come home." *Newsweek,* November 9.

Gelles, R. J., and M. A. Straus. 1988. *Intimate Violence.* New York: Simon and Schuster.

Gellhorn, M. 1959. *The Face of War.* New York: Simon and Schuster.

Gelsema, T. I., et al. 2006. "A longitudinal study of job stress in the nursing profession." *Journal of Nursing Management* 14:289–99.

Gentry, C. S. 1991. "Pornography and rape: An empirical analysis." *Deviant Behavior* 12 (July–September):277–88.

Gerber, A. S., D. P. Green, and R. Shachar. 2003. "Voting may be habit-forming." *American Journal of Political Science* 47:540–50.

Gibson, J. W. 1994. *Warrior Dreams: Violence and Manhood in Post-Vietnam America.* New York: Hill and Wang.

Gillen, M., E. Lefkowitz, and C. Shearer. 2006. "Does body image play a role in risky sexual behavior and attitudes?" *Journal of Youth and Adolescence* 35:230–42.

Gilliard, D. K. 1999. *Prison and Jail Inmates at Midyear 1998.* Washington, DC: Government Printing Office.

Gilligan, J. 2001. "The last mental hospital." *Psychiatric Quarterly* 72:45–61.

Gilman, S. E., I. Kawachi, G. M. Fitzmaurice, and S. L. Buka. 2002. "Socioeconomic status in childhood and the lifetime risk of major depression." *International Journal of Epidemiology* 31:359–67.

Gips, M. A. 1998. "Where has all the money gone?" *Security Management* 42 (February):32–6.

Glantz, S. A., K. W. Kacirk, and C. McCulloch. 2004. "Back to the future: Smoking in the movies in 2002 compared with 1950 levels." *American Journal of Public Health* 94:261–63.

Glosser, G., et al. 2000. "Psychiatric aspects of temporal lobe epilepsy before and after anterior temporal lobectomy." *Journal of Neurological and Neurosurgical Psychiatry* 68 (1):53–8.

Glover, C., and C. E. Behrens. 2006. "Energy: Selected Facts and Numbers." *CRS Report for Congress,* November 29.

Goeders, N. E. 2003. "The impact of stress on addiction." *European Neuropsychopharmacology* 13:435–41.

Gohm, C. L., S. Oishi, J. Darlington, and E. Diener. 1998. "Culture, parental conflict, parental marital status, and the subjective well-being of young adults." *Journal of Marriage and the Family* 60 (May):319–34.

Golant, S. M., and A. J. La Greca. 1994. "Differences in the housing quality of white, black, and Hispanic U.S. elderly households." *Journal of Applied Gerontology* 13 (December):413–37.

Goldberg, W. A., E. Greenberger, S. Hamill, and R. O'Neil. 1992. "Role demands in the lives of employed single mothers with preschoolers." *Journal of Family Issues* 13 (May):312–33.

Golde, J. A., D. S. Strassberg, C. M. Turner, and K. Lowe. 2000. "Attitudinal effects of degrading themes and sexual explicitness in video materials." *Sex Abuse* 12:223–32.

Goldman, N., et al. 2004. "Sex differentials in biological risk factors for chronic disease." *Journal of Women's Health* 13:393–403.

Goldsmith, M. 2004. "Resurrecting RICO: Removing immunity for white-collar crime." *Harvard Journal on Legislation* 41:281–317.

Golge, Z. B., M. F. Yavuz, S. Muderrisoglu, and M. S. Yavuz. 2003. "Turkish university students' attitudes toward rape." *Sex Roles* 49:653–61.

Gomez, O. L., and G. Carrasquilla. 1999. "Factors associated with unjustified Caesarean section in four hospitals in Cali, Colombia." *International Journal of Quality Health Care* 11 (October):385–89.

Goode, S. 2004. "What's behind the hatred of America?" *Insight on the News,* January 6.

Gooden, A. M., and M. A. Gooden. 2001. "Gender representation in notable children's picture books: 1995–1999." *Sex Roles* 45:89–101.

Goodgame, D. 1993. "Welfare for the well-off." *Time* (February 22):36–37.

Goodman, M. 2001. "Making computer crime count." *Law Enforcement Bulletin* 70:10–17.

Goodyear, S. 2001. "Give me shelter." *Ms. Magazine,* April–May, pp. 38–42.

Gordon, J. 2002. "Cool war: Economic sanctions as a weapon of mass destruction." *Harper's Magazine,* November, pp. 43–49.

Gordon, M. T., and S. Riger. 1989. *The Female Fear.* New York: Free Press.

Gorman, C. 1992. "Danger overhead." *Time* (October 26):70.

Gottman, J., et al. 2003. "Correlates of gay and lesbian couples' relationship satisfaction and relationship dissolution." *Journal of Homosexuality* 45:23–44.

Gottschalck, A. O. 2006. "Dynamics of economic well-being: Spells of unemployment 2001–2003." U.S. Census Bureau Web site.

Gould, J. B. 2002. "Playing with fire: The civil liberties implications of September 11th." *PAR* 62:74–79.

Gove, W. R., and M. P. Geerken. 1977. "The effect of children and employment on the mental health of married men and women." *Social Forces* 56 (September):66–76.

Goyette, K., and Y. Xie. 1999. "Educational expectations of Asian American youths." *Sociology of Education* 72 (January):22–36.

Grabe, S., and J. S. Hyde. 2006. "Ethnicity and body dissatisfaction among women in the United States." *Psychological Bulletin* 132:622–40.

Graefe, D. R., and D. T. Lichter. 1999. "Life course transitions of American children." *Demography* 36 (May):205–17.

Graham, H. D., and T. R. Gurr, eds. 1969. *The History of Violence in America.* New York: Bantam.

Graham, K., D. W. Osgood, S. Wells, and T. Stockwell. 2006. "To what extent is intoxication associated with aggression in bars?" *Journal of Studies on Alcohol* 67:382–90.

Graham-Bermann, S. A., and A. A. Levendosky. 1998. "Traumatic stress symptoms in children of battered women." *Journal of Interpersonal Violence* 13 (March):111–28.

Grant, B. F., et al. 2004. "The 12-month prevalence and trends in DSM-IV alcohol abuse and dependence." *Drug and Alcohol Dependence* 74:223–34.

Gray, G. C., et al. 2002. "Self-reported symptoms and medical conditions among 11,868 Gulf War–era veterans." *American Journal of Epidemiology* 155:1033–44.

Gray, M., and J. Tudball. 2003. "Family-friendly work practices." *Journal of Industrial Relations* 45:269–91.

Green, R. 1987. *The "Sissy Boy Syndrome" and the Development of Homosexuality.* New Haven, CT: Yale University Press.

Greenberg, E. S., and L. Grunberg. 1995. "Work alienation and problem alcohol behavior." *Journal of Health and Social Behavior* 36 (March):83–102.

Greenfeld, L. A. 1998. *Alcohol and Crime.* Washington, DC: Government Printing Office.

Grieco, E. M., and R. C. Cassidy. 2001. "Overview of race and Hispanic origin." U.S. Census Bureau Web site.

Griffin, K. W., J. G. Rabkin, R. H. Remien, and J. B. W. Williams. 1998. "Disease severity, physical limitations, and depression in HIV-infected men." *Journal of Psychosomatic Research* 44 (February):219–27.

Grimmett, R. F. 2006. "Conventional arms transfers to developing nations, 1998–2005." *CRS Report for Congress,* October 23.

Gringlas, M., and M. Weinraub. 1995. "The more things change . . . single parenting revisited." *Journal of Family Issues* 16 (January):29–52.

Grodsky, E., and D. Pager. 2001. "The structure of disadvantage: Individual and occupational determinants of the black-white wage gap." *American Sociological Review* 66: 542–67.

Grogan, S., and H. Richards. 2002. "Body image: Focus groups with boys and men." *Men and Masculinities* 4:219–32.

Grogan-Kaylor, A., and M. D. Otis. 2003. "Effect of childhood maltreatment on adult criminality." *Child Maltreatment* 8:129–37.

Grogger, J., and L. A. Karoly. 2005. *Welfare Reform: Effects of a Decade of Change.* Cambridge, MA: Harvard University Press.

Gross, D., A. Sambrook, and L. Fogg. 1999. "Behavior problems among young children in low-income urban day care centers." *Research in Nursing Health* 22 (February):15–25.

Gross, J. 1998. "In quest for the perfect look, more girls choose the scalpel." *The New York Times,* November 29.

Grossman, A. H., and M. S. Kerner. 1998. "Self-esteem and supportiveness as predictors of emotional distress in gay male and lesbian youth." *Journal of Homosexuality* 35 (1):25–39.

Grossman, D., and S. Shulman. 1990. "Down in the dumps." *Discover,* (April):36–41.

Grosswald, B. 2003. "Shift work and negative work-to-family spillover." *Journal of Sociology and Social Welfare* 30:30–42.

Grubb, W. N., and M. Lazerson. 2004. *The Education Gospel: The Economic Power of Schooling.* Cambridge, MA: Harvard University Press.

Grunberg, L., R. Anderson-Connolly, and E. S. Greenberg. 2000. "Surviving layoffs." *Work and Occupations* 27 (February):7–31.

Gryparis, A., et al. 2004. "Acute effects of ozone on mortality from the 'Air Pollution and Health: A European Approach' project." *American Journal of Respiratory and Critical Care Medicine,* e-published ahead of print date, AJRCCM Web site.

Grzywacz, J. G., D. M. Almeida, S. D. Neupert, and S. L. Ettner. 2004. "Socioeconomic status and health: A micro-level analysis of exposure and vulnerability to daily stressors." *Journal of Health and Social Behavior* 45:1–16.

Guidubaldi, J., J. D. Perry, and B. K. Nastasi. 1987. "Growing up in a divorced family: Initial and long-term perspectives on children's adjustment." In *Family Processes and Problems: Social Psychological Aspects,* ed. S. Oskamp, pp. 202–37. Beverly Hills, CA: Sage.

Guilamo-Ramos, V., J. Jaccard, R. Turrisi, and M. Johansson. 2005. "Parental and school correlates of binge drinking among middle school students." *American Journal of Public Health* 95:894–99.

Guimont, C., et al. 2006. "Effects of job strain on blood pressure." *American Journal of Public Health* 96:1436–43.

Gullette, E. C. D., et al. 1997. "Effects of mental stress on myocardial ischemia during daily life." *Journal of the American Medical Association* 277 (May 21):1521–26.

Gunn, R. A., et al. 1995. "Syphilis in San Diego County 1983–1992: Crack cocaine, prostitution, and the limitations of partner notification." *Sexually Transmitted Diseases* 22 (1):60–6.

Guo, G. 1998. "The timing of the influences of cumulative poverty on children's cognitive ability and achievement." *Social Forces* 77 (September):257–88.

Guo, J., J. D. Hawkins, K. G. Hill, and R. D. Abbott. 2001. "Childhood and adolescent predictors of alcohol abuse and dependence in young adulthood." *Journal of Studies on Alcohol* 62:754–62.

Gurr, T. R. 1969. "A comparative study of civil strife." In *The History of Violence in America,* ed. H. D. Graham and T. R. Gurr, pp. 572–632. New York: Bantam.

Gussler-Burkhardt, N. L., and P. R. Giancola. 2005. "A further examination of gender differences in alcohol-related aggression." *Journal of Studies on Alcohol* 66:413–22.

Gutierrez-Lobos, K. 2000. "The gender gap in depression reconsidered." *Social Psychiatry and Psychiatric Epidemiology* 35:202–10.

Haddad, S. 2003. "Islam and attitudes toward U.S. policy in the Middle East." *Studies in Conflict and Terrorism* 26:135–54.

Hagan, J., and H. Foster. 2001. "Youth violence and the end of adolescence." *American Sociological Review* 66:874–99.

Hagerman, E. 1990. "California's drive to mass transit." *World Watch* (September–October):7–8.

Haines, M. M., S. L. Brentnall, S. A. Stansfeld, and E. Klineberg. 2003. "Qualitative responses of children to environmental noise." *Noise Health* 5:19–30.

Halcon, J. J., and M. de la Luz Reyes. 1991. " 'Trickle-down' reform: Hispanics, higher education, and the excellence movement." *Urban Review* 23 (June):117–35.

Haley, R. W., A. M. Maddrey, and H. K. Gershenfeld. 2002. "Severely reduced functional status in veterans fitting a case definition of Gulf War syndrome." *American Journal of Public Health* 92:46–47.

Hall, H. 1987. "The homeless: A mental-health debate." *Psychology Today* (February):65–66.

Hall, Z. W. 2007. "California dreaming? A new start for regenerative medicine in the Golden State." *Regenerative Medicine* 2:25–28.

Hallman, W. K., and A. Wandersman. 1992. "Attribution of responsibility and individual and collective coping with environmental threats." *Journal of Social Issues* 48 (4):101–18.

Halpern-Felsher, B. L., and S. G. Millstein. 2002. "The effects of terrorism on teens' perceptions of dying." *Journal of Adolescent Health* 30:308–11.

Hamilton, M., D. Anderson, M. Broaddus, and K. Young. 2006. "Gender stereotyping in children's picture books." *Sex Roles* 55:757–65.

Hammarstrom, A. 1994. "Health consequences of youth unemployment." *Social Science and Medicine* 38 (March):699–709.

Hampton, T. 2006. "Scientists, ethicists ponder challenges in moving stem cell research forward." *Journal of the American Medical Association* 296:2542–43.

Hanenberg, R., and W. Rojanapithayakorn. 1998. "Expressions of distrust: Third-party voting and cynicism in government." *Political Behavior* 20 (March): 17–34.

Hansell, S., and H. R. White. 1991. "Adolescent drug use, psychological distress, and physical symptoms." *Journal of Health and Social Behavior* 32 (September):288–301.

Hansen, J. 2004. "Defusing the global warming time bomb." *Scientific American,* March, pp. 68–77.

Hanson, S. L. 1994. "Lost talent: Unrealized educational aspirations and expectations among U.S. youths." *Sociology of Education* 67 (July):159–83.

Hanson, T. L. 1999. "Does parental conflict explain why divorce is negatively associated with child welfare?" *Social Forces* 77 (June):1283–316.

Hardesty, P. H., and K. M. Kirby. 1995. "Relation between family religiousness and drug use within adolescent peer groups." *Journal of Social Behavior and Personality* 10 (1):421–30.

Hardin, G. 1971. "The tragedy of the commons." In *Man and the Environment,* ed. W. Jackson, pp. 243–54. Dubuque, IA: Wm. C. Brown.

Harford, T. C., H. Wechsler, and B. O. Muthen. 2003. "Alcohol-related aggression and drinking at off-campus parties and bars." *Journal of Studies on Alcohol* 64:704–11.

Harford, T. C., H. Wechsler, and M. Seibring. 2002. "Attendance and alcohol use at parties and bars in college." *Journal of Studies on Alcohol* 63:726–33.

Harlow, C. W. 2005. "Hate crime reported by victims and police." *Bureau of Justice Statistics Special Report.* Washington, DC: Government Printing Office.

Harmless, A. 1990. "Developmental impact of combat exposure: Comparison of adolescent and adult Vietnam veterans." *Smith College Studies in Social Work* 60 (March):185–95.

Harrell, E. 2005. "Violence by gang members, 1993–2003." Bureau of Justice Statistics Crime Data Brief, June.

Harrington, M. 1962. *The Other America.* Baltimore: Penguin.

Harrison, B. 1994. *Lean and Mean: The Changing Landscape of Corporate Power in the Age of Flexibility.* New York: Basic Books.

Harrison, C., and K. Dautrich. 1999. "The modern American worker." *Public Perspective,* August–September.

Harrison, P. J., I. P. Everall, and J. Catalan. 1994. "Is homosexual behavior hard-wired? Sexual orientation and brain structure." *Psychological Medicine* 24 (November):811–16.

Harry, J. 1989. "Parental physical abuse and sexual orientation in males." *Archives of Sexual Behavior* 18 (June):251–61.

———. 1995. "Sports ideology, attitudes toward women, and anti-homosexual attitudes." *Sex Roles* 32 (January):109–16.

Hart, H. 1957. "Acceleration in social change." In *Technology and Social Change,* ed. F. R. Allen et al., pp. 27–55. New York: Appleton-Century-Crofts.

Hart, L. E., L. Mader, K. Griffith, and M. DeMendonca. 1989. "Effects of sexual and physical abuse: A comparison of adolescent inpatients." *Child Psychiatry and Human Development* 20 (Fall):49–57.

Hartley, C. C. 1998. "How incest offenders overcome internal inhibitions through the use of cognitions and cognitive distortions." *Journal of Interpersonal Violence* 13 (February):25–39.

Harvey, M. R. 1985. *Exemplary Rape Crisis Programs.* Rockville, MD: National Institute of Mental Health.

Hashemian, F., et al. 2006. "Anxiety, depression, and posttraumatic stress in Iranian survivors of chemical warfare." *Journal of the American Medical Association* 296:560–66.

Hashim, A. S. 2007. "Iraq's civil war." *Current History* 106:3–10.

Hassan, N. 2001. "An arsenal of believers: Talking to the 'human bombs.' " *New Yorker,* November 19, pp. 36–42.

Haug, M. R., and S. J. Folmar. 1986. "Longevity, gender, and life quality." *Journal of Health and Social Behavior* 27 (December):332–45.

Hawdon, J. E. 2001. "The role of presidential rhetoric in the creation of a moral panic." *Deviant Behavior* 22:419–45.

Hawkins, D. 1996. "Homeschool battles." *U.S. News and World Report* (February 12):28–29.

Hayeslip, D. W., Jr. 1989. "Local-level drug enforcement: New strategies." *NIJ Reports* 213 (March–April):1–6.

Hayman, P. M., and D. J. Scaturo. 1993. "Psychological debriefing of returning military personnel: A protocol for post-combat intervention." *Journal of Social Behavior and Personality* 8 (5):117–30.

Haywood, M. D., E. M. Crimmins, T. P. Miles, and Y. Yang. 2000. "The significance of socioeconomic status in explaining the racial gap in chronic health conditions." *American Sociological Review* 65:910–30.

Hazelwood, R. R., R. Reboussin, and J. I. Warren. 1989. "Serial rape: Correlates of increased aggression and the relationship of offender pleasure to victim resistance." *Journal of Interpersonal Violence* 4 (March):65–78.

He, J., et al. 1999. "Passive smoking and the risk of coronary heart disease." *New England Journal of Medicine* 340 (March 25):920–26.

Heaney, C. A., B. A. Israel, and J. S. House. 1994. "Chronic job insecurity among automobile workers: Effects on job satisfaction and health." *Social Science and Medicine* 38 (May):1431–37.

Hearn, J. C. 1991. "Academic and nonacademic influences on the college destinations of 1980 high school graduates." *Sociology of Education* 64 (July):158–71.

Heaton, R. B. 2002. "Factors contributing to increasing marital instability in the United States." *Journal of Family Issues* 23:392–409.

Hecker, D. E. 2005. "Occupational employment projections to 2014." *Monthly Labor Review* 128:70–101.

Heilman, M. E. 2001. "Description and prescription: How gender stereotypes prevent women's ascent up the organizational ladder." *Journal of Social Issues* 57:657–74.

Heim, N. 1981. "Sexual behavior of castrated sex offenders." *Archives of Sexual Behavior* 10 (1):11–19.

Helfand, I. 1999. "Moving the world back from nuclear brink." *San Diego Union-Tribune,* October 18.

Helwig, A. A. 1998. "Gender-role stereotyping: Testing theory with a longitudinal sample." *Sex Roles* 38 (5–6):403–24.

Helwig, R. 2001. "Worker displacement in a strong labor market." *Monthly Labor Review* 124:13–28.

Henn, M., M. Weinstein, and S. Forrest. 2005. "Uninterested youth? Young people's attitudes toward party politics in Britain." *Political Studies* 55:556–78.

Henning, K., et al. 1996. "Long-term psychological and social impact of witnessing physical conflict between parents." *Journal of Interpersonal Violence* 11:35–51.

Henry, W. A., III. 1994. "Pride and prejudice." *Time* (June 17):54–59.

Herring, C. 2002. "Is job discrimination dead?" *Contexts* 1:13–18.

Herrnstein, R. J., and C. Murray. 1994. *The Bell Curve: Intelligence and Class Structure in American Life.* New York: Free Press.

Hersey, J. 1946. *Hiroshima.* New York: Alfred A. Knopf.

Hershberger, S. L., N. W. Pilkington, and A. R. D'Augelli. 1997. "Predictors of suicide attempts among gay, lesbian, and bisexual youth." *Journal of Adolescent Research* 12 (October):477–97.

Hesse-Biber, S. 1996. *Am I Thin Enough Yet? The Cult of Thinness and the Commercialization of Identity.* New York: Oxford University Press.

Hetherington, E. M. 1993. "An overview of the Virginia longitudinal study of divorce and remarriage with a focus on early adolescence." *Journal of Family Psychology* 7:39–56.

Hetherington, M. J. 1999. "The effect of political trust on the presidential vote, 1968–96." *American Political Science Review* 93 (June):311–23.

Heymann, J. 2000. "What happens during and after school: Conditions faced by working parents living in poverty and their school-aged children." *Journal of Children and Poverty* 6:5–20.

Hibbard, J. H., and C. R. Pope. 1991. "Effect of domestic and occupational roles on morbidity and mortality." *Social Science and Medicine* 32 (7):805–11.

Hicks, M. H. 2006. "The prevalence and characteristics of intimate partner violence in a community study of Chinese American women." *Journal of Interpersonal Violence* 21:1249–69.

Hill, E. J., A. J. Hawkins, V. Maartinson, and M. Ferris. 2003. "Studying 'working fathers.' " *Fathering* 1:239–62.

Hill, E. J., V. Martinson, and M. Ferris. 2004. "New-concept part-time employment as a work-family adaptive strategy for women professionals with small children." *Family Relations* 53:282–92.

Hilton, J. M., and K. Kopera-Frye. 2006. "Loss and depression in cohabiting and nonco-habiting custodial single parents." *The Family Journal* 14:28–40.

Himmelstein, D. U., S. Woolhandler, I. Hellander, and S. M. Wolfe. 1999. "Quality of care in investor-owned vs. not-for-profit HMOs." *Journal of the American Medical Association* 282 (July 14):159–63.

Hing, B. O. 1998. "Don't give me your tired, your poor: Conflicted immigrant stories and welfare reform." *Harvard Civil Rights–Civil Liberties Law Review* 33 (1):159–82.

Hingson, R. W., T. Heeren, and M. R. Winter. 2006. "Age of alcohol-dependence onset." *Pediatrics* 118:755–63.

Hingson, R., T. Heeren, R. Zakoes, M. Winter, and H. Wechsler. 2003. "Age at first intoxication, heavy drinking, driving after drinking, and risk of unintentional injury among U.S. college students." *Journal of Studies on Alcohol* 64:23–31.

Hinze, S. W. 2004. " 'Am I being over-sensitive?' Women's experience of sexual harassment during medical training." *Health* 8:101–27.

Hipp, J. R., D. J. Bauer, P. J. Curran, and K. A. Bollen. 2004. "Crimes of opportunity or crimes of emotion? Testing two explanations of seasonal change in crime." *Social Forces* 82:1333–72.

Hirschman, R. S., H. Leventhal, and K. Glynn. 1984. "The development of smoking behavior: Conceptualization and supportive cross-sectional survey data." *Journal of Applied Social Psychology* 14 (May–June):184–206.

Hobfoll, S. E., D. Canetti-Nisim, and R. J. Johnson. 2006. "Exposure to terrorism, stress-related mental health symptoms, and defensive coping among Jews and Arabs in Israel." *Journal of Consulting and Clinical Psychology* 74:207–18.

Hobson-Horton, L. D., and L. Owens. 2004. "From freshman to graduate: Recruiting and retaining minority students." *Journal of Hispanic Higher Education* 3:86–107.

Hochschild, J. L., and N. Scovronick. 2003. *The American Dream and the Public Schools.* New York: Oxford University Press.

Hodson, R. 2001. *Dignity at Work.* New York: Cambridge University Press.

Hofstadter, R., and M. Wallace, eds. 1970. *American Violence.* New York: Vintage.

Hogan, M. J., M. A. Long, P. B. Stretesky, and M. J. Lynch. 2006. "Campaign contributions, post-war reconstruction contracts, and state crime." *Deviant Behavior* 27:269–97.

Hogan, R., and C. C. Perrucci. 1998. "Producing and reproducing class and status differences: Racial and gender gaps in U.S. employment and retirement income." *Social Problems* 45 (November):528–49.

Hoge, C. W., A. Terhakopian, C. A. Castro, S. C. Messer, and C. C. Engel. 2007. "Association of posttraumatic stress disorder with somatic symptoms, health care visits, and absenteeism among Iraq war veterans." *American Journal of Psychiatry* 164:150–53.

Holahan, C. J., R. H. Moos, C. K. Holahan, R. C. Cronkite, and P. K. Randall. 2001. "Drinking to cope: Emotional distress and alcohol use and abuse." *Journal of Studies on Alcohol* 62:190–98.

Holcomb, D. R., L. C. Holcomb, K. A. Sondag, and N. Williams. 1991. "Attitudes about date rape: Gender differences among college students." *College Student Journal* 25 (December):434–39.

Holland, J. J. 2002. "Federal suits to be filed over 2000 vote." *San Diego Union-Tribune,* May 22.

Hollingshead, A. B. 1949. *Elmtown's Youth.* New York: John Wiley & Sons.

Hollingworth, W., et al. 2006. "Prevention of deaths from harmful drinking in the United States." *Journal of Studies on Alcohol* 67:300–308.

Holmes, T. H., and M. Masuda. 1974. "Life change and illness susceptibility." In *Stressful Life Events,* ed. B. S. Dohrenwend and B. P. Dohrenwend, pp. 45–72. New York: John Wiley & Sons.

Holt, T. J. 2003. "Examining a transnational problem: An analysis of computer crime victimization in eight countries from 1999 to 2001." *International Journal of Comparative and Applied Criminal Justice* 27:199–220.

Hong, J., and M. M. Seltzer. 1995. "The psychological consequences of multiple roles." *Journal of Health and Social Behavior* 36 (December):386–98.

Hood, E. 2005. "Investigating indoor air." *Environmental Health Perspectives* 113:158.

Horos, C. V. 1974. *Rape.* New Canaan, CT: Tobey.

Horowitz, J. M. 1999. "Bad news on formaldehyde." *Time,* January 18, p. 94.

Horvath, M., and A. M. Ryan. 2003. "Antecedents and potential moderators of the relationship between attitudes and hiring discrimination on the basis of sexual orientation. *Sex Roles* 48:115–30.

Horwitz, A. V., and L. Davies. 1994. "Are emotional distress and alcohol problems differential outcomes to stress? An exploratory test." *Social Science Quarterly* 75 (September):607–21.

Hossler, D., J. Schmit, and N. Vesper. 1999. *Going to College: How Social, Economic, and Educational Factors Influence the Decisions Students Make.* Baltimore, MD: Johns Hopkins University Press.

House, J. S. 2002. "Understanding social factors and inequalities in health." *Journal of Health and Social Behavior* 43:125–42.

Householder, J., R. P. Hatcher, W. J. Burns, and I. Chasnoff. 1982. "Infants born to narcotic-addicted mothers." *Psychological Bulletin* 9 (September):453–68.

Howard, G., et al. 1998. "Cigarette smoking and progression of atherosclerosis." *Journal of the American Medical Association* 279 (January 14):119–24.

Howell, J. C. 1998. "Youth gangs: An overview." *Juvenile Justice Bulletin*, August.

Hu, M., M. Davies, and D. B. Kandel. 2006. "Epidemiology and correlates of daily smoking and nicotine dependence among young adults in the United States." *American Journal of Public Health* 96:299–308.

Huang, M., and R. Hauser. 1998. "Trends in black-white test-score differentials." In *The Rising Curve: Long-Term Gains in IQ and Related Measures,* ed. U. Neisser, pp. 303–32. Washington, DC: American Psychological Association.

Huesmann, L. R., J. Moise-Titus, C. Podolski, and L. D. Eron. 2003. "Longitudinal relations between children's exposure to TV violence and their aggressive and violent behavior in adulthood: 1977–1992." *Developmental Psychology* 39:201–21.

Huff, D. D. 1992. "Upside-down welfare." *Public Welfare* 50 (Winter):36–40.

Hughes, A. 2004. "Researchers study 'sick' buildings." *Civil Engineering,* May 4, p. 33.

Hugick, L., and J. Leonard. 1991. "Job dissatisfaction grows: 'Moonlighting' on the rise." *Gallup Poll Monthly,* no. 312 (September):2–15.

Hummer, R. A., et al. 1999. "Race/ethnicity, nativity, and infant mortality in the United States." *Social Forces* 77 (March):1082–118.

Hurst, S. R. 2006. "Health official estimates 150,000 civilian deaths." *The San Diego Union-Tribune,* November 10.

Hussey, J. M., J. J. Chang, and J. B. Kotch. 2006. "Child maltreatment in the United States." *Pediatrics* 118:933–42.

Hutchinson, P. 1962. *The Christian Century Reader.* New York: Association Press.

Hyde, J. S. 1986. *Understanding Human Sexuality,* 3d ed. New York: McGraw-Hill.

———. 2005. "The gender similarities hypothesis." *American Psychologist* 60:581–92.

Ianni, F. A. J. 1998. "New Mafia: black, Hispanic, and Italian styles." *Society* 35 (January–February):115.

Iceland, J., and R. Wilkes. 2006. "Does socioeconomic status matter? Race, class, and residential segregation." *Social Problems* 53:248–73.

Ickovics, J. R., and J. Rodin. 1992. "Women and AIDS in the United States: Epidemiology, natural history, and mediating mechanisms." *Health Psychology* 11 (1):1–16.

Incrocci, L., W. C. Hop, A. Wijnmaalen, and A. K. Slob. 2002. "Treatment outcome, body image, and sexual functioning after orchiectomy and radiotherapy for Stage I–II testicular seminoma." *International Journal of Radiation Oncology* 53:1165–73.

Ingersoll, S., and D. LeBoeuf. 1997. "Reaching out to youth out of the educational mainstream." *Juvenile Justice Bulletin* (February).

Ingmar-Paul, K., and K. Moser. 2006. "Incongruence as an explanation for the negative mental health effects of unemployment." *Journal of Occupational and Organizational Psychology* 79:595–621.

Institute on Taxation and Economic Policy. 2003. *Who Pays? A Distributional Analysis of the Tax System in All 50 States.* 2nd ed. Washington, DC: Institute on Taxation and Economic Policy.

Isaac, R. J., and V. C. Armat. 1990. *Madness in the Streets: How Psychiatry and the Law Abandoned the Mentally Ill.* New York: Free Press.

Ising, H., H. Lange-Asschenfeldt, H. J. Moriske, J. Born, and M. Eilts. 2004. "Low frequency noise and stress." *Noise Health* 6:21–28.

Jackson, L. A., D. A. Lewandowski, J. M. Ingram, and C. N. Hodge. 1997. "Group stereotypes: Content, gender specificity, and affect associated with typical group members." *Journal of Social Behavior and Personality* 12 (2):381–96.

Jackson, P. B., and S. Mustillo. 2001. "I am woman: The impact of social identities on African American women's mental health." *Women's Health* 32:33–59.

Jackson, P. B., P. A. Thoits, and H. F. Taylor. 1995. "Composition of the workplace and psychological well-being:

The effects of tokenism on America's black elite." *Social Forces* 74 (December):543–57.

Jacobs, D., and J. T. Carmichael. 2002. "The political sociology of the death penalty." *American Sociological Review* 67:109–31.

Jacobs, G. D. 2001. "The physiology of mind-body interactions." *Journal of Alternative and Complementary Medicine* 7:83–92.

Jacobs, G. S. 1998. *Getting around Brown, Desegregation, Development, and the Columbus Public Schools.* Columbus: Ohio State University Press.

Jacobs, J. W. 1982. "The effect of divorce on fathers: An overview of the literature." *American Journal of Psychiatry* 139 (October):1235–41.

Jacobs, L. A. 2001. "What makes a terrorist?" *State Government News* 44:10–14.

Jacobs, N., and D. Harvey. 2005. "Do parents make a difference to children's academic achievement? Differences between parents of higher and lower achieving students." *Educational Studies* 31:431–48.

Jacobsen, P. B., et al. 2002. "Predictors of posttraumatic stress disorder symptomatology following bone marrow transplantation for cancer." *Journal of Consulting and Clinical Psychology* 70:235–40.

James, D. J., and L. E. Glaze. 2006. "Mental health problems of prison and jail inmates." *Bureau of Justice Statistics Special Report,* September.

James, J., and N. J. Davis. 1982. "Contingencies in female sexual role deviance: The case of prostitution." *Human Organization* 41 (4):345–50.

Jamieson, A., H. B. Shin, and Jennifer Day. 2002. *Voting and Registration in the Election of November 2000.* Washington, DC: Government Printing Office.

Jaret, C. 1991. "Recent structural change and US urban ethnic minorities." *Journal of Urban Affairs* 13 (3):307–36.

Jarvis, K. L., E. E. Gordon, and R. W. Novaco. 2005. "Psychological distress of children and mothers in domestic violence emergency shelters." *Journal of Family Violence* 20:389–402.

Jencks, C. 1992. *Rethinking Social Policy: Race, Poverty, and the Underclass.* Cambridge, MA: Harvard University Press.

———. 1994. *The Homeless.* Cambridge, MA: Harvard University Press.

Jennison, K. M., and K. A. Johnson. 1998. "Alcohol dependence in adult children of alcoholics." *Journal of Drug Education* 28 (1):19–37.

Jensen, L., and T. Slack. 2003. "Underemployment in America." *American Journal of Community Psychology* 32:21–31.

Jessor, R., F. M. Costa, P. M. Krueger, and M. S. Turbin. 2006. "A developmental study of heavy episodic drinking among college students." *Journal of Studies on Alcohol* 67:86–94.

Jeynes, W. H. 2006. "The impact of parental remarriage on children." *Marriage & Family Review* 40:75–102.

Jimerson, S., B. Egeland, L. A. Stroufe, and B. Carlson. 2000. "A prospective longitudinal study of high school dropouts." *Journal of School Psychology* 38:525–49.

Jin, R. L., C. P. Shah, and T. J. Svoboda. 1995. "The impact of unemployment on health." *Canadian Medical Association Journal* 153 (September 1):529–40.

Jiobu, R. M., and T. J. Curry. 2001. "Lack of confidence in the federal government and the ownership of firearms." *Social Science Quarterly* 82:77–88.

Joe, K. A. 1994. "The new criminal conspiracy? Asian gangs and organized crime in San Francisco." *Journal of Research in Crime and Delinquency* 31 (November):390–415.

Johnson, B. D., E. D. Wish, J. Schmeidler, and D. Huizinga. 1991. "Concentration of delinquent offending: Serious drug involvement and high delinquency rates." *Journal of Drug Issues* 21 (Spring):205–29.

Johnson, B. R., S. J. Jang, D. B. Larson, and S. De Li. 2001. "Does adolescent religious commitment matter?" *Journal of Research in Crime and Delinquency* 38:22–44.

Johnson, C. 2004. *The Sorrows of Empire: Militarism, Secrecy, and the End of the Republic.* New York: Metropolitan Books.

Johnson, C. K. 2005. "Obesity goes from no. 2 killer to no. 7." *The San Diego Union-Tribune,* April 20.

Johnson, D. P., and J. Friedman. 1993. "Social versus physiological motives in the drug careers of methadone clinic clients." *Deviant Behavior* 14 (January–March):23–42.

Johnson, E. S., and B. Vinick. 1981. "When an adult son or daughter divorces." *Journal of Divorce* 5 (Fall–Winter):69–77.

Johnson, J. G., P. Cohen, E. M. Smailes, S. Kasen, and J. S. Brook. 2002. "Television viewing and aggressive behavior during adolescence and adulthood." *Science* 295:2468–71.

Johnson, N. J., P. D. Sorlie, and E. Backlund. 1999. "The impact of specific occupation on mortality in the U.S. national longitudinal mortality study." *Demography* 36 (August):355–67.

Johnson, P. R., and J. Indvik. 1994. "Workplace violence." *Public Personnel Management* 23 (Winter):515–23.

Johnson, R. A., and D. R. Gerstein. 1998. "Initiation of use of alcohol, cigarettes, marijuana, cocaine, and other substances in U.S. birth cohorts since 1919." *American Journal of Public Health* 88 (January):27–33.

Johnston, D. D., and D. H. Swanson. 2003. "Invisible mothers: A content analysis of motherhood ideologies and myths in magazines." *Sex Roles* 48:21–33.

Johnston, L. D., P. M. O'Malley, and J. G. Bachman. 2003. *Monitoring the Future: National Results on Adolescent Drug Use.* Bethesda, MD: National Institute on Drug Abuse.

Johnston, L. D., P. M. O'Malley, J. G. Bachman, and J. E. Schulenberg. 2006. *Monitoring the Future: National Results on Adolescent Drug Use.* Bethesda, MD: National Institute on Drug Abuse.

Jonas, B. S., and R. W. Wilson. 1997. "Negative mood and urban versus rural residence." National Center for Health Statistics Web site.

Jones, S., and D. Myhill. 2004. "Seeing things differently: Teachers' constructions of under-achievement." *Gender and Education* 16:531–46.

Jorgenson, A. K. 2006. "Global warming and the neglected greenhouse gas." *Social Forces* 84:1779–98.

Kalleberg, A., B. F. Reskin, and K. Hudson. 2000. "Bad jobs in America: Standard and nonstandard employment relations and job quality in the United States." *American Sociological Review* 65 (April):256–78.

Kalmuss, D. 1984. "The intergenerational transmission of marital aggression." *Journal of Marriage and the Family* 46 (February):11–19.

———. 2004. "Nonvolitional sex and sexual health." *Archives of Sexual Behavior* 33:197–209.

Kandel, D., K. Chen, and A. Gill. 1995. "The impact of drug use on earnings: A life-span perspective." *Social Forces* 74 (September):243–70.

Kane, E. W. 1995. "Education and beliefs about gender inequality." *Social Problems* 42 (February):74–89.

Kang, S. Y., S. Magura, and J. L. Shapiro. 1994. "Correlates of cocaine/crack use among inner-city incarcerated adolescents." *American Journal of Drug and Alcohol Abuse* 20 (4):413–29.

Kaplan, R. M., and R. G. Kronick. 2006. "Marital status and longevity in the United States population." *Journal of Epidemiology and Community Health* 60:760–65.

Katz, J. 1988. *Seductions of Crime: Moral and Sensual Attractions of Doing Evil.* New York: Basic Books.

Keane, C. 1998. "Evaluating the influence of fear of crime as an environmental mobility restrictor on women's routine activities." *Environment and Behavior* 30:60–74.

Kellermann, A., et al. 1992. "Suicide in the home in relation to gun ownership." *New England Journal of Medicine* 327 (August):467–72.

Kelloway, E. K., and B. H. Gottlieb. 1998. "The effect of alternative work arrangements on women's well-being." *Womens Health* 4:1–18.

Kemper, P., J. D. Reschovsky, and H. T. Tu. 2000. "Do HMOs make a difference?" *Inquiry* 36 (Winter):419–25.

Kendler, K. S., L. M. Thornton, and C. A. Prescott. 2001. "Gender differences in the rates of exposure to stressful life events and sensitivity to their depressogenic effects." *American Journal of Psychiatry* 158:587–93.

Kennedy, L. W., and S. W. Baron. 1993. "Routine activities and a subculture of violence: A study of violence on the street." *Journal of Research in Crime and Delinquency* 30 (February):88–112.

Kenworthy, L. 1999. "Do social-welfare policies reduce poverty? A cross-national assessment." *Social Forces* 77 (March)1119–39.

Kerley, K. R., and H. Copes. 2004. "The effects of criminal justice contact on employment stability for white-collar and street-level offenders." *International Journal of Offender Therapy and Comparative Criminology* 48:65–84.

Kershaw, T. 1992. "The effects of educational tracking on the social mobility of African Americans." *Journal of Black Studies* 23 (September):152–69.

Kessler, R. C., and J. D. McLeod. 1984. "Sex differences in vulnerability to undesirable life events." *American Sociological Review* 49 (October):620–31.

Kessler, R. C., et al. 2005. "Lifetime prevalence and age-of-onset distributions of DSM-IV disorders in the National Comorbidity Survey replication." *Archives of General Psychiatry* 62:593–602.

Kessler, R. C., W. T. Chiu, O. Demler, and E. E. Walters. 2005. "Prevalence, severity, and comorbidity of 12-month DSM-IV disorders in the National Comorbidity Survey replication." *Archives of General Psychiatry* 62:617–27.

Khattak, S., et al. 1999. "Pregnancy outcome following gestational exposure to organic solvents." *Journal of the American Medical Association* 281 (March 24–31):1106–09.

Kheifets, L., A. A. Afifi, and R. Shimkhada. 2006. "Public health impact of extremely low-frequency electromagnetic fields." *Environmental Health Perspectives* 114:1532–37.

Kilmer, J. R., et al. 2006. "Misperceptions of college student marijuana use." *Journal of Studies on Alcohol* 67:277–81.

Kilpatrick, D. G., et al. 2000. "Risk factors for adolescent substance abuse and dependence." *Journal of Consulting and Clinical Psychology* 68:19–30.

Kim, H., and H. Kim. 2005. "Incestuous experience among Korean adolescents." *Public Health Nursing* 22:472–82.

Kim, R., K. K. Nakamura, G. Fong, R. Cabarloc, B. Jung, and S. Lee. 1992. "Asian immigrant women garment workers in Los Angeles." *Amerasia Journal* 18 (1):69–82.

Kimm, S. Y. S., et al. 2002. "Decline in physical activity in black girls and white girls during adolescence." *New England Journal of Medicine* 347:709–15.

King, C. E. 1989. "Homelessness in America." *Humanist* 49 (May–June):8.

King, D. Y. 1998a. "Qualifications of Indonesia's civil servants: How appropriate to the dynamic environment?" *Journal of Political and Military Sociology* 26 (Summer):23–38.

———. 1998b. "Reforming basic education and the struggle for decentralized educational administration in Indonesia." *Journal of Political and Military Sociology* 26 (Summer):83–95.

Kinnier, R. T., A. T. Metha, J. L. Okey, and J. M. Keim. 1994. "Adolescent substance abuse and psychological health." *Journal of Alcohol and Drug Education* 40 (Fall):51–56.

Kirby, J. A. 1996. "Big Apple excises X-rated rot." Chicago Tribune, April 19.

Kirby, J. B., and T. Kaneda. 2005. "Neighborhood socioeconomic disadvantage and access to health care." *Journal of Health and Social Behavior* 46:15–31.

Kirsh, S. J., and P. V. Olczak. 2002. "The effects of extremely violent comic books on social information processing." *Journal of Interpersonal Violence* 17:1160–78.

Kitzmann, K. M., N. K. Gaylord, A. R. Holt, and E. D. Kenny. 2003. "Child witnesses to domestic violence." *Journal of Consulting and Clinical Psychology* 71:339–52.

Klamen, D. L., L. S. Grossman, and D. R. Kopacz. 1999. "Medical student homophobia." *Journal of Homosexuality* 37:53–64.

Klaus, P., and C. M. Rennison. 2002. *Age Patterns in Violent Victimization, 1976–2000.* Washington, DC: Bureau of Justice Statistics.

Klein, E. J., H. J. Davies, and M. A. Hicks. 2001. *Child Pornography: The Criminal-Justice System Response.* National Center for Missing and Exploited Children Web site.

Klerman, G. L., ed. 1986. *Suicide and Depression among Adolescents and Young Adults.* Washington, DC: American Psychiatric Press.

Kliewer, S. 2004. "Allowing spirituality into the healing process." *Journal of Family Practice* 53:616–24.

Kline, M., J. R. Johnston, and J. M. Tschann. 1991. "The long shadow of marital conflict: A model of children's post-divorce adjustment." *Journal of Marriage and the Family* 53 (February):297–309.

Klose, M., and F. Jacobi. 2004. "Can gender differences in the prevalence of mental disorders be explained by sociodemographic factors?" *Archives of Women's Mental Health* 7:133–48.

Kluegel, J. R. 1987. "Macro-economic problems, beliefs about the poor and attitudes toward welfare spending." *Social Problems* 34 (February):82–99.

Klug, B. J., and P. T. Whitfield. 2002. *Widening the Circle: Culturally Relevant Pedagogy for American Indian Children.* New York: Routledge/Falmer.

Knee, J. A. 2004. "Is that really legal?" *The New York Times,* May 2.

Knoke, D., and Y. Ishio. 1998. "The gender gap in company job training." *Work and Occupations* 25 (May):141–67.

Knudsen, H. K., P. M. Roman, J. A. Johnson, and L. J. Ducharme. 2005. "A changed America? The effects of September 11th on depressive symptoms and alcohol consumption." *Journal of Health and Social Behavior* 46:260–73.

Koepke, L., J. Hare, and P. B. Moran. 1992. "Relationship quality in a sample of lesbian couples with children and child-free lesbian couples." *Family Relations* 41:224–29.

Kogevinas, M., et al. 1998. "Respiratory symptoms, lung function and use of health services among unemployed young adults in Spain." *European Respiratory Journal* 11 (June):1363–68.

Kolbert, E. 2002. "Bad environments." *New Yorker,* May 20, pp. 35–36.

———. 2006. "Untransformed." *The New Yorker,* September 25, pp. 64–65.

Komarovsky, M. 1940. *The Unemployed Man and His Family.* New York: Dryden Press.

Kopecki, D. 2006. "On the hunt for fraud." *Business Week,* October 11, p. 11.

Koretz, G. 1997. "The downside of downsizing." *BusinessWeek,* April 28.

Koss, M. P., and J. A. Gaines. 1993. "The prediction of sexual aggression by alcohol use, athletic participation, and fraternity affiliation." *Journal of Interpersonal Violence* 8 (March):94–108.

Kozaryn, L. D. 2002. "Bush says Saddam Hussein 'must be stopped.' " U.S. Department of Defense website.

Kozol, J. 1967. *Death at an Early Age.* New York: Bantam Books.

———. 1992. *Savage Inequalities: Children in America's Schools.* New York: Crown Publishers.

Krajick, K. 2001. "Long-term data show lingering effects from acid rain." *Science* 292:195–97.

Kramer, L. A., and E. C. Berg. 2003. "A survival analysis of timing of entry into prostitution." *Sociological Inquiry* 73:511–28.

Kramer, R. 1999. "Weaving the public into public administration." *Public Administration Review* 59 (January–February):89–92.

Krassas, N. R., J. M. Blauwkamp, and P. Wesselink. 2001. "Boxing Helena and corseting Eunice: Sexual rhetoric in *Cosmopolitan* and *Playboy* magazines." *Sex Roles* 44:751–71.

Kreeger, K. Y. 2002. "Deciphering how the sexes think." *Scientist,* January 21, pp. 28–33.

Krieg, E. J. 1998. "The two faces of toxic waste: Trends in the spread of environmental hazards." *Sociological Forum* 13 (1):3–20.

Kristiansen, S., and M. Ramli. 2006. "Buying an income: The market for civil service positions in Indonesia." *Contemporary Southeast Asia* 28:207–33.

Kristof, N. D. 2006. "Iraq and your wallet." *The New York Times,* October 24.

Krugman, P. 2006. "Broken promises." *The New York Times,* August 28.

Kruks, G. 1991. "Gay and lesbian homeless/street youth: Special issues and concerns." *Journal of Adolescent Health* 12 (November):515–18.

Kruttschnitt, C. 1989. "A sociological, offender-based study of rape." *Sociological Quarterly* 30 (2):305–29.

Kruttschnitt, C., J. D. McLeod, and M. Dornfeld. 1994. "The economic environment of child abuse." *Social Problems* 41 (May):299–315.

Kryzanek, M. J. 1999. *Angry, Bored, Confused: A Citizen Handbook of American Politics.* Boulder, CO.: Westview.

Kuhr, S., and J. M. Hauer. 2001. "The threat of biological terrorism in the new millenium." *American Behavioral Scientist* 44:1032–41.

Kull, S., C. Ramsay, and E. Lewis. 2003. "Misperceptions, the media, and the Iraq war." *Political Science Quarterly* 118:569–98.

Kuo, F. E., and W. C. Sullivan. 2001. "Environment and crime in the inner city." *Environment and Behavior* 33:343–67.

Kuo, L. 2002. *Prostitution Policy: Revolutionizing Practice through a Gendered Perspective.* New York: New York University Press.

Kuo, M. 2000. "Asia's dirty secret." *Harvard International Review* 22:42–45.

Kurdek, L. A. 1990. "Divorce history and self-reported psychological distress in husbands and wives." *Journal of Marriage and the Family* 52:701–08.

Kushel, M. B., et al. 2005. "Revolving doors: Imprisonment among the homeless and marginally housed population." *American Journal of Public Health* 95:1747–52.

Kuttner, R. 1998. "Must good HMOs go bad?" *New England Journal of Medicine* 338 (May 21):16–22.

———. 2005. "Generous to a fault?" *The San Diego Union-Tribune,* January 6.

Lacayo, R. 2003. "The war comes back home." *Time,* May 12, pp. 30–34.

Lacey, M. 2005. "Beyond the bullets and blades." *The New York Times,* March 20.

LaCroix, A. Z., et al. 1991. "Smoking and mortality among older men and women in three communities." *New England Journal of Medicine* 324 (June 6):1619–25.

Ladwig, K. H., B. Marten-Mittag, B. Formanek, and G. Dammann. 2000. "Gender differences of symptom reporting and medical health care utilization in the German population." *European Journal of Epidemiology* 16:511–18.

Laffaye, C., C. Kennedy, and M. B. Stein. 2003. "Post-traumatic stress disorder and health-related quality of life in female victims of intimate partner violence." *Violence and Victims* 18:227–38.

Lamb, H. R. 1998. "Deinstitutionalization at the beginning of the new millennium." *Harvard Review of Psychiatry* 6 (May–June):1–10.

Landolt, M. A., et al. 2004. "Gender nonconformity, childhood rejection, and adult attachment: A study of gay men." *Archives of Sexual Behavior* 33:117–28.

Langstrom, N., and M. C. Seto. 2006. "Exhibitionistic and voyeuristic behavior in a Swedish national population survey." *Archives of Sexual Behavior* 11:23–35.

Lanier, C. A. 2001. "Rape-accepting attitudes." *Violence against Women* 7:876–85.

Lankoande, S., et al. 1998. "Prevalence and risk of HIV infection among female sex workers in Burkina Faso." *International Journal of STD and AIDS* 9 (March):146–50.

Lantz, P. M., et al. 1998. "Socioeconomic factors, health behaviors, and mortality." *Journal of the American Medical Association* 279 (June 3):1703–08.

Lantz, P. M., J. S. House, R. P. Mero, and D. R. Williams. 2005. "Stress, life events, and socioeconomic disparities in health." *Journal of Health and Social Behavior* 46:274–88.

Lanza-Kaduce, L., K. F. Parker, and C. W. Thomas. 1999. "A comparative recidivism analysis of releases from private and public prisons." *Crime and Delinquency* 45 (January):28–47.

Larcinese, V., L. Rizzo, and C. Testa. 2006. "Allocating the U.S. federal budget to the states." *Journal of Politics* 68:447–56.

Lareau, A. 2003. *Unequal Childhoods: Class, Race, and Family Life.* Berkeley: University of California Press.

LaRossa, R., C. Jaret, M. Gadgil, and G. R. Wynn. 2001. "Gender disparities in Mother's Day and Father's Day comic strips." *Sex Roles* 44:693–718.

Larson, M. S. 2003. "Gender, race, and aggression in television commercials that feature children." *Sex Roles* 48:67–75.

Latorre, R. A., and K. Wendenburg. 1983. "Psychological characteristics of bisexual, heterosexual, and homosexual women." *Journal of Homosexuality* 9 (Fall):87–97.

Lauer, J. C., and R. H. Lauer. 1986. *'Til Death Do Us Part: How Couples Stay Together.* New York: Haworth.

Lauer, R. H. 1971. "The middle class looks at poverty." *Urban and Social Change Review* 5 (Fall):8–10.

———. 1974. "Rate of change and stress: A test of the 'future shock' thesis." *Social Forces* 52:510–16.

———. 1976. "Defining social problems: Public opinion and textbook practice." *Social Problems* 24 (October):122–30.

———. 1991. *Perspectives on Social Change.* 4th ed. Boston: Allyn and Bacon.

Lauer, R. H., and J. C. Lauer. 1983. *The Spirit and the Flesh: Sex in Utopian Communities.* Netuchen, NJ: Scarecrow.

———. 1988. *Watersheds: Mastering Life's Unpredictable Crises.* New York: Little, Brown.

———. 1999. *Becoming Family: How to Build a Stepfamily That Really Works.* Minneapolis, MN: Augsburg.

———. 2007. *Marriage and Family: The Quest for Intimacy.* 6th ed. New York: McGraw-Hill.

Laumann, E. O., R. T. Michael, J. H. Gagnon, and S. Michaels. 1994. *The Social Organization of Sexuality.* Chicago: University of Chicago Press.

Lauzen, M. M., and D. M. Dozier. 2005. "Maintaining the double standard: Portrayals of age and gender in popular films." *Sex Roles* 52:437–46.

Law, W. 1906. *A Serious Call to a Devout and Holy Life.* New York: E. P. Dutton.

Lawlor, D. A., et al. 2006. "Family socioeconomic position at birth and future cardiovascular disease risk." *American Journal of Public Health* 96:1271–77.

Lawyer, S. R., K. J. Ruggiero, H. S. Resnick, D. G. Kilpatrick, and B. E. Saunders. 2006. "Mental health correlates of the victim-perpetrator relationship among interpersonally victimized adolescents." *Journal of Interpersonal Violence* 21:1333–53.

Leary, W. E. 1996. "No evidence power lines a threat." *San Diego Union-Tribune,* November 1.

Leatherdale, S. T., P. W. McDonald, R. Cameron, and K. S. Brown. 2005. "A multilevel analysis examining the relationship between social influences for smoking and smoking onset." *American Journal of Health Behavior* 29:520–30.

Lebeque, B. 1991. "Paraphilias in U.S. pornography titles: 'Pornography made me do it' (Ted Bundy)." *Bulletin of the American Academy of Psychiatry and Law* 19 (1):43–48.

Lee, B. A., C. R. Farrell, and B. G. Link. 2004. "Revisiting the contact hypothesis: The case of public exposure to homelessness." *American Sociological Review* 69:40–63.

Lee, B. A., and C. J. Schreck. 2005. "Danger on the streets: Marginality and victimization among homeless people." *American Behavioral Scientist* 48:1055–81.

Lee, D. J., S. J. Niemcryk, C. D. Jenkins, and R. M. Rose. 1989. "Type A, amicability and injury: A prospective study of air traffic controllers." *Journal of Psychosomatic Research* 33 (2):177–86.

Lee, G. R., and J. R. Bulanda. 2005. "Change and consistency in the relation of marital status to personal happiness." *Marriage and Family Review* 38:69–84.

Lee, J., and F. D. Bean. 2003. "Beyond black and white: remaking race in America." *Contexts* 2:26–33.

Lee, M. R., and G. C. Ousey. 2001. "Size matters: Examining the link between small manufacturing socioeconomic deprivation and crime rates in nonmetropolitan communities." *Sociological Quarterly* 42:581–602.

Lee, V. E., and D. Burkam. 2002. *Inequality at the Starting Gate: Social Background Differences in Achievement as Children Begin School.* Washington, DC: Economic Policy Institute.

Lehman, W. E. K., D. J. Farabee, M. L. Holcom, and D. D. Simpson. 1995. "Prediction of substance use in the workplace: Unique contributions of personal background and work environment variables." *Journal of Drug Issues* 25 (2):253–74.

Lehmann, J. B., C. U. Lehmann, and P. J. Kelly. 1998. "Development and health care needs of lesbians." *Journal of Women's Health* 7 (April):379–88.

Leiber, M., and K. C. Fox. 2005. "Race and the impact of detention on juvenile justice decision making." *Crime and Delinquency* 51:470–97.

Leidholdt, D., and J. G. Raymond. 1990. *The Sexual Liberals and the Attack of Feminism.* New York: Pergamon.

Leigh, B. C., M. T. Temple, and K. F. Trocki. 1993. "The sexual behavior of US adults: Results from a national survey." *American Journal of Public Health* 83:1400–1408.

Lemonick, M. D. 1996. "What's wrong with our sperm?" *Time,* March 18, pp. 78–79.

Lenski, G. E. 1966. *Power and Privilege.* New York: McGraw-Hill.

Lenssen, N. 1993. "Providing energy in developing countries." In *State of the World 1993*, ed. L. Brown, pp. 101–19. New York: W. W. Norton.

Leonhard, D. 2002. "Out of a job and no longer looking." *The New York Times*, September 29.

Leshner, A. I. 1998. "Addiction is a brain disease— and it matters." *National Institute of Justice Journal*, October, pp. 2–6.

Leslie, M. 2003. "Acid rain collection." *Science* 301:899.

LeVay, S. 1991. "A difference in hypothalamic structure between heterosexual and homosexual men." *Science* 253 (August 30):1034–37.

Leveille, S. G., C. C. Wee, and L. I. Iezzoni. 2005. "Trends in obesity and arthritis among baby boomers and their predecessors, 1971–2002." *American Journal of Public Health* 95:1607–13.

Levi, M. 1998. "A state of trust." In *Trust and Governance*, ed. V. Braithwaite and M. Levi, pp. 77–98. New York: Russell Sage Foundation.

Levin, H. 2006. "Worker democracy and worker productivity." *Social Justice Research* 19:109–21.

Levine, C. 1995. "Orphans of the HIV epidemic: Unmet needs in six U.S. cities." *AIDS Care* 7 (February):57–62.

Levy, C. J. 1999. "More power was supposed to grease these skids." *The New York Times*, June 27.

Levy, J. A., C. P. Gallmeier, and W. W. Wiebel. 1995."The outreach assisted peer-support model for controlling drug dependency." *Journal of Drug Issues* 25 (3):507–29.

Lewin, T. 1990. "Too much retirement time? A move is afoot to change it." *The New York Times*, April 22.

Lewis, D. O., R. Lovely, C. Yeager, and D. Della-Femina. 1989. "Toward a theory of the genesis of violence: A follow-up study of delinquents." *Journal of the American Academy of Child and Adolescent Psychiatry* 28 (May):431–36.

Lewis, R. 2002. "Race and the clinic: Good science?" *Scientist* 16 (February 18):16.

Lichter, S. R., L. S. Lichter, D. R. Amundson, and J. M. Fowler. 1987. "The truth about Pravda: How the Soviets see the United States." *Public Opinion* (March–April):12–13.

Lieberman, B. 2004. "Rising CO_2 levels threaten oceans, scientists say." *San Diego Union-Tribune*, July 16.

Light, P. C. 1999. *The True Size of Government*. Washington, DC: Brookings Institution Press.

Lii, J. H. 1995. "Week in sweatshop reveals grim conspiracy of the poor." *The New York Times*, March 12.

Link, B. G. 1987. "Understanding labeling effects in the area of mental disorders: An assessment of the effects of expectations of rejection." *American Sociological Review* 52 (February):96–112.

Link, B. G., et al. 1989. "A modified labeling theory approach to mental disorders." *American Sociological Review* 54:400–423.

Link, B. G., J. Mirotznik, and F. T. Cullen. 1991. "The effectiveness of stigma coping orientations: Can negative consequences of mental illness labeling be avoided?" *Journal of Health and Social Behavior* 32 (September):302–20.

Linz, D., and N. Malamuth. 1993. *Pornography*. Newbury Park, CA: Sage.

Liptak, A., N. A. Lewis, and B. Weiser. 2002. "After Sept. 11, a legal battle on the limits of civil liberty." *The New York Times*, August 4.

Liskow, B. I., et al. 2000. "Mortality in male alcoholics after ten to fourteen years." *Journal of Studies on Alcohol* 61:853–61.

Litrownik, A. J., R. Newton, W. M. Hunter, D. English, and M. D. Everson. 2003. "Exposure to family violence in young at-risk children." *Journal of Family Violence* 18:59–73.

Liu, L. 2006. "Quality of life as a social representation in China." *Social Indicators Research* 75:217–40.

Liu, X., and H. B. Kaplan. 1996. "Gender-related differences in circumstances surrounding initiation and escalation of alcohol and other substance use/abuse." *Deviant Behavior* 17 (1):71–106.

Livingston, D. W. 1998. *The Education-Jobs Gap: Underemployment or Economic Democracy*. Boulder, CO: Westview Press.

Lo, S., R. Stone, and C. W. Ng. 2003. "Work-family conflict and coping strategies adopted by female married professionals in Hong Kong." *Women in Management Review* 18:182–90.

Locke, B. D., and J. R. Mahalik. 2005. "Examining masculinity norms, problem drinking, and athletic involvement as predictors of sexual aggression in college men." *Journal of Counseling Psychology* 52:279–83.

Locke, M. 1996. "Suicide, natural causes: How most inmates die on death rows." *Chicago Tribune*, March 6.

Locke, S., and D. Colligan. 1986. *The Healer Within: The New Medicine of Mind and Body*. New York: New American Library.

Lockhart, L. L., B. W. White, V. Causby, and A. I. 1994. "Letting out the secret: Violence in lesbian relationships." *Journal of Interpersonal Violence* 9 (December):469–92.

Loeber, R., and D. P. Farrington. 1998. *Serious and Violent Juvenile Offenders: Risk Factors and Successful Interventions*. Newbury Park, CA: Sage.

Loftus, J., 2001. "America's liberalization in attitudes toward homosexuality, 1973 to 1999." *American Sociological Review* 66:762–82.

Long, S. H., and M. S. Marquis. 1999. "Geographic variation in physician visits for uninsured children: The role of the safety net." *Journal of the American Medical Association* 281 (June 2):2035–41.

Longres, J. F. 1991. "An ecological study of parents of adjudicated female teenage prostitutes." *Journal of Social Service Research* 14 (1–2):113–27.

Lonsway, K. A., and L. F. Fitzgerald. 1995. "Attitudinal antecedents of rape myth acceptance." *Journal of Personality and Social Psychology* 68 (April):704–11.

Lopata, H. Z. 1984. "Social construction of social problems over time." *Social Problems* 31 (February):249–72.

Lorenz, F. O., K. A. Wickrama, R. D. Conger, and G. H. Elder, Jr. 2006. "The short-term and decade-long effects of divorce on women's midlife health." *Journal of Health and Social Behavior* 47:111–25.

Loring, M., and B. Powell. 1988. "Gender, race, and DSM-III: A study of the objectivity of psychiatric diagnostic behavior." *Journal of Health and Social Behavior* 29 (March):1–22.

Louie, M. C. 1992. "After sewing, laundry, cleaning and cooking, I have no breath left to sing." *Amerasia Journal* 18 (1):1–26.

Loury, G. C. 2005. "Racial stigma and its consequences." *Focus* 24:1–6.

Loveless, T., 1999. "Will tracking reform promote social equity?" *Educational Leadership* 56 (April):28–32.

Lovering, D. 2001. "Taming the killing fields of Laos." *Scientific American,* August, pp. 67–71.

Lowi, T. J., and J. Romance. 1998. *A Republic of Parties? Debating the Two-Party System.* Lanham, MD: Rowman and Littlefield.

Lowman, J., C. Atchison, and L. Fraser. 1997. *Sexuality in the 1990s: Survey Results.* Vancouver, BC: British Columbia Ministry of the Attorney General.

Loxton, D., M. Schofield, and R. Hussain. 2006. "Psychological health in midlife among women who have ever lived with a violent partner or spouse." *Journal of Interpersonal Violence* 21:1092–1107.

Lucas, J. L., and R. B. Heady. 2002. "Flextime commuters and their driver stress, feelings of time urgency, and commute satisfaction." *Journal of Business and Psychology* 16:565–71.

Lundwall, R. A. 2002. "Parents' perceptions of the impact of their chronic illness or disability on their functioning as parents and on their relationships with their children." *The Family Journal* 10:300–307.

Lung, F. W., T. J. Lin, Y. C. Lu, and B. C. Shu. 2004. "Personal characteristics of adolescent prostitutes and rearing attitudes of their parents." *Psychiatry Research* 125:285–91.

Luthar, S. S., and G. Cushing. 1997. "Substance use and personal adjustment among disadvantaged teenagers." *Journal of Youth and Adolescence* 26 (June):353–72.

Lynch, J. W., G. A. Kaplan, and S. J. Shema. 1997. "Cumulative impact of sustained economic hardship on physical, cognitive, psychological, and social functioning." *New England Journal of Medicine* 337 (December 25):1889–95.

McAdams, D. P., and F. B. Bryant. 1987. "Intimacy motivation and subjective mental health in a nationwide sample." *Journal of Personality* 55:395–413.

McBroom, J. R. 1992. "Alcohol and drug use by third, fourth, and fifth graders in a town of 20,000." *Sociology and Social Research* 76 (April):156–60.

McCabe, M. P. 1987. "Desired and experienced levels of premarital affection and sexual intercourse during dating." *Journal of Sex Research* 23:23–33.

McCall, L. 2001. "Sources of racial wage inequality in metropolitan labor markets." *American Sociological Review* 66:520–41.

McCarthy, B., and J. Hagan. 1992. "Mean streets: The theoretical significance of situational delinquency among homeless youths." *American Journal of Sociology* 98 (November):597–627.

McClam, E. 2005. "Role in tax scam admitted by KPMG." *San Diego Union-Tribune,* August 30.

McCleese, C. S., and L. T. Eby. 2006. "Reactions to job content plateaus." *Career Development Quarterly* 55:64–76.

McCloskey, L. A., and E. L. Lichter. 2003. "The contribution of marital violence to adolescent aggression across different relationships." *Journal of Interpersonal Violence* 18:390–412.

McConkey, D. 2001. "Whither Hunter's culture war? Shifts in evangelical morality, 1988–1998." *Sociology of Religion* 61:149–74.

McCormick, C. M., and S. F. Witelson. 1994. "Functional cerebral asymmetry and sexual orientation in men and women." *Behavioral Neuroscience* 108 (June):525–31.

McDevitt, J., J. Balboni, L. Garcia, and J. Gu. 2001. "Consequences for victims: A comparison of bias- and non-bias-motivated assaults." *American Behavioral Scientist* 45:697–713.

MacDonald, M., and D. Nierenberg. 2003. "Linking population, women, and biodiversity." In *State of the World 2003,* ed. L. Starke, pp. 38–61. New York: W. W. Norton.

McDonald, R., et al. 2006. "Estimating the number of American children living in partner-violent families." *Journal of Family Psychology* 20:137–42.

McDonough, P., and P. Berglund. 2003. "Histories of poverty and self-rated health trajectories." *Journal of Health and Social Behavior* 44:198–214.

McDowall, D., C. Loftin, and B. Wiersema. 2000. "The impact of youth curfew laws on juvenile crime rates." *Crime and Delinquency* 46 (January):76–91.

MacEachern, D. 1990. *Save the Planet: 750 Ways You Can Help Clean Up the Earth.* New York: Dell.

McFarlane, J., P. Willson, A. Malecha, and D. Lemmey. 2000. "Intimate partner violence." *Journal of Interpersonal Violence* 15 (February):158–69.

McFarlin, S. K., W. Fals-Stewart, D. A. Major, and E. M. Justice. 2001. "Alcohol use and workplace aggression." *Journal of Substance Abuse* 13:303–21.

McGarva, A. R., M. Ramsey, and S. A. Shear. 2006. "Effects of driver cell-phone use on driver aggression." *The Journal of Social Psychology* 140:133–46.

McGinn, A. P. 1999. "Charting a new course for oceans." In *State of the World 1999,* ed. Lester R. Brown et al., pp. 78–95. New York: W. W. Norton.

———. 2000. *Why Poison Ourselves?* Washington, DC: Worldwatch Institute.

———. 2002. "Reducing our toxic burden." In *State of the World 2002,* ed. Linda Starke, pp. 75–100. New York: W. W. Norton.

McGruder-Johnson, A. K., et al. 2000. "Interpersonal violence and posttraumatic symptomatology." *Journal of Interpersonal Violence* 15 (February):205–21.

MacKay, N. J., and K. Covell. 1997. "The impact of women in advertisements on attitudes toward women." *Sex Roles* 36 (9–10):573–84.

McKee, M., and V. Shkolnikov. 2001. "Understanding the toll of premature death among men in Eastern Europe." *British Medical Journal* 323:1051–55.

McKeganey, N. 1994. "Why do men buy sex and what are their assessments of the HIV-related risks when they do?" *AIDS Care* 6 (3):289–301.

McKellar, J., E. Stewart, and K. Humphreys. 2003. "Alcoholics Anonymous involvement and positive alcohol-related outcomes." *Journal of Consulting and Clinical Psychology* 71:302–8.

McLanahan, S., and G. Sandefur. 1994. *Growing Up with a Single Parent: What Hurts, What Helps.* Cambridge, MA: Harvard University Press.

McLaughlin, D. K., and C. S. Stokes. 2002. "Income inequality and mortality in U.S. counties." *American Journal of Public Health* 92:99–104.

McLoyd, V. C. 1998. "Socioeconomic disadvantage and child development." *American Psychologist* 53 (February):185–204.

McMenamin, B., and J. Novack. 1999. "The white-collar gestapo." *Forbes,* December 1, pp. 82–91.

McQuaid, J. R., et al. 2000. "Correlates of life stress in an alcohol treatment sample." *Addictive Behaviors* 25 (January–February):131–37.

McWhirter, D. P., and A. M. Mattison. 1984. The *Male Couple: How Relationships Develop.* Englewood Cliffs, NJ: Prentice-Hall.

Mack, J. E., and J. Z. Rubin. 1991. "Is this any way to wage peace?" *Los Angeles Times,* January 31.

Maguire, K., and A. I. Pastore, eds. 2006. *Sourcebook of Criminal Justice Statistics.* Bureau of Justice Statistics Web site.

Maher, T. 1998. "Environmental oppression." J*ournal of Black Studies* 28 (3):357–67.

Mahtesian, C. 1999. "So much politics, so little time." *Governing,* August, pp. 22–26.

Maier, T. W. 1998. "Entrapping the whistle-blowers." *Insight on the News,* February 2, pp. 8–12.

Major, V. S., K. J. Klein, and M. G. Ehrhart. 2002. "Work time, work interference with family, and psychological distress." *Journal of Applied Psychology* 87:427–36.

Makela, K., et al. 1996. *Alcoholics Anonymous as a Mutual-Help Movement: A Study in Eight Societies.* Madison: University of Wisconsin Press.

Malamuth, N. M., T. Addison, and M. Koss. 2000. "Pornography and sexual aggression." *Annual Review of Sex Research* 11:26–91.

Maloff, D. 1981. "A review of the effects of the decriminalization of marijuana." *Contemporary Drug Problems* 10 (Fall):307–22.

Mandel, H., and M. Semyonov. 2006. "A welfare state paradox: State interventions and women's employment opportunities in 22 countries." *American Journal of Sociology* 111:1910–49.

Mann, A. 1998. "This place makes me sick." *Time,* December 21, pp. 38–40.

Mann, R. E., R. F. Zaleman, R. G. Smart, B. R. Rush, and H. Suurvali. 2006. "Alcohol consumption, alcoholics anonymous membership, and suicide mortality rates, Ontario, 1968–1991." *Journal of Studies on Alcohol* 67:445–53.

Manning, W. E., P. J. Smock, and D. Majumdar. 2004. "The relative stability of cohabiting and marital unions for children." *Population Research and Policy Review* 23:135–59.

Mansour, S. A. 2004. "Pesticide exposure—Egyptian scene." *Toxicology* 198:91–115.

Marano, H. E. 1996. "Why they stay." *Psychology Today,* May–June, pp. 57–78.

Marano, H. E., and E. Strand. 2003. "Points of departure." *Psychology Today* July/August, pp. 48–49.

Marcon, R. A. 1999. "Impact of parent involvement on children's development and academic performance." Paper presented at the Southeastern Psychological Association meeting.

Marjoribanks, K. 2003. "Learning environments, family contexts, educational aspirations, and attainment." *Learning Environments Research* 6:247–65.

Markey, C., and P. Markey. 2005. "Relations between body image and dieting behaviors." *Sex Roles* 53:519–30.

Markham, D. 2003. "Attitudes towards patients with a diagnosis of 'borderline personality disorder.' " *Journal of Mental Health* 12:595–612.

Markowitz, F. E. 2003. "Socioeconomic disadvantage and violence." *Aggression and Violent Behavior* 8:145–54.

Marks, A. 2006. "Prosecutions drop for U.S. white-collar crime." *Christian Science Monitor,* August 31.

Marks, N. F. 1995. "Midlife marital status differences in social support relationships with adult children and psychological well-being." *Journal of Family Issues* 16 (January):5–28.

Markward, M. J. 1997. "The impact of domestic violence on children." *Families in Society* 78 (January–February):66–71.

Marsch, L. A. 1998. "The efficacy of methadone maintenance interventions in reducing illicit opiate use, HIV risk behavior and criminality." *Addiction* 93 (April):515–32.

Marsh, B. 2006. "The nation: Plentiful, productive—and illegal." *The New York Times,* April 2.

Martell, R. F., C. Parker, and C. G. Emrich. 1998. "Sex stereotyping in the executive suite." *Journal of Social Behavior and Personality* 13 (1):127–38.

Martin, C. S., P. R. Clifford, and R. L. Clapper. 1992. "Patterns and predictors of simultaneous and concurrent use of alcohol, tobacco, marijuana, and hallucinogens in first-year college students." *Journal of Substance Abuse* 4 (3):319–26.

Martin, J. K., and P. M. Roman. 1996. "Job satisfaction, job reward characteristics, and employees' problem drinking behaviors." *Work and Occupations* 23 (February):4–25.

Martin, P. S. 2003. "Voting's rewards: Voter turnout, attentive publics, and Congressional allocation of federal money." *American Journal of Political Science* 47:110–27.

Martinez, M. D., and D. Hill. 1999. "Did motor voter work?" *American Politics Quarterly* 27 (July):296–315.

Marullo, S. 1987. "The functions and dysfunctions of preparations for fighting nuclear war." *Sociological Focus* 20 (April):135–53.

Mason, J. O. 1993. "Violence, alcohol and other drugs." *Public Health Reports,* January–February, pp. 1–3.

Mason, W. A. 2001. "Self-esteem and delinquency revisited (again)." *Journal of Youth and Adolescence* 30:83–102.

Massey, D. S., G. A. Condran, and N. A. Denton. 1987. "The effect of residential segregation on black social and economic well-being." *Social Forces* 66 (September):29–56.

Mathews, D. 2006. "The Rescue Foundation." *New Internationalist* 390:33.

Matthies, E., R. Hoger, and R. Guski. 2000. "Living on polluted soil." *Environment and Behavior* 32:270–86.

Mattingly, M. J., and S. M. Bianchi. 2003. "Gender differences in the quantity and quality of free time." *Social Forces* 81:999–1030.

Maxwell, N. L. 1994. "The effect on black-white wage differences in the quantity and quality of education." *Industrial and Labor Relations Review* 47 (January):249–64.

May, P. A. 1991. "Fetal alcohol effects among North American Indians." *Alcohol Health and Research World* 15 (3):239–48.

May, P. A., and J. R. Moran. 1995. "Prevention of alcohol misuse." *American Journal of Health Promotion* 9 (4):288–99.

Mayall, A., and D. E. Russell. 1993. "Racism in pornography." *Feminism and Psychology* 3 (2):275–81.

Mayer, E. A., M. Craske, and B. D. Naliboff. 2001. "Depression, anxiety, and the gastrointestinal system." *Journal of Clinical Psychiatry* 61:28–36.

Mayer, J. 2005. "High stakes." *The New Yorker,* September 19, pp. 37–38.

Mazerolle, L., C. Kadleck, and J. Roehl. 2004. "Differential police control at drug-dealing places." *Security Journal* 17:61–69.

Mazzeo, S. E. 1999. "Modification of an existing measure of body image preoccupation and its relationship to disordered eating in female college students." *Journal of Counseling Psychology* 46 (January):42–50.

Meadows, R. J., and K. L. Anklin. 2002. "Study of the criminal motivations of sentenced jail inmates." In *Visions for Change: Crime and Justice in the Twenty-First Century,* 3rd ed., ed. R. Muraskin and A. R. Roberts, pp. 287–302. New York: Prentice-Hall.

Mechanic, D., D. McAlpine, S. Rosenfield, and D. Davis. 1994. "Effects of illness attribution and depression on the quality of life among persons with serious mental illness." *Social Science and Medicine* 39 (July):155–64.

Meckler, L., 1998. "Blacks in America get sick more than whites, die sooner." *San Diego Union-Tribune,* November 27.

Medler, A. 2002. "The maturing politics of education choice." *Teachers College Record* 104:173–95.

Mehio S., A., N. Shaar Sameer, and S. el Yassir. 2000. "Impairments, disabilities and needs assessment among nonfatal war injuries in South Lebanon, Grapes of Wrath, 1996." *Journal of Epidemiology and Community Health* 54 (January):35–39.

Menaghan, E. G. 1991. "Work experiences and family interaction processes: The long reach of the job?" *Annual Review of Sociology* 17:419–44.

Menard, K. S., A. H. Phung, M. F. Ghebrial, and L. Martin. 2003. "Gender differences in sexual harassment and coercion in college students." *Journal of Interpersonal Violence* 18:1222–39.

Mendell, M. J., et al. 2006. "Indicators of moisture and ventilation system contamination in U.S. office buildings as risk factors for respiratory and mucous membrane symptoms." *Journal of Occupational & Environmental Hygiene* 3:225–33.

Mendoza, M., and C. Sullivan. 2006. "Uncle Sam struggling to collect on fines." *San Diego Union-Tribune,* March 19.

Menke, E. M., and J. D. Wagner. 1998. "A comparative study of homeless, previously homeless, and never homeless school-aged children's health." *Issues in Comparative Pediatric Nursing* 20 (July–September):153–73.

Meredith, D. 1986. "Day-care: The nine-to-five dilemma." *Psychology Today,* February, pp. 36–44.

Merton, R. K. 1957. *Social Theory and Social Structure.* New York: Free Press.

Mesch, G. S. 2000. "Women's fear of crime." *Violence and Victims* 15:323–36.

Meurer, J. R., H. Yang, C. E. Guse, M. C. Scanlon, and P. M. Layde. 2006. "Medical injuries among hospitalized children." *Quality and Safety in Health Care* 15:202–207.

Meyer, I. H. 2003. "Prejudice, social stress, and mental health in lesbian, gay, and bisexual populations." *Psychological Bulletin* 129:674–97.

Meyer, L. B. 2003. "Economic globalization and women's status in the labor market." *Sociological Quarterly* 44:351–83.

Meyers, C. 1988. *Discovering Eve: Ancient Israelite Women in Context.* New York: Oxford University Press.

Michalos, A. C., B. D. Zumbo, and A. Hubley. 2000. "Health and the quality of life." *Social Indicators Research* 51:245–86.

Michelson, M. R. 2003. "Getting out the Latino vote: How door-to-door canvassing influences voter turnout in rural central California." *Political Behavior* 25:247–63.

Mickelson, R. A. 1990. "The attitude-achievement paradox among black adolescents." *Sociology of Education* 63 (January):44–61.

———. 2001. "Subverting Swann: Tracking as second generation segregation in Charlotte, North Carolina." *American Educational Research Journal* 38:215–52.

Milburn, M. A., R. Mather, and S. D. Conrad. 2000. "The effects of viewing R-rated movie scenes that objectify women on perceptions of date rape." *Sex Roles* 43:645–64.

Miller, A. B., T. To, D. A. Agnew, C. Wall, and L. M. Green. 1996. "Leukemia following occupational exposure to 60-Hz electric and magnetic fields among Ontario electric utility workers." *American Journal of Epidemiology* 144 (July 15):150–60.

Miller, J. 2001. *One of the Guys: Girls, Gangs, and Gender.* New York: Oxford University Press.

Miller, J., and D. Jayasundara. 2001. "Prostitution, the sex industry, and sex tourism." *Sourcebook on Violence against Women,* ed. C. M. Renzetti, J. L. Edleson, and R. K. Bergen, pp. 459–80. Thousand Oaks, CA: Sage.

Miller, M. C. 2005. *Fooled Again.* New York: Basic Books.

Miller, T. R., D. T. Levy, R. S. Spicer, and D. M. Taylor. 2006. "Societal costs of underage drinking." *Journal of Studies on Alcohol* 67:519–28.

Miller, W. R., and P. L. Wilbourne. 2002. "Mesa Grande: A methodological analysis of clinical trials of treatments for alcohol use disorders." *Addiction* 97:265–77.

Millett, K. 1971. "Prostitution: A quartet of female voices." In *Woman in Sexist Society,* ed. V. Gornick and B. K. Moran, pp. 60–125. New York: Mentor Books.

Mills, C. W. 1956. *The Power Elite.* New York: Oxford University Press.

———. 1959. *The Sociological Imagination.* New York: Oxford University Press.

Mills, T. C., et al. 2004. "Distress and depression in men who have sex with men." *American Journal of Psychiatry* 161:278–85.

Minino, A. M., and B. L. Smith. 2001. "Deaths: Preliminary data for 2000." *National Vital Statistics Reports,* October 9.

Minton, H. L., and G. J. McDonald. 1984. "Homosexual identity formation as a developmental process." *Journal of Homosexuality* 9 (Winter 1983–Spring 1984):91–104.

Mintz, E. 1998. "Members' diligence in casting ballots climbs to a 45-year high." *Congressional Quarterly Weekly Report,* January 3, p. 24.

Mirowsky, J., and C. E. Ross. 1995. "Sex differences in distress: Real or artifact?" *American Sociological Review* 60 (June):449–68.

Mishel, L., J. Bernstein, and S. Allegretto. 2006. *The State of Working America.* Ithaca, N.Y.: Cornell University Press.

Mitchell, A. 1983. *The Nine American Lifestyles.* New York: Macmillan.

Mitchell, R. S. 1969. *The Homosexual and the Law.* New York: Arco.

Moen, P., D. Dempster-McClain, and R. M. Williams, Jr. 1992. "Successful aging: A life-course perspective on women's multiple roles and health." *American Journal of Sociology* 97 (May):1612–38.

Moen, P., and Y. Yu. 2000. "Effective work/life strategies." *Social Problems* 47:291–326.

Mohler-Kuo, M., G. W. Dowdall, M. P. Koss, and H. Wechsler. 2004. "Correlates of rape while intoxicated in a national sample of college students." *Journal of Studies on Alcohol* 65:37–45.

Mokdad, A. H., J. S. Marks, D. F. Stroup, and J. L. Gerberding. 2004. "Actual causes of death in the United States, 2000." *Journal of the American Medical Association* 291:1238–45.

Molitor, F., and K. W. Hirsch. 1994. "Children's toleration of real-life aggression after exposure to media violence." *Child Study Journal* 24(3):191–207.

Monastersky, R. 1999. "China's air pollution chokes crop growth." *Science News,* March 27. Science News website.

Monroe, L. M., et al. 2005. "The experience of sexual assault." *Journal of Interpersonal Violence* 20:767–76.

Montemurro, B., C. Bloom, and K. Madell. 2003. "Ladies night out: a typology of women patrons of a male strip club." *Deviant Behavior* 24:333–52.

Montgomery, M. B. 1989. "The decision to have children: Women faculty in social work." *Affilia* 4 (Summer):73–84.

Monto, M. A. 2001. "Prostitution and fellatio." *Journal of Sex Research* 38:140–45.

———. 2004. "Female prostitution, customers, and violence." *Violence against Women* 10:160–88.

Monto, M. A., and N. McRee. 2005. "A comparison of the male customers of female street prostitutes with national samples of men." *International Journal of Offender Therapy and Comparative Criminology* 49:505–29.

Moore, A. A., et al. 2005. "Longitudinal patterns and predictors of alcohol consumption in the United States." *American Journal of Public Health* 95:458–65.

Moore, P. 1999. "New evidence links air pollution with lung cancer." *Lancet* 353 (February 27):729.

Moos, R. H., and B. S. Moos. 2004. "Long-term influence of duration and frequency of participation in Alcoholics Anonymous on individuals with alcohol use disorders." *Journal of Consulting and Clinical Psychology* 72:81–90.

Morain, D. 1990. "Complex, costly cleanups may snarl base closings." *Los Angeles Times,* June 19.

Moran, C. 2002. "Federally mandated school choice has few takers locally." *San Diego Union-Tribune,* September 3.

Morgan, L. A. 1991. *After Marriage Ends: Economic Consequences for Midlife Women.* Newbury Park, CA: Sage.

Moritsugu, K. 2001. "U.S. economy struggles to bear brunt of terrorism's costs." Knight Ridder/Tribune News Service, Knight Ridder/Tribune Web site.

Morrell, S. L., R. J. Taylor, and C. B. Kerr. 1998. "Unemployment and young people's health." *Medical Journal of Australia* 168 (March 2):236–40.

Morris, E. W. 2005. "'Tuck in that shirt!' Race, class, gender, and discipline in an urban school." *Sociological Perspectives* 48:25–48.

Morrongiello, B. A., and K. Hogg. 2004. "Mothers' reactions to children misbehaving in ways that can lead to injury." *Sex Roles* 50:103–18.

Morse, J. 2002. "Learning while black." *Time,* May 27, pp. 50–52.

Mosher, D. L., and R. D. Anderson. 1986. "Macho personality, sexual aggression, and reactions to guided imagery of realistic rape." *Journal of Research in Personality* 20 (March):77–94.

Moskowitz, J. M. 1989. "The primary prevention of alcohol problems: A critical review of the research literature." *Journal of Studies on Alcohol* 50 (January):54–88.

Motivans, M. 2003. "Money laundering offenders, 1994–2001." *Bureau of Justice Statistics Special Report.* Washington, DC: Government Printing Office.

Moulder, J. E., K. R. Foster, L. S. Erdreich, and J. P. McNamee. 2005. "Mobile phones, mobile phone base stations and cancer." *International Journal of Radiation Biology* 81:189–203.

Mukamal, K. J., and E. B. Rimm. 2001. "Alcohol's effects on the risk for coronary heart disease." *Alcohol Research and Health* 25:255–61.

Muldoon, O. T., and K. Wilson. 2001. "Ideological commitment, experience of conflict and adjustment in Northern Irish adolescents." *Medicine, Conflict, and Survival* 17:112–24.

Mulkey, L. M., R. L. Crain, and A. J. C. Harringon. 1992. "One-parent households and achievement: Economic and behavioral explanations of a small effect." *Sociology of Education* 65 (January):48–65.

Mullins, B. 2006. "U.S. lobbying tab hits a record." *Wall Street Journal,* February 14.

Mullins, L. C., K. P. Brackett, D. W. Bogle, and D. Pruett. 2004. "The impact of religious homogeneity on the rate of divorce in the United States." *Sociological Inquiry* 74:338–54.

Mumola, C. 2005. "Suicide and homicide in state prisons and local jails." *Bureau of Justice Statistics Special Report,* August.

Murbeth, S., M. Rousarova, H. Scherb, and E. Lengfelder. 2004. "Thyroid cancer has increased in the adult populations of countries moderately affected by Chernobyl fallout." *Medical Science Monitor* 10:300–306.

Murdaugh, C., S. Hunt, R. Sowell, and I. Santana. 2004. "Domestic violence in Hispanics in the Southeastern United States." *Journal of Family Violence* 19;107–15.

Murty, K. S., J. B. Roebuck, and G. R. Armstrong. 1994. "The black community's reactions to the 1992 Los Angeles riot." *Deviant Behavior* 15:85–104.

Musser, G., and S. Nemecek. 2000. "A new kind of war." *Scientific American,* June, p. 47.

Mustanski, B. S., M. L. Chivers, and J. M. Bailey. 2002. "A critical review of recent biological research on human sexual orientation." *Annual Review of Sex Research* 13:89–140.

Myerson, J., M. R. Rank, F. Q. Raines, and M. A. Schnitzler. 1998. "Race and general cognitive ability." *Psychological Science* 9 (March):139–42.

Myhill, D., and S. Jones. 2006. "'She doesn't shout at no girls': Pupils' perceptions of gender equity in the classroom." *Cambridge Journal of Education* 36:99–113.

Myrdal, G. 1944. *An American Dilemma.* New York: Harper and Bros.

Nader, R. 1990. "Corporate state is on a roll." *Los Angeles Times,* March 5.

Nansel, T. R., et al. 2001. "Bullying behaviors among U.S. youth." *Journal of the American Medical Association* 285:2094–2100.

Napoli, M. 1998. "Hormone-disrupting chemicals." *HealthFacts,* November, p. 1.

National Center for Education Statistics. 2000a. *The Condition of Education 1999.* Washington, DC: U.S. Department of Education.

———. 2000b. "Percentage distribution of the highest postsecondary attainment of 1992 12th-graders who were likely postsecondary participants, by race/ethnicity, sex, and socioeconomic status." NCES Web site.

———. 2001. *The Condition of Education 2001.* Washington, DC: U.S. Department of Education.

———. 2004. *The Condition of Education 2004.* Washington, DC: Government Printing Office.

———. 2006a. *The Condition of Education 2006.* NCES Web site.

———. 2006b. *Digest of Educational Statistics.* NCES Web site.

National Center for Health Statistics. 2000. "Puerto Ricans' health fares worse than other U.S. hispanics." Press release. NCHS Web site.

———. 2006. *Health, United States, 2006.* Hyaattsville, MD: National Center for Health Statistics.

National Center on Addiction and Substance Abuse at Columbia University. 1998. *Back to School 1998: The CASA National Survey of American Attitudes on Substance Abuse.* Washington, DC: National Center on Addiction and Substance Abuse.

National Coalition for the Homeless. 2000. *Welfare to What II?* Washington, DC: NCH.

———. 2003a. "People need affordable housing." NCH Web site.

———. 2003b. "People need livable incomes." NCH Web site.

———. 2006a. "A dream denied: The criminalization of homelessness in U.S. cities." NCFH Web site.

———. 2006b. "Hate, violence, and death: Street USA, 2005." NCFH Web site.

———. 2006c. "How many people experience homelessness?" NCFH Web site.

———. 2006d. "Who is homeless?" NCFH Web site.

National Election Studies. 2004. *The NES Guide to Public Opinion and Electoral Behavior.* NES Web site.

National Environmental Trust. 2002. *First in Emissions, Behind in Solutions.* Washington, DC: National Environmental Trust.

National Institute of Justice. 1996a. "Alternative sanctions in Germany: An overview of Germany's sentencing practices." *Research Preview,* February.

———. 1996b. "The cycle of violence revisited." *Research Preview,* February.

National Institute of Mental Health. 1982. *Television and Behavior: Ten Years of Scientific Progress and Implications for the Eighties,* Vol. 1, Summary Report. Washington, DC: Government Printing Office.

———. 1988. The 14 *Worst Myths about Recovered Mental Patients.* Washington, DC: Government Printing Office.

———. 2004. "Fiscal year 2005 president's budget request for NIMH." National Institute of Mental Health Web site.

National Institute on Alcohol Abuse and Alcoholism. 2001. *Alcohol: Getting the Facts. Bethesda,* MD: NIAAA.

National Institute on Drug Abuse. 1998. *Marijuana: Facts for Teens.* NIDA Web site.

———. 2004. *Preventing Drug Use among Children and Adolescents.* National Institute on Drug Abuse Web site.

———. 2005. "NIDA infofacts: Methamphetamine." NIDA Web site.

National Study of Charter Schools. 2000. *The State of Charter Schools 2000.* National Study of Charter Schools Web site.

National Survey on Drug Use and Health. 2004. "Religious beliefs and substance use among youths." *The NSDUH Report,* January 30.

National Victims Resource Center. 1991. *Juvenile Prostitution: Fact Sheet.* Rockville, MD: Victims Resource Center.

Nearing, S. 1969. *Black America.* New York: Schocken.

Neckerman, K. M., and J. Kirschenman. 1991. "Hiring strategies, racial bias, and inner-city workers." *Social Problems* 38 (November):433–47.

Needle, R. H., S. S. Su, and W. J. Doherty. 1990. "Divorce, remarriage, and adolescent substance use: A longitudinal study." *Journal of Marriage and the Family* 52:157–69.

Nelson, A., C. Dawkins, and T. Sanchez. 2004. "Urban containment and residential segregation." *Urban Studies* 41:423–39.

Nelson, C. M. 2004. "Internet becomes source of political information for more people." *Dallas Morning News,* January 11.

Nelson, S. H., G. F. McCoy, M. Stetter, and W. C. Vanderwagen. 1992. "An overview of mental health services for American Indians and Alaska natives in the 1990s." *Hospital and Community Psychiatry* 43 (March):257–61.

Neria, Y., et al. 2000. "Posttraumatic residues of captivity." *Journal of Clinical Psychiatry* 61 (January):39–46.

Nesbitt, P. D. 1997. *Feminization of the Clergy in America.* New York: Oxford University Press.

Ness, E. 2003. "Federal government's program in attacking the problem of prostitution." *Federal Probation* 67:10–12.

Ness, R. B., et al. 1999. "Cocaine and tobacco use and the risk of spontaneous abortion." *New England Journal of Medicine* 340 (February 4):333–39.

Netemeyer, R. G., J. C. Andrews, and S. Burton. 2005. "Effects of antismoking advertising-based beliefs on adults smokers' consideration of quitting." *American Journal of Public Health* 95:1062–66.

Netter, W. J. 2003. "Curing the unique health identifier." *Jurimetrics* 43:165–86.

Newman, K., C. Fox, D. Harding, J. Mehta, and W. Roth. 2004. *Rampage: The Social Roots of School Shootings.* New York: Basic Books.

Newman, R. J. 1998. "A U.S. victory, at a cost of $5.5 trillion." *U.S. News and World Report,* July 13.

Newport, F. 1998a. "Americans remain more likely to believe sexual orientation due to environment, not genetics." *Gallup Poll Archives.* Gallup Poll Web site.

———. 1998b. "No single problem dominates Americans' concerns today." *Gallup Poll Archives.* Gallup Poll Web site.

Newton, J. 1998. "White guys: Hegemonic masculinities." *Feminist Studies* 24:11–20.

Nicaise, V., G. Cogerino, J. E. Bois, and A. J. Amorose. 2006. "Students' perceptions of teacher feedback and physical competence in physical education classes." *Journal of Teaching in Physical Education* 25:36–57.

Nierenberg, D. 2006. "Population continues to grow." Pp. 74–75 in L. Starke, ed., *Vital Signs:* 2006–2007. New York: W.W. Norton.

Nieves, E. 1999. "For patrons of prostitutes, remedial instruction." *The New York Times,* March 18.

Nijhof, G. 1995. "Parkinson's disease as a problem of shame in public appearance." *Sociology of Health and Illness* 17 (March):193–205.

Niskar, A. S., et al. 1998. "Prevalence of hearing loss among children 6 to 19 years of age." *Journal of the American Medical Association* 279 (April 8):1071–76.

Nixon, K., L. Tutty, P. Downe, K. Gorkoff, and J. Ursel. 2002. "The everyday occurrence: Violence in the lives of girls exploited through prostitution." *Violence against Women* 8:1016–43.

Noble, K. G., M. J. Farah, and B. D. McCandliss. 2006. "Socioeconomic background modulates cognition-achievement relationships in reading." *Cognitive Development* 21:349–68.

Nock, S. L. 1995. "A comparison of marriages and cohabiting relationships." *Journal of Family Issues* 16 (January):53–76.

Noll, J. G., L. A. Horowitz, G. A. Bonanno, P. K. Trickett, and F. W. Putnam. 2003. "Revictimization and self-harm in females who experienced childhood sex abuse." *Journal of Interpersonal Violence* 18:1452–71.

Noonan, M. C., M. E. Corcoran, and P. M. Courant. 2005. "Pay differences among the highly trained." *Social Forces* 84:831–51.

Noonberg, A., G. Goldstein, and H. A. Page. 1985. "Premature aging in male alcoholics: 'Accelerated aging' or 'increased vulnerability'?" *Alcoholism: Clinical and Experimental Research* 9 (July–August):334–38.

Nord, M., M. Andrews, and S. Carlson. 2005. "Household food security in the United States, 2004." *Economic Research Report No. (ERR11),* October.

Norton-Hawk, M. A. 2002. "Lifecourse of prostitution." *Women, Girls, and Criminal Justice* 3:1–9.

———. 2004. "Comparison of pimp- and non-pimp-controlled women." *Violence against Women* 10:189–94.

Nossiter, A. 2006. "New Orleans population is reduced nearly 60%." *The New York Times,* October 7.

Oakes, J. 2005. *Keeping Track: How Schools Structure Inequality.* 2nd ed. New Haven, CT: Yale University Press.

Obach, B. K. 2002. "Labor-environmental relations." *Social Science Quarterly* 83:82–100.

Obot, I. S., F. A. Wagner, and J. C. Anthony. 2001. "Early onset and recent drug use among children of parents with alcohol problems." *Drug and Alcohol Dependence* 65:1–8.

O'Brien, R. M., J. Stockard, and L. Isaacson. 1999. "The enduring effects of cohort characteristics on age-specific homicide rates, 1960–1995." *American Journal of Sociology* 104 (January):1061–95.

Occupational Safety and Health Administration. 1996. *Information about OSHA.* OSHA Web site.

———. 2002. "Occupational injury and illness incidence rates per 100 full-time workers." OSHA Web site.

O'Connor, R. E., R. J. Bord, B. Yarnal, and N. Wiefek. 2002. "Who wants to reduce greenhouse gas emissions?" *Social Science Quarterly* 83:1–17.

Office of Juvenile Justice and Delinquency Prevention. 2006. "Teen dating violence awareness and prevention week." *OJJDP's E-Mail Information Resource.*

Office of National Drug Control Policy. 2003a. *Cocaine.* Washington, DC: Government Printing Office.

———. 2003b. *What Americans Need to Know about Marijuana.* Washington, DC: Government Printing Office.

———. 2004. *The Economic Costs of Drug Abuse in the United States.* Washington, DC: Government Printing Office.

——— 2006. *Girls and Drugs.* Washington, DC: Government Printing Office.

Ogden, C. L., et al. 2006. "Prevalence of overweight and obesity in the United States, 1999–2004." *Journal of the American Medical Association* 295:1549–55.

Ohshige, K., et al. 2000. "Cross-sectional study on risk factors of HIV among female commercial sex workers in Cambodia." *Epidemiology of Infections* 124 (February):143–52.

Okagaki, L., and P. A. Frensch. 1998. "Parenting and children's school achievement." *American Educational Research Journal* 35 (Spring): 123–44.

O'Keefe, M. 1994. "Linking marital violence, mother-child/father-child aggression, and child behavior problems." *Journal of Family Violence* 9 (March):63–78.

Okie, S. 2005. "Fat chance." *Natural History,* February, pp. 34–38.

Olds, D. L., C. R. Henderson, Jr., and R. Tatelbaum. 1994. "Prevention of intellectual impairment in children of

women who smoke during pregnancy." *Pediatrics* 93 (February):228–33.

Oliver, C. 1995. "Defending pornography: Free speech, sex, and the fight for women's rights." *Reason,* April, pp. 3–6.

Olson, M. R., and J. A. Haynes. 1993. "Successful single parents." *Families in Society* 74 (April):259–67.

Ong, P. M. 1991. "Race and post-displacement earnings among high-tech workers." *Industrial Relations* 30 (Fall):456–68.

Opp, R. D. 2002. "Enhancing program completion rates among two-year college students of color." *Community College Journal of Research and Practice* 26:147–63.

Orfield, G., and C. Lee. 2005. *Why Segregation Matters: Poverty and Educational Inequality.* Cambridge: The Civil Rights Project at Harvard University.

Orsagh, T., and J. Chen. 1988. "The effect of time served on recidivism: An interdisciplinary theory." *Journal of Quantitative Criminology* 4 (June):155–71.

Osberg, L., and T. Smeeding. 2006. "'Fair' inequality? Attitudes toward pay differentials." *American Sociological Review* 71:450–73.

Ostrow, R. J. 1991. "Asian organized crime problem growing, study says." *Los Angeles Times,* October 3.

Ouweneel, P. 2002. "Social security and well-being of the unemployed in 42 nations." *Journal of Happiness Studies* 3:167–92.

Overpeck, J. T., et al. 2006. "Paleoclimatic evidence for future ice-sheet instability and rapid sea-level rise." *Science* 311:1747–50.

Overpeck, M. D., R. A. Brenner, A. C. Trumble, L. B. Trifiletti, and H. W. Berendes. 1998. "Risk factors for infant homicide in the United States." *New England Journal of Medicine* 339 (October 22):1211–12.

Oxman, T. E., D. H. Freeman, Jr., and E. D. Manheimer. 1995. "Lack of social participation or religious strength and comfort as risk factors for death after cardiac surgery in the elderly." *Psychosomatic Medicine* 57 (January–February):5–15.

Padilla, M. T. 1999. "Race violence leads to rise in anti-racism groups." *Salt Lake Tribune,* August 22.

Pager, D. 2003. "The mark of a criminal record." *American Journal of Sociology* 108:937–75.

Paige, J. M. 1971. "Political orientation and riot participation." *American Sociological Review* 36 (October): 810–20.

Paige, S. 1998. "Babylon rides high-tech wave." *Insight on the News,* September 28.

Palmer, C. 1989. "Is rape a cultural universal? A reexamination of the ethnographic data." *Ethnology* 28 (January):1–16.

Palzkill, B., and A. Fisher. 1990. "Between gymshoes and high-heels: The development of a lesbian identity and existence in top class sport." *International Review for the Sociology of Sport* 25 (3):221–34.

Pape, R. 2005. *Dying to Win: The Strategic Logic of Suicide Terrorism*. New York: Random House.

Parent, M., M. Rousseau, P. Boffetta, A. Cohen, and J. Siemiatycki. 2007. "Exposure to diesel and gasoline engine emissions and the risk of lung cancer." *American Journal of Epidemiology* 165:53–62.

Parents Television Council. 2006. "Wolves in sheep's clothing." PTC Web site.

Park, C. L., S. Armeli, and H. Tennen. 2004. "The daily stress and coping process and alcohol use among college students." *Journal of Studies on Alcohol* 65:126–35.

Parker, F. 1975. "What's right with American education." In *Myth and Reality,* 2d ed., ed. G. Smith and C. R. Kniker, pp. 29–36. Boston: Allyn and Bacon.

Parker, R. E. 1994. *Flesh Peddlers and Warm Bodies: The Temporary Help Industry and Its Workers.* New Brunswick, NJ: Rutgers University Press.

Parker, S., and H. Parker. 1991. "Female victims of child sexual abuse: Adult adjustment." *Journal of Family Violence* 6 (June):183–97.

Parks, M. 1991. "Cherynobyl." *Los Angeles Times,* April 23.

Paschall, M. J., M. Bersamin, and R. L. Flewelling. 2005. "Racial/ethnic differences in the association between college attendance and heavy alcohol use." *Journal of Studies on Alcohol* 66:266–74.

Pasley, K., J. Kerpelman, and D. E. Guilbert. 2001. "Gendered conflict, identity disruption, and marital instability." *Journal of Social and Personal Relationships* 18:5–27.

Pastor, M., J. L. Sadd, and R. Morello-Frosch. 2004. "Waiting to inhale: The demographics of toxic air release facilities in 21st-century California." *Social Science Quarterly* 85:420–40.

Paternoster, R. 1989. "Absolute and restrictive deterrence in a panel of youth: Explaining the onset, persistence/desistance, and frequency of delinquent offending." *Social Problems* 36 (June):289–309.

Paternoster, R., and P. Mazerolle. 1994. "General strain theory and delinquency: A replication and extension." *Journal of Research in Crime and Delinquency* 31 (August):235–63.

Patterson, C. J. 2000. "Family relationships of lesbians and gay men." *Journal of Marriage and the Family* 62:1052–69.

Patterson, J., and P. Kim. 1991. *The Day America Told the Truth.* New York: Prentice-Hall.

Paul, P. 2004. "The porn factor." *Time,* January 19.

Pavalko, E. K., K. N. Mossakowski, and V. J. Hamilton. 2003. "Does perceived discrimination affect health? Longitudinal relationships between work discrimination and women's physical and emotional health." *Journal of Health and Social Behavior* 44:18–33.

Pawel, D. J., and J. S. Puskin. 2004. "The U.S. Environmental Protection Agency's assessment of risks from indoor radon." *Health Physics* 87:68–74.

Pearce, L. D., and D. L. Haynie. 2004. "Intergenerational religious dynamics and adolescent delinquency." *Social Forces* 82:1553–72.

Peaslee, A. L. 1969. "Education's role in development." *Economic Development and Cultural Change* 17:293–318.

Peek, C. W., G. D. Lowe, and L. S. Williams. 1991. "Gender and God's word: Another look at religious fundamentalism and sexism." *Social Forces* 68 (June):1205–21.

Peleg-Oren, N., and M. Sherer. 2001. "Cancer patients and their spouses." *Journal of Health Psychology* 6:329–38.

Peleman, R. A. 2004. "New and re-emerging infectious diseases." *Current Opinion in Anaesthesiology* 17:265–70.

Penna, M. L., and M. P. Duchiade. 1991. "Air pollution and infant mortality from pneumonia in the Rio de Janeiro metropolitan area." *International Journal of Health Services* 21 (2):199–227.

Peplau, L. A. 1981. "What homosexuals want." *Psychology Today* (March):28–37.

Pereira, L. A., et al. 1998. "Association between air pollution and intrauterine mortality in Sao Paulo, Brazil." *Environmental Health Perspectives* 106 (June):325.

Peretti, P. O., and A. di Vitorrio. 1993. "Effect of loss of father through divorce on personality of the preschool child." *Social Behavior and Personality* 21:33–38.

Perina, K. 2002. "Covenant marriage: A new marital contract." *Psychology Today,* March–April, p. 18.

Perkins, C. 2003. "Weapon use and violent crime." *Bureau of Justice Statistics Special Report.* Washington, DC: Government Printing Office.

Perkins, H. W., M. P. Haines, and R. Rice. 2005. "Misperceiving the college drinking norm and related problems." *Journal of Studies on Alcohol* 66:470–78.

Perl, R. F. 2006. "International terrorism: Threat, policy, and response." *CRS Report for Congress,* August 16.

Perlini, A. H., and T. L. Boychuk. 2006. "Social influence, desirability and relationship investment." *Social Behavior and Personality* 34:593–602.

Perry, S. W. 2004. *American Indians and Crime.* Washington, DC: Bureau of Justice Statistics.

Perry-Jenkins, M., R. L. Repetti, and A. C. Crouter. 2000. "Work and family in the 1990s." *Journal of Marriage and the Family* 62:981–98.

Persson, K., J. Bengtsson, A. Kjeilberg, and S. Benton. 2001. "Low frequency noise 'pollution' interferes with performance." *Noise and Health* 4:33–49.

Pescosolido, B. A., E. Grauerholz, and M. A. Milkie. 1997. "Culture and conflict: The portrayal of blacks in U.S. children's picture books through the mid-and late-twentieth century." *American Sociological Review* 62 (June):443–64.

Petersen, R. C. 1981. "Decriminalization of marijuana— A brief overview of research-relevant policy issues." *Contemporary Drug Problems* 10 (Fall):265–75.

Peterson, J. L., and N. Zill. 1986. "Marital disruption, parent-child relationships, and behavior problems in children." *Journal of Marriage and the Family* 48 (May):295–307.

Petoskey, E. L., K. R. Van Stelle, and J. A. De Jong. 1998. "Family variables in substance-misusing male adolescents." *American Journal of Drug and Alcohol Abuse* 24 (1):61–84.

Petrill, S. A., A. Pike, T. Price, and R. Plomin. 2004. "Chaos in the home and socioeconomic status are associated with cognitive development in early childhood." *Intelligence* 32:445–60.

Petry, N. M., and B. Martin. 2002. "Low-cost contingency management for treating cocaine- and opioid-abusing methadone patients." *Journal of Consulting and Clinical Psychology* 70:398–405.

Petterson, S. M., and A. B. Albers. 2001. "Effects of poverty and maternal depression on early child development." *Child Development* 72:1794–813.

Pettit, B., and B. Western. 2004. "Mass imprisonment and the life course: Race and class inequality in U.S. incarceration." *American Sociological Review* 69:151–69.

Peugh, J., and S. Belenko. 2001. "Alcohol, drugs, and sexual function." *Journal of Psychoactive Drugs* 33:223–32.

Pew Research Center. 2006a. "Are we happy yet?" Pew Research Center Web site.

———. 2006b. "Little consensus on global warming." Pew Research Center Web site.

Pfaff, D., ed. 2002. *Hormones, Brain and Behavior.* San Diego, CA: Academic.

Pfefferbaum, B., et al. 2001. "Traumatic grief in a convenience sample of victims seeking support services after a terrorist incident." *Annals of Clinical Psychiatry* 13:19–24.

———. 2002. "Exposure and peritraumatic response as predictors of posttraumatic stress in children following the 1995 Oklahoma City bombing." *Journal of Urban Health* 79:354–63.

Pfiffner, L. J., K. McBurnett, and P. J. Rathouz. 2001. "Father absence and familial antisocial characteristics." *Journal of Abnormal Child Psychology* 29:357–67.

Phelan, J. C., E. J. Bromet, and B. G. Link. 1998. "Psychiatric illness and family stigma." *Schizophrenia Bulletin* 24 (1):115–26.

Phillips, D. P., T. E. Ruth, and L. M. Wagner. 1993. "Psychology and survival." *Lancet* 342 (November 6): 1142–45.

Phillips, G., and R. Over. 1992. "Adult sexual orientation in relation to memories of childhood gender conforming and gender nonconforming behaviors." *Archives of Sexual Behavior* 21 (December):543–58.

Phillips, J. A. 2006. "The relationship between age structure and homicide rates in the United States, 1970 to 1999." *Journal of Research in Crime and Delinquency* 43:230–60.

Physicians for Human Rights. 2002. "War-related sexual violence in Sierra Leone." Physicians for Human Rights Web site.

Pierce, J. 2002. "Poll: 8 of 10 want Internet obscenity laws enforced." *American Center for Law and Justice Newsletter,* March 18.

Pierce, J. P., et al. 1998. "Tobacco industry promotion of cigarettes and adolescent smoking." *Journal of the American Medical Association* 279 (February 18):511–15.

Pilippo, S., L. Mustaniemi, H. Lenko, R. Aine, and J. Maenpaa. 1999. "Surgery for ovarian masses during childhood and adolescence." *Journal of Pediatric and Adolescent Gynecology* 12 (November):223–27.

Pine, J. C., B. D. Marx, and A. Lakshmanan. 2002. "An examination of accidental-release scenarios from chemical-processing sites: The relation of race to distance." *Social Science Quarterly* 83:317–31.

Pinkerton, J. P. 2003. "A grand compromise." *The Atlantic Monthly,* January/February, pp. 115–16.

Pinkleton, B. E., Y. Fujioka, and E. W. Austin. 2000. "The role of interpretation processes and parental discussion in the media's effects on adolescents' use of alcohol." *Pediatrics* 105:343–49.

Piotrkowski, C. S. 1998. "Gender harassment, job satisfaction, and distress among employed white and minority women." *Journal of Occupational Health Psychology* 3 (January):33–43.

Piquero, N. L., S. G. Tibbetts, and M. B. Blankenship. 2006. "Examining the role of differential association and techniques of neutralization in explaining corporate crime." *Deviant Behavior* 26:159–88.

Pitcavage, M. 2001. "Camouflage and conspiracy: The militia movement." *American Behavioral Scientist* 44:957–81.

Pittman, L. D., and P. L. Chase-Lansdale. 2001. "African American adolescent girls in impoverished communities." *Journal of Research on Adolescence* 11:199–224.

Plane, D. L., and J. Gershtenson. 2004. "Candidates' ideological locations, abstention, and turnout in U.S. midterm Senate elections." *Political Behavior* 26:69–93.

Plant, E. A., and N. Sachs-Ericsson. 2004. "Racial and ethnic differences in depression." *Journal of Consulting and Clinical Psychology* 72:41–52.

Platt, A. 1969. *The Child Savers: The Invention of Delinquency.* Chicago: University of Chicago Press.

Pochagina, O. 2006. "The sex business as a social phenomenon in contemporary China." *Far Eastern Affairs* 34:118–34.

Pollack, H. A. 2001. "Sudden infant death syndrome, maternal smoking during pregnancy, and the cost-effectiveness of smoking cessation intervention." *American Journal of Public Health* 91:432–36.

Pollard, C. A., H. J. Pollard, and K. J. Corn. 1989. "Panic onset and major events in the lives of agoraphobics: A test of contiguity." *Journal of Abnormal Psychology* 98 (August):318–21.

Polling Report, Inc. 2007. Polls. Polling Report Web site.

Pollock, C. 1987. "Realizing recycling's potential." In *State of the World 1987,* ed. Lester R. Brown, pp. 101–21. New York: W. W. Norton.

Pollock, J. M., J. L. Mullings, and B. M. Crouch. 2006. "Violent women." *Journal of Interpersonal Violence* 21:485–502.

Pool, R. 1993. "Evidence for homosexuality gene." *Science* 261 (July 16):291–92.

Popenoe, D., and B. D. Whitehead. 1999. *Should We Live Together?* Rutgers, NJ: National Marriage Project.

Portegies, P., and N. R. Rosenberg. 1998. "AIDS dementia complex." *CNS Drugs* 9 (January):31–40.

Posner, R. A. 2001. "Security versus civil liberties." *Atlantic Monthly,* December, pp. 46–47.

Postel, S. 1987. "Stabilizing chemical cycles." In *State of the World 1987,* ed. L. R. Brown, pp. 157–76. New York: W. W. Norton.

Potter, L. B. 2001. "Influence of homicide on racial disparity in life expectancy—United States, 1998." *Journal of the American Medical Association* 286:1212.

Potterat, J. J., et al. 2004. "Mortality in a long-term open cohort of prostitute women." *American Journal of Epidemiology* 159:778–85.

Potterat, J. J., D. E. Woodhouse, J. B. Muth, and S. Q. Muth. 1990. "Estimating the prevalence and career longevity of prostitute women." *Journal of Sex Research* 27 (May):233–43.

Potterfield, J. E., and M. B. Pace. 1992. "Working class children and middle class schools: Teacher training to resolve this volatile combination." *Education* 113 (Fall):149–53.

Powell, W. E. 1994. "The relationship between feelings of alienation and burnout in social work." *Families in Society* 75 (April):229–35.

Pratt, T. C., and J. Maahs. 1999. "Are private prisons more cost-effective than public prisons?" *Crime and Delinquency* 45 (July):358–71.

Presser, H. B. 2004. "The economy that never sleeps." *Contexts* 3:42–49.

Prigerson, H. G., P. K. Maciejewski, and R. A. Rosenheck. 2002. "Population attributable fractions of psychiatric disorders and behavioral outcomes associated with combat exposure among US men." *American Journal of Public Health* 92:59–63.

Prince, D. A. 1986. "A psychological profile of prostitutes in California and Nevada." Unpublished Ph.D. dissertation, United States International University, San Diego, CA.

Princiotta, D., S. Bielick, and C. Chapman. 2005. "1.1 million homeschooled students in the United States in 2003." *Education Statistics Quarterly* 6:1–2.

Pringle, P. 1997. "Remembering while building for the future." *San Diego Union-Tribune,* April 27.

Prior, M. 2006. "The incumbent in the living room." *Journal of Politics* 68:657–63.

Proctor, B. D., and J. Dalaker. 2003. *Poverty in the United States: 2002.* Washington, DC: Government Printing Office.

Prokhorov, A. V., et al. 2006. "Youth tobacco use." *Pediatrics* 118:890–903.

Proulx, R. J., and L. Jimerson. 1998. "Business as usual? Not in Vermont." *School Business Affairs* 64 (April):9–14.

Quadagno, D., D. F. Harrison, K. G. Wambach, P. Levine, A. Imershein, J. Byers, and K. Maddox. 1991. "Woman at risk for human immunodeficiency virus." *Journal of Psychology and Human Sexuality* 4 (3):97–110.

Quadagno, J. 2005. *One Nation Uninsured: Why the U.S. Has No National Health Insurance.* New York: Oxford University Press.

Quillian, L. 1995. "Population, perceived threat, and prejudice in Europe." *American Sociological Review* 60 (August):586–611.

Radkowsky, M., and L. J. Siegel. 1997. "The gay adolescent: Stressors, adaptations, and psychosocial interventions." *Clinical Psychology Review* 17 (2):191–216.

Rahn, W. M., and T. J. Rudolph. 2005. "A tale of political trust in American cities." *Public Opinion Quarterly* 69:530–60.

Raine, A., P. Brennan, and S. A. Mednick. 1994. "Birth complications combined with early maternal rejection at age 1 year predispose to violent crime at age 18 years." *Archives of General Psychiatry* 51 (December):984–88.

Rainwater, L. 1967. "Crisis of the city: Poverty and deprivation." *Washington University Magazine* (Spring):17–21.

Raloff, J. 1999. "Formaldehyde: Some surprises at home." *Science News,* January 9, p. 22.

Rank, M. R. 1994. *Living on the Edge: The Realities of Welfare in America.* New York: Columbia University Press.

———. 2001. "The effect of poverty on America's families." *Journal of Family Issues* 22:881–903.

———. 2003. "As American as apple pie: Poverty and welfare." *Contexts* 2:41–49.

Rank, M. R., H. Yoon, and T. A. Hirschl. 2003. "American poverty as a structural failing." *Journal of Sociology and Social Welfare* 30:3–29.

Rankin, J. H., and R. M. Kern. 1994. "Parental attachments and delinquency." *Criminology* 32 (November):495–515.

Ranson, G. 2001. "Men at work: Change—or no change?—in the era of the 'new father.' " *Men and Masculinities* 4:3–26.

Rantala, R. R. 2004. "Cybercrime against businesses." *Bureau of Justice Statistics Technical Report.* Washington, DC: Government Printing Office.

Raphael, J., and D. L. Shapiro. 2004. "Violence in indoor and outdoor prostitution venues." *Violence against Women* 10:126–39.

Ratnesar, R. 2002. "Revenge: Arafat—and why the rage keeps burning." *Time,* April 8.

Rau, R., and A. Triemer. 2004. "Overtime in relation to blood pressure and mood during work, leisure, and night time." *Social Indicators Research* 67:51–73.

Ray, B. D. 1999. *Home Schooling on the Threshold.* Salem, OR: National Home Education Research Institute.

Ray, J. 1990. "Interactional patterns and marital satisfaction among dual-career couples." *Journal of Independent Social Work* 4:61–73.

Ray, K. C., J. L. Jackson, and R. M. Townsley. 1991. "Family environments of victims of intrafamilial and extrafamilial child sexual abuse." *Journal of Family Violence* 6 (December):365–73.

Rearden, J. J., and B. S. Markwell. 1989. "Self concept and drinking problems of college students raised in alcohol-abused homes." *Addictive Behaviors* 14 (2):225–27.

Reckard, E. S. 1994. "Study shows S&L fraud artists get less prison time than burglars do." *San Diego Union-Tribune,* November 18.

Rehnquist, W. H. 1998. *All the Laws but One: Civil Liberties in Wartime.* New York: Alfred A. Knopf.

Reichman, L., and J. H. Tanne. 2001. *Timebomb: The Global Epidemic of Multi-Drug Resistant Tuberculosis.* New York: McGraw-Hill.

Reid, J., P. Macchetto, and S. Foster. 1999. *No Safe Haven: Children of Substance-Abusing Parents.* Washington, DC: National Center on Addiction and Substance Abuse.

Reilly, D. M. 1984. "Family therapy with adolescent drug abusers and their families: Defying gravity and achieving escape velocity." *Journal of Drug Issues* 14 (Spring):381–91.

Reine, I., M. Novo, and A. Hammarstrom. 2004. "Does the association between ill health and unemployment differ between young people and adults?" *Public Health* 118:337–45.

Reinhardt, J. M., P. Meadows, and J. M. Gillette. 1952. *Social Problems and Social Policy.* New York: American Book.

Reinherz, H. A., R. M. Giaconia, A. M. Hauf, M. S. Wasserman, and A. D. Paradis. 2000. "General and specific childhood risk factors for depression and drug disorders by early adulthood." *Journal of the American Academy of Child Adolescent Psychiatry* 39 (February):223–31.

Reitzel-Jaffe, D., and D. A. Wolfe. 2001. "Predictors of relationship abuse among young men." *Journal of Interpersonal Violence* 16:99–115.

Remery, C., A. van Doorne-Huiskes, and J. Schippers. 2003. "Family-friendly policies in the Netherlands." *Personnel Review* 32:456–73.

Renner, M. 1991. "Military victory, ecological defeat." *World Watch* July–August):27–34.

———. 1993a. *Critical Juncture: The Future of Peacekeeping.* Washington, DC: Worldwatch Institute.

———. 1993b. "Preparing for peace." In *State of the World 1993,* ed. L. Brown, pp. 139–57. New York: W. W. Norton.

———. 1997. *Small Arms, Big Impact.* Washington, DC: Worldwatch Institute.

———. 1999. "Ending violent conflict." In *State of the World 1999,* ed. Lester R. Brown et al., pp. 151–68. New York: W. W. Norton.

———. 2002. "Breaking the link between resources and repression." In *State of the World 2002,* ed. Linda Starke, pp. 149–73. New York: W. W. Norton.

———. 2006a. "Conflict and peace trends." Pp. 81–87 in L. Starke, ed., *Vital Signs: 2006–2007.* New York: W. W. Norton.

———. 2006b. "Vehicle production continues to expand." Pp. 64–65 in L. Starke, ed., *Vital Signs: 2006–2007.* New York: W. W. Norton.

Rennison, C. M. 2003. "Intimate partner violence, 1993–2001." *Bureau of Justice Statistics Crime Data Brief.* Washington, DC: Government Printing Office.

Reskin, B. 1998. *The Realities of Affirmative Action in Employment.* Washington, DC: American Sociological Association.

Resnick, M. D., et al. 1997. "Protecting adolescents from harm." *Journal of the American Medical Association* 278 (September 10):823–32.

Revelle, R. 1971. "Pollution and cities." In *The Survival Equation: Man, Resources, and His Environment,* ed. R. Revelle, A. Khosla, and M. Vinovskis, pp. 382–414. Boston: Houghton Mifflin.

Revicki, D. A., and H. J. May. 1989. "Organizational characteristics, occupational stress, and mental health in nurses." *Behavioral Medicine* 15 (Spring):30–36.

Revkin, A. C. 1989. "Crack in the cradle." *Discover* (September):62–69.

———. 2001. "EPA ties tiniest soot particles to early deaths." *The New York Times,* April 21.

Reynal-Querol, M. 2002. "Ethnicity, political systems, and civil wars." *Journal of Conflict Resolution* 46:29–54.

Reynolds, J. 2004. "When too much is not enough: Actual and preferred work hours in the United States and Abroad." *Sociological Forum* 19:89–120.

Reynolds, K., et al. 2003. "Alcohol consumption and risk of stroke." *Journal of the American Medical Association* 289:579–88.

Ricchiardi, S. 1998. "Double vision." *American Journalism Review* 20 (3):30–36.

Rice, R. W., M. R. Frone, and D. B. McFarlin. 1992. "Work-nonwork conflict and the perceived quality of life." *Journal of Organizational Behavior* 13 (March):155–68.

Richards, M., R. Hardy, and M. Wadsworth. 1997. "The effects of divorce and separation on mental health in a national UK birth cohort." *Psychological Medicine* 27:1121–28.

Richards, M., M. J. Jarvis, N. Thompson, and M. E. J. Wadsworth. 2003. "Cigarette smoking and cognitive decline in midlife." *American Journal of Public Health* 93:994–98.

Richardson, J. W. 2002. "Poor, powerless and poisoned." *Journal of Children and Poverty* 8: 141–57.

Rieker, P. P., and E. (Hilberman) Carmen. 1986. "The victim-to-patient process: The disconfirmation and transformation of abuse." *American Journal of Orthopsychiatry* 56 (July):360–70.

Rinfret-Raynor, M., A. Riou, S. Cantin, C. Drouin, and M. Dube. 2004. "A survey on violence against female partners in Quebec, Canada." *Violence against Women* 10:709–28.

Ripley, A., and S. Steptoe. 2005. "Inside the revolt over Bush's school rules." *Time,* May 9, pp. 30–33.

Ritzer, G. 1995. *Expressing America: A Critique of the Global Credit Card Society.* Thousand Oaks, CA: Pine Forge Press.

Rivara, F. P., et al. 1997. "Alcohol and illicit drug abuse and the risk of violent death in the home." *Journal of the American Medical Association* 278 (August 20):569–75.

Roan, S. 1990. "Air sickness." *Los Angeles Times,* April 3.

Roane, K. R. 1998. "Prostitutes on wane in New York streets but take to Internet." *The New York Times,* February 23.

Roark, A. C. 1988. "Day care." *Los Angeles Times,* October 31.

Robelen, E. W. 2006. "NAEP reanalysis finds lag in charter school scores." *Education Week,* Education Week Web site.

Roberts, D. F., L. Henriksen, and P. G. Christenson. 1999. *Substance Use in Popular Movies and Music.* Washington, DC: Government Printing Office.

Roberts, J. T. 1993. "Psychosocial effects of workplace hazardous exposures: Theoretical synthesis and preliminary findings." *Social Problems* 40(February):74–89.

Robins, L. N., and D. A. Regier. 1991. *Psychiatric Disorders in America.* New York: Free Press.

Robinson, J., and G. Godbey. 1997. *Time for Life: The Surprising Way Americans Use Their Time.* University Park: Pennsylvania State University Press.

Robinson, T. N., M. L. Wilde, L. C. Navracruz, K. F. Haydel, and A. Varady. 2001. "Effects of reducing children's television and video game use on aggressive behavior." *Archives of Pediatric and Adolescent Medicine* 155:17–23.

Robison, K. K., E. M. Crenshaw, and J. C. Jenkins. 2006. "Ideologies of violence: The social origins of Islamist and leftist transnational terrorism." *Social Forces* 84:2009–26.

Rodgers, H. R., Jr., and C. S. Bullock. 1972. *Law and Social Change.* New York: McGraw-Hill.

Rodgers, J. E. 1994. "Addiction—A whole new view." *Psychology Today,* September–October, pp. 32–39.

Rodriguez, E. 2001. "Keeping the unemployed healthy." *American Journal of Public Health* 91: 1403–11.

Rogers-Dillon, R. 1995. "The dynamics of welfare stigma." *Qualitative Sociology* 18 (4):439–56.

Rogge, R. D., and T. N. Bradbury. 1999. "Till violence does us part." *Journal of Consulting and Clinical Psychology* 67 (June):340–51.

Rolland, J. S. 1987. "Chronic illness and the life cycle: A conceptual framework." *Family Process* 26 (2):203–21.

Romero-Daza, N., M. Weeks, and M. Singer. 2003. " 'Nobody gives a damn if I live or die': Violence, drugs, and street-level prostitution in inner-city Hartford, Connecticut." *Medical Anthropology* 22:233–59.

Romo, H. D. 1999. "Tracking programs derail minority and disadvantaged students' success." *Community College Journal* 69 (January):12–17.

Roodman, D. M. 1999. "Building a sustainable society." In *State of the World 1999,* ed. Lester R. Brown et al., pp. 169–88. New York: W. W. Norton.

Roosevelt, M. 2004. "The tragedy of Tar Creek." *Time,* April 26, pp. 42–47.

Rorabaugh, W. J. 1979. *The Alcoholic Republic: An American Tradition.* New York: Oxford University Press.

Roscigno, V. J. 1998. "Race and the reproduction of educational disadvantage." *Social Forces* 76 (March):1033–60.

Roscigno, V. J., D. Tomaskovic-Devey, and M. Crowley. 2006. "Education and the inequalities of place." *Social Forces* 84:2121–45.

Rose, K. M., et al. 2004. "Women's employment status and mortality." *Journal of Women's Health* 13:1108–18.

Rosen, J. 2000. "Talk is cheap—Campaign finance reform meets the Internet." *New Republic,* February 14, pp. 20–24.

Rosen, K. H., and S. M. Stith. 1995. "Women terminating abusive dating relationships." *Journal of Social and Personal Relationships* 12 (February):155–60.

Rosenbaum, E., and D. B. Kandel. 1990. "Early onset of adolescent sexual behavior and drug involvement." *Journal of Marriage and the Family* 52 (August):783–98.

Rosenbaum, J. E., S. J. Popkin, J. E. Kaufman, and J. Rusin. 1991. "Social integration of low-income black adults in middle-class white suburbs." *Social Problems* 38 (November):448–61.

Rosenberg, D. 2002. "Stem cells: Slow progress." *Newsweek,* August 12.

Rosenblum, J. D. 1995. *Copper Crucible: How the Arizona Miners' Strike of 1983 Recast Labor-Management Relations in America.* Ithaca, NY: ILR Press.

Rosenbluth, S. C., J. M. Steil, and J. H. Whitcomb. 1998. "Marital equality: What does it mean?" *Journal of Family Issues* 19 (May):227–44.

Rosenfeld, R. 2002. "Crime decline in context." *Contexts* 1:25–34.

Rosenfield, S. 1997. "Labeling mental illness: The effects of received services and perceived stigma on life satisfaction." *American Sociological Review* 62 (August):660–72.

Rosenman, R. H. 1990. "Type A behavior pattern: A personal overview." *Journal of Social Behavior and Personality* 5 (1):1–24.

Rosenthal, J. 2006. "Precisely false vs. approximately right." *The New York Times,* August 27.

Rosenthal, N. H. 1989. "More than wages at issue in job quality debate." *Monthly Labor Review* 112 (December):4–8.

Rosenthal, R., and L. Jacobson. 1968. "Self-fulfilling prophecies in the classroom: Teachers' expectations as unintended determinants of pupils' intellectual competence." In *Social Class, Race, and Psychological Development,* ed. M. Deutsch, I. Katz, and A. R. Jensen, pp. 219–53. New York: Holt, Rinehart, and Winston.

Roskes, E., R. Feldman, S. Arrington, and M. Leisher. 1999. "A model program for the treatment of mentally ill offenders in the community." *Community Mental Health Journal* 35: 461–72.

Rosoff, S. M., H. N. Pontell, and R. H. Tillman. 2002. *Profit without Honor: White-Collar Crime and the Looting of America.* 2nd ed. New York: Prentice-Hall.

Ross, C., and J. Mirowsky. 1992. "Households, employment, and the sense of control." *Social Psychology Quarterly* 55 (3):217–35.

Ross, C. E., and J. Mirowsky. 1988. "Child care and emotional adjustment to wives' employment." *Journal of Health and Social Behavior* 29 (June):127–38.

Ross, C. E., J. Mirowsky, and J. Huber. 1983. "Dividing work, sharing work, and in-between: Marriage patterns and depression." *American Sociological Review* 48 (December):809–23.

Ross, M. W. 2005. "Typing, doing, and being: Sexuality and the internet." *Journal of Sex Research* 42:342–52.

Ross, S. L., and M. A. Turner. 2005. "Housing discrimination in metropolitan America." *Social Problems* 52:152–80.

Roston, E., and J. F. O. McAllister. 2004. "Humiliation in an Iraqi jail." *Time,* May 10, p. 20.

Roth, J. A., and C. S. Koper. 1999. *Impacts of the 1994 Assault Weapons Ban: 1994–96.* Washington, DC: National Institute of Justice.

Roth, L. M. 2003. "Selling women short: Gender differences in compensation on Wall Street." *Social Forces* 82:783–802.

Rovner, S. 1990. "Age-bashing: Past and present." *Los Angeles Times,* November 22.

Roxburgh, A., L. Degenhardt, and J. Copeland. 2006. "Post-traumatic stress disorder among female street-based sex workers in the greater Sydney area, Australia." *BMC Psychiatry* 24:6–24.

Roy, A. 2003. "Distal risk factors for suicidal behavior in alcoholics." *Journal of Affective Disorders* 77:267–71.

Ruback, R. B., and D. L. Ivie. 1988. "Prior relationship, resistance, and injury in rapes: An analysis of crisis center records." *Violence and Victims* 3 (Summer):99–111.

Rudalevige, A. 2005. "Reform or séance? Seeking the 'spirit' of no child left behind." *Teachers College Record,* TCR Web site.

Rudner, L. M. 1999. "Scholastic achievement and demographic characteristics of home school students in 1998." *Education Policy Analysis Archives* 7 (8):1–39.

Ruggles, P. 1990. *Drawing the Line: Alternative Poverty Measures and Their Implications for Public Policy.* Washington, DC: Urban Institute Press.

Ruo, B., et al. 2003. "Depressive symptoms and health-related quality of life." *Journal of the American Medical Association* 290:215–21.

Russell, D. E. H. 1982. *Rape in Marriage.* New York: Macmillan.

———. 1986. *The Secret Trauma: Incest in the Lives of Girls and Women.* New York: Basic Books.

———. 1998. *Dangerous Relationships: Pornography, Misogyny, and Rape.* Newbury Park, CA: Sage.

Ryan, W. 1971. *Blaming the Victim.* New York: Pantheon Books.

Saad, L., and F. Newport. 2001. "Blacks and whites differ about treatment of blacks in America today." *Gallup Poll Monthly,* no. 430, pp. 58–63.

Sabin, M., R. L. Cardozo, L. Nackerud, R. Kaiser, and L. Varese. 2003. "Factors associated with poor mental health among Guatemalan refugees living in Mexico 20 years after civil conflict." *Journal of the American Medical Association* 290:635.

Sacco, V. F. 2003. "Black hand outrage: A constructionist analysis of an urban crime wave." *Deviant Behavior* 24:53–77.

Sacks, J. J., T. R. Simon, A. E. Crosby, G. Shelley, and M. P. Thompson. 2001. "Attitudinal acceptance of intimate partner violence among U.S. adults." *Violence and Victims* 16:115–26.

Sadker, M., and D. Sadker. 1994. *Failing at Fairness: How America's Schools Cheat Girls.* New York: Charles Scribner's Sons.

Saenz, R., and J. K. Thomas. 1991. "Minority poverty in nonmetropolitan Texas." *Rural Sociology* 56 (Summer):204–23.

Salam, M. T., Y. F. Li, B. Langholz, and F. D. Gilliland. 2004. "Early-life environmental risk factors for asthma." *Environmental Health Perspectives* 112:760–65.

Salvendy, J. T. 1989. "Brief group psychotherapy at retirement." *Group* 13 (Spring):43–57.

Samaan, R. A. 2000. "The influences of race, ethnicity, and poverty on the mental health of children." *Journal of Health Care for the Poor and Underserved* 11 (February):100–10.

Samet, J. M., et al. 2000. "Fine particulate air pollution and mortality in 20 U.S. cities, 1987–1994." *New England Journal of Medicine* 343:1742–49.

Sampat, P. 2000. *Deep Trouble: The Hidden Threat of Groundwater Pollution.* Washington, DC: Worldwatch Institute.

Sampson, R. J., S. W. Raudenbush, and F. Earls. 1997. "Neighborhoods and violent crime: A multilevel study." *Science* 277 (August 15):918–24.

Sanchez-Jankowski, M. 1991. *Islands in the Street: Gangs and American Urban Society.* Berkeley: University of California.

Sandell, J., and E. Plutzer. 2005. "Families, divorce and voter turnout in the U.S." *Political Behavior* 27:133–62.

Sandelowski, M., C. Lambe, and J. Barroso. 2004. "Stigma in HIV-positive women." *Journal of Nursing Scholarship* 36:122–28.

Sandler, B. R. 1984. "The quiet revolution on campus: How sex discrimination has changed." *Chronicle of Higher Education* (February):72.

San Francisco Bureau. 2001. "New program hits racist property deeds." *Sun Reporter,* May 24, p. 3.

San Francisco Task Force on Prostitution. 1996. *Final Report.* San Francisco, CA: San Francisco Task Force on Prostitution.

Sang, B., J. Warshow, and A. J. Smith, eds. 1991. *Lesbians at Midlife: The Creative Transition.* San Francisco: Spinsters.

Saphores, J. M., H. Nixon, O. A. Ogunseitan, and A. A. Shapiro. 2006. "Household willingness to recycle electronic waste." *Environment and Behavior* 38:183–208.

Saporito, S., and D. Sohoni. 2006. "Coloring outside the lines: Racial segregation in public schools and their attendance boundaries." *Sociology of Education* 79:81–105.

Sarafino, E. P., M. E. Paterson, and E. L. Murphy. 1998. "Age and impacts of triggers in childhood asthma." *Journal of Asthma* 35 (2):213–17.

Sarche, J. 2004. "Colorado court rules against school vouchers." *The America's Intelligence Wire,* June 28.

Sargent, J. D., T. A. Wills, M. Stoolmiller, J. Gibson, and F. X. Gibbons. 2006. "Alcohol use in motion pictures and its relation with early-onset teen drinking." *Journal of Studies on Alcohol* 67:54–65.

Sashkin, M. 1984. "Participative management is an ethical imperative." *Organizational Dynamics* 12 (4):5–22.

Sausner, R. 2003. "Young children bring pot to school." *District Administration* 39:13.

Savitz, D. A., E. A. Whelan, and R. C. Kleckner. 1989. "Self-reported exposure to pesticides and radiation related to pregnancy outcome—Results from national natality and fetal mortality surveys." *Public Health Reports* 104 (September–October):473–77.

Sawin, J. L. 2004. "Making better energy choices." In *State of the World 2004,* ed. L. Starke, pp. 24–45. New York: W. W. Norton.

Scarpa, A. 2003. "Community violence exposure in young adults." *Trauma, Violence, and Abuse* 4:210–27.

Schachter, S., and J. E. Singer. 1962. "Cognitive, social, and psychological determinants of emotional state." *Psychological Review* 69 (September):379–99.

Scheff, T. 1966. *Being Mentally III.* Chicago: Aldine.

Scher, R. K. 1997. *The Modern Political Campaign.* New York: M. E. Sharpe.

Scherer, J., and E. Slawski. 1981. "Desegregation: Advantages to whites." *Urban Review* 13 (Winter):217–25.

Schlosser, E. 1997. "The business of pornography." *U.S. News and World Report,* February 10.

Schmidley, D. 2003. The *Foreign-Born Population in the United States:* March 2002. Washington, DC: Government Printing Office.

Schmidt, G. L. 1989. "Reversible mental illness: The role of the family in therapeutic context." *Journal of Psychotherapy and the Family* 5 (1–2):89–96.

Schnake, M. E., S. C. Bushardt, and C. Spottswood. 1984. "Internal work motivation and intrinsic job satisfaction: The effects of goal clarity, goal difficulty, participation in goal setting, and task complexity." *Group and Organization Studies* 9 (June):201–19.

Schneider, J. P. 2003. "The impact of compulsive cybersex behaviours on the family." *Sexual and Relationship Therapy* 18:329–54.

Schneider, W., and I. A. Lewis. 1984. "The straight story on homosexuality and gay rights." *Public Opinion* (February–March):16–60.

Schnurr, P. P., A. Spiro 3d, and A. H. Paris. 2000. "Physician-diagnosed medical disorders in relation to PTSD symptoms in older male military veterans." *Health Psychology* 19 (January):91–97.

Schofer, E., and J. W. Meyer. 2005. "The worldwide expansion of higher education in the twentieth century." *American Sociological Review* 70:898–920.

Schonfeld, A. M., S. N. Mattson, and E. P. Riley. 2005. "Moral maturity and delinquency after prenatal alcohol exposure." *Journal of Studies on Alcohol* 66:545–54.

Schorr, L. B. 1989. "Early interventions to reduce intergenerational disadvantage: The new policy context." *Teachers College Record* 90 (Spring):362–74.

Schulman, K. A., et al. 1999. "The effect of race and sex on physicians' recommendations for cardiac catheterization." *New England Journal of Medicine* 340 (February 25):618–26.

Schulz, A. J., et al. 2006. "Discrimination, symptoms of depression, and self-rated health among African American women in Detroit." *American Journal of Public Health* 96:1265–70.

Schwarez, S. K., and G. W. Rutherford. 1989. "Acquired immunodeficiency syndrome in infants, children and adolescents." *Journal of Drug Issues* 19 (Winter):79–92.

Schwartz, F. N. 1989. "Management women and the new facts of life." *Harvard Business Review* 67 (January–February):64–76.

Schwartz, J. 2004. "Air pollution and children's health." *Pediatrics* 113:1037–43.

———. 2006. "A scarred region mends, with help from many friends." *The New York Times,* November 13.

Scott, D. 1999. "Equal opportunity, unequal results." *Environment and Behavior* 31 (March):267–90.

Scott, J. 1988. "Study links nine common medical errors to deaths." *Los Angeles Times,* October 1.

———. 1990a. "Job-related illness called America's invisible killer." *Los Angeles Times,* August 31.

———. 1990b. "Parents' smoking linked to children's lung cancer." *Los Angeles Times,* September 6.

Scott, J., and D. Leonhardt. 2005. "Class in America: Shadowy lines that still divide." *The New York Times,* May 15.

Scott, M. S., and C. F. Delgado. 2005. "Identifying cognitively gifted minority students in preschool." *Gifted Child Quarterly* 49:199.

Scott, W. A., R. Scott, and M. McCabe. 1991. "Family relationships and children's personality: A cross-cultural, cross-source comparison." *British Journal of Social Psychology* 30 (March):1–20.

Scully, D., and J. Marolla. 1984. "Convicted rapists' vocabulary of motive: Excuses and justifications." *Social Problems* 31 (5):530–45.

Seccombe, K., K. B. Walters, and D. James. 1999. " 'Welfare mothers' welcome reform, urge compassion." *Family Relations* 48 (April):197–206.

Seeman, M., A. Z. Seeman, and A. Budros. 1988. "Powerlessness, work, and community: A longitudinal study of alienation and alcohol use." *Journal of Health and Social Behavior* 29 (September):185–98.

Seivewright, N. 1987. "Relationship between life events and personality in psychiatric disorder." *Stress Medicine* 3 (July–September):163–68.

Selke, W. L., and H. E. Pepinsky. 1982. "The politics of police reporting in Indianapolis, 1948–1978." *Law and Human Behavior* 6 (3–4):327–42.

Sell, R. L., J. A. Wells, and D. Wypij. 1995. "The prevalence of homosexual behavior and attraction in the United States, the United Kingdom and France: Results of national population-based samples." *Archives of Sexual Behavior* 24 (June):235–48.

Semple, S. J., T. L. Patterson, and I. Grant. 2002. "Gender differences in the sexual risk practices of HIV+ heterosexual men and women." *AIDS and Behavior* 6:45–54.

Senanayake, S. N., and M. J. Ferson. 2004. "Detention for tuberculosis: Public health and the law." *Medical Journal of Australia* 180:573–76.

Senn, C. Y., and H. L. Radtke. 1990. "Women's evaluations of and affective reactions to mainstream violent pornography, nonviolent pornography, and erotica." *Violence and Victims* 5 (3):143–55.

Sennett, R., and J. Cobb. 1972. *The Hidden Injuries of Class.* New York: Vintage Books.

Settles, I. H., L. M. Cortina, J. Malley, and A. J. Stewart. 2006. "The climate for women in academic science." *Psychology of Women Quarterly* 30:47–58.

Shackelford, T. K., and J. Mouzos. 2005. "Partner killing by men in cohabiting and marital relationships." *Journal of Interpersonal Violence* 20:1310–24.

Shanker, A. 1990. "A proposal for using incentives to restructure our public schools." *Phi Kappa Delta* 71 (January):345–57.

———.1993. "The debate on grouping." *The New York Times,* January 31.

———. 1994. "The crab bucket syndrome." *The New York Times,* June 19.

———. 1996. "Where we stand." *The New York Times,* March 24.

———. 1997. "Where's the evidence?" *The New York Times,* February 2.

Shapiro, B. 1997. "When justice kills." *The Nation,* June 9.

Sharpe, R. 1993. "Losing ground: In latest recession, only blacks suffered net employment loss." *The Wall Street Journal,* September 14.

Shehan, C. L., M. A. Burg, and C. A. Rexroat. 1986. "Depression and the social dimensions of the full-time housewife role." *Sociological Quarterly* 27:403–21.

Sheinberg, M., and P. Fraenkel. 2001. *The Relational Trauma of Incest.* New York: The Guilford Press.

Shelton, B. A., and D. John. 1999. "Who does what and how much do they do? Gender and total work time." *Sociological Focus* 32:287–302.

Sherman, L. W., et al. 1998. *Preventing Crime: What Works, What Doesn't, What's Promising.* Washington, DC: Government Printing Office.

Shipler, D. K. 2004. *The Working Poor: Invisible in America.* New York: Alfred K. Knopf.

Shishehbor, M., D. Litaker, C. E. Pothier, and M. S. Lauer. 2006. "Association of socioeconomic status with functional capacity, heart rate recovery, and all-cause mortality." *Journal of the American Medical Association* 295:784–92.

Shojania, K. G., E. C. Burton, K. M. McDonald, and L. Goldman. 2003. "Changes in rates of autopsy-detected diagnostic errors over time." *Journal of the American Medical Association* 289:2849–56.

Shope, J. H. 2004. "When words are not enough: The search for the effect of pornography on abused women." *Violence against Women* 10:56–72.

Siegrist, J. 1995. "Emotions and health in occupational life." *Patient Education and Counseling* 25 (July):227–36.

Signorielli, N. 1989. "Television and conceptions about sex roles: Maintaining conventionality and the status quo." *Sex Roles* 21 (September):341–60.

Silberg, J., M. Rutter, B. D'Onofrio, and L. Eaves. 2003. "Genetic and environmental risk factors in adolescent substance use." *Journal of Child Psychology and Psychiatry and Allied Disciplines* 44:664–76.

Silbert, M., and A. M. Pines. 1981. "Occupational hazards of street prostitutes." *Criminal Justice and Behavior* 8 (4):395–99.

Sills, Y. G. 1994. The AIDS *Pandemic: Social Perspectives.* Westport, CT: Greenwood.

Silverstein, C. 1981. Man to Man—*Gay couples in America.* New York: William Morrow.

Simcha-Fagan, O., J. C. Gersten, and T. S. Langner. 1986. "Early precursors and concurrent correlates of patterns of illicit drug use in adolescents." *Journal of Drug Issues* 16 (Winter):7–28.

Simon, H. B. 2006. "Old bugs learn some new tricks." *Newsweek,* December 11.

Simon, T., J. Mercy, and C. Perkins. 2001. *Injuries from violent crime, 1992–98.* Washington, DC: Government Printing Office.

Simon, T., et al. 2001. "Attitudinal acceptance of intimate partner violence among U.S. adults." *Violence and Victims* 16:115–26.

Simone, A., and B. H. Kleiner. 2004. "Practical guide to workplace reduction." *Management Research News* 27:125–32.

Simons, R. L., and L. B. Whitbeck. 1991. "Sexual abuse as a precursor to prostitution and victimization among adolescent and adult homeless women." *Journal of Family Issues* 12 (September):361–79.

Simpson, G. E., and M. Yinger. 1965. *Racial and Cultural Minorities.* New York: Harper and Row.

Singer, J. L., D. G. Singer, and W. S. Rapaczynski. 1984. "Family patterns and television viewing as predictors of children's beliefs and aggression." *Journal of Communication* 34 (Spring):73–89.

Singer, L. T., et al. 2002. "Cognitive and motor outcomes of cocaine-exposed infants." *Journal of the American Medical Association* 287:1952–60.

Singh, V. P. 1991. "The underclass in the United States: Some correlates of economic change." *Sociological Inquiry* 61 (Fall):505–21.

Sirgy, M. J., D. Efraty, P. Siegel, and D. J. Lee. 2001. "A new measure of quality of work life (QWL) based on need satisfaction and spillover theories." *Social Indicators Research* 55:241–302.

Skanberg, A., and E. Ohrstrom. 2002. "Adverse health effects in relation to urban residential soundscapes." *Journal of Sound and Vibration* 250:151–55.

Skinner, K. B., S. J. Bahr, D. R. Crane, and V. R. A. Call. 2002. "Cohabitation, marriage, and remarriage." *Journal of Family Issues* 23:74–90.

Skrla, L., P. Reyes, and J. J. Scheurich. 2000. "Sexism, silence, and solutions." *Educational Administration Quarterly* 36:44–75.

Sleegers, J. 2000. "Similarities and differences in homelessness in Amsterdam and New York City." *Psychiatric Services* 51 (January):100–04.

Slevin, P., and S. F. Kovaleski. 2000. "Outside Palm Beach, complaints growing." *Washington Post,* November 11.

Sloan, J. H., A. L. Kellermann, and D. T. Reay. 1988. "Handgun regulations, crime, assaults, and homicide." *New England Journal of Medicine* 319 (November):1256–62.

Sloan, M. 2006. "Election shows corruption still matters." *The San Diego Union-Tribune,* December 6.

Smart, R. G. 1991. "Crack cocaine use: A review of prevalence and adverse effects." *American Journal of Drug and Alcohol Abuse* 17 (March):13–26.

Smedley, B. D., A. Y. Stith, and A. R. Nelson, eds. 2002. *Unequal Treatment: Confronting Racial and Ethnic Disparities in Health Care.* Washington, DC: Institute of Medicine.

Smeeding, T. M. 2005. "Public policy, economic inequality, and poverty." *Social Science Quarterly* 86:955–83.

Smith, D. 2006. "Offshoring: Political myths and economic reality." *The World Economy* 29:249–56.

Smith, D. W., et al. 2000. "Delay in disclosure of childhood rape." *Child Abuse and Neglect* 24 (February):273–87.

Smith, P. D., P. C. Rivers, and K. J. Stahl. 1992. "Family cohesion and conflict as predictors of drinking patterns: Beyond demographics and alcohol expectancies." *Family Dynamics of Addiction Quarterly* 2 (2):61–69.

Smith, R. A. 1997. "Race, income and authority at work." *Social Problems* 44 (February):19–32.

———. 2005. "Do the determinants of promotion differ for white men versus women and minorities?" *American Behavioral Scientist* 9:1157–81.

Smolowe, J. 1995. "Enemies of the state." *Time,* May 8, pp. 58–69.

Snow, D. L., et al. 2006. "The role of coping and problem drinking in men's abuse of female partners." *Violence and Victims* 21:267–85.

Snyder, H. N., and M. Sickmund. 1999. *Juvenile Offenders and Victims: 1999 National Report.* Washington, DC: Office of Juvenile Justice and Delinquency Prevention.

———. 2006. *Juvenile Offenders and Victims: 2006 National Report.* Washington, DC: National Center for Juvenile Justice.

Sobel, E., et al. 1995. "Occupations with exposure to electromagnetic fields: A possible risk factor for Alzheimer's disease." *American Journal of Epidemiology* 142 (September 1):515–24.

Socall, D. W., and T. Holtgraves. 1992. "Attitudes toward the mentally ill: The effects of label and beliefs." *Sociological Quarterly* (3):435–45.

Soine, L. 1995. "Sick building syndrome and gender bias." *Social Work and Health Care* 20 (3):51–65.

Solomon, S. D., and Jonathan R. T. Davidson. 1997. "Repairing the shattered self: Recovering from trauma." *Journal of Clinical Psychiatry* 58:5–11.

Solowij, N., et al. 2002. "Cognitive functioning of long-term heavy cannabis users seeking treatment." *Journal of the American Medical Association* 287:1123–31.

Somers, M. R., and F. Block. 2005. "From poverty to perversity: Ideas, markets, and institutions over 200 years of welfare debate." *American Sociological Review* 70:260–87.

Sorenson, J., R. Wrinkle, V. Brewer, and J. Marquart. 1999. "Capital punishment and deterrence: Examining the effect of executions on murder in Texas." *Crime and Delinquency* 45 (October):481–93.

Sorokin, P. A. 1942. *The Crisis of Our Age.* New York: E. P. Dutton.

South, S. J. 2001. "Time-dependent effects of wives' employment on marital dissolution." *American Sociological Review* 66:226–45.

Specter, M. 1996. "10 years later, through fear, Chernobyl still kills in Belarus." *The New York Times,* March 31.

Spector, P. E. 2002. "Employee control and occupational stress." *Current Directions in Psychological Science* 11:133–36.

Spelke, E. S. 2005. "Sex differences in intrinsic aptitude for mathematics and science?" *American Psychologist* 60:950–58.

Spergen, I. A., and G. D. Curry. 1990. "Strategies and perceived agency effectiveness in dealing with the young gang problem." In *Gangs in America,* ed. C. R. Huff, Newbury Park, CA: Sage.

Spilerman, S., and T. Lunde, 1991. "Features of educational attainment and job promotion prospects." *American Journal of Sociology* 97 (November):689–720.

Spix, C., et al. 1998. "Short-term effects of air pollution on hospital admissions of respiratory diseases in Europe." *Archives of Environmental Health* 53 (January–February):54–64.

Sprang, G. 1999. "Post-disaster stress following the Oklahoma City bombing." *Journal of Interpersonal Violence* 14 (February):169–83.

St. George-Hyslop, P. H. 2000. "Piecing together Alzheimer's." *Scientific American,* December, pp. 76–83.

St. Jean, Y., and J. R. Feagin. 1998. *Double Burden: Black Women and Everyday Racism.* Armonk, NY: M. E. Sharpe.

Stack, S. 1990. "Execution publicity and homicide in South Carolina: A research note." *Sociological Quarterly* 31 (4):599–611.

Stack, S., I. Wasserman, and R. Kern. 2004. "Adult social bonds and use of Internet pornography." *Social Science Quarterly* 85:75–88.

Staines, G. L., K. J. Pottick, and D. A. Fudge. 1986. "Wives' employment and husbands' attitudes toward work and life." *Journal of Applied Psychology* 71:118–28.

Stanley, S. M., S. W. Whitton, and H. J. Markham. 2004. "Maybe I do: Interpersonal commitment and premarital or nonmarital cohabitation." *Journal of Family Issues* 25:496–519.

Stansfeld, S. A., and M. P. Matheson. 2003. "Noise pollution: Non-auditory effects on health." *British Medical Bulletin* 68:243–57.

Stanton, A. H., and M. S. Schwartz. 1961. "The mental hospital and the patient." In *Complex Organizations,* ed. A. Etzioni, pp. 234–42. New York: Holt, Rinehart and Winston.

Steele, J., J. B. James, and R. C. Barnett. 2002. "Learning in a man's world." *Psychology of Women Quarterly* 26:46–50.

Steelman, L. C., and B. Powell. 1991. "Sponsoring the next generation: Parental willingness to pay for higher education." *American Journal of Sociology* 96 (May):1505–29.

Steenland, K., S. Hu, and J. Walker. 2004. "All-cause and cause-specific mortality by socioeconomic status among employed persons in 27 U.S. states, 1984–1997." *American Journal of Public Health* 94:1037–42.

Stefanko, M., and J. Horowitz. 1989. "Attitudinal effects associated with an environmental hazard." *Population and Environment* 11 (Fall):43–57.

Steffensmeier, D., and S. Demuth. 2000. "Ethnicity and sentencing outcomes in U.S. federal courts." *American Sociological Review* 65:705–29.

Stein, B. D., et al. 2004. "A national longitudinal study of the psychological consequences of the September 11, 2001, terrorist attacks." *Psychiatry* 67:105–17.

Stein, M. B., et al. 2004. "Relationship of sexual assault history to somatic symptoms and health anxiety in women." *General Hospital Psychiatry* 26:178–83.

Steinberg, L., B. B. Brown, and S. M. Dornbusch. 1997. *Beyond the Classroom: Why School Reform Has Failed and What Parents Need to Do.* New York: Touchstone.

Sternberg, R. J., E. L. Grigorenko, and K. K. Kidd. 2005. "Intelligence, race, and genetics." *American Psychologist* 60:46–59.

Stets, J. E. 1993. "The link between past and present intimate relationships." *Journal of Family Issues* 14 (May):236–60.

Stetz, M. 1999. " 'Driving while black' no crime, but ..." *San Diego Union-Tribune,* March 14.

Stevens, D. J. 1994. "Predatory rapists and victim selection techniques." *Social Science Journal* 31 (4):421–33.

Stevens, M. L. 2001. *Kingdom of Children: Culture and Controversy in the Homeschooling Movement.* Princeton, NJ: Princeton University Press.

Stewart, W. F., J. A. Ricci, E. Chee, S. R. Hahn, and D. Morganstein. 2003. "Cost of lost productive work time among U.S. workers with depression." *Journal of the American Medical Association* 289:3135–44.

Stewart, W. F., J. A. Ricci, E. Chee, D. Morganstein, and R. Lupton. 2003. "Lost productive time and cost due to common pain conditions in the U.S. workforce." *Journal of the American Medical Association* 290:2443–54.

Stice, E., and S. K. Bearman. 2001. "Body-image and eating disturbances prospectively predict increases in depressive symptoms in adolescent girls." *Developmental Psychology* 37:597–607.

Stiles, B. L., X. Liu, and H. B. Kaplan. 2000. "Relative deprivation and deviant adaptations." *Journal of Research in Crime and Delinquency* 37 (February):64–90.

Stine, S. M. 1998. "Opiate dependence and current treatments." In *New Treatments for Chemical Addictions,* ed. Elinore F. McCance-Katz, pp. 75–111. Washington, DC: American Psychiatric Association.

Stires, L. K. 1991. "The Gulf 'war' as a sanctioned massacre." *Contemporary Social Psychology* 15 (December): 139–43.

Stith, S. M., et al. 2000. "The intergenerational transmission of spouse abuse." *Journal of Marriage and Family* 62:640–54.

Stix, G. 2006. "A climate repair manual." *Scientific American,* September, pp. 46–49.

Stockholm International Peace Research Institute. 2007. "Recent trends in military expenditures." Stockholm International Peace Research Institute Web site.

Stoll, B. M., G. L. Arriaut, D. K. Fromme, and J. A. Felker-Thayer. 2005. "Adolescents in stepfamilies." *Journal of Divorce & Remarriage* 44:177–89.

Stone, B. 1999. "Get a life!" *Newsweek,* June 7.

Stone, P. H. 2006. *Heist: Superlobbyist Jack Abramoff, His Republican Allies, and the Buying of Washington.* New York: Farrar, Straus & Giroux.

Stoneman, B. 1999. "Un-happy workers." *American Demographics,* May.

Story, L. B., and R. Repetti. 2006. "Daily occupational stressors and marital behavior." *Journal of Family Psychology* 20:680–89.

Stratigos, A. J., and A. D. Katsambas. 2003. "Medical and cutaneous disorders associated with homelessness." *Skinned* 2:168–72.

Straus, M. A. 2001. "New evidence for the benefits of never spanking." *Society* 38:52–60.

Straus, M. A., D. B. Sugarman, and J. Giles-Sims. 1997. "Spanking by parents and subsequent antisocial behavior of children." *Archives of Pediatrics and Adolescent Medicine* 151 (August):761–67.

Strecher, V. J., M. W. Kreuter, and S. C. Kobrin. 1995. "Do cigarette smokers have unrealistic perceptions of their heart attack, cancer, and stroke risks?" *Journal of Behavioral Medicine* 18 (February):45–54.

Streissguth, A. P. 1992. "Fetal alcohol syndrome: Early and long-term consequences." In *Problems of Drug Dependence* 1991, ed. L. Harris, Rockville, MD: National Institute on Drug Abuse.

Stretesky, P., and M. J. Hogan. 1998. "Environmental justice: An analysis of superfund sites in Florida." *Social Problems* 45 (May):268–87.

Strohschein, L. 2005a. "Household income histories and child mental health trajectories." *Journal of Health and Social Behavior* 46:359–75.

———— 2005b. "Parental divorce and child mental health trajectories." *Journal of Marriage and Family* 67:1286–1300.

Strossen, N. 1995. "The perils of pornophobia." *Humanist,* May–June, pp. 5–7.

Stroul, B. A. 1989. "Community support systems for persons with long-term mental illness: A conceptual framework." *Psychosocial Rehabilitation Journal* 12 (January):9–26.

Stuart, G. L., T. M. Moore, S. E. Ramsey, and C. W. Kahler. 2003. "Relationship aggression and substance use among women court-referred to domestic violence intervention programs." *Addictive Behaviors* 28:1603–10.

————. 2004. "Hazardous drinking and relationship violence perpetration and victimization in women arrested for domestic violence." *Journal of Studies on Alcohol* 65:46–53.

Stuart, J. A., and P. D. Bliese. 1998. "The long-term effects of Operation Desert Storm on the psychological distress of U.S. Army Reserve and National Guard veterans." *Journal of Applied Social Psychology* 28 (January):1–22.

Sturm, J. J., K. Yeatts, and D. Loomis. 2004. "Effects of tobacco smoke exposure on asthma prevalence and medical care use in North Carolina middle school children." *American Journal of Public Health* 94:308–13.

Substance Abuse and Mental Health Services Administration. 2003. *Results from the 2002 National Survey on Drug Use and Health.* Rockville, MD: DHHS.

Sullivan, D. A. 2001. *Cosmetic Surgery: The Cutting Edge of Commercial Medicine in America.* New Brunswick, NJ: Rutgers University Press.

Sung, H., et al. 2005. "Major state tobacco tax increase, the master settlement agreement, and cigarette consumption." *American Journal of Public Health* 95:1030–35.

Surratt, H. L., J. A. Inciardi, S. P. Kurtz, and M. C. Kiley. 2004. "Sex work and drug use in a subculture of violence." *Crime and Delinquency* 50:43–59.

Sutherland, E. H. 1968. "White collar criminality." In *Radical Perspectives on Social Problems,* ed. Frank Lindenfeld, pp. 149–60. New York: Macmillan.

Sutherland, E. H., and D. R. Cressey. 1955. *Principles of Criminology.* 5th ed. Philadelphia: J. B. Lippincott.

Swaab, D. F., and M. A. Hofman. 1990. "An enlarged suprachiasmatic nucleus in homosexual men." *Brain Research* 537 (1–2):141–48.

Swaim, R. C., E. R. Oetting, R. W. Edwards, and F. Beauvais. 1989. "Links from emotional distress to adolescent drug use: a path model." *Journal of Consulting and Clinical Psychology* 57 (April):227–31.

Swanson, J. W., et al. 2002. "The social-environmental context of violent behavior in persons treated for severe mental illness." *American Journal of Public Health* 92:1523–31.

Swartz, R. 2002. "Redefining a case in the postreform era." *Focus* 22:16–21.

Swers, M. L. 2002. *The Difference Women Make: The Policy Impact of Women in Congress.* Chicago, IL: University of Chicago Press.

Symanski, R. 1974. "Prostitution in Nevada." *Annals of the Association of American Geographers* 64 (September):357–77.

Sypnowich, C. 2000. "The culture of citizenship." *Politics and Society* 28:531–55.

Szymanski, A. 1976. "Racism and sexism as functional substitutes in the labor market." *Sociological Quarterly* 17 (Winter):67–73.

Taft, C. T., et al. 2006. "Examining the correlates of psychological aggression among a community sample of couples." *Journal of Family Psychology* 20:581–88.

Taft, P., and P. Ross. 1969. "American labor violence: Its causes, character, and outcome." In *The History of Violence in America,* ed. H. D. Graham and T. R. Gurr, pp. 281–395. New York: Bantam.

Talbot, M. 2003. "Catch and Release." *Atlantic Monthly,* January/February, pp. 97–100.

Tanner, J. C. 2006. "XXX adult content: Coming to a phone near you?" *America's Network,* June, pp. 26–32.

Tavernise, S., and D. G. McNeil. 2006. "Researchers estimate 600,000 dead in Iraq since U.S. invasion." *The San Diego Union-Tribune,* October 11.

Taylor, M. J., A. S. Barusch, and M. B. Vogel-Ferguson. 2006. "Heterogeneity at the bottom: TANF closure and long-term welfare recipients." *Journal of Human Behavior in the Social Environment* 13:1–14.

Teicher, M. H. 2002. "Scars that won't heal: The neurobiology of child abuse." *Scientific American,* March, pp. 68–75.

Terkel, S. 1972. *Working.* New York: Avon Books.

Teti, D. M., M. E. Lamb, and A. B. Elster. 1987. "Long-range socioeconomic and marital consequences of adolescent marriage in three cohorts of adult males." *Journal of Marriage and the Family* 49 (August):499–506.

Thabet, A. A., and P. Vostanis. 2000. "Posttraumatic stress disorder reactions in children of war." *Child Abuse and Neglect* 24 (February):291–98.

Thombs, D. L., J. Ray-Tomasek, C. J. Osborn, and R. S. Olds. 2005. "The role of sex-specific normative beliefs in undergraduate alcohol use." *American Journal of Health Behavior* 29:342–51.

Thompson, M. P., I. Arias, K. C. Basile, and S. Desai. 2002. "The association between childhood physical and sexual victimization and health problems in adulthood in a nationally representative sample of women." *Journal of Interpersonal Violence* 17:1115–29.

Thompson, M. P., J. B. Kingree, and S. Desai. 2004. "Gender differences in long-term health consequences of physical abuse of children." *American Journal of Public Health* 94:599–604.

Thomson, E., and U. Colella. 1992. "Cohabitation and marital stability: Quality or commitment?" *Journal of Marriage and the Family* 54 (May):259–68.

Thomson, E., T. L. Hanson, and S. S. McLanahan. 1994. "Family structure and child well-being: Economic resources vs. parental behaviors." *Social Forces* 73:221–42.

Thoreau, H. D. 1968. *Walden and the Essay on Civil Disobedience.* New York: Lancer.

Thornberry, T. P., and M. Farnworth. 1982. "Social correlates of criminal involvement: Further evidence on the relationship between social status and criminal behavior." *American Sociological Review* 47 (August):505–17.

Thornberry, T. P., D. Huizinga, and R. Loeber. 2004. "The causes and correlates studies." *Juvenile Justice* 9:3–19.

Thornberry, T. P., M. D. Krohn, A. J. Lizotte, and D. Chard-Wierschem. 1993. "The role of juvenile gangs in facilitating delinquent behavior." *Journal of Research in Crime and Delinquency* 30 (February):55–87.

Thornberry, T. P., C. A. Smith, C. Rivera, D. Huizinga, and M. Stouthamer-Loeber. 1999. "Family disruption and delinquency." *Juvenile Justice Bulletin,* September.

Thorne, P. S., et al. 2001. "Indoor environmental quality in six commercial office buildings in the Midwest United States." *Applied Occupational and Environmental Hygiene* 16:1065–77.

Thottam, J. 2004. "When execs go." *Time,* April 26, pp. 40–41.

Throop, D. R. 1997. "What are men's issues?" World Wide Web Virtual Library: Men's Page Web site.

Thrupp, L. A. 1991. "Sterilization of workers from pesticide exposure: The causes and consequences of DBCP-induced damage in Costa Rica and beyond." *International Journal of Health Services* 21 (4):731–57.

Thun, M. J., et al. 1997. "Alcohol consumption and mortality among middle-aged and elderly U.S. adults." *New England Journal of Medicine* 337 (December 11):1705–14.

Tickell, C. 1992. "The quality of life: What quality? Whose life?" *Environmental Values* 1 (Spring):65–76.

Tierney, J. 1998. "Calling all noisebusters." *The New York Times Magazine,* February 22, p. 24.

Tiet, Q., et al. 2001. "Relationship between specific adverse life events and psychiatric disorders." *Journal of Abnormal Child Psychology* 29:153–64.

Tilly, C., and R. Albelda. 1994. "It's not working: Why single mothers can't work their way out of poverty." *Dollars and Sense* 196 (November–December):8–10.

Ting, Y. 1997. "Determinants of job satisfaction of federal government employees." *Public Personnel Management* 26 (Fall):313–34.

Tivnan, E. 1987. "Homosexuals and the churches." *The New York Times Magazine,* October 11, pp. 84–91.

Tjaden, P., and N. Thoennes. 2006. "Extent, nature, and consequences of rape victimization: Findings from the national violence against women study." NIJ Web site.

Toffler, A. 1970. *Future Shock.* New York: Random House.

Tolbert, C. J., J. A. Grummel, and D. A. Smith. 2001. "The effects of ballot initiatives on voter turnout in the American states." *American Politics Research* 29:625–48.

Tomaskovic-Devey, D., and V. J. Roscigno. 1996. "Racial economic subordination and white gain in the U.S. South." *American Sociological Review* 61(August):565–89.

Tomaskovic-Devey, D., et al. 2006. "Documenting desegregation: Segregation in American workplaces by race, ethnicity, and sex, 1966–2003." *American Sociological Review* 71:565–88.

Toner, R., and S. G. Stolberg. 2002. "Decade after health care crisis, soaring costs bring new strains." *The New York Times,* August 11.

Tonry, M. H. 1995. *Malign Neglect: Race, Crime, and Punishment in America.* New York: Oxford University Press.

Tonry, R. 1999. "Fevered issue, second opinion." *The New York Times,* October 10.

Torpy, J. M., and R. M. Glass. 2006. "Anorexia nervosa." *Journal of the American Medical Association* 295:2684.

Torres, K. C., and C. Z. Charles. 2004. "Metastereotypes and the black-white divide." *Du Bois Review* 1:115–49.

Torrey, E. F. 1994. "Violent behavior by individuals with serious mental illness." *Hospital and Community Psychiatry* 45 (July):653–62.

Tower, R. B., and M. Krasner. 2006. "Marital closeness, autonomy, mastery, and depressive symptoms in a U.S. Internet sample." *Personal Relationships* 13:429.

Tracy, P. E., and J. A. Fox. 1989. "A field experiment on insurance fraud in auto body repair." *Criminology* 27 (August):589–603.

Traeen, B., T. S. Nilsen, and H. Stigum. 2006. "Use of pornography in traditional media and on the internet in Norway." *Journal of Sex Research* 43:245–54.

Treas, J., and D. Giesen. 2000. "Sexual infidelity among married and cohabiting Americans." *Journal of Marriage and the Family* 62 (February):48–60.

Troisi, A., A. Pasini, M. Saracco, and G. Spalletta. 1998. "Psychiatric symptoms in male cannabis users not using other illicit drugs." *Addiction* 93 (April):487–92.

Trotter, A. 1997. "Inequities in access to technology documented." *Education Week,* May 21.

Tsang, M. C., R. W. Rumberger, and H. M. Levin. 1991. "The impact of surplus schooling on worker productivity." *Industrial Relations* 30 (Spring):209–28.

Tu, H. T., P. Kemper, and H. J. Wong. 2000. "Do HMOs make a difference? Use of health services." *Inquiry* 36 (Winter):400–10.

Tu, H. T., and J. D. Reschovsky. 2002. "Assessment of medical care by enrollees in for-profit and nonprofit health maintenance organizations." *New England Journal of Medicine* 346:1288–93.

Tucker, J., S. L. Nock, and D. J. Toscano. 1989. "Employee ownership and perceptions of work." *Work and Occupations* 16 (February):26–42.

Turner, H. A., and K. Kopiec. 2006. "Exposure to interparental conflict and psychological disorder among young adults." *Journal of Family Issues* 27:131–58.

Turner, R. J., and D. A. Lloyd. 1999. "The stress process and the social distribution of depression." *Journal of Health and Social Behavior* 40 (December):374–404.

Turnipseed, D. 1992. "Anxiety and perceptions of the work environment." *Journal of Social Behavior and Personality* 7 (3):375–94.

Tuxill, J. 1999. *Nature's Cornucopia.* Washington, DC: Worldwatch Institute.

Tween, S. H., and C. D. Ryff. 1991. "Adult children of alcoholics: Profiles of wellness amidst distress." *Journal of Studies on Alcohol* 52 (March):133–41.

Twenge, J. M. 2000. "The age of anxiety? Birth cohort change in anxiety and neuroticism, 1952–1993." *Journal of Personality and Social Psychology* 79:1007–21.

Tyack, D. 2003. *Seeking Common Ground: Public Schools in a Diverse Society.* Cambridge: Harvard University Press.

Tyler, K. A., and K. A. Johnson. 2006. "Trading sex: Voluntary or coerced?" *Journal of Sex Research* 43:208–16.

Tyler, P. E. 1995. "China's war zone." *New York Times,* November 16.

Uchitelle, L. 1996. "More downsized workers are returning as rentals." *The New York Times,* December 8.

Uchitelle, L., and N. R. Kleinfield. 1996. "On the battlefields of business, millions of casualties." *The New York Times,* March 3.

Uggen, C. 2000. "Work as a turning point in the life course of criminals." *American Sociological Review* 67:529–46.

Uggen, C., and A. Blackstone. 2004. "Sexual harassment as a gendered expression of power." *American Sociological Review* 69:64–92.

Ullman, S. E. 1998. "Does offender violence escalate when rape victims fight back?" *Journal of Interpersonal Violence* 13 (April):179–92.

Ullman, S. E., and L. R. Brecklin. 2003. "Sexual assault history and health-related outcomes in a national sample of women." *Psychology of Women Quarterly* 27:46–57.

Ullman, S. E., and H. H. Filipas. 2001. "Correlates of formal and informal support seeking in sexual assault victims." *Journal of Interpersonal Violence* 16:1028–47.

Ullman, S. E., and R. A. Knight. 1992. "Fighting back: Women's resistance to rape." *Journal of Interpersonal Violence* 7 (March):31–43.

Ungar, S. 1992. "The rise and (relative) decline of global warming as a social problem." *Sociological Quarterly* 33 (4):483–501.

United Nations. 1992. *Long-Range World Population Projection: Two Centuries of Population Growth, 1950–2150.* New York: United Nations.

United Nations Environment Programme. 2006. *GEO: Global Environment Outlook.* United Nations Environment Programme Web site.

United Nations General Assembly. 2006. "Report of the special representative of the Secretary-General for children and armed conflict." United Nations Web site.

United Nations Population Fund. 2001. *Population Issues Briefing Kit 2001.* New York: UNFPA.

Unsworth, M. E. 1999. "Freedom of information: Its ebb and flow." *American Libraries,* June–July, pp. 82–86.

U.S. Census Bureau. 1975. *Historical Statistics of the United States, Colonial Times to 1970.* Washington, DC: Government Printing Office.

———. 1990. *Statistical Abstract of the United States.* Washington, DC: Government Printing Office.

———. 1996. *Statistical Abstract of the United States.* Washington, DC: Government Printing Office.

———. 2003. *Statistical Abstract of the United States: 2003.* Washington, DC: Government Printing Office.

———. 2004. "Poverty 2003." Census Bureau Web site.

———. 2004/2005. *Statistical Abstract of the United States.* Washington, DC: Government Printing Office.

———. 2005. "Annual social and economic supplement." Census Bureau Web site.

———. 2007. *Statistical Abstract of the United States.* Washington, DC: Government Printing Office.

U.S. Department of Education. 1993. *National Excellence: A Case for Developing America's Talent.* Washington, DC: Government Printing Office.

———. 2006. *The Condition of Education 2006.* Washington, DC: Government Printing Office.

U.S. Department of Health and Human Services. 1995. "Preliminary estimates from the 1994 national household survey on drug abuse." *Advance Report Number 10.* September.

U.S. Department of Justice. 1992. *Drugs, Crime, and the Justice System.* Washington, DC: Government Printing Office.

———. 1996. *Capital Punishment, 1994.* Washington, DC: Government Printing Office.

———. 2001. *Federal Criminal Case Processing, 1999.* Washington, DC: Government Printing Office.

———. 2003. *Federal Crime Case Processing, 2001.* Washington, DC: Government Printing Office.

U.S. Department of Labor. 2003. *National Compensation Survey: Occupational Wages in the United States, July 2002.* Washington, DC: Government Printing Office.

———. 2004. *National Compensation Survey: Employee Benefits in Private Industry in the United States, March 2003.* Washington, DC: Government Printing Office.

———. 2006a. *Charting the U.S. Labor Market in 2005.* U.S. Department of Labor Web site.

———. 2006b. "National compensation survey: Employee benefits in private industry in the United States, March 2006." U.S. Department of Labor Web site.

———. 2006c. "Union members summary." U.S. Department of Labor Web site.

U.S. Department of Labor, Women's Bureau. 1998. "Facts on working women." Department of Labor Web site.

———. 2000. "OPA press release: Statement by Secretary of Labor Alexis M. Herman on job-related injuries and illnesses data." Press release. Department of Labor Web site.

U.S. Department of State. 2002. *Patterns of Global Terrorism 2001.* Department of State Web site.

———. 2006. "Country reports on terrorism." U.S. Department of State Web site.

U.S. Public Health Service. 1995. *Healthy People 2000.* Washington DC: Government Printing Office.

U.S. Riot Commission. 1968. *Report of the National Advisory Commission on Civil Disorders.* New York: Bantam.

Useem, M., and J. Karabel. 1986. "Pathways to corporate management." *American Sociological Review* 51 (April):184–200.

Valera, E. M., and H. Berenbaum. 2003. "Brain injury in battered women." *Journal of Consulting and Clinical Psychology* 71:797–804.

Valera, R. J., R. G. Sawyer, and G. R. Schiraldi. 2001. "Perceived health needs of inner-city street prostitutes." *American Journal of Health Behavior* 25:50–59.

Van Deerlin, L. 2003. "Abandoning the bill of rights." *San Diego Union-Tribune,* June 11.

Vandepitte, J., et al. 2006. "Estimates of the number of female sex workers in different regions of the world." *Sexually Transmitted Infections* 82:8–25.

Vandervalk, I., E. Spruijt, M. De Goede, W. Meeus, and C. Maas. 2004. "Marital status, marital process, and parental resources in predicting adolescents' emotional adjustment." *Journal of Family Issues* 25:291–317.

van Hook, M. P., E. Gjermeni, and E. Haxhiymeri. 2006. "Sexual trafficking of women." *International Social Work* 49:29–40.

Van Koppen, P. J., and R. W. J. Jansen. 1999. "The time to rob: Variations in time of number of commercial robberies." *Journal of Research in Crime and Delinquency* 36 (February):7–29.

van Vianen, A. E. M., and A. H. Fischer. 2002. "Illuminating the glass ceiling." *Journal of Occupational and Organizational Psychology* 75:315–37.

Vaughan, K. K., and G. T. Fouts. 2003. "Changes in television and magazine exposure and eating disorder symptomatology." *Sex Roles* 49:313–20.

Vazsonyi, A. T., L. M. Belliston, and D. J. Flannery. 2004. "Evaluation of a school-based universal violence prevention program." *Youth Violence and Juvenile Justice* 2:185–206.

Vedantam, S., A. Epstine, and B. Geiger. 1997. "Tobacco firm says smoking is addictive." *San Diego Union-Tribune,* March 21.

Venkatesh, S. A. 1994. "Getting ahead: Social mobility among the urban poor." *Sociological Perspectives* 37 (Summer):157–82.

Ventegodt, S., et al. 2005. "Global quality of life (QOL), health and ability are primarily determined by our consciousness." *Social Indicators Research* 71:87–122.

Vera, M. N., J. Vila, and J. F. Godoy. 1994. "Cardiovascular effects of traffic noise." *Psychological Medicine* 24 (November):817–27.

Verbrugge, L. M., and J. H. Madans. 1985. "Women's roles and health." *American Demographics* 7 (March):36–39.

Verdurmen, J., et al. 2005. "Alcohol use and mental health in adolescents." *Journal of Studies on Alcohol* 66:605–9.

Verger, P., et al. 2004. "The psychological impact of terrorism." *American Journal of Psychiatry* 161:1384–89.

Villaveces, A., et al. 2000. "Effect of a ban on carrying firearms on homicide rates in two Colombian cities." *Journal of the American Medical Association* 283 (March 1):1205–09.

Vinokur, A., and M. L. Selzer. 1975. "Desirable versus undesirable life events: Their relationship to stress and mental distress." *Journal of Personality and Social Psychology* 32 (August):329–39.

Vinson, D. C., M. Maclure, C. Reidinger, and G. S. Smith. 2003. "A population-based case-crossover and case-control study of alcohol and the risk of injury." *Journal of Studies on Alcohol* 64:358–66.

Visaria, L., and P. Visaria. 1995. "India's population in transition." *Population Bulletin* 50 (3):1–43.

Vitaliano, P. P., J. James, and D. Boyer. 1981. "Sexuality of deviant females: Adolescent and adult correlates." *Social Work* 26 (November):468–72.

Vivar, M. A., 1982. "The new anti-female violent pornography: Is moral condemnation the only justifiable response?" *Law and Psychology Review* 7 (Spring):53–70.

Vlahov, D., S. Galea, J. Ahern, H. Resnick, and D. Kilpatrick. 2004. "Sustained increased consumption of cigarettes, alcohol, and marijuana among Manhattan residents after September 11, 2001." *American Journal of Public Health* 94:253–54.

Vogel, R. D. 2006. "Harder times." *Monthly Review* 58:29–39.

Vora, E. A., and J. A. Vora. 2002. "Undoing racism in America." *Journal of Black Studies* 32:389–404.

Voss, M., L. Nylen, B. Floderus, F. Diderichsen, and P. D. Terry. 2004. "Unemployment and early cause-specific mortality." *American Journal of Public Health* 94:2155–61.

Voydanoff, P. 2004. "The effects of work demands and resources on work-to-family conflict and facilitation." *Journal of Marriage and Family* 66:398–412.

Vrij, A., and F. W. Winkel. 1991. "Characteristics of the built environment and fear of crime: A research note on interventions in unsafe locations." *Deviant Behavior* 12 (April–June):203–15.

Wade, T. J., and D. J. Pevalin. 2004. "Marital transitions and mental health." *Journal of Health and Social Behavior* 45:155–70.

Wagner, M. B. 1990. *God's Schools: Choice and Compromise in American Society.* New Brunswick, NJ: Rutgers Unversity.

Wagstaff, M. C., and B. E. Wilson. 1988. "The evaluation of litter behavior modification in a river environment." *Journal of Environmental Education* 20 (Fall):39–44.

Wahl, O. F. 2003. "News media portrayal of mental illness." *American Behavioral Scientist* 46:1594–1600.

Wainwright, J. L., and C. J. Patterson. 2006. "Delinquency, victimization, and substance use among adolescents with female same-sex parents." *Journal of Family Psychology* 20:526–30.

Wallerstein, J. S. 1986. "Women after divorce: Preliminary report from a ten-year follow-up." *American Journal of Orthopsychiatry* 56 (January):65–77.

Wallis, C. 2004. "Hidden scars of battle." *Time,* July 12, p. 35.

Walsh, M. 2001. "Public sees role for religion in schools." *Education Week*. Education Week Web site.

Walt, S. M. 2005. *Taming American Power: The Global Response to U.S. Primacy.* New York: W. W. Norton.

Walter, H. J., et al. 1995. "Sexual, assaultive, and suicidal behaviors among urban minority junior high school students." *Journal of the American Academy of Child and Adolescent Psychiatry* 34:73–80.

Walters, P. B. 1984. "Occupational and labor market effects on secondary and postsecondary educational expansion in the United States: 1922 to 1979." *American Sociological Review* 49 (October):659–71.

Wang, P. S., O. Demler, and R. C. Kessler. 2002. "Adequacy of treatment for serious mental illness in the United States." *American Journal of Public Health* 92:92–98.

Wang, P. S., et al. 2005. "Twelve-month use of mental health services in the United States." *Archives of General Psychiatry* 62:629–40.

Warr, M. 1993. "Parents, peers, and delinquency." *Social Forces* 72 (September):247–64.

Watson, D. L. 2002. "The terrorist threat confronting the United States." FBI Web site.

Watt, T. T. 2002. "Marital and cohabiting relationships of adult children of alcoholics." *Journal of Family Issues* 23:246–65.

Wauterickx, N., A. Gouwy, and P. Bracke. 2006. "Parental divorce and depression." *Journal of Divorce & Remarriage* 45:43–68.

Weaver, C. N. 1997. "Has the work ethic in the USA declined? Evidence from nationwide surveys." *Psychological Reports* 81:491–95.

Weaver, C. N., and M. D. Matthews. 1990. "Work satisfaction of females with full-time employment and full-time housekeeping: 15 years later." *Psychological Reports* 66:1248–50.

Webb, J. T. 2000. "Mis-diagnosis and dual diagnosis of gifted children." Paper presented at the Annual Conference of the American Psychological Association.

Wechsler, H. 2002. "Trends in college binge drinking during a period of increased prevention efforts." *Journal of American College Health* 50:203–18.

Weidenbaum, M. L. 1999. "A key driver for the U.S. economy: The global economy: Superpowers to supermarkets." *Vital Speeches* 65 (June 1): 506–510.

Weinberg, A., and L. Weinberg, eds. 1963. *Instead of Violence.* New York: Grossman.

Weinberg, N. S., and W. B. Stason. 1998. "Managing quality in hospital practice." *International Journal of Quality Health Care* 10 (August):295–302.

Weisbrot, M. 2000. "Globalism for dummies." *Harper's Magazine,* May, pp. 15–19.

Weisburd, D., and L. G. Mazerolle. 2000. "Crime and disorder in drug hot spots." *Police Quarterly* 3:331–49.

Weismantle, M. 2001. "Reasons people do not work." *Current Population Reports*. Washington, DC: Government Printing Office.

Weiss, H. E., and L. W. Reid. 2005. "Low-quality employment concentration and crime." *Sociological Perspectives* 48:213–32.

Weiss, R. S. 1990. Staying the Course: *The Emotional and Social Lives of Men Who Do Well at Work*. New York: Free Press.

Weissman, M. M., et al. 1996. "Cross-national epidemiology of major depression and bipolar disorder." *Journal of the American Medical Association* 296 (July 24):293–99.

Weisz, M. G., and C. M. Earls. 1995. "The effects of exposure to filmed sexual violence on attitudes toward rape." *Journal of Interpersonal Violence* 10 (March):71–84.

Weitzer, R., and S. A. Tuch. 2004. "Race and perceptions of police misconduct." *Social Problems* 51:305–25.

Weitzman, E. R., and I. Kawachi. 2000. "Giving means receiving: the protective effect of social capital on binge drinking on college campuses." *American Journal of Public Health* 90:1936–39.

Welsh, W. N. 2002. "Court-ordered reform of jails." In *Visions for Change: Crime and Justice in the Twenty-First Century,* 3rd ed., ed. R. Muraskin and A. R. Roberts, pp. 390–407. New York: Prentice-Hall.

Welte, J. W., and E. L. Abel. 1989. "Homicide: Drinking by the victim." *Journal of Studies on Alcohol* 50 (May):197–201.

Werum, R., and B. Winders. 2001. "Who's 'in' and who's 'out:' State fragmentation and the struggle over gay rights, 1974–1999." *Social Problems* 48:386–410.

Western, B., M. Kleykamp, and J. Rosenfeld. 2006. "Did falling wages and employment increase U.S. imprisonment?" *Social Forces* 84:2291–2311.

Weston, C. 2004. "SFA survey finds crime cost to business soars to [euro] 1 bn." *Europe Intelligence Wire,* February 12.

Whatley, M. A. 2005. "The effect of participant sex, victim dress, and traditional attitudes on causal judgments for marital rape victims." *Journal of Family Violence* 20:191–200.

Wheaton, B., and P. Clarke. 2003. "Space meets time: Integrating temporal and contextual influences on mental health in early adulthood." *American Sociological Review* 68:680–706.

Wheeler, D. L. 1994. "An ominous legacy of the atomic age." *Chronicle of Higher Education,* January 12.

Whipple, E. E., and C. Webster-Stratton. 1991. "The role of parental stress in physically abusive families." *Child Abuse and Neglect* 15 (3):279–91.

Whisman, M. A. 2006. "Childhood trauma and marital outcomes in adulthood." *Personal Relationships* 13:375.

Whisman, M. A., L. A. Uebelacker, and M. L. Bruce. 2006. "Longitudinal association between marital dissatisfaction and alcohol use disorders in a community sample." *Journal of Family Psychology* 20:164–67.

Whitam, F. L. 1983. "Culturally invariable properties of male homosexuality: Tentative conclusions from cross-cultural research." *Archives of Sexual Behavior* 12 (June):207–26.

Whitam, F. L., and R. M. Mathy. 1991. "Childhood cross-gender behavior of homosexual females in Brazil, Peru, the Philippines, and the United States." *Archives of Sexual Behavior* 20 (April):151–70.

White, G. F., J. Katz, and K. E. Scarborough. 1992. "The impact of professional football games upon violent assaults on women." *Violence and Victims* 7 (2):157–71.

White, J. M. 1987. "Premarital cohabitation and marital stability in Canada." *Journal of Marriage and the Family* 49 (August):641–47.

———. 1989. "Reply to comment by Trussell and Rao: A reanalysis of the data." *Journal of Marriage and the Family* 51 (May):540–44.

White, L., and B. Keith. 1990. "The effect of shift work on the quality and stability of marital relations." *Journal of Marriage and the Family* 52 (May):453–62.

White, L. K., and A. Booth. 1985. "Stepchildren in remarriages." *American Sociological Review* 50 (October): 689–98.

White, R. K. 1966. "Misperception and the Vietnam war." *Journal of Social Issues* 22 (July):1–19.

Whitehead, B. D., and D. Popenoe. 2001. *The State of Our Unions: The Social Health of Marriage in America.* National Marriage Project Web site.

Whitfield, C. L., R. F. Anda, S. R. Dube, and V. J. Felitti. 2003. "Violent childhood experiences and the risk of intimate partner violence in adults." *Journal of Interpersonal Violence* 18:166–85.

Whitlock, E. P., M. R. Polen, C. A. Green, T. Orleans, and J. Klein. 2004. "Behavioral counseling interventions in primary care to reduce risky/harmful alcohol use by adults." *Annals of Internal Medicine* 140:557–68.

Whittle, J. C., P. K. Whelton, A. J. Seidler, and M. J. Klag. 1991. "Does racial variation in risk factors explain black-white differences in the incidence of hypertensive end-stage renal disease?" *Archives of Internal Medicine* 151 (July):1359–64.

Whooley, M. A. 2006. "Depression and cardiovascular disease." *Journal of the American Medical Association* 295:2874–81.

Whyte, M. K. 1990. *Dating, Mating, and Marriage.* New York: Aldine de Gruyter.

Wickrama, K., et al. 1995. "Role identity, role satisfaction, and perceived physical health." *Social Psychology Quarterly* 58:270–83.

Widom, C. S., and A. M. Ames. 1994. "Criminal consequences of childhood sexual victimization." *Child Abuse and Neglect* 18 (April):303–18.

Wild, T. C. 2002. "Personal drinking and sociocultural drinking norms." *Journal of Studies on Alcohol* 63:469–75.

Wilens, T. E., et al. 2002. "A family study of the high-risk children of opioid- and alcohol-dependent parents." *American Journal on Addictions* 11:41–51.

Wilensky, H. L. 1967. *Organizational Intelligence.* New York: Basic Books.

Williams, C. L. 1995. *Still a Man's World: Men Who Do "Women's Work."* Berkeley and Los Angeles: University of California Press.

Williams, D. R., H. W. Neighbors, and J. S. Jackson. 2003. "Racial/ethnic discrimination and health." *American Journal of Public Health* 93:200–208.

Williams, D. R., D. T. Takeuchi, and R. K. Adair. 1992. "Socioeconomic status and psychiatric disorder among blacks and whites." *Social Forces* 71 (September):179–94.

Williams, J. 2004. "Facts that should change the world." *New Statesman,* May 10, p. 21.

Williams, R. 1989. *The Trusting Heart: Great News about Type A Behavior.* New York: Random House.

Williams, R., and R. Nesiba. 2005. "The changing face of inequality in home mortgage lending." *Social Problems* 52:181–208.

Williams, T., and W. Kornblum. 1985. *Growing Up Poor.* Lexington, MA: DC Heath.

Williamson, C., and T. Cluse-Tolar. 2002. "Pimp-controlled prostitution." *Violence against Women* 8:1074–92.

Willis, B. M., and B. S. Levy. 2003. "Child prostitution increasing." *Southern Medical Journal* 96:69.

Wilson, E. O. 2000. *Sociobiology: The New Synthesis.* Cambridge, MA: Harvard University Press.

Wilson, G. 2005. "Race and job dismissal." *American Behavioral Scientist* 48:1182–99.

Wilson, G. C. 2002. "Truth be told, they do lie." *National Journal,* March 2, p. 636.

Wilson, W. J. 1987. *The Truly Disadvantaged: The Inner City, the Underclass, and Public Policy.* Chicago: University of Chicago Press.

Wingspread Group on Higher Education. 1993. *An American Imperative: Higher Expectations for Higher Education.* Racine, WI: Johnson Foundation.

Winick, C., and P. M. Kinsie. 1971. *The Lively Commerce.* Chicago: Quadrangle.

Wiseman, J. P. 1991. *The Other Half: Wives of Alcoholics and Their Social-Psychological Situation.* New York: Aldine de Gruyter.

Witt, H. 2004. "9 years after Oklahoma City blast, militias remain shadowy groups in U.S." Knight Ridder/Tribune News Service, April 18.

Witt, S. D. 1997. "Parental influence on children's socialization to gender roles." *Adolescence* 32 (Summer):253–59.

Woellert, L. 2002. "Soft money: Is it the end—or the end run?" *Business Week,* July 8, p. 47.

Wolfinger, N. H. 1998. "The effects of parental divorce on adult tobacco and alcohol consumption." *Journal of Health and Social Behavior* 39 (September):254–69.

———. 2005. *Understanding the Divorce Cycle: The Children of Divorce in Their Own Marriages.* New York: Cambridge University Press.

Wolfner, G. D., and R. J. Gelles. 1993. "A profile of violence toward children." *Child Abuse and Neglect* 17 (March):197–212.

Wong, W. C. W., E. A. Holroyd, A. Gray, and D. C. Ling. 2006. "Female street sex workers in Hong Kong." *Journal of Women's Health* 15:390–99.

Woo, D. 2000. *Glass Ceilings and Asian Americans.* Walnut Creek, CA: AltaMira Press.

Wood, D. 2004. "Defense spending a threat to world economic stability." *San Diego Union-Tribune,* January 19.

Wood, P. B., and J. P. Bartkowski. 2004. "Attribution style and public policy attitudes toward gay rights." *Social Science Quarterly* 85:58–74.

Woodruff, S. I., and T. L. Conway. 1992. "A longitudinal assessment of the impact of health/fitness status and health behavior on perceived quality of life." *Perceptual and Motor Skills* 75 (August):3–14.

Woods, N. F., and F. M. Lewis. 1995. "Women with chronic illness: Their views of their families' adaptation." *Nursing Journal* 16 (March–April):135–48.

Woody, B. 1991. "Recent employment experience of black women workers in the services economy." *Sociological Practice Review* 2 (July):188–99.

Worden, A. P., and B. E. Carlson. 2005. "Attitudes and beliefs about domestic violence." *Journal of Interpersonal Violence* 20:1219–43.

Work and Family Newsbrief. 2003. "Telework found to reduce conflict: Those who work from home at least two to three days a week report having lower levels of work-family conflict than those who don't." *Work and Family Newsbrief,* p. 3.

Worklife Report. 2003. "Vacation advantage for European workers." *Worklife Report* 14:12–13.

World Health Organization. 2005. "Indoor air pollution and health." World Health Organization Web site.

World Resources Institute. 1999. *World Resources 1998–1999.* New York: Oxford University Press.

Wren, C. S. 1997. "Ex-addicts find methadone more elusive than heroin." *The New York Times,* February 2.

Wright, E. R., G. Avirappattu, and J. E. Lafuze. 1999. "The family experience of deinstitutionalization." *Journal of Behavioral Health Service Research* 26 (August):289–304.

Wright, H. I., J. S. Gavaler, and D. Van Thiel. 1991. "Effects of alcohol on the male reproductive system." *Alcohol Health and Research World* 15 (12):110–14.

Wright, P. J., R. H. Fortinsky, K. E. Covinsky, P. A. Anderson, and C. S. Landefeld. 2000. "Delivery of preventive services to older black patients using neighborhood health centers." *Journal of the American Geriatric Society* 48 (February):124–30.

Wu, Z., and C. M. Schimmele. 2005. "Food insufficiency and depression." *Sociological Perspectives* 48:481–504.

Wurdinger, S. D. 2005. *Using Experiential Learning in the Classroom.* New York: Rowman & Littlefield.

Wyatt, G. E., and M. Riederle. 1995. "The prevalence and context of sexual harassment among African American and white American women." *Journal of Interpersonal Violence* 10 (September):309–21.

Wynn, R. L., and J. Bowering. 1990. "Homemaking practices and evening meals in married and separated families with young children." *Journal of Divorce and Remarriage* 14:107–23.

Yardley, J. 2002. "The 10 percent solution." *The New York Times,* April 14.

Yates, J. 2006. "Unions and employee ownership." *Industrial Relations* 45:709–33.

Yip, P. S., and J. Thorburn. 2004. "Marital status and the risk of suicide." *Psychological Reports* 94:401–7.

Yoder, J. D., and L. L. Berendsen. 2001. "Outsider within the firehouse." *Psychology of Women* 25:27–36.

Young, M. L. 1998. "A plethora of paradoxes." *USA Today,* March, p. 15.

Youth, H. 2003. "Watching birds disappear." In *State of the World 2003,* ed. L. Starke, pp. 14–37. New York: W. W. Norton.

Yu, T. 2006. "Challenging the politics of the 'model minority' stereotype." *Equity and Excellence in Education* 39:325–33.

Yuan, N. P., M. P. Koss, M. Polacca, and D. Goldman. 2006. "Risk factors for physical assault and rape among six Native American tribes." *Journal of Interpersonal Violence* 21:1566–90.

Yung, K. 2004. "Job stresses starting to take toll." *San Diego Union-Tribune,* May 24.

Zautra, A. J., M. A. Okun, S. E. Robinson, and D. Lee. 1989. "Life stress and lymphocyte alterations among patients with rheumatoid arthritis." *Health Psychology* 8 (1):1–14.

Zimiles, H., and V. E. Lee. 1991. "Adolescent family structure and educational progress." *Developmental Psychology* 27:314–20.

Zimmerman, T. S., S. A. Haddock, and C. R. McGeorge. 2001. "Mars and Venus: Unequal planets." *Journal of Marital and Family Therapy* 27:55–68.

Zlotnick, C., D. M. Johnson, and R. Kohn. 2006. "Intimate partner violence and long-term psychosocial functioning in a national sample of American women." *Journal of Interpersonal Violence* 21:262–75.

Zuckerbrod, N. 2002. "Number of military ousted for homosexuality rose in '01." *San Diego Union-Tribune,* March 14.

Zuger, A. 1998. "Prostitutes' stress is greater than soldiers'." *San Diego Union-Tribune,* August 19.

Zuravin, S., and G. L. Greif. 1989. "Normative and child maltreating AFDC mothers." *Social Casework* 70 (February):76–84.

Zvonkovic, A. M. 1988. "Underemployment: Individual and marital adjustment to income loss." *Lifestyles* 9 (Summer):161–78.

Zwerling, C., and H. Silver. 1992. "Race and job dismissals in a federal bureaucracy." *American Sociological Review* 57 (October):651–60.

Chapter 1—**chapter opener:** © SuperStock; **page 12:** © Viviane Moos/Corbis; **16:** © Bettmann/Corbis; **20:** © Michael Newman/PhotoEdit; **29:** © Rick Gomez/Corbis

Chapter 2—**chapter opener:** © Royalty-Free/Corbis; **page 41:** © Debra Reid/AP Wide World Photos; **49:** © Lebrun Didier/Gamma

Chapter 3—**chapter opener:** © Stockbyte/Corbis; **page 60:** © Hogan Jeremy/Gamma; **76:** © James Pickerell/The Image Works; **84:** © Bill Aron/PhotoEdit; **87:** © John Griffin/The Image Works

Chapter 4—**chapter opener:** © Andrew Lichtenstein/Aurora; **page 98:** © Reuters/Corbis; **101:** © A. Ramey/Woodfin Camp; **115:** © Joel Gordon; **120:** © Mike Fender/AP Wide World Photos

Chapter 5—**chapter opener:** © SW Production/Picture Quest/Jupiter Images; **page 128:** © Hannah Gal/Corbis; **134:** © Brian Hendrickson/AP Wide World Photos; **140:** © Peter Byron/Photo Researchers, Inc.; **144:** © John Birdsall/The Image Works

Chapter 6—**chapter opener:** © Robin Nelson/PhotoEdit; **page 162:** © Nathan Benn/Corbis; **169:** © Andy Levin/Photo Researchers; **177:** © Lynne Sladky/AP Wide World Photos; **180:** © Rubber Ball Collection/Creatas

Chapter 7—**chapter opener:** © Tim Pannell/Corbis; **page 189:** © Alan Carey/The Image Works; **198:** © Alistair Berg-FSP/Gamma; **199:** © The Image Bank/Getty Images; **203:** © AP/Wide World Photos; **207:** © Bob Daemmrich; **209:** © Paul Conklin/PhotoEdit

Chapter 8—**chapter opener:** © Masterfile; **page 225:** © Jim West/The Image Works; **234:** © Alan Oddie/PhotoEdit; **240:** © Ralf-Finn Hestoft/Corbis; **244:** © Chip Somodevilla/Getty Images

Chapter 9—**chapter opener:** © Hisham F. Ibrahim/Getty Images; **page 255:** © Rommel Pecson/The Image Works; **260:** © Bob Daemmrich; **263:** © Michael Newman/PhotoEdit; **272:** © Jim Cole/AP Wide World Photos

Chapter 10—**chapter opener:** © Michael Newman/PhotoEdit; **page 287:** © Michael S. Yamashita/Corbis; **294:** © Grant Le Duc/Stock Boston; **301:** © David Paul Morris/Getty Images; **305:** © Atlanta Constitution/ SYGMA

Chapter 11—**chapter opener:** © Corbis; **page 323:** © Rod Morata/Stone/Getty Images; **325:** © Mary Kate Denny/PhotoEdit; **331:** © Mike Derer/AP Wide World Photos; **336:** © James Marshall/The Image Works

Chapter 12—**chapter opener:** © Rolf Bruderer/Masterfile; **page 352:** © Yellow Dog Productions/Getty Images; **356:** © David Young-Wolff/PhotoEdit; **361:** © Brand X Pictures/Getty Images; **367:** © Gary Watts/The Image Works

Chapter 13—**chapter opener:** © Ric Feld/AP Wide World Photos; **page 379:** © Matt Herron/Black Star; **389:** © Michael Newman/PhotoEdit; **393:** © Philip Mark/AP Wide World Photos; **399:** © Jana Birchum/Black Star

Chapter 14—**chapter opener:** © Ahmad Al-Rubaye/AFP/Getty Images; **page 414:** © Peter Turnley/Corbis; **417:** © AP/Wide World Photos; **423:** © Royalty-Free/Corbis; **435:** © Parent/Heidemedia/Contrast/Gamma

Chapter 15—**chapter opener:** © Gautam Singh/AP Wide World Photos; **page 447:** © Pete Seaward/Stone/Getty Images; **450:** © Norman R. Rowan/Stock Boston; **458:** © Bruce Forster/Stone/Getty Images; **461:** © David Sailors/Corbis

subject index